LA
636.4
.S5
1979

LARRY A. JACKSON LIBRARY
Lander College
Greenwood, S. C. 29646

EDUCATION AND SOCIETY IN TUDOR ENGLAND

EDUCATION AND SOCIETY IN TUDOR ENGLAND

BY

JOAN SIMON

236011

CAMBRIDGE UNIVERSITY PRESS
CAMBRIDGE
LONDON · NEW YORK · MELBOURNE

ARRY A. JACKSON LIBRARY
Lander College
Greenwood, S. C. 29646

Published by the Syndics of the Cambridge University Press
The Pitt Building, Trumpington Street, Cambridge CB2 1RP
Bentley House, 200 Euston Road, London NW1 2DB
32 East 57th Street, New York, NY 10022, USA
296 Beaconsfield Parade, Middle Park, Melbourne 3206, Australia

© Cambridge University Press 1966

Library of Congress catalogue card number: 65-14850

First published 1966
First paperback edition 1979

First printed in Great Britain at the University Press, Cambridge
Reprinted in Great Britain at the Alden Press, Oxford

ISBN 0 521 22854 9 hard covers
ISBN 0 521 29679 X paperback

CONTENTS

PREFACE

Much has been written about education in Tudor England but there is no straightforward account of developments at the Reformation. In nearly all discussions of the subject for the past half century it has been accepted that the keynote of this period was destruction, that grammar schools were crippled or swept away and elementary schooling obliterated during the reign of Edward VI. It is to remove this misconception, which has obscured the nature of educational change at a turning point in English history, that this book has been written.

There is no need to recapitulate detailed criticisms of the case made by A. F. Leach in *English Schools at the Reformation*, published in 1896. But it may be noted that this was drawn up at a time when old endowments, having been assessed by a series of commissions, were more purposefully applied to foster a system of secondary schools—a matter with which Leach, as an assistant charity commissioner, was intimately concerned. That the benefactions of an earlier age should survive for this use seemed to a Victorian, bred in the tradition of Stubbs, no less than the purpose of providence and it was in this context, rather than in historical perspective, that Leach assessed the effect of Reformation legislation and castigated Tudor kings. Moreover, his analysis rested on so high an estimate of the schooling provided by the medieval church that change could only seem a change for the worse. In the circumstances the main point escaped attention, namely that the chantry commissioners of the 1540's were engaged in much the same kind of undertaking as the charity commissioners of three centuries later. In other words it was at the Reformation—not, as is still universally taught, in the nineteenth century—that state intervention in English education began; to recognise this is to see all subsequent developments in a new light.

As the whole question has been re-opened the task now is to marshal the available evidence afresh.[1] In so doing educational programmes and practice must be related to wider social movements since it is in large

[1] For comments on two articles criticising Leach's case, Joan Simon, 'A. F. Leach: A Reply', *British Journal of Educational Studies*, XII, no. 1 (1963). For the original articles 'A. F. Leach on the Reformation', III, no. 2, IV, no. 1 (1955); see also 'The Reformation and English Education', *Past and Present*, no. 13 (1957).

part failure to do this that invalidates former assessments. But it is one thing to be aware of the need, quite another to fulfil it. Education has affiliations with almost every aspect of life and is in a special sense both a resultant and determinant of social attitudes and aspirations. Yet text-books of educational history often treat the changes of this period as an uncontrolled reaction to two abstract forces 'the renaissance' and 'the Reformation' and the essential questions are seldom asked, let alone answered. Standard histories either discuss educational as an adjunct of ecclesiastical affairs or cover the subject in a chapter which also takes in literature, the arts and other matters extraneous to the mainstream of events. On the other hand the relevant specialist literature is vast and incorporates very various approaches; by the medieval or modern historian, for instance, classicists or critics of English literature, protagonists of the different churches each with its martyrs for a faith. Even particular schools and colleges evoke strong loyalties while the university in its peculiarly English form tends to be an article of belief. There is probably no subject about which so much has been written as 'humanism' and 'the renaissance', or the age of Shakespeare, nor any which engenders more heat among historians of the period than the composition of social classes in the Tudor age.

Through all this one must steer a course as best one may, making points that arise from the evidence or are necessary to the discussion, though I am only too aware of the crudities that result from treating large issues, about which volumes have been written, in single paragraphs. At the same time on some relevant matters there is all too little guidance, and points can only be tentatively advanced. But it has been a chief concern, in questioning too easy generalisations, to suggest the scope there is for inquiry along new lines.

Since this book has been written as a contribution to the history of education—for those unfamiliar with the period or unable to keep abreast of all that is written about it—I have attempted an account framed in the light of more recent research which includes well-known with lesser-known material to provide a reasonably comprehensive picture. The discussion must be conducted with former interpretations in mind, and to bring neglected matters to attention, but particular points of controversy are usually raised at the outset of different sections to allow for straightforward presentation of the contemporary evidence; there are frequent references to secondary sources where further information and discussion may be found. If many of the facts were first brought to light or together by Leach there have been valuable contributions by W. H. Woodward, J. W. Adamson, above all Foster Watson on whose researches this survey so heavily depends. More generally there is a debt to Sir Fred Clarke's cogent argument in *Education and Social Change* (1940), that ideas about English education are endlessly reiterated but seldom examined in the light of the social forces which have shaped them and that the century after the Reformation particularly invites historical investigation in this sense.

The starting point was an inquiry into the background of educational developments during the Commonwealth which brought to light how far Leach's findings conflicted with later evidence. The same conclusion emerged from some research into local developments in the midlands, taking as a background the picture of this region provided by Dr W. G. Hoskins. In turning to the period of the Reformation, I owe much to some advice from the late R. H. Tawney. I am also indebted to others who commented on the papers published and suggested that the case might be filled out in a book, notably Dr G. R. Elton. Among those with whom I have had discussions over the years, Mr Christopher Hill made useful criticisms of the first draft of these chapters in 1959. At this point there appeared the first of Professor W. K. Jordan's surveys of charitable bequests during the decades 1480–1660; this and the subsequent volumes, establishing beyond dispute an increase rather than decrease in the number of schools at and after the Reformation, made superfluous a great deal of detailed argument. So, too, did the volume of Professor David Knowles's history of monasticism covering the dissolution, which assesses evidence that has been the subject of much controversy, while various publications by Professor A. G. Dickens undermined accepted views about the period of the Reformation and provided materials for a re-assessment. Other more recent studies, including Professor M. H. Curtis's re-interpretation of the role of the universities, could also be taken into account when this book was redrafted in 1963.

It will be clear from the references how many and various are my debts, though there is no exhaustive bibliography of works consulted; instead the main sources drawn upon are listed and there is a selected bibliography to supplement the many others available. This last, intended primarily for students of education, covers reprints of contemporary writings which are comparatively easily available; in the text the titles of books have been modernised, as also the spelling of quotations. For my own part I have been largely dependent on the London Library whose open shelves are both an invitation to widen inquiries and a warning against imagining any inquiry complete. There is, in fact, a considerable addendum of books throwing more light on matters discussed here which appeared after the present study had been brought to a close.

I cannot hope to have avoided errors in so complex a field, but an examination of this particular part of the record may open the way to the more general re-assessment of early educational history that is long overdue. I owe to Brian Simon of Leicester University School of Education an introduction to investigating school provision locally, which underlined how much remains to be discovered, while his studies of developments in the nineteenth century stimulated an attempt to make sense of earlier educational changes. Without his constant intervention this book would never have reached completion, in the intervals of work of quite another kind. Without the support of the Syndics of the Cambridge University Press it could not have been published and I am grateful for the help given in seeing it through the press.

J.S.

October 1964

NOTE ON 1979 REISSUE

Since this book was first published much has been written about the nature and importance of changes in the economic and social, as well as the political and religious, spheres during the century after 1540. This underlines a thesis turning on the extent and significance of educational change at this period, rather than calling the argument in question, although some detailed points are open to correction. Meanwhile the bibliography at the close of the volume has been updated in my sections on education in *The New Cambridge Bibliography of English Literature*, ed. George Watson, Vol. I, *600–1660* (1974), pp. 627–39, 2381–2418.

J.S.

January 1979

ABBREVIATIONS

APC	*Acts of the Privy Council*, ed. J. R. Dasent
Athenae	*Athenae Cantabrigiensis*, ed. C. H. and T. Cooper
CHEL	*Cambridge History of English Literature*
CPR	*Calendar of Patent Rolls*
CSPD	*Calendar of State Papers, Domestic*
ECD	*Educational Charters and Documents*, ed. A. F. Leach
E.E.T.S.	*Early English Text Society*
EGS	*English Grammar Schools to 1660*, by Foster Watson
ESR	*English Schools at the Reformation, 1546–48,* by A. F. Leach
L & P	*Calendar of Letters and Papers, Henry VIII*
T.R.H.S.	*Transactions of the Royal Historical Society*
VCH	*Victoria History of the Counties of England*

Full details are given in the check-list of sources at the end of the book.

PART I

THE FIFTEENTH-CENTURY BACKGROUND AND HUMANIST INNOVATIONS

I

THE FIFTEENTH-CENTURY BACKGROUND

A necessary preliminary to discussing educational change in the sixteenth century is some account of developments in preceding years. There has been considerable controversy about the nature and extent of schooling in the later middle ages, but the most recent assessment is that made by W. K. Jordan in the course of a detailed study of educational benefactions. He suggests that, if the ten counties covered may be regarded as in any way typical, there has been a 'gross over-estimate of the number of grammar schools actually in existence and functioning in say 1480'. The evidence seems rather to suggest 'that the number of medieval foundations in which lay children might gain instruction was limited indeed and that by 1480 most of these foundations had been gravely weakened or had been closed'. Or, again: 'Men of the later fifteenth century began their building of educational resources upon most limited foundations left from the ruin of the medieval world.'[1] This last may, perhaps, convey too sweeping an impression; historians have long ceased to suppose that the medieval world ground to a close in 1485, that 'modern times' then arose like a phoenix from the ashes. But the criticism of assessments by A. F. Leach is just, that he tended to reckon any and every reference to schooling as evidence of an established school which remained continuously in being down the centuries.[2]

On the other hand it has recently been restated, after Leach, that fifteenth-century England was well provided with grammar schools, and that these were clearly distinguished from more elementary schools

[1] *Philanthropy in England, 1480–1660* (1959), pp. 285–6; *The Charities of Rural England, 1480–1660* (1961), p. 301.

[2] This kind of approach has been questioned elsewhere. A school is mentioned in Carlisle in 1188, 'other references to it occur in the next two centuries; the last in 1370–1. Then there is a blank. No school is recorded in the Valor of 1535. Thus by normal genealogical standards, it cannot be said that the school founded by the statutes of 1545 has a proved pedigree from that mentioned in 1188' (C. M. L. Bouch, *Prelates and People of the Lake Counties. A History of the Diocese of Carlisle*, Kendal, 1948, p. 38).

teaching song, reading and writing.[1] Distinctions were not, in practice, as rigid as this. The established school may have set out to teach Latin, but reading as well as grammar. Lesser schools were often kept by chantry priests who themselves had only a smattering of Latin; they were expected to teach children to participate in the Latin mass but no doubt taught the elements in the vernacular as well. Writing, which rarely figures, was less an elementary than a semi-vocational subject, linked with ciphering.

There will be no attempt here to enumerate fifteenth-century schools, but it should be recalled that in earlier centuries the endowed foundation was the exception rather than the rule, so that the main schools documented are those connected with a monastic house or major church. Later, and most notably after 1480, information about endowments begins to accumulate and by the close of the sixteenth century contemporaries affirmed that there was a grammar school in every market town and many another besides.[2] Here, evidently, is an important new trend and it was accompanied by a new educational outlook. But this is not to say that old institutions and ideas were on all sides in ruins, that new foundations and theories filled a gaping void; there is evidence enough of the survival of medieval institutions, no less than methods of teaching, to this day.

What it does suggest is that educational developments in the sixteenth century broke away from the pattern prevailing in earlier years, that there began to emerge a system of education in the modern sense in place of forms of upbringing designed to fit men for different estates of society. If the course and direction of change is to be traced the starting point must be the overall provision for education in the later middle ages. When the organised grammar school is taken as the norm it is usually inferred that the church alone sponsored educational facilities. But the medieval church was only an estate of society, however much it may have aspired to control every aspect of social life, and if the grammar school originally developed to educate those entering on

[1] E. F. Jacob, *The Fifteenth Century* (Oxford, 1961), p. 667.

[2] A recently compiled list of Yorkshire schools provides evidence of, perhaps, 10 established schools at the close of the fourteenth century (besides occasional mentions of masters elsewhere) and more than 25 additional endowments for, or used for, education from 1480 to 1525, with an accumulating number of grammar school foundations after this last date (P. J. Wallis and W. E. Tate, 'A Register of Old Yorkshire Grammar Schools', *Researches & Studies*, no. 13, University of Leeds Institute of Education, 1956, pp. 64–104).

this estate, there were also other forms of education. The best way to assess these is to consider briefly the social trends which gave rise to particular educational needs and provision. Against this background the extent of the church's monopoly over education may be considered, as also the nature of the main foundations of the period, before turning to developments in education itself which also prepared the way for the changes of the sixteenth century.

(1) *Education and society in the later middle ages*

In *Feudal Society* Marc Bloch discusses an age in depth, taking in ties of kinship and the length of folk memory as well as more developed social bonds and the learning of the schools. There emerges a picture of a social process at work, a process which, reduced to its essence, is the history of human education. An example is the way the development of law is treated, in terms not merely of institutions but inculcation of 'the habit of reasoned argument no matter what the subject under discussion', so that 'towards the end of the twelfth century men of action had at their disposal a more efficient instrument of mental analysis than that which had been available to their predecessors'. While the chief judicial functions centred on the royal court and the households of great magnates, men of lesser rank had enough to do with administrative matters locally 'to make the legal spirit one of the earliest cultural influences to be diffused in knightly circles'. Indeed this influence antedated the more self-conscious cultivation of noble qualities, associated with the main knightly function of military service, from which resulted that whole code of conduct termed 'courtesy'. At the same time attention is drawn to the fact that legal terminology was for long handicapped by an archaic vocabulary at a time when popular tongues, in a variety of dialects, lacked precision and stability. Hence the key importance to medieval society of Latin, a developed language which served as a means of communication between the educated. This was not only the language of teaching but the only language taught; to be able to read was simply to be able to read Latin, thereby acquiring the designation *litteratus*. None the less, to many men who used it Latin remained, as it were, an external language so that they were 'forced to resort to perpetual approximations in the expression of their thoughts'.[1]

[1] Marc Bloch, *Feudal Society* (1961), pp. 77–8, 108, 303, 305.

This conveys essentials which may pass unnoticed when medieval education is discussed in terms of certain well-defined categories, for instance, the chivalric training of young nobles in the household as contrasted with the systematic schooling of clerks. In this context an impression is often gained that the nobility was more or less illiterate, that churchmen alone commanded Latin and the knowledge necessary for the conduct of government. But from very early times sovereigns took great care to educate their heirs and it was generally held that 'a leader of men should have access to the treasure-house of thoughts and memories to which the written word, that is to say Latin, alone provided the key'.[1] It has been suggested that the ever-increasing use of written documents in the administrative system of twelfth-century England presupposes that leading laymen were then literate, though it was clerks who, 'little more than nominally in the service of the church, undertook the humbler tasks of royal and private administration'. There were also, of course, the prelates who filled key posts in the royal service, but this only underlines the point that needs making: if the lay nobility had been so unlettered as is sometimes implied the clerk would have been master rather than what he was, the servant of the state.[2]

These are useful reminders when it comes to discussing the fifteenth and sixteenth centuries which provide some interesting similarities with the 'renaissance' of the eleventh and twelfth; for instance, in the fact that the spread of learning among wider sections of the lay order contributed necessary support to a new form of monarchy, while it was also a main concern of the learned to promote mastery of language as a means to self-expression.

The extent to which the nobility dominated medieval society is illustrated by the contemporary picture of the social order, as a community of those who fought, those who prayed and those who laboured on the land. If the peasantry were tenants, or serfs, the monasteries were essentially the creation of landowners, endowed with lands in free alms in return for the service of offering perpetual prayers for their founders. From the time when Anglo-Saxon kings accepted missionaries as bishops, according them the same status as lay lords, and noblemen founded churches in their territories granting certain rights, the

[1] Bloch, p. 79.

[2] H. G. Richardson and G. O. Sayles, *The Governance of Mediaeval England from the Conquest to Magna Carta* (Edinburgh, 1963), pp. 282–3.

ecclesiastical system had necessarily developed within the framework of the social order.[1] Though the church gained a well-defined legal status and administered powerful courts, as well as a diocesan and parish organisation, it was not an estate standing rigidly apart whose affairs were regulated solely by canon law under the guidance of the papacy. Rather the clerical mingled closely with the lay order at every level. Bishops owed allegiance and military service to the crown as lords of temporal estates, besides exercising spiritual jurisdiction; the poorest parish priests shared much the same conditions as the peasantry and were often immediately dependent on lay patrons. Diocesan affairs were administered not from a cathedral church but the episcopal palace, with the aid of officials of a personal household, as affairs of state were administered by the king. Secular cathedrals and collegiate churches developed, like the monasteries, as closed corporations with extensive property and their own jurisdictions; though they were seldom communities in the same sense as those of the regulars because most of the prebends supported clerks employed in royal or episcopal administration who resided not in the close but in the great households. Taken as a whole, the church was a complex of institutions which had accumulated privileges and obligations over the centuries, a body which as the greatest of feudal landowners was 'implicated to the hilt in the economic fabric'. This was a church which, in R. H. Tawney's words, aspired to be 'not a sect, but a civilisation' and was accordingly guardian of a patriarchal doctrine which represented 'a softened reflection of the feudal land system'.[2]

The great religious communities were the centres of learning in the earlier middle ages and provided organised instruction for young entrants in the Latin and singing needed to participate in services in church; instruction which became available also to outsiders once regular schools became established. But the great households, the focus of government and administration, were the centres providing an education for lay pursuits. Drawing men together in the performance of a wide variety of duties, they provided training for many functions in the form of an apprenticeship in service, a form which extended to cover the upbringing of young men of birth.[3] The knightly code

[1] David Knowles, *The Monastic Order in England* (Cambridge, 1949), pp. 561 ff.

[2] R. H. Tawney, *Religion and the Rise of Capitalism* (1944 ed.), pp. 19, 25, 56.

[3] The custom was specifically sanctioned by the church, 'inasmuch as according to the truth of the gospel, the heir, so long as he is a child, differeth nothing from a servant,

which to a large extent governed the training of the nobility became crystallised when followers congregated round king or baron and courtly forms of life became established. Later, when urban communities brought together men of the same occupation, professional codes likewise took shape which governed new forms of education. The first associations formed were the gilds of scholars engaged in teaching which arose in northern Europe in connection with the great urban cathedrals and achieved recognition as universities. There followed in time gilds of lawyers and doctors, tradesmen and craftsmen, all integrally concerned with setting a standard of entry to a profession which implied regulating the conditions of training. In the later middle ages lay education rested mainly on the social structure of the gilds.

In England developments took a course somewhat different from that on the continent. Since the monastic order for long held a pre-eminent position, secular cathedrals were less wealthy and influential than their continental counterparts and did not have the same stake in education.[1] The university that became established at Oxford owed nothing to any great church and much, it would seem, to royal interest at a time when there was a pressing need for the services of the educated; in any case the subsequent rise of Cambridge was 'very pleasing and acceptable' to Henry III 'since no little advantage to our kingdom and honour to us accrues therefrom'.[2] The universities in turn gained less influence than those abroad because of the system of common law which was exclusive to England and of immediate interest to the crown. By the fourteenth century the common lawyers were developing their own system of education centred at the inns of court and lesser inns of chancery, which were situated between the king's courts at Westminster and the city of London. Within the city itself the better trades established a form of apprenticeship in service under gild supervision at this time which spread to provincial towns in the fifteenth century; this form of apprentice training, like that of the upper classes,

though he be lord of all', as a fifteenth-century bishop put it (*Visitations of Religious Houses in the Diocese of Lincoln*, ed. A. Hamilton Thompson, Lincoln Record Society, 1918), II, i, p. 77.

[1] 'England's scholastic development virtually skips the age of great cathedral schools, and learning passes from the monasteries to the universities without any break in time' (R. W. Southern, 'England in the Twelfth Century Renaissance', *History*, XLV, no. 155, 1960, p. 204).

[2] Quoted in Doris Mary Stenton, *English Society in the Early Middle Ages* (1951), p. 262.

was concerned with manners and morals as well as instruction in the relevant skills.

Once forms of education became institutionalised the facilities offered were sought after by others besides entrants to a profession. Schools administered by religious corporations in or near towns drew others besides prospective clerks and to this extent developed as local schools. When the universities gained recognition with the aid of privileges granted by king and pope, and the right to grant degrees which constituted a licence to teach, clerks of all grades were drawn there, members of all the religious orders, most notably the friars. Parish priests could gain leave to study and Oxford was particularly patronised by the Benedictine order, which founded its own houses of scholars; but other students made their way to university without intending to take a degree in the preliminary faculty of arts, let alone the main higher faculties of theology or canon law. If the universities were of interest to the church, the inns of court provided particularly for the lay nobility concerned with questions of landownership and administrative and judicial matters. By the fifteenth century they also exercised an attraction, not only for those intent on qualifying in law but also others seeking a modicum of legal knowledge and some experience of life in communities at the hub of affairs.

To turn to the fifteenth century is inevitably to draw on the evidence of Sir John Fortescue, who, describing the laws and government of England in about 1470, pays considerable attention to education. His book was written for the instruction of a prince, a task that had formerly fallen to clerics,[1] and it is on the education of the prince that Fortescue first insists, particularly the need for him to be learned in the laws. Then, passing to the training of the nobility for their social duties, he makes clear that the legal backbone of upbringing in the household was the feudal system of wardship. When lands were held in knight service heirs who succeeded under age became wards of the lord of the fee, who took control of their estates and might arrange their marriage but was bound to provide his wards with a training suitable to their station and future responsibilities. Fortescue frankly extols the system because it assures minors of a sound training in the military arts in a household of higher social standing. The lord is naturally interested in training his follower well and what could be more useful

[1] For earlier works, J. E. Mason, *Gentlefolk in the Making* (Philadelphia, 1935), pp. 10–14; Jacob, pp. 305–7.

to the minor 'who by reason of his tenure will expose his life and fortune to the dangers of war in the service of his lord, than to be trained in military and warlike exercises...since he will not be able to shun such activities in mature age'?[1] This was the underlying theory rather than a description of current practice, in an age when feudal bonds had been much loosened. But if the gentry had long ceased to render service in person, turning to develop their own estates and take their own part in affairs, the principle of patronage still ruled and it was necessary to seek a powerful protector;[2] within this framework sons were often placed in the service of a lord for their upbringing whether or not wardship was in question.

Household upbringing comprised much else than military exercises as Fortescue himself noted when he referred to training in music, dancing and other accomplishments, particularly in the royal household; and, since the wardship of heirs of all tenants-in-chief fell to the king, he saw the court as 'the supreme academy of the realm, and a school of vigour, probity and manners'. Ordinances issued in the 1460's for the household of Edward IV illustrate the traditional form of chivalric training. It was the duty of the master of the henchmen to teach young men to ride, joust and wear armour and to instruct them in the formalities of courtly tenure and household service, with particular attention to their manners at table. They were also to be taught 'sundry languages and other learnings virtuous, to harping, to pipe, sing, dance', while each should practise 'that thing of virtue that he shall be most apt to, with remembrance daily of God's service accustomed'.[3]

It would be mistaken, however, to envisage the upbringing of the nobility solely in these terms. Writing in the early fourteenth century Robert Holcot, Dominican friar and student of the classics, underlined that magnates kept resident tutors for their sons because application to study and continuity of influence were considered important; just as nobles of old sought out the best philosophers to teach boys and form their character.[4] If tutors were available in some of the great lay

[1] Sir John Fortescue, *De Laudibus Legum Anglie*, ed. S. B. Chrimes (Cambridge, 1942), pp. 17, 107–9; H. E. Bell, *An Introduction to the History and Records of the Court of Wards and Liveries* (Cambridge, 1953), p. 119.

[2] Jacob, pp. 338–43.

[3] *The Household of Edward IV*, ed. A. R. Myers (Manchester, 1959), pp. 126–7.

[4] Beryl Smalley, *English Friars and Antiquity in the Early Fourteenth Century* (Oxford, 1960), pp. 192–3.

households, the episcopal household was particularly well suited to provide education; for younger sons a place among the clerks of a diocesan bishop was not to be despised since patrons could be looked to for assistance to attend a university and obtain a benefice. In general boys were sent from home at an early age—and girls as well—if not to join the following of noble or bishop then into some household of higher social standing, to grandparents, or to a neighbouring monastery. The heads of the more considerable houses, who now lived apart from their communities, frequently had the sons of one or another county family under their care.

The monastic order had long ceased to hold its former dominant position and contributed little to the higher ranges of government; indeed the religious orders held no political power within the ecclesiastical system, which made it the easier to isolate them for destruction. But older county families retained close links with local houses which had often been founded by their forbears and were ruled by relatives. The historian of the Berkeley family writes of religious communities in three counties at which the lords of this house were always with solemn processions and honourable ceremonies 'received as founders'; which offered prayers for the family at over forty chantries, owed 'many annual rents and services' including feudal aids on the marriage of daughters or knighting of sons, and 'brought up and instructed divers of their children, received and kept as corrodies many of their old unserviceable servants...with other like duties incident to a founder's right'.[1] Though smaller houses were often insolvent and down-at-heel at this time, the greater abbeys remained influential in their localities and could offer inmates a standard of life which compared favourably with that of most lay landowners. Rules were much less strictly kept than formerly and possessions no longer shared in common; there was a division of income among the inmates with larger sums going to holders of offices, who often prepared for their duties by a period at university, and the lion's share to an abbot who might spend much of the year residing on his various manors.[2] The monastic life itself was not, therefore, without appeal to younger sons of the gentry, though most entrants were sons of lesser men in the

[1] J. Smyth, *Lives of the Berkeleys*, ed. J. Maclean (Bristol and Gloucestershire Archaeological Society, 1883), II, pp. 249–50.

[2] M. D. Knowles, *The Religious Orders in England* (Cambridge, 1959), III, pp. 111, 457–8.

countryside or the towns;[1] novices received a training in the rule and the education that went with it within the house.

Younger sons of the nobility also sought a career in the church, as a road to office and status, not least because under the system of primogeniture they remained commoners and relatively unprovided for; the privileges of earldoms and baronies were attached to the 'honour' and could be handed down only to elder sons.[2] In the fifteenth century most of the old earldoms and baronies came into the hands of a few families, all closely related, opening up the way for dynastic struggles for the crown. But taken as a whole the English nobility did not constitute a closed hereditary caste, as tended to be the case on the continent where all sons of nobles inherited that rank. Rather it was a relatively flexible body which could be recruited from below and from the thirteenth century the degree of knighthood could be attained by acquiring landed wealth.[3] Since rank and its privileges were so closely associated with landed possessions the later dispersal of landownership was to have far-reaching repercussions, bringing into being below the knights of the shire a growing body claiming the honourable status of gentleman.

During the fifteenth century the gentry were acquiring a more prominent place in the economy, as the great landed demesnes broke up under various pressures and farms were leased out rather than worked directly. While tenant farmers multiplied, and some prospered, the smaller estates of the gentry were also well adapted to produce for the market.[4] It was, therefore, lesser men who profited from economic expansion while the great landowner, whether lay or ecclesiastical, tended to become a *rentier* deriving only a static income. As the powers of feudal magnates and the old religious corporations correspondingly declined, the more substantial gentry in the counties undertook additional duties, administering the law for the crown. This marked a new stage in a long history of participation in local government which

[1] Most of the canons of Leicester Abbey in the fifteenth century had distinctively local names—Wigston, Belgrave, Saddington, Rothley, Ashby, Shepshed (A. Hamilton Thompson, *The Abbey of St Mary...Leicester*, Leicester, 1949, p. 61).

[2] Bloch, p. 331.

[3] While old families could die out 'into the ranks of the barons and knights there was always a steady influx of aspirants to gentility including not only the war heroes and those who earned the gratitude of a powerful patron, but also sons of successful lawyers ...kinsmen of influential bishops...prosperous traders' (M. McKisack, *The Fourteenth Century*, Oxford, 1959, p. 264).

[4] Jacob, pp. 370 ff.

helped to transform the squire into the country gentleman,[1] and a considerable contribution to hastening the process was the spread of legal education.

The inns of court emulated universities; though they did not award the same kind of degrees, wrote Fortescue, they conferred 'a certain estate not less eminent or solemn than the degree of doctor...called the degree of serjeant-at-law', accorded at a complex and dignified ceremony.[2] Serjeants left their inns once they acquired the office but otherwise older members of the profession who had begun to practise taught the younger, as at universities. There was also instruction available in music, dancing, and 'all games proper to nobles' such as was given in the royal household. During vacations young men applied themselves 'to the study of legal science, and at festivals to the reading, after the divine services, of Holy Scripture and of chronicles'. This, observed Fortescue, 'is indeed a cultivation of virtues and a banishment of all vice' and so 'knights, barons, and also other magnates' sent heirs to the inns for a time to ensure a good upbringing, though they would later live by their patrimonies.[3]

According to Fortescue residence at the inns was expensive, especially if a servant was kept as was usual, and most men could not afford the outlay of some £13. 6*s.* 8*d.* a year; 'poor and commonplace people' had not the wherewithal and 'merchants rarely desire to reduce their stock by such annual burdens. Hence it comes about that there is scarcely a man learned in the laws to be found in the realm who is not ...sprung of noble lineage.' This, again, was precept, illustrating the extent to which law was associated with the nobility, rather than an accurate assessment of current practice. In the fifteenth century yeomen's sons acquired a legal education while sons of merchants figured prominently in the profession, several rising to the highest offices.[4] But though the first great lay profession gained growing importance during the century, it was not recognised as such; rather the practice of knighting judges brought it within the scope of honour

[1] F. M. Powicke, *Mediaeval England 1066–1485* (1931), pp. 207–11.

[2] It is described as a stage in a contemporary lawyer's career by Joan Wake, *The Brudenells of Deene* (1954 ed.), pp. 15–16.

[3] Fortescue, pp. 117–19, 121.

[4] B. H. Putnam, *Early Treatises in the Practice of the Justices of the Peace* (Oxford, 1924), p. 130. Even monks followed the prevailing trend and registered for a period at the inns; e.g. in 1492 John Islip, chaplain to the abbot of Westminster, who later became warden of some of the abbey's manors (Knowles, p. 96).

in the upper ranges while other levels were assimilated to lesser degrees in the social order.[1]

Boroughs took their place within the feudal order as communal owners of property, owing services and payments as a community, and developed social sanctions which often derived from a pre-feudal age; for instance, under the practice known as Borough English the youngest son inherited, in which case it was the elder son of a merchant or tradesman who was likely to seek an outlet in the law or the church.[2] The corporate body of the borough acted as the guardian of heirs of burgesses who succeeded under age and this had its effect on social habits. Since the powerful court of orphanage of the city of London provided a surety that children's interests and property would be looked after in the event of a father's early death London merchants did not force children into marriage before the age of free consent, nor into their own trade. As a result they were interested in education as a preparation for other careers; already in the late fourteenth century an alderman could suggest that his elder son take up the common law, the younger go to a university or if he wished enter trade.[3] By comparison, gentlemen's heirs had no freedom of choice and early entry into the marriage-market to secure a suitable alliance was general,[4] with consequent effects on the duration of education. Moreover, the feudal form of wardship could be more of a threat than a safeguard since the minor's lands might be exploited and his education neglected by a guardian who had no direct interest in his welfare,[5] a

[1] The status attained by common lawyers, as also the intermingling of clerical and lay rankings, is well illustrated in a table of precedence given in a text-book by the usher of Humphrey, duke of Gloucester. The pope takes precedence of all, followed by emperor and king; the cardinal precedes prince of the blood royal, then come archbishop and royal duke. In the second rank, bishop, marquis and earl are co-equal. In the third come viscount, legate, baron, suffragan bishop, mitred abbot; with the chief baron of the exchequer, the three chief justices and the lord mayor of London. Fourth are the knight's equals: abbot without mitre, priors, deans, archdeacons, the mayor of Calais (the Staple), doctors of divinity. Finally the esquire's equals are doctors of civil and canon law, serjeants-at-law and masters of Chancery; the rest to be placed at the esquire's table being masters of arts, members of religious orders, parsons or vicars with cure, heralds, merchants, gentlemen and gentlewomen (F. J. Furnivall, ed., *Early English Meals and Manners*, E.E.T.S., 1894, pp. 170–1).

[2] Cf. Joan Thirsk, 'Industries in the Countryside', *Essays in the Economic History of Tudor and Stuart England* (Cambridge, 1961), pp. 77–8.

[3] Sylvia Thrupp, *The Merchant Class of Mediaeval London, 1300–1500* (Chicago, 1948), pp. 192, 204–5.

[4] Jacob, pp. 324–6.

[5] Wardship rights became chattels to be sold and were treated as a source of revenue from the thirteenth century (Joel Hurstfield, *The Queen's Wards*, 1958, pp. 4–5).

point that Fortescue conveniently overlooked but which was to become of growing moment in the sixteenth century.

As the towns gained increasing control over their affairs—the administration of justice, rights over markets and trade and eventually hospitals and schools—they encroached on functions which had formerly belonged to the great households and religious communities; this widening experience of municipal government constituted a long process of training for the urban middle class.[1] The fifteenth century was an age when the richer citizens gained the ascendant, government became more organised and oligarchic and incorporation was increasingly sought after[2]—a movement that was to be accelerated at the Reformation. It is at this period that the apprenticeship system became established so that control of the number of apprentices and conditions of binding were used to restrict lucrative trades in the interests of already established men; measures were taken to curb this and other restrictive practices, but it is doubtful whether they had much effect.[3]

As time went on entrants to the better trades were expected to have a reasonable standard of education and this stimulated demands for a more effective schooling than that obtainable from parish clerk or chantry priest. By 1478 the Goldsmiths' Company had a rule that no apprentice be taken 'without he can write and read'. At a higher level regulations made by the gild of scriveners in 1497 refer to apprentices lacking grammar 'wherethrough oftentimes they err, and their acts and feats been incongruous, and not perfectly done to the great reproach and slander of the said fellowship'; it is laid down that every master taking an apprentice should present him for examination before the wardens of the gild and if found wanting the boy must be set 'to grammar school unto such time as he have or by reasonable capacity may have positive grammar'.[4] It is at this time that borough schools begin to come to light in some of the more considerable towns.

[1] G. Unwin, *Studies in Economic History* (1927), pp. 93–7.

[2] M. Weinbaum, *The Incorporation of Boroughs* (Manchester, 1937), pp. 63 ff.

[3] O. J. Dunlop and R. D. Denman, *English Apprenticeship and Child Labour* (New York, 1912), pp. 28 ff., 43–8.

[4] Cited in *The Case of the Free Scriveners of London* (1749), pp. 25–6. Even in provincial towns indentures might include a proviso that an apprentice be put to school; in 1447 a Leicester tailor bound himself to pay for an apprentice's education 'ad scolas literatura' during the first year of his term (*Calendar of Charters and other Documents...Hospital of William Wyggeston at Leicester*, ed. A. Hamilton Thompson, Leicester, 1933, p. 348).

On the whole, however, towns remained relatively small; there were not, as on the continent, highly developed urban communities set in a backward countryside with an impassable barrier between. The key wool and cloth trades took root in rural areas where gild restrictions did not operate and the labour of peasant families could be called upon; for the poorer peasantry now held their lands as copyholders, or existed as cottagers, and could supplement work on the land with spinning or weaving in the home in which even small children were engaged. New centres of population developed, therefore, which in time vied with chartered boroughs, but, London and a few leading ports apart, towns merged into the countryside. Though London merchants dominating overseas trade grew to great wealth, and in provincial centres merchants of the Staple were much richer than the majority of townsmen, these men did not found merchant dynasties as did their counterparts in Italy in different circumstances. Rather, at a time when there was no secure long-term investment except land, they bought up landed property; if they became successfully established on a country estate their descendants ranked as gentry while the family's leading place in the urban community was taken by others.[1]

If merchants could become landlords the gentry were often engaged in producing for the market, and set younger sons to a profession or trade in the towns; an interest in education for secular occupations was a particular bond, among many, between merchants and gentlemen.[2] In general there was considerable fluidity in the middle ranges of the social order, notably in the home counties and midlands; Wales and the northern counties saw much less change. Marriage was a particular aid to advancement in an economic or social sense, status being fair exchange for a dowry provided out of the profits of trade. So, too, was training as a common lawyer at a time when legal business—in connection with dealings in land and arranging of marriages, the supervision of wardships and wills—was steadily expanding. It could on occasion pave the way to a fortune, transforming a yeoman's son

[1] 'The continued mobility of both urban and rural population in the fifteenth and sixteenth centuries is very evident'. Sons of the lesser gentry or yeomen who became established as merchants in a town founded a family which often remained only for two more generations before moving back into the county to take its place among the gentry (W. G. Hoskins, 'English Provincial Towns in the Early Sixteenth Century', reprinted in *Provincial England*, 1963, p. 76).

[2] Thrupp, pp. 160–1, 247.

into a knight who was likely in turn to seek a legal education for more than one son.[1]

In many districts of fifteenth-century England, including outlying counties, there was a considerable number of freeholders who, like the gentry, had established a position at the expense of both the poorer peasantry and the great landlords; sometimes whole villages were composed of free tenants whose forefathers had bought up moieties of manors which had been entirely dismembered. Freeholders held their land by socage tenure, but though a relief might be due when an heir succeeded there was no feudal dependency.[2] Fortescue, comparing the government of England in his day with customs on the continent, had much to say of the small sheep-farmer, his outlook and social contribution. Such men, by comparison with peasants labouring on the land, were 'not very much burdened with the sweat of labour' and so 'more apt and disposed to investigate causes which require searching examination than men who, immersed in agricultural work, have contracted a rusticity of mind from familiarity with the soil'. Here, in his view, lay the basis of the unique English jury system, for in England alone were such men to be found, 'free tenants and many yeomen, sufficient in patrimony to make a jury', whereas in continental states the nobility so dominated society that there was hardly a man of any substance in the villages.[3] So also the yeomanry were of sufficient liveliness of mind to seek education, and schools were to be found not only in boroughs but also in country districts, taught by the priests supported by parochial gilds. Sons of yeomen were often said to provide the backbone of the church.

Another contemporary observer, John Rous—one of the first antiquaries, whose duties as agent to a magnate aroused interest in topographical studies—commented on a negative phenomenon in the countryside. This was the depopulation of many villages, a result not only of the extension of grazing and wool production but also of changes in the location of the cloth industry and the concentration of workers employed by prosperous clothiers in new centres of population.[4] The

[1] William Paston (b. 1378), son of a Norfolk yeoman, attended the inns of court and rose to become a judge; his heir and fourth son were trained in the law (*The Paston Letters*, Everyman ed., p. xvi).

[2] If a minor inherited he became the ward, not of any lord, but according to traditional custom sanctioned by common law of his kindred (Fortescue, p. 107).

[3] *Ibid.* p. 68.

[4] Jacob, pp. 365–9.

obverse side of the picture of prospering farmers, traders, clothiers, is therefore a swelling number of dependent poor. The poverty-stricken peasant, without land to sustain his family, tended to drift into the towns and by the early sixteenth century a third of the population of larger towns could be written off as worth nothing in terms of worldly goods, while another third were wage earners who paid subsidies at the minimum rate. In all, then, up to two-thirds of the urban population lived near or below the poverty line; the top third constituted a social pyramid rising to a needle-like point—through prosperous artificers, tradesmen and professional men to the single merchant who might alone pay up to a third of the subsidy due from the community.[1]

While some of the older chartered boroughs were declining in the fifteenth century, in centres where the wool trade flourished merchants kept house on a generous scale, beautified the streets of their native place with new public buildings and family houses, endowed schools, enlarged churches.[2] The familiar letters of such merchant families as the Stonors and the Celys show that men and women in this walk of life, including apprentices, could read and write; while the Paston letters, passing between members of a family which rose from the peasantry to the status of landed gentry during the century, indicate both literacy and a fund of practical knowledge, if little of academic learning.[3]

English was, of course, the language these people used in their correspondence, as in the business of life. The development of a national language out of a number of regional dialects, which was closely associated with the emergence of a national economy, greatly widened the horizons of the middle class. Up to the fifteenth century, while Latin was the language of scholarship and ecclesiastical affairs French had frequently been used among the upper classes and in branches of business and administration. This was the language used in state offices, legal deeds, petitions, wills, inventories, instructions to reeves and bailiffs. The mayor and aldermen of London even corre-

[1] Hoskins, pp. 83–5.

[2] 'The remarkable line of churches...Chipping Camden, Winchcombe, Northleach Chedworth, Fairford, Cricklade' in the Cotswolds 'pay their tribute to the capitalist entrepreneurs who extended and in some cases rebuilt the villages of an earlier manorial age' (Jacob, p. 647).

[3] Eileen Power, *Mediaeval People* (1951 ed.), pp. 126–8. It has been suggested that perhaps 40 per cent of lay male householders in London could read Latin, many more than this, therefore, English (Thrupp, pp. 157–8).

sponded in French with provincial towns and issued proclamations in that language to citizens of the capital, while French was the language used in schools—the medium through which Latin was taught—until almost the close of the fourteenth century.[1]

Only at this period did English come into its own in pleadings at law and in parliament, at a time when the language was being developed by Langland and Chaucer in poetry, by Wycliffe in prose. Eventually what had been the dialect of the south-eastern region, where both court and capital were situated and the great vernacular writers originated, became transformed into the King's English. In the early decades of the fifteenth century the vernacular gained ground in every quarter. The development of Lollardy, which initially drew considerable support from the gentry and urban middle class, contributed much to its spread as a written language, a development hastened too by incipient national feeling and contemporary hostility towards France. When, in 1455, Bishop Pecock published his refutation of Lollard attacks on the church, *The Repressor of Over Much Blaming of the Clergy*, this was the first important theological work to be written in the vernacular since Anglo-Saxon days. It was an eloquent tribute to the growth to literacy and consciousness of the lay order at large.

It may be noted that Pecock set out to vindicate the church and its teaching under six heads: (i) the use of images, (ii) the going on pilgrimage, (iii) the holding of landed possessions, (iv) the retention of the various ranks of the hierarchy, (v) the framing of ecclesiastical laws with papal and episcopal authority, and (vi) the institution of the religious orders.[2] This list, set out from the opposite angle—as ecclesiastical privileges and practices to be abolished or severely curtailed—constituted the programme of the English Reformation.

(2) *The challenge to the church's monopoly of schoolkeeping*

The spread of literacy among laymen, accompanied by a growing demand for regular schooling, constituted a new challenge to a church which had for centuries monopolised the means to education in this sense. Nor was this merely tacit. There was a direct assault on the monopoly of schoolkeeping exercised by certain of the great religious

[1] Helen Suggett, 'The use of French in England in the later Middle Ages', *T.R.H.S.*, fourth series, XXVIII (1946), pp. 61 ff.

[2] Reginald Pecock, *The Repressor of Over Much Blaming of the Clergy*, ed. C. Babington (1860), I, p. xxiii.

corporations, monastery and secular church alike, and a new initiative in providing schools.

It has usually been assumed by historians of education that the medieval church sponsored an organised system of schools and exercised an unchallenged jurisdiction over educational affairs.[1] But the chief schools sponsored by the church were adjuncts of semi-autonomous religious corporations rather than units in a system under diocesan control. Episcopal powers in practice by no means corresponded to the position as laid down by canon law, and the greater abbeys and cathedral churches exercised wide powers, including ordinary powers. The universities had early encroached on the episcopal right of granting a licence to teach; on the other hand there is no evidence that bishops exercised this ancient prerogative in the later middle ages—it was to be revived under Mary and continued under the Elizabethan settlement.[2] Meanwhile the range of ecclesiastical jurisdiction was progressively narrowed while the powers of the royal courts were correspondingly extended.[3] At the Reformation the operation of canon law and the activities of ecclesiastical courts were curtailed, the church became subject to the crown and there was no longer any question of exclusive control over education.

When an abbey or cathedral claimed the right to a monopoly of schoolkeeping in a certain area this was in much the same sense as towns claimed a monopoly of trade. A corporation had gained the privilege of keeping school and with this went the right of licensing other schoolmasters in the vicinity or preventing them from teaching if they provided undue competition.[4] It was this form of granting

[1] 'For close on eleven hundred years, from 598 to 1670, all educational institutions were under exclusively ecclesiastical control. The law of education was a branch of canon law. The church courts had exclusive jurisdiction over schools and universities and colleges...' (*ECD*, p. xii).

[2] N. Wood, *The Reformation and English Education* (London, 1931), p. 53.

[3] For instance, the common law claimed jurisdiction over advowsons. A ruling of 1343 prohibited the hearing of pleas relating to the patronage of grammar schools in the ecclesiastical courts (J. E. G. de Montmorency, *State Intervention in English Education*, Cambridge, 1902, p. 41).

[4] The abbot of St Albans approved statutes in 1310 which empowered the master of the school sponsored by the abbey to 'suppress, annul, destroy and eradicate all adulterine schools within our territory and jurisdiction, by inhibiting...under pain of excommunication, any person from resorting to or presuming to keep any schools held without the will and assent of the master of our grammar school, within our aforesaid jurisdiction'. The statutes also conferred powers over scholars on the master similar to those granted to universities though on a limited scale (*ECD*, pp. 241–52).

a licence to teach that was the subject of controversy in the fifteenth century. The relevant privileges were upheld by the ecclesiastical courts but appeals to abrogate them were made in the secular courts and to the king in parliament; attempts to break the ecclesiastical monopoly of schoolkeeping were, therefore, one aspect of a wider conflict, endemic for many years, which came to a head at the Reformation.

A considerable extension of educational facilities could, of course, take place without interference. A lay centre of higher education had in fact come into being at the inns of court, quite apart from the established universities, but though churchmen might regard the growing power of common lawyers with reserve and apprehension, as a challenge to ecclesiastical powers on the highest plane, there was nothing to be done to prevent this. Otherwise new facilities for teaching were provided within the existing framework. At Oxford, for instance, private teachers of practical subjects became established in considerable numbers and the university regulated their position in 1432. They provided, for students following the arts course and possibly others, instruction in the art of writing, accounting, elementary French, the drafting of charters, conveyancing—instruction of a kind relevant to various employments, as for example the post of steward in a household.[1]

In the larger towns new demands for education were no doubt met by private teachers in the same way; the scrivener naturally gravitated to teaching of this kind.[2] At the more elementary level it was possible to call further on the services of the parish clerk, who was traditionally expected to teach, or any other clerk who was available. In time, as a result, founders of chantries, hospitals, almshouses, began to make teaching children one of the duties of clerks or chaplains of their foundations. Gilds could also freely initiate schools in newer centres which lacked any major ecclesiastical foundation, while the authorities of boroughs where there had never been an established school could invite a teacher to set up in the town. In this case inducements would be offered, such as a rent-free house, a room in which to teach and a guarantee that no other teacher would be allowed to set up as rival; if the venture was successful a borough school came into being. Thus

[1] *ECD*, pp. 397–9; H. G. Richardson, 'Business Training in Mediaeval Oxford', *American Historical Review*, XLVI (1940–1), pp. 259–60; *idem*, 'An Oxford Teacher of the Fifteenth Century', *Bulletin of the John Rylands Library*, XXIII (1939), pp. 436–9.

[2] Thrupp, p. 159.

in Hull by the middle of the fifteenth century 'the schoolhouse is town property, repaired and furnished at the corporation's expense, and the master is a public official wearing the town livery, dwelling in one of the corporation's houses and receiving an annual stipend from the chamberlains'; this last being small, in the nature of a retainer, he charges fees on a scale 'fixed by the corporation and in order to maintain his income at an acceptable level...possesses a monopoly of Latin teaching, both in grammar and reading, within the borough'.[1]

The monopoly of teaching exercised by some of the great secular churches had originated in a similar way. In theory all the greater churches were supposed to provide free teaching; in practice fees were universally charged both in their grammar schools and for granting a licence to teach to other masters. It devolved on the chancellor of the chapter to appoint a master to teach grammar, who was usually awarded some office in the church carrying a small stipend which could then be made up by fees;[2] the precentor, responsible for the music of the church, held the right to appoint a master to teach singing. Where cathedral chapters had an extensive jurisdiction and were highly organised these officials gained powers to license masters in these categories teaching elsewhere. The area over which rights were exercised varied and there is direct evidence in only a few cases. The best documented example is that of Lincoln where the chancellor enforced a monopoly over grammar teaching in the county (or archdeaconry) as well as in the city, and the precentor exercised a like control over song schools. Besides assertion of these rights against outsiders there was even strife at Lincoln over the respective rights (and dues) of the choristers' master and the grammar master of the cathedral in the early fifteenth century.[3]

When the matter was internal to the church, bishops, aware of the need to extend education and protect the rights of parishes, were

[1] John Lawson, *A Town Grammar School through Six Centuries* (Oxford, 1963), pp. 17–19. The scale of fees fixed in 1454 was '8*d*. a quarter for teaching grammar (*grammatica*) and 6*d*. a quarter for teaching reading (*lectura*)'; the petty scholars learning the ABC and graces were specifically excluded from the monopoly.

[2] K. Edwards, *The English Secular Cathedrals in the Middle Ages* (Manchester, 1949), p. 197. Early endowments were of the 'magister scolarum', an office which evolved into that of chancellor of the chapter, the endowments then financing this office, not a school or master. No English secular cathedral (let alone collegiate church) operated the Lateran decree of 1215 requiring that one of the prebends be reserved to finance a grammar master to teach freely.

[3] Edwards, p. 200; *ECD*, pp. 387–93.

prepared to resist the claims of old and influential foundations. Thus in 1439 Bishop Alnwick—who was much engaged at this time in regulating violent disputes within the Lincoln chapter—issued a firm order at a visitation. The precentor 'might appoint and prefer' the song-master in the city and others within his purview in the county, but he was not to interfere with schools

which certain curates hold for their own parishioners, in their own parishes, or which are held by parish clerks in the same, for we will not that such persons be hindered by the precentor from educating and instructing the small boys of their parishes in song.[1]

It was another matter when outsiders stressed the harm done by the monopoly of teaching and sought a remedy in the secular courts; this churchmen were bound to resist. The issue was mainly fought out in London where the population was rapidly growing and masters set up to teach Latin grammar without seeking a licence from the three ancient foundations which held a monopoly in the city—the cathedral church of St Paul's, the church of St Mary-le-Bow and the royal free chapel of St Martin's-le-Grand. In 1393 several schoolmasters were summoned before the ecclesiastical courts on these grounds, but they retaliated by seeking an inhibition in the mayor's court and an upholding of their right to keep school without the assent of the officials concerned. This outright challenge brought a response from the ecclesiastical authorities at the highest level, in the form of a petition to the crown from the archbishop of Canterbury, the bishop of London and the chief dignitaries of the three churches; it was requested that the mayor and aldermen of London be commanded not to act in the matter to the prejudice of the ecclesiastical courts.[2] There is no record of the outcome but the case suggests a readiness not merely to evade but to undermine ecclesiastical jurisdiction in this matter.

Not long after, in 1411, the judges of the king's bench pronounced on the question when a case was brought before them on a plea of trespass. On this occasion a schoolmaster and his assistant, appointed by the abbot and convent of Llanthony Abbey to teach in Gloucester, sought damages against a rival master; they pleaded serious loss through competition which had forced them to reduce their fees from 3*s.* 4*d.*

[1] A. Hamilton Thompson, *Song Schools in the Middle Ages* (1942), p. 14. There is evidence that the precentor successfully exercised this right, at least in Lincoln, in 1305 (*ECD*, p. 237).

[2] de Montmorency, p. 41.

or 2*s*. to 1*s*. a quarter. The common lawyers expressed astonishment that they should be asked to penalise a man for teaching youth which 'is a virtuous and charitable thing to do, helpful to the people, for which he cannot be punished by our law'. There was no question of trespass since the abbot's title did not derive from any freehold or estate; the question as to whether or not he held a monopoly over education in the sense claimed was a 'spiritual' matter, one for the ecclesiastical courts, but there was no remedy at common law and the case was dismissed. It would, it was adjudged, 'be contrary to reason that a master could be disturbed from holding a school where he pleased save in the case of a university or school of ancient foundation'. The common law was, then, on the side of the laity, against ecclesiastical pretensions to enforce a monopoly of teaching, and this evidently served as a test case since no other figures.[1] The next evidence relates to attempts to eliminate the privileges of schools of ancient foundation.

Meanwhile in 1406 the right to attend school had been generally extended by a statute of labourers. Formerly those of villein status must obtain their lord's consent before setting children to school, and this affected men who had long ceased to be serfs but were still legally villeins. Under the statute men with less than 20*s*. a year were forbidden to apprentice children to a craft, a measure designed to safeguard the agricultural labour force;[2] but it was laid down that 'every man or woman of what state or condition that he be shall be free to set their son or daughter to take learning at any school that pleaseth them within the realm'. It would almost seem that this provision served as an invitation to defy any monopoly of teaching. Certainly much the same phraseology was used by the common council of Coventry, one of the most flourishing boroughs at this time but partly under monastic rule, when it questioned the right of the abbot of the cathedral priory to interfere with plans in the town in 1439.[3]

[1] de Montmorency, pp. 50–9, where this judgement, so often misread, is explained (for the text, pp. 241–2).

[2] *Ibid.* p. 29. London evaded this condition and eventually gained exemption from it, an indication that apprentices often came from the poorer strata at this time (Thrupp, p. 215).

[3] A grammar master had been invited and accommodation provided but this evidently produced the customary objections; the council, ceding the prior's right 'to occupy a school of grammar if he like to teach his brethren and children of the almonry', argues that he should 'not grudge nor move the contrary but that every man of this city be at his free choice to set his child to school to what teacher of grammar that he liketh, as reason asketh' (*The Coventry Leet Book*, ed. M. D. Harris, E.E.T.S. 1907–13, p. 190).

Whatever the desire to maintain ancient privileges there were no longer only three but five recognised schools in London by the 1440's, one additional one being connected with the newly constituted hospital of St Anthony. This comes to light in 1445 when the ecclesiastical authorities again called on the crown for aid in stemming the tide of unauthorised teaching. On this occasion it was affirmed that 'many and divers persons' insufficiently learned in grammar were presuming to hold 'common grammar schools', and laid down that five schools were quite sufficient, there must be no others. This is set out and assented to in an ordinance issued by Henry VI, who was much influenced by his ecclesiastical advisers, and all citizens were commanded not to 'trouble nor hinder the masters of the said schools...but rather to help and assist them'.[1]

Probably at the first opportunity, in February of the following year, a concerted protest against this edict was presented to the king in parliament. This time it came from churchmen of some standing, namely the rectors of four city churches, who, it must be assumed, spoke also for leading London citizens. Their plea was a general one, for the needs of a capital with a growing population which acted as a magnet to the young; lack of schools meant that not only the clergy, to their shame, were often ignorant, but also the laity who needed to be competently learned for various callings.

Evidence relating to the preceding years shows that teachers setting up in the city had found support and made a place for themselves. There was at least one group of scholars in London in the early decades of the century who, besides teaching school, met together to discuss matters of scholarly and literary interest. One of these, John Seward—educated at Oxford and in contact with other university scholars—figures as master of the school connected with St Peter's, Cornhill, for many years, up to his death (at the age of 71) in 1435.[2] A colleague was William Relyk who taught at a tavern in Lombard Street which

[1] *ECD*, pp. 416–18. Six years earlier Henry VI had proclaimed a monopoly of teaching for the school of his college at Eton within a ten miles radius (*ibid.* pp. 413–15).

[2] V. H. Galbraith, 'John Seward and his Circle', *Mediaeval & Renaissance Studies*, I (1943), pp. 85 ff. One of the king's wards was at school at Cornhill in 1419–20 (*ECD*, p. 397). St Peter's, Cornhill, was under the patronage of the common council and the church had a library attached; Stow records Seward's mastership in 1422 as also that in his own day a grammar school was held in this building (John Stow, *Survey of London*, Everyman ed., pp. 174–5).

was later owned by an influential London alderman, Simon Eyre, who was interested in promoting education.[1]

The historian of London enumerates various benefactions at this period which bear on education; notably the funds left by Richard Whittington, mercer and three times lord mayor, to build a library at the Guildhall and establish a college of priests, and by John Carpenter, clerk to the common council, for the maintenance and education of four poor boys.[2] The wills of other citizens also evince a growing interest in education, sums quite often being left to maintain sons at school and one testator in ten naming as executor a city priest who might be expected to assist in such a matter.[3] In 1439 William Bingham, rector of a city parish and closely acquainted with Carpenter and other leading citizens, established a college at Cambridge intended to provide teachers of grammar for local schools; associated with this initiative were William Lichfield, former fellow of Peterhouse, rector of All Hallows the Great, and Gilbert Worthington, rector of St Andrew's Holborn.[4] These were two of the four rectors who drew up the petition to the crown in 1446, calling for an end to the monopoly of teaching in the capital; the other two being John Neal, master of St Thomas Acon Hospital under the patronage of the Mercers' Company, and John Cote, rector of St Peter's Cornhill.

London, their petition ran,[5] had 'a great multitude of young people, not only born and brought up in the same city, but also of many other parts of this land', who came there for work and schooling. There must be sufficient schools, otherwise the interests of youth were grievously damaged for the benefit of two or three schoolmasters: for

> where there is a great number of learners, and few teachers, and all the learners be compelled to go to the same few teachers, and to none other, the masters wax rich in money and the learners poor in cunning, as experience openly sheweth, against all virtue and order of weal public.

[1] Eyre built Leadenhall chapel and on his death left a large sum to establish a college of priests there, three of whom were to teach grammar, writing and song, but the directive was not carried out by his executors (Stow, pp. 139–40).

[2] Stow, pp. 99–100. Carpenter was executor of Whittington's will (1421) responsible for carrying out the directive; his own bequest took effect in 1440, the four boys probably being choristers of the Guildhall chapel (A. E. Douglas-Smith, *The City of London School*, Oxford, 1937, pp. 9–11, 24).

[3] Thrupp, pp. 160, 187–8.

[4] A. H. Lloyd, *The Early History of Christ's College* (Cambridge, 1934), pp. 11, 397, 399–400.

[5] *ECD*, pp. 418–20.

It was requested that four additional schools be established, the four rectors concerned and their successors being empowered to nominate the masters, and the royal assent was given so long as the bishop of London or the archbishop of Canterbury were consulted. It has been maintained that this order must have been ineffective since the ecclesiastical authorities would never have given their consent, while there is no evidence that the schools were established.[1] The failure of the petition has likewise been cited as evidence of the inadequacy of provision in London—such schools as there were being 'too hopelessly unimpressive to elicit any considerable help from merchant donors' who were beginning at this time to endow schools elsewhere.[2] But it is reasonable to suppose that influential merchants would have found a way of remedying matters nearer home and this démarche probably marks a turning point in a long struggle to break down restrictive monopolies.

There were, in fact, schools connected with three of the churches concerned at a later date, if they had not been in existence before.[3] Moreover, in subsequent years no more is heard of any monopoly of teaching in London and the schools of the three ancient foundations which claimed this right had either disappeared or been replaced by 1510. They were presumably open to competition not only from other recognised schools—and St Anthony's was one that came particularly to the fore at this time[4]—but also from private masters on whom there can no longer have been the same restrictions. There is no good reason to suppose that education in London was at a low ebb in the second half of the fifteenth century.[5]

[1] A. F. Leach, 'The Ancient Schools in the City of London', in W. Besant, *London The City* (1910), p. 428. [2] W. K. Jordan, *The Charities of London* (1960), p. 210.

[3] As St Peter's, Cornhill, evidently was—this was rated by later chroniclers among leading schools (*Stow's Annals*, ed. E. How, 1631, p. 1067). The other two were St Thomas Acon, refounded as the Mercers' School in 1540, and St Andrew's Holborn (M. McDonnell, *Annals of St Paul's School*, 1959, p. 28).

[4] There is an account of St Anthony's school by Leach (*loc. cit.* pp. 407 ff.) who also bears witness to the lack of information about those of St Martin's-le-Grand and St Mary-le-Bow. St Paul's was 'scola nullius plane momenti', in Colet's words, in the first decade of the sixteenth century—manifestly of no importance (McDonnell, p. 31).

[5] There was, perhaps, less need for endowments here than elsewhere. Apart from schools in the city—which held regular disputations somewhat on the university model at St Bartholomew's, Smithfield, and Holy Trinity, Aldgate—there were others connected with monastic houses without the walls; for instance the almonry school of Westminster Abbey which was attended by sons of citizens and for which a new schoolhouse was built in 1422 (L. E. Tanner, *Westminster School*, 1954, p. 13).

Ancient foundations in other parts of the country seem also progressively to have relinquished attempts to maintain a monopoly, even the conduct of their own schools. The chapter of Beverley Minster was energetically suppressing adulterine masters in the fourteenth century; in the fifteenth the master of Beverley School itself was not an official of the minster but a layman, steward of one of the gilds and a governor of the town. Another major collegiate church with some fifty clergy, Ripon, evidently did not control the school at the Reformation; this, held in the town, seems to have been administered by the leading gild to which the schoolhouse belonged.[1] Elsewhere borough schools became more firmly established. At Ipswich, as at Hull, a master subject to the authority of the borough taught throughout the fifteenth century, taking fees on an approved scale; the school was endowed in 1483, as were other borough schools already in existence at this time.[2]

In towns other than chartered boroughs the tasks of local administration were undertaken by gilds. It is necessary to differentiate leading local gilds, which exercised such functions, both from craft gilds and from a wide variety of lesser fraternities which merely maintained one priest, or if very small contributed to keep a light before an altar.[3] The larger gilds drew revenues from lands and tenements which were administered by the masters, or wardens; after outgoings for repairs, the stipend of chaplains was usually a first charge on these and then various payments towards the repair of roads, bridges, seawalls, or for aid to the poor. In Essex, East Anglia, the Cotswolds, where there were flourishing towns engaged in the wool and cloth trades, one of the gild chaplains often kept school.[4] When a wealthy member left an

[1] A. F. Leach, *Early Yorkshire Schools*, I (1899), pp. xliii–xlviii; *VCH Yorks.* I, pp. 426–7, 432–3. The process can be seen at work at Lincoln at a later date (*VCH Lincs.* II, pp. 434 ff.).

[2] I. E. Gray and W. E. Potter, *Ipswich School, 1400–1950* (Ipswich, 1950), p. 5; *ECD*, p. 423. In 1477 the scale of fees was 10*d.* a quarter for grammarians (8*d.* if they were burgesses' sons), 8*d.* a quarter for those learning the psalter, 4*d.* for those entering on the primer, petties learning their alphabet being excluded.

[3] The best brief discussion of a complex question remains that in W. J. Ashley, *An Introduction to English Economic History and Theory* (1893), II, pp. 136–9, cf. H. F. Westlake, *The Parish Gilds of Mediaeval England* (1919). Some urban gilds were responsible for pageants or mystery plays, others simply groups living in a parish and centred on its church, often formed to maintain a particular altar or chapel which had been falling into neglect (A. Hamilton Thompson, *The English Clergy and their Organisation in the Later Middle Ages*, Oxford, 1947, p. 135, cf. Jacob, pp. 400–5).

[4] At Finchingfield and Maldon in Essex; Eye and Lavenham, in Suffolk; Boston and Louth in Lincolnshire (*VCH Essex*, II, pp. 516, 666; *VCH Suffolk*, II, p. 338; *VCH Lincs.* II, pp. 453, 460).

endowment to provide a stipend for a special schoolmaster, or a sum to erect a schoolhouse, the gild school became firmly established; such, for instance, was the case at Stratford-on-Avon in the 1480's.[1] Elsewhere schools might simply be held in the gild's hall and in this case, as with borough schools, there is no record of a foundation.

In rural areas men came together in parochial gilds, contributing to a common stock which might consist of lands or money but also of a herd of cattle or flock of sheep. These also maintained a priest where funds allowed who could be called upon to teach the children of the parish. Such, at any rate, was the case by the 1540's; for instance, at Eccleshall in Staffordshire two small gilds were then maintaining a priest with a stipend of just over £3 who taught children freely.[2] It may be added that parishes universally held a fund deriving from bequests and collections for the use of the church, a first call on this being for repairs to the fabric of the nave for which parishioners were responsible; this was administered by the two churchwardens and if repairs did not swallow it up was used for other purposes.[3] There was here an aspect of parish organisation ready to hand for development, and when gilds ceased to figure schoolmasters were often paid out of a general parish fund; as also, where communal lands were held, out of the income of the 'town estate'.

Individual founders also endowed chantry priests at particular altars or in the chapels of parish churches. The development of the chantry movement has been ascribed in part to the increasing emphasis laid by the church on the doctrine of the last judgement and on Christ as an unrelenting judge of sinners; the concomitant was the cult of the Virgin Mary and the saints who might be called upon to intercede with this stern judge on men's behalf.[4] Accordingly particular priests were endowed to perform this office, to offer specified prayers at

[1] *ECD*, pp. 377–87. A schoolmaster was endowed as such at Chipping Norton in 1450, another at Chipping Camden in the 1480's (*VCH Oxon.* II, p. 467; *VCH Glos.* II, p. 418).

[2] *ESR*, II, pp. 201, 209. This was evidently on a very different scale from the regular schoolmaster kept by the Palmers' Gild of Ludlow at a stipend of £10 (*ibid.* pp. 185–6). The point is made because Leach, when analysing the chantry certificates, threw together every reference to a gild; since, with one or two exceptions, he only printed certificates mentioning a school his often quoted statement (Unwin, p. 99; Jacob, p. 667) that of 33 gilds investigated 28 kept grammar schools is hardly meaningful. There is no mention of provincial craft gilds maintaining schools.

[3] Hamilton Thompson, *The English Clergy*, p. 130.

[4] A. R. Myers, *The Later Middle Ages* (1956 ed.), pp. 160–1.

altars dedicated to the saints or in Lady Chapels. But the majority of funds were left only for a term of years, not in perpetuity, and by the fifteenth century the impulse was perceptibly waning.[1]

Only a small proportion of chantry priests in this category was bound by a foundation deed to keep school.[2] But others engaged in teaching where there was a demand for their services, though their qualifications, like their stipends in many cases, may have been small enough and they usually charged fees. That schools were connected with chantries does not, however, imply that they were under ecclesiastical control.[3] The funds of chantries were usually administered by lay feoffees; gild chaplains and incumbents of the many 'priest's services' were stipendiaries who received a wage and were removable at will—canonical institution was not required any more than it was for domestic chaplains employed in a household. Since stipendiaries were quite often required not only to teach but to assist in parochial duties some efforts were made to bring them within the discipline and system of taxation of the church, but without much success. It seems probable that the control exercised by laymen over the revenues and incumbents of chantries contributed to preparing the ground for the Reformation.[4] Certainly the civic officials of York in the fifteenth century had no doubt about their rights, claiming on one occasion when rebutting ecclesiastical intervention: 'all the chantries of this

[1] One calculation gives some 280 chantries established in London parish churches by individual founders in the fourteenth century but only 133 founded from 1403 onwards; of all these barely 200 were being maintained by the 1540's, since besides those which had ceased others had fallen into desuetude (G. H. Cook, *Mediaeval Chantries and Chantry Chapels*, 1947, p. 39). Much the same pattern emerges in the case of obits endowed at York Minster. There were in the thirteenth century 15, in the first half of the fourteenth century 17, in the second half about 50, throughout the fifteenth century 24, in 1500–35 only 4. By 1548 at least 25 chantries had lapsed, 18 remained (F. Harrison, *Life in a Mediaeval College*, 1952, pp. 165, 197).

[2] E.g. in 1446 Robert Gryndour settled lands to maintain a priest at Newland, to pray for his soul and teach a grammar school. The stipend was £11 but the incumbent might take the usual fees of 8*d*. a quarter from those learning grammar, 4*d*. from those learning to read; he was also bound to maintain a scholar as assistant, providing his keep, and to distribute 5*s*. 4*d*. annually to the poor (*ESR*, II, pp. 82–4). Provisions were rarely as detailed as this.

[3] The registry of the archbishop of York shows 'little concern about the numerous chantry priests who...conducted small schools, and there is nothing to show whether they were expected to be licensed or not, or to exhibit at visitations' (J. S. Purvis, ed., *Educational Records*, York, 1959, p. 2).

[4] K. L. Wood-Legh, 'Some Aspects of the History of Chantries in the Later Middle Ages', *T.R.H.S.*, fourth series, XXVIII (1946), p. 60.

city have been and are founded by the citizens and notabilities of this city: therefore both the priests of this city and its suburbs, having chantries, are the special orators of the citizens, their patrons and masters'.[1] The logical outcome of this attitude is to be observed in the next century when, to relieve a hard-pressed exchequer, nine chantries were suppressed and their funds turned to civic uses—this nearly a decade before the passage of the first chantries act.[2]

The educational benefactions of London merchants during the fifteenth century—made, as was the custom, at their birthplace, which was frequently a provincial town or township—usually took the form of endowing a chantry priest and making teaching one of his duties. There is one notable exception, the endowment made by William Sevenoaks in 1432 to maintain a master 'sufficiently advanced and expert in the science of grammar, B.A., by no means in holy orders, to keep a grammar school' and teach all poor boys freely.[3] But this, which ties in with developments in London itself at the time, finds no other parallel. In 1487 Sir Edmund Shaw of the Goldsmiths' Company was content to endow only a chantry school with the proviso that the master be an honest priest, 'a discreet man, and cunning in grammar'.[4] At the turn of the century the emphasis begins to change and some merchant founders establish schools more tenuously connected with chantry observances, under the governance of their own livery company or a specially constituted governing body. At this period such schools were not intended to serve a parish, let alone the needy poor; rather it was for the sons of merchants and gentlemen that founders wished to provide, or at the least respectable citizens—though some of these might qualify as poor. The school founded in 1503 at Macclesfield by Sir John Percival, rich merchant tailor and onetime lord mayor, was to amend the shortage of teachers in the district and provide teaching in grammar for 'gentlemen's sons and other good men's children of the town and country thereabouts'. The school at Cromer, placed under the Goldsmiths' Company in 1505 by Sir Bartholomew Rede, was designed 'for gentlemen's sons and good men's

[1] Jacob, p. 404.

[2] A. G. Dickens, *Lollards and Protestants in the Diocese of York, 1509–1558* (Oxford, 1959), p. 206. There was also direct disciplining of chantry priests; the London courts, empowered to impose fines or imprisonment on the lesser clergy, did so on occasion for idleness and neglect of duty (Thrupp, pp. 186–7).

[3] *ECD*, p. 401.

[4] B. Varley, *History of Stockport Grammar School* (Manchester, 1957), p. 23.

children and especially poor men's children'; the master was to be an M.A. and preferably educated at Eton or Winchester.[1]

In these various ways laymen established an increasing stake in education and the monopoly of teaching exercised by ancient ecclesiastical foundations had been broken well before the close of the century. All this explains why John Colet could found, in place of the cathedral school which had for centuries dominated teaching in London, a public school placed squarely under the control of the leading city company. It was also in the first decade of the sixteenth century that the town of Bridgnorth set its school on a firm foundation, laying down that all children seeking education must attend it; that is, no priest might keep school, except for one child to help him say mass, on pain of a fine, but all children must go to the common school of the borough.[2] So in one town at least the practice of centuries was reversed by the assertion of a lay monopoly of schoolkeeping at the expense of the church.

(3) *The church, collegiate foundations and the universities*

While the standard of lay education steadily rose during the later middle ages there was no like improvement in the education of the clergy.[3] Little has so far been said about recruitment to the church and there is not much information about the background of the majority of parish priests. The way to a good living was to gain the interest of a patron, and 'the university student and rising clerk sought out those who could maintain or "exhibit" them by presenting them to benefices'.[4] But many looked to enter the church who could not hope to reach a university, while there were innumerable benefices too poor to attract those who had acquired an education. The poverty of the parish clergy can be overestimated—there were men of some status and learning among incumbents in the fifteenth century;[5] but it remains true that hundreds of parish churches were appropriated to religious corporations which accordingly received all the revenues and paid only a small fixed stipend to a priest to serve the cure. This had become a major abuse, whereby ancient foundations were underpinned at the expense of the parishes, but it continued throughout the

[1] Jordan, *Charities of London*, pp. 221–2; D. Wilmot, *A Short History of the Grammar School, Macclesfield* (Macclesfield, 1910).

[2] *ECD*, p. 439.

[3] G. R. Potter, 'Education in the Fourteenth and Fifteenth Centuries', *Cambridge Mediaeval History*, VIII (1936), p. 698.

[4] Jacob, p. 338.

[5] *Ibid.* pp. 286–8.

century; by the Reformation, to take two examples, 392 of the 622 parish churches in Yorkshire and half the 628 churches of Lincolnshire were exploited in this way.[1] Another anomaly was that, while there were diminishing opportunities of obtaining a competent benefice and many parishes were poorly served, auxiliary chantry priests had been endowed in considerable numbers to maintain private masses; though, on the other hand, 'priest's services' were quite often established specifically to provide assistance for an incumbent serving a large cure—that is to say, some of those classified as chantry priests acted as curates.

The poorer clergy have been described as the 'ecclesiastical proletariat'; most were 'ordained on titles provided by religious houses and they progressed from being chaplains of chantries to employment as parish priests with a vicarage as the summit of their practicable ambitions'.[2] In other words the monasteries provided one of the main means to entering the priesthood by dispensing benefices to those seeking ordination and, since the educational standard set was not high, it may well be that the necessary instruction was often gained, together with the interest that would lead to preferment, in almonry schools.[3] The almonries were at the gates of monasteries, outside the precinct proper, and schools held there could be attended by boys from the locality as well as those maintained by the house. This was also one way of recruitment to the religious orders themselves.[4]

It is usually affirmed that regulars were uninterested in teaching and unable to engage in it outside the precinct, but the Augustinians quite often appointed one of the canons to serve the cure of churches appropriated to the house, particularly in outlying counties, and there is indirect evidence that regulars acted as masters of schools.[5] The strictly

[1] Hamilton Thompson, *The English Clergy*, p. 115.

[2] R. L. Storey, *Thomas Langley and the Bishopric of Durham, 1406–37* (1961), p. 181.

[3] *Visitations*, I, p. 22; Knowles, p. 409; cf. *The Book of William Morton, Almoner of Peterborough Monastery 1448–67*, ed. C. N. L. Brooke, Northants Record Soc. XVI (1954), p. xxvi.

[4] Bradwell Priory was ordered at a visitation to maintain 'some teachable children' on 'the broken meat of your tables' and instruct them 'in reading, song and the other elementary branches of knowledge, that they may serve the monks at the celebration of masses and be admitted as brethren...of the said priory according to their manners and deserts' (*Visitations*, I, p. 22).

[5] In 1515 Bishop Hugh Oldham stipulated that the master of a school in Lancashire should be 'a fit person, secular or regular, learned and fit to be master' (A. A. Mumford, *The Manchester Grammar School*, 1929, p. 471). It was laid down that the master of

enclosed monastery, it may be recalled, was a product of the Counter-Reformation, an amendment of the prevailing practice for monks to be too much in the world. When bishops inquired into the provision of education at visitations it was sometimes found that obligations were generally neglected; there was no teacher of grammar for the novices at St Mary's Abbey, Leicester, in 1440, nor one in the town 'where the abbot is bound to furnish such a teacher...for the instruction both of the clerks of the almonry and others in the neighbourhood'.[1] At Kyme Priory the young canons were instructed in grammar in the nave of the priory church, which served also as a parish church, though they had to pay for the privilege out of their *peculium*.[2] But an additional endowment could be gained to support a master to teach both novices and boys in the almonry; as at Evesham in 1462 when the diocesan bishop authorised appropriation of yet another parish church to maintain a master of grammar, 'very necessary and very much in request to teach the monks, especially the novices of the said monastery, and other boys and youths, in the same'.[3] The number of boys maintained by the larger houses tended to increase at this time because of the growing demand for boy singers in the churches.

It was once supposed that monasteries were the only educational centres throughout the middle ages; it has since been held that their contribution was negligible by comparison with that of secular churches. But the greater houses, besides financing houses for scholars at Oxford and maintaining almonry schools, sometimes controlled other local schools and provided accommodation for the master, or acted as trustees of school endowments with the right to present the masters. A rapid glance across England gives an idea of the distribution of foundations, all of which administered education in one or another of these ways. Moving south from the Vale of Evesham there were houses of Benedictines or Augustinians at Worcester, Evesham, Tewkesbury, Winchcombe, Gloucester, Cirencester, Bath, Bristol, and further west at Bridgewater and Sherborne. Moving north through the midlands there were Reading, Abingdon and Bicester, Bedford, Coventry, Leicester and Derby. In the fenland and East Anglia were Peterborough, Ely, Norwich and Bury St Edmunds, and further south

Blackburn chantry school must be 'a secular and no regular priest', implying that the regulars also served chantries (G. A. Stocks, ed., *Records of Blackburn Grammar School*, Chetham Society, 1909, p. xv).

[1] *Visitations*, II, i, p. 208.

[2] *Ibid.* pp. 169, 171; cf. Purvis, p. 11.

[3] *VCH Worcs.* IV, p. 500.

the great houses of Colchester and St Albans, Westminster and Canterbury. In the north-west a wealthy foundation such as Furness Abbey, with its numerous dependencies, exercised an influence not only in Lancashire but also Yorkshire, Cumberland and Westmorland, while in the north-east Durham had an extensive jurisdiction.

Because of the predominance of the monastic order in an earlier age, eight of the seventeen cathedrals were served by monks up to the Reformation so that there were only nine secular cathedrals, several of them comparatively distant.[1] It should be emphasised again that these were served by communities bound to maintain a continuous round of services, as were the regulars, while 'outside church the interests of a corporation whose members were by their training for the most part better lawyers than theologians were occupied largely by matters of financial and legal business'.[2] Much the same was true of collegiate churches. It was forcibly argued by Leach that these were the mainstay of education up to the Reformation, indeed that they approximated to colleges at the universities and universally administered grammar and elementary (or song) schools as well. But, though evidence of schools is forthcoming in some cases, in general prebends were disposed of within a system of patronage which neither favoured the cause of learning nor an interest in sponsoring local education, beyond assuring established rights and dues.[3] Since the majority of canons were non-resident, ancient collegiate churches, particularly those which originated as royal free chapels, often had little corporate life or local influence.[4] On the other hand, a few of the large ones and the cathedrals accumulated

[1] Besides York, Lincoln, Salisbury, London (St Paul's), there were lesser bodies at Lichfield, Chichester and more distantly Wells, Exeter, Hereford—the last remained exempt from episcopal visitation until well after the Reformation (Edwards, pp. 133–4). Three large collegiate churches—Beverley, Ripon and Southwell—acted as proto-cathedrals in the vast diocese of York.

[2] Such as care of the church fabric, building projects, the management of large endowments and estates, defence of the rights of the church against importunate litigants, the exercise of jurisdiction over tenants—all things which, 'emerging from and dependent upon the main object for which the church was founded, implied a preoccupation with interests which, highly local and circumscribed...were mainly secular' (Hamilton Thompson, *The English Clergy*, p. 98).

[3] As bishop of Durham, Thomas Langley disposed of all the 36 prebends of the five collegiate churches in the diocese; the only graduates preferred were canon lawyers needed in diocesan administration, otherwise those presented were officials of his household or candidates favoured by influential local magnates (Storey, pp. 176, 179).

[4] Hamilton Thompson, *The English Clergy*, pp. 81–2.

dozens of lesser members, to become primarily communities of minor clergy ruled by the small nucleus of resident canons who held the chief offices. The absentee canons paid a vicar-choral to take their place in choir and the vicars, their numbers thus swollen, sometimes formed corporations of their own to defend their particular interests; there were also many chantry priests serving altars besides clerks of various grades and choristers.

This was a community in need of education and cathedral grammar schools—though usually held in the town rather than the close and acting as a local school—evidently provided to a considerable extent for members of the foundation; in any case clerks and younger vicars were often required to attend the grammar school.[1] As for the 'song schools' these catered particularly for boy choristers, who were increasingly employed at this time, and usually provided for their education in grammar as well as singing.[2] Since a body of young choristers needed supervision there were some moves to provide a special house in the close with a resident master to supervise upbringing; at Wells Cathedral, for instance, where an elaborate régime was laid down.[3]

Some of the later collegiate churches also had their choristers but these were usually boarded with the canons and visitation injunctions suggest that their education often went by default. The Newarke College, Leicester—a rich, semi-royal foundation initiated in 1330—had licence (like other royal chapels) to choose for its six choristers 'boys that are fit and learned in song and compel them to do service'; it fell to the sacrist to supervise these boys but in 1440 'the choristers, roaming about as it were without a leader, spent their time gadding about and in other unruly deeds, making no progress in virtues'.[4] There was no school of any sort connected with this college. In so far as such foundations did sometimes provide elementary instruction for local inhabitants it was given by a minor clerk, or a bellringer with

[1] Edwards, pp. 196–7, 287.

[2] The song school 'fluctuated throughout its history between the standing of a school of music and a grammar or preparatory school. It was never an elementary school in the modern sense, a type of different origin' (J. W. Adamson in *The Legacy of the Middle Ages*, ed. C. G. Crump and E. F. Jacob, Oxford, 1926, p. 256).

[3] Edwards, p. 322.

[4] A. Hamilton Thompson, *History of...the New College in the Newarke, Leicester* (Leicester, 1937), pp. 115, 183–4. In the view of the author, who spent many years studying the history of collegiate churches, 'there is none which presents so complete a picture of the life of a college of secular canons in theory and practice' as this.

time on his hands, just as elsewhere chantry priests were called upon to teach.[1]

In the fifteenth century there were added new foundations which have sometimes been ranked with collegiate churches but should more properly be regarded as multiple chantries. In other words, while lesser men established a chantry with one or at most two priests, kings, bishops and noblemen founded on a lavish scale, sometimes erecting special chapels for their tombs and endowing whole 'colleges' of priests to pray for their souls. Lay nobles, on occasion, adopted a practical approach, endowing foundations which could take over the charge of retired retainers as monasteries had been forced to do.[2] But bishops were inclined to see the collegiate pattern in a traditional light, as a way of bringing scattered chantry priests together under discipline and educating them, so that they in turn might be useful teachers.[3]

Colleges of priests were usually superimposed on a parish church, adapted and enlarged for the purpose, and there was at this time a development of choral music which required the services of trained musicians; consequently a 'master of the choristers' figures on some foundations—but this was a professional musician with the duty of training the whole choir, not a schoolmaster. Sometimes a local school was taken over. At Higham Ferrars, for instance, a school held in a chantry chapel adjacent to the church was incorporated with the collegiate body established by Henry Chichele, archbishop of Canterbury from 1414 to 1443; this consisted of eight chaplains, four clerks, six choristers, for whom special quarters were built round a quadrangle, on a pattern also adopted in university towns.[4] Such foundations

[1] Sometimes the duty was laid down. A small college at Sibthorpe (1342) was required to employ a clerk instructed in reading and song to serve the altars, wait on the chaplains, ring the bells, sleep in the church, and teach small boys of the parish and any others who wanted to learn their letters for a reasonable fee; his wages were 13*s.* 4*d.* (Hamilton Thompson, *Song Schools*, pp. 22–3).

[2] E.g. the 'college' at Staindrop, Durham, founded in 1412 by an earl of Warwick for 8 chaplains, 4 clerks, 6 esquires, 6 yeomen, 6 other poor men, to which three parish churches were appropriated (Storey, p. 188).

[3] 'Desiring with all my heart...to reform the chantry priests of the church', ran Archbishop Rotherham's deed founding a small college in 1483, 'who, hitherto commoning and lodging in different places to the scandal of themselves and of the church, have been given over to ease and idleness, we decree...that they shall live in my college' and there devote themselves to study 'to the praise of God and health of their souls'; three of the four priests were required to teach grammar, music, writing (*ECD*, p. 427).

[4] Cook, p. 77; *VCH Northants*, II, p. 217.

enhanced the dignity of particular churches and their services but made the ecclesiastical system even more top heavy, while conditions in the majority of parishes remained unamended. A great deal too much has been made of the contribution of both older collegiate churches and chantry colleges to education, and it is as well to recall that 'if slackness was a common feature of the life of monasteries at this period, the life of secular colleges was even more careless'.[1]

There was, of course, no easy way of remedying abuses which derived from the church's whole position in society and corresponding social pressures, not least the direct demands made by lay patrons. Landowners quite often retired in old age to quarters reserved in a monastic house, with their wives and a retinue of servants, and this was hardly calculated to raise the tone of the community's life. If country squires found nunneries a useful haven for unmarriageable daughters, there were likely to be nuns with no vocation. Equally, at a time when noblemen were finding it difficult to provide for younger sons, these were literally quartered on the church; even boys of ten and upwards were presented to a benefice so that the income might finance them through school or university—a convenient adaptation of the practice whereby beneficed priests were given leave of absence to attend grammar school or university.

In particular the church alone could not do away with plurality, which was deeply rooted and indeed had had far-reaching social effects.[2] So long as kings, lacking an adequate treasury, could only conduct affairs of state by calling on the services of churchmen, so long would there be non-residence, neglect of local duties, deflection of funds intended for religious and charitable purposes to this end. Precisely because this was the end, ecclesiastics could put up a strong defence.

[1] Hamilton Thompson, *History of...the New College...Leicester*, p. 105. Another authority, referring to the usual view that colleges fostered education at large while monasteries were sunk in a cloistered life, notes that closer study of particular areas might suggest an opposite view: 'in Suffolk the life and work of the monasteries would compare favourably with that of the colleges. The promotion of learning was little advanced by these collegiate establishments and certainly the monasteries were doing something in that direction' (*VCH Suffolk*, II, p. 55).

[2] The emoluments so provided 'paved the way of poor students, maintained promising men in the standard of comfort to which they had been accustomed, rewarded the services of clerks, officials, family physicians, and others employed in royal and episcopal households; and, most important of all, by strengthening the ties between the local gentry, the schools, and the great households, they gave more coherence to English society as a whole' (Sir Maurice Powicke, *The Thirteenth Century*, Oxford, 1953, pp. 487–8).

The church was the nursery of statesmen and as such must command rich benefices and permit pluralism; otherwise it could not attract the sons of men of birth into its service by offering them a suitable standard of life. It was in this context that attacks on plurality were always regarded, now and later, as direct attacks on the status of the church. In particular, bishops and abbots must maintain the same state as the lay nobility if the church's position in the social order was to be upheld. Nevertheless there were members of the episcopate who attempted to reform the worst abuses in ancient foundations and to bring order to diocesan administration. Royal control over the chief ecclesiastical appointments was extended when the papacy was discredited and weakened by the great schism and kings advanced men of proved worth; besides the noblemen who held high ecclesiastical office there were, therefore, men of relatively humble origin who had risen by virtue of legal knowledge and administrative ability.[1] These were the bishops who did what they could at visitations to raise the educational standard in monastery and secular church alike and who were instrumental in founding new colleges, not only up and down the country but also for those studying at the universities.

If little could be done to prevent encroachment on ancient rights, these foundations represented, in large part at least, an ecclesiastical counter-measure against growing lay influence. It may be recalled that anti-clericalism had reached a climax in the Lollard movement which initially gained noble patrons and found support in the towns, as also at the university of Oxford where Wycliffe was an influential teacher. Though the movement was driven underground by severe repressive measures, to persist mainly among the poorer clergy and artisans, bishops remained preoccupied with the need to combat heresy.[2] Particular measures were taken to bring Oxford to order, culminating with the constitutions of Archbishop Arundel in 1406.[3]

[1] The episcopal bench became more noteworthy in the fifteenth century 'as it grew more representative of the class of able graduates who had made their career in ecclesiastical administration and were to prove valuable public servants' (Jacob, p. 272).

[2] According to Pecock the Lollards held that all moral law is grounded in the scriptures, that all humble Christian men and women can arrive at the true sense of the bible and that consequently all should have access to this in their own tongue and the education enabling them to study it (Jacob, pp. 282–3, Thrupp, p. 155). One of the four principal points Lollards were still advancing in the early sixteenth century was 'reading of Scripture Books in English' (Dickens, pp. 8–9).

[3] Though as late as 1414 the university drew up articles for presentation to a general council of the church which recapitulate the main Lollard criticisms, including

One of the last Lollard petitions, presented to the king in parliament in 1410, called for confiscation of the lands of the higher clergy and their use to succour the poor and improve the conditions of parish priests. It had, of course, no outcome, but the following year an official step was taken which had considerable implications for the future. At a time of war with France the alien priories, offshoots of French monasteries in England, were dissolved—on the grounds that they had links with the king's enemies—and their property passed into the hands of the crown. In the years to come it acted as a treasury on which royal and episcopal founders of colleges drew.[1] The main foundations financed from this source were at Oxford and Cambridge.

The universities were of the closest concern to the church. It was not merely that heresy must be combated; at a time when the influence of the monastic order was declining and the powers of common lawyers presented a new challenge, it was particularly important to extend opportunities for secular clerks to qualify in canon and civil law. The main foundations at Oxford belonged to the orders of monks and friars who had played a considerable part in establishing the university, including the houses for students maintained by the great Benedictine monasteries—Gloucester Hall, Durham College, Canterbury College. By comparison existing houses for secular clerks were few and relatively insignificant, though the average student needed support during the long years of study combined with teaching in the university schools, necessary to obtain a higher degree.

The basic course in the arts faculty—in grammar, logic and dialectic—was of four years and crowned by the degree of bachelor of arts. But the course leading to an M.A. involved three years' further study, mainly of Aristotelian philosophy, and then two years' teaching as a regent master in the schools. The same principle applied to the higher faculties—of medicine, canon and civil law, theology. In medicine the master of arts must study an additional four years to become bachelor, a further two to become doctor and then teach for at least two more years; though in practice the faculties of medicine and civil law at

charging 'the whole order of prelates with nepotism and avarice' (H. C. Maxwell Lyte, *A History of the University of Oxford*, 1886, pp. 280–4, 302; cf. J. A. Robson, *Wycliffe and the Oxford Schools*, Cambridge, 1961, pp. 244–6).

[1] And when it was exhausted prospective founders began to look around for 'decayed' monasteries which might likewise be turned to a new use (Knowles, p. 157; cf. Donald Matthew, *The Norman Monasteries and their English Possessions*, Oxford, 1962).

Oxford were so weak that there was sometimes only one doctor in residence and inadequate provision for teaching or examining. Three years' study of civil law was also necessary for the intending doctor of canon law who then read and lectured in the latter for five years. In the highest faculty, theology, seventeen years of study was theoretically required to qualify as doctor of divinity.[1] Hence the need for colleges providing board and keep for scholars reading for higher degrees who also constituted the teaching body of the university.

The university was governed by its graduates; that is by a house of regent masters who taught in the schools and a house of non-regent masters made up of all the other doctors and graduates resident at the university as members of convents, colleges or halls. But little enough supervision could be exercised over young men and boys who—at a time when there was no fixed age nor specific qualification for entry—simply registered their names and announced an intention to follow courses, finding for themselves a lodging in hostels, inns or houses in the town. Many of these profited little from their studies and there was all too often brawling in the streets and trouble with the townspeople. There was, therefore, fault to be found both with the discipline and the standard of education, particularly in the arts faculty which provided the necessary groundwork for higher studies. While attention had become concentrated on disciplines which paved the way to the heights of scholastic theology—logic, dialectic, moral philosophy—the other traditional liberal arts of grammar and rhetoric were neglected. Though schooling had by no means always been thorough, students often spent only a term on grammar before launching into logic and dialectic on an insecure foundation.

One way whereby influence could be brought to bear within the university, to improve both discipline and teaching, was by founding colleges for which specific rules and forms of study were laid down and to which bishops were appointed as visitors. Such was New College, founded in the 1370's by William of Wykeham, ecclesiastical statesman, the greatest pluralist of his day and incumbent of the richest bishopric. This was for seventy fellows,[2] twenty of whom were required to study civil or canon law. Wykeham was also concerned to improve the teaching of grammar, but the way he chose to do so

[1] Lyte, pp. 205 ff.

[2] The later term 'fellows' is used to avoid confusion, though in fact those on college foundations were usually called 'scholars' at this time.

was to the benefit of his own foundation rather than of the university as a whole, for he established a second college with grammar school attached under his own eye at Winchester. All entrants to New College must be chosen from among the seventy scholars on this foundation; they were to be supervised during their first two years by older fellows and some disputations were to be held within the college walls—an innovation possibly intended to protect younger students from heretical ideas.[1] The warden of New College was assigned a substantial stipend, sufficient to enable him to vie with the heads of monastic houses, and considerable powers in ruling the community in conjunction with thirteen senior fellows who held specified offices.

This college—much larger, more highly organised and more richly endowed than the six existing colleges for secular clerks—marked a new stage in the development of foundations which in time usurped many of the functions of teaching and eventually came to dominate the government of the university itself. At this period Balliol housed a master and twenty-two fellows, Exeter a rector and twelve fellows, Oriel a provost and ten fellows with a limited additional number of bachelors of arts. The titular heads of these communities, elected as were all college heads by the members, commanded no extensive powers. Fellows usually received an allowance for commons, a small stipend, a livery or gown, and had the benefit of the use of a library and room to work. But though they had duties as regent masters in the university their college imposed no teaching duties; here their obligation was to attend the requisite masses in chapel and pray for the souls of the founder and other benefactors on specified occasions. Beneficed clergy who returned to the university to study, and often remained for years, could hire a room and pay for their keep, so becoming pensioners of the foundation; laymen of standing also took rooms on occasion taking their meals with the community as fellow-commoners. But fellowships were clearly intended for young men in orders (either minor or holy orders) whose future career lay in the church, in particular for 'poor clerks' who could not otherwise maintain themselves during the long years of study. For such they were very desirable but the communal life according to a semi-monastic régime did not exercise a general appeal. When provision was made by later founders for young men of birth to reside in colleges for

[1] H. Rashdall and R. Rait, *New College* (1901), pp. 23–6, 40–7. The attempt to make of Wykeham 'an "educationist" of great and original ideas' is here rejected as fanciful.

tuition it was not as members of the foundation but as a specially treated class of 'pensioner' or 'fellow-commoner'.

Meanwhile the first fifteenth-century foundation for seculars at Oxford, endowed in 1429 by a bishop of Lincoln, was specifically intended to combat Lollard ideas; the 'College of the Blessed Mary and All Saints of Lincoln' was designed as a small body of theologians dedicated to defending 'the mysteries of the sacred page against those ignorant laics who profaned with swinish snouts its most holy pearls'.[1] Nine years earlier the university had passed a statute requiring all scholars to reside in a licensed inn or hall and this was re-enacted in 1432.[2] In subsequent years new facilities were provided for those religious orders which had no house for students in the university; St Mary's College for Augustinian canons was settled in 1435 and St Bernard's for the Cistercian order, with Archbishop Chichele's help, in 1437.[3] The following year the same prelate—who had been prominent both in promoting the war with France and securing suppression of the alien priories—founded the 'College of the Souls of all the Faithful Departed', securing for its endowment some of the confiscated monastic lands and naming the king as co-founder. This was for forty fellows, the majority to be theologians, sixteen canon or civil lawyers, but it was also designed as a vast chantry from which prayers would daily ascend for the souls of the founders and all 'the Dukes, Earls, Barons, Knights, and others who fell in the wars for the Crown of France'.[4] This strong emphasis on the chantry element approximated a foundation at the university to colleges of chantry priests at large.[5]

Colleges designed to enforce orthodoxy or engage in a round of observances were not best fitted to enhance Oxford's status as a centre of learning. It also suffered from the economic pressures consequent on continuing war and increasingly, since papal powers to provide to

[1] J. Wells, *Oxford and its Colleges* (1897), p. 133. Even the revised statutes drawn up by Thomas Rotherham in the 1480's required every fellow admitted to swear that he would neither openly nor secretly favour 'that pestilent sect, which reviving ancient heresies, attacks the sacraments, and the position, and the endowments of the church'; if any transgressed he was to be cast out of the college fold 'as a diseased sheep' within eight days (Lyte, p. 349).

[2] When it was decreed that only graduates might be principals of halls (Lyte, pp. 336, 201).

[3] *Ibid.* pp. 341–3. The Benedictine houses were also added to, Gloucester College acquiring a library and chapel with the aid of funds provided by the abbot of St Albans and a chapel being added to Durham College.

[4] Wells, p. 147.

[5] Hamilton Thompson, *The English Clergy*, pp. 147–8.

English benefices had been curtailed, from a system of patronage whereby benefices were awarded regardless of qualifications.[1] When, in 1438, the king drew attention to the marked decrease in the number of students, Oxford, comparing the university to Rachel weeping for her children, complained that while dependants of the powerful secured advancement the claims of men of learning were overlooked. But the university itself conferred degrees by grace on those lacking academic qualifications and in 1453 elected as chancellor the scion of a noble family who had no scholarly attributes.[2]

At a time when Oxford was subject to various pressures attention focused on the second university in eastern England which had hitherto been more local in character. In 1430 Cambridge had its exemption from the jurisdiction of the diocesan bishop, and so its status as a university, confirmed by a fresh papal bull. Like the orders of monks and friars, which owed direct allegiance, universities had always been of particular interest to the papacy; now when papal influence must be upheld in face of encroachments by the civil power the establishment of new universities was actively encouraged and immunities freely granted—over twenty were founded in the chief states of Europe while others, like Cambridge, were awarded fresh rights.[3] The universities, however, also owed more than has sometimes been recognised to the intervention of kings, Oxford in various ways from its inception, Cambridge particularly in the fourteenth and fifteenth centuries.[4]

Though the friars were there in considerable strength there were no large monastic colleges at Cambridge while lay initiative in founding

[1] For the Statute of Provisors, re-enacted in more stringent form in the 1390's, see Jacob, pp. 198–200, 234–6. Popes, while often providing foreigners to the richest benefices, had tended to choose university men if there was a choice between English candidates, a course that even bishops could not be relied upon to take (J. B. Mullinger, *The University of Cambridge*, 1873, I, p. 284; cf. G. Barraclough, *Papal Provisions*, Oxford, 1935, p. 161).

[2] George Neville was at the time barely twenty and though his name had been inscribed on the books of Balliol had no degree, yet three years later he was bishop of Exeter with a dispensation against taking holy orders for four years and in 1464 became archbishop of York (Lyte, p. 315).

[3] Mullinger, I, p. 282. Among new universities were Leipzig (1409), Turin (1412), Louvain (1426), Florence (1438), Basle (1460) and also, though these were little more than colleges of arts, St Andrews (1411), Glasgow (1451), Aberdeen (1494), while one of many abortive attempts to establish a university at Dublin was made in 1475.

[4] Pearl Kibre, *Scholarly Privileges in the Middle Ages* (Mediaeval Academy of America, 1961), pp. 319–24; cf. A. C. Chibnell, *Richard de Badew and the University of Cambridge 1315–1340* (Cambridge, 1963).

others had been noteworthy by comparison with Oxford, where almost the sole founders were bishops. Since the university itself was not so highly developed, the colleges were also less tied to the higher faculties and made more provision for younger students. To the first established college for secular clerks, Peterhouse, seven others had been added in the years between 1324 and 1360. These included Clare Hall, endowed by a wealthy heiress and granddaughter of Edward I, for twenty fellows and ten poor youths studying grammar and logic; Pembroke Hall, founded by a countess of Pembroke allied to the royal houses of England and France, for twenty-four fellows and six minor scholars of grammar; King's Hall which began as a house of scholars supported by the crown and, as the statutes drawn up by Richard II made clear, was designed for young men of some standing. In addition, Trinity Hall, founded in 1350 by a worldly ecclesiastical statesman, Bishop Bateman of Ely, was mainly intended to train canon and civil lawyers 'for the advantage, rule and direction of the commonwealth' as well as the service of the diocese. The same bishop later augmented the revenues and revised the statutes of Gonville Hall (1349) so that studies should also be mainly directed to law as a necessary preparation for men of affairs.[1]

The first fifteenth-century foundation here was Buckingham College, endowed in 1428 for the monks of Croyland Abbey, which in 1480 was provided with a new building by the then duke of Buckingham, Henry Stafford, and opened also to seculars.[2] In 1439 God's House was initiated by the London rector, William Bingham, familiar with the demand for an extension of schooling. He laid down that lectures in the college were to be on works appropriate to the study of the Latin language and literature in order to prepare masters to teach; every fellow, unless elected as a reader or presented to a cure, must accept an appointment as master of any grammar school which offered a competent salary. Here was an attempt to supply additional teachers able to teach in a new way, and the first lecturer appointed contracted to read 'lectures upon the poets and orators' in the college hall.[3] But though the house was intended to support twenty-five fellows there were only four on the foundation when it was swallowed up by a

[1] H. E. Maldon, *Trinity Hall* (1902), p. 18; J. Venn, *Gonville and Caius College* (1901), pp. 6–7.

[2] Mullinger, II, p. 64.

[3] Lloyd, pp. 134–5. The statutes are printed in H. Rackham, *Early Statutes of Christ's College, Cambridge* (Cambridge, 1927).

new college half a century later, and evidence as to its influence is lacking.

In 1440 the young and hapless Henry VI, inspired by his ecclesiastical advisers, began to put in hand a vast new college at Cambridge. This was designed to have a related college with a school at Eton, on the pattern introduced by Wykeham, and both were endowed in large part with lands earlier confiscated from the great French abbeys of Fécamp, Fontenay, Yvry and Bec. In welcoming this initiative churchmen were still preoccupied with Lollardy, the bishop of Lincoln, in whose diocese Eton then stood, extolling the king's goodness towards 'our Holy Mother the Church of England, which in these last days the sons of Belial would have destroyed' but for the royal protection.[1] In the outcome, churchmen declined any part in the foundation of the 'King's College of Our Lady and St Nicholas at Cambridge' and the university itself deplored the turn of events; for Henry obtained papal bulls exempting his college from the jurisdiction of archbishop of Canterbury, diocesan bishop and chancellor of the university alike. With this form of independence, formerly the mark of friaries and monasteries, went regulations framed on the monastic model; all the seventy fellows must wear the clerical tonsure and study theology, except for six permitted to study law, two medicine, two astronomy.[2]

Six acres of heavily populated ground, bordering on the river where commerce centred, were gradually wrested from the reluctant inhabitants of Cambridge to make room for this royal foundation. Not long after its establishment Henry's queen gave her patronage to another new college, which thereby came under court influence; this eventually became known as Queens', when the favour of a Yorkist queen was sought to perpetuate it, and became the royal residence at the university, its buildings resembling those of a country house rather than following the ecclesiastical pattern.[3] It is seldom remarked that Henry also made sufficiently large donations to Pembroke Hall to rank as a second founder, added to the endowments of God's House which thus became recognised as a royal foundation, presented two tenements and a hostel to Clare Hall which had fallen on evil days, and recompensed Trinity Hall so handsomely for relinquishing some interests in

[1] H. C. Maxwell Lyte, *A History of Eton College* (1877), p. 5.

[2] This exemption from university authority operated to keep what was for long the largest college outside the mainstream of university life (Mullinger, I, pp. 305 ff.).

[3] J. H. Gray, *The Queens' College* (1899), pp. 4 ff.

favour of King's that it was able to establish two additional fellowships.[1] All in all this contributed considerably to the development of the university and in future Cambridge looked to both queens and kings for special patronage.

Soon after receiving its new benefactions Pembroke Hall established control over one of the student hostels in the town, making this into an annexe of the college where fellows lectured in return for fees.[2] The extension on these lines of the scope and powers of colleges seems to have taken place at both universities during the remainder of the century. There were thirty-four students in Pembroke's hostel each paying 8*d.* a term to the college, and a second hostel was shortly purchased to be used in the same way. Gonville Hall likewise acquired the Physwick hostel, a house given by a benefactor in which thirty to forty students were accommodated, each paying 16*d.* a quarter chamber rent and a like sum to the two principals of the hostel, who supervised studies and lectured.[3] So some fellows became directly concerned with teaching undergraduates attached to their college. Future founders were to take account of this, notably the lady Margaret Beaufort when, regarding herself as trustee of Henry VI's good intentions, she enlarged God's House into Christ's College at the turn of the century.

The royal 'College of our Lady of Eton beside Windsor' was also planned on a grand scale, being designed as a corporation of priests and clerks who would intercede for the king's soul in a chapel larger than Salisbury Cathedral. The school attached to this, besides catering for scholars on the foundation, was charged to admit day boys freely (having been granted a local monopoly of teaching) and also required to extend free instruction to twenty sons of nobles who boarded at their own cost. The master of Winchester School, William Wainfleet, was brought to Eton with thirty-five of his scholars to start the school, a step which brought him further rapid preferment.[4] It was in 1448, the year after becoming bishop of Winchester, that Wainfleet initiated the

[1] A. Attwater, *Pembroke College* (Cambridge, 1936), pp. 17–18; Lloyd, p. 88; J. R. Wardale, *Clare College* (1899), p. 22; Maldon, pp. 56–8, 62–3.

[2] That there had earlier been regular lecturing in hostels is suggested by the statute of God's House laying down that the college reader should lecture 'on every day on which lectures are usually read in hostels' (Lloyd, pp. 133–4).

[3] The internal principal was a resident fellow of the college chosen by the master, the external principal, elected by him and the hostel students conjointly, resided in the hostel itself (J. Venn, *Biographical History of Gonville and Caius College*, Cambridge, 1901, III, p. 201).

[4] Lyte, *Eton*, p. 17.

foundation of Magdalen College at Oxford which eventually, like Eton, was required to reserve special rooms for twenty young noblemen who might reside at their own expense under the care of tutors.[1] Closely analogous were the privileges offered in colleges to founder's kin. Here was a new way of providing for those who were otherwise brought up in the royal or episcopal households often directly at their patrons' expense. The universities were, of course, only too ready to welcome noblemen's sons; indeed they petitioned for the favour of receiving them. Thus Oxford in 1480 entreated Edward IV to send his nephew, Edward Pole, son of the duke of Suffolk, and having obtained the favour wrote fulsome letters reporting on the young man's remarkable progress in learning.[2]

(4) *Trends in education*

Discussing education in the 1550's Thomas Becon recalled some old common proverbs, such as 'a child were better unborn than untaught' and 'manners make a man'.[3] These were homely sayings, since it was primarily in the household and family that children received an upbringing according to their station and the occupation they would take up in life. The countryman's son learned agricultural practices in the course of work on the land. The sons of urban craftsmen had their training as apprentices in the family of the master to whom they were bound; and masters stood *in loco parentis* being responsible for feeding, clothing, disciplining apprentices and seeing that they were instructed in the elements as well as in skills. The nobleman's son was likewise brought up in the household where he was trained in the course of various activities and benefited to a greater or lesser degree from some formal instruction. Regular schooling, in short, was incidental rather than central to upbringing except in the case of those who from an early age looked to enter the church and attended grammar school before registering at the university. Even here a period at local or university schools was often fitted into the framework of household upbringing.

This served well enough during an age when society devolved duties requiring specialised learning mainly onto a single estate, the church. It was no longer adequate when a good deal more than simple literacy

[1] Lyte, *Oxford*, p. 367. [2] *Ibid.* p. 330.

[3] *Catechism etc.* (Parker Society, 1844), p. 383.

became necessary in expanding lay callings. More schools were needed and more were established, sometimes directly at the expense of the church, but there is little evidence of any change in the form of education; just as schools were for the most part established within a traditional framework, and connected with chantries, so teaching continued to be associated with ecclesiastical ritual.

It has often been argued that there had long been independent schools, with all that this implied for the development of education, Winchester and Eton being cited as examples.[1] But the schools concerned were, of course, adjuncts of colleges of priests and though scholars were not constantly engaged in observances, as were senior members of the foundation, they yet had considerable duties in church. Eton scholars said the same prayers on rising as fellows, chaplains and choristers; then while the latter sang matins in church scholars must do likewise as they made their beds before 5 a.m. School opened with prayers and later boys must leave their lessons when a bell rang to announce the elevation of the host during mass, attend this part of the service and remain to join in prayers for the foundation. After school closed, with further prayers, scholars joined in saying vespers and before retiring again joined others on the foundation in further specified observances.[2]

In the small chantry school teaching was directly linked to participation in the mass. As late as 1526 the statutes of Childrey school, framed by a Berkshire gentleman, enjoin the priest

> to teach children the Alphabet, the Lord's prayer, the Salutation of the Blessed Virgin, the Apostles' Creed and all other things which are necessary to enable them to assist the priest in the celebration of the Mass, together with the psalm De Profundis and the usual prayers for the dead.

The former requirements reproduced the standard instructions to parish priests about the teaching of their flock; the relevance of the latter is clear from contemporary wills.[3] All these prayers, in Latin,

[1] The status of Winchester 'as a self-governing independent body was far superior to that enjoyed by any other existing school' and it may 'thus fairly be said to mark an epoch in the development of English education' (McKisack, p. 500, drawing on A. F. Leach, *A History of Winchester College*, 1899).

[2] *EGS*, p. 39.

[3] Jacob, p. 280. The will of the merchant founder of Wolverhampton School, proved in 1523, called for 24 boys at his funeral bearing tapers being 'poor men's children such as can say our lady matins or the psalm De Profundis'; sums of from 2*d.* to 6*d.* were usually left for each child (G. P. Mander, *A History of Wolverhampton School*, Wolverhampton, 1913, p. 6).

must be learned parrot-fashion though it was also laid down by this sixteenth-century founder that religious instruction be given in the vernacular and children taught 'to fear God and keep his commandments'. Only after all this has been set out is it briefly required that if any are 'apt and disposed to learn grammar' the chantry priest should 'teach them what is most useful and expedient'.[1]

Regulations for borough schools suggest that teaching followed a similar pattern, if more systematically and at one remove, passing from the primer of Latin prayers through the psalter to grammar rules. These last were expounded orally and learned by heart, from grammars which had been in use for centuries. Where teachers possessed other books they were evidently of the compendium type, collections of elegant extracts or commentaries rather than the text of authors; but books at this time were essentially a luxury product, costing more than the average teacher could well afford.[2] Even merchant benefactors did not require teaching of any specific kind beyond instruction in grammar. The one indication of a more worldly approach derives from an ecclesiastical statesman, Thomas Rotherham, who required one of the priests of his chantry college to teach writing; this since there were many able youths in Yorkshire 'who do not all wish to attain the dignity...of the priesthood, that these may be better fitted for the mechanical arts and other concerns of this world'.[3]

It was also primarily bishops, whose duties had taken them abroad and widened horizons, who fostered at this time a new interest in the classics which was communicated to the universities. Some lay nobles contributed to this development. Humphrey, duke of Gloucester, assisted scholars to travel to Italy, invited Italian scholars to England and eventually left his extensive library to Oxford. The example was followed by John Tiptoft, earl of Worcester, who had fallen under the spell of the Italy of the *quattrocento*, and these gifts stimulated the building of a university library, completed in 1488.[4] Individual colleges received a like stimulus. William Grey, bishop of Ely, who himself studied in Italy under the famous scholar Guarino, left his library to his former college Balliol. This college, mainly reserved to northerners, profited from the patronage of the Yorkist nobility; young noblemen,

[1] N. Carlisle, *Endowed Grammar Schools* (1818), I, p. 32.

[2] *EGS*, pp. 229–30; H. E. Bell, 'The Price of Books in Mediaeval England', *The Library*, fourth series, XVII (1937), pp. 312–32.

[3] *ECD*, p. 425.

[4] Lyte, *Oxford*, pp. 319–23.

making a career in the church, inscribed their names on the college books and hired a fellow to tutor them and the fees so gained, with further funds solicited from Greys, Nevilles, Tiptofts, enabled the college to build a library for Bishop Grey's collection.[1]

A scholar of Balliol who later rose to high office was John Morton, archbishop of Canterbury, in whose household Thomas More received an early training before being sent by his patron to Oxford where he probably resided at Canterbury College. The latter was a dependency of the great priory of Christchurch which became acquainted with Italian scholarship when William Selling was prior. Here was another who had travelled in Italy, studied under Guarino and returned with many books, and Selling was probably responsible for the early training of a young man who in turn travelled and was to exercise considerable influence at Oxford, Thomas Linacre. Another prelate who, towards the close of the century, took a close interest in the education of young men in his household was Thomas Langton, bishop successively of Salisbury and Winchester and master of Queen's College, Oxford—for bishops now quite frequently held the mastership of colleges. Himself educated at Padua and Bologna, he 'so highly prized the study of humanity', as one of his dependants later wrote, 'that he had boys and youths instructed in it at a school in his house; and he was vastly delighted to hear the scholars repeat to him at night the lessons given by the teachers during the day'. The writer was Richard Pace who himself attended Padua University at his patron's expense and rose to high office in the state under Henry VIII.[2]

If teaching on new lines became available in some of the great households, there is less evidence that it was prevalent at the universities. Endowments made earlier in the century at Oxford had done nothing to improve teaching in the arts faculty and the university itself was evidently not in a sufficiently prosperous state to amend matters, even if its petitions are not literally credited.[3] There were hardly any

[1] H. W. C. Davis, *Balliol College* (1898), pp. 43–5. For Grey's aims and achievements as patron of letters, R. A. B. Mynors (ed.), *Catalogue of the Manuscripts of Balliol College* (Oxford, 1963).

[2] Furnivall, pp. xix–xx. Another bishop who encouraged classical studies was John Chelworth, whose nephew of the same name studied at Padua and was complimented by Oxford University for his endeavours to restore 'grammatical literature' (R. J. Mitchell, 'English Students at Padua, 1460–75', *T.R.H.S.*, fourth series, XIX, p. 109).

[3] In 1435 the university reported that lectures had altogether ceased, in 1480 that learning 'is well nigh extinct' (Kibre, pp. 317–19).

foundations in the years between 1450 and 1480 while, with the disturbances of the time, those of the 1440's were long in the making. Building at Eton virtually ceased after the downfall of the house of Lancaster and was never realised on the scale intended though Wainfleet took up the task in the 1470's; there were then only four fellows and far less than the statutory number of seventy scholars.[1] Wainfleet, however, initiated a more important development in 1480 when he augmented his own foundation Magdalen College and connected with it a school of grammar. Places were now provided for thirty demies, young students who might be admitted from the age of twelve, and for two masters of grammar on the foundation. But the new schoolhouse, built on the north side of the great gateway, was not reserved to members of the college; it was a centre for the teaching of grammar open to the university at large.[2]

The work of this school marked an important stage in the revival and re-orientation of grammar teaching at Oxford, but its importance to schools elsewhere was at least as great. John Ankwyll, the first master, and his assistant John Stanbridge, were prominent in popularising more enlightened methods of teaching grammar to schoolboys, based on Italian examples. There was, moreover, a regulation which brought to fulfilment the intention behind the earlier God's House, namely that some scholars prolong their studies in grammar to perfect themselves as teachers. It was after attending Magdalen College that William Horman became head successively of the schools of Eton and Winchester colleges and William Lily first high master of the new school of St Paul's. Others who passed through this college over the years were greatly to influence educational developments—William Grocyn, Richard Fox, John Colet, Thomas Wolsey, William Tyndale.

But up to the end of the fifteenth century, in so far as the universities remained oriented to the ecclesiastical system, improvements in teaching operated to underpin the prevailing studies and outlook rather than to initiate any new departure.[3] Thus better teaching of grammar could provide better-grounded clerks for episcopal chanceries, a new acquaintance with the humanities could contribute to legal and theological studies, but there are few signs of any fresh thinking: more,

[1] Lyte, *Eton*, pp. 74–7. It remained for Henry VII to complete the chapel of King's.

[2] R. G. Stanier, *Magdalen School* (Oxford, 1958), pp. 8–9.

[3] R. Weiss, *Humanism in England in the Fifteenth Century* (1957), pp. 179–83.

at Oxford in particular, of a renewed cultivation of Duns Scotus.[1] Though there were greater opportunities of studying civil and canon law than formerly, ambitious young men who could gain assistance went if they could direct to Padua, Bologna, Ferrara, whose degrees provided a passport to office of a kind that Oxford and Cambridge could not emulate.[2] At home, in the absence of any influential demand, there were no major innovations; the general structure of scholarship remained unchanged and the requirements of scholastic theology continued to overshadow courses. There was as yet no trace of what was becoming known as the 'new learning'—that is, the critical and historical study of the scriptures in the original texts and of patristic writers, as opposed to the old learning which confounded divinity with the pagan philosophies of the ancient world. The first acquaintance with this outlook came in 1497 when John Colet returned from Italy to lecture at Oxford on the Pauline epistles.

That there was little outside pressure to re-orientate university courses, that humanist studies made so little headway, was mainly because the only influential lay element in society was provided for at the inns of court. The system of common law had early been influenced by civil and canon law but it was essentially medieval in origin and constantly developed in use; this was the body of law studied while, by the same token, the stimulus to study the heritage of Roman law—which operated with such effect among the powerful civilians of contemporary Italy—was absent.[3] But, though there was no particular interest in cultivating the humanities at the inns of court, there were important developments in what was by now a century-old system of lay education, closely integrated with an expanding legal apparatus.[4]

The legal training at the inns was highly technical and at an advanced level, requiring a knowledge of Latin and also of law French. Lecturers, or readers, expounded the law from standard works and readings were followed by 'moots', or debates, in the course of which principles were applied and students' abilities could be assessed. This presupposed an adequate grounding which must have been acquired in the household or by attendance at school, particularly the university schools. By the

[1] Jacob, pp. 680–2. [2] Mitchell, p. 116. [3] Smalley, pp. 310–12.

[4] To the courts of exchequer and common pleas there had been added in the early fourteenth century the court of the king's bench; in the fifteenth century the court of chancery was established to deal with civil cases by a system of law known as equity, the cases of humbler suitors were heard in an embryo court of requests, while the development of parliament presaged a great extension of statute law.

fifteenth century the inns of chancery, which initially brought together pupils of the senior clerks of the chancery studying the nature and drafting of writs, had begun to act in part as preparatory schools for the greater inns established by the pleaders, or barristers. This was the cheapest way of entering the law, as Fortescue noted, but there was also direct entry to the greater inns.[1] Leading lawyers of the fifteenth century had spent a time at Oxford or Cambridge, usually in one of the halls or hostels patronised by civil and canon lawyers, then directly entering one of the inns of court. Thus, Robert Rede is said to have been resident at Buckingham College and fellow of King's Hall, Cambridge, before entering Lincoln's Inn; William Coningsby, son of an eminent lawyer, went from Eton to King's College in 1497 before entering the Inner Temple.[2] There are many later instances and in default of other evidence it may perhaps be surmised there were earlier ones; some knowledge of civil and canon law, as well as a grounding in Latin, was very necessary to the common lawyer and could be obtained at university without going through the whole degree course. It may also be recalled that Thomas More, son of another leading lawyer, spent two years at Oxford between the ages of fourteen and sixteen and later, when he seemed to be wasting time on such extraneous matters as Greek and philosophy, was deprived of his allowance and set to study at an inn of chancery before entering Lincoln's Inn.[3]

The needs of both students and practitioners stimulated the preparation of many compilations and guides to study at this time which went to make up a growing corpus of legal literature. Thomas Lyttelton wrote his *Tenures* as a summary of medieval land law for the instruction of his son and it became a standard text. But Fortescue—chief justice of the king's bench and chancellor of the realm—was concerned rather

[1] Michael Birks, *Gentlemen of the Law* (1960), pp. 40–1, 102; P. Anstie Smith, *A History of Education for the English Bar* (1860), pp. 9–10.

[2] *Athenae*, I, pp. 20, 76. Laymen who rose to become royal counsellors in the early sixteenth century had often begun in the same way. Thomas Audley was at Cambridge, probably Buckingham College, before entering the Inner Temple; Thomas Wriothesley, son of a court official, was sent to Cambridge, probably Trinity Hall, and then Gray's Inn (*ibid.* pp. 83, 98).

[3] R. W. Chambers, *Thomas More* (1963 ed.), pp. 61–3. Though belonging to a later date the account by Sir James Whitelocke, a merchant's son, of how he made his way to an inn of chancery and then an inn of court via study of civil law at Oxford is relevant (J. Bruce, ed., *Liber Famelicus of Sir James Whitelocke*, Camden Society, 1858, pp. 13–15).

with public law and the instruction of a king and takes a more comprehensive view. Since the scope of common law had been rapidly extending he could see this as a developing system and, though he evinces all the conservatism associated with a law grounded in precedent, Fortescue adopts a critical and historical approach which may reasonably be classed as humanist. He derives legal theories from observation and practice and, making a comparative analysis of political institutions in different states, relates differences to underlying differences in economic and social structure; in so doing he stresses the role of the English parliament which serves to make the monarchy, by contrast with more absolute monarchies on the continent, a limited monarchy, limited because of its parliamentary character.[1]

This and other written texts provided a body of knowledge which not only served legal training but contributed much towards the coherent development of case law in the courts and statute law in parliament. When the time came for a frontal attack on the church the common lawyers came into their own; it was they who contributed most to the development of parliamentary procedure, the carrying through of the Reformation by statute and the building up of a new governmental apparatus which took over tasks of administration formerly performed by churchmen. There were, then, developments in legal knowledge and education at this period which had an immediate effect and were of much import for the future. It is usual to account the Elizabethan age as the time when the inns of court became leading educational institutions because they then attracted so many young gentlemen; but this influx and other pressures operated to undermine traditional forms of training and it was rather before it took place, in the fifteenth century, that the inns had their golden age as centres of legal education.

'The study of English law is as far removed as can be from true learning', wrote Erasmus, bred on the classics, at the turn of the century, 'but in England those who succeed in it are highly thought of. And there is no better way to eminence there; for the nobility are mostly recruited from the law.'[2] While the lawyers achieved growing prominence there was a decline in the military arts during a period when England was for long at peace abroad. The fact that during the second half of the century there were no major foreign wars meant

[1] S. B. Chrimes (ed.), *De Laudibus Legum Anglie*, pp. xvi–xviii.

[2] Quoted in Chambers, pp. 79–80.

that the nobility lost a chief means to fame and lesser men opportunities to rise.[1] Many of those of noble and gentle birth, complained William of Worcester, onetime secretary to that great adventurer Sir John Fastolf, 'learn the practice of law or custom of land, or of civil matter', wasting their time ruling the commons rather than cultivating traditional skills. The same tendency is illustrated by the publication in 1481 of a translation of Cicero, designed 'for noble wise and great lords, gentlemen and merchants that have been and daily been occupied in matters touching the public weal'.[2]

In sum, there were no spectacular developments in fifteenth-century England comparable to those in the city states of the Italian peninsula, but there was a slow maturing of change in institutions and attitudes which laid the foundation for a durable advance in the next century. In this context a much more important phenomenon than the particular school and college foundations which usually command attention was the steady expansion of lay education at various levels. This received an immense impetus from application of the main technical discovery of the century, the effect of which was felt when William Caxton of the Mercers' Company returned from thirty years' trading in the Low Countries to begin printing books at Westminster. The printed book did not at first make much impact, and traditional texts were the first to appear in this form, but it heralded a revolution in education and self-education. Not only could there be serious and sustained textual study, in place of the prevailing oral teaching, but a vastly increased range of subject matter became available to scholars, in relatively accurate form by comparison with the vagaries of scriveners.[3] So far as the layman was concerned access to knowledge became immeasurably easier once printed books multiplied. Hitherto there had been libraries in only a few centres of learning; whereas the abbeys of Canterbury or Bury owned some two thousand volumes, scholarly compilations accumulated over centuries, the library of Cambridge University had only some three hundred. Within a century individual scholars owned

[1] 'The most splendid opportunities for established families to increase their wealth or for new ones to rise quickly to fame and fortune were offered by war, and this was an important factor, not only in the moral code but also in the economics of the nobility' (G. Holmes, *The Later Middle Ages*, 1962, p. 162).

[2] *Ibid.* pp. 134, 164.

[3] The printer's art 'made possible a standard of critical accuracy which was so much higher than what was known before as to be almost a new creation' (P. S. Allen, *The Age of Erasmus*, Oxford, 1914, p. 258).

collections thrice this size for their own use, while country gentlemen had sizeable libraries covering a variety of subjects.[1]

Inevitably books were the chief agents in the spread of new ideas, for the printing-presses were in the towns of Europe and, under lay control, constituted a new kind of weapon against which the established order had no means of defence. The influence of a scholar like Erasmus, the very nature of his work, depended directly on the availability of the printing-press outside the jurisdiction of the church, or that of any learned community jealous of privileges and resistant to change. Though presses were established in the university towns it was rare for them to take firm root and flourish there; it was in the great commercial metropolises of Europe that printing was carried forward.[2]

This new stimulus to literacy and learning had barely been felt in England by the turn of the century. But when Erasmus came over in 1499, and again six years later, he met with a few men—five or six in number, all of whom had studied abroad—who could be ranked with Italian scholars for knowledge of Latin and Greek, though they were to be found not at a university but in the capital. 'No place in the world has given me such friends as your city of London', Erasmus wrote to Colet in 1507 from Paris,[3] from which he was shortly to return to assist in founding a new kind of school and to teach for a while at Cambridge. The time was ripe for a move to re-orientate education. Those who travelled on the continent, not only to universities in Italy but also as merchants to Antwerp and other leading cities, could not but become aware how far England lagged behind. Moreover, there were new prospects in the air, even though men did not grasp the significance of overseas discoveries nor of trends in economic and social change at home; indeed it was the dislocation produced that was noticed above all, especially the poverty and ignorance brought to light, but this in itself was a stimulus to action.

At the close of the fifteenth century, England, with a population of

[1] The inventory of one such in 1556 records 140 printed books of which 100 were in English; these comprised translations from the Latin, chronicles, medical and veterinary treatises, volumes on geometry, surveying and cosmography, legal works bearing on the duties of a J.P., works by English poets and the latest drama, with volumes by French and Italian authors as well—Boccaccio, Petrarch, Machiavelli, Froissart (R. Irwin, *The Origins of the English Library*, 1958, pp. 163–4).

[2] Curt F. Bühler, *The Fifteenth Century Book* (Philadelphia, 1960), pp. 55–6; cf. E. P. Goldschmidt, *The First Cambridge Press in its European Setting* (Cambridge, 1955).

[3] Allen, pp. 128–30.

between two and three millions, was still a country rooted in the land with no great centres of civilisation comparable to the cities of Italy, Germany and the Low Countries. Politically her standing in Europe was not high, intellectually there was little to boast about. If the new ideas now revolutionising education in Florence, Padua, Ferrara, had barely penetrated it was the same with new techniques which promoted the spread of learning; by 1500 there were printing-presses in only 4 English cities as compared with 73 in Italy, 50 in Germany, and a Greek press had been set up in Milan before Caxton issued his first book from Westminster.[1] English culture itself, the English language and literature, were undeveloped and almost unheard of in Europe, for few visitors crossed the channel. One who did, a cultivated Venetian, observed that laymen had little scholarship and learning was still virtually monopolised by the church; adding that even well-born Englishmen, instead of educating their children in a civilised way, sent them to be trained in service in the households of others.[2]

Educational institutions were to be increasingly questioned by native critics. Apprenticeship was too often restricted to sons of men of substance while others had no access to any form of training, though poverty was directly related to lack of skill and employment. The church had for long been neglecting its educational duties and the standards of the parish clergy were scandalously low, while the universities were becoming obscurantist in their devotion to scholasticism. The traditional way of bringing up the nobility was no longer adequate now that laymen were increasingly occupied with matters of state and local government; even the common law was hardly a suitable vehicle of training, despite the achievements of the inns of court, since it lacked the coherence and system of civil law and was couched in a mixture of English and bowdlerised French. So criticism was to range in the coming years over the whole field of education and all the medieval institutions were called in question. In the formulation of these criticisms, no less than of measures for reform, a small body of humanist scholars played a key part.

[1] H. Guppy, 'The Evolution of the Art of Printing', *Bulletin of the John Rylands Library*, XXIV (1940), p. 233.

[2] *A Relation of the Island of England...about the year 1500*, ed. C. A. Sneyd (Camden Society O.S. XXXVII), pp. 24–5.

II

HUMANISTS, THE NEW LEARNING AND EDUCATIONAL CHANGE

The brief outline given of trends in the fifteenth century has suggested that this was an age of educational expansion rather than advance. More schools became available, but teaching remained on traditional lines and text-books were as yet few. One or two 'schools' in the great households apart, humanist programmes of study and teaching methods were all but unknown.[1] The same was true of all the states of northern Europe; their schools and universities 'knew only the first tentative flickers of humanism before 1500'.[2] Humanist ideas did not cross frontiers unless the way had been prepared, unless new demands made them relevant.

Before turning to the evidence in England it is as well to discuss the term 'humanist' and the related term 'renaissance' which has been used by historians to cover a wide variety of changes in Europe over widely varying periods of time.[3]

The concept of a renaissance of classical antiquity was first adopted and spread by Italian scholars of the *trecento* and *quattrocento* who were engaged in quarrying the artistic, literary and learned heritage of the ancient world to new ends—in particular those aspects that had been neglected by earlier scholars, but which bore closely on contemporary concerns. Classical scholarship had never been lacking.[4]

[1] For a description of prevailing practice at school and university, Allen, pp. 33 ff., 104 ff.; cf. *EGS*, pp. 229–30, where it is pointed out that Leach's reconstruction of a curriculum for Winchester is purely hypothetical.

[2] R. R. Bolgar, *The Classical Heritage and its Beneficiaries* (Cambridge, 1954), p. 342.

[3] A standard educational history is entitled *Studies in Education during the Age of the Renaissance 1400–1600*. The recent first volume of the New Cambridge Modern History is entitled *The Renaissance (c. 1493–1520)*, its chronological successor being *The Reformation (c. 1520–1559)*.

[4] The humanists, in the words of a medievalist, 'constituted themselves the ungrateful heirs of centuries of classical culture' in claiming to be the first to rediscover antiquity (Smalley, p. 291).

But for centuries the schoolmen had adapted Roman law to tune in with the needs of a civilisation based on the land; they had adapted pagan philosophies to Christian doctrine in vast semi-secular theological systems; they had borrowed words and phrases from vernacular languages to turn Latin into an instrument serving the needs of their time. In the process classical Latin was much adulterated, original works buried under commentaries. When, therefore, the political and philosophical works of the ancient world were studied in their original form, by laymen living in communities which were setting a new standard of urban culture, scholastic learning began to seem an anachronism, a descent into confusion and darkness from the light of the ancient world.

Those who first took up and fostered classical studies in the Italian city states were not, as has often been represented, itinerant and dependent scholars, but men of influence and standing. Nearly all were lawyers, trained in university schools where the professors of civil law were married laymen active in affairs, or the sons of legal families which in the conditions of city life easily built up fortunes and attained a predominant position.[1] The study of Roman law helped to prepare the ground for an intense cultivation of classical literature which had much of relevance to offer to the modern city state. Everything was grist to the humanist mill, the scientific works of the Greeks as well as treatises by Roman orators, and critical examination of these was one of the prerequisites of a new scientific outlook. The educational writings of Plutarch, of Cicero and Quintilian—left aside by scholars who had been uninterested in man as an individual, seeking a guide to use of his powers in a civic context—exercised great influence. Not least, comparative and historical studies brought a new clarity and lent a new authority to demands for ecclesiastical reform, for they illustrated that the church had grounded doctrine and law on faulty texts and how far it had moved from the primitive simplicity of early Christianity. Greek, which had been relatively little studied of late, attracted new interest, and a profound admiration for the width and depth of Greek learning took root; Plato's works were re-assimilated and it was comparison of Aristotle's original writings with the imperfect versions

[1] Smalley, pp. 280–1. Florentine humanists belonged almost exclusively to, or managed to enter, the ranks of the upper or upper-middle class, the effective ruling class of the city state (Lauro Martinez, *The Social World of the Florentine Humanists 1390–1460*, Princeton, 1963, pp. 267 ff.).

commented upon by generations of schoolmen that contributed most to the development of a critical attitude of mind.

While the continuity of these studies with much that had gone before must be recognised, none the less a movement was under way in fifteenth-century Italy to which it is warrantable to apply a new term, humanist.[1] In its narrowest sense, as it was first used by contemporaries, this term covered scholars who championed literary as against scholastic studies, rhetoric and declamation as against logic and disputation in the schools; it therefore bore directly and specifically on the content and methods of education. But this move was both a symptom and a cause of much wider developments in the whole range of the arts, vernacular literatures, scientific and political ideas, psychological attitudes which marked an age of transition from the medieval to the modern world, from an ecclesiastically dominated to a lay culture. It is these developments, in all their complexity, that historians subsume under the term 'renaissance'. In this context the humanist writers who popularised classical learning and literature and new forms of education helped materially to pioneer a new outlook; more specifically they advocated an approach to and methods of learning and exposition which in time became the general material of intellectual exchange and production. The term 'humanist' can reasonably be stretched to cover this whole trend. It can be used to indicate not merely advocacy of literary studies, which could be introduced in a traditional setting with no great repercussions, but an outlook on learning generally and the relation of learning to life which, in tune with social developments, held the key to the future; which comprised, in a concern for the affairs of this world and the use of learning to influence these affairs, a new interest in individual human beings, their potentialities and aspirations.

It was in this sense that humanist ideas were first brought to bear in

[1] Historians now classify as 'pre-humanist' the group centred on Padua in the late thirteenth and fourteenth centuries, as 'early humanist' the activities of Petrarch and his contemporaries, and as 'humanist' the movement in the fifteenth and early sixteenth centuries (Smalley, pp. 6–7). 'When the fourteenth century gives way to the fifteenth, we seem to pass from the gloom of a passage into the brilliant light of a sunlit room.... The widened interests of scholarship embrace for the first time the whole of the classical heritage. Not only is the movement started by Petrarch for the recovery of Roman eloquence and the Roman way of life brought to a triumphant conclusion, but the work of earlier ages in law, medicine and philosophy is once again examined, criticised and completed....Greek studies which had so long wilted in obscurity take their place alongside Latin, their long hidden treasures accessible at last to a multitude of scholars' (Bolgar, p. 265).

England in the early sixteenth century. But in the particular circumstances of the time they were largely directed to the matter that must condition all educational, intellectual and social advance—reform of the church. This has created further misunderstandings, though it has long since been pointed out that there is no good reason arbitrarily to distinguish the revival of letters from the revival of religion.[1] The matter has been confused afresh by introduction of the term 'humanism', one not in contemporary use and which carries so many overtones that it is necessary to make a qualification; so we arrive at the heading 'renaissance humanism' which appears in the text-books, to make confusion worse confounded. It is not surprising that those who operate with such a terminology, at several removes from the contemporary facts, find themselves at odds with the men on the spot in sixteenth-century England. Classicists, for instance, using the term 'humanism' to cover interest in classical studies and what these had to offer, complain that English humanists were not sufficiently single-minded in this respect. 'We might expect a kind of manifesto of humanism,' writes one authority of the statutes of St Paul's; 'what we find is in some respects out of keeping with what humanism normally involved.'[2] The assumption is that 'humanism' normally involved concentration on the classics and admiration for classical example almost in an eighteenth-century sense; and this idea is in turn often connected with another, that humanist educational plans related primarily to the upbringing of the aristocracy or governing classes.

Colet is necessarily a stumbling-block here since it was his overriding concern to promote a Christian education and the school he founded was designed primarily for the children of the citizens of London. For his failure to fit into the categories adopted by historians Colet has been the target of some ill-considered abuse.[3] It is true that the writings of English humanists reflect the state of English learning,

[1] 'The distinction is neither formally correct nor materially exact. The renaissance was not necessarily secular and classical—it might be, and often was, both religious and Christian; nor was the Reformation essentially religious and moral—it might be and often was political and secular' (A. M. Fairbairn, 'Tendencies in European Thought in the Age of the Reformation', *Cambridge Modern History*, 1903, II, p. 691).

[2] M. L. Clarke, *Classical Education in Britain, 1500–1900* (Cambridge, 1959), p. 5.

[3] A recent critic has gone so far as to say that 'in his capacity as humanist we see Colet at his worst', that 'no more deadly and irrational scheme could have been propounded' than the directives he issued for teaching in his school (C. S. Lewis, *English Literature in the Sixteenth Century*, Oxford, 1954, p. 160).

with its strong scholastic tendency. But attempts to present the founder of St Paul's as a backward-looking conservative underline limitations not so much in his outlook as in understanding of what it represented in relation to contemporary conditions inside and outside the schools. It is vital to an appreciation of educational development to recognise that this approach implied important innovations, both in teaching the classics and religious teaching, which evoked much abuse from the conservative in 1510. This must be the excuse for covering again some well-trodden ground.

The chief protagonists of educational reform in northern Europe, Erasmus and Vives in particular, advanced a whole philosophy in which education, in the widest sense of the term, took a key place. The question of interest is how these ideas were presented and applied, what was specifically new about the organisation and curriculum of St Paul's by comparison with what had gone before, and the parallel innovations advocated by humanists at the universities. More difficult to determine, but important to an evaluation of the position on the eve of the Reformation, is the extent to which the example of St Paul's was followed by other schools. The point of departure, before turning to these questions, must be the climate in which humanist ideas were advanced, for this in large part determined the extent of their influence.

(1) *The new learning and education*

The traditional outlook on education, reflecting the practice of centuries, persisted more or less unchallenged up to the sixteenth century. The sons of noblemen must be brought up as men of action, trained in military skills, since their primary obligation to society was a military one, though there were also courtly arts and knowledge to be acquired. Since it was held that nobility originally stemmed from prowess in war rewarded by a king, that therefore the hereditary nobility owed their dominant position to qualities of courage and leadership, and that the longer the lineage whereby these were passed down the greater the worth,[1] education was a subsidiary matter of adding polish to a finished product esteemed on its own account. On the other hand, the repository of learning, the nursery of administrators, was the church, preparation for which involved application to learning of an academic

[1] Ruth Kelso, *The Doctrine of the English Gentleman in the Sixteenth Century* (Univ. of Illinois, 1929), pp. 24–5.

kind. Such learning carried no great esteem in itself, since it led in the main to employment in a dependent, clerkly, capacity. It could on occasion carry its possessor to high status but this was bestowed not so much in honour of learning as the services whereby it had been brought to bear in the interests of the crown.

The humanists roundly affirmed that education and learning themselves confer nobility, a nobility of mind ranking higher than any nobility of blood. At the same time they insisted, drawing on examples from the civic life of the ancient world, that the true evidence of nobility in this sense is quality of service to the public good. This concept was of particular relevance in England at a time when a new breach was being made in the wall of feudal privilege, when good service to the crown was frequently rewarded not only by advancement in the church but by conferring noble rank. In the circumstances the traditional view that honour and worth rested on long lineage began to appear manifestly out of date and in need of replacement. As new sanctions were sought it was becoming ever clearer that the right kind of education contributed much to successful careers and social advancement, and also that suitable forms of education were often less readily available to men of birth than to others. All this prepared the soil for humanist ideas to take root and spread. In the outcome no subject provoked more continuous discussion than the origin and nature of gentility and the extent to which gentlemanly qualities can be formed by education.[1]

Under the first Tudor, while faithful servants of the crown were ennobled, the crown itself was raised to a higher and more lonely state. Henry VII followed the example of his predecessor in seeking to consolidate the monarchy on traditional lines but, having a doubtful title to the throne, found it advisable to eliminate magnates related to the royal house. As a result a new distance began to be established between king and nobility, which was further widened by insistence on the royal prerogative and, too, by raising court life to a new dignity with impressive ceremonies and display. When the next reign opened there was only one duke and one marquis in England and the crown wielded a new influence from new heights.[2] But the nucleus of a new nobility had been created, made up of men whose rapid rise to high

[1] Kelso, *passim*. The relation of the sixteenth-century literature to earlier tracts and manuals is discussed by Mason, ch. 1.

[2] A. F. Pollard, *Henry VIII* (1905), p. 37.

rank was consolidated by the acquisition of extensive estates and the adoption of a style of life emulating that of the Tudor court. The sons of such men were ready candidates for new forms of education.

In parallel, able men who had made a career in the church now predominated in the ecclesiastical hierarchy at the expense of the aristocrats who had remained influential in the previous century. Henry VIII's chief bishops were all men of this kind. William Warham, John Fisher, Richard Fox, Cuthbert Tunstall, Hugh Oldham, came from families of the lesser gentry or yeomanry, so also did Hugh Latimer and Thomas Cranmer while the great Thomas Wolsey was the son of an Ipswich burgess. All these were patrons of scholars, founders or supporters of schools and colleges, men keenly interested in humanist ideas which bore closely on the reform of the church and learning as well as on lay education.

Humanist scholars usually met with opposition at the universities, of whose scholarship they were very critical, but found their services much in demand elsewhere as diplomats and advisers; while those who continued to concentrate on scholarship found patrons among leading statesmen, both lay and ecclesiastical, and employment as tutors. Not only could kings and bishops make good use of their knowledge but it enhanced the reputation of the newly ennobled to extend protection to scholars of European standing. The humanists, for their part, saw it as a primary task to guide the kings who now wielded growing powers in the states of Europe as also their influential counsellors. This was not so much an end in itself as a means to the wider end of promoting enlightened government and reforms in the ecclesiastical and social order.

Books of various kinds were devoted to this matter. The Spanish humanist Juan Luis Vives wrote a brief guide for the son of Lord Mountjoy in 1523 and followed it with a book on the Christian upbringing of girls, dedicated to Catherine of Aragon, before addressing his major work to the king of Portugal. Erasmus dedicated *The Institution of a Christian Prince* to Charles of Spain, later the emperor Charles V, in 1516. The previous year the great French scholar Budé had drawn up a similar treatise in the vernacular at the accession of Francis I and Melanchthon framed another for the guidance of German princes. These were in the nature of political tracts, in particular urging princes to keep the peace and abstain from disastrous military adventures; humanists were overtly contemptuous of the chivalric code and martial glories, and it is a mistake to envisage them as advocates of courtly education. Indeed, concerned to investigate the actual origins of government, they had no particular veneration for princes;[1] unless, that is, they acquired a knowledge of the arts of peaceful government and characteristics ensuring the wise exercise of ruling powers.

This, however, was only one aspect of promoting education. Humanists could also use their influence at court to further developments in school and university which would serve to undermine scholasticism and civilise the church. All in all a Christian commonwealth could only be brought into being if the church devoted its attention to spiritual and social duties, the direction of secular affairs was in the hands of wise lay governors and the people too were lifted out of ignorance. Vital to all these ends was an extension and re-orientation of the education given to the rising generation.

New opportunities for pursuing these aims seemed to open out when in 1509 Henry VIII succeeded. Here was a new ruler who had himself been admirably brought up and who respected men of learning.[2] Among many loud in their praises was William Blount, Lord Mountjoy, who had studied with Erasmus in Paris and was known as the most learned among the noble and the most noble among the learned. He invited his former tutor to come and see for himself the opening of a new era; Erasmus accepted the invitation, so renewing for five years his association with Colet and others while receiving the patronage of Archbishop Warham and Bishop Fisher of Rochester, chancellor of Cambridge University. A decade later, writing of the king's application to study, Erasmus is holding up the English court as a model of learning and piety which can boast more scholars than any university. How strange it is, he reflects, that religious men in monasteries now care only for ease and luxury while the love of learning has gone from them to secular princes, the court and the nobility.[3]

By this time Wolsey, onetime fellow of Magdalen College, had risen by rapid preferment to become archbishop of York and the

[1] 'What power and sovereignity soever you have,' Erasmus told them, 'you have it by the consent of the people. And if I be not deceived, he that hath authority to give hath authority to take away again' (quoted in Christopher Morris, *Political Thought in England. Tyndale to Hooker*, 1953, p. 21).

[2] He had had two poets laureate as tutors in his grandmother's household and gained a reputation for speaking modern languages, as a Latin scholar, a skilled executant in music, and adept at the more active courtly arts including the game of tennis (Pollard, pp. 19–25).

[3] J. Strype, *Ecclesiastical Memorials* (Oxford, 1822), I, i, pp. 53–4.

king's chief minister. The king's secretary was Richard Pace, former student at Padua and friend of Erasmus and More. Mountjoy was a member of Catherine of Aragon's household which reflected the humanist tradition as it had developed in Spain and to which in 1523 Vives was appointed as tutor to the princess, Mary. Thomas More, who had seen his *Utopia* published some years before in Louvain under Erasmus's supervision, had made a reputation at the bar and latterly become a member of the privy council. Thomas Linacre was physician to the king and president of the Royal College of Physicians newly incorporated in 1518. John Colet had long been dean of St Paul's and in the royal favour. It was through the influence of such men that two foundations dedicated to the new learning had been successfully established in the previous decade, a school in the capital and a college at Oxford, stronghold of scholasticism.

Many of the ideas advanced by the humanists, Erasmus in particular, were radical. But their emphasis on civilised learning, the kind of challenge they presented to scholasticism and traditional forms of education—and with this to the church itself—were in tune with the prevailing outlook at court; leading bishops were among those most acutely aware of the need for some reform, particularly of the old religious communities and the universities. At the same time humanist ideas were congenial to an urban middle class risen to positions of responsibility but accorded little recognition in the social order and particularly resentful of ecclesiastical pretensions and interference. Indeed these ideas were fundamentally a product of the development of urban culture and the rise to economic and social influence of the middle class.[1]

Colet, Erasmus and More all had their origin in the towns. Colet was a citizen of London by birth, son of a prominent member of the leading city company. More, son of a common lawyer, followed his father's profession and his first employment at the bar was in commercial cases. He subsequently became under-sheriff of the city, freeman of the Mercers' Company, and was sent to Flanders in 1514 at the request of London merchants to settle a dispute with the Hanseatic League. The first book of *Utopia*, written the following year, suggests

[1] 'The Italian intelligenzia, that found itself so strongly pressed to provide the ideological superstructure of a specifically capitalist culture, can be seen to have put into words the aspirations not only of their compatriots but of the rising middle-class throughout the West. Their writings were in the fullest sense representative of the changing world of their time' (Bolgar, p. 246).

how Bruges and Antwerp, with their fine buildings and wide streets, impressed a Londoner familiar with wood and plaster houses in crowded yards and alleys.[1]

Erasmus, born in Rotterdam, subsequently sampled most aspects of the scholar's life. At first an Augustinian canon, he supplemented the regulation theological studies by reading all the chief classical poets and eventually escaped to take up the post of secretary to a princely bishop. He thus became acquainted with the life of the towns in which in turn the household resided and with public affairs. Receiving a stipend from his patron to attend the university of Paris he supplemented this, as did many scholars, by teaching younger students while continuing his own studies.[2] But it was his aquaintance with Colet, when he first visited England in 1499, that set Erasmus on the road to becoming the chief advocate of the new learning. It was from this time that he began to publish open criticism of the church, not least of monasticism which he knew from the inside, and of scholastic learning which he had once admired but had now outgrown.

Colet and Erasmus set the new learning in the centre of the picture, advocating study of the classical tongues and literatures as a means to deeper knowledge, in particular of the scriptures. Closely coupled with teaching in this sense was their outright condemnation of the lack of learning, worldliness and corruption of the church as an institution. In his early works Erasmus voiced what was fundamentally a bourgeois anti-clericalism. 'I marvel a great deal', he wrote in 1503 in a book intended for the general reader,

> how these ambitious names of power and dominion were brought in, even unto the very popes and bishops, and that our divines be not ashamed no less indiscreetly than ambitiously to be called everywhere our masters, when Christ forbade his disciples that they should not suffer to be called either lords or masters.

To challenge the rights of spiritual lords in this way was ultimately to challenge also the pretensions of lay lords, to set up a new code of conduct which conceded nothing to those of high degree:

> Whoso thinketh it not everywhere to be an excellent thing...if a man descend of worshipful stock and of honourable ancestors, which thing they call

[1] *The Utopia of Sir Thomas More*, ed. J. H. Lupton (Oxford, 1895), pp. xxi, xxvi–xxvii.

[2] J. Huizinga, *Erasmus of Rotterdam* (1952 ed.), pp. 4–9, 16–19, 26–8.

nobleness? Let it not move thee one whit when thou hearest the wise men of this world...so earnestly disputing of the degrees of their genealogy or lineage...thou, laughing at the error of these men after the manner of Democritus, shalt count (as true it is indeed) that the only and most perfect nobleness is to be regenerate in Christ.

Here was a new basis for private judgement, a creed for a class seeking a recognised position. 'Think it not therefore well or aright because that great men or because that most men do it, but this wise only shall it be well and right, whatsoever is done, if it agree to the rule of Christ.' These passages come from *The Manual of the Christian Knight*[1] as it was translated by William Tyndale shortly before he left England for Germany in 1534 to embark on his translation of the bible into the vernacular. First published in English in 1533 and often reprinted, this book was widely read. So also was Erasmus's *Little Book of Good Manners for Children*, a tract in the form of earlier manuals but with a different content, which was translated in 1532: 'Let others paint on their escutcheons lions, eagles, bulls, leopards. Those are the possessors of true nobility who can use on their coats of arms ideas which they have thoroughly learned from the liberal arts.'[2]

It was in the same spirit that the schoolmen were arraigned. Colet's advice to students was 'Study the bible and the Apostles' Creed and let divines if they will dispute about the rest'. Of Aquinas, the greatest schoolman of them all and idol of the church, Colet remarked: 'If he had not been very arrogant indeed, he would not surely so rashly and proudly have taken upon himself to define *all* things. And unless his spirit had been somewhat worldly, he would not surely have corrupted the whole teaching of Christ, by mixing it with his profane philosophy.'[3] Erasmus concentrated his attack on Duns Scotus who had a greater following than Aquinas in the universities. More generally he pointed to the disputations over points of grammar which never reached a clear conclusion, the endless commentaries each more obscure and further from the original than the last, as well as the confusion of divinity with philosophy in the monuments to scholastic theology. All this and more he held up to ridicule in a book which shook the church throughout Europe—*In Praise of Folly* (1509) written in More's house in London and dedicated to his host—and later challenged seriously and in detail.

[1] *Enchiridion Militis Christiani* (1905 ed.), pp. 193, 222.

[2] *EGS*, pp. 105–6.

[3] F. Seebohm, *The Oxford Reformers* (1887 ed.), pp. 105–6, 107.

The counterpart of this was insistence on a return to study of the bible itself and the early fathers of the church—Paul, Origen, Ambrose, Jerome, Augustine—a standpoint which aroused strong opposition in the universities. 'I have heard some men myself which stood so greatly in their own conceit...', wrote Erasmus in the *Enchiridion*, 'that they despised the interpretation of old doctors that were nigh unto Christ and his apostles both in time and living also...and Master Dunce gave them such confidence that notwithstanding they never once read the holy scripture, yet thought they themselves to be perfect divines.'[1]

So far as scholarship was concerned this approach set a number of positive tasks upon which Erasmus embarked; for instance, the task of clarifying grammar, which had been drawn into the orbit of scholastic dispute, of studying the languages in which the scriptures were originally written, notably Greek. Presenting his edition of *Valla's Annotations on the New Testament* (1505), Erasmus insisted that theologians must be sound grammarians, for the scriptures could not be interpreted by divine inspiration but only by sound learning.[2] Valla had shown that there were many passages in the Vulgate which were a bad rendering of the original Greek or manifestly corrupted, and Erasmus followed this up with his own translation of the New Testament into Latin (*Novum Instrumentum*, 1516) which drove the lesson home, not least by way of pungent annotations. This was a fundamental challenge to the authority of the church.

In the humanist view, however, it was not only future theologians who must study, not only those who aspired to direct affairs in church or state, but also every man who desired to live wisely and well. In More's rational republic government fell to the learned; boys were selected in early youth for their promise and carefully educated for future responsibilities, particularly in the wisdom of Greece, but all children were taught in the vernacular and given training in husbandry or crafts.[3] Erasmus laid emphasis on the duty of heads of families to provide and supervise a Christian education for their children, an insistence on the family's role which owed little to the tradition of the feudal nobility and much to the practice of the towns. Men of means should also exercise liberality to provide for the education of the less wealthy by founding schools, and Erasmus wrote eloquently of the

[1] *Loc. cit.* p. 66.

[2] Seebohm, pp. 177–8.

[3] *Utopia* (Everyman ed.), pp. 63–4, 82–3.

need to spread education so that ordinary men and women might have access to the scriptures in their native tongue.[1]

This last plea was voiced most clearly in *An Exhortation to Diligent Study of Scripture*—the title under which the introduction to the revised New Testament was translated into English in 1529—in words which were to be echoed by Tyndale in the preface to his English bible, by Coverdale and many another. Closely analogous were objections to the ritual of church services conducted in a language incomprehensible to the people, music being elevated above words to which no one listened, sermons but rarely given and the educative function generally neglected. Such criticism fell most heavily on the monks, as one of Erasmus's annotations to the New Testament illustrates.[2] He complained that boys were kept in the Benedictine monasteries 'solely and simply to sing morning hymns to the Virgin'; they 'do not understand what they are singing, yet according to priests and monks it constitutes the whole of religion....Money must be raised to buy organs and train boys to squeal and to learn no other thing that is good for them.'

The worldliness and corruption of the higher clergy were also castigated, in particular by Colet, in the light of a comparison with the simplicity of the primitive church. A notable example is his sermon before convocation in 1513, made at the invitation of Archbishop Warham and published in English shortly afterwards, which suggests a planned intention. In this Colet condemned the breathless race for promotion from benefice to benefice, the proud dominion of leading churchmen, the covetousness which led to exaction of endless dues from birth to burial, the corruption of ecclesiastical courts in caring only for those laws which were lucrative while amendment of the people's way of life was neglected. Bishops and priests lowered their office when they were invariably subservient to worldly pressures. It was this that induced opposition from the laity; nothing, not even heresy, Colet affirmed, is 'so pestilent and pernicious' to church and people 'as the evil and wicked life of priests'. The essential reforms he urged were: that only the fit and educated be admitted to the priesthood,

[1] Seebohm, pp. 327, 444.

[2] 'The laity are burdened to support miserable, poisonous corybantes, when poor, starving creatures might be fed at the cost of them. They have so much of it in England that the monks attend to nothing else. A set of creatures who ought to be lamenting their sins fancy they can please God by gurgling in their throats' (J. A. Froude, *Life and Letters of Erasmus* (1895), pp. 130–1).

that the monasteries be reformed, non-residence ended, and episcopal wealth properly used not on pomp and luxury but for the good of the diocese and the poor.[1]

Such views could now be widely disseminated to a growing audience of the literate. With the printing-press at his disposal Erasmus issued a continuous stream of treatises, text-books and frankly popular tracts, which were published in all the chief cities of Europe—in Antwerp, Basle, Cologne, Cracow, Vienna, as well as Paris and London. Among his most influential works were the *Colloquies*, first written for Froben's young son; published in 1515 the book was promptly banned by the university of Paris but, constantly reprinted with new additions, it eventually became a popular text in the reformed schools of Germany. The reason is not far to seek. With his clarity, wit and rational approach Erasmus cut through the stuffy overgrowth of sophistry and superstition, bringing in the necessary lessons on the way. Here he is on a shipwreck.

What, asks the interlocutor, did the passengers do? 'There you would have seen a miserable face of things. The sailors singing *salve regina* implored the virgin mother, calling her the star of the sea, the queen of heaven, lady of the world, harbour of safety, and flattering her with many other titles, which the holy scriptures nowhere attribute to her.' What, interpolates the first speaker, 'has she to do with the sea, who never sailed, I believe?' Erasmus explains that Venus once took care of sailors but, having now ceased so to do, 'the virgin mother is substituted for this mother, not a virgin'. More banter follows, further cuts at 'ridiculous superstition', with a suggestion that remembrance of Paul the apostle who did know something about the sea and shipwreck would have been more to the point, until the interlocutor asks: 'What did you in the meantime, did you make vows to none of the saints?'—'Not at all.'[2]

Despite their far-reaching criticisms of the ecclesiastical order the humanists did not envisage a rift in the unity of the universal church. The idea of a European community of states, welded together by a common language, learning and creed, was central to their thought.

[1] S. Knight, *Life of Dean Colet* (Oxford, 1823), pp. 251–64.

[2] This translation, which captures the spirit of the original, is given in G. A. Plimpton's survey of school books, *The Education of Shakespeare* (1933), pp. 96–102. It will be clear from quotations given here that allowance must be made for the difference between contemporary and modern translations; in Tyndale's version Erasmus speaks in a different style but the one most Englishmen read.

Nevertheless their telling criticisms of monasticism, the worship of saints and relics, pilgrimages to shrines, their consistent exposure of the abuse of ecclesiastical powers and neglect of charitable duties, voiced feelings that had been gathering strength and paved the way for more thoroughgoing reformers. Not least was this so in their call for the spread of a Christian education, in the first instance in the vernacular.

(2) *St Paul's School*

It was in the light of this general outlook that St Paul's school was founded, on a new model and with a radically new curriculum. Here was a public school of the kind that all humanist writers advocated: a school open to all comers, placed in the city and not shut away in a monastic precinct, held in a building of its own and under the control of a public authority. For the dean of St Paul's, having taken careful steps to nullify all rights formerly exercised by the chapter of the cathedral, placed his foundation under the governance of the city company to which his father had belonged. As Erasmus wrote, the school was entrusted 'not to the clergy; not to the bishop, not to the chapter; nor to any great minister at court; but amongst the married laymen; to the Company of Mercers, men of probity and reputation'. And Colet did this because 'he found less corruption in such a body of citizens than in any other order or degree of mankind'.[1]

In establishing his school Colet did not express concern to improve the education of the clergy, nor to provide especially for gentlemen's sons, nor to meet the practical needs of merchants; rather he was interested in the enlightened education of children, 'my countrymen, little Londoners especially'. During the preparation of his project he called in many of the humanist circle to help in drawing up a new plan of studies—Linacre, William Lily, who after leaving Magdalen had studied in Italy and learned Greek in Rhodes, above all Erasmus. It was the practical necessity of producing text-books and directions for the teachers of his friend's foundation that first caused Erasmus to bend his keen brain and extensive knowledge to detailed educational problems.

The records of the Mercers' Company include a reference to the building of a schoolhouse in 1508, the following year Colet first ear-marked lands for the endowment and on 12 April 1510 the court was

[1] Carlisle, II, p. 83.

informed that he was waiting on the king to discuss making over lands in mortmain. Subsequently, having heard in some detail of the dispositions the dean proposed to make, they 'were well content and gave him thanks and were also well content to go further with him in the said matter'.[1] Colet evidently went to great pains to involve members of the company in planning the school for there is a minute that six of the court were chosen 'which shall weekly attend upon Master dean of St Pauls at such time as he shall appoint them to come unto the new schoolhouse at Pauls when as he and they shall devise for to devise, make and ordain such ordinances, rules and constitutions as shall be needful'.[2] That July, Lily—a layman and married—was appointed high master and presented with the ordinances, and soon took possession of the special house being built adjoining the schoolhouse; the usher also had his own dwelling. The stipend of the former was £35, of the latter £18, sums two or three times as great as was customary so that they might teach freely all the 153 boys for whom the school was planned.[3]

Colet added a chapel and chaplain to the foundation but this was no chantry priest, nor were the children to engage in repetition of offices. Instead of praying for the founder the chaplain was to 'pray for the children to prosper in good life and in good literature to the honour of God and our lord Christ Jesu'. When the bell rang to announce the elevation of the host during the daily celebration of mass in chapel the pupils were to kneel up in their seats in school and say a prayer, after which 'they shall sit down again to their learning'.[4]

The school was dedicated to the child Jesus and Colet hung a picture of Christ teaching over the master's chair, as also at Erasmus's suggestion another of God the Father with the legend 'Hear ye Him'. This in itself was a manifesto—the humanists particularly deprecated the cult

[1] McDonnell, pp. 32–5; the complicated procedure whereby Colet ensured the status of the school and endowed it is detailed here with fresh information from the company's records (pp. 38–57).

[2] *Acts of Court of the Mercers' Company* (Cambridge, 1936), p. 401.

[3] Colet spent nearly the whole of his patrimony on building and endowing the school, the buildings costing some £3000, the endowment nearly £2500. By comparison the wealthy merchant tailor Sir John Percival, who left a total of some £2780 for religious and charitable purposes, earmarked £1100 to endow a chantry with one priest to pray for his soul, a second to keep school (Jordan, *Charities of London*, pp. 211, 325).

[4] This is specified in the founder's statutes, printed with annotations in R. B. Gardiner, *Admission Registers of St Paul's School* (1884), pp. 375–84.

of the virgin and the saints with which schools had so often been associated. The other arrangements Erasmus described in this way:

He divided the school into four apartments. The first, viz., the porch and entrance is for catechumens, or the children to be instructed in the principles of religion; where no child is to be admitted, but what can read and write. The second apartment is for the lower boys, to be taught by the second master or usher; the third, for the upper forms, under the headmaster: which two parts of the school are divided by a curtain to be drawn at pleasure....The boys have their distinct forms, or benches, one above another. Every form holds sixteen; and he that is head or captain of each form has a little kind of desk by way of pre-eminence.[1]

The detailed description suggests that the arrangements were novel, in particular the standard set for entry and the division into forms implying a desire for planned teaching up the school. While this principle was of first importance the actual number of forms specified for this and later schools was not, perhaps, of such moment as is sometimes suggested but it may be noted that nine were planned for St Paul's, not eight as has been calculated.[2]

Colet himself drew up an accidence for the earliest stage of teaching and a short guide in English called *Institution of a Christian Man*.[3] These made up an elementary text, known as the *Æditio*. Lily framed a simple syntax in English which was published under the title *Rudimenta*, sometimes as a separate volume but also in one volume with Colet's *Æditio*. This was the basic text-book for St Paul's, one in the vernacular. There was much more difficulty in framing a Latin grammar. Linacre, whose assistance was engaged, responded with a long treatise which Colet found unsuitable. Lily then prepared a Latin syntax which was considerably amended by Erasmus; since neither was prepared to claim authorship, this appeared anonymously under the title *De*

[1] Carlisle, II, p. 82.

[2] By T. W. Baldwin, *William Shakspere's Small Latine and Lesse Greeke* (Urbana, 1944), II, pp. 702–5. Colet's statutes say clearly that the school is for 153 boys 'according to the number of seats' and Erasmus describes forms for 16 pupils with a desk for the head boy of each, making 17. Though the chaplain was enjoined to teach the catechism he evidently did no more than instruct individual entrants as they came before admission to the school proper; the practice of teaching a regular class of petties in the porch developed later but the company put a stop to it in 1561 (McDonnell, p. 83). Ten years later there was an under-usher teaching a petty class and eight forms under the master and usher.

[3] It consisted of the articles of the faith, the seven sacraments and precepts of living in English; there followed the apostles' creed, pater noster and a prayer to the child Jesus in Latin (Knight, pp. 381–8).

Constructione, the first known edition being that printed by Pynson in 1513. Lily also composed grammar rules in verse (*De generibus nominum*) which long remained current and became generally known under the opening words of the two sections as 'Propria quae maribus' and 'As in praesenti'.[1] Meanwhile Erasmus translated Colet's moral precepts into Latin verse for the use of the school; the verses were printed as a preface to his new edition of Cato's distichs, also published in 1513, as was his edition of Aesop's fables. These were standard elementary texts and underline again concern for the first stage of learning.

In addition Erasmus compiled, expressly for the school, a text-book of quite a new kind intended to foster new methods of teaching. This was in two parts—the *De Copia Verborum* and *De Copia Rerum*—and designed as an aid to studying the content of Latin authors, giving directions for the taking and classifying of notes.[2] He also wrote at this time a manual for teachers, *De Ratione Studii*, which dealt with 'the right method of instruction' to be followed by schoolmasters, and so also with their own qualifications in learning. The master should 'acquaint himself with authors of every type, with a view to contents rather than to style', wrote Erasmus, going on to stress that such knowledge could be consolidated by taking and ordering notes as recommended in the *De Copia*. To illustrate the kind of knowledge a teacher should have and be able to impart, he points out that to understand classical poets and historians it is necessary to introduce some geography and discusses how this can lead on to other things:

> This subject includes two parts, a knowledge, first of the names ancient and modern, of mountains, rivers, cities; secondly, of names of trees, plants, animals, of dress, appliances, precious stones, in which the average writer of today shows a strange ignorance. Here we gain help from the works which have come down to us upon agriculture, architecture, the art of war, cookery, precious stones and natural history. We can make good use in the same subject of etymology....We can trace word-change in names through modern Greek, or Italian and Spanish.

After illustrating this technique of learning further, by reference to other subjects, Erasmus concludes:

> a genuine student ought to grasp the meaning and force of every fact or idea that he meets with in his reading, otherwise the literary treatment

[1] *EGS*, pp. 247–50, as corrected and supplemented by C. G. Allen, 'The Sources of "Lily's Latin Grammar"', *The Library*, fifth series, IX (1954), pp. 85–8.

[2] For a description of this, *EGS*, pp. 437–9.

through epithet, metaphor or simile will be to him obscure and confused. There is thus no discipline, no field of study...which may not prove of use in expounding the poets and orators of antiquity. 'But', you rejoin, 'you expect all this of your scholar?' Yes, if he proposes to become a teacher; for he thus secures that his own erudition will lighten the toil of acquisition for those under his charge.[1]

That Colet, far from deprecating such close attention to what classical authors had to say, warmly approved this approach is indicated in a letter welcoming the newly published book in 1511. Would that he could find such teachers, he wrote. 'When I came to that point at the end of the letter, where you say that you could educate boys up to a fair proficiency in both tongues in fewer years than it takes those pedagogues to teach their babble, O Erasmus, how I longed that I could make you the master of my school!' Colet expressed the hope that on leaving Cambridge, where he then was, Erasmus would 'give us a helping hand in teaching our teachers', enjoining also 'do not give up looking for an undermaster, if there should be anyone in Cambridge who would not think it beneath his dignity to be under the head-master'.[2]

A school planned on such lines could not but attract attention and from some quarters critical comment. It was not surprising Thomas More remarked that some people should bear malice for, like the great horse which hid armed Greeks for the attack on the Trojans, the school was bound to bring forth men who would expose their ignorance. This was an old humanist tag, first applied to Vittorino da Feltre's famous school at Mantua, but it was relevant. In fact Colet was assailed both for his outspokenness about ecclesiastical corruption and his new foundation, not the least of his critics being his immediate superior the bishop of London. He himself described one incident to Erasmus, lightheartedly enough, in 1512:

Now listen to a joke! A certain bishop, who is held, too, to be one of the wiser ones, has been blaspheming our school before a large concourse of people, declaring that I have erected what is a useless thing, yea a bad thing—

[1] W. H. Woodward, *Desiderius Erasmus Concerning the Aim and Method of Education* (Cambridge, 1904), pp. 166–8.

[2] Seebohm, pp. 218–19. The first undermaster, whether from Cambridge is not known, was unsatisfactory since he had no knowledge of teaching method. The second, appointed in 1515, was a bachelor of grammar of Magdalen College School who left to become tutor to Wolsey's natural son (McDonnell, p. 60).

yea more (to give his own words) a temple of idolatry. Which, indeed, I fancy he called it because the poets are to be taught there. At this, Erasmus, I am not angry, but laugh heartily.

Colet added, reminded of more important matters: 'do not forget the verses for our boys, which I want you to finish with all good nature and courtesy. Take care to let us have the second part of your *Copia*.' The latter was soon forthcoming, with a dedicatory preface extolling Colet and turning guns on his enemies. 'He must be envious indeed', declared Erasmus, 'who does not back with all his might the man who engaged in a work like this. He must be wicked, indeed, who can gainsay or interrupt him. That man is an enemy to England who does not care to give a helping hand where he can.' Such references in a text-book reprinted five times during the next three years and used throughout Europe made both school and founder widely known.[1]

At home, however, Colet was for a time under a cloud, threatened with excommunication and loss of office. Tyndale later affirmed that his chief crime was to have published a paraphrase of the paternoster in the vernacular,[2] and that he was only saved from the wrath of conservative ecclesiastics by that patron of humanist scholars Archbishop Warham: 'the bishop of London would have made dean Colet of Paul's a heretic for translating the paternoster in English had not the bishop of Canterbury helped the dean'.[3] But Colet also had the favour of the young king who was neither averse to the aims of his school nor criticism of the church and who would even himself accept criticism from the dean of St Paul's.

Shortly before his death Colet drafted a final set of statutes for the school he had so carefully planned and successfully brought to birth. In these he does not set out a detailed curriculum; he was, after all, expressing his intentions to a body of London citizens and, exceptionally, was aware that the passage of time and advancement of knowledge would make changes necessary—these he fully authorises. Meanwhile he formulates his own ideas about the teaching of boys briefly in general terms. 'I would they were taught always in good literature, both Latin and Greek, and good authors such as have the very Roman eloquence joined with wisdom'; he added, 'especially Christian authors

[1] Seebohm, pp. 252–3. Another book dedicated to Colet, which extolled the school and was evidently intended for use in it, was *De Fructu* by Richard Pace, published in Basle in 1517 (Knight, pp. 231, 391–4).

[2] Knight, p. 388.

[3] Seebohm, pp. 254–5.

that wrote their wisdom in clean and chaste Latin' and later specified certain names in this category as Erasmus had specified the best classical authors. But he himself was more eloquent, in so far as the vernacular in which his directions were written allowed, about what was not to be taught—the 'Latin adulterate' of scholasticism; 'all such abusion which the later blind world brought in which more rather may be called blotterature than literature I utterly abanish and exclude out of this school'. He would substitute the true Latin speech and 'the very Roman tongue' used by Cicero and Sallust, Virgil and Terence, the pure Latin also used by the fathers of the church. In the preface to the school grammar he clearly indicated that this was to be used in conjunction with reading classical authors. All who wish to understand, speak and write Latin well must

> busily learn and read good Latin authors of chosen poets and orators, and note widely how they wrote and spake, and study always to follow them, desiring none other rules but their examples. For in the beginning men spake not Latin because such rules were made but contrariwise because men spake such Latin, upon that followed the rules and were made. That is to say Latin speech was before the rules, not the rules before the Latin speech.

So also the masters were enjoined to concentrate on speaking Latin to the pupils rather than on expounding grammar rules; for reading good books, 'hearing eloquent men speak, and finally busy imitation with tongue and pen' is a far better means of attaining 'true eloquent speech, than all the traditions, rules and precepts of masters'.[1]

Lily later wrote a tract on manners for the boys of the school, *Carmen de Moribus*, comprising some eighty Latin verses setting out rules of conduct. A boy should wash well and come to school tidy, salute his master, have his quills, ink and paper ready, take pains in learning, speak Latin clearly, help other less advanced pupils and study the best Latin authors—again Virgil, Terence, Cicero are specified—conscientiously. Never imitate those who trifle away their time, nor boast of nobility and denigrate the parentage of other men, counsels Lily; this is bad manners. Do not sell or exchange; leave money, which is an incitement to evil, to others. Shun lies and contention and never take the name of God in vain.[2] There was nothing notably new about this kind of advice which figured in much the same way in earlier medieval manuals.

[1] Knight, p. 390. [2] *EGS*, p. 107.

What was new about Colet's approach was the clear severing of school teaching from ecclesiastical ritual and the attempt to permeate education with Christian principle. His primary aim, as set out in the statutes, was 'by this school specially to increase knowledge and worshipping of God and Our Lord Christ Jesu and good Christian life and manners in the children'. To this end he directed that education begin with the catechism in English, that the first Latin book should be Erasmus's translation of his simple precepts for living, that afterwards Christian authors be included with classical and their content taken to heart on the lines advocated in *De Copia* which was specified for use. Just as the religious observances of the medieval church were external and mechanical—so mechanical that men hired priests to repeat standard prayers for them and, as the humanists also complained, thoughtlessly worshipped painted images while themselves remaining unchanged—so in the schools stock prayers and grammar rules were learned and repeated by rote; they remained unrelated to the heritage of literature and learning as to the purposes of life. It was Colet's central idea that learning be turned to promote a Christian way of living, that children so educated would seek to put principle into practice in their daily affairs.[1] Essential to this end was a rational approach to learning, a clearing away of scholastic confusion so that grammar became a science of service to understanding, a full comprehension of those works of classical and Christian writers which incorporated the sum of human wisdom in lay and religious matters. These works were to be studied in a planned order, under the guidance of skilled teachers able to extract every ounce of knowledge from them, knowledge extending to cover geography, history and other fields. Thus Colet set out to place learning at the service of living, to present it as a means of preparing the individual to live well himself and do good in society. In maintaining that it was the function of the school to impart learning in this way he set an essentially new educational aim; embodying this approach in text-books, statutes, the actual organisation of his foundation, Colet provided a model humanist school.

[1] The same intention lies behind *A Right Fruitful Monition concerning the Order of a Good Christian Man's Life*, a short tract written in 1515 which achieved wide popularity.

(3) *Colleges at Cambridge and Oxford*

While humanist plans for schooling were designed to provide a better general education for laymen, matters stood differently so far as the universities were concerned. Here the main task set by humanist aims was to improve facilities for the education of the clergy, to train men who would be able and ready to minister in a new way. This was the particular concern of John Fisher, patron of Erasmus, who became chancellor of the university of Cambridge in 1503, bishop of Rochester in the following year, and did much to influence developments in his former university. Fisher, like Colet, looked to reform the abuses of the church from within, by raising educational standards among the clergy and promoting preaching of an evangelical kind. An ascetic and scholar, whose outlook contrasted strongly with that of the worldly politician Wolsey, Fisher found favour with Henry VII's mother, the pious Lady Margaret Beaufort. As her chaplain he was able to turn her attention from the monasteries she favoured—notably the wealthy abbey of Westminster to which the king was devoting large sums for his chapel—to the need for preachers, the study of divinity and more facilities for students. In the outcome Lady Margaret readers in divinity were endowed at both universities and at Cambridge also a preacher—charged to deliver six sermons annually in London and other towns at a time when preaching had long been at a discount—and two colleges.[1]

Christ's College, which replaced God's House in 1506, made large allowance for younger students on the foundation. Besides the twelve fellows, who must all be in holy orders, there were to be forty-seven disciples, or scholars; pensioners might only be taken if they strictly observed the discipline of the college. In deference to the earlier foundation scholars proficient in grammar were to be encouraged to continue in this discipline and also to study methods of teaching.[2] Other scholars were to study arts and theology and a lecturer was appointed to deliver four lectures daily in the college hall—on dialectic, logic, philosophy and, as the first lecturer of God's House had contracted for, on Latin poets and orators. The second college, St John's, suffered considerable vicissitudes since it had not been settled when the

[1] Mullinger, I, pp. 440–1.

[2] The proviso that they take up posts as schoolmasters being repeated from the God's House statutes (J. Peile, *Christ's College*, 1900, p. 19).

foundress died and her executors contrived to retain the lands allotted for the benefit of her heir, the young Henry VIII; only by Bishop Fisher's efforts was an alternative endowment arranged and buildings secured.[1] The statutes issued in 1516 closely followed those of Christ's. Here, too, there was provision for some pensioners. One of the earliest entrants was the only son of a Kentish gentleman in the royal service, Thomas Wyatt, who took an M.A. in 1522 at the age of nineteen; he had a reputation as a Latin scholar as well as for other attributes when he in turn took service under the king.[2]

The endowments of 'decayed' monasteries were frequently used to finance colleges at this period. In 1496 Jesus College, founded by Bishop Alcock, had taken the place of a Benedictine nunnery,[3] Christ's derived some of its endowment from a Norfolk abbey, St John's took over the site and lands of an Augustinian hospital. Ideas at Oxford turned in the same direction and an unsuccessful attempt was made to persuade the Lady Margaret to benefit that university by transforming the ancient priory of St Frideswide's into a college; an idea that evidently remained in the mind of Thomas Wolsey. There had been no new foundation at Oxford since 1448—except for the transformation of Brasenose Hall into a college in the year of Henry VIII's accession—but this position was remedied in 1517 when Richard Fox, bishop of Winchester, and Hugh Oldham, bishop of Exeter, founded Corpus Christi. It had been Fox's original intention to found a college for the young inmates of a monastery in his diocese as a step towards the necessary reform of the monastic order. But his associate is said to have exclaimed: 'What, my lord, shall we build houses and provide livelihoods for a company of buzzing monks, whose end and fall we ourselves may live to see; no, no, it is more meet a great deal that we should have a care to provide for the increase of learning and for such as by their learning shall do good in church and commonwealth'.[4] So plans for a college of secular clerks were substituted, and its statutes set out in detail a humanist curriculum.

[1] This early example of the alienation of lands intended to endow education and other problems attending the foundation are detailed in Thomas Baker, *History of St John's College, Cambridge*, ed. J. E. B. Mayor (Cambridge, 1869), I, pp. 55 ff.

[2] *Athenae*, I, pp. 80–1.

[3] Though this, in sharp contrast to the foundations a decade later, was a chantry college with school attached—similar to the small Jesus College established by Archbishop Rotherham in Yorkshire.

[4] A. A. Mumford, *Hugh Oldham* (1936), pp. 107–8.

Designed for twenty fellows and twenty disciples, students between the ages of twelve and nineteen, Corpus Christi, like the new Cambridge colleges, had a minimum of ancillary members—two chaplains, two clerks, two choristers. All candidates for fellowships must be acquainted with the works of Latin poets, orators and historians and be able readily to compose verse and write epistles in classical Latin. Three lectureships were attached to the college, the lectures to be delivered publicly in the university. Wainfleet had earlier made a like provision at Magdalen, one lecture to be in theology, two in philosophy.[1] One of the Corpus Christi lectureships was in theology but the other two were in Latin, or 'humanity', and Greek. It was the special task of the Latin lecturer to extirpate all barbarism from 'our beehive', as Fox, using a well-worn simile, consistently called his college. Lectures should cover the poets—Virgil, Ovid, Lucan, Juvenal, Terence, Plautus—and among other authors Cicero, Sallust, Valerius Maximus, Suetonius, Pliny, Livy, Quintilian; students were also recommended to study such Italian classicists as Valla and Politian under whom Linacre had studied. The Greek lecturer, the first to be established at either university, was required to lecture three times a week throughout the year on grammar and authors; on the works of Isocrates, Lucian, Aristophanes, Theocritus, Euripides, Sophocles, Pindar, Hesiod, Demosthenes, Thucydides, besides Aristotle. The theology lecturer was to cover the scriptures, the Old Testament and the New, and in his interpretation 'ever as far as possible follow the ancient and holy doctors both Latin and Greek, and especially Jerome, Augustine, Ambrose, Origen, Hilary, Chrysostom, John Damascene and others of that sort, not Nicholas of Lyra, not Hugh of Vienne, and the rest, who, as in time so in learning, are far below them'. So the schoolmen were dethroned in favour of patristic writers.[2]

Rules of conduct were detailed and strict, designed to enforce a simple life and eliminate corrupt practices. There were no special arrangements for housing young noblemen, the number of pensioners being limited to six who must be men of birth or knowledgeable in the law and so able to assist the community in an emergency. Many of the original fellows of Corpus were imported from Magdalen, with which the new college was linked in various ways, but the first lecturer in

[1] Lyte, *Oxford*, p. 367.

[2] T. Fowler, *History of Corpus Christi College* (Oxford, 1893), pp. 37 ff.; Lyte, *Oxford*, pp. 407–13.

humanity was one of Colet's followers, educated by Lily, Thomas Lupset. The second was the Spanish humanist Vives, appointed in 1523; he was already well known in England by reputation and the previous year had dedicated his commentaries on Augustine's *Civitas Dei* to Henry VIII. Erasmus, writing shortly after the foundation of the college to its first master, John Claymond, speaks of the great interest shown by the king and Cardinal Wolsey. It will, he predicts, with his customary enthusiasm, be regarded as one of the chief ornaments of Britain, and the trilingual library—of Latin, Greek and Hebrew works—will attract more scholars to Oxford than were formerly attracted to Rome.[1]

This view was not generally shared in the university; indeed the reaction against the new foundation was violent enough to suggest that, whatever interest in the humanities there had been at Oxford, study of classical poets was a startling innovation. But a whole course of study was now being advanced as an alternative to the traditional teaching of logic and dialectic and this was likely to antagonise teachers of the latter. While the disaffected could dub all classical literature as pagan, Greek could also be counted heretical since it was associated with the eastern church. Tyndale, in a later exchange with Thomas More, had vivid memories of the controversy, recalling how

> the old barking curs, Duns' disciples and like draff called Scotists, the children of darkness, raged in every pulpit against Greek, Latin and Hebrew, and what sorrow the schoolmasters that taught the true Latin tongue had with them, some beating the pulpit with their fists for madness, and roaring with open and foaming mouth, that if there were but one Terence or Virgil in the world, and that same in their sleeves, and a fire before them, they would burn them therein, though it should cost them their lives.[2]

At a Lenten sermon, delivered in the spring of 1518, a university preacher assailed the study of classical literature probably somewhat in this manner, and there had been brawls in the streets between clerks who banded together under the name of Trojans to offer organised opposition to the Grecians of Corpus. Shortly afterwards the court moved to Abingdon and Thomas More and Richard Pace, who were in attendance, took steps to bring royal influence to bear. Meanwhile, More addressed his own rebuke to the university authorities in what

[1] Fowler, p. 59; cf. J. R. Liddell, 'The Library of Corpus Christi College, Oxford, in the Sixteenth Century', *The Library*, fourth series, XVIII (1938), pp. 385–416.

[2] S. L. Greenslade (ed.), *The Work of William Tindale* (1938), p. 93.

was a manifesto of the humanist outlook. Theology, though the highest study, was not the only subject recognised by universities, he pointed out; an acquaintance with polite literature was useful and necessary to lawyers, who were in turn essential to the state, and much knowledge of human affairs could be gained from classical poets, orators and historians. Moreover, worldly learning could lead men on to higher things. As for theologians they must study Latin, Greek and Hebrew, unless theology was to be restricted to the minute *questiones* about which the schoolmen and their followers disputed in their barbarous idiom; but this was not the method of the great fathers of the church who themselves studied Greek, the language in which the New Testament was originally written and which the Council of Vienne had ordered to be taught in the principal universities. More concluded by contrasting the conduct of Oxford with that of Cambridge which was contributing towards the support of a Greek lecturer recently established by Bishop Fisher. He ended with a warning that further opposition would alienate the favour of their chancellor, Archbishop Warham, their great patron Cardinal Wolsey, and their king.[1]

According to Erasmus's account there followed a peremptory order from the king himself that students of Greek be allowed to prosecute their studies unmolested which, if it did not appease objections, served to quieten the outcries. But perhaps a more potent influence was that of Wolsey who visited Oxford at about this time and seems to have taken the public lectures under his own protection, while announcing an intention of promoting more. It was evidently Wolsey who sent Vives, Lupset and others to lecture at Oxford in subsequent years, though they held the Corpus Christi lectureships. The university responded to this benevolent interest on the part of the man who held the reins of power with many protestations of gratitude and, despite the warnings of its chancellor, delivered up its statutes to the cardinal for revision. This example was followed by Cambridge in 1524 and it is clear that Wolsey was contemplating a considerable re-organisation of the universities.[2]

Oxford was not flourishing at this time; recurrent epidemics of the sweating sickness emptied the colleges while there are also references to the mounting cost of living discouraging students. Writing to Thomas More in 1523 the university complained in its usual sweeping

[1] Lyte, *Oxford*, pp. 436–7.

[2] Mullinger, I, p. 549.

fashion—enumerating those to whom it had always looked to supply students—that abbots had almost ceased to send their monks to the schools, nobles their sons, beneficed clergy their relations and parishioners, so that the old halls were falling into ruin and only endowed colleges retained a semblance of prosperity.[1] Though Magdalen and Corpus Christi developed as centres of classical scholarship, humanist studies were only followed side by side with a traditional learning which had as yet barely been challenged. In relation to the established university disciplines of medicine and law the humanists offered little enough, while a great deal more than they had provided was necessary to undermine the vast edifice of scholastic theology and philosophy.[2] Meanwhile there was still much to be gained from the traditional legal studies, particularly if, as seems probable, more attention was being paid to civil law. William Petre, son of a Devonshire freeholder, who qualified in this faculty at Oxford in the 1520's, was one of a number who found that this took them far.[3]

Nevertheless, there is evidence that the classics were widely read,[4] and students kept up their interests later. A young monk who left Oxford in 1528 to return to Evesham Abbey, and thereafter conducted a voluminous correspondence with other Oxford men in Benedictine houses, and various parish priests known to him, shows a familiar acquaintance with such writers as Virgil, Horace, Ovid, Juvenal, Cato, the younger Pliny; he was also conversant, among Christian doctors, with Jerome and Lactantius, among contemporaries with Budé, Lily, Pace, Baptista Mantuan; and he had a rudimentary knowledge of Greek. This young monk was in charge of teaching the novices and was a close friend of the master of the grammar school who was accommodated in the house.[5]

[1] Lyte, *Oxford*, pp. 433–4.

[2] Bolgar, pp. 282 ff.

[3] Entered at Exeter College as a commoner at 14, Petre became fellow of All Souls in 1523, graduated bachelor of law in 1526 and was then elected principal of Vine Hall, a hall of civil lawyers. Shortly after he became tutor and companion to the son of the earl of Wiltshire and was later subsidised from the privy purse to travel abroad, gaining his first office in 1536 (F. G. Emmison, *Tudor Secretary*, 1961, pp. 2–6).

[4] The records of the leading university bookseller in 1520 show that more copies of Terence and Cicero were sold that year than of Aristotle; Virgil and Ovid ranking next, then Lucan, Aristophanes, Lucian, Horace, Pliny, Sallust. Small popular tracts apart, one in seven book buyers bought a work by Erasmus (*CHEL*, III, pp. 21–2).

[5] In his letters he writes 'an excellent, idiomatic, conversational Latin which derives its vocabulary from Plautus and Terence rather than Cicero. His style...immediately proclaims him for what he is, a fervent disciple of Erasmus' (Knowles, pp. 101–2, 106).

Cambridge continued to draw the majority of its students from nearby counties—monks from Norfolk and Suffolk houses, the sons of merchants, yeomen and gentlemen. Thomas Bilney, Hugh Latimer, Thomas Cranmer, Thomas Becon, are among well-known names of those in residence in the decade 1510–20, during the first years of which Erasmus was teaching in the university; so also Edward Crome, Nicholas Shaxton, John Skip, all fellows of Gonville Hall for up to twenty years, all later leading reformers.[1] Young men studying in the faculty of civil and canon law with the prospect of office in government were more likely to adopt a conservative standpoint, but they too imbibed aspects of Erasmian teaching. Stephen Gardiner, son of a Bury clothier, was at Trinity Hall; his first step on the road to the bishopric of Winchester came when, as tutor to the duke of Norfolk's son, he engaged Wolsey's favour. Of other future bishops Nicholas Heath, son of a London cutler, became fellow of Christ's in 1521 and shortly after one of Wolsey's chaplains; Rowland Lee, son of a Northumberland gentleman, commenced doctor of civil law in 1520 and became commissary general to Wolsey some years later.[2]

Prominent among those pursuing new studies were the inmates of monasteries and friaries—the Augustinian friar Robert Barnes, the Gilbertine Robert Holgate, a future archbishop of York, the Dominican friar John Hilsey and the Benedictine Henry Holbeach, both later to become bishops. Besides those who resided to take higher degrees, monks from neighbouring houses frequently spent a year or so at the university. The small Gonville Hall, for instance, received inmates of all the greater monasteries in East Anglia, including Norwich and Bury, and from such lesser houses as Wheatacre and Butley Priory which kept a school.[3] Returned from Cambridge such students, like the young monk of Evesham, often taught in turn and helped to spread humanist learning.

The latest works of Erasmus were eagerly studied at Cambridge, in particular the New Testament. One college, it is true, banned this, solemnly forbidding any person to bring a copy into the precinct by horse, boat, cart or porter. On hearing this he did not know whether

[1] H. C. Porter, *Reformation and Reaction in Tudor Cambridge* (Cambridge, 1958), pp. 42–3.

[2] A comparative list of reforming and conservative bishops, with information about their education, is given in L. Baldwin Smith, *Tudor Prelates and Politics 1536–58* (Princeton, 1953), pp. 306–7.

[3] J. Venn, *Early Collegiate Life* (Cambridge, 1913), pp. 65–79.

to laugh or cry, Erasmus wrote to a Cambridge friend, but it was 'pitiful for men to condemn and revile a book which they have not even read, or having read, cannot understand'. No doubt, having heard gossip about it, they immediately exclaimed '"O Heavens, O earth! Erasmus has corrected the Gospels"; when it is they themselves who have *depraved* them'. What did the authorities fear? That new interests would draw away their scholars and empty lecture-rooms?

Why do they not examine the facts? Scarcely thirty years ago, nothing was taught at Cambridge but the 'parva logicalia' of Alexander, antiquated exercises from Aristotle, and the '*questiones*' of Scotus. In process of time improved studies were added—mathematics, a new, or, at all events, a *renovated* Aristotle, and a knowledge of Greek.... What has been the result of all this. Now the university is so flourishing, that it can compete with the best universities of the age. It contains men, compared with whom theologians of the old school seem only the ghosts of theologians.[1]

In sum, Erasmus concluded, his critics were grieved because students, instead of indulging in frivolous quibbles, 'study with more and more earnestness the gospels and the apostolic epistles'. He himself had found two years of Cambridge enough; apart from the climate, teaching interfered with other work. But in 1516 one of his closest associates there, Henry Bullock of Queens', was lecturing in the university on the Gospel of St Matthew, using Erasmus's notes as guide, while another disciple, John Bryan of King's, lectured on Aristotle without reference to the schoolmen.[2] In 1518, with Bishop Fisher's aid, a readership in Greek was established. Richard Croke, the first to hold it, had studied with Grocyn at Oxford, under Erasmus at Cambridge and after some time at Paris and various German universities, had returned in 1517 to find favour at court and become preceptor in the Greek tongue to the king. It was shortly after this that he became fellow of St John's where he laid the foundations of Greek scholarship later built upon by John Cheke. In his first public oration Croke urged that Oxford should not be allowed to outstrip Cambridge in Greek. The scholars he mentioned were, in fact, no longer members of that university but making a mark in public life—Richard Pace, Cuthbert Tunstall, also

[1] Seebohm, pp. 399–400.

[2] Porter, pp. 31–2. During his time at Cambridge Erasmus, as he wrote to Colet, had conducted 'pitched battles on your behalf with these Thomists and Scotists'. He had also been engaged in much else, including editing a Greek grammar (*ibid.* pp. 34–5).

a former student at Padua, now rising fast in the church, Thomas More—but these examples and his own experience enabled Croke to stress the value of Greek as a passport to office. At the same time he carefully avoided undue criticism of the schoolmen and proposed only that Greek authors be added to other studies.[1]

While new subjects gained something of a foothold in the university course it was outside this that the gospels were earnestly studied. The Augustinian friary, exempt from episcopal jurisdiction, became the centre of the new learning in this sense. Robert Barnes, having left here to study under Erasmus at Louvain University, returned to become prior and gathered many students around him, not only for readings of Terence and Cicero but also, in the tradition of Colet, to hear lectures on the Pauline epistles. This led on, and with the most far-reaching effect, to direct study of the bible itself.

(4) *Developments up to 1530*

It is not easy to assess how far the example of St Paul's, where humanist educational plans were at first so thoroughly put into practice, influenced other schools. But some idea can be gained of general trends in the first decades of the sixteenth century.

The basic course of education had been built round the Latin primer of prayers, the psalter, then the 'Donat', the generic term for all elementary grammars. Some instruction was given in English, as the example of Childrey School suggests, and children must have learned to read in the vernacular, but the school course began with Latin. Here the first printed text-books to become available—to the more organised schools with competent masters—were those of the Magdalen College grammarians. But John Stanbridge and Robert Whittinton, both prolific authors of text-books designed particularly for boys, adhered to the method of using Latin phrases and extracts to illustrate grammar rules—the method to which Colet so objected as putting the cart before the horse. One of the features of these books was that the material was adapted to schoolboy interests; thus Stanbridge's *Vulgaria* consisted of short commonplace phrases in English and Latin such as 'Sit away or I shall give thee a blow', or 'Would God we might go play'.[2] This kind of thing, though suitable to the needs of a time when Latin had

[1] Mullinger, I, pp. 527 ff.

[2] W. Nelson, *A Fifteenth Century Schoolbook* (Oxford, 1956), pp. x–xi.

been colloquially spoken, was by no means the best introduction to Latin as the language of literature and scholarship. Indeed, though it long remained a general rule that Latin be spoken on school premises some scholars were soon deprecating this as a hindrance rather than a help.

Colet laid emphasis on an ordered approach to learning from the earliest stage in the vernacular and Lily, with the assistance of Linacre's work and of Erasmus, prepared an elementary Latin grammar designed to be used concurrently with reading authors. Some later text-books begin to move in this direction. The *Vulgaria* (1519) of William Horman —educated at Magdalen, master of the schools at Eton and Winchester colleges successively—had passages arranged under subject matter according to Erasmian directives; these, though often homely enough, were less colloquial and intended as a bridge to reading authors. The book was prefaced with commendatory verses by Lily and by Robert Aldrich, formerly of King's and acquainted with Erasmus at Cambridge, who was master at Eton from 1515 to 1521. But Robert Whittinton challenged the Lily approach and upheld his own views in the *Vulgaria* he published in 1520 and a considerable controversy ensued.[1] If Lily's methods eventually emerged victorious the process seems to have been a long one. During these and later years only one or two English editions of his grammar are to be traced, and it may well be that it became better known abroad, where it was associated with Erasmus's name, than at home; meanwhile there were innumerable editions of books by Stanbridge and Whittinton up to 1530.[2]

It is probable that Magdalen College school itself early adopted the Lily grammar since it was no longer known as the home of the Stanbridge method in 1515; a school endowed at Manchester in that year was required to follow this method as used at Banbury, where Stanbridge himself had moved to become master of St John's Hospital which had a school attached.[3] Whittinton became master of the hospital at Lichfield where there was also a school which would have adhered to his method. The schools of Eton and Winchester colleges were also apparently still using the grammars of Stanbridge and Whittinton up to the late 1520's.

[1] Stanier, pp. 37–8.

[2] For lists, correcting S.T.C., Eloise Pafort, 'A group of Early Tudor School Books', *The Library*, fourth series, XXVI (1946), pp. 227–61; and H. S. Bennett, 'A Check-List of Whittinton's Grammars', *ibid.*, fifth series, VII (1952), pp. 1–14.

[3] Stanier, p. 44.

In 1519 Richard Fitzjames, bishop of London—who was, of course, well acquainted with Colet's school if no supporter of his more advanced ideas—was instrumental in founding a school in connection with the Augustinian abbey of Bruton.[1] It was directed that the scholars be freely taught grammar 'after the good new form used in Magdalen College in Oxford or in the school of Paul's in London', the aim set being that boys should become 'after their capacities perfect Latin men'. This probably implied use of Lily's grammar but in any case was plainly a reference to the two schools of the day which had set new standards in teaching Latin. Other founders, however, looked to more familiar models. John Leach, vicar of Walden, directed that the school for which he left funds in 1517 should adopt methods of teaching grammar used at Eton and Winchester. The school at Rolleston, founded by a bishop of Chichester in 1520, was directed to look to Winchester practice generally, while another cleric who augmented Cuckfield school in 1528 required that the Eton timetable be followed. Roger Lupset, provost of Eton, was content to direct that his school at Sedbergh should teach grammar 'after the manner, form and use of some laudable, notable and famous school' when he issued orders for it in 1528 and placed it under the supervision of St John's College, Cambridge.[2]

All this is evidence of a desire to improve teaching and school organisation rather than of intentions to start a humanist school. There seems to be only one foundation directly modelled on St Paul's at this period, Berkhamsted school, initiated by Colet's successor as dean of St Paul's, John Incent. This was founded in conjunction with the local gild which in 1523 decided to devote its lands to the support of a school; Incent added some of his own, a schoolhouse was built to accommodate 144 boys and three masters were appointed—but there is no evidence of the curriculum followed.[3]

The following year the school endowed at Manchester by Bishop Hugh Oldham before his death was re-organised to safeguard its endowments; these were placed in the hands of lay trustees, rules were

[1] Associated in conveying lands to the abbey to endow this were his nephew, a judge, and the chancellor of St Paul's, John Edmonds, D.D.; the abbot provided site and schoolhouse, was accorded the right to appoint the master and bound to pay him £10 a year (J. D. Tremlett, ed., *Calendar of the MSS. belonging to the King's School, Bruton, 1286–1826*, pp. 5–6).

[2] *Sedbergh School Register*, ed. B. Wilson, (Leeds, 1909), p. 5.

[3] *VCH Herts.* II, pp. 71 ff.

drawn up based on those of St Paul's and appointment of the master was vested in Corpus Christi College. The school now looked towards both the main humanist foundations but none the less the Stanbridge grammar is still specified for use, possibly in deference to the founder who had earlier laid this down. There is no further information apart from Oldham's original intentions, voiced indirectly in the statutes of 1524, which are couched in somewhat traditional terms.[1] More schools were founded in the north in subsequent years. In Lancashire another was endowed at Farnworth by Bishop Smyth, also founder of an Oxford college.[2] Others established, mostly in connection with chantries, were at Blackburn, Liverpool, Leyland, Bolton, Warrington —the latter intended by Sir Thomas Boteler 'to be a very clear lantern of good example and virtuous living to all the county thereabouts' according to orders issued in 1526.[3] In Yorkshire the chantry schools at Sedbergh and Giggleswick (1507) seem early to have had a master's house with room to board and lodge pupils coming from a distance.[4]

Otherwise it is noteworthy that schools were still placed under the control of monastic houses, the most convenient repositories for endowments and directives, or endowments made to raise the standard of teaching within them. A fund was entrusted to Winchcombe Abbey in 1521 for payments to a master of grammar to be lodged and boarded in the precinct; in 1527 John Cole, warden of All Souls, Oxford's chantry college, conveyed lands to Faversham Abbey to finance a master to teach the novices grammar. On the other hand the abbot of Milton Abbey, when he endowed a free school there in 1521, placed it under the control of lay feoffees.[5]

As the example of Evesham has shown, there was an interest in humanist studies in some monastic houses at this time, fostered by inmates who had been at university and had leisure to pursue the

[1] His concern was to bring up children 'in good learning and manners', beginning with grammar as 'the gate by which all other be learned and known'; such teaching was needed in Lancashire where the common people were poor and schoolmasters scarce 'so that the children...having pregnant wit, have been, most part, brought up rudely and idly, and not in virtue, cunning, erudition, literature and in good manners' (Mumford, pp. 127–8).

[2] Bishop Fox, co-founder of Corpus Christi, also paid due attention to schools, building a schoolhouse at Taunton in 1522 and endowing a school at Grantham, his birthplace, in 1528 (Carlisle, I, p. 804).

[3] *VCH Lancs.* II, p. 601.

[4] E. A. Bell, *History of Giggleswick School* (Leeds, 1912), p. 15.

[5] *VCH Glos.* II, p. 421; Carlisle, I, pp. 374, 573.

interests acquired there. Indeed humanist teachers were more likely to be found in a monastic community with an enlightened head than in a small provincial town with a grammar school supervised by local men. When in 1525 Robert Whitgift, brother of a Grimsby merchant, became abbot of the nearby Augustinian priory at Wellow he was a zealous supporter of the new learning; among the pupils he took in for schooling were the sons of neighbouring gentlemen and his nephew, John Whitgift.[1] At Reading by 1530 the school administered by the abbey had as headmaster Leonard Cox, one of many itinerant humanist scholars, who had taught at Cracow University for a considerable time. He was author of the first English rhetoric, published during these years, which was specifically intended as a schoolbook, and to assist 'all such as will either be advocates or proctors in the law or...teachers of God's word, in such manner as may be most sensible and acceptable to their audience'. This was dedicated to his patron who took much interest in the school, Abbot Hugh Farington.[2]

In the provinces it was usual for local people who endowed schools to make a monastic house in some way responsible. The widow of a wealthy bellfounder, famous throughout the midlands, endowed Nottingham school in 1513, putting the borough in charge of administration under the oversight of the neighbouring priory. Another wealthy widow left £20 to provide stipends for a master and usher at Lewes in 1512; the local prior was to appoint the master who must be 'a priest able to teach grammar having no cure of souls' or other duties 'whereby he might draw his attendance from the said school'—a proviso Colet had made explicit and which from now on was more frequent.[3] In 1527 Adam Pennington left lands to endow a school in his home town Kendal, to be administered by the abbot of Risby or the alderman of the Corpus Christi gild to find a priest 'to keep and teach a free school'.[4]

Merchant benefactors continued to show an interest in promoting education but Colet's example was not one that could easily be followed. He had not only devoted to his school the whole of a substantial patrimony, inherited as sole surviving child of a wealthy citizen, but had specially trained teachers and provided a set of new text-books. The

[1] P. M. Dawley, *John Whitgift and the Reformation* (1955), p. 4.

[2] Leonard Cox, *The Arte or Crafte of Rhethoryke*, ed. F. I. Carpenter (Chicago, 1899), p. 41. In part a translation of a treatise by Melanchthon it was reprinted in 1532.

[3] A. W. Thomas, *History of Nottingham High School* (Nottingham, 1957); *VCH Sussex*, II, p. 411.

[4] Bouch, pp. 38–9.

average London merchant could hardly aim so high, even if he wished to emulate all this study of classical literature, and such founders continued to establish schools much on the old model in the provincial towns of their origin. It was, according to the historian of the city, a longstanding and 'laudable custom' of London for citizens to divide up their personal estate and leave half to charities of various kinds.[1] Estates could now be considerable, but education must still take its place on a list which usually included bequests to monasteries or friaries for masses or endowments of a chantry priest, as well as sums for hospitals, lazarhouses and prisons, the parish church, the poor, repair of bridges and highways. Merchant founders, however, more frequently set aside sums to build a schoolhouse which had its implications for improved education. For instance, Sir Stephen Jennings, a rich merchant tailor, provided a schoolroom and lodgings for the master and usher of Wolverhampton school, endowed during his lifetime in 1513 and placed under the control of his own company.[2] One London founder at this period specified the kind of teaching he had in mind when leaving lands in 1507 to endow a chantry priest at Enfield; he was to teach children 'to know and read their alphabet letters, to read Latin and English and understand grammar, and to write their Latins according to the use and trade of grammar schools'. In 1524 ten children were being taught by a writing master, retained for twelve weeks, besides receiving normal instruction in the school.[3]

In London itself the chief schools besides St Paul's were those connected with St Anthony's Hospital and St Thomas Acon Hospital. The historian of the city, John Stow, who was born in about 1525, witnessed as a boy the traditional disputations between scholars of these and other schools, held annually according to long custom at St Bartholomew's Priory in Smithfield. He recalled, for a later generation to which the practice was unfamiliar, that in the churchyard 'upon a bank boarded about under a tree some one scholar hath stept up, and there hath opposed and answered, till he were by some better scholar overcome and put down; and then the overcomer taking the place, did like as the first; and in the end the best opposers and answerers had rewards'.[4] This indicates that the university method of disputation

[1] Half went to masses and charity, half to the widow if there were no children; otherwise the latter had a third, the widow a third, charity the remaining third (Thrupp, p. 199).

[2] Mander, p. 29.

[3] L. B. Marshall, *A Brief History of Enfield Grammar School* (Richmond, 1958), pp. 11–12.

[4] Stow, p. 68.

over points of grammar was still followed by leading schools and Stow recalled that St Anthony's came out best though pupils from the school of St Peter's Abbey, Westminster, and from St Paul's were also engaged. The latter would hardly have been practised in disputation since teaching at their school was on very different lines; indeed Colet had specifically forbidden his scholars to participate in the Bartholomew's Day disputations designating these as 'but foolish babbling and loss of time'. But custom and considerations of prestige no doubt weighed more than rules, and though in 1534 the Mercers attempted to prevent the school from participating, calling on the statutes for authority,[1] it may well have continued to do so until the annual event itself ceased after the Reformation.

It must be inferred that in other matters St Paul's soon made its mark for scholars were coming from outside London from an early date and in 1525 the statutory number was exceeded.[2] Thomas More's adopted son, John Clement, who became the first Greek lecturer at Corpus Christi, and Colet's protégé Thomas Lupset, the first lecturer in Latin, were both known as Lily's pupils, while another, John Leland, the antiquary, helped to spread his master's fame. John Ritwise, Lily's son-in-law, succeeded as high master in 1522; he was boarding two scholars at the king's expense at the rate of some £15 a year in the early 1530's and by this time the school had several times been called upon to present plays at court. Ritwise himself wrote a tragedy which he acted with his scholars before Wolsey and in 1528 the Venetian ambassador, a cultured critic, recorded that a play by Terence had been executed by the boys with skill and grace at an official banquet. All this suggests that St Paul's was for the time in fashion, possibly more than Colet would have desired.

Among Lily's pupils who were later to rise to high office were Anthony Denny, son of a baron of the exchequer, and William Paget, son of a minor official, both of whom went on to Cambridge. But except for a few names—Sir William Carew brought a truant son, Peter, up from Devon but Ritwise had no success with him—there is little record of those who attended. The mercers, of course, patronised the school. Roger North sent his only son Edward who went on to

[1] McDonnell, p. 68.

[2] That year it was reported to the company that 'the school is surcharged with scholars and in especial them that come out of the country'; it was ordered that the latter be excluded to keep to the statutory number (*ibid.* p. 65).

Peterhouse before entering the inns of court and embarking on a career in public life. Richard and John Gresham also sent sons, one of whom was later to initiate another notable educational foundation in London; Thomas Gresham left St Paul's in 1530 to become a pensioner at Gonville Hall, Cambridge, for a year or so before being apprenticed for eight years to his uncle.[1] No doubt the school continued to be filled in subsequent years but even one so well provided for could have its ups and downs, if good masters were not easily available and governors unpractised, and matters did not go so well with St Paul's after the departure of Ritwise in 1532. Saddled with an inadequate master, who in the end remained seventeen years, the Mercers' Company ignored requests from the highest quarters to appoint a qualified scholar; evidently no Greek was taught in the school from 1532 to 1558.[2]

By contrast Magdalen College school, after a succession of undistinguished masters, came in 1526 under the guidance of Thomas Robertson who contributed a section to the version of Lily's grammar published in 1532;[3] he was succeeded in 1534 by Richard Sherry, later translator of one of Erasmus's educational tracts and author of a textbook on rhetoric.[4] The school of Eton College, which had no master of note after Aldrich left in 1521, came in 1528 under Richard Cox, a young man who had taken his M.A. at Cambridge four years before when the new learning was abroad. He was succeeded in 1534 by Nicholas Udall who the previous year had published *Flowers for Latin Speaking...gathered out of Terence* which included notes on vocabulary and grammar—one of the first collections of this kind paving the way for later rhetorics—and who also wrote one of the first plays in English to survive, a fully fledged five-act comedy inspired by Plautus.[5] Whether or not plays in English were acted in school at this time

[1] McDonnell, p. 67; Venn, *Biographical History of Caius*, I, p. 28. As he later noted, apprenticeship was unnecessary for one who could have become free of the company by patrimony, but his father wisely insisted on this necessary preparation for a merchant adventurer's career.

[2] McDonnell, pp. 69–71, 80. Colet had only specified that the high master should be acquainted with Greek 'if such may be gotten'.

[3] *EGS*, pp. 241–2. He later had many preferments and was one of those engaged in preparing the Bishop's Book of 1537.

[4] From 1542 to 1548 the master was John Harley, a reformer, subsequently tutor to the duke of Northumberland's sons (Stanier, pp. 71–8).

[5] Lyte, *Eton*, pp. 114–19. Udall may have had a hand in translating Terence's *Andria*, published by More's brother-in-law John Rastell, himself author of an English interlude (R. F. Jones, *The Triumph of the English Language*, Oxford, 1953, pp. 83–4 n.).

remains in doubt but it was a short step from the dialogues in *vulgaria* to elementary drama.[1]

If there was difficulty in getting a master for St Paul's clearly good teachers were at a premium elsewhere. There was some choice in the larger towns and a boy might pass from one master to another. In Norwich, second largest city of the country, Matthew Parker, eldest surviving son of a worsted weaver, was taught to read by two priests, to write by the parish clerk, and learned grammar from yet another master, either at school or at home, before entering a Cambridge college at the age of sixteen in 1521. But students still entered the university young after only an elementary grounding. Thomas Cranmer, second son of a Nottinghamshire gentleman, often recalled in later life how little he learned from a severe teacher who terrorised and dulled the wits of his scholars before he went to Cambridge at fourteen.[2]

The average schoolmaster, still more the parish clerk or chantry priest, lacked all the equipment necessary to approach the classics as literature with grammar as a subsidiary and stuck to the old ways of expounding grammar rules and learning by rote.

> I remember when I was young in the north [wrote Roger Ascham, born in Yorkshire in 1515] they went to the grammar school little children; they came from thence great lubbers; always learning, and little profiting; learning without book, everything, understanding within the book, little or nothing: their whole knowledge, by learning without the book, was tied only to their tongue and lips and never ascended up to the brain and head and therefore was soon spit out of the mouth again.

Ascham himself, the son of a steward to a Yorkshire nobleman, had the good fortune to be taught in the household of a gentleman—Sir Humphrey Wingfield, a lawyer and landholder in Suffolk—who kept a tutor for his own three sons and others of the household. His early education was of mind and body before, in about 1530, he was sent to Cambridge by his patron, as Thomas More and Richard Pace had earlier received their opportunities at the hands of bishops.[3]

[1] For some observations on this, Nelson, pp. xxvi–xxix.

[2] *Athenae*, I, pp. 145, 327–8.

[3] Ascham wrote of his patron 'to whom next God I ought to refer for his manifold benefits bestowed on me' that he 'ever loved and used, to have many children brought up in learning in his house....For whom at term times he would bring down from London both bow and shafts', going with them into the field to see them shoot (*English Works*, ed. W. Aldis Wright, Cambridge, 1904, pp. 97, 239).

Private tutors engaged by noblemen or gentlemen, to whom and to whose patrons humanist scholars often addressed themselves, evidently had more opportunity and encouragement to teach the classics than most. But in the education of the gentleman aspiring to life at court other studies took an important place. French, in particular, remained an essential accomplishment at a time when more and more foreign diplomats were coming to the English court but few knew the English tongue. Here the royal household set the tone with several French tutors in attendance, including Giles Duwes who had taught the king in youth and continued to teach young noblemen up to his death in 1535, while many great households had a resident or visiting French master as well as a master of Latin grammar.[1]

Another noted French tutor was John Palsgrave who taught the king's sister before her marriage to Louis of France and later the duke of Richmond, Henry's natural son by a sister of Lord Mountjoy; though he found the latter task a thankless one since the duke's attendants distracted him from his books, considering these an unsuitable concern for a young nobleman, and soon relinquished the post to Richard Croke.[2] In 1530, Palsgrave published a monumental grammar which set out to place French on the same footing as Latin, addressing a commendatory foreword to Thomas Howard, brother of the earl of Surrey, and Charles Blount, heir of Mountjoy, who were probably also his pupils. Teachers of modern languages had a considerable influence on methods of teaching and furtherance of the vernacular. Palsgrave, dedicating to the king in 1540 an English translation of a newly written Latin play intended for schools, took the opportunity to stress that many difficulties in teaching resulted from imperfect English usage. Even those who came from a university with a scholarly knowledge of Latin could not easily translate into nor express themselves in the vernacular; some had to put themselves through a course of reading English before taking up administrative posts while others, called from the universities 'to instruct any of your grace's noblemen's

[1] Girls were taught French more readily than Latin; it was Anne Boleyn's fluency in the language that led to her rapid advancement at court (K. Lambley, *The Teaching and Cultivation of the French Language in England during Tudor and Stuart Times*, Manchester, 1920, pp. 71, 86 ff.).

[2] Croke was engaged to teach a small school assembled for the benefit of the duke composed of such of his young gentlemen attendants 'as by example of good education as well in nurture as good learning, might the more fairly induce him to profit by his learning' (J. G. Nichols, *Literary Remains of Edward VI*, Roxburghe Club, 1867, I, p. xli).

children', found their imperfections in English so great as to hinder the pupils 'they have taken charge to instruct and bring forward'.[1] This was a point that Vives, another experienced teacher, also underlined.

The great household continued to exercise an overriding attraction. From 1515, when he became chancellor and cardinal, Wolsey's household acted as a magnet to young men seeking preferment. It was also cited as a model in that masters acquainted with the latest developments in classical learning were provided to instruct young gentlemen in the cardinal's service and he kept a master of the wards, as did the king himself. For his natural son, Thomas Winter, Wolsey secured a former master of Magdalen College school who had also taught at St Paul's, and later Thomas Lupset.[2] It was still in the households of bishops or abbots that such tutors were most likely to be found, among the following of such as Cuthbert Tunstall, bishop of London from 1522, or that of the abbot of Glastonbury, Richard Whiting, elected at Wolsey's instigation in 1525, who achieved the reputation of bringing up some three hundred sons of the nobility within a decade, besides fitting others for entry to university.[3]

These two categories were still clearly differentiated for the universities remained what they had always been, predominantly centres for the education of intending churchmen. Now that humanist learning was well regarded at court, and an aid to achieving office, gentlemen with court connections were likely to seek a competent tutor to supervise their sons' education at home, or even in one of the newer colleges. Those who intended sons to qualify as lawyers had long accepted some academic study as a necessary preliminary. But this did not mean that the idea of learning as proper to clerks, something that gentlemen should leave to inferiors, was a thing of the past, particularly in more provincial circles. Richard Pace, who himself owed office as a diplomat to education, drew the moral in the preface of his book dedicated to the founder of St Paul's school. Here he relates a possibly apocryphal but instructive exchange with a country squire who exclaims that such scholars as Erasmus remain beggars and he would rather his son should hang than study; it is for gentlemen to learn how

[1] Palsgrave was well acquainted with More, who presented him to several livings, and also Erasmus (P. L. Carver, ed., *The Comedy of Acolastus translated from the Latin of Fullonius by John Palsgrave*, E.E.T.S., 1937, pp. xvi, 6).

[2] A. F. Pollard, *Wolsey* (1929), pp. 308–10.

[3] *Athenae*, I, p. 71.

to hawk and hunt skilfully leaving the study of letters to the sons of peasants. This provides the necessary opening for Pace to observe that, should the king be attended by a foreign ambassador who required an answer on some matter of policy, 'your son, if he were educated as you wish, could only blow his horn, and the learned sons of peasants would be called to answer, and would be far preferred to your hunter or fowler son'.[1]

This argument, though by no means new,[2] had particular force at a time when learning was taking men of common parentage—such as a Wolsey and a Thomas Cromwell—to positions which enabled them to dispose of the honour and fortunes of the hereditary nobility. The hunting, hawking, nobleman became a staple of later treatises on education and the duties of public service. That the phenomenon was not unknown is suggested by an account of the sixteenth-century representative of the ancient house of Berkeley. Born in the 1530's, Henry, Lord Berkeley, spent long hours 'in his best age at bowls, tennis, cockpit, "shufgrote", cards and dice, especially when he liked the company'. In addition, 'his chief delights wherein he spent near three parts of the year were, to his great charges, in hunting the hare, fox and deer, red and fallow, not wanting choice of as good hunting horses as yearly he could buy at fairs in the north; and in hawking both at river and at land'.[3]

Some young noblemen were, however, to be found at the universities at this period, not merely as formerly with the intention of seeking the highest offices in the church, but for a spell of education in colleges which provided special accommodation for young men of birth and offered some tutoring in civilised studies. It was as a result of teaching the sons of the marquis of Dorset when at Magdalen that Wolsey got his first preferment.[4] It was also to Magdalen, to reside in rooms in the

[1] Furnivall, p. xiii.

[2] 'We commonly see', wrote Robert Holcot in the early fourteenth century, 'that the sons of the rich and powerful do not learn, and that the sons of simple poor men are raised to the highest ecclesiastical dignities by reason of their character and science' (Smalley, p. 198).

[3] The relation is made somewhat apologetically by the seventeenth-century historian of the family, compiling his chronicle specifically for the instruction of its latest heir: 'the hours may seem too long which this lord spent in his best age' at his pleasures (Smyth, II, p. 363).

[4] 'It pleased the said Marquis against a Christmas season to send as well for the schoolmaster as for his children home to his house for their recreation', and, finding the latter well learned, 'he having a benefice in his gift being at that time void gave the

president's lodging, that the king's kinsman and ward Reginald Pole was sent in 1512 or the following year; he was then about thirteen and had spent the previous six years learning grammar at the Carthusian priory at Sheen in Surrey[1]—but this was a young nobleman destined for the church.

If humanist studies could be followed in a few colleges, promising young scholars were much in demand as tutors in the great households, an employment which not only deprived the universities of their teaching but also restricted opportunities for work.[2] Equally there were few enough teachers able or encouraged to adopt new methods in the schools; though the example of St Paul's was followed in some quarters the majority of schools were in no position to profit from it and St Paul's itself did not live up to all the founder's hopes. Colet's school, crowning a long history of lay initiative in providing educational facilities, charted the necessary next step to meet lay needs, a recasting of the curriculum. But it was not until teaching at the universities was more generally re-oriented and schools prised from their ecclesiastical shell that a general move in this direction became possible.

same to the schoolmaster in reward for his diligence' (W. Cavendish, *Life of Wolsey*, ed. R. S. Sylvester, E.E.T.S., 1959, p. 5). Stephen Gardiner took his first steps to office by the same means, as also Croke and others.

[1] W. Schenk, *Reginald Pole* (1950), pp. 1–2.

[2] Thomas Lupset, recalled to Wolsey's service in 1529, voices what was a general complaint among scholars that the duties of office in a household precluded serious study. 'I am in such a place', he writes to a former pupil from the cardinal's palace in Hertfordshire, 'where I have no manner of books with me to pass the time after my manner and custom. And though I had here with me plenty of books, yet the place suffereth me not to spend in them any study. For you shall understand, that I lie waiting on my lord cardinal, whose hours I must observe, to be always at hand, lest I be called when I am not by: the which should be straight taken for a fault of great negligence' (J. A. Gee, *Life and Works of Thomas Lupset*, Yale, 1928, p. 235).

III

ERASMUS AND VIVES ON EDUCATION

It is worth while at this point to turn aside and examine humanist ideas in more detail, to consider why they were so relevant to social needs. The main innovation of humanist writers on education, from the very outset of the fifteenth century in Italy, was that they laid emphasis on 'the formation of character and not on the acquisition of knowledge', that they saw the great figures of Greece and Rome not as paragons of learning but 'as paragons of human excellence'.[1] This was fundamentally a lay approach corresponding to the social changes of the age and contrasting sharply with earlier attitudes. The emphasis laid on rhetoric at the expense of concentration on logic was particularly significant in this connection; while logic was the particular sphere of the philosopher, rhetoric was proper to the populariser, the link whereby learning was communicated to men at large.[2]

Humanist precepts were translated into practice by scholars called upon—as were their English counterparts later—to educate boys who would enter on lay pursuits. This is not to say that education lost its Christian connotation but new subjects were introduced and efforts consciously directed to developing character—the ability to make the most of gifts and learning in the world of affairs.[3] By the sixteenth century there was greater emphasis on the more courtly aspects of education, in scholarship there was developing a mannered 'Ciceronianism', in politics that secular spirit associated with the name of Machiavelli, while a church which was one of the most corrupt in Europe failed to promote essential reforms. It was not, therefore, to contem-

[1] Bolgar, pp. 258, 281.

[2] 'Over and over again in logical and rhetorical treatises of the English Renaissance, logic is compared to the closed fist and rhetoric to the open hand, this metaphor being borrowed from Zeno through Cicero and Quintilian to explain the preoccupation of logic with the tight discourses of the philosopher, and the preoccupation of rhetoric with the more open discourses of orator and popularizer' (W. S. Howell, *Logic and Rhetoric in England, 1500–1700*, Princeton, 1956, p. 4).

[3] The educational aims and methods of this age are discussed in detail in W. H. Woodward, *Vittorino da Feltre and other Humanist Educators* (Cambridge, 1921).

porary Italy that the northern humanists looked but to the more relevant example of an earlier age, while also returning to the classics then brought to light.

The educational writings that attracted most attention and admiration were those of Plutarch, Quintilian and Cicero. Plutarch's treatise on upbringing, first translated from the Greek into Latin by Guarino in 1411, brought a new recognition of the potentialities of education and so of the importance it should be accorded and the respect due to teachers. It gave detailed advice about early upbringing in the home, the proper age to begin formal studies, the function of games in education, the right use of rewards and punishment. Quintilian's *Education of the Orator*, first published in full by Poggio in 1417, had an equally profound effect, for in fifteenth-century Venice and Florence, as in the age of Quintilian, public speaking was the chief means whereby knowledge and personality were brought to bear in the conduct of affairs; this work, giving a new insight into the aims and organisation of Roman education and the teaching methods used, underlined the citizen's obligation to place his knowledge and powers at the service of the community. Finally Cicero's *De Oratore*, recovered in the original in 1422, added to the works of the most admired writer of Latin a treatise concerned with education as a preparation for active life in a civilised urban society.

These were the humanist guide-books to educational reform in northern Europe in the early sixteenth century, as they had been in Italy a century before. Erasmus, indeed, could apologise for dealing with the aims and methods of teaching since 'Quintilian has said, in effect, the last word on the matter'.[1] This was to do himself an injustice for he added much that was new, in particular relating to the techniques of learning and scholarship, while his follower Vives was a highly original thinker. Like their Italian forerunners, the northern humanists consistently emphasised that close and detailed study of classical tongues and authors, both as regards form and content, was the best and most useful preparation for life, whether active or scholarly. They also insisted that schools should treat children as human beings, paying attention to individual qualities, and give due time to recreation and exercise as an essential aspect of education, though there was less elaboration of this last point than in Italy. All this underlined the need

[1] W. H. Woodward, *Studies in Education during the Age of the Renaissance, 1400–1600* (Cambridge, 1924), p. 10.

to improve the status of teachers, for masters who could give an education of the kind envisaged, not merely imparting knowledge but moulding character, must combine integrity and civilised manners with sound learning. Since the emphasis was on the dissemination of education to meet lay needs, it also raised the question of establishing schools in every locality under public control.

These were the lessons that Erasmus and Vives passed on in the context of their own views on the relation between religion and learning, learning and life. 'Let a school be established in every township', wrote Vives, provided with masters of proven learning and uprightness who are 'paid from the public treasury'. He added, 'let boys and youths learn from these men those arts which are suited to their age and tastes' and underlined the importance of discovering individual inclinations and abilities.[1] 'It is a duty incumbent on statesmen and churchmen alike to provide that there be a due supply of men qualified to educate the youth of the nation. It is a public obligation in no way inferior, say, to the ordering of the army', declared Erasmus. If the community were backward in this respect, 'yet should every head of a household do all that he can to provide for the education of his own'. Addressing himself to parents Erasmus insisted that 'no man is born to himself, no man is born to idleness. Your children are begotten not to yourself alone, but to your country; not to your country alone, but to God.' Neglectful parents do 'wrong to their country, to which...they give pestilent citizens. They do equally a wrong against God, at whose hands they receive their offspring to bring it up in his service.'[2] Such views were closely related to the humanist aim of promoting the good society which was seen as essential before education could come fully into its own. Vives quotes the lessons drawn by Xenophon from the education of Cyrus, that most states confine themselves to punishing wrongdoing but the Persians tried to prevent it by providing a sound education; note also, he adds, Xenophon's apt conclusion, for children to become good it is 'only necessary that they should be placed in a well-directed state'.[3]

Both Erasmus and Vives tirelessly demonstrated that Latin, combined with Greek, was the most suitable and desirable medium of learning, as also the gateway to literatures comprehending the accumulated

[1] *Vives: On Education*, a translation of the *De Tradendis Disciplinis* with detailed introduction, ed. Foster Watson (Cambridge, 1913), pp. 72 ff.

[2] Woodward, *Erasmus*, pp. 187–8, 209–10. [3] *Vives: On Education*, pp. 266–7.

wisdom of mankind. Dealing in detail with techniques of teaching and works to be covered, they advanced a coherent defence of the contention that the classics must constitute the central core of studies, facing squarely—if they did not altogether resolve—the problem of reconciling a pagan literature with Christian doctrine. If the immediate influence of Erasmus was the greater, because his published text-books concretely embodying these ideas were very widely used, Vives was the more profound thinker, more sensitive to the new developments of the age. A Spaniard of good birth, he had grown up in a country with a developing pride in its native language and literature; later he settled in Bruges where, living as a layman in one of the more progressive urban communities, he was in contact with commercial enterprise and the nascent scientific outlook associated with navigation and new discoveries overseas. Here was a man equipped to consider education as a social function, to bring rational methods of analysis to bear in a field hitherto dominated by precept, as Thomas More recognised when reading some of his work in 1519. 'I rejoice that my estimate of him agrees with yours', Erasmus replied in a letter. 'He is one of the number of those who will overshadow the name of Erasmus. There is no one to whom I am better inclined... he has a wonderful philosophical mind.'[1] The most advanced humanist ideas on education may, then, best be illustrated by drawing on Vives's major work, published in Antwerp in 1531, in which he sums up a long experience of scholarship and teaching.

It may be recalled here that Vives spent a considerable time in England, more continuously than Erasmus; he was at Oxford and in London, in More's circle and at court, from 1522 to 1528. A minor work covering some of the theme of the *De Tradendis* was composed at Oxford in 1523 and probably known there. Both works were certainly known later—to Roger Ascham and Richard Mulcaster, for instance, to Francis Bacon and to Ben Jonson who incorporated whole passages in his *Timber or Discoveries*, a commonplace book compiled according to humanist principles.[2] Yet, possibly because he does not easily fit into the usual picture, Vives has often been overlooked when the humanist tradition is discussed.[3]

[1] *Ibid.* pp. xxii–xxiii.
[2] *Ibid.* pp. xxxi–xlii, lxxiii–lxxxii.
[3] He has, for instance, only one incidental mention in a generally accepted interpretation, Fritz Caspari, *Humanism and the Social Order in Tudor England* (Chicago, 1954), but his work has more recently received attention in H. A. Mason, *Humanism and Poetry in the Early Tudor Period* (1959).

(1) *The classics and education for the good life*

Language, writes Vives, outlining the essentials of education, is 'the treasury of culture and the instrument of society'. It would be a good thing for the human race if there were only a single language common to all nations, a language 'sweet, learned and eloquent'; this is what is needed as an instrument of education.

> The educative value of a language is in proportion to its apt suitability for supplying names of things. Its eloquence consists in its variety and abundance of words and formulae; all of which should make it a pleasure for men to use. It should have the capacity to explain most aptly what they think. By its means much power of judgment should be developed.

Such a language is Latin, one already diffused through many nations and among all scholars. 'Almost all sciences are committed to its literature....It is like a wise and brave man who has the good fortune to be born in a well-taught state.' This language must, then, be preserved and cultivated. 'If it were lost, there would result a great confusion of all kinds of knowledge, and a great separation and estrangement of men.' Having established the central importance of Latin, Vives goes on to underline that it must be learned exactly and not in a corrupt form. 'For if corrupted, the language forthwith ceases to be a unity', it becomes mingled with local dialects and cannot be universally understood. 'We have found by experience', Vives adds, 'that this has already happened.'[1] Here was a primary reason for the insistence of humanist writers on a return to classical Latin at a time when vernacular languages were in process of rapid development and so lacked a settled vocabulary and recognised grammatical structure, let alone dictionaries and grammars.

The humanists also advocated that Greek, though begun after Latin, should be taught concurrently with it throughout most of the educational course. The argument here was the close affinity of the two tongues and the essential interdependence of their literatures; to Latin authors Greek was a second language, and they drew on Greek sources for vocabulary, literary forms, mythology. But for all their enthusiasm for Greek, and realisation of its key importance for higher studies, Erasmus and Vives did not give great attention to methods of teaching Greek in school; suitable books, let alone teachers, were almost

[1] *Vives: On Education*, pp. 91–3.

entirely lacking. It was rather by his translations from Greek into Latin that Erasmus made his main contribution towards furthering knowledge of Greek literature, life and thought. Himself of humble origin, he was early attracted by the works of Lucian which were concerned with the practical problems and affairs of the ordinary man, and he followed up translations of individual authors with his *Adagia*, dedicated to Mountjoy, a compendium of extracts illustrating the traditional and often homely wisdom of the Greeks and giving concrete descriptions of all aspects of public and domestic life in town and country. This was a new way of making classical knowledge available to the literate in palatable form, in this case between the covers of a single book which could be used in schools.[1]

The chief reason for studying the classical languages was that they were the gateway to the most significant body of knowledge; it followed that literature must be studied for its content, not merely its form or style. When the student has a working knowledge of the two tongues, wrote Erasmus in the *De Ratione Studii* with adult scholars in mind, he can devote his attention to 'the *content* of ancient literature'. He added:

> It is true, of course, that in reading an author for purposes of vocabulary and style the student cannot fail to gather something besides. But I have in mind much more than this when I speak of studying 'contents'. For I affirm that with slight qualification the whole of attainable knowledge lies enclosed within the literary monuments of ancient Greece.[2]

This argument, repeated in many ways in different works, disposes of the superficial view that humanists placed a polished style before any other educational aim. Nevertheless, they were inevitably concerned with ensuring complete mastery of the classical languages (in practice, of Latin), for this was essential not only to a full understanding of what was read but also to ensure clear exposition, to provide the means to self-expression. Here the necessary proficiency was to be attained primarily by imitation. But the term imitation in the humanist vocabulary had not a passive but rather an active connotation. It

[1] Bolgar, pp. 299–300.

[2] Woodward, *Erasmus*, p. 164. The lesson was duly learned and passed on. 'Let Italian, and Latin itself, Spanish, French, Dutch, and English bring forth their learning, and recite their authors, Cicero only excepted, and one or two more in Latin, they be all patched clouts and rags, in comparison of fair woven broadcloths. And truly, if there be any good in them, it is either learned, borrowed, or stolen, from some one of those worthy wits of Athens' (Ascham, *English Works*, p. 213).

involved, as has already been suggested, the picking out and noting of similes, metaphors, turns of phrase, rhetorical devices, wise sayings, not merely for contemplation, but for subsequent use and adaptation by the teacher, writer, orator or even ordinary conversationalist. It was thus integrally concerned with the actual techniques of literary composition and so, besides being used in Latin, could be turned to the end of enhancing vernacular writing and speaking in a language which remained to be polished and perfected. Hence, besides its educational importance, the wide cultural repercussions of this method.

Vives advises that as many authors as possible be studied for each employs a different style for different purposes. 'From all these authors, the scholar will choose what is useful to the aims of his work, and he will follow the method of painters, who, from the aspect of fields and plains, transfer all the most pleasing sights on to their own canvas.' To attain true imitation, however, 'there is need of a quick and keen judgment, as well as a certain natural and hidden dexterity' and teachers should be careful not to allow pupils to outrun their limitations. If a student imitates a model in a stupid, passive, manner, or simply pilfers examples from an original, then the teacher should correct him 'and induce him to follow his own bent, so that he may be true to himself when another's example will not suit his purpose'.[1] The emphasis is, of course, on study for creative use, not learning as an ornament.

How was the school to set about its tasks? Detailed instructions were provided which were widely followed. Boys should learn Latin between the ages of seven and fifteen when as yet unfitted to understand other branches of knowledge, wrote Vives, a reference to the fact that they were often drawn into study of logic much too early. They should first learn to read, initially single vowel sounds, then the combination of sounds, then syllables, and after this learn to name letters. Then, after acquiring the first elements of grammar, boys should be given a Latin text. 'Let this be in free conversational style, pleasant, easy and of terse discourse.' Vives himself supplied just such a book in his colloquies—published under the title *Latinae Linguae Exercitatio* in 1539—which were written round subjects familiar and interesting to schoolboys but in classical, and not colloquial, Latin.[2] The colloquy became an essential ingredient of the school curriculum. Those of

[1] *Vives: On Education*, pp. 194–5.

[2] Translated by Foster Watson under the title *Tudor School-boy Life* (1908).

Erasmus, though hardly so suitable for the schoolboy, were also used and there were later added versions by Sebastian Castellion (1543) and the Calvinist Mathurin Cordier (1564).

As for grammars, Vives recommended Linacre and Lily, but he is bound to note the lack of suitable dictionaries for use in school. This was not remedied in England until Sir Thomas Elyot published his Latin–English dictionary in 1538, a work which, corrected and expanded by Thomas Cooper of Magdalen College, was much used in English grammar schools; it was supplemented in the 1550's by the first children's dictionary arranged according to subject matter.[1] Meanwhile pupils must make up their own vocabularies of words and phrases and for the purpose Vives advised the use of special note-books, or paper-books.

The paper-book, however, was much more than a substitute dictionary, and an innovation at a time when schools were chiefly concerned with oral exposition and learning by heart. In the first place, Vives argued, it is a necessary part of education to teach pupils to write correctly and quickly. 'Let them be convinced that nothing conduces more truly to wide learning than to write much and often and to use up a great deal of paper and ink.'[2] Then, to keep note-books was to have at their disposal, in an ordered and systematic form stamped by personal taste, an essential core of knowledge; this could then be thoroughly memorised and mastered. Vives suggests divisions in the book for vocabulary, history notes, anecdotes, weighty judgments, witty or acute sayings, proverbs, names of well-known men or famous towns, of animals or plants or strange stones, and a special section for difficult or doubtful passages. Pupils should also have another large book in which to take down notes dictated by the teacher, or to note passages they have themselves picked out of the best authors. All note-books should be indexed for easy reference.

Erasmus had first popularised this technique in his *De Copia*, which explained the principle of collecting extracts under different heads and provided a wealth of examples, advocating that teachers pursue this method for the purpose of self-education. Vives reduced more effectively

[1] *EGS*, pp. 388–9, 392–3.

[2] *Vives: On Education*, p. 108. The emphasis was also on writing well; English scholars such as John Cheke, Thomas Smith, Roger Ascham, sedulously cultivated the italic hand. The first thing the master of Wolsey's school at Ipswich thought to send to its patron in 1529 was specimens of the boys' handwriting (C. Caine, 'Cardinal Wolsey's College, Ipswich', *British Archaeological Assoc. Journal*, N.S. XX (1914), pp. 231–2).

to the pupil's level a technique which humanist scholars had perfected in setting out to master the whole corpus of classical literature. This concentration on the detailed content of the classics meant a first step towards the teaching of other subjects. Like Erasmus, Vives outlines how a skilled exposition by the teacher should take him far afield into history, geography, natural philosophy, ethics. He should, wherever possible, lighten his exposition with stories and fables; when there comes up the name of a man renowned for wisdom or even 'notorious for his hateful deeds' the main facts of his life should be given. If a place is mentioned it should be noted 'what special products are to be found there, then if anything remarkable has happened in that place'; or 'an animal, or plant, or stone, should be briefly described, and anything concerning its nature and qualities should—as far as possible and in the most attractive way—be noted and described'.[1] A useful model for teaching of this kind were the colloquies which ranged over a variety of topics, including contemporary themes. Those of Erasmus discussed manners and piety in children, the futility of pilgrimages, the failings of monks, the problems of marriage, the nature of childbirth, the excesses of the nobility, the ignorance of grammarians and much else by the way.

Vives envisages that the further teaching of grammar should continue in the framework of reading authors so that grammar is always seen as a means to an end. The order of study should be, first, the meaning of words and the rules of speech, next an understanding of the idea the author is conveying so that 'the boy may learn to bring out the sense of those passages which are written obscurely...this sharpens the judgment greatly'. After come more detailed grammar rules. As for the authors to be chosen, Vives frankly admits the difficulty. It is better

> to accept the Christian teaching handed down through the Christian tradition from Christ than to learn from the monumental works of the impious, even if we cut out those things which might injure the integrity of good morals. If this cannot be done, at least, let some man show us the way, a man not only well furnished with learning, but also a man of honour and of practical wisdom whom we trust as a leader.[2]

Such a man was Erasmus who had named the authors that could properly be used in school, those to be excluded and those which must

[1] *Vives: On Education*, p. 105. Such studies later came under the heading of cosmography.

[2] *Ibid.* p. 52.

be duly expurgated before admission. Moreover, Erasmus had argued the case for the resulting curriculum thoroughly, justifying in particular the study of Greek authors. He pointed out that Christian culture in fact developed out of the Greek, that the early fathers of the church owed much to Greek philosophy and that even the doctrine of the church reflected the influence of pagan thought.[1] This led to the further argument that the best classical writers, though pagan, had taught a morality which closely approximated to the Christian ethic; which bore on this a good deal more closely, at any rate, than did contemporary scholasticism.[2] It followed that active study of classical literature in the right spirit could uphold and foster virtue. The case was then demonstrated in detail and practical aids provided for transforming theory into practice by the editing and preparation of texts and directives for teaching.[3]

In the light of this approach Vives advanced a selection of texts for different stages of the school course;[4] similar lists, with various modifications, figure in many of the statutes framed for English schools in later decades. A beginning should be made with some simple verses, such as the *Distichs* of Cato, a traditional text.[5] Then, after an exposition of Erasmus's *De Copia Verborum*, figures of speech can be taken from Quintilian, while Mosellanus (a contemporary German teacher from whom Lily borrowed for sections of his grammar) has 'prepared for use a table of figures of speech which can be hung on the wall so that it will catch the attention of the pupil as he walks past it, and force itself upon his eyes'. Thus from grammar the pupil passes not to logic but to rhetoric. Vives advocates next the *De Copia Rerum* and a general survey of history with 'divisions into some well-known periods' and with history links geography.

After this the pupils can proceed to the best writers from the point of view of style as well as content: Caesar, Cicero's familiar letters, Terence and, suitably expurgated, Plautus. In poetry there are Seneca's

[1] A theme followed up by a recent book which 'endeavours to present medieval or scholastic philosophy as a direct continuation of Greek thought' (David Knowles, *The Evolution of Mediaeval Thought*, 1962, p. ix).

[2] Erasmus wrote that he never read Cicero on old age, or friendship, or his *De Officiis* 'without pausing now and then to kiss the page and pay homage to that holy soul whom God's spirit has so manifestly possessed'.

[3] For these arguments, and the great influence of Erasmus's works, see Bolgar, pp. 273–5, 297–300, 336–40.

[4] *Vives: On Education*, pp. 134 ff.

[5] *EGS*, pp. 121–2.

tragedies, Virgil's *Bucolics* and *Georgics*, the odes of Horace; to these Vives adds the Christian authors Colet had advocated for St Paul's, Prudentius and the modern Baptista of Mantua whose *Eclogues* became a standard school text. The pupil can then begin to make verses himself and later the teacher can expound some of Ovid's fables, Martial's epigrams, Persius, and finally the *Aeneid*. But the poets are only the spice of learning, it is the historians who provide solid nourishment; Vives advocates, in particular, Livy and Valerius Maximus but also Caesar, Sallust, Tacitus.[1] Finally, Cicero's orations must have a place in the studies of every boy for they embody 'grace, insight and all the qualities of good style'. When these authors have been expounded and the pupil has mastered the first elements, he can read more widely on his own—Cato who wrote on the country, Vitruvius on architecture and so on.

Turning briefly to Greek, Vives recommends Theodore Gaza's grammar, though his rules are 'very unsuitable for teaching'; he also notes that 'a Greek dictionary is still a desideratum'. The best elementary text to translate is Aesop—with which the Greeks themselves used to begin—and then 'some oration from a pure and easy writer, e.g. of Isocrates or Lucian, should be put into the pupil's hand'. Discussing authors, Vives insists particularly on Homer: 'His sense of common human feeling is so strong, and everything that he says is so much in accord with the actuality of life that, after all these centuries, with their altered customs and habits...his words...are still suitable to our age and for every other'. In history a chief text should be Xenophon's *Hellenica* 'for you will find nothing purer and more unaffected on the subject'.[2]

Vives also includes modern authors in his lists, though with older students and private reading in mind. Laurentius Valla 'affords the chief help for choice of elegant words', and Budé has done 'a great service for Latin' in his books on Roman law and the coinage. Boccaccio on the genealogy of the gods is useful and modern writers who 'can add something to the pupil's style' include Pontano (though he does ape Cicero too much), Politian who 'has great brightness' and Erasmus who 'has wonderful fluency and lucidity'. The student can study geography in Strabo. 'Let him also consider the maps of Ptolemy, if

[1] English school statutes were inclined to place Sallust and Caesar first, then Livy, Justin, Valerius Maximus (Baldwin, II, p. 564).

[2] *Vives: On Education*, pp. 142–8.

he can get a corrected edition. Let him add the discoveries of our countrymen on the borders of the East and the West.' These, says Vives, returning elsewhere to Spanish voyagers and their discovery of the new world, 'cannot but seem fabulous to our posterity, though they are absolutely true'.[1]

Modern historians are also in good estimation even though they wrote in the vernacular; notably 'the Spanish Valera, Froissart, Monstrelet, Philip de Comines, of whom there are many not less worthy to be known and read than the majority of Greek and Latin historians'. And Vives expatiated at length on the delight and utility of history, the need for a historical approach to all subjects and how history could best be studied.[2] In this he was well ahead of Erasmus, who tended to regard history as a repository of anecdotes and moral precepts, reflecting more closely the tendencies of his age.[3] An intense, if not always critical, interest in the historical past, the publication of vernacular chronicles, a new emphasis on the importance of history as a study for men of affairs, the application of scholarly methods in this field, were typical features of the coming stage of development in England.

Similarly Vives went beyond Erasmus in laying great stress on the importance of the vernacular in teaching. 'If the teacher does not know how to express aptly and exactly in the vernacular what he wishes to speak about, he will easily mislead the boys....Nor do boys sufficiently understand the use of their own language unless things are explained to them one by one with the greatest clarity.' Every teacher, therefore, should know the history of his mother tongue, be conversant with old words that have gone out of use and new that have recently been introduced. 'Let him be as a prefect of the treasury of his language', Vives urges,[4] and many English tutors and schoolmasters saw matters in this light, from Cheke and Palsgrave in the 1540's to Mulcaster in the 1580's. At the same time others made the classical heritage available in English translation and in so doing laid the foundations for a new development of the language preparing the way for writers of poetry and prose. This development Vives also foresaw and fostered. To imitate the ancients in elegance, he wrote, 'is not so much bad and

[1] *Ibid.* pp. 139–41, 169, 246.

[2] *Ibid.* pp. 231–49.

[3] In the preface to his *Res Germanicae* (1531), Beatus Rhenanus argues 'that German history is as important as Roman, modern as much worth studying as ancient' (P. S. Allen, p. 275).

[4] *Vives: On Education*, p. 103.

blameworthy as dangerous, for fear lest we depart from our own strength and fall into absurdities'. It is far better to 'write in the vernacular languages, in which the great mass of the people are themselves authorities, teachers, judges'.[1]

Throughout his exposition of educational methods, Vives constantly emphasises the importance of involving the pupil, of making him practise himself instead of merely listening and memorising. In practical matters, he says, 'unless at some time or other you have yourself gone through the experience, however much precepts may be expounded to you', you will differ little from a novice who has never heard of the matter before. The same applies in education; only by practice can pupils really master skills and knowledge, make these their own. Boys, having been taught to speak correctly, should constantly practise speaking; having been taught how to compose letters and make verses, they should constantly write letters, verses, compositions. They should do double translations from Latin into the vernacular and back again to perfect their command and understanding of the language.[2] This method was later popularised in England by Ascham, who has received much credit for it, while school statutes often insisted on teaching pupils to speak clearly and the school play was largely cultivated to this end.

In general, by advocating the simple teaching of syntax in place of formal study of grammar rules, the humanists made a place for and reinstated rhetoric in the school and university curriculum, emphasising its practical application. Rhetoric, Vives insisted, drawing conclusions more far-reaching than those who saw this as a vocational training for the cleric, courtier or statesman, 'is necessary for all positions in life'. Men's emotions and their reason are inflamed and moved by speech which 'holds in its possession a mighty strength which it continually manifests'. Rhetoric is not, therefore, the empty use of words, not merely the cultivation of an elegant style; the object of studying it is to avoid impure and inaccurate speech, to ensure that men give expression to practical wisdom. So, Vives advocates, 'let young men declaim, before their teachers, on those matters which may afterwards be useful in life; and not as was the habit of the ancients in the philosophical schools, on matters which never occurred in real life'. Or again, 'let all eloquence stand in full battle array for goodness and piety, against crime and wickedness'.[3]

[1] *Vives: On Education*, p. 197. [2] *Ibid.* pp. 113–14. [3] *Ibid*, pp. 180, 185, 186.

(2) *The psychology and philosophy of education*

New concern for the individual and the part he could play in life necessarily brought into question not only methods of teaching, but also attitudes to learning on the part of the pupil which had hitherto gone more or less unrecognised. The medieval school imparted a defined body of knowledge; this the teacher expounded and the pupil was supposed to absorb, though his wits were later exercised in disputation. As laymen increasingly sought education, and an education relevant to particular functions in society, teachers were required both to cover new subjects and to ensure that they were learned to good effect. The questions how do children learn, how therefore may their talents best be developed, inevitably arose, as some of the preceding arguments have illustrated.

Here the humanists substituted for the traditional outlook of feudal society—that 'virtue' is innate only in those of long and noble lineage—ideas imbibed from the literature of the classical world. According to these, men are distinguished from the animals by three main instincts or qualities. Implanted by nature is a striving towards perfection—this is virtue. As an aid to realising this, men, in place of the instincts proper to animals, are endowed with reason. Further, they have a social instinct which causes them to unite together in societies. It follows that it is by exercising their reason in society—in the first place through education—that men realise their innate virtue, attain virtue in practice. In the light of this general outlook Erasmus postulates three conditions determining individual progress: nature, training and practice.

By *Nature*, I mean partly innate capacity for being trained, partly native bent towards excellence. By *Training*, I mean the skilled application of instruction and guidance. By *Practice*, the free exercise on our own part of that activity which has been implanted by and is furthered by Training. Nature without skilled Training must be imperfect, and Practice without the method which Training supplies leads to hopeless confusion.[1]

Vives went more deeply into the subject, in a way that brings to mind Hobbes and Locke rather than any of his predecessors or contemporaries. He affirmed that 'the senses open up the way to all knowledge', that memory is the faculty whereby the mind retains percepts apprehended through sensation, that the retention of impressions

[1] Woodward, *Erasmus*, p. 191.

is effected through association and is greatly assisted if interest is aroused.[1] These psychological theories were the fruit of comprehensive study of the theory and practice of education, the fruit also of an independent mind and a fundamentally rational outlook. Vives, indeed, flatly rejected the then prevailing view, which reflected the passing of a traditional social order, that nature was decaying in her old age and contemporaries could never aspire to match the great philosophers of the past. A citizen of a busy and lively community, his eyes were wide open to the present scene and potentialities for the future; accordingly he is on the side of the moderns against the ancients as Bacon, Milton and many another were later to be in what became a veritable battle of ideas:

Nature is not yet so effete and exhausted as to be unable to bring forth, in our times, results comparable to those of earlier ages. She always remains equal to herself, and not rarely...comes forward more strongly and powerful than in the past, as if mustering together all her forces. So we must regard her in this present age as reinforced by the confirmed strength which has developed, by degrees through so many centuries....If we only apply our minds sufficiently, we can judge better over the whole round of life and nature than could Aristotle, Plato, or any of the ancients.[2]

Vives goes on to ask what, in effect, was Aristotle's method and what are the lessons to be drawn from it:

Did he not dare to pluck up by the root the received opinions of his predecessors? Is it, then forbidden to us to...investigate, and to form our own opinions?...Truth stands open to all. It is not yet taken possession of. Much of truth has been left for future generations to discover.

Here, prefacing a discussion of educational purposes and methods, is an affirmation of faith in human capacities, a support for the new spirit of inquiry which provides the foundation for a scientific approach to education. Having rejected all *a priori* opinions, Vives proceeds to make use of the Aristotelian method to inquire into the origins and nature of learning.

His book opens with the words: 'Man has received from God a great gift, viz. a mind, and the power of inquiring into things'; and he goes on to trace man's development in society as a prelude to

[1] Woodward, *Studies*, pp. 185–8; *Vives: On Education*, pp. cxx–cxxii; see also Foster Watson, *Vives, Father of Modern Psychology*, an offprint from *Psychological Review*, XXII (1915).

[2] *Vives: On Education*, pp. 8–9.

discussing his educational needs. In other words he establishes that man is a social animal and human knowledge a social product; an educational programme must, therefore, take account of both the nature of man's mind and the structure of knowledge, which are closely interrelated. In considering this aspect Vives insists on the fundamental importance of speech. In primitive societies, he writes, men first looked after bodily needs and later established communities with forms of government, laws, means of defence; it was in these societies that the human mind developed, primarily with the aid of speech.

> Daily business brought men together, and speech bound them to move as closely as possible amongst one another in an indivisible perpetual society. By the help of speech, their minds, which had been hidden by concentration on bodily needs, began to reveal themselves; single words were attended to, then phrases and modes of speaking, as they were appropriate for use, i.e. as they were marked by public agreement of opinion, which is, as it were, what a mint is to current coin. It is a great advantage to have a common language, for it is a bond which holds society together.

As men began to master their environment, 'the human mind passed from necessities to conveniences...for while the whole of man's nature was oppressed by the vast power and uncertainty of necessity, everything had been changed into an enemy; nor could man think of anything except raising this blockade'. Once it was raised men actively sought knowledge, but 'because the human mind, provided with its small lamp, is not able to attain to the conception of that ultimate end, unless it has been enlightened by the end itself...therefore there was need of God, not only to teach us how to come to Him, but also to lead us by the hand, since we are weak, and constantly liable to fall'. This is the function of religion 'and piety is, of all things, the most necessary for perfecting man'. But God, once mentioned, remains poised above what is essentially a rational exposition. Indeed Vives has announced in his preface an express intention of producing reasons 'from nature, not out of divine oracles, so that I should not leap across from philosophy to theology'.[1]

He goes on to inquire, in what is a valuable survey of contemporary learning, how the human arts developed and their present position; the relevance of this analysis to the educational methods advocated will be clear.[2]

[1] *Ibid.* pp. 7, 11, 14–18.

[2] *Ibid.* pp. 23 ff.

In the beginning first one, then another experience, through wonder at its novelty, was noted down for use in life; from a number of separate experiments the mind gathered a universal law, which, after it was further supported and confirmed by many experiments, was considered certain, and established. Then it was handed down to posterity. Other men added subject matter which tended to the same use and end. This material, collected by men of great and distinguished intellect, constituted the branches of knowledge, or the arts.

It is clear, says Vives, that all that is in the arts was first in nature, though the men who first noted these things are honoured as discoverers, just as those men are honoured who collect rules from experience, as did Hippocrates in the sphere of medicine. In brief, experience through various applications makes up arts. But experiences are casual unless ruled by reason; if there is no judgment arts may degenerate into fraud, as for example in necromancy. Vives concludes:

I call that knowledge which we receive when the senses are properly brought to observe things...in a methodical way to which clear reason leads us on, reason so closely connected with the nature of our mind that there is no one who does not accept its lead; or our reasoning is 'probable', when it is based on our own experiences or those of others, and confirmed by judgment, resting upon probable conjecture. The knowledge in the former case is called science, firm and indubitable, and in the latter case, belief or opinion.

What, Vives goes on to ask, are suitable Christian arts? And answers: 'What other than those which are necessary for the aims of either this or the eternal life', which 'will either advance piety or be of service to...the uses of life'. All learning is empty unless applied to use. Languages, for instance, are not an end in themselves but only the entrance hall to knowledge, the object of studying them is to penetrate to facts and ideas—the conception that Montaigne popularised and the great seventeenth-century educationist Comenius so ardently propagated. Vives, too, insists that there are other ways of acquiring knowledge than through books. Young people can, for instance, more easily attain a knowledge of nature than abstract knowledge for this 'can be acquired by the sharpness of the senses and the power of observation'. The student can 'observe the nature of things in the heavens, in cloudy and in clear weather, in the plains, on the mountains, in the woods'; he can seek the advice of 'gardeners, husbandmen, shepherds and hunters', as Pliny and other great authors did. To do so is to 'bring great advantage to husbandry, for the culture of palatable fruits, for foods and drinks, and in remedies and medicines for the recovery of health'.[1]

The practical bearing of other subjects is similarly stressed. The applications of arithmetic are clear and from geometry 'we proceed to all measurement, proportion, movement and position of heavy weights', to study of the measurement of 'fields, mountains, towers and buildings'; and only consider, Vives requests his readers, how useful are the resulting arts, for instance what 'great comfort architecture brings to us in our dwellings'.[2] But while clearly recognising the practical relevance of newly developing branches of mathematics, Vives could hardly advocate that these be taught in school; few books were available besides folios of Euclid and crabbed abridgements, useless for teaching purposes, until the works of Robert Recorde and others began to appear in the 1540's. In fact Vives warns against too much concern with mathematical abstractions which may 'withdraw the mind from the practical concerns of life and render it less fit to face concrete and mundane realities'. Here he was evidently referring to forms of study prevailing at the universities, and incidentally making a point about current methods of education unfitting men for life which Bacon later elaborated.[3]

Astronomy Vives also recommends as an essential study which

> should be applied to descriptions and determinations of time and seasons, without which rustic toil, on which all life is dependent, could not be carried on; then to the positions of places, showing what is the longitude and latitude of each, and to questions of distance. All this is very useful for cosmography and absolutely necessary to the general theory of navigation; without this knowledge the sailor would wander in uncertainty amidst the greatest and most grievous dangers.[4]

[1] *Vives: On Education*, pp. 170–1. [2] *Ibid.* p. 204.

[3] Ascham seems to be echoing this forty years on when he deplores undue sharpening of the wits and remarks 'mark all mathematical heads, which be only and wholly bent to those sciences, how solitary they be themselves, how unfit to live with others, and how unapt to serve in the world' (*English Works*, p. 190). But by this time mathematics had advanced on new lines and Richard Mulcaster retaliates that they are both useful and of educational value; those with understanding of the subject 'may boldly mislike the mislikers and oppose the whole ancient philosophy, and all well appointed commonweals against such mockmathematicals without whose help they could not live, nor have houses to hide their heads, though they thank not their founders' (*Positions*, 1887, pp. 240–3).

[4] *Vives: On Education*, p. 205.

The need for navigational aids was, of course, the greatest stimulus to study of geography and astronomy, studies later much cultivated in the great port and trading centre of London.

Vives directs particular attention to the practical arts. The student 'should not be ashamed to enter shops and factories, and to ask questions from craftsmen, and get to know about the details of their work'. Recently learned men had disdained to inquire into these things so that they have remained undiscovered; 'we know far more of the age of Cicero and Pliny than of that of our grandfathers, in respect of their food, attire, worship and dwellings'. This leads Vives to exclaim: 'How much wealth of human wisdom is brought to mankind by those who commit to writing what they have gathered on the subject of each art from the most experienced therein!' Such inquiries are a pleasant recreation for students and, too, 'a most honourable occupation and one clearly worthy of a good citizen. By such observation in every walk of life, practical wisdom is increased to an almost incredible degree; those who make such observations should hand them down and let them serve posterity for whom we ought to care as we do for our own sons.'[1] This course was taken by men whose experience led to the same conclusions. Emphasis on observation and practice, attention to the needs of posterity in the light of a belief that knowledge could be advanced, these were among the innovations of an outlook which squarely substituted this world for the next and essential prerequisites for the development of modern science.

This, then, is the true end of all studies, Vives affirms, 'this is the goal. Having acquired our knowledge we must turn it to usefulness, and employ it to the common good.'[2] With this goal in view and using the test of practice Vives does not hesitate to criticise the ancients, even Aristotle to whom he owes so much. 'It is far more profitable to learning', he argues, 'to form a critical judgment on the writings of great authors, than merely to acquiesce in their authority and to receive everything on trust from others.' Students of Aristotle are therefore advised to leave out 'those tiresome disputes, or rather invectives, against the ancient philosophers'; in any case 'Aristotle does not always quote correctly for he twists the sense or the words, and does not give all the counter arguments. He does not offer valid confutations and he replies to them by answering ideas which are invented by himself.'[3] Again Aristotle's physics and metaphysics,

[1] *Vives: On Education*, pp. 209–10. [2] *Ibid.* p. 283. [3] *Ibid.* pp. 8, 165.

though containing much of value, include also much that is obscure. 'His subtleties which are often drawn out to fine distinctions, render blunt and dull the keenest intellect. He has shown an inclination in some matters to ask questions where there was never any occasion to do so, and through his excessive care and attention he has believed himself to have discovered something which he never saw, and which never even existed.'[1] This was to question the philosopher who was the idol, above all criticism, of the university schools, to criticise in particular those aspects of his work over which contemporary scholars frequently lingered.

In all these things—his questioning of authority, use of the inductive method, insistence on the relation of knowledge to human welfare, support for vernacular tongues—Vives points the way to the empirical materialist philosophy of the seventeenth century and the activities of those who founded the first scientific societies. His arguments show that there was a closer relation than is often recognised between promotion of scholarly study on humanist lines and the beginning of scientific inquiry, just as, paradoxical though it may appear on the surface, concentration on the Latin language and literature did not hinder, but provided a direct lead towards the enrichment and study of English.

The extent of Erasmus's influence in this sense should also be recalled. He was the chief populariser of the technique of literary imitation, the means whereby the knowledge and ideas of the ancient world were absorbed and adapted to the needs of developing national cultures. The whole technique of translation of the classics, as it developed in subsequent years, rested on this principle. Translations were not literal and exact but of a creative kind, rendering classical works—and later Italian and French—into English terms, not merely English words. Poets such as Wyatt used this method of translation as a staff to support steps towards creative writing in the vernacular, as a guide to experimenting with new forms; as many another later experimented with, adapted and then transcended, various classical models in the drama and the writing of history. While some revived old expressions or borrowed from other languages to enrich English, others, trained in disciplined study of the classics, turned to systematising it—compiled dictionaries and grammars and attempted to regularise the chaos of orthography.

[1] *Ibid.* p. 173.

In addition, Erasmus's writings on moral themes, in tracts addressed to the ordinary reader, bridge the gap between medieval manuals and what became a vast literature on manners, callings, religious duties, family life, which exercised much influence in forming attitudes at a time of social change. At the same time humanists enjoined rulers to study well and govern wisely, gentlemen to be worthy of their status, churchmen to attend to their proper functions in such a way as to win respect; these themes too remained actual and were taken up. Through the changes of the coming years men adhering to different standpoints could, therefore, often find relevant material in early humanist writings, make it their own and draw it into what became a recognisable English tradition in educational literature—much as the humanists had drawn on the resources of the classics.

The use made of humanist precepts in English education, the extent to which some were developed and applied and others superseded, depended on the purposes for which education was sought and promoted by men of differing aspirations. As the Reformation advanced new problems came to the forefront, new names were invoked, and those of Erasmus and Vives tended to recede into the background. Otherwise it is the very thoroughness with which the humanist approach and methods were adopted that has obscured the extent of their influence. Just as, in the light of humanist teaching, some men went on to read the bible and, adopting reforming views, are thereafter identified as reformers, so others turned directly to the classics as they had been exhorted to do; it is, therefore, to classical authors that later writers above all express an obligation while themselves writing in English. But this does not mean, as is so often suggested, that humanist ideas had only a brief hearing in England before being overwhelmed and thrust from the scene. Rather through the medium of education and self-education they became the very tools of scholarship and creative work.

On the other hand there was much in the humanist programme to encourage concentration on books, to reinforce an already prevailing tendency for studies to remain of the study, preoccupied with words. So long as humanist subjects were cultivated within the old framework at the universities they themselves were likely to become restricted rather than leavening the rest. In the schools there were teachers who used new grammars and expounded classical authors formally and without understanding so that Lily and Cicero in time became bywords for boredom and loss of time. A new generation could, therefore, once more find educational methods totally at fault as too linguistic and literary and would attempt to rotate the stress from words to things. This has sometimes been taken to imply that humanist programmes were inherently one-sided and out of touch with life and so fastened a dead hand on education.

Here it is relevant to note that one classical writer, above all others, came to represent the humanist approach and appeal to men of the world in Tudor England—as to Italian forerunners from Petrarch onwards. This was Marcus Tullius Cicero. It was not only Cicero's speeches at the height of his influence and the works he wrote in a period of retirement from the stormy politics of his day that became hand-books; there were also the familiar letters which opened up a new range of experience for they combined sympathetic understanding of human feelings and doings with much psychological self-revelation in discussing the springs of action.[1] Cicero's musings on conflicting duties to a tyrannous ruler, one's country, family claims, were immensely actual, as were the activities of a knight and country gentleman who was also lawyer, statesman and, as it might be said, member of parliament. No doubt English schools did not set essay questions of the kind Cicero tended to set himself—'Should one remain in one's country even under a tyranny?', 'Should a man who has done great service to his country, and thereby incurred envy and injury, go out of his way to run risks for it, or should he be permitted eventually to take thought for himself and his loved ones, abandoning endless struggles against those who have the power?' But these were the kind of questions posed by life in Tudor England and eventually explored by its greatest dramatist. The Elizabethans were for ever quoting Tully, a historian of the period has remarked.[2] This one man's writings literally informed an age when politics and personalities were closely interwoven and knowing the way of the world depended much on understanding the hearts and minds of men, including one's own. Once more, in this case, works which might seem remote in time and relevance bore directly on the deepest contemporary needs.

[1] 'There is probably no human document comparable with Cicero's letters until we come to those works, among which Rousseau's *Confessions* should perhaps be counted the first, that have caused and catered for the modern preoccupation with motives and states of mind' (L. P. Wilkinson, ed., *Letters of Cicero*, 1949, pp. 13, 19).

[2] A. L. Rowse, *The England of Elizabeth* (1950).

IV

EDUCATION AND THE STATE

The humanists emphasised the key part played by education in society and, drawing on the example of the classical world, argued that state intervention was necessary to direct it wisely and well. Whatever attention may or may not have been given to this argument, with the advent of the Reformation education became a matter of directly political concern. Schools and universities were enlisted either in the cause of reform or to uphold the established order and there was a strong impetus towards developing organised systems of education with more uniform curricula and teaching methods. While divergences between states meant that schooling and scholarship developed along different lines, there was a mutual interaction of these trends, since the framework of European learning remained, though the international world of scholarship no longer survived in the form that had obtained for centuries under the aegis of a universal church.

It was in the autumn of 1517, the year Corpus Christi College was founded, that Martin Luther nailed ninety-five theses to the church door at Wittenberg, framed in Latin after the university form of a challenge to debate. The particular target of his attack was papal indulgences which typified the corruption of the church, the manner of his questioning such as to challenge the supreme authority of its head. His action precipitated into new channels what had been longstanding contradictions and dissensions and in the outcome the power of the medieval church was irretrievably broken. The papacy had of late been increasingly subjected to political ends in the struggle between France and Spain to dominate the Italian peninsula; the revolt against its jurisdiction was one aspect of the emergence from a European system of nation states, at a time when the focus of trade was shifting from the Mediterranean and inland waterways to the Atlantic seaboard and northern coasts. Subsequent years saw the growth to maturity of vernacular languages and literatures, while the needs of navigation in the service of trade, and new forms of industrial production, brought to birth modern science. As a man attuned to the currents of his time Vives apprehended something of all this. It was not easy to see clearly in the coming years, through the clouds of religious controversy and preoccupation with pressing practical affairs. But so far as education was concerned advice and to spare had been provided which could be adapted to use as occasion served.

In 1521 the Diet of Worms marked the severance of the German church from Rome, but it is important to realise that a quarter of a century passed before men finally gave up hope of a reconciliation. It did not seem to contemporaries, as it does to some modern historians, that humanist ideas and Reformation principles fell into quite separate categories, that the former essentially survived in isolation from the latter.[1] Luther claimed with some justice that he had only hatched the egg Erasmus laid; the latter, while sympathising with the initial protest, complained that from the hen's egg laid Luther had hatched a fighting cock. But if Erasmus had profound differences with the reformers and his later writings became more conservative, nothing could undo the effect of earlier works which still circulated widely.[2] It was men trained to their outlook who directed the measures of the Reformation in different countries of northern Europe.

Hitherto humanist scholars had found a welcome at court and in great households but had usually held posts at universities for comparatively brief periods through the influence of patrons; while their ideas aroused enthusiasm among the young they met with strong opposition from older members of established centres of learning. Similarly when humanist teachers took charge of schools their efforts were turned to improving methods of teaching grammar and introducing classical texts but could hardly extend to complete re-organisation. This is why St Paul's was of such significance as a prototype humanist school.[3] As the Reformation swept through northern and

[1] It is here that the term 'renaissance', with the particular connotations it carries, becomes a barrier to understanding; when used in relation to Elizabethan England it should be with the proviso that 'what gave the English Renaissance its peculiar and distinctive character...was the English Reformation' (F. Smith Fussner, *The Historical Revolution*, 1962, p. 17).

[2] 'The extent of the influence of Erasmus in creating a critical, untraditional climate of mind can scarcely be exaggerated' (Knowles, p. 147).

[3] This has been obscured by a tendency to backdate humanist developments to the fifteenth century. There was very little humanist influence in the schools and universities of northern Europe before 'the theoretical work of Erasmus and the foundation in England of St Paul's which demonstrated that the *pietas litterata* could work in practice'; after 1520 'the methods and aims of the new movement effectively began to transform the German schools' (Bolgar, p. 342).

western Germany—and spread into eastern Europe, the Baltic states, Scandinavia—the re-organisation of schools became a key question, an indispensable aspect of establishing a protestant state. Scholars and teachers must now translate educational theory into practice on a large scale, drawing up not only general guides to planning but also detailed timetables and directives for presentation of subject matter. New text-books began to pour from printing-presses, to be distributed far beyond the borders of German states. At the same time existing universities were re-organised and new established. In 1523 the first protestant educational treatise appeared when Ulrich Zwingli published *The Christian Education of Boys* not long before his untimely death.

Elsewhere humanist ideas were brought into the mainstream of scholarship in various ways. In France the university of Paris was implacably opposed to new studies and humanists worked outside it. At the French court, as at the English, a ruler who aspired to emulate Italian princes appointed learned humanists as ambassadors and officials, but Francis I—who had come to the throne at the age of twenty amid hopes as high as those greeting the young Henry VIII—also took measures to advance scholarship. In 1522 he appointed the famous scholar Guillaume Budé as royal librarian, in 1526 the royal press was established under Robert Estienne to publish the growing corpus of work by French scholars; four years later chairs of Greek and Hebrew were established at Paris University, followed by chairs of Latin and mathematics, to lay the foundations for the Collège de France. During these and subsequent years, when Italian scholarship was foundering after the sack of Rome, Budé's great works on the Greek language, Roman law, the coinage—to which Vives refers with such respect—brought French scholarship to a leading position.[1] There were added works in the vernacular, particularly historical and legal studies on humanist lines.[2] At the school level the most notable foundation was the Collège de Guyenne, established in 1534 by the municipality of Bordeaux, the great commercial and administrative centre of the south-west.[3] Mathurin Cordier played a part in organising this, on the model of German schools, before with the growing intolerance towards reformers he left for Geneva. It was to this school that Michel Montaigne was sent, already speaking Latin fluently at the age of six as a result of his father's methods of upbringing, in 1539. One of his

[1] Bolgar, pp. 376–7; cf. Elizabeth Armstrong, *Robert Estienne, Royal Printer* (Cambridge, 1954). [2] Fussner, pp. 27–8. [3] Woodward, *Studies*, pp. 139 ff.

teachers was George Buchanan, gaining experience which led to employment as tutor of the heir to the throne of Scotland—and, as it turned out, of England too.

Some years earlier, in 1515, a wealthy layman had founded at Louvain University the Collegium Trilingue for study of the three learned languages. Here Erasmus worked for five years to establish a humanist centre of learning but the college was drawn into developing religious controversies and he left for Basle to find the peace necessary to write, remaining there among a circle of scholars until his death in 1536. In that same year John Calvin, a refugee from persecution in his native France, settled in Geneva. He had already published the first version of his *Institutes of the Christian Religion* and at Geneva, and later for a time at Strasburg, turned his mind to questions of education and school organisation.

Meanwhile the papal council, whose failure to remedy abuses had provoked the Lutheran challenge, still found no constructive response. But there was in Italy a considerable movement for reform of the church on Erasmian, though essentially conservative, lines; the main educational product was Cardinal Sadoleto's *De Liberis Recte Instituendis* (1530) which had a considerable influence on later catholic programmes.[1] An associate of this movement was Reginald Pole, now resident in Padua where his household was a centre for English scholars. Padua, as state university of the Venetian republic which was tolerant in religious matters, drew many scholars of international standing at this time when other universities were tending to become more narrowly national. Its schools of medicine and civil law, in particular, achieved a leading position.[2]

Italy also offered for emulation the first vernacular literature of distinction, including Machiavelli's analyses of the realities of statecraft and diplomacy and Castiglione's guide to courtly politics, relationships, learning—*Il Cortegiano*, published in 1528 though written over a decade earlier. The fruit of Italy's past achievements, rather than mirroring the disordered present, this influential book left aside the tyrannies that underpinned princely courts; the courtiers who conversed in its pages, real men and women though in an idyllic setting, combined learning with sensibility and taste, wit and judgement, to provide an example of truly civilised human beings.[3]

[1] *New Cambridge Modern History*, II, pp. 257–9; Woodward, *Studies*, pp. 167 ff.

[2] Kibre, p. 83.

[3] Woodward, *Studies*, pp. 244 ff.

In England in the 1520's it was not the king who stood out as chief patron of learning. It was Cardinal Wolsey—lord chancellor, papal legate and effective ruler of both church and kingdom—who planned a college at Oxford intended to outshine every other foundation in Christendom and also took up the cause of promoting humanist methods in the schools. But though his ideas might be large Wolsey epitomised the limitations of the church he served with its emphasis on outward show and preoccupation with secular politics. When by embroiling England in upholding the papal cause abroad he paved the way to his own downfall the age of great ecclesiastical statesmen came to a close. Events moved swiftly in the direction of a break with Rome and as the church in England became subject to the crown education also came under lay direction. Henry VIII could now step into his minister's shoes both as ruler of the church in England and promoter of professorships and colleges.

By 1530 a new generation had taken the place of the early humanist circle in England. Colet died in 1518, Lily and Linacre in the early 1520's, Lupset in 1530, while Vives left the English court in disgrace for his support of Catherine of Aragon in 1528 and Thomas More, who succeeded Wolsey as the first lay chancellor, became involved in the disputes of the day. Of the second generation some, notably at Cambridge, were moving steadily towards a reforming standpoint and this conditioned their attitude to education and learning. Others who had taken up careers in public life—effectively in Wolsey's household and subsequently as servants of the king or his new chief minister—became concerned with education as an instrument of policy, the politics of education. This was a time when, over and above the complex business of dissolving and reforming ecclesiastical institutions, the apparatus of central and local government was reconstructed to encompass new tasks. Once more, therefore, young scholars were drawn from their studies into various forms of public work. This meant a stimulus to learning in specific directions but militated against profound textual scholarship of the kind pursued in France and the reformed German universities, or cultivation of medicine and civil law of the kind that brought fame to Padua. English scholars must still, therefore, go to school to the continent if they wished to keep abreast of developments in learning.

In the 1520's Englishmen were expected to look askance at the progress of the German Reformation, including its educational measures, and the new learning began to look like heresy. Fifteen years later England had also thrown off papal authority, the dissolution of the monasteries was being planned and educational change on the order of the day. At this time humanist ideas were embodied in plans for reform specifically related to English needs.

(1) *The example of Germany*

The year after Luther voiced his challenge to papal authority a young humanist scholar, Philip Melanchthon, self-educated in Latin and Greek and an ardent adherent of Erasmus, was invited to fill a new chair of Greek at Wittenberg. Founded at the turn of the century this was one of the many contemporary universities established by princes and Melanchthon's invitation came from the elector of Saxony. Humanist studies had a foothold at Wittenberg but, as elsewhere, only side by side with the traditional, and Melanchthon's inaugural address dealt with the need for further development on humanist lines; he also established a private school in his own house to enable experiment with different methods of organising an educational course. The new professor immediately came under the influence of Martin Luther who dominated the intellectual life of the town and, having received some concentrated tuition, was soon appointed also professor of theology. Together these two men changed the face of the university. A chair of Hebrew had also been founded and during the next few years the study of languages proceeded apace as also the development of Lutheran doctrine. When statutes for the university were drawn up in 1536 they openly proclaimed its humanist and protestant character.[1]

Events took much the same course in other states and cities of Reformation Germany, concurrently with the establishment of a reformed church and under Luther's energetic leadership. Directly after the Diet of Worms Luther began his translation of the bible into German, following this up with catechisms for teaching purposes. In 1523 he was assisting in the drafting of local plans for the organisation of education and poor relief and the following year circulated a *Letter to the Burgomasters and Councillors of all Towns in German Lands* urging the establishment and maintenance of Christian schools.

However significant the theological points at issue, it was still a relatively short step from the teachings of Erasmus to those of Luther.

[1] Woodward, *Studies*, pp. 214–15.

Melanchthon easily transferred his allegiance, so also Zwingli before going on to take up an independent stand. Such divergences early made their appearance in the reforming movement and Calvin was to effect another. But the most fundamental beliefs were held in common; all reformed churches adhered to the doctrine of justification by faith and had passed from direct study of the scriptures to accepting the bible as the sole authority in spiritual matters. These doctrines, rendering superfluous the ritual and hierarchy of the medieval church, set fresh educational aims.

The effect reforming doctrines had on education, the way they themselves developed, depended much on the conditions in which they were formulated and gained acceptance. When, after 1517, Luther began preaching in the vernacular, in a tradition common to the friars throughout the middle ages, he denounced ecclesiastical corruption and the tyranny of Rome with an ardour which strongly appealed to laymen—to princes who wished to be master in their own house, to nobles with an eye on monastic property, to the people at large who from birth to burial must pay endless dues to the church. But, like Erasmus's popular writings, Luther's developing doctrine had a particular appeal for the burghers of the great autonomous cities on whose support he so largely depended. The doctrine and organisation of the medieval church reflected and upheld the traditional order within states as well as in Europe as a whole. Protestantism in all its varieties not only satisfied long latent anti-papal and anti-clerical feelings but gave expression to a social and moral outlook which had hitherto lacked recognition; moreover, proclaiming men's freedom to make their own terms with their God without the intervention of a priesthood, it inferred a new equality on the social plane.

Outright attacks on ecclesiastical powers and wealth were, therefore, likely to bring the hierarchy of lay authority and property relations into question in so far as it paralleled that of the church and bore as hardly on the people. Once Luther had provided the spark, in what was already an explosive situation in Germany, there arose from among the peasantry men who demanded full Christian equality in the community, as earlier leaders of peasant revolts had done, with the vernacular bible in their hands.[1] As events began to move towards

[1] There were no social strata in the German countryside corresponding to English gentlemen and yeomen to 'take the strain at the middle levels of the social pyramid. Between princes and peasants were great inequalities and festering wrongs...' (E. G.

a general rebellion prosperous burghers became circumspect and Luther himself turned from exhortations to action to preaching the need for consolidation of government, the church, education. If in theory men were free to put their own interpretation on the scriptures, in practice it was clear that they needed guidance. When peasant uprisings spread widely, to reach a climax in the wars of 1525, Luther was the first to call for reprisals and urge the obligation of obedience to the civil power. This was the period when he laid his educational plans before the rulers of the towns with earnest pleas to put them into practice.

Before the peasant wars Germany was a conglomeration of lay princedoms, ecclesiastical sovereignities, autonomous cities and the estates of nobles wielding sovereign powers. In the outcome the princes profited most from the conflict; the power of the church was broken, that of the lay nobility reduced and provincial territories were established within which cities effectively came under princely rule. Lutheranism, therefore, emerged from the struggle as the accepted religion of a number of small states and recognising the superior rights of the secular prince. As such, though anathema to the medieval church with its key doctrine of papal supremacy, it proved in time a relatively congenial example to English rulers, at least by comparison with papal intransigence and the more radical and republican doctrine of Calvin. Meanwhile English observers could note that in Germany the old ecclesiastical order was in ruins—the monasteries, in particular, had been laid waste—leaving place for the establishment of a church with a limited authority; and that ecclesiastical lands, which the popular movement had sought to share out among tenants, had fallen mainly to princes and the patricians of the towns. Also to be observed were sustained efforts to build up a new system of education and to make provision for the growing numbers reduced to extreme poverty.

During these years Luther's projects for education and poor relief had begun to be translated into practice. A model scheme was first provided when he assisted the city of Leisnig to draw up an ordinance in 1523, providing for a public fund to be devoted to the poor and education.[1] In order 'that this our faith may be suitably expressed in

Rupp, 'Luther and the German Reformation', *New Cambridge Modern History*, II, p. 86). There is no account in this volume of the wider social movements such as that of A. F. Pollard, *Cambridge Modern History*, II (1903), pp. 174 ff. See also for the popular movements and doctrines which accompanied the 'Magisterial Reformation' in the years 1516–80, George Hunston Williams, *The Radical Reformation* (1962).

[1] It is printed in F. R. Salter (ed.), *Some Early Tracts on Poor Relief* (1926).

brotherly love', ran the prologue, we 'have ordered, raised and set up, in complete unanimity, a common chest'. This would receive sums formerly donated to the church, stocks held by parishes and gilds, offerings of alms, legacies, and be controlled by ten overseers or guardians. It would be used to pay the minister, the sacristan and a schoolmaster, all to be appointed by the guardians. The master, who must value his office and be 'pious, blameless, well-educated', would receive quarterly payments from the common chest and in return teach freely, except for taking a small sum from 'foreigners' coming from outside the town. The guardians were also charged to choose a woman to give girls under twelve instruction in the faith, reading in the vernacular, writing. In addition they were to maintain all orphaned children, setting them to school if they showed ability and otherwise apprenticing them to trade and providing dowries for the girls. The remaining funds were to be expended on the poor—all begging being prohibited—and on maintaining public buildings.

A new system of education was one of the necessary foundations of the Lutheran church. If the clergy generally were to preach they must be both knowledgeable and trained in the techniques of oratory; if the people were to understand they must be literate. But Luther was not merely concerned to make the new church take over the educational functions ascribed to the old, to provide schools for intending clergy on the one hand, elementary teaching of the faith on the other. It was his aim to promote a system of education financed and administered by the secular power. In advocating this Luther threw his great influence into the balance in support of the humanist programme of linguistic and literary studies to be provided in public schools under public control.

This is the sense of his letter to the rulers of German cities.[1] 'It is a great and solemn duty that is laid upon us,' he wrote, 'a duty of immense moment to Christ and to the world, to give aid and council to the young. And in so doing we likewise promote our own best interests.' Continuing to frame his argument to his audience, Luther went on to detail the variety of services on which the cities spent large sums and asked—'ought we not to expend on the poor suffering youth therein, at least enough to provide them with a schoolmaster or two?' The

[1] Translated, with extracts from other relevant documents, in *Readings in the History of Education*, ed. E. P. Cubberley (Cambridge, Mass., 1920), pp. 241–3; also in *Early Protestant Educators*, ed. F. Eby (New York, 1931).

opportunity was there, for many knowledgeable young scholars were available as teachers who had already demonstrated that boys could learn more in three years than the old schools had ever been able to impart; that same argument with which Erasmus had delighted Colet. With this, Luther went on, few could disagree but some might well ask: 'What will it profit us to have Latin, Greek, Hebrew, and your other liberal arts taught to them? Will not German suffice to teach us all of the Bible and the word of God that is essential to salvation?' Luther had his answer to this practical objection, that languages are both useful and, a glorious gift of God, necessary to the true religion. 'The prince of darkness is shrewd enough to know that, where the languages flourish, there his power will soon be so rent and torn that he cannot readily repair it....For, as the light of the sun dispels the shadows of the night, so do the languages render useless all the glosses of the fathers.' A knowledge of Hebrew and Greek not only would render the old epitomes, with all their errors, obsolete, but was indispensable to a right understanding of the scriptures. 'Since now, it becomes Christians to regard the scriptures as the one and only book, which is all their own, and since it is a sin and shame for us not to be familiar with our own book, nor with the language and the word of our God;—so it is a still greater sin and shame, for us not to learn the languages' especially when God offers new opportunities.

Luther then turns to another practical objection, that many children are needed at home and cannot be spared for school. He has not in mind, he explains, such schools as formerly took twenty years to teach the rudiments. 'I ask no more than this, namely, that boys shall attend upon such schools as I have in view, an hour or two a day, and none the less; spend the rest of their time at home, or in learning some trade, or doing whatever else you will; thus both these matters will be cared for together, while they are young and opportunities are favourable.' 'So, too,' he adds, 'your little girls may easily find time to go to school an hour a day, and yet do all their household duties; for they now devote more than that to overmuch play, dancing and sleep.' To train youth aright, Luther concludes, coming at last to the heart of the matter, is essential not only for their own sake 'but also for the welfare and stability of all our institutions, temporal and spiritual alike'. There is need to 'begin at once, and in good earnest, to attend to this matter'.

While Luther preached the need for education in homely and

downright terms,[1] and gave his powerful support to humanist learning in schools and universities, Melanchthon worked out the details in terms of programmes of teaching and provided practical assistance in educational organisation. In 1524 he was invited to re-organise the Nuremberg high school and for the next thirty-six years he so dominated the educational scene as to earn the title 'preceptor of Germany'. The Nuremberg Academy opened in 1526 amid high hopes. Inaugurating it Melanchthon affirmed that it was the purpose of providence that children be brought up in virtue and religion and that this obligation 'extends to the entire youth of the state whose training demands corporate provision'; this because the ultimate aim must be 'not private virtue alone but the interest of the public weal'.[2] Whereas Erasmus had once commended the English court for supplanting the church in the promotion of learning, Melanchthon commends a city's zeal; bishops were no longer on the side of letters, princes were not always enlightened patrons, but Nuremberg was like Florence which had welcomed Greek exiles as honoured guests. In the event the rich merchants of Nuremberg hardly lived up to the encomium for, rather than keeping sons destined for commerce on at school, they sent them away to finish their education by learning modern languages—to Bruges or Venice, Swiss or English cities. It was rather grammar schools for younger boys that developed widely.

In 1527 Melanchthon was surveying schools in Saxony at the elector's request and drawing up plans for an organised system of education extending from vernacular school to university.[3] Already the foundations had been laid in Wittenberg of the system which provided a model for all the reformed German states.[4] At the base were free vernacular schools teaching reading, writing, music and the elements

[1] A particular example is his 'Sermon on the Duty of Sending Children to School', a lengthy discourse sent out to all pastors to be read to the people in 1530 (Eby, pp. 100–51).

[2] Woodward, *Studies*, p. 224.

[3] 'If there is a town or village which can do it, your Grace has the power to compel it to support schools...', Luther wrote to the elector of Saxony in 1526. 'If they are unwilling...then your Grace is the supreme guardian of the youth and of all who need his guardianship, and ought to hold them to it by force, so that they must do it. It is like compelling them by force to contribute and to work for the building of bridges and roads, or any other of the country's needs.' He added, 'If they cannot do it and are overburdened with other things, there are the monastic properties which were established chiefly for the purpose of relieving the common man, and ought still to be used for that purpose' (Eby, p. 85).

[4] It is outlined in a school ordinance which was incorporated in the Wittenberg Church Ordinance of 1559 (Eby, pp. 213–27).

of religion, then came Latin schools for those aged nine to sixteen, leading in turn to the state university. Besides re-organising the university at Wittenberg, Melanchthon also influenced, at Heidelberg and Tübingen, changes which paved the way for the new protestant foundations of Marburg (1527), Königsberg (1544) and Jena (1558).

Higher schools were in due course successfully established in some cities, the most notable being that at Strasburg which Johann Sturm was called in to organise in 1535. Bringing together a lower and upper school into an academy of ten classes, for which the order of teaching was carefully planned, he provided an institution particularly suitable to the needs of the great city, one which acted as a model as St Paul's had earlier done. The sons of Zwingli of Zurich and Oecolampadius of Basle were educated under Sturm at Strasburg; here Calvin learned much which he adapted to use when founding the Geneva Academy, while from England Roger Ascham maintained a correspondence with Sturm over many years and passed on his teaching methods to an English audience.[1]

As this great task of re-organisation was undertaken the Erasmian educational outlook was modified. Methods of imparting elementary education in the vernacular claimed more attention. In the school curriculum the reading of classical authors was curtailed to make place for study of the scriptures, so that the authors for whom Melanchthon found place were considerably fewer in number than Erasmus and Vives had recommended. At the university level the aim of widening knowledge and cultivating literary appreciation and skill likewise gave place to acquisition of the techniques of profound study, in particular in Hebrew and Greek; so the way was prepared for the great contributions to scholarship of succeeding generations.

During these years the Reformation spread far beyond the confines of German states, and additional examples were provided of associating educational reconstruction with reform of the ecclesiastical system. For instance, in Denmark ecclesiastical property was first secularised in 1536, the income of the crown being trebled, and bishops were confined to purely spiritual duties; subsequently the Church Ordinance of 1539 laid down a detailed policy for schools. In Sweden king and nobility combined to denude bishops and cathedrals of much property and the church's political and legal powers were abrogated in 1527; later, with the consolidation of a reformed church went steps to organise

[1] J. W. Adamson, *A Short History of Education* (Cambridge, 1919), pp. 159–66.

an educational system.[1] There is little or no evidence that these developments had any direct influence in England. Of events in Germany, however, Englishmen soon became aware.

(2) *Wolsey, the universities and the royal supremacy*

In May 1521 there was a ritual burning of Luther's works at Paul's Cross, presided over by Cardinal Wolsey with the papal nuncio, the archbishop of Canterbury and the bishop of London in attendance while Bishop Fisher preached a sermon denouncing heresy. Plans were put in hand for the prosecution of all merchants or stationers who imported heretical books and for the summary excommunication of any found to possess one. Some months later Henry forwarded to the pope the refutation of Luther's opinions which he had prepared at Wolsey's instigation and was rewarded with the title 'defender of the faith'. A body of theologians was required to go more deeply into Luther's works, which had already been condemned by both universities, and after meeting at Oxford responded with treatises defending indulgences and papal supremacy which were forwarded to the cardinal and the king.[2] There were renewed efforts along the same lines after the upheavals of 1525 in Germany and it was with this policy of upholding ecclesiastical authority and combating heresy that the chief educational project of this period was connected, as is illustrated by a long letter addressed to Wolsey in January 1526 by his close adherent John Longland, bishop of Lincoln.[3]

The bishop wrote that he had conveyed to the king the cardinal's obligation for permission to found a college 'which ye took to be of the highest recompense that he could do unto you, for the service your Grace hath done unto him'. Plans for the new foundation had been duly delivered and the king 'marvellously rejoiceth with many words and thanks to you for the same'. With such encouragement the bishop had dilated on the great good the cardinal's college could do, both 'in bringing up youth in virtue' and in 'the maintenance of Christ's church and his faith', adding that many educated there would be able

[1] *New Cambridge Modern History*, II, pp. 140–3, 148.

[2] Pollard, *Henry VIII*, p. 125; Lyte, *Oxford*, pp. 456–7.

[3] Sir Henry Ellis, *Original Letters Illustrative of English History* (1825), I, pp. 179–84. The letter, dated only 5 January, is here ascribed to 1523, in *L & P* to 1525; but since it includes a reference to securing Fisher to preach against Luther at Paul's Cross, which he did again in February 1526, it seems to belong to that year.

to render the king honourable service. The king had been much gratified by this, as also by the plans to refute Luther's works, forbid merchants to import them, excommunicate the disobedient. 'His Highness is as good and gracious in this quarrel of God as can be thought, wished, or desired', affirmed Bishop Longland, who had improved the occasion by assuring Henry, 'what power and name he hath obtained by his notable work made against Luther, and in what estimation he is in throughout Christendom...and that now in this suppression of Luther his adherents and disciples should get much more laud, praise and honour.' After dinner, the bishop went on to relate, the king led up the queen saying 'Madame, my lord of Lincoln can show of my lord cardinal's college at Oxford, and what learning there is and shall be, and what learned men in the same', upon which a new hearer was given an exposition of the prospects: students would come from all parts of Christendom to the college, the younger would each have a tutor, there would be many lecturers, and every member of the community would be bound to pray for king and queen.

All this, which throws light on the church's dealings with the king as well as educational projects, bore on a scheme that had been in the air since 1518, one on which the cardinal's plans for university reform now centred. Wolsey entertained many and various projects during his years of ascendancy from 1515 to 1529—purging and streamlining the monastic order, establishing new bishoprics, codifying the complex statutes of the universities—but most served as models for others in later years; only a college came briefly into being during his lifetime, intended to turn humanist learning to upholding the authority of the church.

Cardinal College, Oxford, was provided for as earlier ones had been by the dissolution of monastic houses, but this time on a considerable scale and in a manner that served as a precedent. In 1524, after persistent pressure at Rome, Wolsey's agents secured papal bulls authorising the suppression of various religious houses and diversion of their endowments to a semi-ecclesiastical community of some two hundred members; the principle established to attain this end was that monasteries with less than seven professed members could not properly celebrate observances and so might legitimately be suppressed.[1] Having also

[1] It was added that diversion of lands was necessary because the apportionment of any more in mortmain to the church would cause grave discontent among the laity (Lyte, *Oxford*, pp. 441–2).

gained the royal assent Wolsey began building on the site of Oxford's most ancient foundation, St Frideswide's Priory, and the new college was already taking shape when the statutes were issued in final form in 1527.

The foundation was for sixty canons and forty petty canons—together with chaplains, choristers and their master, a large number of servants and lay officials—and places were to be reserved for twenty young noblemen. The petty canons, to be chosen from the grammar schools Wolsey intended to found, must be at least fifteen and all those under twenty must be supervised by tutors from among the seniors.[1] To the college were attached six public professorships of the kind Wolsey had already been promoting, in the traditional disciplines of theology, philosophy, medicine, canon law, but also civil law and humanity. Wolsey laid down that the professors be appointed by the dean and senior canons, university officials and the heads of other secular colleges in Oxford. This ruling is noteworthy in that, while leaving monastic colleges aside, it accords other college heads a specific status in a university matter for the first time; they had recently been playing a more prominent part in university affairs, notably in putting down Lutheran opinions.

The cardinal also announced his intention of rebuilding the university schools to provide an adequate setting for the new professors, and laid down the subject matter lectures should cover. The professor of theology must expound the bible, both the Old and New Testaments, but also the *questiones* of Duns Scotus—the schoolman most abhorred by Erasmus but valued as a source of subtle arguments for the refutation of heresy. Philosophy lectures must cover Plato as well as Aristotle, the professor of humanity was to lecture twice daily on such Latin rhetoricians as Cicero and Quintilian and on Greek poets and orators, lectures on civil law must pay particular attention to meaning rather than mere phraseology.[2] Here was a judicious promotion of humanist studies side by side with the traditional, with due emphasis on civil law which was regarded as of particular relevance to the service of the state at home and abroad.

Meanwhile a reforming movement was beginning to take shape in England. To ideas which had long been in the air, to the persisting

[1] This was not a major innovation; it was a longstanding practice in the monasteries that, as a visitation order of 1441 puts it, 'to the young canons who have not attained the condition of priesthood certain other canons of riper age and discretion be assigned and appointed as caretakers', having the guardianship of allowances and so on (*Visitations*, II, i, p. 77).

[2] Lyte, *Oxford*, pp. 452–3.

traditions of Lollardy below the surface, there was now added a growing acquaintance with and discussion of developing Lutheran tenets. This, though most intensive in places where young men of education were brought together—as at Cambridge—also went on in the great households and at the board of country gentlemen whose interests extended beyond local affairs. One example is the Gloucestershire knight, Sir John Walsh, with whom, in the early 1520's, William Tyndale took a post as tutor, having taken an M.A. at Oxford and later studied Greek at Cambridge. Since his patron kept open house the tutor met many churchmen—abbots, deans, learned doctors—who commonly discussed the works of Erasmus and Luther and exchanged opinions. Tyndale took up a radical position and, required to justify it, responded by translating Erasmus's *Enchiridion*. This brought a charge of heretical opinions but it came to nothing and in 1523 the young man went to London with the idea of embarking on further translations, seeking support from Bishop Cuthbert Tunstall, who was highly respected by humanist scholars for his piety and learning.[1] The bishop of London had no place in his household for a young man anxious to translate the New Testament but a rich London merchant heard Tyndale preach, took him in and shortly financed a journey to Germany. It was from Worms that the English Testament eventually reached England, in April 1526. By October Bishop Tunstall was ordering his archdeacons to secure all copies in the diocese and in November the book was publicly burned, once more at Paul's Cross.[2] Similar action was taken elsewhere and a year or so later Thomas More, to whom the bishop of London forwarded heretical books with a licence to read them, was composing his *Dialogue... touching the pestilent sect of Luther and Tyndale*.

Tyndale had by this time published his important work *The Obedience of a Christian Man* in which, among much else, he fired some of the first shots in a century-long controversy about the efficacy of the English tongue to express thought and convey knowledge. Primarily concerned to uphold translation of the scriptures, Tyndale argued that the apostles had preached in their mother tongue, St Jerome translated

[1] Greenslade, pp. 6–7, 97.

[2] Tunstall's prohibition on reading the translation described its authors as 'children of iniquity, maintainers of Luther's sect, blinded through extreme wickedness, wandering from the way of truth and the Catholic faith', who 'craftily have translated the New Testament into our English tongue, intermeddling therewith many heretical articles, and erroneous opinions, pernicious and offensive, seducing the simple people' (*Complaint and Reform in England*, ed. W. H. Dunham and S. Pargellis, Oxford, 1938, p. 99).

the bible into his vernacular: why, then, should not Englishmen have it in theirs? In so doing he turned on those who held that English was too undeveloped a language, that the bible 'cannot be translated into our tongue it is so rude'. 'It is not so rude as they are false liars', affirmed Tyndale roundly. Having himself translated the New Testament from the Greek of Erasmus's text, and then the Old Testament directly from the Hebrew, he maintained that 'the Greek tongue agreeth a thousand times more with the English than with the Latin'; even more so Hebrew.[1]

As Tyndale's translations and works filtered into England by devious means, to be passed from hand to hand, Hugh Latimer was preaching in English at Cambridge. Here, too, Robert Barnes drew large audiences until in 1525 he was imprisoned for a time by Wolsey for too outspoken a denunciation of the avarice and ostentation of the higher clergy. On his release Barnes travelled to Germany to make acquaintance with that prominent member of his order, Martin Luther, and embraced his views, remaining at Wittenberg until 1535 when Thomas Cromwell called on his services. This was the way ideas were moving among many younger Cambridge men who discussed much the same matters as had earlier engaged Sir John Walsh's guests and reached much the same conclusions as Tyndale.

By this time the new learning had gained a foothold in the official university course. George Stafford, fellow of Pembroke and well versed in Greek and Hebrew, lectured in the schools on the scriptures, leaving the schoolmen altogether aside, up to his early death in 1529. Latimer was official university preacher. According to Thomas Becon —who attended his sermons as a boy of sixteen 'very desirous to have the knowledge of good letters' in the true humanist spirit—there was still a common saying in Cambridge twenty years later, 'When master Stafford read and master Latimer preached, then was Cambridge blessed'. Stafford, Becon recalled,[2] was a man of perfect life with 'singular knowledge in the mysteries of God's most blessed word'. As Colet had done before him, he threw new light on the Pauline epistles and expounded in his lectures 'the native sense and true understanding of the four evangelists'. Latimer proved in his sermons 'with manifest authorities of God's word and arguments invincible, besides the allegations of doctors' that all Christian people, whether priests or laymen, should read the scriptures in the English tongue.

[1] Greenslade, p. 89.
[2] *Catechism, etc.*, pp. 424–6.

Further he inveighed against images, relics and pilgrimages which diverted attention from 'works of mercy' and strongly criticised the traffic in benefices and the promotion to livings of men 'unlearned and ignorant in the law of God'. Of all these sermons the young Becon took careful notes, as a generation later all schoolboys were expected to do, and they remained imprinted on his memory; nor, as he remembered, was he alone in this.

Cambridge was, then, a centre of the new learning at this time, and beginning to be more in that Lutheran books, imported through the eastern ports, had a considerable circulation. It was indirectly owing to Wolsey that the infection spread to Oxford, when a group of Cambridge students was recruited to man Cardinal College; these were chosen as 'scholars of ripe wits and abilities' for Wolsey intended to congregate the best brains of Europe on his foundation. The Cambridge contingent joined with Oxford scholars and young men from the cardinal's household—Thomas Starkey and Richard Morison were two of these—to make up a community of some thirty under the newly appointed dean.[1] This had hardly become established when, in 1528, a sheaf of anxious letters—from an Oxford head to the bishop of Lincoln, from the chancellor of the university to the cardinal—brought disturbing news; that an adept Lutheran propagandist, Thomas Garret, former Oxford scholar, had descended on the university and been fruitfully at work, particularly among the cardinal's canons. 'Pity it were', wrote the aging Archbishop Warham, patron of Erasmus, 'that through the lewdness of one or two cankered members which, as I understand, have induced no small number of young and incircumspect fools to give ear unto them, the whole university should run in the infamy of so heinous a crime, the hearing whereof should be right delectable and pleasant to open Lutherans beyond the sea and secret behither, whereof they would take heart and confidence that their pestilent doctrines should increase and multiply, seeing both the universities of England infected therewith.' 'Whereof', he added, harking back to the days of Lollardy, 'the one hath many years been void of all heresies, and the other afore now taken upon her praise that she never was defiled, and nevertheless now she is thought to be the original occasion and cause of the fall of Oxford.'[2]

[1] W. G. Zeeveld, *Foundations of Tudor Policy* (Cambridge, Mass., 1948), pp. 26–9.

[2] Lyte, *Oxford*, pp. 457–9. Garret had taken his B.D. at Cambridge not long before, subsequently acting as distributor of Lutheran books and Tyndale's translations; he was

Bishops and heads rounded up and incarcerated offenders, the chief being Cambridge men, but to their consternation the cardinal was not disposed to take action. It was not Wolsey's way to hound scholars as heretics; nor indeed were there any burnings during his ascendancy, unless of books to prevent the spread of disaffection among the lower orders. Even the radical Thomas Bilney of Cambridge had so far only received a warning, as also had Latimer though his licence to preach was renewed. Towards his own canons Wolsey was equally lenient, evidently setting more store on retaining the allegiance and services of promising young men than making an example of them; in any case all were acquitted, some to return to Cardinal College with protestations of devotion to their patron.[1]

Wolsey was, indeed, quite single-minded about promoting his college and the way he accumulated funds for it aroused mounting criticism. Monastic houses expected to donate large sums secured various privileges in return. Individual abbots found that a substantial contribution might stave off an enforced retirement or pave the way to promotion; the inmates of St Bartholomew's Smithfield, foreseeing the death of their prior and wishing to elect a successor (a privilege frequently usurped by the cardinal), offered £300 towards the building of his college. The bishop of Lincoln, active in encouraging such offers from others by threat or flattery, himself profferred £200 if Wolsey would look after his nephew's preferments. All this tended to make the cardinal a personification of ecclesiastical abuses; the king himself heard it said, as he informed his minister, that 'the college is a cloak for covering all mischiefs'.[2]

Earlier there had been local protests against the dissolution of small monasteries whose endowments were needed to finance the college. When the inmates of a Sussex house were ejected, gentlemen of the locality came to their support against the cardinal's agents. Archbishop Warham, charged to discover whether the inhabitants of Tonbridge

clearly 'amongst the earliest and most effective of Lutheran propagandists', converting and instructing young men who later took a leading part in prosecuting the Reformation (Dickens, pp. 58–9). For a contemporary description of his influence at Oxford, John Foxe, *Acts and Monuments*, ed. J. Pratt, v, pp. 421–9.

[1] There are many grateful references to Wolsey by scholars, not all fulsome or sycophantic. Vives, who was lecturing at Oxford at this time, dedicated a Latin translation of Isocrates to the cardinal referring to his incredible 'kindness and goodwill to students' (*Vives: On Education*, p. lxxviii).

[2] Pollard, *Wolsey*, pp. 201–4.

were prepared to see their priory go in favour of a free school for forty scholars, linked with Cardinal College, replied in the negative. The idea that they were, he informed Wolsey in July 1525, had been propagated by two or three people involved in a lawsuit with the prior who would be glad to see the priory go; as for the inhabitants at large they would rather 'have the said place not suppressed than the contrary, if it might stand with the king's highness pleasure and your grace's'.[1]

Possibly there were difficulties elsewhere, though objections did not save the Tonbridge house. In any event, instead of founding a number of grammar schools up and down the country as he had originally intended, Wolsey established a second, smaller, Cardinal College in his native city, on the ruins of St Peter's Priory, Ipswich. The borough authorities were persuaded to add the endowments of their school which was accordingly annexed to the new foundation. There was a special opening ceremony in September 1529 for which the cardinal's chief agent, Thomas Cromwell—who had organised the dissolutions preparing the ground for the cardinal's colleges—came down from London with copes and vestments, altar cloths and plate, and assisted in the disposition of hangings and furniture. A solemn procession was made through the town by the dean, sub-dean, six chaplains, eight clerks and nine choristers of the foundation, attended—as the dean informed the founder—by 'all the honourable gentlemen of the shire', the bailiffs and leading townsmen, the priors of neighbouring houses and many clergy, all of whom were afterwards entertained to a banquet.[2] This was something very different from Colet's unostentatious foundation of a city school.

Nevertheless, Wolsey modelled the curriculum of the school he had taken over on that worked out for St Paul's. It was presumably at his instigation that the clergy in convocation in 1529, after deploring that there were so many different methods of teaching grammar—with consequent hindrance to boys who must change methods when they changed masters—directed that only one grammar be used in all schools, to be prescribed within the year.[3] This was published the same year under the title *Rudimenta Grammatices*, prescribed by Cardinal Wolsey to be taught in the school of Ipswich and 'all other schools throughout England'. The volume is prefaced by a plan for the

[1] S. Rivington, *Tonbridge School* (1925), pp. 3–6.

[2] Ellis, 1825, I, pp. 185–90.

[3] *ECD*, p. 447.

organisation of Ipswich School, directing that it be divided into eight forms and specifying the authors to be used at each stage. Wolsey notes that he has founded the school and provided text-books 'on the instruction of boys, on the method and theory of teaching principally necessary for such youth... knowing full well that hope for the commonwealth must rest upon that age, even as the corn from the seed'.[1] But the texts in fact set forth for general use are those of Colet, Erasmus and Lily, while the programme of authors advocated closely approximates to that in use at St Paul's.[2]

Wolsey's grammar may never have circulated widely, since he was disgraced before the close of the year it appeared.[3] But there is evidence that the school of Eton College, which formerly used the texts of Stanbridge and Whittinton, had made a change to Lily's grammar by 1530; the then headmaster was Richard Cox, one of the Cambridge immigrants to Cardinal College, and other text-books now used were Erasmus's *De Copia* and his manual on letter writing *De Conscribendis Epistolis* published in 1522.[4] And it is from about 1530 that the Stanbridge and Whittinton grammars cease to be published. In 1532 Whittinton turned to translating, one of the first books he produced being Erasmus's *Little Book of Good Manners for Children*; the same year a new edition of Lily's grammar appeared.

Whatever the use Wolsey made of humanist text-books, his educational aims differed profoundly from those of Colet. He was not

[1] Compare Erasmus's letter to Colet from Cambridge, reporting his part in an argument, when he affirmed that childhood was an age 'from which the richest harvest might be expected, as indeed it was the seedplot and planting-ground of the commonwealth' (*The Epistles of Erasmus*, ed. F. M. Nichols, II, 1904, p. 37; *EGS*, pp. 250–2; Baldwin, pp. 123–6).

[2] In 1549, a year for which information is newly available (McDonnell, p. 76), Wolsey's plan assigned Aesop and Terence to the third form, Virgil to the fourth, the upper school programmes being:

	St Paul's, 1549	*Ipswich, 1529*
V	Mantuan, Terence	Cicero's Letters
VI	Cicero's Letters, Virgil	Sallust or Caesar
VII	Sallust, *Aeneid*	Horace, Ovid
VIII	Caesar, Horace, Ovid, and Cicero *de Officiis*	Valla and other higher studies

[3] There is only one known copy of the 1529 edition and one of an edition published in Antwerp dated 1535 (V. J. Flynn, ed., *A Shorte Introduction of Grammar by William Lily*, New York, 1945).

[4] No books by Erasmus find mention in a timetable for the school of Winchester College at this date, though this may be because pages relating to higher forms are missing from the record (*ECD*, pp. 448–51).

concerned to further learning among laymen so much as to counteract the effect of growing literacy. His argument for establishing new colleges was that 'as printing could not be put down, it were best to set up learning against learning and, by introducing able persons to dispute, suspend the laity betwixt fear and controversy, as this, at the worst, would yet make them attentive to their superiors and teachers'.[1] This was the policy that was to animate the Counter-Reformation and pave the way to its success in countries where ecclesiastical control over education was never broken. But it could not now prevail in England. Soon, after the cardinal's fall and with his college at Oxford reduced, the universities were called upon to renounce the authority of the bishop of Rome.

The taking over of Wolsey's vast possessions was a rehearsal for what was to come. In the year of life that remained to him, while submitting to all else, he made strenuous efforts to preserve his colleges, relying on the good offices of his servant Thomas Cromwell, 'my only refuge and aid'.[2] But Wolsey had failed to make over the endowments accumulated with such care to his foundations so that they counted as personal property and were, despite Cromwell's efforts, dispersed with the rest.[3] As the cardinal's palaces became those of the king, Henry announced in April 1530 his intention of dissolving the Ipswich college and putting the property to his own use; a few months later the Oxford college was also suppressed and most of the lands granted away. Not until 1532 did Henry establish in the building at Oxford, itself a fragment of what had been planned, a small collegiate body—laying down that it was subject neither to bishop, archbishop, nor legate but to the king alone.[4]

Having dispensed with a minister who had failed to move the papacy to grant the divorce he sought, Henry now took the offensive. The

[1] This is how, aptly enough, Lord Herbert of Cherbury paraphrased Wolsey's representations to the papacy. 'All which being maturely weighed by his Holiness, it was not doubted but he would advise and commend to all Christian princes, the erecting of new colleges and seminaries for the advancement of learning' (*The Life and Raigne of King Henry the Eighth*, 1649, pp. 157–8).

[2] *State Papers Henry VIII* (1830), I, p. 355. Cromwell had entered the cardinal's service as legal adviser in 1514; he gathered influence after Wolsey became chancellor and a key position in managing his affairs after his fall, entering parliament and the king's service the following year (G. R. Elton, *The Tudor Revolution in Government*, Cambridge, 1953, pp. 76–86).

[3] Pollard, *Wolsey*, pp. 325–6.

[4] C. E. Mallet, *History of the University of Oxford* (1924), II, p. 38.

support of parliament was invited to demonstrate the strength of his following to observers abroad, and the Commons responded with anti-clerical statutes expressing long-felt resentment of the powers of ecclesiastical courts over the laity and attacking simony and plurality in the church.[1] Henry also sought the advice of the chief university centres of Europe on the canonical rights and wrongs of his marriage and received support for his case from various universities abroad as well as those at home. It was in helping to convince Cambridge of the rightness of the king's cause that a fellow of Jesus College, Thomas Cranmer, first came to the royal notice and at once found himself cast in the role of travelling diplomat to convince Europe as well.[2] Direct intimidation of the church followed, in the form of a threat to indict the whole body of clergy for præmunire for exercising independent jurisdiction in the ecclesiastical courts. No sooner had this threat been waived, by buying the royal pardon with large sums, than the king was found to be demanding the title of 'supreme head of the church'.

During this period Thomas More, who had stepped into Wolsey's place, was undertaking only the narrower duties of the chancellor's office—he would not meddle with the divorce to which he was unalterably opposed—and found time to turn his learning and literary skill to polemics against the Lutheran position. In 1529 his attack on Tyndale was published at a time when the bishops, freed from Wolsey's restraining hand, had begun to burn heretics. The man who had once advocated the spread of literacy in the vernacular must now oppose this in so far as it was taking place in direct association with the spread of heretical ideas.[3] Among Lutheran books imported at this time there were various primers in English. 'We have', wrote More,

the ABC for children and because there is no grace therin, lest we should lack prayers, we have the *Primer* and the *Ploughman's Prayer* and a book of

[1] G. R. Elton, *England under the Tudors* (1955), pp. 123 ff. Included among grievances against the bishops was the accusation that they 'do daily confer and give sundry benefices unto certain young folks, calling them their nephews or kinsfolk, being in their minority' and so unable to serve a cure; accordingly the revenues are taken 'and the poor silly souls' of the people 'for lack of good curates do perish without good example, doctrine or any good teaching' (*The Tudor Constitution* (Cambridge, 1960), p. 326).

[2] Jaspar Ridley, *Thomas Cranmer* (1962), pp. 26–7, where it is pointed out that the idea of consulting universities did not originate with Cranmer.

[3] Tyndale's New Testament translated key words from the Greek (by comparison with the version in the Latin Vulgate) as follows: congregation (church), elder (priest), love (charity), favour (grace), knowledge (confession), penance (repentance). There were also annotations in the manner of Erasmus.

other small devotions, and then the whole *Psalter*, too. After the *Psalter*, children were wont to go straight to their *Donat* and their *Accidence*, but now they go straight to Scripture. And for this end we have as a Donat the book of the *Pathway to Scripture* in a little book, so that after these books are learned well we are ready for...Tyndale's *Testament* and all the other high heresies. Of all these heresies the seed is sown and prettily sprung up in these little books before. For the *Primer* and *Psalter*, prayers and all, were translate and made in this manner for heretics only.[1]

According to this testimony there was a range of text-books available to make up a regular course of schooling in the vernacular, on lines now familiar in the reformed states of Germany. This could only have provided a new stimulus to literacy while there was a growing knowledge of reforming doctrine among the literate. Learning might be on the side of the established order, while the reformers had as yet an incompletely worked out system of ideas, but these ideas chimed in with long-felt aspirations. Moreover, as Colet had once warned, the corruption of the church provided arguments far stronger than theologians could devise in its defence, and so the reforming party gained adherents in the universities. Thomas Bilney, who had resumed preaching at large, now fell victim to the ecclesiastical authorities and was burned as a heretic in the Lollard's pit at Norwich in August 1531. But Latimer once more escaped molestation and continued the preaching which affronted churchmen and university authorities, this time on the royal intervention because he upheld the king's cause in the matter of the divorce.

Within little more than a year of Bilney's death this cause was won, Henry had remarried, Cranmer was his new archbishop of Canterbury, More had resigned the chancellorship and Thomas Cromwell had taken the first steps to power. During the next two years control over the church was extended and consolidated, under Cromwell's guidance, by statutes which, though dealing with specific matters, had far-reaching implications.[2] For instance, at the first session of the parliament of 1534 ecclesiastical courts were made subject to the king's courts and the throne was secured to the children of Anne Boleyn by the act of succession—this, involving recognition of the divorce, implied rejection of papal authority. The second session saw the passage of the act of supremacy proclaiming that the king 'justly and rightfully is and ought to be Supreme Head of the Church of England'—a recognition

[1] *EGS*, p. 33. [2] Elton, *England under the Tudors*, pp. 130–6.

which, however vaguely formulated, implied the right to visit ecclesiastical foundations which had formerly belonged to the spiritual power embodied in the church. In addition first-fruits—the first year's income on all benefices which had formerly been due to Rome—were secured to the crown and a new annual tax of 10 per cent was levied on the net income of all benefices including fellowships at the universities.[1]

It was by this train of events—both rapid and confusing—that the universities were shorn of their papal immunities; deprived also of the support of a church under heavy attack they were now open to royal visitation. In 1534 Oxford, a decade after it had upheld papal indulgences, found that the 'bishop of Rome' had no greater jurisdiction in England than any other such bishop. In 1535 the only two leading figures who had resisted the royal policy were executed after the passage of a new treasons act. More had been high steward of both universities, Fisher chancellor of Cambridge for many years; his successor was Cromwell, while Bishop Longland of Lincoln took office as chancellor of Oxford. Earlier in the year commissioners had been appointed to value the property of all monasteries, collegiate churches and colleges at Oxford and Cambridge for the purpose of levying the new tax due to the crown; their returns were put together to make up the *Valor Ecclesiasticus*. By the autumn another set of visitors was conducting a visitation of both universities. The stage was set for a reformation in England which, though developments had taken a course very different from that in Germany, might also extend to include educational reform.

(3) *Some proposals for reform*

In the early 1530's humanist educational ideas were taken up and adapted in various ways. The first humanists had taken everything relating to education for their province. Colet wrote in English for the ordinary man's child, upheld the cause of enlightened teaching in public schools and preached the need for learning among the clergy. Erasmus wrote for the general reader and compiled many text-books besides addressing innumerable tracts on education and learned works to princes, nobles, leading churchmen. After Erasmus had praised the folly of the schoolmen Thomas More, taking Plato as guide, wrote

[1] Knowles, pp. 241–2.

a book of wit and insight praising the follies of the world; a book which used as framework the description by Amerigo Vespucci of his new discoveries, referred directly to the social problems of contemporary England and advocated universal education. Vives, who went deeply into the psychology and philosophy of education, was also interested in the development of the vernacular literatures and science and wrote a notable treatise on provision for the poor. When, however, a new generation took over there were differentiated trends.

The writing of popular works in the vernacular now became the province of the growing body of reformers. In the sermons of such as Latimer the language of the common people became a more flexible instrument for the communication of ideas, while the translators of the bible, profiting from affinities between Greek or Hebrew and English, brought to birth a work which above all else moulded the speech and thought of later generations. It was in the cities, primarily by the common council of London, that schemes were evolved for the care and training of the children of the poor.

On the other hand the humanist programme of studies was now advocated less in educational and more in political terms, by men closely engaged in operating the royal policy at a critical time. When Wolsey's household was dispersed the talent he had fostered, in what was an embryo civil service, became available to the king and under Cromwell's direction young men were set to the task of formulating concrete policies and fostering a new outlook. In place of Wolsey's attempts to promote educational reform under the aegis of the church there were now moves to do so in the interests of the state. While in Germany appeal was made to patricians of the towns to assist in reorganising the church and extending education, in England much depended on enlisting the support of the gentry who held a key place in local administration. But if the country gentry were to be called upon more widely to consolidate secular forms of government it was urgently necessary to remedy their educational deficiencies.[1] In the prevailing circumstances the call tended to take the form of exhorting gentlemen to educate themselves.

[1] A writer familiar with contemporary records contrasts 'the fumbling incoherencies which emanated from the average semi-educated gentry and middle classes in the reign of Henry VIII' with the 'scholarly grasp of Latin, strong legal and theological interests, and above all... mastery of lucid and forceful English' shown by a Yorkshire gentleman, Francis Bigod, a ward of Wolsey sent to Cardinal College who probably also spent a period at the inns of court (Dickens, p. 59).

The early humanists had provided various guides to the proper upbringing of young men of birth and Sir Thomas Elyot now compiled a native version. One tract was, however, addressed rather to the middle class, by Colet's pupil Thomas Lupset. His *Exhortation to Young Men persuading them to walk in the path of honesty and goodness* (1530) was evidently much read, since it was reprinted five times within fourteen years, but, like More's later works, it sadly reflects the dilemma of the conservative humanist at this juncture. Critical faculties, the search for knowledge, are at a discount. In this tract, addressed to the son of a London merchant he had once tutored, Lupset urging study of Erasmus's New Testament immediately enjoins:

Presume not in no case to think that there you understand aught: leave devising thereupon: submit yourself to the expositions of holy doctors; and ever conform your consent to agree with Christ's church. This is the surest way you can take, both before God and man. Your obedience to the universal faith shall excuse you, before God, although it might be in a false belief: and the same obedience shall also keep you out of trouble in this world, where you see, how foolish meddlers be daily sore punished...it is your part to obey and follow the church.[1]

Formerly, when gentlemen had been advised to secure competent tutors and bring up their children aright, Sir Thomas More's household was often held up as a pattern. Not only did he employ brilliant young scholars as tutors, so that even his daughters achieved an extraordinary reputation for learning, but also the happy family life in his home, where grandchildren congregated together with learned scholars, was held to epitomise the combination of Christian brotherhood in learning with daily life. Even before More's name became unmentionable all this was on rather a special plane, removed from the realities of most men's lives, certainly from the way of life in a great household or at court. This provided other examples for emulation. Many of Henry VIII's lay advisers, those employed in diplomacy particularly, were men whose education had been finished abroad; so far was this recognised as necessary and desirable that promising young men were sent on their travels at the expense of the privy purse.[2] A notable example of

[1] Gee, p. 244.

[2] William Petre has already been mentioned; another example is John Mason, picked out as a notable orator on an Oxford occasion and sent as king's scholar to Paris in 1530; first employed as secretary to an ambassador he was later ambassador himself (Zeeveld, pp. 71–2).

private upbringing at this time, if the record is exact, is that provided for Anthony St Leger, eldest son of a Kentish squire. Born in 1496, he was sent from home at the age of twelve 'for his grammar learning with his tutor into France, for his carriage into Italy, for his philosophy to Cambridge, for his law to Gray's Inn; and for that which completed all, the government of himself, to court'—all this forming a man, in the words of a later writer, who 'was neither soldier, nor scholar nor statesman, yet he understood the way how to dispose of all these to his country's service and his master's honour'.[1]

This kind of model of the all-round man was first clearly advanced for imitation by Castiglione's book, copies of which were circulating in England soon after its publication in Italian in 1528. *Il Cortegiano* provided instruction and examples to be followed in a variety of ways. Advice on how wit may be exercised within the bounds of taste suggests how cultivation of the art of conversation prepared the way for imaginative writing; within a few pages one might find the fanciful tale of the Lucca merchant bargaining with Muscovites for sables over an iced-up Polish river when the very words froze solid in the air above, and the story of the ape brought back by one of Vasco da Gama's men from India who took on his master at chess at the Portuguese court, had him checkmate and showed intelligence in avoiding the consequences.[2] On a more serious plane were the disquisitions on women and Platonic love and the dispassionate debate on statecraft. The influence of this book can be traced in much of the work of the first great poet of the century, Thomas Wyatt, who made acquaintance with the author in the course of travels to Rome, Ferrara, Bologna, Florence, Venice, on the king's business.[3] Wyatt was a courtier in Castiglione's sense of the term—of good birth yet scholarly, with a knowledge of modern languages and a reputation for wit, diplomat and member of Cromwell's entourage, courtly yet Christian, a poet whose sonnets were supplemented by versions of the penitential psalms in English metre. It was the poets who first made the English language a more polished instrument and held up native models of conduct. Their work for many years circulated only verbally or in manuscript

[1] *Athenae*, I, p. 192, quoting from Lloyd's *State Worthies*.

[2] B. Castiglione, *The Book of the Courtier* (Everyman, 1948), pp. 146–8. To add to its topicality there was the author's impression of Henry VIII as a boy, gained on an embassy to England in 1506, and the citing of the king with Francis I and Charles V as hopes of the age (*ibid.* p. 290).

[3] A. K. Foxwell (ed.), *The Poems of Sir Thomas Wiat* (1913), II, pp. vi–viii, xxii.

but it could none the less be of influence.[1] Henry Howard, earl of Surrey, extolled his friend as an example to young men who wished to take the path of virtue:

A tongue that served in foreign realms his king:
  Whose courteous talk to virtue did enflame.
Each noble heart: a worthy guide to bring
  Our English youth, by travail unto fame.

This flowering was short. Wyatt died in 1542 at the early age of thirty-nine, disillusioned with court life and politics; Surrey fell victim five years later after Henry VIII had turned against the Howards. But already in 1536, with the disgrace and execution of Anne Boleyn, an era at court had ended. It is not until English literature blossoms into sudden maturity in the closing decades of the century that the tradition to which Castiglione's work gave rise can be traced in Sidney's *Arcadia*, Lyly's *Euphues*, Spenser and Shakespeare. Meanwhile the times dictated that more workaday models of conduct be held up to gentlemen.

Elyot, an associate of More's circle, was well placed to provide such a model; trained in the common law, appointed clerk to the council by Wolsey, he was after associated with Cromwell, being knighted in 1530. His book, published in 1531 by the royal printer, had no doubt received official encouragement and was duly dedicated to the king:

I have enterprised to describe in our vulgar tongue the form of a just public weal.... And for as much as this present book treateth of the education of them that hereafter may be deemed worthy to be governors of the public weal under your highness (which Plato affirmeth to be the first and chief part of a public weal; Solomon saying also where governors be not the people shall fall into ruin) I therefore have named it The Governor, and do now dedicate it to your highness.[2]

Elyot drew widely on the writings of Italian and northern humanists, on the bible as well as the classics, to embroider the theme of the worth of learning and the duty of applying it to the public good. But again, at a time when events and ideas were unfolding apace, the tone of this

[1] Wyatt's poems made up much of at least one court album which served for the education of a younger generation and circulated widely; this first belonged to his follower the earl of Surrey and the king's natural son the duke of Richmond, who were brought up together, and passed later through various hands (Foxwell, pp. 241–6).

[2] *The Boke named the Governour*, ed. Foster Watson (Everyman, 1907). It has often been discussed, e.g. by Woodward, *Studies*, pp. 260 ff. and by Caspari who emphasises Elyot's indebtedness to Erasmus and More and discusses his social philosophy with reference to other works.

book is conservative.[1] Humanist precepts had once seemed to provide an excellent justification for social mobility but now, when dangerous ideas about the equality of men before God were circulating, Elyot used them to preach stability, to renew the outlook inherited from a traditional society. This, summarily outlined, held that God's primary purpose had been to ordain both the natural and social order in perfect balance; just as the sun and stars, birds and animals, keep to their proper spheres and concerns so must each estate in society. Elyot purposely leaves aside the familiar term 'commonweal' and substitutes 'public weal' which enables heavy emphasis on the supremacy of the prince. In this context it is his main objective to re-interpret traditional obligations with the aid of the ideal of citizenship to be found in classical authors. In particular, for the obligation of service to an immediate lord which had been built into the practice of an earlier age but was now notably weakened, for the authority of the pope now discarded, there must be substituted the obligation of service to the state and obedience to the crown.

Before the Reformation broke loose Erasmus had freely stressed that learning confers nobility of mind and character, that this could be acquired by the ordinary man, while on the other hand the corruption of the church and the tyranny of princes was castigated. But the uprisings in Germany burned deeply into men's minds and the post-Reformation Erasmus proclaimed that princely tyranny was preferable by far to anarchy. Protestant reformers likewise put their trust in princes, to support the Lutheran church where it was becoming established and elsewhere to subdue the old church whose corruption was held ultimately responsible for all dislocation and disorder; to this end Tyndale also stressed obedience to the prince, if with some important qualifications, while Cranmer was to carry belief in the royal supremacy to its logical conclusion. But the king could not rule alone; there must be a substitute for an ecclesiastical hierarchy which had so largely fulfilled the responsibilites of government but was now being relegated to spiritual and lesser administrative duties. This implied, in England as elsewhere, a new emphasis on lay education for secular occupations along humanist lines.

[1] It has been suggested that the first three sections on 'The Form of a Just Public Weal' were prefixed to an already drafted treatise on education to provide a relevant tract for the times (Stanford E. Lehmberg, *Sir Thomas Elyot. Tudor Humanist*, Texas University, 1960, p. 39).

Elyot did not, however, set a completely new pattern of education before his fellow gentlemen, as has often been suggested; rather he proposed refurbishing a familiar form of upbringing by giving a humanist content to instruction in the household and at the inns of court. He likewise adapted other humanist ideas. According to humanist philosophy, as has been seen, virtue is innate; learning and training realise it, by these means it can be brought to bear in action, the living proof of virtue being thoroughness of application to the public good. In his exposition Elyot stresses the initial point in such a way as to argue that virtue is primarily innate in men of birth.[1] The rest then fell into place and, much moralising and elaboration of the humanist programme of studies apart, Elyot's advice to gentlemen is straightforward enough. Bring up your sons at home and supervise their education carefully since this is of great account; it should combine sound instruction with enlightened and suitable recreation, healthy and useful exercises. Obtain a good tutor, without counting the cost too meanly as some parents do; retain him until his pupils are twenty-one—far too many parents dispense with tutors when boys are only fourteen leaving them to idle away their time at the most formative age. Have no fear that learning will make your son a clerk; properly directed, study will rather turn him into a leader and governor of men.

When advocating particular studies Elyot stresses their relevance in this sense. Caesar, for instance, is an excellent guide to war, giving instructions relevant to contemporary wars against Irishmen and Scots who are 'of the same rudeness and wild disposition that the Swiss and Britons were in the time of Caesar'. This was to adapt humanist techniques to a subject which Erasmus held in singular aversion. Vives, while suggesting that studies of war merely equip the mind with examples of doing evil and injury, reluctantly concedes them some place in history.[2] Elyot advises that note be taken of the cause of wars,

[1] The essence of his complex argument, deducing intellectual inequality from social inequality, is stated briefly by Castiglione: 'Nobleness of birth, is as it were a clear lamp that sheweth forth and bringeth into light, works both good and bad, and inflameth and provoketh to virtue, as well with the fear of slander, as also with the hope of praise.' Therefore, though there is virtue wherever there is personal merit in action, 'it chanceth always in a manner, both in arms and other virtuous acts, that the most famous men are gentlemen. Because nature in every thing hath deeply sowed that privy seed, which giveth a certain force and property of her beginning unto whosoever springeth of it, and maketh it like unto herself' (p. 34).

[2] 'We cannot help noticing briefly, who took up arms, who were the leaders on either side, where the conflict took place, who were beaten, and what happened to them.

'the counsels and preparations on either part, the estimation of the captains, the manner and forms of their governance, the continuance of the battle, the fortune and success of the whole affair'. There is also much emphasis on government in peace though the republicanism of the ancients is here an embarrassment, as their paganism elsewhere, and this prompts the occasional gloss; the government of Rome, for instance, must be recognised as imperfect because 'the insolence and pride of Tarquin...excluded kings out of the city'. Nevertheless, Elyot can easily conclude that if a nobleman reads history rightly 'there is no study or science for him of equal commodity and pleasure'.[1]

When boys have been thoroughly grounded parents should send them to the inns of court. Legal training is certainly impaired because the law is couched in barbarous Anglo-Norman; laws must be reduced to greater order, framed in 'a more clean and elegant style', either in English, Latin or good French, while methods of pleading need civilising to concur with classical rhetoric. But in general, Elyot affirms, as Fortescue had done before him, English law draws on the best practice of all other countries and study of it, preceded by a wide study of the classics, can produce 'men of so excellent wisdom that throughout all the world shall be found in no commonweal more noble counsellors'.[2]

Elyot's complicated programme of classical studies—he even advocated that Greek might be learned before Latin—may be compared with the tuition actually given to Cromwell's son, as the boy's tutor described it to his employer a few years after publication of *The Governor*. Gregory Cromwell's occupations included training in the use of arms and playing musical instruments, but also serious study of French and learning arithmetic. His tutor daily heard him read in English, correcting his pronunciation and also expounding the etymology and significance of words borrowed from Latin or French. One day's work is described which faithfully reflects humanist teaching method. After hearing mass the boy studied one of Erasmus's colloquies, being asked not only to read it through but also to reflect on the precepts; he also compared the Latin with an English translation made by his tutor. Afterwards he practised writing for an hour or two and then

But whatever is said or read in history, wars should be recognised not otherwise than as cases of theft, as indeed they usually were.... Let the student then give his attention to peaceful affairs, a far more satisfactory and fruitful study....' (*Vives: On Education*, p. 236).

[1] *Loc. cit.* pp. 45–7.

[2] *Ibid.* p. 64.

for as long again read Fabyan's *Chronicles*.[1] This left the rest of the day for playing upon the lute and virginals, for riding (when his tutor recounted some Roman or Greek history by the way which the boy retailed again in the form of a story), for hawking, hunting and shooting with the long bow.

Thomas Cromwell was, perhaps, an exceptional parent and had secured as tutor a young scholar who had been among the community around Pole in Padua. But while he was in power his household was the one in which men most wished to place their sons, and on all counts it seems likely that the kind of education outlined was more usually provided than anything approaching the elaborate classical régime propounded by Elyot. The latter has sometimes been represented as restoring the balance to an over-scholarly approach because of his disquisitions on games and exercises, but this is to overlook that in this connection as in others he administered a heavier dose of scholarship than most. His contribution in this sense was considerable since he also wrote on medicine and health, the education of women, translated Plutarch's treatise on upbringing and did a signal service in compiling a dictionary. It was with this last that he contributed most to developments in the schools, a subject left altogether aside in *The Governor*.

It was in the nature of Elyot's thesis that he should also leave aside problems which prevented gentlemen from securing the best upbringing for their sons. This point was taken up by Thomas Starkey, once member of Cardinal College and subsequently secretary in Pole's household in Padua where Richard Morison, also formerly of Cardinal College, and Thomas Lupset were also resident at various times. Starkey and Morison returned to England in 1534 to place themselves at Cromwell's disposal and both were employed on writing tracts for the times. Starkey also made a comprehensive review of English government and society—framed in the form of a dialogue between Pole and Lupset—in which education receives particular attention.[2] In this he pinpoints the bad upbringing of the nobility as the worst of all 'ill customs' in England, painting a picture blacker than Elyot had done. Young men of birth are 'customarily brought up in hunting and hawking, dicing and carding, eating and drinking...in all vain

[1] Published in 1515 under the title *The New Chronicles of England and France* but concentrating on the affairs of London (Ellis, 1846, I, pp. 341–5).

[2] It was never published, if for no other reason than that Pole eventually turned squarely against Henry's policies (*A Dialogue between Reginald Pole and Thomas Lupset*, ed. K. M. Burton, 1948; discussed in Caspari, pp. 110–31).

pleasure, pastime and vanity' as though 'to nothing else in this world of nature brought forth'. Rather than merely blaming parents, however, Starkey looks for an underlying reason for this state of affairs and finds it in primogeniture and wardship. The former he accepts as necessary, to preserve the nobility above the commons and provide heads or governors, though younger brothers should have some rights and prospects if they are to take life seriously. But the system of wardship he finds against all reason. In practice the lord has little regard for the 'bringing up in learning and virtue' of the minor, however good his birth, may well mishandle his lands and even has the power to marry off his ward according 'to his own pleasure and profit'.[1]

This was to raise a burning question. When, some sixty years earlier, Fortescue had extolled the system of wardship for its educational benefits, he left out of account the fact that rights of wardship no longer fell to an immediate lord who stood in a patriarchal relationship to his dependant and cared for him as his own. Now, largely centred in the crown since the reign of Henry VII, they were usually sold to the highest bidder to secure an important addition to the royal revenues. In 1526 there was a new tightening of the reins as steps were taken towards establishing a regular court of wards; after 1536 the situation was to be greatly aggravated in so far as the feudal tenure by knight service was imposed when monastic lands were sold by the crown. There was, therefore, growing criticism of a burden which had long been unpopular, criticism sharpened by a new awareness of the importance of educating gentlemen.

Starkey declares that, if noblemen's sons are to be properly educated, all the old and barbarous customs of wardship must be abrogated. Everyone who has charge of a ward must render account to a judge, not only of his revenues but also, much more, 'of the ordering and institution of his ward both in virtue and learning'. Whereas Elyot advocated upbringing in the household, Starkey puts the humanist argument that it is limiting to bring up youth privately with no regard to 'common discipline and exercises'; tutors may be kept in households to give formal instruction while other necessary exercises pertaining to nobility are neglected. What is needed is a form of education drawing the two together, and here Starkey advocates Italian practice, the setting up of public academies specifically designed for young men of birth. 'As we have in our universities colleges and common places to

[1] *Dialogue*, pp. 109–10, 123.

nourish the children of poor men in letters', he writes, so much more should there be 'certain places appointed for the bringing up together of the nobility' to which 'the nobles should be compelled to set forward their children and heirs, that in a number together they might the better profit'. Some of the great monastic houses, of which there are plainly too many supporting idle and ignorant men, could be turned to this use—Westminster, for instance, or St Albans. Teachers should be appointed from among 'the most virtuous and wise men of the realm', to instruct young men of birth not only in virtue and learning but also in all feats of war and in the laws since they will in future be military leaders and governors of the common sort. From such an education would 'spring the fountain of all civility and politic rule'.[1]

While Starkey sees the proper upbringing of the nobility as a key question more and better education is his remedy for most other social problems as well. Twenty years earlier Thomas More had drawn a vivid picture of contemporary social evils, concluding that 'rich men, not only by private fraud but by common laws do every day pluck and snatch away from the poor some part of their daily living—God help me, I can perceive nothing but a certain conspiracy of rich men procuring their own commodities under the name and title of a commonwealth'. Starkey's criticisms are on broadly similar lines. Following More in stressing the dignity of work he affirms, after Erasmus, that no man is born for his own pleasure—every man should labour according to his estate, particularly the well born. It is one of the chief diseases of the body politic that princes, lords and bishops seek only their own profit and pleasure while even judges seek bribes. With the head of the state so disordered, no wonder that ploughmen and craftsmen are negligent; hence high prices, penury and the growing army of beggars. English cities seem to Starkey dirty and dilapidated so that gentlemen fly into the country; there they enclose arable for pasture, gather for themselves, and in an attempt to emulate princes build great houses and keep armies of followers. Altogether there are far too many unproductive serving men in England, and, also over many idle monks, friars and canons while good religious men are too few.[2]

His educational proposals follow directly from these criticisms. Education is of such key importance in forming positive qualities that it should be compulsory not only for the nobility but for all. 'Every

[1] *Dialogue*, pp. 169 ff. [2] *Ibid.* pp. 84–5, 92–3.

man, under a certain pain, after he has brought his children to seven years of age, should set them forth either to letters or a craft, according as their nature requireth, after the judgment and power of their friends.' In every town and village there should also be 'a common place appointed' for young people to take exercise.[1]

If the standards of the clergy are to be raised there must be better local schools. Starkey does not so much suggest a shortage of schools as the inadequacy of many when he writes, 'it were nothing amiss to put two or three...small schools of £10 a year together and make one good, with an excellent master'. Moreover, in every town the priest should instruct youth and see that the most promising go to universities 'there to be instructed in the liberal sciences and so to be made preachers of the doctrine of Christ'; like others, Starkey saw the reform of the universities as an aspect of reform of the church. But educational institutions must be imbued with the aim of imparting virtue as well as learning since learning without the ability and desire to apply it is 'pernicious and pestilent'. University studies particularly need reform; it is because standards are so low, affirms Starkey fresh from Padua, that 'we have few great learned men in our country' and if they are not amended all letters and learning will fail.[2]

As for the wider educational influence of the church the problem here is that priests 'patter up their matins and mass...nothing understanding'; their flocks understand even less. Music is used in a fashion 'more convenient to minstrels than to devout ministers of the divine service', the words being so diversely descanted that 'it is more to the outward pleasure of the ear, and vain recreation, than to the inward comfort of the heart and mind, with good devotion'. Should divine service, then, be in the vulgar tongue and the gospel also translated into English? In giving his answer to this question Starkey is bound to disclaim identity with the Lutheran position; 'heretics be not in all things heretics', he therefore remarks, and on this point the Lutherans may well be right.[3] The church's educational influence will also be greatly increased if plurality and non-residence are curbed, if bishops reside in their dioceses and, keeping only a quarter of their income, use the rest to build churches and maintain the poor; this was what Colet had urged in his sermon of 1512, a return to the early practice of the church which required this 'due distribution of the patrimony of Christ'.

[1] *Ibid.* pp. 142, 148. [2] *Ibid.* pp. 180–2. [3] *Ibid.* pp. 126–8, 189.

In sum, Starkey is inclined to trace back most shortcomings to 'the ill and idle bringing up of youth' in the great households; they prefer 'pleasant living in service with the nobility spiritual and temporal' to learning and performing their duties.[1] It is, then, vital to establish a viable system of education and the state should make the requisite forms of training compulsory for all. Let the heads, officers and rulers pay due attention to this matter, Starkey insists, for 'the good education of youth in virtuous exercises is the ground of the remedying all other diseases in this our politic body' without which other medicines can be of little avail; in this matter, 'the chief key' to other reforms, 'all diligence is required'.[2]

This trenchant argument was probably submitted to the king and Cromwell late in 1535.[3] That same year another of Cromwell's able assistants, William Marshall, translated and published in London the ordinances on poor relief issued by the town of Ypres, outlining a scheme which derived directly from a treatise by Vives. In many European states the incidence of extreme poverty had reached a level which impelled fresh thinking and action. The traditional view—that sickness, famine, beggary, were acts of God, to be relieved by alms distributed by religious bodies—no lònger covered the contemporary facts any more than existing agencies met the needs; many of the poor were men lacking work for ascertainable causes, or whole families uprooted from the land whose plight under prevailing laws More had so feelingly described in his *Utopia*. Vives must have discussed these problems in England since it was at Oxford that the Spanish magistrate of Bruges, there on a visit in 1523, approved the idea of a treatise on the subject; a treatise that Vives eventually dedicated to the governing body of his home town in 1526.

It was his aim to advance practical measures, he wrote in a prefatory letter. The town, recognising the problem, was heartily disposed to relieve the needs of the wretched, as indeed was right—'it was the original cause of cities that there should be opportunity in each of them where love should unite citizens in the giving and receiving of benefits

[1] Colet disapproved of English educational institutions because they fostered idleness, wrote Erasmus. 'Ever for your soul's sake flee from idleness' wrote Colet's pupil, Lupset, 'the which is not only in him that doth nothing, but also in him that doth not well; and idle you be when you be not well occupied' (Gee, p. 246).

[2] *Dialogue*, p. 144.

[3] For Starkey's correspondence with Cromwell, *L & P*, VIII, pp. 80–7; Caspari, p. 111.

and in mutual help'.[1] While, therefore, in Germany appeal was made to a new witness of brotherly love in the reformed church, Vives appealed to a traditional corporate spirit. In the body of his book he sets out clearly the principles that should govern different forms of aid by the community. Advancing the thesis that poor relief is the keystone of the bridge between rich and poor, and must be carefully planned, he advocates a census of all the poor in every town, whether in the streets, in almshouses or at home. A detailed analysis should then be made of different classes of poverty and treatment provided accordingly in the light of three principles. Begging should be prohibited and all paupers fit to work set to useful labour; the sick, infirm and helpless should be provided for in hospitals; the children of the poor should be educated to save them from becoming paupers in turn.[2]

On this last point Vives advocates: 'Let there be a hospital where abandoned children may be nurtured, to whom appointed women shall act as mothers.' Children should remain there until six, then move on to a public school providing maintenance as well as education and training. The authorities should spare no expense in selecting suitable teachers; 'they will secure for the city over which they rule a great boon at small cost'. Boys should learn to read and write but 'let them first of all learn Christian piety and the right way of thinking'. The quicker learners should stay on in school, help to teach younger children and prepare themselves to enter a seminary to train as priests. Others should move into workshops, in accordance with their individual bent, and girls should be taught spinning, sewing, weaving, embroidery, cookery, household management; though Vives, always an advocate of education for women, also advises that 'if any girl show herself inclined for and capable of learning, she should be allowed to go further with it'.[3]

It was not easy for this kind of project, which had much in common with those of Lutheran and Swiss towns, to be put into practice in the Spanish Netherlands, where the friars and other religious orders felt their interests threatened. Ypres came nearest to doing so and its ordinances became known throughout Europe. So also did Vives's tract which circulated widely.[4] Such leading London citizens as Richard Grafton—who combined authorship and translation with publishing and was active in the city's government—must have been acquainted

[1] Salter, p. 5.
[2] *Ibid.* pp. 10–11.
[3] *Ibid.* pp. 18–19.
[4] Ashley, II, pp. 347–9.

with it; in any case they later helped to put the principles outlined into practice when the London hospitals came under the city's control. Meanwhile William Marshall, called upon to frame a poor law, produced a comprehensive plan advocating that the parish, supervised by justices of the peace, be adopted as the basic unit for administering relief. In the event the poor law of 1536 was only a perfunctory measure but this work was to be taken up later.[1]

Such were the proposals advanced in the early 1530's at a time when a reformation of the church and learning, of social institutions, seemed in sight. After the visitation of the monasteries had taken place Thomas Starkey addressed a letter to the king putting the case for a dissolution and use of the proceeds to better ends. The pious laymen who first established these houses, he wrote, would wish their gifts, now so misused, to be taken away. Indeed they might well cry with one voice:

> We thought to establish houses of virtue, learning and religion, the which now...we see turned to vice, blindness and superstition. We thought to establish certain companies to live together in pure and Christian charity, wherein we see now reigneth much hate, rancour and envy, much sloth, idleness and gluttony, much ignorance, blindness and hypocrisy, wherefore we cry, alter these foundations and turn them to better use; provide they may be as common schools to the education of youth in virtue and religion.

If there was disquiet about a possible dissolution, Starkey advised the king, this was because it was generally thought that 'the farm and occupation' of monastic property would be leased 'unto great lords and gentlemen...which have thereof no great need at all'. This, if it came about, would 'greatly diminish the profit of your act' whereas to assist younger sons 'living in service unprofitably and...those of lower state and degree...would greatly help to set forward Christian civility'.[2]

[1] Jordan, *Philanthropy*, p. 85.

[2] S. J. Herrtage (ed.), *Starkey's Life and Letters* (E.E.T.S. 1878), pp. lv, lviii.

PART II

THE REFORMATION IN ENGLAND, 1536–53

V

THE PROGRESS OF THE HENRICIAN REFORMATION

The writings of English humanists underline what historians of education have sometimes overlooked, that the early sixteenth century was an age of economic and social as well as political and religious change. There has been a tendency to present educational plans as the product of two great international movements in thought, whereas it was in meeting contemporary social needs that Englishmen drew in one way or another on Italian example or that of the German Reformation. The practical measures adopted must be judged in the same light. It is arbitrary, for instance, to make the Erasmian programme of classical studies into a yardstick and criticise anything that fell short of it. Contemporaries did not look at things in this way but took up and modified ideas in the service of immediate ends so that deviations from original programmes, rather than being regarded as a regrettable departure from principle, may be taken as an interesting pointer to current concerns. In this sense there was a much closer relation between theory and practice than is sometimes allowed.

It has often been held that in the early decades of the sixteenth century humanist learning was in its heyday, only to be abruptly cut off at the Reformation, but it would seem that so far as the educational system was concerned it had gained only a foothold and had yet to make its way. Attempts to suggest that there was an 'English Renaissance' at this time are associated with the idea that the European renaissance as a whole represented 'the gradual flowering of the seeds of Western culture sown in the Middle Ages', a growth fostered in the early Tudor age only by 'men of enduring faith'.[1]

It has been suggested here that the educational aims advanced by the early humanists were furthered by the reforming movement.

[1] From the preface to *The Thought and Culture of the English Renaissance. An Anthology of Tudor Prose 1481–1555*, ed. E. Nugent (Cambridge, 1956), which makes much of St Thomas More but virtually ignores protestant thinking and writing though it extends to cover the reign of Edward VI.

It is impossible to assign Colet and Erasmus to one era, 'the renaissance', and consign their immediate successors to the wholly different era of the Reformation. The problem is sometimes evaded by discounting Colet as an oddity and leaving aside the wider aspects of programmes advanced by Erasmus and Starkey to concentrate on one particular field in which humanist ideas were applied, the education of the gentleman. It then appears that the main line of development to be traced is from the writings of Erasmus, Elyot and Starkey to such leading figures of what is usually called the 'English Renaissance' as Sidney and Spenser.[1]

What has helped to make this kind of approach possible is the belief that the Reformation in England had a wholly negative effect on education, notably that legislation to abolish chantries had the indirect result of destroying or crippling innumerable grammar schools. The best to be said of such a period is, perhaps, that earlier educational ideas were not altogether obliterated but survived to inform developments in the Elizabethan age. It is now clear, however, that the author of *English Schools at the Reformation* is not a reliable guide. In analysing the chantry certificates he threw together indiscriminately, except in terms of designating each as an elementary or grammar school, every mention of teaching to be found; bellringers who taught the ABC and choristers' masters of collegiate churches, chantry priests teaching on their own account in return for fees and stipendiaries instructing parish children (as private schoolmasters and curates were later to do), all these qualified as regular schools in common with others specifically endowed as such. There are no good grounds for the finding that local grammar schools were swept away wholesale; when Leach himself investigated foundations in a particular county he found that 'most of them escaped', a conclusion much nearer the truth.[2]

[1] This is the general thesis advanced by Caspari. An influential paper published in 1950 by J. H. Hexter, concerned to examine why 'beginning some time in the reign of Henry VIII' the sons of men of birth swarmed into the 'citadels of clerkly training', did so without mention of the Reformation ('The Education of the Aristocracy in the Renaissance', reprinted in *Reappraisals in History*, 1961, pp. 45–70). In the same tradition is a study of the universities which takes the reign of Elizabeth as starting point, M. H. Curtis, *Oxford and Cambridge in Transition, 1558–1642* (Oxford, 1959).

[2] Though, in the circumstances, it was somewhat wrapped up: 'Like the collegiate churches, the chantries, and the monasteries, most...ancient schools were submerged in the great revolutionary deluge we call the Reformation; but unlike them, though many were swept away, most of them escaped, and many of them, refitted and repaired from time to time, have floated proudly ever since' (*Early Yorkshire Schools*, I, 1899, p. v).

But while, to arrive at his figures, Leach counted in the smallest of chantry schools—regardless of the size of the place or the remuneration of the priest which was sometimes as low as 13*s.* 4*d.*—he tended to brush aside almonry schools, though some, like that of Westminster Abbey, were of considerable standing and possessed a special schoolhouse. In general he ascribed to monasteries alone strictures applied by contemporaries to all the old religious corporations alike and invariably inferred that secular churches and their schools retained all the importance of a much earlier age—unless unnecessarily interfered with by such as Colet. As a result, though he sometimes linked Henry VIII with his son as a destroyer of schools, Leach was more inclined to stress the virtues of dissolving monasteries to augment the number of cathedral schools.[1] The last point has quite recently been taken up again, in the course of a more general controversy, and Henry duly lauded as the greatest of school founders.[2] This has served to fasten the obloquy of damaging education even more firmly on the reign of Edward VI, the time when, so far as doctrinal change was concerned, the English Reformation came into its own.

Here the Henrician and the Edwardian Reformation will be considered separately, since they constitute two distinct stages, and the closest attention will be given to the latter because developments during this period have been much misrepresented. But the main point to be borne in mind before considering Reformation legislation and its effect is that, however many schools were still technically connected with the old religious communities or with chantries, education had long ceased to be the prerogative of the church. A growing lay demand for schooling had been met in the fifteenth century, often directly at the expense of the church. The trend continued in the early sixteenth

[1] Thus, when concerned to emphasise the extent of the devastation at the Reformation, he wrote that of some 300 schools in being in 1535, most 'were swept away either under Henry or his son; or, if not swept away, plundered and damaged' (*ESR*, I, pp. 5–6). But elsewhere Henry VIII figures as a notable improver of old schools, 'on a scale which entitles him to the praise of being, in a sense, the greatest of school founders....The schools which Henry abolished in abolishing the monasteries were the small and insignificant almonry schools of a few charity boys, and these he more than replaced by the great schools which he established in the new cathedral foundations' (*Schools of Mediaeval England*, pp. 310–11).

[2] Caspari, pp. 132–4, referring to Douglas Bush, *The Renaissance and English Humanism* (Toronto, 1939), which sets out to challenge Chambers's thesis that humanist ideas suffered, after More's day, a 'frustration and arrest which blights the fair promise of the early sixteenth century' (Chambers, p. 181).

century when humanist innovations brought a new adaptation of education itself to lay needs. Reformation legislation, following on a long and gradual undermining of ecclesiastical jurisdiction, cleared the ground for much more widespread and rapid developments on these lines, not least so far as the universities were concerned. Whereas one new school planned according to humanist principles had replaced an ancient cathedral school there might now be many others; in place of monastic houses there might be more colleges, even humanist academies. Of this some contemporaries were very much aware, as they were also acutely aware how difficult it would be to ensure that resources were in fact turned to this end. It is here that—instead of lamenting that Tudor monarchs failed to establish the system of secondary education which was still wanting in the nineteenth century[1]—account should be taken of the more general trends of the time. These, though well known, may be briefly summarised.

The stage was set for the Reformation in England by a series of steps directed to a particular end—gaining recognition for the royal divorce—but these led directly on to policies designed to reduce the powers and wealth of the church. Such measures were bound to affect social life at many points; that they were superimposed on an already disrupted economy meant that changes were far-reaching. England had not shared in the expansion of production and commerce which took place on the continent from 1460 to 1540, rather in the face of new competition the cloth trade was prone to extreme fluctuation with consequent underemployment and distress. Economic dislocation was brought into sharp relief by the rise in prices which increased by 50 per cent in the first forty years of the century and more than doubled in the critical decades from 1540 to 1560.[2] The rising cost of living penalised anew landlords drawing a fixed income from rents—the nobility, religious corporations, the crown itself; it also bore hardly on those of the clergy who subsisted on stipends and further impoverished cottagers who owned no land the product of which could supplement meagre day wages. On the other hand high prices favoured those who produced for the market—the gentry and yeomanry, tenant

[1] 'If all, or even half, the endowments of masses for the dead had been devoted to schools...England would soon have had the best secondary education in the world, and the whole history of England and of the world might have been changed for the better' (G. M. Trevelyan, *English Social History*, 1944, p. 114).

[2] Elton, *England under the Tudors*, pp. 224 ff.; cf. Peter J. Bowden, *The Wool Trade in Tudor and Stuart England* (1962).

farmers, who were in a favourable position to supply towns with food, clothiers and tanners with raw materials.

All this provided a new stimulus to increase productivity and extend holdings; there was enclosure of open fields, the engrossing of small farms, and in the process rents and fines were raised, efforts made to transform copyholds into leaseholds, tenants evicted. When contemporaries complained that the extension of sheepruns left a trail of deserted villages they were commenting on the enclosures of the previous century, but later complaints bear witness to a more profound upheaval. It was only in some districts, particularly parts of the midlands, that the face of the countryside was considerably changed,[1] but the whole proceeding cut at the roots of a way of life based on land tenure and production by each household of the necessaries of life. The raising of rents affected men able to speak for themselves, who put their case in petitions and eventually more forcibly; the paupers by their very number forced on attention a new problem, that of the landless 'masterless' man with no fixed place in the social order.

At the other end of the scale noblemen sought more land to increase their revenues, so also did men making careers in public life where expenses were considerable and rewards often sporadic. Land was, of course, not only a direct source of wealth but also the source of patronage and power, indeed the very foundation of the social order. In particular, the economic upheaval of the early sixteenth century seriously reduced the revenues of the monarchy, at a time when other sources of income were becoming ever harder to tap but responsibilities were steadily increasing. This, in the broadest outline, was the position when the possessions of the monastic and religious orders were taken over to be administered by a new Court for the Augmentation of the Revenues of the King's Crown. The annual value of the lands acquired has been assessed at £136,000 by comparison with the £40,000 a year which constituted the former royal revenue from landed property; in addition well over £1 million accrued in the form of valuables. With ecclesiastical lands went also rights of patronage which were an important source of influence, including the right to present to those

[1] The trends are summarised in Joan Thirsk, *Tudor Enclosures* (Historical Association, 1959). In Leicestershire, where there was the greatest outcry, 60 villages and hamlets disappeared between 1450 and 1600. There remained 300 where life and methods of production continued much as before; there was little production for the market, mainly subsistence farming without much use of money until the closing decade of the century (W. G. Hoskins, *The Midland Peasant*, 1957, pp. 175–9).

church livings which had been appropriated to monasteries—some two-fifths of all benefices.[1] As the crown was pressed for funds for immediate use most of these possessions at which the laity had long looked askance—as also in due course the property of chantries and gilds—came into the market to be dispersed more at large. It has been calculated that up to two-thirds of the monastic lands had passed out of the hands of the crown by the close of Henry's reign, most of them in the years 1540–5; though these were sold, not given away as once suggested, it was for the most part below market value and purchasers profited at the expense of the crown from the subsequent steep rise in land values.

While it is not until the later years of the century that the social outcome of the dissolution can be assessed in this sense, opportunities and the demand for education were immediately affected in a number of ways. There was, of course, no more recruitment to monasteries, indeed recruitment to the church itself fell away for some twenty years. At the same time there was a new body of 'augmentations men' supervising monastic and chantry property to add to a growing body of lay administrators. From 1536 steps were taken towards re-organising the apparatus of government; departments of the royal household began to give place to something more like departments of state, the inner circle of councillors became a formal body, the privy council, while the king's principal secretary took on a new executive importance as secretary of state.[2] As a result leading officials, instead of being solely personal servants of the king, began to control a developing machinery of state and there were fresh calls for men with legal training. Young men could now look for promotion not only in the households of prominent statesmen but also through service in departments of government,[3] though here as elsewhere patronage continued to rule.

Changing economic circumstances, new openings in some fields and fewer in others, movements of population, all this necessarily affected educational institutions. There was also another major factor. At the close of the fifteenth century John Colet had been sole survivor of a family of twenty-two and though this may be a particular example

[1] Christopher Hill, *Economic Problems of the Church* (Oxford, 1956), pp. 3–4.

[2] Elton, *England under the Tudors*, pp. 180–4.

[3] 'A good job in any one of the new revenue courts was virtually a guarantee of a promising future' (W. C. Richardson, *History of the Court of Augmentations, 1536–54*, Baton Rouge, 1961, pp. 44–5).

there is evidence that the merchant class of London was barely replacing itself during the century.[1] When Sir Thomas Brudenell, son of a lawyer turned landowner, died in 1549 he was survived by ten of his eleven children; again it is a particular example, infant mortality remained high, but the trend is plain in evidence of population increase.[2]

In considering the availability of education and the stimulus to seek it at this time, it should also be recalled that the impact of printing began now to be felt in widening circles. From 1525, to take one example, there were up to twenty-five printers issuing law books alone; by 1550 a standard work such as Lyttelton's *Tenures*, first printed in 1475, had run through seventeen editions.[3] This had its effect on traditional forms of legal training; a knowledge of law could henceforth be attained without serving all the stages of a lengthy apprenticeship. At the universities, too, education could extend the more easily beyond the official course and standard academic exercises. Indeed with books more and more readily available there could be self-education at various social levels on a growing scale. As Milton later proclaimed books, far from being dead things, 'contain a potency of life in them to be as active as that soul was whose progeny they are'.[4] It was from the 1530's that Erasmus's works began to circulate in English at a time when those of reformers were being added and it became official policy to print and distribute the bible in the vernacular.[5]

These are some of the more general trends to be borne in mind when considering changes in educational supply and demand at the Reformation. The measures taken during the decade 1536 to 1546 which have a general bearing on education may first be outlined before considering the schools and universities in turn. The dissolution of the monasteries, following on earlier legislation to restrict ecclesiastical jurisdiction, was one aspect of a concerted policy to reduce the church's influence and wealth and add a permanent increment to the royal revenues. Various factors at home and abroad influenced the actual unfolding of this policy, and in the end partially frustrated it, but the general lines seem

[1] Thrupp, p. 204.

[2] Wake, p. 47. For a discussion of population figures and an estimate of a 40 per cent rise in the sixteenth century, Jordan, *Philanthropy*, pp. 26–9.

[3] Birks, pp. 102–3.

[4] *Milton's Prose* (World's Classics, 1925), pp. 279–80.

[5] Knowles, p. 153. The *Enchiridion* first published in English in 1533 was reprinted in 1534, 1540, 1541, twice in 1544, again in 1548 and 1550.

to have been clear; plans even extended to confiscation of episcopal lands so that bishops would be deprived of their semi-feudal status and become stipendiaries of the civil power.[1] A necessary accompaniment of such a policy was a purging and reshaping of religious doctrine, an implementation of humanist ideas which in the circumstances represented a considerable step in a protestant direction. Thus the Ten Articles required preaching and teaching in English and commanded the clergy to educate themselves and perform their duties; at the same time images and pilgrimages were forbidden, the practice of invoking saints deprecated and the doctine of purgatory—which underlay all chantry foundations—modified.

Thomas Cromwell, appointed vice-gerent in spirituals early in 1535 by a king who was now the church's ruler, directed policies for a further five years, drawing on the assistance both of humanist scholars and reformers, recalled from abroad in the critical days when Spanish intervention was expected. This crisis prompted determined action to preach the royal supremacy which extended to instructions to schoolmasters.[2] One of those who readily complied was Stephen Gardiner, bishop of Winchester, who sent to Cromwell some verses which he had delivered 'to be learned to the scholars of Winchester', adding 'To other petty teachers I gave commandment in general. This is done onward and more shall be, if ye think necessary.'[3] When the dissolution of the monasteries was shortly put in hand the principle advocated by Starkey—that the king might legitimately take over religious houses which were not fulfilling their proper functions—was applied.[4] The pretexts cited were also those Starkey had advanced; that is, the depravity of the monasteries, established by visitation and asserted in the statute of 1536 which dissolved lesser houses, and a vaguer promise that the proceeds would be turned to good account. The complex story of the various visitations has recently been outlined; so also the steps taken to set up the court of augmentations which was directed

[1] A. F. Pollard, *Political History of England, 1547–1603* (1910), p. 17; Knowles, p. 202.

[2] The imperial ambassador reported on 16 June that the king had commanded that the gospels be read in English in all churches to infect the people with Lutheranism and make them more obstinate in repelling a foreign invasion; schoolmasters also had orders to instruct their scholars to revile apostolic authority (*L & P*, VIII, p. 345).

[3] *The Letters of Stephen Gardiner*, ed. J. A. Muller (Cambridge, 1933), p. 66.

[4] The Lollards had advanced this argument, extending to cover the church the feudal doctrine that lands escheated if service defaulted (Knowles, p. 291). Wolsey's dissolutions, carried out mainly by Cromwell, provided a precedent for the argument that small houses could not adequately perform the necessary duties.

to preserve some lands incorporated, the only indication of any intention to make some refoundations.[1] But of this aspect no more is heard until 1539.

Meanwhile in August 1536 Cromwell issued injunctions to the clergy which made the newly formulated Ten Articles binding, thereby imposing cautious modifications of doctrine. Some of these injunctions closely reflect ideas expressed by Starkey in that they enjoin all parents, masters and governors to avoid the social evils of idleness by setting their children and servants 'even from their childhood, either to learning or to some other honest exercise, occupation or husbandry'. Parish priests should exhort, counsel and use every means to ensure that the young do not remain idle lest for lack of a trade or skill they 'fall to begging, stealing or some other unthriftiness'.[2] In addition it was laid down, to ensure 'that learned men may hereafter spring the more', that the higher clergy for every £100 received from a benefice should maintain a scholar at university or school. Here, too, there was a secular emphasis: such educated men could serve their patrons and the kingdom well both in preaching and generally in the execution of their offices, 'or may, when need shall be, otherwise profit the commonwealth with their counsel and wisdom'.[3]

Enforcement of the religious provisions of these injunctions and the first dissolutions brought a variety of grievances to a head, sparking off a storm of opposition in the north which culminated in the Pilgrimage of Grace; there were also uprisings in Lincolnshire. It is noteworthy that in an answer to the rebels' case Richard Morison pressed for educational provision on the lines of the 1536 injunctions as an essential ingredient of *A Remedy for Sedition*. This was no time to bewail social evils, as Starkey had recently done, and Morison affirmed that the commonalty had little of which to complain since they lived much better than their counterparts abroad. The real root of their rebellious activity was 'evil education', which was 'a great cause of these and other mischiefs that grow in a common wealth', and Morison reinforced

[1] Knowles, pp. 270–90; Elton, *Tudor Revolution*, p. 204; cf. Richardson, pp. 30 ff.

[2] The relevant article is lengthy. How often, it is said, do valiant men fail because their parents brought them up idly, which 'if they had been educated and brought up in some good literature, occupation or mystery, they should, being rulers of their own family, have profited, as well themselves as divers other persons, to the great commodity and ornament of the Commonwealth' (W. H. Frere and W. M. Kennedy, *Visitation Articles and Injunctions of the Period of the Reformation*, Alcuin Club, 1910, II, pp. 6–8).

[3] *Ibid.* pp. 10–11.

the demand for adequate education for different callings and upbringing in a common faith to secure unity of outlook.[1]

When the northern rising was put down abbots who had lent their support were executed and their houses dispersed. Thereafter other monasteries in the north gradually surrendered to the king, including the greater ones expressly excluded from the act of 1536. From 1538 a special form of surrender was submitted to the remainder by a new set of commissioners and by the close of 1540 not only nunneries, friaries and lesser foundations but all the greater houses had been dissolved. The whole operation had been completed in five years, under the pressure of events rather than according to plan, though procedures were well ordered and inventories of possessions and obligations carefully made.[2] During these years reformers such as Latimer—whose nomination as bishop of Worcester by the king was reported by the imperial ambassador as a great blow to the party of the old religion—preached freely against survivals of popery, and there could be new efforts to instruct the people at large. An injunction issued by Latimer in his diocese in 1537 ran: 'That ye and every one of you that be chantry priests, do instruct and teach the children of your parish such as will come to you at the least to read English, so that thereby they may the better learn how to believe, how to pray, and how to live to God's pleasure'.[3] Other injunctions followed those issued by Cromwell in requiring the clergy to study the bible, parents to teach children the ten commandments and the Lord's Prayer in English.

Already in 1535 William Marshall, also concerned at this time with poor relief, had prepared a reformed primer which included directions for reading the bible; this was a revised edition of the Lutheran primer by George Joye which had earlier figured among heretical books.[4] In 1537 there was a major step towards clarifying doctrine when a guide drawn up under Cranmer's supervision was published; this had the familiar humanist title *Institution of a Christian Man* but, failing to receive the royal sanction, became known as 'the Bishops' Book'. At the same time the English bible, prepared by Coverdale on the

[1] Zeeveld, pp. 218–19. *A Remedy for Sedition* was rushed through the press by the king's printer Berthelet in October–November 1536 (*ibid.* pp. 173–5).

[2] Knowles, pp. 350–9; Richardson, pp. 98–102.

[3] Frere, II, p. 17.

[4] E. Burton (ed.), *Three Primers put forth in the Reign of Henry VIII* (Oxford, 1834); Edwin Birchenough, 'The Primer in English', *The Library*, fourth series, XVII (1937), p. 182.

basis of Tyndale's translation, was published with Cromwell's active aid.[1]

The royal injunctions issued in September 1538 reiterating those of two years before, now also required that every parish church purchase an English bible and lay it in the choir. Before this last order became operative, in June, special injunctions were evidently sent to the bishops for circulation to every incumbent in their dioceses, framed to be read to the parishioners to inform them about the bible.[2] Injunctions issued by Cranmer this same year again insist on the clergy's duty to educate themselves. All must have the whole bible in Latin and English within a year, or at least the New Testament, and study a chapter daily working through from beginning to end. None of the clergy 'shall discourage any layman from the reading of the bible in Latin or English, but encourage them to it, admonishing them that they so read it, for reformation of their own life and knowledge of their duty'. No young people might be admitted to the sacrament unless they could say in English the paternoster, the creed and the ten commandments.[3]

The theme was enlarged upon by Cranmer in a preface to the second edition of the 'Great Bible', published in 1540, in which he set out the arguments in favour of making the scriptures available in the vernacular while warning both those who objected to this step and those who might abuse it by introducing contention over points of doctrine.[4] His argument for serious study of the bible by all derived, like that of Erasmus, mainly from St John Chrysostom but he went further than Erasmus had done.

[1] Writing to Cromwell in August 1537 Cranmer extended 'the most hearty thanks that any heart can think...for your diligence at this time in procuring the king's highness to set forth...God's word and his gospel by his grace's authority' (*Miscellaneous Writings and Letters*, Parker Society, 1846, p. 346). For the various editions, see J. F. Mozley, *Coverdale and his Bibles* (1953).

[2] R. B. Merriman, *Life and Letters of Thomas Cromwell* (Oxford, 1902), II, 144–7. The need for this is underlined by an anecdote, still current in Elizabeth's day, about an old mass priest reading for the first time from the English bible the miracle of the loaves and fishes: when 'he came to the verse that reckoneth the number of guests or eaters of the banquet, he paused a little and at last said, they were about five hundred; the clerk that was a little wiser, whispered into the priest's ear that it was five thousand, but the priest turned back and replied with indignation, "Hold your peace, sirra, we shall never make them believe they were five hundred"' (M. St Clair Byrne, *Elizabethan Life*, 1954 ed., pp. 121–2).

[3] Cranmer, p. 81.

[4] *Ibid.* pp. 120–1.

The Holy Ghost hath so ordered and attempered the scriptures [he wrote] that in them as well publicans, fishers, and shepherds may find their edification as great doctors their erudition; for those books were not made to vain-glory like as were the writings of Gentile philosophers and rhetoricians, to the intent the makers should be had in admiration for their high styles and obscure manner of writing, whereof nothing can be understand without a master or an expositor. But the apostles and prophets wrote their books so that their special intent and purpose might be understand and perceived of every reader, which was nothing but the edification or amendment of the life of them that readeth and heareth it.

Take the book into your hands, the archbishop went on, outlining a course of self-education: 'read the whole story, and that thou understandest keep it well in memory; that thou understandest not, read it again and again: if thou can neither so come by it, counsel with some other that is better learned...and I doubt not but God, seeing thy diligence and readiness (if no man else teach thee) will himself vouchsafe with his holy Spirit to illuminate thee'. The bible had in it to teach all men all things. 'Herein may princes learn how to govern their subjects; subjects obedience, love and dread to their princes: husbands, how they should behave them unto their wives; how to educate their children and servants....' Everyone, 'of what estate or condition soever they be, may in this book learn all things, what they ought to believe...as also concerning themselves and all other'.

The church had hitherto been guardian and expositor of the faith, armed with powers to discipline all who deviated from official doctrine. Now, at a time of change and upheaval, doctrine was in doubt and men invited to judge for themselves were all too likely to differ. While some confidently expected an advance towards the standpoint of the reformed churches,[1] for others events were moving, and far too swiftly, in a dangerous direction. It was the king who put the engines into reverse early in 1539 complaining of contention over points of doctrine which was bringing religion itself into disrepute. The defacing and removal of the chief shrines and relics the previous year, the destruction of monastic buildings by royal commissioners and local residents, the transference of others to lay purposes, all this, condoned in the highest quarters, produced undesirable reactions at large; coupled as it was with mockery

[1] For the spread of the doctrine of justification by faith in sermons and primers, pamphlets and plays, David Broughton Knox, *The Doctrine of Faith in the Reign of Henry VIII* (1963).

of former religious practices it encouraged popular iconoclasm of a kind which alarmed ecclesiastical and lay authorities alike. Henry, demanding uniformity in religion, now required it on traditional lines and parliament passed an 'act for abolishing diversity of opinions' which embodied in six articles a full catholic doctrine—including belief in transubstantiation, the practice of confession, the illegality of clerical marriage.[1]

With this, persecutions began afresh and some reformers again took refuge abroad. The translation of the bible issued at this time had been pruned of the Lutheran annotations of the earlier version but soon only men of substance were permitted to read it. A *Manual of Prayers or The Primer in English set out at Length*, published over the name of John Hilsey, bishop of Rochester, considerably modified the version of Marshall. It was at this point that steps were at last taken to turn some of the proceeds of the dissolution to the strengthening of the church and promotion of education. But before plans could be completed the failure of another royal marriage, coupled with a switch in foreign policy from seeking Lutheran alliances to alliance with France, enabled Cromwell's enemies to bring about his fall. The chief promoter of the Reformation and patron of reformers was attainted without a hearing, as both heretic and traitor, in June 1540. He was sincerely mourned by men of sense and feeling, including close friends such as Thomas Wyatt and Thomas Cranmer.[2] Both these, and many another, were endangered by Cromwell's attainder. His radical action in matters of state as well as religious policy had consolidated a powerful opposition and it was a conservative faction that now gained control, supported by Bishop Stephen Gardiner representing conservatism in the church. It was under such auspices that the educational refoundations of this reign were made.

Measures to uphold the mass and restrict reading of the bible could not, however, stem the tide of change. Since the renunciation of the papacy stood, the church in England was essentially a reformed church

[1] *Tudor Constitution*, pp. 389–92.

[2] 'The pillar perished is whereto I leant:
The strongest stay of mine unquiet mind;
The like of it no man again can find,
From East to West, still seeking though he went.'

Cranmer deplored the king's loss of a servant such 'in wisdom, diligence, faithfulness, and experience, as no prince in this realm ever had' (*Misc. Writings*, p. 401). For an assessment of Cromwell's role, A. G. Dickens, *Thomas Cromwell and the English Reformation* (1959).

and it was not now so much revolutionary as logical to envisage further steps ahead.[1] What had been a diffuse desire for an end to ecclesiastical abuses had begun to be channelled into a knowledgeable demand for doctrinal reform. More generally many were abandoning practices and beliefs condemned by humanists and reformers alike, as also implicitly by the injunctions of 1536.[2] Laymen welcomed the curbing of ecclesiastical powers and the opportunity of obtaining ecclesiastical lands whatever their doctrinal preferences; the chief officials of the court of augmentations were not reformers but traditionalists in religious outlook. Even those who had conspired to bring down the commoner Cromwell, and aspired to undo much of his work, were by no means disposed to see another cardinal on the English stage. Henry himself no longer put his trust in bishops as political advisers and evidently recognised that his son's reign must inaugurate new steps, for he handed the boy over to tutors of a strongly protestant bent and the guidance of Cranmer; with whom, though the archbishop had lost influence in government—and was indeed assailed as a heretic—his own relations in the last years remained close.

While Cromwell was in power, grants and sales of monastic lands were controlled in the interests of retaining a much needed supplement to the regular income of the crown. After 1540 monastic property was increasingly sold away to cover the crippling cost of war.[3] At the same time there were influential demands for the confiscation of more ecclesiastical lands while patrons increasingly dissolved chantries and resumed the revenues until the property of all colleges and chantries was taken into the hands of the crown late in 1545. This measure closely affected the schools and universities as the dissolution of the monasteries had also done.

[1] M. M. Knappen, *Tudor Puritanism* (Chicago, 1939), p. 65.

[2] 'From about 1540, or rather earlier, wills and other records from the diocese of York illustrate the rising tide of disbelief in Purgatory, masses for the dead, chantries, the cult of the Virgin and of the saints. Most of these wills naturally derive from the gentry and middle classes; their waning piety also appears in numerous resumptions or embezzlements of chantry endowments' (Dickens, *Lollards and Protestants*, p. 238).

[3] Sales reached a peak figure of over £165,000 in 1545 (Richardson, p. 235).

VI

SCHOOLS AT THE DISSOLUTION OF THE MONASTERIES

There has been no detailed survey of the number of schools connected in one way or another with monastic houses and what happened to them at the dissolution. But broadly speaking, as has been seen, they fell into two main classes; schools held in the almonries and belonging directly to the house, which sometimes had a specific endowment but usually not, and outside schools whose endowments were held in trust. Abbots also often had the right to present masters or exercise some kind of oversight over local schools. All such rights lapsed to the crown at the dissolution and lands held in trust for schools went with other property, though there was usually recompense in the form of a stipend paid by the court of augmentations. But there was no recognition for almonry schools nor were allowances made for the children boarded. The commissioners responsible for the *Valor* made a clear distinction between alms for the poor and provision for educating children which Gardiner outlined to Cromwell.

The title of *alms*, although in our judgment we understand it, and have made allocations thereafter, in the finding and nourishing of old and impotent and lame men; yet we have not so deemed it in the finding of young children to school; and yet it is so called also as the other is, *alms*. We used herein a distinction of *finding*. Which in poor and impotent men is without other shift necessary to live by. But in children no such necessity to find them to school.[1]

It was mainly the greater houses that boarded boy choristers and other clerks in the almonry, sometimes providing teaching in schools which were also open to others. But in one set of returns relating to forty-seven lesser houses there are listed, besides the three hundred inmates, ninety-seven children who were evidently boarded; these

[1] Strype, *Ecc. Mem.* I, i, p. 327. That the general principle adopted by the lawyers operated to exclude allowances for almonry schools was pointed out by A. Savine, *English Monasteries on the Eve of the Dissolution* (Oxford, 1909), and the point stands despite the criticisms of Leach, *Schools of Mediaeval England*, pp. 230–4.

would have gained an education of some kind, at least as good as that provided by small chantry schools. 'While the old myth of the Tudor monasteries as a great educational force has rightly been exploded', writes Dom David Knowles, 'the real if unspectacular service of the monasteries in providing free education must not be forgotten.' The education may not always have been free but the point is a material one now it is recognised that in the closing decades of their long history some of the monasteries housed humanist scholars and those of a reforming turn of mind.[1] It should also be recalled that monastic houses were agencies for recruiting the parish clergy. It seems probable that when almonry schools as such disappeared (whether or not there were substitutes), and churches appropriated to monasteries were scattered under lay patronage, a whole system of recruitment to the church was undermined. Inadequate though this may have been there was nothing to replace it. For some fifteen years after 1535 many diocesan bishops held next to no ordinations and there was 'an almost complete drying up of the stream of ordinands' after the disappearance of the foundations from which titles had so often been obtained.[2] When a system of recruiting the clergy was eventually built up it was on the foundation of a school and university education.

It was, however, gentlemen who first commented that useful places of education were disappearing as the act of 1536 was implemented. While many monastic houses took in a few gentlemen's sons as boarders one or two nunneries ran regular girls' schools on which the county commissioners concerned reported with sympathy and feeling. One, exceptionally, gained a brief reprieve—St Mary's, Winchester, where there were twenty-six daughters of 'lords, knights and gentlemen brought up in the same monastery', as the return noted, reciting the names. There were also some small boys in nunneries; even Cromwell sent his son with a tutor to the nunnery of Little Marlow for a time. But there seems to have been only one other regular school for girls, at Polesworth, Warwickshire; the commissioners referred to 'the gentlemen's children and students that there do live, to the number sometime of thirty and sometime forty and more, that there be right

[1] Knowles, p. 265; Dickens, pp. 138–53. For the number of boys monastic houses were bound to retain, see M. D. Knowles and R. N. Hadcock, *Mediaeval Religious Houses* (1953). Schoolmasters were sometimes boarded as well, and scholars; St Mary's Abbey, York, maintained thirty poor scholars studying at the cathedral school and fed twenty more daily (A. Raine, *History of St. Peter's School, York*, 1926, p. 65).

[2] Knowles, p. 409.

virtuously brought up'.[1] Less tangible were the additional losses detailed by the leader of the northern rebels, Robert Aske, when he wrote of the useful services abbeys performed for gentlemen: 'their young sons there succoured, and in nunneries their daughters brought up in virtue; and also their evidence and money left to uses of infants in abbey's hands, always sure there'. An example illustrating the latter point is the sum left in the hands of the prior of Durham in 1532 by a donor; it was to be used to find '3 scholars next of his kin to their learning', one at the inns of court for up to sixteen years, one at Oxford to study civil and canon law, one to be maintained for thirteen years until he found a benefice.[2]

On the other hand some monastic buildings were retained for or put to the use of a school. Robert Whitgift, who at the dissolution received a pension of £16 as prior of Wellow, Lincolnshire, continued to teach the sons of neighbouring gentlemen in part of the remaining buildings; these, with the lands, passed to Sir Thomas Heneage who originated in Grimsby and was well acquainted with the Whitgift family established there as merchants.[3] At Hitchin a school was set up in the dissolved Carmelite house by Ralph Radcliffe, a Cambridge M.A., who had acted as a private tutor to noblemen and obtained a grant of the premises; he kept one room for dramatic performances to give practice in good speaking and is said to have grown rich on the profits of a successful school which continued to his death in 1559.[4] There were to be many more such private enterprises in the coming decades. Moreover, the majority of monks found benefices at a time when recruitment to the church was falling away; perhaps one in twelve obtained chantries, as many as two in three office of some kind in the church. Of those who became chantry priests several of good education figure as keeping school a decade later.[5]

When it came to the turn of the greater houses there were at stake such schools as Reading and Evesham, which were considerably more

[1] Eileen Power, *Mediaeval English Nunneries* (Cambridge, 1922), pp. 266, 570, 579.

[2] Knowles, p. 328; Purvis, p. 21.

[3] Dawley, p. 25.

[4] The description derives from John Bale, an active proponent of the drama for didactic purposes, who lists some of the plays performed by this school which he visited in 1552 (*Athenae*, I, pp. 203–4).

[5] Knowles, pp. 410–11. In 1548 a schoolmaster at Penrhyn was drawing a pension of £10 out of the Bridgettine abbey of Syon; a chantry priest at Braintree had been an Augustinian canon of Waltham; another, an M.A. teaching in the Isle of Wight, had £6 out of the Cistercian abbey of Hailes; one teaching at Malmesbury had been an inmate of the Benedictine abbey there (*ESR*, II, pp. 42, 67, 91, 259).

important than the average chantry school. But as the dissolutions gained momentum in 1538 there were still no plans forthcoming for any refoundations. Towards the close of this year there were petitions for the reconstitution of particular houses. Robert Ferrar, a reformer recently placed by Cromwell as prior of an important Yorkshire house, urged that this be re-established as 'a college for the nourishment of youth in virtue and learning to the increase and advancement of the lively word of God, diligently, sincerely and truly to be preached to God's people and the king's in these parts'.[1] This petition met with no success, nor did Latimer's attempt to save Malvern Priory to the end that 'learning, preaching, study' might be maintained there together with 'praying and good housekeeping'.[2] Latimer petitioned Cromwell again the same year for lands from some of the dissolved friaries to be granted to the gild at Worcester, notably for support of its school. He had himself been subsidising the master 'because he is honest and bringeth up their youth after the best sort', but funds were also needed for the relief of the poor; if these were granted the people would see 'popishness changed into holiness, beggars unbeggared to avoid beggary'. This suit met with better success,[3] but soon Latimer was obliged to relinquish his bishopric with the enforcement of the Six Articles, while Cranmer lost much of his influence as reformers were thrust into the background.[4]

In May 1539 the French ambassador reported rumours that the recent parliament, having given a cold reply to the king's demand for subsidies for the defence of the realm, had turned to discussion of the reduction of certain abbeys of which they wished to make bishoprics, the foundation of schools for children and hospitals for the poor. An act passed at this session in fact vested all monastic possessions surrendered

[1] Dickens, p. 149.

[2] *Sermons and Remains* (Parker Society, 1845), pp. 410–11. Alexander Nowell was to request in 1563 that it should not be forgotten 'which before at the suppression of abbeys had been foreseen—that but two houses in every shire might have been maintained, the one for the reward of soldiers and the other for scholars'.

[3] So also did a request for assistance in getting a landed endowment for the Crypt School at Gloucester founded by a merchant (*ibid.* pp. 402–3, 418).

[4] Cranmer made an interesting intercession with Cromwell in 1538 on behalf of a good teacher, a Cambridge man, in charge of the gild school at Ludlow; he wished to renounce his priesthood for reasons of conscience but feared to lose office and begged that Cromwell write to the gild on his behalf—being a priest 'was no furtherance but rather an impediment to him in the applying of his scholars' and there was no rule that the schoolmaster be in orders (Cranmer, p. 380).

since the statute of 1536 in the crown, and another, with a preamble written by Henry himself, enumerated the good causes to which monastic revenues might be put and empowered the king to erect new bishoprics to any number he thought fit.[1] Whether or not parliament advanced any propositions, plans were now drawn up for transforming some of the greater abbeys into cathedral churches, reconstituting the cathedral priories, and establishing some new collegiate bodies—all these to have schools attached. Bishops Stephen Gardiner and Cuthbert Tunstall seem to have been mainly responsible for working out the details of whole establishments, down to the names of those who would fill the chief offices, while the number of scholars to be maintained by the proposed refoundations was also specified. One draft plan proposes sixty scholarships at St Albans, thirty at Shrewsbury, twenty at Dunstable and Waltham, and also the appointment of masters with stipends of £20 at Colchester, Bodmin, Launceston, St Germains, Fountains.[2] It is evident that bishops had held their hand during the earlier dissolutions expecting a considerable proportion of monastic wealth to pass to the secular church.

The cathedral corporations proposed were much smaller and more straightforward in organisation than those of the old secular cathedrals, but they were not sufficiently simple for Cranmer. In November 1539 the archbishop returned to Cromwell a plan for the reconstitution of Canterbury. This proposed a provost and twelve prebendaries, six preachers, five readers—in Greek, divinity in Hebrew, divinity and humanity in Latin, medicine, civil law—and the maintenance of ten students at either university as well as a grammar school. Of this Cranmer had specific criticisms. The 'sect of prebendaries', he wrote to his colleague and friend, is not 'a convenient state or degree to be maintained and established', for 'commonly a prebendary is neither a learner, nor teacher, but a good viander', yet he dominates the life of the community and leads younger members astray. 'I would wish', wrote Cranmer, who does not appear to have been consulted by his fellow bishops, 'that not only the name of a prebendary were exiled his grace's foundations but also the superfluous conditions of such persons', for though originally intended, like the monks, to maintain

[1] *L & P*, XIV (i), p. 454; Knowles, p. 358. This was a plan Wolsey had entertained, obtaining a papal bull in May 1529, permitting the erection of new sees (*ibid.* p. 164).

[2] There were various plans, one of the main ones endorsed as coming from the bishop of Winchester, *L & P*, XIV (ii), pp. 151–2 (see H. Cole, *Henry VIII's Scheme of Bishoprics*, 1838).

good learning they had offended as greatly as the latter so that it 'maketh no great matter if they perish both together'; to tell the truth, the archbishop added, forecasting the later puritan case, the prebendary 'is an estate which St Paul...could not find in the church of Christ'. It would be better for the Christian religion if, in place of twelve prebendaries each receiving £40, there were 'twenty divines with £10 apiece, like as it is appointed to be at Oxford and Cambridge; and forty students in the tongues, and sciences, and French to have ten marks apiece; for if such a number be not there resident, to what intent should so many readers be there?' There would, in practice, be none to listen to their lectures for the grammar master would be busy teaching in his school and the prebendaries busy eating; 'surely it were great pity', concludes Cranmer, 'that so many good lectures should be there read in vain'.[1]

The intention may have been to maintain readers as well as scholars at the universities themselves, a use of cathedral revenues in line with the requirement that the richest ecclesiastical benefices be in part turned to the cause of learning. In any case when the wealthy abbey of Westminster was refounded as a secular cathedral provision was made for five readers and twenty students of theology to be maintained at the universities out of its possessions; there were similar arrangements elsewhere on a lesser scale but they did not operate for long.[2] In the event the cathedrals of the new foundation came into being in a haphazard way after Cromwell's fall, and all the plans for additional refoundations fell by the wayside; none of the places mentioned earlier secured a school through the agency of the crown.

Cranmer evidently managed to supervise the statutes and orders relating to the grammar school at Canterbury Cathedral, though he failed to get his nominee—the reformer Edward Crome—as dean and it was saddled with prebendaries. Moreover, when it came to nominating scholars for the foundation he had to contend with fellow commissioners who had begun to see education as an essential buttress of the social order; not hitherto greatly interested in schooling for their sons, gentlemen were now disposed to think that future governors

[1] *Misc. Writings*, pp. 396–7.

[2] Canterbury began with a scheme to support six students of divinity at either university but it shortly petered out, as also a like scheme at Winchester. Though the abbeys refounded were some of the wealthiest of all, with a net income constituting 15 per cent of the total for monastic houses, by no means all this was made over (Knowles, pp. 389–92).

should properly be educated at the expense of the church to the exclusion of the lower orders.[1] Cranmer gave a humanist lecture to his colleagues: 'none of us here, being gentlemen born (as I think), but had our beginning that way from a low and base parentage: and through the benefit of learning and other civil knowledge, for the most part all gentles ascend to their estate'. It was not an argument they were disposed to accept and the traditional view of nobility was urged together with current obligations and the dangers of educating the poor above their station. But Cranmer insisted that 'utterly to exclude the ploughman's son and the poor man's son from the benefit of learning' is to challenge God's liberty 'to bestow his great gifts of grace'; rather, 'if the gentleman's son be apt to learning, let him be admitted; if not apt, let the poor man's child apt enter his room'. It may be supposed that this was a concession forced by circumstances rather than Cranmer's considered opinion; in any case when reformers gained the upper hand the emphasis was different.

It is noteworthy that the relevant statute makes no overt suggestion that a cathedral school should be concerned with providing entrants to the church. It lays down, 'that piety and good letters may in our church aforesaid for ever blossom, grow and flower and in their time bear fruit for the glory of God and the adornment of the commonwealth', there should always be in the school fifty boys 'poor and destitute of the help of their friends, to be maintained out of the possessions of the church, and of native genius as far as may be and apt to learn'. Boys should not be admitted under nine years of age nor after fifteen, except for choristers whose voices had broken, who should have preference.[2] The headmaster should be 'learned in Latin and Greek, of good character and pious life, endowed with the faculty of teaching'. The organisation and curriculum laid down also recall

[1] Part of a discussion on the subject was recorded many years later by the archbishop's secretary, Ralph Morice, who recalled that gentlemen among the commissioners (including the chancellor of the court of augmentations, the newly risen Richard Rich) claimed that only younger sons and gentlemen's heirs should be put to school; that it was proper 'for the ploughman's son to go to plough, and the artificer's children to apply the trade of his parent's vocation, and the gentlemen's children are meet to have the knowledge of government and rule of the commonwealth' (Cranmer, pp. 398–9). It was the actual election of scholars that was at issue; for the names of those nominated, C. E. Woodruff and H. J. Cape, *Schola Regia Cantuariensis* (1908), pp. 62–3.

[2] The cathedral, like others of the new foundation, was required to maintain ten choristers and to nominate to instruct them one of the twelve adult clerks on the foundation who served the choir (*ECD*, p. 435).

Colet and are in the direct humanist tradition. The school is to be divided into six classes and before admission to the first boys should learn 'as it were out of class' the Lord's Prayer, the apostles' creed, the ten commandments. In the first class they should study the rudiments of grammar in English and practise turning short phrases into Latin; in the second, Cato, Aesop, and some familiar colloquies; in the third, Terence, the *Eclogues* of Mantuan and the like, while translating sentences into Latin and writing them down carefully in their parchment books. Both masters are enjoined to work out a plan of teaching and to teach their pupils 'to speak openly, finely and distinctly'. In the fourth form familiar letters of learned men and stories from the poets should be studied; in the fifth 'the chastest poets and the best historians', in the top form, Erasmus's *De Copia*, Horace, Cicero and similar authors. There is no mention of Greek.[1]

While a number of 'king's schools' thus made their appearance these were rarely altogether new. Rather already functioning schools now became an integral part of the foundation of secular churches, for instance at Westminster and Canterbury, at Durham and Ely where former masters remained in office.[2] This was usual, monks also being transformed into prebendaries, abbots into bishops or deans, mainly to save on pensions; there was hardly logic in the step after all that had been said about the depravity and lack of learning of the monastic order.[3] There were less places for scholars on these foundations than had originally been planned; Canterbury alone had fifty, Westminster and Worcester forty, Chester and Ely twenty-four, Rochester and Peterborough twenty, Durham eighteen, Carlisle and Gloucester none.[4] At Worcester the king's school vied with the gild school Latimer had

[1] *ECD*, pp. 457–9, 465–9. The directives were probably carried out as the first headmaster was John Twyne, formerly of Oxford where he studied civil law and attended Vives's lectures at Corpus Christi; he was also a zealous antiquarian (Woodruff & Cape, pp. 60–1). Orders exactly following those of Canterbury were adopted for the school at Worcester Cathedral (*VCH Worcs*. IV, pp. 482–3).

[2] *VCH Durham*, I, p. 375; R. G. Ikin, *Notes on the History of Ely Cathedral Grammar School* (Cambridge, 1931), p. 16.

[3] Knowles, pp. 415–16. Abbots had, of course, often been recently appointed as men who would be ready to accept the dissolution. At Carlisle all the four prebendaries and eight canons were former inmates of the monastery; the first Elizabethan bishop was bitterly to complain that his cathedral was still staffed by 'old unlearned monks' put in at the Reformation (J. Strype, *Life of Edmund Grindal*, Oxford, 1821, p. 105).

[4] A. Monroe Stowe, *English Grammar Schools in the Reign of Queen Elizabeth* (New York, 1908), p. 191. No schools had been proposed at Oxford or at Winchester, already provided for.

been supporting though both remained in existence. But at Norwich no cathedral grammar school found place—the city took the matter in hand in the next reign aided by a proviso in Henry's will—while at Gloucester and Bristol cathedral schools failed to compete effectively with developing borough schools.

In effect, while official policy was directed to establishing schools connected with ecclesiastical foundations on traditional lines, lay founders—and almost exclusively London and provincial merchants at this period—were actively supporting and endowing as many again under the control of boroughs and city companies. The schools which forestalled the royal foundations at Gloucester and Bristol had been endowed in 1528 and 1531 by merchants[1] and endowments were similarly settled at Newcastle, Stamford and elsewhere. Foundations continued in the early 1540's as the cathedral schools were being settled. Nicholas Gibson of the Grocers' Company built a school in Stepney in which sixty boys were being educated freely when he died in 1540, leaving his wife to maintain the school which she subsequently made over to the Coopers' Company.[2] In 1541 Thomas Chipsey, a grocer, endowed the borough school at Northampton vesting the lands in the corporation. The same year Sir George Monnoux made his own company, the Drapers, responsible for the school he established at Walthamstow and in 1543 the Mercers' Company became responsible for West Lavington school founded by one of their leading members.[3] In London itself the Mercers' Company, having raised a loan from Sir Richard Gresham and others and borrowed from the school chest of St Paul's, purchased St Thomas Acon Hospital from the crown guaranteeing to maintain the school there; the Mercers' school opened in 1542 with places for twenty-five free scholars.[4] Meanwhile the common council of London obtained dissolved houses to turn into hospitals for the sick and aged.

Despite the official turn towards the catholic faith and the renewal of persecution the middle class were being enjoined to promote and patronise good schools by the more radical reformers. Thomas Becon, who had absorbed Latimer's sermons at Cambridge in the 1530's, was forced to tear up his published works at Paul's Cross in 1543 and abjure his opinions but these had already been broadcast. His educational

[1] *VCH Glos.* II, pp. 344 ff.

[2] Jordan, *Charities of London*, p. 211.

[3] T. C. Lees, *Short History of Northampton Grammar School* (1947), pp. 9–11; Jordan, p. 224.

[4] *Ibid.* p. 212.

ideas are fully set out in the comprehensive *New Catechism* in which he urged that it was the duty of rulers to set up schools 'where the youth of the Christian commonweal may be brought up in good letters and godly manners but specially in the knowledge of God's true religion' and to see that schoolmasters were adequately rewarded. He likewise reminded parents of their duty, to see that children were well grounded in religion by sending them to school from the age of seven under 'such a schoolmaster as feareth God, is learned, well-mannered, and is able with discretion to judge of the nature and capacity of the children, and so according to the same to teach, instruct...rule and govern them'.[1]

In other matters as well Becon faithfully followed humanist precepts, from his insistence that mothers nurse babies themselves to his adjurations that schoolmasters treat children with kindness and spare the rod. But he outlines a course of study which reflects the adaptation of the humanist curriculum in reformed schools abroad. Schoolmasters should first of all teach some 'godly and learned catechism'; then, when the principles of religion are understood, read each day a lesson from the New Testament. It should be made clear that the scriptures apply to daily living in order to 'kindle and stir up the minds of the scholars, both unto the love of virtue, and also unto the hate of vice', arming them against the errors of papists on the one hand and anabaptists on the other.[2] While upholding the kind of preliminary course earlier denounced by More, Becon also advocates that children be taught 'good letters', the 'poets, orators, historiographers, philosophers', this

> not that they should be mates with God's word, but rather handmaids unto it, and serve to set forth the honour and glory thereof. For unto this end ought all liberal sciences to be studied and learned, even that they might not depress but advance the true religion of God. For eloquence without godliness is as a ring in a swine's snout.

If eloquence is to be safely learned from the classics, Becon affirms as Erasmus and Vives had done before him, careful choice must be made of authors; and he refers to a dictum of 'our countryman, master Lily, sometime schoolmaster of Paul's in London' that children should

[1] *Catechism, etc.* pp. 306–7, 350. Though this was not published until 1559–60 it may reasonably be considered here since it was an extension of an earlier work and the influence is almost entirely Lutheran (D. S. Bailey, *Thomas Becon and the Reformation of the Church of England*, Edinburgh, 1952, pp. 136–7).

[2] *Ibid.* pp. 378–9.

only come into contact with what is good and honest. Of all authors Cicero is by the judgment of learned men the 'most worthy to be embraced'.[1] Children should also be taught their manners and, following Luther, Becon stresses the claims of girls, pours scorn on current methods of teaching them merely to dance, dress up and do fine needlework, and commends the founding of schools to bring them too up in godliness and virtue.[2] If all schoolmasters and parents did their duty in these respects

> we should have a blessed commonweal, replenished with all knowledge, godliness, wisdom, learning, innocency of life, civility of life, civility of manners; all barbarousness, rudeness, ignorancy, superstition, papistry, idolatry, utterly banished and driven out of the bounds of Christianity.[3]

Henry Brinkelow preached in much the same vein. Another of those inmates of monastic houses who early embraced reforming doctrine, he had taken up residence among the merchants of London and become freeman of the Mercers' Company. In the year the company established its school he was pillorying rich Londoners who left large sums for superstitious practices, while giving only coppers to the poor, and telling them to turn the profits of chantries to amending poverty. In a tract published in 1545 Brinkelow called for almshouses and free grammar schools in all urban centres, where the children of the poor might be educated freely, and for the use of episcopal lands as well as monastic property to promote these ends.[4]

Whether or not this lead was being followed there was considerable local initiative in salvaging schools left without status as official plans for refoundation lapsed. At Sherborne the town bought the abbey church for the parish from Sir John Hersey, who had received a grant of the whole property, and rented the schoolhouse in which the former master continued to teach.[5] At Abingdon, the former master continued to keep school with support from the town; this was one of a number of monastic boroughs which lacked status with the removal of abbots who had been their lords and was temporarily under the

1 *Ibid.* pp. 382–3, 386. Reformers consistently stressed Cicero at the expense of Terence and Plautus, earlier much favoured.

2 *Ibid.* p. 377.

3 *Ibid.* p. 384.

4 Jordan, *Philanthropy*, pp. 161–2.

5 W. B. Wildman, *A Short History of Sherborne* (Sherborne, 1902), p. 59. Where local inhabitants could claim parochial rights allowance was made for the return of church buildings or part of them.

governance of officials of the court of augmentations.[1] Local support may also have been forthcoming to maintain the school at St Albans, until it was later refounded by the agency of the former abbot. At Coventry, the reformer John Hales gained a grant of the friary and maintained a school in the choir of its former church.[2]

There were difficulties elsewhere if complaints to the chantry commissioners a decade later about schoolhouses or endowments lost at the dissolution were well grounded. These indicate that there were no settled schools at Bury, Tewkesbury, Bridgewater, where there had formerly been facilities in connection with monasteries; the people of Cirencester specified loss of an endowment held by Winchcombe Abbey so that the school ceased, 'to the great discommodity' of the town, until the inhabitants transferred a chantry endowment in 1545.[3] On the other hand stipends of £10 were awarded in respect of Winchcombe school itself, Farnworth school, whose endowment had been held by Launde Abbey, and Evesham. At Bruton the schoolhouse was also retained but the master shortly left treating the stipend as a personal annuity and the school ceased 'to the heavy loss', as it was later officially admitted, of town and county.[4] At Reading the humanist master of the school Leonard Cox was granted a personal annuity of £10 and use of the schoolhouse, but he seems at this time to have returned to his home country, Wales, to keep school at Caerleon.

Cox, like so many others now in Cromwell's service, was one of a number of scholars engaged during these years in the revision of Lily's grammar, and he sent the results of his efforts to Cromwell in April 1540.[5] It was probably mainly owing to Cromwell that an official Latin grammar was published, later in the year. Though this incorporated Lily's rhymed rules it had otherwise been so much expanded, drawing on Linacre but also in particular on Melanchthon, as to constitute a new work; two years later a simple introduction to

[1] Rowse, p. 493. [2] Jordan, *Charities of London*, p. 224.

[3] *ESR*, II, pp. 84–5.

[4] Carlisle, I, pp. 464, 653; II, pp. 414, 754. Schools whose endowments were held by lay feoffees, though an abbey had power to present the master, naturally retained these, e.g. Lewes, Sussex. On the other hand the endowment left to Faversham Abbey for instructing novices in grammar naturally went (*ibid.* I, pp. 573–4).

[5] This was 'Commentaries on Will. Lily's Construction of the Eight Parts of Speech' and Cromwell ordered Berthelet to print it (*L & P*, XV, pp. 299, 329). A similar tract had been printed by Berthelet in 1537 (C. G. Allen, p. 95). This may have been by Henry Prime who, according to a later account, also produced a commentary on Lily (*EGS*, p. 254).

it in English appeared which was likewise prescribed for universal use. What became, and remained for many years, the standard text-book was not, therefore, the early humanist version which constituted only a beginning; it was, rather, a product of the Reformation.[1]

Once more what had been envisaged by Wolsey was performed by Henry who proclaimed that the king's grammar was intended to make learning of the rudiments of Latin easier 'without the great hindrance, which heretofore hath been, through the diversity of grammars and teachings'. The royal proclamation prefacing the English introduction required all

> schoolmasters and teachers of grammar within this our realm and other our dominions, as ye intend to avoid our displeasure, and have our favour, to teach and learn your scholars this English introduction here ensuing, and the Latin grammar annexed to the same, and none other, which we have caused for your ease and your scholars' speedy preferment briefly and plainly to be compiled and set forth.[2]

It was less easy to prescribe teaching of the faith despite the issue of the King's Book in 1543 to replace that of the bishops; this was hardly a moment when the doctrine of the English church could be formulated in a few simple words. But the place of a catechism was to some extent filled by *The Primer in English most necessary for the education of children* based on Hilsey's full primer; it was issued with an injunction that 'every schoolmaster in bringing up of young beginners in learning, next after their ABC now by us also set forth do teach this primer or book of ordinary prayers unto them in English'.[3] Thus by the early 1540's a complete set of official text-books, on the same general lines as earlier ones, had been published and prescribed for general use—an ABC, a primer of prayers now in English, a Latin grammar with an English introduction.

By 1545 many of the larger collegiate churches had surrendered their charters to the crown in the hope of securing a refoundation and to

[1] The nature of the revision, which may have been supervised by Richard Cox, now tutor to Prince Edward, has been discussed by V. J. Flynn and by C. G. Allen. The Latin version became known as the *Brevissima institutio*, the title under which it was re-issued in 1549, the English version as *A Short Introduction of Grammar*; these were published separately until 1574 when an edition appeared in which the second prefaced the former and the whole was printed as one work; it is this that (however inaccurately) passed down the centuries as 'Lily's Grammar'.

[2] *EGS*, pp. 252–3.

[3] *Ibid.* pp. 34–5. The King's Primer was not issued until 1545 and was not specifically for schools.

guard against depredations; not only were individual patrons beginning to dissolve chantries and resume the revenues but there were growing demands at large for college lands. One collegiate church was refounded at the same time as the cathedrals, Brecon, and another created out of a monastic house with a school attached, Thornton, Lincolnshire.[1] Southwell Minster, one of the proto-cathedrals in the diocese of York, had its rights and property restored in 1543 without alteration of the foundation.[2] Other ancient collegiate churches did not, but it is clear from returns that the great majority did not maintain a schoolmaster on the foundation so that their passing constituted no loss to education. Some special endowments for schooling find mention but they were comparatively recent. At Wimborne Minster, a royal free chapel, a stipend was granted to the priest of the Lady Margaret Beaufort's chantry, established in 1510, to continue as schoolmaster, while four of the vicars choral were appointed as curates to the parish.[3] When, however, the collegiate bodies founded by two fifteenth-century archbishops went, the schools attached were continued only by the uncertain means of imposing an annuity on the former lands payable by the new possessors; at Higham Ferrars in 1542, Wye in 1545.[4]

Elsewhere, once more, local inhabitants intervened and at this stage two settlements were achieved. At Warwick the gild of Holy Trinity and St George bought back some of the lands of the collegiate church and the building itself for a parish church, securing a refoundation of the school in connection with this in 1545.[5] The same took place at Ottery St Mary where, of the former endowments amounting to a yearly value of £303, lands to the value of £45 were secured to endow afresh the parish church and school. Here, too, there was a royal refoundation, and the preamble to the letters patent of 1545 is typical of the Henrician attitude to the church and learning:

We, being led by the particular love and affection with which we greatly favour the young subjects of our kingdom, within our said county of Devon,

[1] Thornton Abbey had been bound to maintain 14 boys; there were 6 choristers on the collegiate foundation which must also maintain 24 bedesmen (*VCH Lincs.* II, p. 461). A collegiate body was also established at Burton-on-Trent but it shortly fell anew when the lands were granted to the king's secretary, Sir William Paget.

[2] W. A. James, *Grammar and Song Schools of Southwell* (Lincoln, 1927), p. 5.

[3] A. L. Clegg, *A History of Wimborne Minster and District* (Bournemouth, 1960), p. 34.

[4] *VCH Northants*, II, p. 221; Carlisle, I, p. 633.

[5] A. F. Leach, *History of Warwick School* (1906), pp. 100–6.

that for the future, they being instructed from their cradles in more polite learning, then before our times were accustomed, may become more learned when they shall arrive at a more advanced age, thus certainly thinking that the church of Christ, whose vice-gerent we are immediately on earth, will not be less adorned and graced by men learned in languages, than by prudent men for the good of the whole kingdom, create, erect, found, ordain, make, and establish a certain free grammar school in the parish.[1]

It was at the close of this year that, expressing its conviction that the king 'of his most godly and blessed disposition intendeth to have the premises used and exercised to more godly and virtuous purposes', parliament passed an act placing all collegiate bodies and chantries—including some recently resumed by patrons—in the king's hands, authorising the issue of special commissions to dissolve them on the pattern adopted for the greater monasteries.[2] Whether or not it had been Henry's intention to suppress all chantries—many, of course, had already gone with monastic churches which were themselves great chantry foundations—he was certainly being forestalled by his subjects. Nor was there any great readiness to make over this property to the crown.[3] But if the Commons would not vote subsidies then at least they must relinquish chantry property at a time when the king was hard pressed to find funds 'for the maintenance of these present wars against the realms of France and Scotland'.

It would have been difficult to justify the step otherwise, since the doctrine of purgatory had been reinstated, and there was no attempt to do so. But some sensed a change in the wind. The imperial ambassador reported on 9 January 1546 that, though the conclusions of the newly risen parliament were (as was usual) kept secret, he heard they had given the king all chantries and colleges for souls departed as also the plate, money, rents, of the gilds; it would be well to inquire into the religious aspect and what was in train.[4] Meanwhile injunctions were still being issued forbidding the ordinary man to read the bible and requiring the destruction of all Lutheran works. In the circumstances there was necessarily confusion.[5] This, far from abating, was aggravated

[1] Carlisle, I, pp. 322–4. [2] *ESR*, I, pp. 59–63.

[3] The bill barely scraped through, William Petre reporting that it 'escaped narrowly and was driven over to the last hour, and yet then passed only by divisions of the house' (Emmison, p. 58). [4] *L & P*, XXI (i), p. 18.

[5] Preaching at the Mercers' Chapel in Lent, 1546, the reformer Edward Crome argued that if chantry masses availed souls in purgatory then parliament had not done

as Henry countenanced the indiscriminate persecution of catholic and reformer alike.

In October 1546 Richard Cox, onetime master of Eton school now almoner of Prince Edward's household, wrote to his friend Paget, the king's secretary, impressing upon him the dangers. Referring to a recent proclamation requiring the burning of heretical books, issued in July, he says this has done much harm. In many places people had burned testaments and bibles taken out of churches and honest men's houses, even the king's books concerning religion and his primers 'which now be utterly despised and not used nor taught the youth....They teach the old Latins with the old ignorance and would that printers should print them again.' In short, some to be on the safe side made away with all, others in their anxiety cast away good and bad, while those who had no books to cast away rejoiced greatly that they might remain in ignorance and superstitious folly.

The commissioners charged to assess gild and chantry property had by now completed their returns and Cox had earlier taken occasion to urge what might be done with this, in particular the need to ensure that laymen did not perpetuate the evils of impropriation while parishes remained unserved. 'The disposition of colleges, chantries etc. is now in hand', he wrote, 'and ye know, I doubt not, the great lack in this realm of schools, preachers, houses and livings for impotent, orphans, widows, poor and miserable; and what lack there shall be, utterly intolerable, if there be not a sufficient number of ministers, priests established in parishes of great circuit and great number.' Let the priests have enough to live on honestly so that beggary did not drive them to the old idolatry. 'This I speak to you, not distrusting of the king's majesty's goodness in this behalf, but because there is such a number of importune wolves that be able to devour colleges, chantries, cathedral churches, universities...and a thousand times as much.' The crying need was to prevent further impropriations. 'Our posterity will wonder at us. The realm will come into foul ignorance and barbarousness when the reward of learning is gone.' Unless, Cox concluded in another letter on the same theme, the king stand strongly 'like a hardy and godly lion' against the wolves, 'hardly anything will be well

well in giving away monasteries, colleges and chantries which served principally for this purpose. But if parliament did well (as no man could deny) in bestowing these on the king, then clearly such private masses did nothing to relieve those in purgatory (Cranmer, pp. 397–8 n.).

bestowed'.[1] Three months later Henry's reign of thirty-seven years had come to a close and Cox's ten-year-old charge succeeded to the throne.

The case was put more roundly by Thomas Becon in *The Jewel of Joy* and so strong was the resentment against the 'wolves' that even the once despised monasteries now appeared in a rosy light. Since gentlemen had become sheepmasters and feeders of cattle, wrote Becon, the poor had neither victuals nor cloth at a reasonable price; for these forestallers of the market had got all things so into their own hands that poor men must either buy at their price 'or else miserably starve for hunger, and wretchedly die for cold: for they are touched with no pity towards the poor'. Indeed, the former preservers of the commonweal 'are now become the caterpillars of the commonweal'; they 'abhor the name of monks, friars, canons, nuns, etc. but their goods they greedily gripe. And yet, where the cloisters kept hospitality...nourished schools, brought up youth in good letters', they did none of these things—thus becoming, in effect, worse than monks or friars. 'The state of England was never so miserable as it is at present.'[2]

A Supplication of the Poor Commons complained both of economic pressures and the prohibition on reading the bible which together reduced all opportunities for education. Either lack of any work meant that children spent the flower of their youth in idleness or the withdrawal of copyholds and raising of rents so impoverished parents that such 'as heretofore were able and used to maintain their own children, and some of ours, to learning, and such other qualities as are necessary to be had in this your highness realm, are now of necessity compelled to set their own children to labour. And all this is little enough to pay the lord's rent and to take the house anew at the end of the year.'[3] Under such circumstances the ordinary man could look for little benefit even from schools offering maintenance by scholarships such as Cranmer had endeavoured to reserve to the needy. As time went on the complaint was to spread that gentlemen's sons obtained such scholarships by patronage while those who wished to study and enter the church could find no place; so that in this way, as in others, the gentry were increasing their privileges at the expense of the welfare and learning of the poor and the church.

[1] *L & P*, XXI (ii), pp. 124, 134, 147. The letters are dated 12, 18 and 29 October 1546, but it has recently been inferred that they belong to the next reign (Richardson, p. 172 n.).

[2] Becon, pp. 434–5.

[3] Strype, *Ecc. Mem.* I, i, pp. 615–16; *Four Supplications 1529–53* (E.E.T.S., 1871), p. 80.

By the close of Henry's reign there had been a wholesale transference of rights over schools to the crown, bringing to a climax a long process of lay encroachment on ecclesiastical powers over education. But no concerted programme for refounding schools had been put into operation and those which were officially established were connected with an ecclesiastical foundation in the traditional way. As a result there were no endowments earmarked for education; cathedral statutes merely specified that certain sums be paid to the masters and scholars on the foundation and these stipends tended to remain at the statutory figure.[1] At Canterbury, Cranmer once more set an example by outlining a humanist curriculum; similar orders were adopted at Worcester, where Latimer had been active, but not necessarily elsewhere at this time. Of the newly constituted cathedrals, eight were required to maintain a number of scholars as well as providing alms for the poor and other services. But there were no longer facilities in the almonries of monasteries for the maintenance and teaching of the poor, nor in the households of abbots for the reception of children of men of means; the question immediately arose as to which category would find a place on the new foundations.

Otherwise schools for which funds had been held in trust usually continued with a stipend from the court of augmentations but those directly maintained by monastic houses lapsed, unless local support was forthcoming. Local efforts secured the refoundation of two schools formerly connected with a collegiate church. During this period London merchants were active in endowing new grammar schools, a course advocated by reformers, though there is no evidence about what was taught. There remained grammar and chantry schools up and down the country—including the schools of the old, unreformed, secular cathedrals—instructed to use the official primer and grammars but with little effect in the prevailing confusion and uncertainty. If education was to be an effective means of unifying the religious outlook and consolidating the social order, further steps were clearly necessary.

[1] For light on the sad later history of cathedral schools, R. C. M. Arnold, *The Whiston Matter: The Rev. Robert Whiston versus the Dean and Chapter of Rochester* (1961).

VII

THE RE-ORIENTATION OF UNIVERSITY LEARNING

Meanwhile there had been considerable changes at Oxford and Cambridge, now subject to the crown. The universities had never been autonomous to the extent that has sometimes been suggested. Privileges always implied obligations and in the previous century Oxford had found that papal immunities could be of little account in times of stress as against the immediate demands of kings. In particular, the consolidation of the chancellor's authority, to reinforce university rights as against those of the town, had been the work of the crown. By the sixteenth century this office was held by leading ecclesiastical statesmen and served as a means of controlling the university from outside, just as colleges helped to exercise authority within. At and after the Reformation the chancellorship was increasingly used to this end while the colleges were looked to as units at the expense of the cumbrous and less easily manageable university body.

In 1530 Archbishop Warham, who had recently been engaged in ordering Cardinal College, brought heavy pressure to bear when Oxford proved recalcitrant in supporting the king's cause. Writing in March of that year to castigate the university for delay, he insisted that answer be made not by the whole body, since 'mighty matters' cannot 'shortly be determined' by a multitude, but by some thirty of 'the wisest and best learned'.[1] A fortnight later the archbishop was obliged to write again, noting that he was well aware of the impediment—'the multitude of regents and non-regents in art' who, not heeding their prince and their chancellor's many requests, 'do daily show more and more their folly, obstinacy and wilfulness, qualities

[1] It is interesting, in view of all that was said now and later about the lack of clarity of the English language by comparison with Latin, that Warham's letter ran: 'I would have written to you in Latin, as I have been accustomed in times past; howbeit because that nothing should be otherwise interpreted than I mean, therefore for this time I write to you in English for Latin words oftentimes may be otherwise interpreted than English words'. The correspondence is printed in N. Pocock, *Records of the Reformation* (Oxford, 1870), I, pp. 248–91.

far unmeet and inconvenient to be in those who should as members in that body...order or rule the same'. This view was upheld by the official emissaries, Bishop Longland and Edward Foxe, who reported in detail to the king the protracted negotiations necessary before a respectable enough majority in his favour could be secured; in the end, with the aid of the heads, they had examined and taken a vote in each college separately. The lessons were learned and applied in future dealings with the universities. Meantime, in thanking Oxford for its support, Henry let it be known that he was cognisant of the cause of delay and that better compliance would ensure better patronage.

Cambridge received a like intimation. The vice-chancellor, William Buckmaster, attending at court with that university's reply, happened to arrive on a day when Latimer was preaching there. Efforts had been made to silence the reformer at Cambridge, as the king well knew having intervened on his behalf, while the university's attitude towards papal prerogative remained questionable. Henry, therefore, seized the occasion to praise Latimer warmly and remark (as the unhappy vice-chancellor retailed to a friend)—'"This displeaseth greatly Mr Vice-chancellor yonder". "Yon same", said he unto the Duke of Norfolk, "is Mr Vicechancellor of Cambridge" and so pointed to me'.[1] After being pilloried before the court, cooling his heels in corridors and taking instructions from officials, the vice-chancellor was sent about his business of keeping the university in step. It was an experience often to be repeated in the coming years.

While vice-chancellors tended to become responsible to chancellors who were now leading lay statesmen the universities also received comprehensive directives by means of visitation. The first injunctions were issued at a critical moment in 1535 when the king, enraged by the elevation of Bishop Fisher to the cardinalate, was ready to countenance any step to denigrate papal pretensions; this was the time when widespread preaching to mobilise public opinion had been ordered because of the danger of Spanish intervention, which Fisher evidently did what he could to promote.[2] It was in the autumn, after both Fisher and More had been executed, that Cromwell's visitors descended on the universities, in the interval of a rapid tour of monastic houses, armed with directives for re-orienting studies and powers to enforce the required changes.

[1] J. Lamb, *Cambridge Documents* (1838), p. 23.

[2] Pollard, *Henry VIII*, p. 305.

Cromwell's injunctions required, in the first place, that all members of either university swear to the king's succession. They then laid down that each college should maintain two daily public lectures in Latin and Greek, that all lectures on scholastic theology be abrogated in favour of lectures 'upon the scriptures of the Old and New Testament according to the true sense thereof', and that all students be permitted to attend these lectures and, also, to read the scriptures privately. Further, since the whole realm had renounced papal rights and acknowledged the king as supreme head of the church, the universities must cease to teach canon law and confer degrees in it. All ceremonies and observances which 'hindered polite learning' should be abolished. Students should be instructed in the liberal arts—in logic and rhetoric, arithmetic, geometry and music; in philosophy the works of Aristotle should be supplemented with those of the early German humanist Agricola and Melanchthon, in place of the frivolous *questiones* and obscure glosses of Duns Scotus and other schoolmen. All statutes of the university and of colleges which were opposed to these injunctions were declared void. All heads and officers of colleges were required to swear due and faithful observance of the articles.[1]

In the recent past some of the newer colleges had been charged by founders to maintain public lectures on specified subjects, both as a means of supplementing the declining system of university teaching and of ensuring the introduction of new studies. Now all colleges at both universities and the universities themselves were enjoined to promote study of the humanities and the bible in this way. Cromwell's commissioners, all of whom were lawyers holding official positions, reported by letter the situation as they found it and what had been done.[2]

From Oxford Richard Layton wrote in September to say that Corpus Christi and Magdalen already kept good public lectures but he had inaugurated a Greek lecture at the latter. Stipends had also been assigned for two public lectures in Greek and Latin at both New College and All Souls and for Latin lectures at Merton and Queen's. The remaining colleges had insufficient revenues but had been told that

[1] Mullinger, I, p. 630.

[2] 'It is a mistake to regard them as a group of unusually odious and brutal persecutors and informers.' The commissioners were 'all men of intelligence who made for themselves careers of some distinction...either canonists, civilians or common lawyers,... used...for every kind of business, administrative, judicial and diplomatic' (Knowles, p. 270).

their members must attend lectures at the larger colleges which were open to all; every student had been enjoined to attend at least one lecture on pain of loss of commons. These measures, Layton concluded, added to the injunction that civil law be read in place of canon law, meant an end to the schoolmen; or, as he elaborated the point with a Rabelaisian touch, 'we have set Duns Scotus in Bocardo [the university gaol] and have utterly banished him Oxford for ever, with all his blind glosses, and is now made a common servant to every man, fast nailed up upon posts in all common houses of easement'. When the visitors returned to New College after declaring the injunctions, they found 'all the great quadrant court full of the leaves of Dunce, the wind blowing them in every corner'. Layton added: 'We find here all men...glad to accomplish all things.'[1]

Dr John Price, writing a month later from Cambridge, was less easily taken in by appearances and warned that, though they outwardly conformed willingly to the royal supremacy, some heads of colleges showed 'great pertinacity in their own blindness'. If, he advised, 'they were gradually removed, learning would flourish there, as the younger sort be of much towardness'. Among the 'old sort' he named the vice-chancellor and Dr Nicholas Metcalfe of St John's with three others.[2] The second Cambridge visitor, Dr Thomas Leigh, formerly of King's College, confirmed that some heads were still much addicted to 'sophistical learning', discontented with what had been done and attempting to gain some relaxation of the visitor's injunctions. He urged Cromwell to see that these were put into execution but also drew attention to the fact that the university had been adversely affected by the recent imposition of the tax of first-fruits on college fellowships which new entrants could not find, while the poorer colleges could not meet the tenths so that the number of fellows was decreasing in several. It would be well if, as chancellor, Cromwell could get the taxes remitted for the colleges had no superfluity and it was a pity to take anything from them.[3]

The visitorial injunctions left by Dr Leigh required that the university institute, at its own expense, a public lecture in either Greek or Hebrew.

[1] *L & P*, IX, pp. 117–18.

[2] *Ibid.* p. 223. 'He was a papist indeed', wrote Ascham of the master of his college, but though 'a man meanly learned himself' he was not 'meanly affectioned to setting forth learning in others'. He procured Ascham a fellowship in 1535 though the latter had received 'grievous rebuke and some punishment' for speaking against the pope (*English Works*, pp. 278–80).

[3] *Ibid.* p. 238.

Otherwise they were concerned mainly with the maintenance of order and the remedying of abuses. Scholars were required to observe rules, factions to compose differences (one measure taken being a reduction in the number of college fellowships reserved to natives of particular counties), and heads and fellows were directed that no money must be taken for the award of fellowships and reception of scholars.[1] The colleges here were also required to institute lectures in Greek and Latin.[2] There was evidently also a concern for standards since one college was ordered to send home scholars who were not properly grounded so that their guardians might put them to grammar school for three years until they were qualified to read arts.[3] Finally, the university was required to deliver up its charters, including all 'papistical muniments' and an inventory of property, to the king's chief minister or his deputy.[4]

On the advice about the newly imposed taxes Cromwell immediately acted, coupling with the concession the chief point in his visitors' injunctions. The colleges, in short, were exempted from paying tenths on condition that all at each university contribute to the support of public lecturers.[5] Another act passed in 1536, at a time when the Commons were much taken up with the question of plurality and non-residence, required all beneficed men over forty residing at university to leave forthwith and attend to their cures; those under forty who remained were directed to attend lectures regularly and take a full part in disputations instead of idling away their time—an indication that beneficed priests formed an appreciable section of the university body and contributed to maintaining academic exercises, as also did monastic residents. If this measure operated to remove some older residents, Cromwell's injunctions of the same year endeavoured to

[1] Mullinger, II, p. 9.

[2] The directive seems to have been carried out; e.g. Gonville Hall which already had a Latin lecture initiated one in Greek, though the stipend was only £3 (Venn, *Biographical History*, III, pp. 245–6).

[3] This information occurs in a letter written by a scholar at St Nicholas Hostel (*L & P*, VIII, p. 388).

[4] So also the colleges. The Pembroke accounts record £1. 2*s*. 4*d*. spent 'for our master's journey to London to deliver the Papistical Muniments' (Attwater, p. 33).

[5] The act exonerating fellows and colleges from first-fruits and tenths referred to the king's recognition that tenuous livings might cause scholars 'to withdraw and give their minds to such other things and fantasies as should neither be acceptable to God nor profitable to his public wealth'; it extended to Eton and Winchester, from this time treated as part of Cambridge and Oxford respectively, though they were required to maintain not lectures but masses (Leach, *Winchester*, pp. 245–6).

ensure a new supply of younger students, by laying on all holders of rich benefices the duty of supporting a student at university.[1]

In subsequent years some heads of colleges who lagged behind events were quietly removed; Metcalfe, for instance, was prevailed upon to retire from St John's in 1537. But opposition to the new measures continued beneath the surface, not least at Corpus Christi, Oxford, one of the centres of that conservative humanist trend which was later to find an outlet in a renovated catholicism. In 1538 Cranmer forwarded to Cromwell complaints received from some members of this college that the injunctions were not being implemented and that those 'which be counted of the new learning' were not 'admitted to any office nor yet to any council of the college business'.[2] Latimer, as active in relation to university matters as others, urged Cromwell to continue with the good work of cleansing colleges; send for the masters and statutes, he writes, and if the latter are not good change them, if the former are mere time-servers change them too.[3] It was from this time that nomination of masters by the crown became usual. One scheme submitted to Cromwell at this point—by John Parkins, a common lawyer and onetime student at Oxford—proposed that all fellows and scholars be appointed by the crown and that laymen be appointed as heads: the master of a college should be 'no priest but a politic wise man'.[4]

The universities had, therefore, received a considerable shaking up before the dissolution of friaries and monastic houses brought further change. At Oxford a dozen houses were swept away, almost as many as remained. The Dominicans and Carmelites had considerable communities, while Durham and Canterbury Colleges were larger than many of the thirteen secular colleges which now joined in the bidding for parcels of land and buildings. But there were also others in the field, including speculators. Gloucester College went first to the new bishop of Oxford, the Cistercian St Bernard's to the embryo 'king's' college which had succeeded Wolsey's foundation; one small house secured by the city became in turn Bridewell prison, almshouse, school while another eventually housed the county gaol.[5] All this removed foundations and a class of scholars which had been part of

1 Mullinger, II, pp. 12–14.
2 *Misc. Writings*, pp. 381–4.
3 *Sermons and Remains*, p. 393.
4 G. R. Elton, *Star Chamber Stories* (1958), pp. 23–6.
5 Mallet, II, pp. 71–7.

the university for centuries and must radically have changed the atmosphere of university life. Some pensioned monks found their way back as individuals but the withdrawal of monastic residents and students depleted numbers and this always meant a disruption of academic exercises. In 1539, in a letter to Cromwell, the university lamented that the number of students had been halved.[1]

Cambridge, with fewer monastic foundations and no special colleges for the religious, saw less dissolution. But, though the Augustinian friary was less important than in the days of Robert Barnes, there had been fifteen members of the Dominican priory under a prior who became chaplain to Cranmer and bishop of Rochester, and twenty-four inmates of the Greyfriars convent.[2] The secular colleges also saw the last of the monks who had resided as paying pensioners. Gonville Hall, a small community of eleven, had housed some sixteen pensioners, most of them supported by East Anglian monasteries; this evidently deteriorated, while Pembroke Hall sold one of its dependent hostels and was shortly letting another, presumably because of lack of demand for places.[3] The Carmelite friary, anticipating events, had already leased land to the neighbouring college of Queens' and in August 1538 this college petitioned Cromwell for the site and buildings of the friary; the point was stressed that the college always provided hospitality when royalty visited the university. Cromwell granted the request within a week and the college was soon at work beautifying the president's lodgings and improving other buildings with stone from the friary.[4]

Shortly after, the university addressed a letter to the king which suggests an infusion of new blood into its councils, for it welcomes the dissolution of monasteries which 'had been unprofitable, nay pernicious to Christian religion' and expresses the hope that the king will 'make excellent use of them by converting them into colleges and places of good literature; that, as before, lazy drones and swarms of impostors were sent out of them, so now by these means, men might be bred up in them to promote solid learning and preach the gospel'.[5] A more

[1] Mullinger, II, p. 49. The Oxford registers from 1505 to 1538 contain the names of 357 religious; many of these were students of theology who proceeded to degrees (Dickens, p. 139).

[2] Here complaints of a fall in numbers were directly linked to the dissolution (Mullinger, II, pp. 25–6).

[3] Venn, *Caius College*, pp. 42–3; Attwater, p. 33.

[4] Gray, *Queens' College*, pp. 61, 88.

[5] Strype, *Ecc. Mem.* I, i, pp. 484–5.

direct petition in September asked for one of the dissolved houses to be refounded as an eternal monument to the king's name and for the grant of the hall of the Greyfriars, where all university assemblies were held, to the university.[1] But for the time no recompense was forthcoming.

In the eyes of the historian of Cambridge University the scattering to the winds of the schoolmen clearly marks the end of an epoch. This was hardly the case, in so far as the scholastic outlook persisted for a century or more, but younger fellows of some Cambridge colleges did now find time to turn attention to the classics and the scriptures. This was the golden age of St John's which had accumulated some notable young men—John Cheke, Roger Ascham, William Bill, James Pilkington, Thomas Lever. Cheke took the lead in an endeavour to turn the college into an all-round centre of learning in which each fellow followed a particular bent. He himself insisted on study of the scriptures and of Greek, holding that, if virtue was to be attained as the true end of learning, the chief authors to be studied were, besides Cicero, Plato, Aristotle, Xenophon, Isocrates and Demosthenes. Some of these he read in his own rooms with his colleagues, together with Homer, Sophocles, Euripides, Herodotus, Thucydides, as Roger Ascham recorded in 1545.[2]

No doubt there was nothing equivalent to the work of leading scholars abroad among these young men, but nor was Ascham merely eulogising a friend when he recalled in later years the work of this generation at St John's under Cheke's guidance. His detailed account of the use and development of humanist imitation shows that there was serious communal scholarship of a kind that was to spread to other fields, while there was also a lively interest in the bearing of studies on writing in the vernacular, on the development of the English language. Some thirty years on Ascham could still plainly recall a tutorial with Cheke who declared that Sallust was not the best author for a young scholar to imitate.

> And what is the cause thereof, Sir, quoth I. Verilie, said he, because in Sallust writing is more art than nature, and more labour than art....And therefore he doth not express the matter lively and naturally with common speech as

[1] Emphasis is again laid on the depletion of numbers, with the assertion that there were hardly any students in residence except in colleges (Mullinger, II, p. 27). Six years later the number in colleges was given as 676.

[2] *English Works*, p. 45.

ye see Xeonophon doth in Greek, but it is carried and driven forth artificially, after too learned a sort, as Thucydides doth in his orations. And how cometh it to pass, said I, that Caesar and Cicero's talk is so natural and plain and Sallust writing so artificial and dull, when all they three lived in one time? I will freely tell you my fancy herein, said he,

and Ascham records the explanation at length.[1]

With Cheke in this matter he couples John Redman, a student at Oxford's humanist college and Paris University before becoming fellow of St John's in 1530, and Thomas Watson, admitted fellow in 1533, who though an unregenerate papist was an excellent Latinist.[2] Ascham names also two young men from other colleges, Walter Haddon, son of a Buckinghamshire gentleman, educated under Richard Cox at Eton, who entered King's in 1533 and studied civil law; and Thomas Smith, son of an Essex gentleman, fellow of Queens' from 1530 and noted for his knowledge of Greek. Both Cheke and Smith were brought to the royal notice and named king's scholars through the agency of the king's physician, William Butts, a Cambridge man himself, friend of Latimer and Cranmer and much in Henry's confidence; another so placed who also helped to advance young scholars was Sir Anthony Denny, himself a former member of St John's.[3]

At Queens' Dr William May, civil lawyer and associate of Cranmer, was elected president in 1537; here a pupil of Smith—a future bishop —was John Ponet, made fellow in 1532, who achieved a reputation not only as a Greek scholar but for knowledge of modern languages and mathematics. Pembroke Hall, the college of George Stafford who had earlier pioneered the new learning, had ever since been known as 'studious, well learned and a great setter forth of Christ's gospel and of God's true word'; so at least it was claimed by Nicholas Ridley, fellow since 1524 and elected master in 1540. Edmund Grindal was a fellow highly thought of here, and Ridley brought into a fellowship John Bradford who had been at the Inner Temple but was converted there to the cause of reform and study of divinity by a fellow student; the latter, Thomas Sampson, in turn came to hold a fellowship at

[1] *English Works*, pp. 297–8.

[2] When Watson 'wrote his excellent tragedy of Absalom', he, Cheke and Ascham 'for that part of true imitation, had many pleasant talks together, in comparing the precepts of Aristotle and Horace *De Arte Poetica*, with the examples of Euripides, Sophocles and Seneca'. They also brought contemporary English poets into the discussion (*ibid.* pp. 284–5, 289).

[3] *Athenae*, I, pp. 87, 99, where other biographical details are also to be found.

Pembroke. One of Ridley's pupils who left the college in 1540 to preach about the country was William Turner who later achieved a reputation as botanist as well as reformer. He recorded that his tutor instructed him in Greek but that, though learned and pious, he was 'without hypocrisy or monkish austerity; for every often he would shoot at the bow and play tennis with me'.[1] Use of the terms teacher and pupil at this period illustrates the re-orientation taking place in those colleges which were setting new standards in learning, though the pupils were often younger fellows.

There were also, however, sons of gentlemen in residence in these colleges who were later to make their mark, in public life rather than the church. William Cecil, only son of a Lincolnshire gentleman holding a minor post at court, left Stamford school in 1535 for St John's where he studied under Cheke and himself read the college Greek lecture at the age of nineteen; but he took no degree, though he remained at Cambridge for six years and married his tutor's sister there before going to study common law at Gray's Inn. Another who profited from Cheke's learning was William Pickering, a close friend of Cecil who also gained office and served as a diplomat but retained the reputation of being a Greek scholar.[2] Walter Mildmay, fourth and youngest son of an Essex gentleman who was auditor of the court of augmentations, was at Christ's College at the same period from which he too went on to Gray's Inn without taking a degree. A decade before this Nicholas Bacon, second son of a Suffolk gentleman, had been at Corpus Christi, taking a B.A. in 1527 before entering Gray's Inn to qualify in law. A decade later Francis Walsingham, third and youngest son of a Kentish squire, registered as fellow commoner at King's.

These young men evidently took their studies seriously enough; though, like many another before them, they did not often have a degree in view they did intend to study law later to some effect. By no means all stayed so long at the university as Cecil, though there were more of them about; or, at any rate, since the departure of the religious they took a more prominent place in the depleted university. They were now more frequently to be found in the colleges, which

[1] Attwater, pp. 35–6, 40.

[2] *Athenae*, I, pp. 325–6. Cecil always refused to be counted a scholar. 'I was once but a simple, small, unlearned and low member' of St John's, as he said, disclaiming ability to decide issues between scholars when chancellor of the university (Porter, p. 113).

had been denuded of monks and beneficed clergy, some tabling with the fellows (as fellow commoners), others tabling with the younger scholars (as commoners, or pensioners). But there was no call for them to attend university exercises, particularly now that lectures were given within colleges, so that though some colleges were lively enough the university as such was hardly flourishing.

Indeed Cambridge could barely find the stipends for the public lecturers it had been bound to support. It was, therefore, more than welcome when the king took it upon himself to endow professorships in Greek and Hebrew, as also three others in civil law, divinity and medicine in 1540.[1] These were financed in the first place out of the revenues of Westminster Cathedral while a number of king's scholars, supported from this and like sources, also made their appearance for a time. The regius professorship of Greek at Cambridge was awarded to John Cheke who now proceeded to lecture in the university at large on the authors studied in St John's.[2] The first professor of medicine was Cheke's brother-in-law, John Blythe of King's, who had studied at Ferrara. Thomas Smith of Queens', appointed professor of civil law, forthwith left for Padua to perfect his knowledge and acquire a doctorate in order to contribute adequately to development of this study. On his return his first oration dealt with new advances in the subject, dwelling particularly—in a way reminiscent of Croke's earlier advocacy of Greek—on its importance to the service of the state and as a passport to office.[3]

It was evidently intended to provide for those of the king's scholars studying law by amalgamating two colleges at Cambridge and making similar dispositions at Oxford. It was no doubt in this connection that Henry sought advice about initiating a new form of training in civil law, a knowledge of which was particularly important for diplomats

[1] No deed of foundation is extant for the regius professorships and the date derives from the letters patent to the professor of Hebrew at Cambridge; this was Thomas Wakefield, brother of Robert Wakefield also of Cambridge and noted as an orientalist (John Willis Clark, *Endowments of the University of Cambridge*, Cambridge, 1904, p. 153).

[2] Mullinger, II, pp. 52–3.

[3] It remained essential to go abroad for higher learning, particularly so far as civil law and medicine were concerned to Padua. The previous year John Caius, fellow of Gonville Hall and a student of Greek and Hebrew, had left to study medicine there; after taking an M.D. and travelling to consult European scholars, he returned in 1547 to put this subject too on a new footing (Venn, *Biographical History*, III, pp. 32–3; Walter Langdon Brown, *Some Chapters in Cambridge Medical History*, Cambridge, 1946, pp. 3–6, 13–14).

and those concerned with matters of foreign trade. Nicholas Bacon, who was attached to the court of augmentations, was charged to provide a detailed account of the course of study and exercises at the inns of court and advance plans for a new house of students, designed to further knowledge of 'the pure French and Latin tongues' as well as of the law so that the king might be better served by his own students of the law both at home and abroad.

Bacon's plan envisaged a foundation whose members would all be elected by the crown, to a number decided by the king, while additional entrants should be admitted as the head of the institution thought fit. The course of study proposed, modelled on that of the inns of court, included pleadings in both Latin and French, orators doing what they could 'to banish the corruption of both tongues' as Elyot had earlier argued was so necessary. Lectures were to be read in Greek and Latin on the first three days of the week, in French on Friday and Saturday. In order that a knowledge of affairs might be gained, two students should always be deputed to attend on ambassadors sent on missions abroad. It was proposed that the study of history be particularly encouraged since it perpetuates good deeds and secures a full awareness of dangerous ones; two of the best students should be deputed to write a history and chronicle of England 'without respect of any person', and selected students permitted to attend and record treason trials.[1]

This project came to nothing, possibly in part because the scholarships themselves soon lapsed, but plans to amalgamate colleges for this purpose were later revived. Meanwhile Cambridge acquired fresh facilities when Buckingham College—a semi-monastic community which had escaped dissolution but was impoverished by the withdrawal of monastic inmates—was refounded by a lawyer and statesman once resident there. Thomas Audley, lord keeper, was one of those lowborn counsellors whom the rebels of 1536 had wished to see cast down—together with Cromwell and Rich—but he had continued to flourish in office and was one who received extensive grants of monastic property. None the less he was concerned at the wholesale disappearance of houses which contributed to relieving the poor, and provided hospitality where there were no other facilities, and in 1538 was urging Cromwell to salvage two priories in Essex and reconstitute them as

[1] The relevant documents are printed in Edward Waterhous, *Fortescutus Illustratus* (1663), pp. 539 ff.

collegiate churches to this end.[1] Four years later he made provision for Magdalene College, to maintain a master and eight fellows, though after his death his executors failed to produce funds to support more than four fellows and the college was not regularly constituted until the reign of Mary.[2]

With the turn to conservatism, intervention in university affairs was of a very different nature from that of Cromwell's day. In 1542 Bishop Gardiner, now chancellor, was adjuring Cheke not to teach the new pronunciation of Greek, which Erasmus had been the first to advocate. If this was generally introduced, the bishop argued, the authority of older scholars would be weakened to the subversion of good order; a warning followed up by a ban which both Cheke and Smith tried in vain to have lifted.[3] Nor did the study of civil law make much progress; the only graduate to proceed to the degree of doctor was Walter Haddon, who became the next professor.[4]

Meanwhile Smith, though he continued to lecture at times, became clerk to the council of Queen Katherine Parr. By 1544 Cheke had left the university for Prince Edward's household, where a school for the prince's henchmen was being established, while a promising younger fellow of St John's, William Grindal, became tutor to the Princess Elizabeth. Roger Ascham deplored the university's loss though it was the kingdom's gain. His own contribution to knowledge at this time was a book in English on the practice of archery, which won warm approval from the king to whom it was dedicated, and on Grindal's early death he in turn became tutor to a princess. So, as Oxford had earlier lost Grocyn and Linacre, Cambridge was now denuded of its most advanced scholars by the court.

Cheke's new status, however, enabled him to supervise a revision of the statutes of St John's. That he did so at the request of the reforming party among the fellows indicates that there were considerable dissensions even within this college. The original statutes had made large provision for northerners on the foundation and a strong contingent of fellows deriving from the north was opposing new developments. Following the lines laid down by the Cromwellian visitors the new

[1] *State Papers. Henry VIII* (1830), I, p. 587. Audley was particularly concerned about Colchester, where there were many poor; he was instrumental in establishing the school there in 1539.

[2] Mullinger, II, pp. 64–7; E. K. Purnell, *Magdalene College* (1904), pp. 30 ff.

[3] Mullinger, II, pp. 59–62; Muller, pp. 100–23.

[4] Mullinger, II, p. 132.

statutes freed fellowships from particular counties. At the same time the master's stipend and powers were increased to allow of greater control and twelve of the thirty-two fellows were designated as seniors with special powers in the college government. It is significant that new rules were also drafted to control the entry of pensioners who had not been a force to be reckoned with in 1516. The 1545 statutes laid down that none be admitted pensioner unless he had a knowledge of Latin sufficient to enable him to profit from the regular course of instruction and ensure that he did not impede the studies of others. Each fellow was to take only one pensioner, the master was permitted four, making a total of thirty-six.[1]

In 1545 Bishop Gardiner was again bringing Cambridge affairs before the privy council and writing to the university in peremptory fashion about a play performed in Lent at Christ's College. This, by a graduate of Wittenberg, was dedicated to Cranmer and depicted the development of the church up to the Reformation; in the chancellor's view it reflected adversely on certain ceremonies, though again he was mainly concerned about upholding authority.[2] But the matter was handled without detriment to the university by the new vice-chancellor, Matthew Parker, master of Corpus Christi College since the previous year. Parker has been recommended to the college by the king because of his 'singular grace and industry in bringing up youth in virtue and learning'; when elected vice-chancellor he received 79 out of 98 votes, Ridley, another candidate, only gaining five.[3]

More serious concerns soon occupied all attention, as the universities became aware that college lands were in jeopardy under the chantries act. In February 1546 the vice-chancellor and university of Cambridge wrote to the king expressing their obligation and readiness to put their possessions at his service. But the same day an anxious letter was dispatched to the king's secretary, Paget (formerly of Trinity Hall), reminding him of the importance of universities to the state and asking

[1] Mullinger, II, p. 39; Baker, I, pp. 118–20.

[2] 'In this play they hiss the Roman pontiff, who fully deserves it, and accordingly by the same token, indicate their derisive rejection of all men of learning', ran his letter to the vice-chancellor, regent masters and non-regent masters, 'with you looking on and not raising your voice' (Muller, p. 139).

[3] One of that early group of Cambridge reformers which included Bilney and Latimer, Parker had afterwards become dean of the collegiate church of Stoke-by-Clare, under the queen's patronage, and revived the school there (V. J. K. Brook, *Life of Archbishop Parker*, Oxford, 1962, pp. 9, 18, 22, 28–31).

his protection for the cause of learning.[1] A letter and documents were also sent to Thomas Smith to lay before the queen, as much perhaps because Cambridge was accustomed to petition queens as patrons as because of Katherine Parr's known favouring of reform.

Whatever might be the king's intentions—and the universities had some cause to express obligation for past benefits and expect more—there were many indications that pressure was being brought to bear, pressure which a ruler with unpaid servants and a failing exchequer must find it hard to resist. There was no question of confiscating lands; rather, as Parker noted later, 'certain officers in the court and others... in authority under the king' were 'importunately suing to him to have the lands and possessions of both universities surveyed, they meaning afterwards to enjoy the best of their lands and possessions by exchange of impropriated benefices and such other improved lands'.[2] This, of course, was merely to follow the example of a monarch who had dealt cavalierly enough with his bishops' lands on precisely these lines and, moreover, had recently taken over college and chantry lands which patrons had looked to resume.

Petitions were of sufficient effect to secure that internal commissions were appointed to assess university possessions which saved the heavy expense attendant on a normal visitation and might be counted upon for sympathetic reports. The Cambridge commission suitably consisted of Parker, William May of Queens', and John Redman who had become master of King's Hall in 1542, assisted by eleven clerks borrowed from the court of augmentations. An encouraging reply was also received from the queen. According to their desires she had 'attempted the king's majesty' and found that, notwithstanding the rights granted by parliament, 'his highness being such a patron to good learning, doth tender you so much that he will rather advance learning and erect new occasion thereof, than to confound those your ancient and godly institutions'.[3]

This forecast of a new foundation came at a time when the commission was already collecting evidence. Accounts for all the colleges were drawn up which showed that all but two had an expenditure exceeding income, the gap being made up by fines for leases, moneys

[1] 'That it should not be handed over to such as know better what money can do than where learning deserves to be, but to such as can rightly esteem both' (*L & P*, XXI (i), p. 99).

[2] Lamb, p. 59.

[3] *Ibid.* p. 71; *L & P*, XXI (i), p. 131.

received for sales of wood and other incidental receipts. Whether or not these were exact, the endowments shown were small enough by comparison with those of the greater abbeys most recently dissolved. At Cambridge, besides King's with over £1000, and St John's with over £500, only Christ's, King's Hall and Queens' had an income over £200; at Oxford also only five colleges had more than this while Balliol, Exeter and University had under £100.[1]

When the report on Cambridge was submitted at Hampton Court the king studied it carefully. Then, according to Parker who was present as chief commissioner, he looked up and 'in a certain admiration said to certain of his lords which stood by, that he thought he had not in his realm so many persons so honestly maintained in living by so little land and rent'. On hearing how difficult it was for colleges to live within their income, he observed, well aware of the kind of claims in view, 'that pity it were these lands should be altered to make them worse'; at which, Parker records, some were grieved, for the wolves were evidently to be disappointed. The commissioners, on the other hand, were encouraged to elaborate the university's case and beg the king 'to be so gracious lord, that he would favour us in the continuance of our possessions such as they were, and that no man by his grace's letters would require to permute with us to give us worse'. The king 'made answer and smiled, that he could not but write for his servants and others doing...service for the realm in wars and other affairs, but he said he would put us to our choice whether we should gratify them or no, and bade us hold our own for after his writing he would force us no further'. With this promise, though it might have proved hard to keep—and indeed amounted to little more than throwing the colleges to the wolves—the commissioners felt 'well armed and so departed'.[2]

Oxford had earlier been relieved to learn that the chief visitor was to be Richard Cox. But there was no welcome for one of the directives

[1] The number maintained in fourteen Cambridge colleges was given as 676, in twelve Oxford colleges as 569, the unincorporated halls being omitted. At Cambridge three fellows were wanting at Peterhouse owing to the cost of repairs the previous year, two at Pembroke for lack of revenues, three at Trinity Hall because of the absence of the master (Bishop Gardiner on a diplomatic mission) and expenditure on the college walls; four fellows were wanting at St John's and two at Clare Hall pending elections (Lamb, pp. 60 ff.). The returns are printed in full in *Documents relating to the University and Colleges of Cambridge* (1852). For a summary of the Oxford return, *L & P* XXI (i), p. 140.

[2] Lamb, pp. 59–60.

he brought, that some colleges be re-organised so that civil lawyers might all be in one, students of medicine in another. Indeed the university appointed a deputation to appeal against this injunction at court, despite the fact that, as at Cambridge, the colleges had received confirmation of their privileges and property. Informing Paget of this in October 1546, Cox wrote: 'I fear the suit to be of little purpose and not gracious, I think they might do well to sue for some endowment for the university which is poor and miserable, and hath scant £5 by the year', by comparison with the annual income of some £50 at Cambridge[1]—an indication of the poverty of the universities by comparison with individual colleges.

In the event there was no time to enforce any unwelcome re-organisation, and before the close of the year both universities had been provided with a royal foundation. At Oxford, Christ Church finally took the place of what had once been Cardinal College, as a cathedral body and college combined, and to it were attached three of the regius professorships; the first dean was Richard Cox and, endowed with the lands of Rowley and Oseney abbeys, the college rent roll amounted to some £2000. On 19 December Cambridge obtained the foundation for which it had first petitioned a decade before. This absorbed the old established colleges of King's Hall and Michaelhouse, dissolved under the chantries act, and also the Physwick hostel belonging to Gonville Hall.[2] The buildings taken over were repaired with stone from the former Franciscan friary, at length obtained for a university use, and the revenues assigned amounted to some £1600. The stipend of the master, whose appointment like that of the dean of Christ Church lay with the crown, was £100, by comparison with £74 for the master of King's, £18 for the master of St John's and less than £6 for older colleges.

Henry, perhaps conscious of his approaching end, did not name the college after himself nor introduce it in the flamboyant fashion of former years but dedicated it

> to the glory and honour of Almighty God, and of the Holy and undivided Trinity, for increase and strengthening of Christianity, extirpation of error, development and perpetuation of religion, cultivation of wholesome study in all departments of learning, knowledge of languages, education of youth

[1] *L & P*, XXI (ii), p. 147.

[2] For an account of the founding of Trinity, W. W. R. Ball, *Cambridge Papers* (1918), pp. 1–25.

in piety, virtue, self-restraint, and knowledge, charity towards the poor, and relief of the afflicted and distressed.

With this foundation a seal was set on the rise of Cambridge which for the remainder of the century surpassed Oxford in influence. But, settled after the old king's death, Trinity College received virtually no lands; these were diverted, as powerful advisers had wished to exchange the lands of established colleges, and impropriations substituted—a presage of problems in the coming reign.

VIII

POLICIES UNDER EDWARD VI

When the ten-year-old Edward succeeded in January 1547 his legacy was a crown heavily in debt, pressing economic problems, general confusion in the matter of religious doctrine and stirrings of popular unrest. The regency council which took up the reins of government was composed almost entirely of representatives of the new nobility. There were only two bishops, one Cranmer, and a single hereditary peer among twenty-six councillors, many of whom had added to their possessions monastic lands of an annual value of £200 or more[1]—a greater amount than sustained most colleges at the universities. The lands of the latter were still in demand but the duke of Somerset—Edward Seymour, raised to the status of Lord Protector—is said to have responded to such pressure with a telling question. 'If learning decay, which of wild men maketh civil; of blockish and rash persons wise and goodly counsellors, of obstinate rebels obedient subjects, and of evil men good and godly Christians; what shall we look for else but barbarism and tumult?' Should college lands go, he added, 'it shall be hard to say whose staff shall stand next the door; for then I doubt not but the state of bishops, rich farmers, merchants, and the nobility shall be assailed'.[2]

There was a new consciousness of dangers from below. The tenant farmer, like the universities, looked to the king for the redress of grievances and had not looked altogether in vain; Somerset favoured a continuation of policies to mitigate economic pressures, in particular legislation to control enclosure. At the same time the Six Articles were repealed, the old laws against heresy abrogated and the doctrinal position of Cromwell's day reasserted. With this went renewed measures to instruct men in the faith and in their duties. The homilies issued in 1547 to be read in parish churches every Sunday, ready-made sermons at a time when preachers were few, introduced modifications of doctrine but ranged well beyond doctrinal matters. 'An Exhortation

[1] A. F. Pollard, *England under Protector Somerset* (1900), pp. 80–2.

[2] W. Harrison, *Description of England* (1877), I, pp. 88–9. Harrison, who studied at both universities, was at Cambridge in 1551.

concerning good order and obedience to rulers and magistrates', developing a theme broached earlier in Marshall's primer, proclaimed this as part of a necessary obedience to God; for God, who created all things, assigned on earth 'kings, princes, with other governors under them, all in good and necessary order'. So also with the other degrees in society, all of which 'have need of other'. No longer was there the familar figure of Henry VIII, able to assert himself as God's viceroy on earth, but men could be persuaded of their good fortune in his son; and that 'it is an intolerable ignorance, madness and wickedness for subjects to make any murmuring, rebellion, resistance, commotion or insurrection, against their most dear and most dread sovereign lord and king, ordained and appointed of God's goodness, for their commodity, peace and quietness'.[1]

The royal injunctions at the outset of the reign required a reformation of church services which included reading the litany in English. Besides the English bible, which might again freely be read, and this meant fresh licence to study Tyndale's version as well as later ones, every parish church must have the English version of Erasmus's paraphrases of the four gospels—a pointer to Somerset's endeavour to maintain a middle road.[2] Once more all chantry priests were called upon to 'exercise themselves in teaching youth to read and write and bring them up in good manners and other virtuous exercises'.[3] But at the close of the year a new chantries act, to replace that which became void on Henry's death, took all chantry possessions into the hands of the crown and forecast their use to aid schools and universities, the parish clergy and the poor.

Exiles who had fled from Henry's last round of persecutions now returned and, with the advent also of ministers from the reformed churches abroad, there resulted an outburst of preaching and discussion. Nor did this bear only on doctrinal matters; the deepest grievances aired were the raising of rents, eviction of poorer tenants, enclosures of all kinds, and these evils were laid at the door of the landlords. Robert

[1] *Certain Sermons or Homilies appointed by the King's Majesty to be declared and read by all Parsons, Vicars, or Curates every Sunday in their Churches where they have Cure* (1547).

[2] Gardiner noted a discrepancy between these and the homilies. 'The injunctions contain a commandment to see taught and learned two books, one of homilies, another of Erasmus's Paraphrases....These books strive one against another directly' (quoted in G. Constant, *The Reformation in England*, 1941, II, p. 230).

[3] Frere, II, pp. 114–30. The injunction of 1536 relating to the upbringing of youth is repeated word for word.

Crowley's *Petition against the Oppressors of the Poor Commons of this Realm*, addressed to parliament in 1548, underlined anew that honest men's children, of good hopes in the liberal sciences and other good qualities, of whom there was a great lack in the realm, were compelled to turn to handicrafts and day labour to sustain their parents and so prevented from completing their education.[1] Leading reformers, in sympathy with protests, helped to voice them. Latimer preached as ardently against the selfish landlord as against popish practices and if the social outlook he expressed was a traditional one it chimed in well enough with the principles of the reformed religion. The theory of a fixed social hierarchy as the necessary framework of order implied that no encroachments should be made from any direction; each estate might justly defend its rights within the social order and landlords stood condemned if they encroached on the estate below their own. With advocacy of popular rights went renewed emphasis on popular education. It was Latimer who was the chief spokesman of what approached a political party, the 'commonwealth's men', the leading member of this group in the Commons being John Hales who promoted a series of bills against enclosure.[2]

These efforts were defeated as the problems inherited from Henry's reign came to a head. War with Scotland continued, half-conquered Irish provinces must be kept in check, and when a consignment of chantry lands was sold in April 1548—at the earliest possible moment and before the full survey was completed—the privy council noted that it was 'specially for the relief of the king's majesty's charges', daily growing by reason of military expenses; adding that subjects had the more willingly granted the chantries 'that they might thereby be relieved of the continued charge of taxes contributions, loans and subsidies'.[3] This was no doubt true of the gentry who were as unwilling to vote subsidies as to countenance any hindrance to enclosure. In fact the Commons rejected all bills intended to regulate enclosures but passed the most savage law of the century, directed against the victims of agrarian upheaval, the dispossessed poor.[4]

[1] Strype, *Ecc. Mem.* II, i, p. 222.

[2] S. T. Bindoff, *Tudor England* (1950), pp. 129–35; R. H. Tawney, *The Agrarian Problem in the Sixteenth Century* (1912), pp. 362–8.

[3] *APC*, II, pp. 184–5.

[4] The measure, passed just before the chantries act, figures in the Commons Journals as 'Bill for Vagabonds and Slaves'. Under it a sturdy beggar might be made a slave for two years or, if he absconded, for life; sons of vagrants could be apprenticed until 24, their daughters until 20, punishment for resistance being slavery. But it is doubtful

Latimer, like Becon, now accused gentlemen of gathering for themselves. Pointing both to the raising of tenants' rents and the exploiting of impropriated benefices, for in this matter lay patrons had simply taken over from the monasteries, he declared that all such proceedings 'do intend plainly to make the yeomanry slavery and the clergy shavery. For such works are all singular, private wealth and commodity. We of the clergy had too much; but that is taken away and now we have too little.' Moreover, the yeomanry were so pressed that they could no longer keep sons to school and this could destroy the realm. 'For by yeomen's sons the faith of Christ is and hath been maintained chiefly. Is this realm taught by rich men's sons? No, no; read the chronicles: ye shall find sometime noblemen's sons which have been unpreaching bishops and prelates, but ye shall find none of them learned men.' This observation brought an accusation of speaking 'opprobriously against the nobility'. But Latimer had no complaints about the chantries act, only a warning that chantry priests be not made ministers, as abbots had been made bishops: 'I would not that ye should put in chantry priests. I speak not against such...as are able to preach; but those that are not able. I will not have them put in; for if ye do this, ye shall answer for it.'[1]

In the spring of 1549 the universities were visited and important reforms initiated. Now, too, a prayer book replaced the Henrician primers and was prescribed for universal use,[2] dethroning the Latin mass in favour of an English service. This, prepared by Cranmer in the closing years of the previous reign, did not go nearly so far as reformers now felt necessary but the change was a profound one for the people at large. Another change in age-old custom was brought about by an act passed in February which legalised clerical marriage. However much other measures may have violated some feelings, this one proved congenial enough to the clergy; within four years a considerable proportion had taken wives.

Meanwhile nothing had been done to remedy popular grievances. There began to be gatherings to express discontent, disturbances ensued, and by the summer the countryside from Norfolk to Worcestershire was in an uproar, Devon and Cornwall no less. Calling for an end to encroachments on their rights, the peasantry on the whole also opposed

whether it ever operated and it was shortly repealed in favour of an earlier measure (Jordan, *Philanthropy*, p. 86).

[1] *Sermons* (1844), pp. 100, 124, 141. [2] *Tudor Constitution*, pp. 392–6.

innovations in religion, though some of the East Anglian marchers spoke as reformers.[1] But to the council and gentlemen in the counties—catholic and reformer alike—this was a revolt of tenants against landlords, which threatened to become countrywide on the German model, and retaliation was swift and severe. Three hundred were executed after the East Anglian movement had been crushed by the earl of Warwick, soon to become duke of Northumberland, and equally rigorous measures were taken in the west. Once the popular movement had been reduced Somerset fell, and in place of protective legislation a series of penal laws made discussion of grievances or combination to remedy them a criminal offence.[2] One of the victims in Oxfordshire was the vicar of Chipping Norton, Henry Joyce, who joined the local revolt because four chantry priests in the parish church had been pensioned off, under the chantries act, and he was left to minister to 800 parishioners without any assistance; the chantry house, gild hall and other property had been bought up by strangers and nothing left but a stipend of £6 for the schoolmaster. Joyce was hanged from his church steeple.[3]

With the danger from below removed, and no restraining hand above, the way was clear for further dispossession of the poor and the church; and, too, of the crown itself in that free grants of land were more often made and chantry property tended to melt away. Whereas Henry had controlled factional struggle among his nobles this now worked itself out in the council so that there was less control over administrative departments and malpractices spread;[4] though they had not been lacking before and the evidence does not suggest any breakdown in such departments as the augmentations. Somerset's downfall had been encompassed by a broad alliance of all who deplored his lenient social policies and there was thereafter a catholic section of the council; but it was eliminated early in 1550 when Northumberland took control and turned to the reforming party for backing.[5] Under his guidance there were new plans to reduce episcopal possessions, in

[1] Tawney, pp. 333, 339–40. The petition of the Norfolk rebels prayed that priests be resident so that 'their parishioners may be instructed with the laws of God' and that every incumbent with a benefice of £10 or over 'shall either by themselves or by some other person teach poor men's children of their parish the book called the catechism and the primer' (F. J. Furnivall, ed., *Ballads from Manuscripts*, Ballad Society, 1868–72, pp. 149–50).

[2] Tawney, pp. 371–2.

[3] Rose Graham, *The Chantry Certificates for Oxfordshire* (Alcuin Club, 1920), p. xxi.

[4] Richardson, p. 168.

[5] A. F. Pollard, in *Cambridge Modern History*, II, pp. 494–9.

particular those of the princely bishopric of Durham. At the same time when reformers replaced conservative bishops their sees were mulcted by the well-tried method of forcing an unequal exchange of lands. None the less the exchequer remained in acute difficulties, despite additional borrowings abroad, and in 1551 the council decided to collect 'such church plate as remaineth to be employed unto his highness use'.[1]

Leading reformers, faced with the realities of popular revolt, condemned it as contrary to the will of God and the duties of Christians, as Luther had once done and according to the teaching of the homilies. This time Cheke wrote a book eloquently denouncing sedition while Cranmer issued severe reproofs as reprisals were carried out in Devon.[2] But in the Lent of 1550 Latimer and Lever were castigating the nobility as sharply for bringing the Reformation into disrepute, stressing particularly that promises to endow education remained unfulfilled. Lever made specific accusations about the despoiling of schools. Latimer, preaching a week later, had nothing to add to a competent account except a fresh warning—'this much I say unto you, magistrates: if ye will not maintain schools and universities ye shall have a brutality'. But his chief concern is again with the upholding of preaching and protection of benefices—'what should secular men do with the livings of preachers?'—and he drives the point home with suitably round figures: 'I think there be at this day ten thousand students less than were within these twenty years, and fewer preachers; and that is the cause of rebellion'.[3] Latimer adds 'if there were good bishops, there should be no rebellion'.

[1] *APC*, III, p. 288. What remained, that is, after depredations encouraged by the council's order of February 1548 that all images in churches be destroyed. The gentry were as ready to resume church plate and vestments as chantry lands; many parishes eventually reported to the commissioners that they had sold most of their plate and given the proceeds to the poor or towards other local uses (Graham, pp. xxiv–xxvi).

[2] One point of the rebels' programme here was that half the abbey and chantry lands in any man's possession, however come by, be given up to found two centres in place of two great abbeys where the devout might pray for king and commonwealth. Cranmer rejected this as extreme arrogance after so great a sedition against king and commonwealth. It would be 'against all justice and equity' to take from the king lands annexed to his crown and 'against all right and reason to take from all other men such lands as they came to by most just title, by gift, by sale, by exchange or otherwise' (Cranmer, p. 186).

[3] *Sermons*, p. 269. The same figure of students lacking, possibly drawn from this source, was advanced by the speaker of the House of Commons in 1563 when dealing with the same theme—the evils of impropriation and the consequent decay of learning,

Good bishops were shortly to replace those inherited from Henry's day—notably Ridley in London, Ponet at Rochester, Hooper at Gloucester—and steps were also taken to investigate maladministration and corruption. There was a growing realisation in some quarters of the gulf between precepts and practice. Sir William Petre, longstanding servant of the crown, wrote to William Cecil in September 1551: 'At the beginning the apostles left their fishing of fishes and became fishers of men, and now we who talk much of Christ and His Holy Word have, I fear me, used a much contrary way; for we leave fishing for men and fish again in the tempestuous seas of the world for gain and wicked mammon.'[1] This was a time when gentlemen, first advanced under Henry, awarded themselves dukedoms; others, to whom the establishment of a family was itself a religion, also profited largely, the disorganised state of financial offices and lack of straightforward payment for services offering opportunity and excuse.[2]

There was little involvement in European affairs during the reign and intellectual contacts were mainly with the Swiss churches. Luther had died the year before Henry VIII, Francis I two months after, and Europe was in flux as Charles V endeavoured to consolidate the Hapsburg empire over Germany by war. It was because of the resultant setback to the Reformation that Oxford and Cambridge profited from the advent of some notable refugees, the chief of them Martin Bucer of Strasburg from whom Calvin learned so much. Meanwhile ambassadors abroad—John Mason, Richard Morison, William Pickering, Henry Wotton and others—kept the council informed of a variety of matters; of the capital made at the French court out of the strictures of English preachers about the decay of grammar schools and universities, of the reconvening of the Council of Trent in 1551 ('A few Italian bishops were there, and invited the Holy Ghost to a mass, which done, he had leave to go whither he would'), of Charles V's angry protest that his cousin Mary was prevented from attending mass by mere councillors.[3]

because scholars were deprived of due reward; Simonds d'Ewes, *Journals* (1682), p. 65A. The point is made because these two statements have often been adduced as evidence of the destruction of hundreds of schools.

[1] Emmison, p. 96.

[2] Cecil later affirmed that he received more in four years under Edward than in twenty-six serving Elizabeth (Hurstfield, p. 279). He was knighted in October 1551, together with John Cheke and Henry Sidney at the same time as John Dudley was created duke of Northumberland, Henry Grey, duke of Suffolk.

[3] *Calendar of State Papers Foreign 1547–53*, pp. 72–3, 106, 137.

Meanwhile the advance towards a reformed doctrine continued, to be sealed when parliament approved the second Edwardian prayer book in 1552, and was accompanied by concerted efforts to establish a protestant system of education. The tightening up of administration during these years enabled policies to be implemented for which the way had long been prepared. Though preachers often pillory the mercenary they also bear witness to a growing support for reform. Becon, travelling about the country after his brush with authority in 1543, found a hundred friends in those who had studied his works and the writings of Tyndale and Frith, including 'both men and women of the nobility which greatly delight in reading the holy scriptures, and do not only love but live the gospel'. He taught for a time in Staffordshire, attempting to the best of his ability to bring up youth 'in the knowledge of good literature and the principles of Christ's doctine'. Later, in Warwickshire, he taught 'divers gentlemen's sons, which I trust, if they live, shall be a beauty to the public weal of England, both for preferment of true religion and for the maintenance of justice'.[1] Latimer also bears witness to a new prevalence of learning, affirming 'There is in this realm...a great sight of laymen, well learned in the scriptures, and of virtuous and godly conversation, better learned than a great sight of us the clergy'. There had, then, been others besides Henry VIII who entrusted sons to protestant teachers or sent them to colleges where the new learning was fostered. Such men begin to come to the fore in the Edwardian age; Walter Mildmay, who rose rapidly in the court of augmentations, was one such, while the chancellor of the court, Richard Sackville—also a gentleman's son, educated at Cambridge and Gray's Inn—was an 'earnest favourer and furtherer of God's true religion'.[2]

All in all there were strong reasons for taking up the tasks left over from Henry's reign, for re-organising schools and colleges into a more effective system of education. Some might see this as a necessary means of consolidating the social order, particularly after recent disturbances, as a bulwark of Reformation policies in the political sense. But others sought, as the early humanists had done, to promote education for the good of society and the welfare of the church, and, too, the salvation of individual souls. These considerations weighed in the balance against the difficulties resulting from a disordered administration and a depleted exchequer.

[1] Becon, pp. 420, 423, 424. [2] Ascham, p. 179.

IX

THE CHANTRIES ACT OF 1547 AND ITS OUTCOME

A bill 'for Chantry lands and Church lands'—an inauspicious title—was introduced in the Commons on 30 November 1547. There had been considerable difficulty in securing the passage of the first chantries act and there was to be more in getting another through both houses

In the Commons, spokesmen for the boroughs of Coventry and Lynn represented so loudly the case for excluding gild lands from confiscation that a planned intervention was necessary to prevent them stampeding the house and securing deletion of the objectionable clause. The privy council, recollecting 'what moment the labour of a few setters-on had been heretofore in like cases' in winning the support of 'free voices'—a comment on the recent development of parliamentary debate—authorised councillors in the house to 'stay and content them of Lynn and Coventry by granting them to have and enjoy their guild lands etc., as they did before', so long as they desisted from advancing further objections or amendments.[1] There may also have been representations about schools; that these would be affected in considerable numbers had been made clear in the returns of the commissioners appointed under the earlier act. When the bill went to the Lords it failed to pass there; even Cranmer voted against, apparently because there was insufficient provision for augmenting church livings. But a 'New Bill for Chantries, Colleges and Free Chapels' passed rapidly through both houses on 21 and 22 December; this time, in the Lords, only five bishops voted against, including Tunstall of London and Skip of Hereford, soon to be replaced.[2] In its final form the act made allowance for funds held for secular objects as also for the allocation of lands to maintain additional parish clergy and school foundations.

[1] *Commons Journals*, p. 2; *Tudor Constitution*, pp. 297–8; cf. Ashley, II, pp. 147–8.

[2] *Lords Journals*, I, pp. 312–13; Pollard, *Political History*, pp. 18–19. Gardiner agreed that chantry masses had been abused: 'I, that allow mass so well, and I, that allow praying for the dead (as indeed the dead are of Christian charity to be prayed for), yet can agree with the realm in that matter of putting down chantries' (Foxe, VI, pp. 89–90).

The preamble recited that superstition and errors in the Christian religion derived from men's ignorance 'of their very true and perfect salvation through the death of Jesus Christ', that these errors centred partly in 'vain opinions of purgatory', which in turn were upheld by the abuse of chantries 'made for the continuance of the said blindness and ignorance'. Since parliament could not conveniently amend chantries and convert them 'to good and godly uses, as in erecting of grammar schools to the education of youth in virtue and godliness, the further augmenting of the universities, and better provision for the poor and needy' it was committed to the king and his council 'to order, alter, convert, and dispose' of the same.[1] The form of this frequently quoted statement should be noted and it should be remembered that preambles were notoriously propagandist; what counted were the actual provisions of the act introduced.

This time the act vested outright in the crown, as from the following Easter, all the possessions of colleges, free chapels and chantries (exception now made of those dissolved by patrons five years or more before) and also of 'all fraternities, brotherhoods and gilds' other than 'fellowships of mysteries or crafts'. But one clause specifically exempted the hostels, halls and colleges at Oxford and Cambridge, and Winchester and Eton, even down to the chantries founded in them.[2] The king was empowered to appoint commissioners to make an inventory of lands and possessions. These, or any two of them, might also be authorised, in cases where the foundation deed of a gild or perpetual chantry specified the keeping of a grammar school or a preacher, to assign lands 'to remain and continue in succession to a schoolmaster or preacher for ever, for and toward the keeping of a grammar school or preaching' and also 'to make ordinances' concerning the service of the schoolmaster and by what name he should be called. They were also to be authorised to grant pensions to the priests of dissolved chantries—and, as it turned out, stipends to those recommended for continuance in office as curates or schoolmasters.

[1] For the main provisions of the act, J. R. Tanner, *Tudor Constitutional Documents* (Cambridge, 1922), pp. 103–7.

[2] Cathedrals or colleges which were the seat of a bishop's see were also exempt, though not their chantries, and chapels of ease with only a small close. There was no mention of hospitals, though some which had chantries within them were dissolved; ancient foundations in this category had often ceased to fulfil their original function and offices were mere sinecures (Jordan, *Philanthropy*, pp. 258–9). Grammar school foundations not connected with a chantry were, naturally, exempt, but some find mention in certificates because they received a small payment out of a chantry endowment.

Commissions were duly appointed to cover groups of counties on the same model as those under the act of 1545, except that bishops now found no place whereas they had formerly headed commissions. Most of the members were gentlemen from the counties concerned with one or two officials of the court of augmentations attached who probably did most of the detailed work. Reports were due for completion by the end of May 1548 and there were two sets of returns. First, there were reports collected from incumbents and churchwardens in the parishes addressed to the commissioners; these were summarised in a certificate to the court of augmentations from the latter with added recommendations for the payment of pensions to priests displaced or of stipends to those recognised as vicars, curates or schoolmasters.[1]

In June 1548 the commission of two was appointed but it was not authorised to assign lands. It was to issue warrants for payment of pensions and the stipends allotted 'until such time as other order and direction shall be taken therein'. The two commissioners were the newly appointed general surveyor of the court of augmentations, Walter Mildmay, and the surveyor of liveries in the court of wards, Robert Keilway, a reputable lawyer who retained this office until his death in 1581.[2] In July they issued continuance warrants for each county authorising the payment to those chantry priests who had been recognised as usefully serving a cure or teaching of the same stipend they had hitherto received, while all the rest were allotted pensions according to a specified scale.[3] Sums left for the poor were usually continued at the same rate but there was not a great deal, just as the chantries in general realised less than expected. Property, in the form of urban tenements, was often deteriorating, little surplus being available for repairs, and income had been diminishing. Many chantries brought in no more than the stipend for one priest and where this was less than £5 it went on a pension and nothing accrued to the crown. Since lands were rapidly sold, pensions became a heavy drain on diminishing capital resources.[4]

It should be made clear, however, that there was no question of two crown officials, placed in a position to decide the fate of schools,

[1] Examples of each are printed in full in Graham, pp. 12 ff., 44 ff.

[2] *APC*, II, pp. 184–6; Richardson, p. 174 n.

[3] Those receiving £5 or under got the whole amount; from £5 to £6. 13*s*. 4*d*.—£5; up to £10—£6; between £10 and £20—£6. 13*s*. 4*d*. (Graham, p. xv).

[4] Richardson, pp. 179–82.

vetoing the recommendations of the county commissioners to save the exchequer from payment of stipends. The county commissions were well leavened with augmentations officials to begin with; their recommendations were simply adopted at the centre, so that the two commissioners could sign a whole series of warrants on a single day.[1] Two points should be stressed here. First, that a stipend was often awarded to a priest found keeping school effectively whether or not the foundation deed of the chantry or gild mentioned a school and whether or not he was said to teach Latin grammar. Secondly that the receivers were required to pay these stipends to the present incumbents, named as schoolmasters, 'and to such other person or persons as shall have and enjoy the rooms and places of the same persons', so that stipends could be, and were, paid over many years to come. Consequently places where there was a reasonably capable chantry or stipendiary priest teaching in 1548 gained a regular annuity from the crown for a schoolmaster though no endowment for education had been made. This was, of course, the only way of keeping schools in being; pensions were a first charge on revenues, many chantries had no more coming in than would pay one priest, and if out of this a pension was awarded little or nothing was left over for an incumbent.

If many of the stipends awarded were very low—under, often well under, £5—this only serves to illustrate how poorly many chantries were endowed. The minimum figure for continuance was 20*s.* a year and priests receiving less seem to have been automatically pensioned even if they professed to teach. At Witney the county commissioners pensioned off an old chantry priest who had once taught but 'doth little service now' and represented the inhabitants' desire for a schoolmaster; in the circumstances no stipend was available, nor in this case was an endowment secured, but this is an isolated instance.[2] For the most part the commissioners seem to have been on the lookout for

[1] Graham, pp. xvii–xviii. This has often been pointed to as evidence of heartless bureaucracy; the fact that many continuance warrants are missing from the records allowed for Leach's inference (not checked against later evidence) that no stipend was awarded to many schools.

[2] The commissions varied in outlook and much of the work in Oxfordshire was done by a zealous deputy-surveyor of augmentations for the county. It may be noted here that population figures given in initial returns and those in later ones incorporating requests for endowments sometimes differed considerably: Witney is first accorded 800 and then 1100, Burford rises from 544 to 1000, Banbury from 460 to 1400. The age of incumbents is given roughly in multiples of ten and the number of pupils in schools likewise in round figures (*ibid.* pp. xii–xiv).

teachers, and ready enough to find those teaching sufficiently competent to continue. Some of the county commissions suggested additional places where schools were needed. Occasionally the income of an endowment was shifted from an out-of-the-way place to a town; that benefactors had usually favoured their own birthplace meant that schools were by no means always settled where the best use could be made of them. Shifts of population had also left some parishes over-provided with churches, other very populous ones served by a single incumbent. Not a few chantry priests were continued in office as vicars or curates, despite Latimer's warning against placing those who could not preach, though others were described as incapable of any useful service. But it is impossible to give any general assessment because this whole subject has attracted so little interest or research.

Before the returns became available, various steps were taken to safeguard the endowments of particular schools, which were frequently at risk when disappointed heirs intervened and particularly so at a time when lands were known to be forfeit to the crown. One or two foundations initiated in Henry's reign were carried through in 1547.[1] Several schools were promoted or protected by private act of parliament in 1548. The former abbot of St Albans took the initiative in refounding the school there at a time when Nicholas Bacon, high steward of the town, was negotiating a charter of incorporation. St Albans school was planned for 144 scholars under three masters, like nearby Berkhamsted which itself was once modelled on St Paul's, and passed under the control of the borough a few years later. Berkhamsted School was also the subject of a private act, protecting the endowments against the founder's heirs,[2] protection of a kind also needed for Pocklington in Yorkshire after a relative of the founder laid claim to the school lands on the plea they had not been properly conveyed.[3]

The lands of Stamford school were secured against a like danger through the agency of William Cecil, once educated there; he saw

[1] At Crediton, Devon, the school was endowed in connection with the parish church, on the pattern adopted at Ottery St Mary (*CPR Ed. VI*, I, 43–5). Ipswich School, formerly drawn into the local Cardinal College, was regained by the borough (Gray & Potter, pp. 33–40). Norwich secured a city grammar school in connection with a hospital granted by the will of Henry VIII (*CPR Ed. VI*, I, pp. 13–17). Grimsby transformed a chantry into a school between one chantries act and another with the aid of Sir Edward North, then chancellor of the court of augmentations (*ibid.* p. 176).

[2] *VCH Herts.* II, pp. 56 ff.

[3] P. C. Sands and C. M. Haworth, *History of Pocklington School* (1951), p. 18. The act of 1548 is recited in letters patent of 1553 (*CPR Ed. VI*, V, p. 234).

that the school was placed under the borough with nomination of the master in the hands of his former college, St John's.[1] But this college, faced with a similar situation in the case of Sedbergh school,[2] took no evasive action until it was learned in 1549 that the school lands were about to be bought up; the proposal being that the master's stipend be secured upon them, the procedure adopted in Henry's reign. The college had a close interest in the matter since it presented the master and there were eight scholarships connected with the school endowed at the college by the same benefactor. The help of a former member now in high office, Sir Anthony Denny, was sought, as also that of Somerset. The latter's intervention stayed the sale but shortly afterwards it went through,[3] at a time when attention was much occupied elsewhere, probably as a result of pressure at the court of augmentations or on local officials in Yorkshire.

This served as a telling example of maladministration of the chantries act, with results opposite to those intended. It was the point Thomas Lever made most of in his hard-hitting sermon before the court in the spring of 1550, describing Sedbergh school as 'sold, decayed and lost', saved once by charity but lost through bribery. However just this last accusation may have been the school had not in fact closed its doors; the master had been receiving a stipend equivalent to the former income since 1548 and did so until a fresh endowment in land was secured by letters patent in 1551.[4]

Roger Ascham, writing to the privy council on behalf of St John's in 1549, cogently argued the case for endowing schools with lands rather than paying stipends to masters. Though a stipend of £10 might be equivalent to the normal income from lands, when a tenant died or a new master succeeded a fine of double the rent was due which increased the average income considerably; the school was by that much the loser. Who, he then asked, would pay the £10? If the king did so, then for perhaps £200 received from a purchaser of land the exchequer might pay out £1000 in annual pensions—as indeed some-

[1] B. L. Deed, *History of Stamford School* (Stamford, 1954), pp. 13–14, 94–6. Colleges now quite often gained the right to present masters, formerly accorded in many cases to monastic houses.

[2] Already in 1544 the feoffees of the school lands had had some designs on these; the help of Archbishop Holgate, president of the council in the north, had been engaged on this occasion (Baker, I, pp. 364, 365).

[3] *Ibid.* pp. 371, 372.

[4] *CPR Ed. VI*, IV, pp. 97–9. Though the lands were not so conveniently situated.

times proved the case. The purchasers were unlikely to maintain a stipend since what with this, the purchase money and the annual payments they would be no gainers. Finally, he warned that the north country, deprived of gratuitous education for its sons, would become disaffected and that charity would wax cold given that not even a time of reformation could repress plunder.[1] It may be noted that charity was not, at the time, falling away in the north. In 1548 the chantry school at Skipton-in-Craven was endowed anew by a private benefactor. Also in Yorkshire three schools founded by Archbishop Holgate were settled early in this reign; these were at his birthplace, Hemsworth, at Old Malton and in the close of the cathedral at York. Holgate, a former Gilbertine monk but an upholder of the new learning, probably since his Cambridge days in the 1520's, laid down that the master of the York school be knowledgeable in Hebrew as well as Greek and Latin, teaching all these to scholars he judged to be apt.[2]

The question of assigning lands to endow schools had yet to be dealt with in detail. But in general, whereas the concern in Henry's reign had been to constitute collegiate bodies with schools attached, now the policy was to strengthen the parish clergy and settle local grammar schools under boroughs or lay governing bodies. Attention concentrated to the end Starkey had advocated, the establishment of one or two good schools, usually with two masters apiece paid a reasonable salary, in each county. The county commissioners were evidently thinking along these lines from the outset as they collected information about existing schools. Those for Gloucestershire, for instance, reported that Newent was a market town with over five hundred inhabitants but 'all the youth of a great distance therehence rudely brought up and in no manner of knowledge and learning, where were a place meet to... erect a school for the better and more godly bringing up of the same youth'. The people of Cheltenham had advanced the claims of their town to the commissioners in the same sense; it was a market town full of children with no other school nearby, 'wherefore it is thought convenient to signify unto your Masterships the same to be a meet place to establish some teacher and erect a grammar school, so it might stand with the Kings Majesty's pleasure'.[3]

[1] Baker, p. 372.

[2] A. M. Gibbon, *The Free Grammar School of Skipton-in-Craven* (Liverpool, 1947); A. G. Dickens, *Robert Holgate* (York, 1955), pp. 22–3; Purvis, p. 13.

[3] *ESR*, II, pp. 83, 85–6.

It may have been the intention to legislate for a general return of lands to school foundations or for the establishment of new schools. In any case a bill was introduced in the Commons in January 1549 'for making schools and giving lands thereto'. It was referred to 'Mr Secretary Smythe', that is Thomas Smith, former Cambridge professor now in office, and figures again later in the month, to be passed on 9 February as the 'bill for the giving of lands to the finding of schools'; but it then disappears after a first reading in the Lords. During the second session of parliament a bill of the same title was read once, in December, but does not figure again;[1] shortly after action was taken by the privy council by way of issuing instructions to the court of augmentations. Meanwhile measures affecting particular schools did go through, in accordance with the promise extracted that gild lands would be returned.

In February 1549 Thomas Smith—knighted in this year—assisted in securing a charter for Saffron Walden, the town of his birth, which granted rights over the local school and returned its endowments. Two other boroughs attained incorporation in the summer covering a similar return of endowments and grant of rights over schools, Maidstone and Wisbech.[2] Towns were now increasingly anxious to gain incorporation which, by conferring exemption from the Statute in Mortmain, enabled them to take advantage of the new market in land.[3] Some were former monastic boroughs, others sought freedom from episcopal control; many had recently lost gild property and in retrieving it sought also to extend possessions and rights. It was the policy to assist these efforts as well as aiding the endowment of churches and schools directly, though the evidence of what was done has yet to be brought together. At Hull, for instance, 'the Edwardian government refounded the hospitals, secured the threatened churches, and subsidised the grammar school and the clergy from the revenues of chantry lands; all this in addition to the very extensive grants made to the town by letters patent in 1551'.[4]

'Further order' was now taken for the refoundation of schools, before Lever and Latimer made their open protests, during the same

[1] Pollard, *England under Protector Somerset*, p. 126; *Commons Journals*, pp. 6, 7.

[2] The latter with the aid of Thomas Goodrich, bishop of Ely, member of the privy council (*CPR Ed. VI*, II, pp. 174–6, 211–12, 340).

[3] Weinbaum, p. 92.

[4] Dickens, p. 210. See also C. G. Parsloe, 'The Growth of a Borough Constitution: Newark-on-Trent, 1549–1688', *T.R.H.S.*, fourth series, XXII (1940), pp. 171 ff.

month that the catholic faction was ousted from the council. In February 1550 a commission was issued to the chancellor of the court of augmentations conferring on him powers to act

in consideration of the regard due to gifts and promises by Henry VIII and the king for the erecting of grammar schools, appointment of livings for preachers and the poor, endowment of vicars...and like godly acts.[1]

It is recited that since the chantries act empowered the king to commission divers persons to erect grammar schools (and endow vicars, appoint preachers and assistants in churches serving large parishes, relieve the poor) the chancellor should 'take order' to this end. The lands made over to any such corporation should not exceed a yearly value of £20, and the chancellor should prescribe conditions for the use of the endowments assigned in the king's name; he was empowered to nominate others 'to erect and examine' the schools and other consignments concerned, allotting reasonable fees where necessary.[2]

It is after this date that evidence of refoundations accumulates. Some of the towns petitioning for lands had lacked a settled foundation since the dissolution of the monasteries but others took the opportunity to request lands to endow a school where there had been none; in some cases only a licence to acquire lands was sought and buildings were also requested for the use of a school. While rights over schools were granted when boroughs were incorporated, under the same letters patent, in other cases schools were handed over to already corporate boroughs or special governing bodies were set up composed of the more substantial inhabitants who were often named in the charter. A review of some of the evidence will show how various counties fared and the composition of the governing bodies appointed to have charge of local schools.

From Shropshire, the recorder of Shrewsbury advanced a special request on behalf of the town in 1548. This was followed in 1550 by a petition for a school subscribed by leading inhabitants of the county as well as the bailiffs and burgesses of the town who had meantime laid out £20 in securing suitable premises. By letters patent of 1552 they secured a grant of lands formerly belonging to one collegiate church in the town and tithes belonging to another, bringing in an income

[1] While this commission extended the authority of the court generally most of its provisions relate specifically to the leasing or alienation of crown lands (Richardson, pp. 176, 192).

[2] *CPR Ed. VI*, III, pp. 214–15.

of £20. 8*s.* annually.[1] The school kept by the Palmers' Gild of Ludlow, which had maintained a schoolmaster with a stipend of £10, was re-established a few months later when the gild lands were returned and the borough's charter confirmed.[2]

In Warwickshire, the Gild of the Holy Cross at Stratford had reported that part of its income went to repair the great bridge over the Avon, relief of the poor and a stipend of £10 to a schoolmaster. This school, too, was re-established in 1553 when the town gained incorporation, nomination of the master resting with the duke of Northumberland and his heirs.[3] Another gild of the Holy Cross at Birmingham, which does not appear previously to have supported a school, successfully petitioned for lands to endow one and received these by letters patent in 1552; no powerful adviser is mentioned here and a single gentleman heads the list of twenty governors.[4] The same year Nuneaton, where a chantry had been turned to the use of a school, also gained a foundation; here the list of twelve governors is headed by Sir Marmaduke Constable, son of a Yorkshire knight attainted after the pilgrimage of grace, the other eleven being designated as 'yeomen'.[5]

The school kept by the Trinity Gild at Worcester, which had been in abeyance on and off and assisted by Latimer in the 1530's, was reported to have over a hundred scholars in 1548, taught in the gild's great hall. In view of the recent establishment of the king's school, the commissioners recommended that the gild school might cease, a suggestion stoutly and successfully resisted.[6] The refoundation in

[1] *CPR Ed. VI*, IV, p. 387; G. W. Fisher, *Annals of Shrewsbury School* (1899), pp. 1–3.

[2] *CPR Ed. VI*, IV, pp. 345–6. The borough was accorded presentation of the preacher and vicar, to be paid out of the income of lands in place of chantry priests, as well as of the schoolmaster.

[3] *ESR*, II, pp. 239–40; *CPR Ed. VI*, V, pp. 279–80.

[4] *CPR Ed. VI*, IV, pp. 40–1; T. W. Hutton, *King Edward's School, Birmingham* (Oxford, 1952), pp. 6–7 (see Conrad Gill, *History of Birmingham*, Oxford, 1952, pp. 40–3).

[5] *CPR Ed. VI*, IV, p. 293. For an endowment bringing in £2. 13*s.* 4*d.* there was substituted lands yielding £10. 15*s.* 8*d.* to support one master (*King Edward VI School, Nuneaton*, 1952, pp. 13–14). The term 'yeoman', officially implying at least a 40*s.* freeholder, designated all who were not gentlemen; those so called in the charter of Wakefield school in 1591 included a deputy steward of the manor who served in a legal capacity, drapers and chapmen (M. H. Peacock, *A History of Wakefield Grammar School*, Wakefield, 1892, pp. 8–10).

[6] F. V. Follett, *A History of the Worcester Royal Grammar School* (1951), pp. 11 ff. An indication of the support given to schools with no legal foundation is that two stipends of £10 and £5 were granted at King's Norton in this county because two stipendiary priests were keeping a good school—it was said to have 120 scholars (*ESR*, II, pp. 268–9, 280). The school at Chaddesley Corbet retained its lands (*VCH Worcs.* IV, p. 474).

this county was at Stourbridge. Here a chantry priest with a stipend of £6. 0*s*. 4*d*. had been bound to teach children freely in addition to his other duties. The new school was for a schoolmaster and usher, the yearly value of the lands assigned for its support £17. 10*s*. 6*d*., and it was placed under the governance of eight of the more substantial inhabitants.[1]

Another school refounded under a special governing body was Macclesfield in 1552. This, founded in 1503 for 'gentlemen's sons and other good men's children', seems to have gained plenty of support for the list of fourteen governors is headed by five esquires and two gentlemen.[2] A petition from Morpeth was backed by William, Lord Dacre; chantry lands were regranted and the bailiffs and burgesses empowered to appoint the master and make statutes with the advice of the bishop of Durham—this was the usual formula for boroughs.[3] Other boroughs which gained control of schools were East Retford and Louth in 1551, the latter gaining incorporation for the purpose with the aid of Richard Goodrich, son of the bishop of Ely and attorney to the court of augmentations.[4] Guildford, on a petition of the borough and neighbourhood, was allotted lands in January 1553.[5] Grantham regained chantry lands in the same year to provide as before a stipend of £12 for the master.[6]

By contrast, Chelmsford school was vested in 1551 in the four leading local families who had headed the petition for a refoundation—Sir William Petre, Sir Walter Mildmay, Sir Henry Tirrel, Thomas Mildmay—and later became known as the 'knight school'.[7] At Spilsby the duchess of Suffolk and her heirs were granted the lands of a former collegiate foundation with the right of presenting the vicar of the parish church and the schoolmaster and the obligation of paying their stipends. The latter is named in the charter; he was to have a dwelling house and £13. 6*s*. 8*d*. a year and the school was to be inaugurated by the Christmas of 1550.[8]

Schools were not only valued for the education they provided but

[1] *CPR Ed. VI*, IV, p. 303. Again only one gentleman is named, Thomas Jerveis of London, to be a governor for life even if not resident in the town.

[2] *Ibid.* pp. 361–2.

[3] *Ibid.* pp. 384–5.

[4] *Ibid.* pp. 47–8, 119–22.

[5] With power to appoint the master and usher taking the advice of William, marquis of Northampton, great chamberlain and keeper of the manor of Guildford (*ibid.* p. 251).

[6] To be appointed with the advice of William Cecil during his life and after the bishop of the diocese or, in a vacancy of the see, the master of St John's College (*ibid.* V, pp. 35–6).

[7] *Ibid.* IV, pp. 116–17; Stowe, p. 43.

[8] *CPR Ed. VI*, III, pp. 263–4.

also for the trade they brought, not least in such outlying counties as Herefordshire. At Ledbury, where a chantry priest kept school on a stipend of under £4 supplemented by fees, the inhabitants represented that this was a poor town and they 'not only had profit and advantage by the keeping of a grammar school there, as in boarding and lodging ... scholars, but also the country thereabouts, in uttering their victuals there by means of the said scholars'.[1] Fifteen chantry priests were returned as teaching in this county, but ten drew stipends of under £5 and for the most part kept small parish schools. At Kinnersley, however, a chantry priest had spent all his time for the past five years keeping a school; he was reported to have sixty scholars and to be well qualified. At Leominster a private schoolmaster held a flourishing school supported solely by the fees of his pupils; this, the largest market town in the county, had been in the hands of the crown since the dissolution of the priory and had no settled school. Here a foundation was established, though it was not completed until 1554 so that it is usually credited to the next reign.[2] The chapter of Hereford Cathedral was also moved to build a schoolhouse.[3]

Staffordshire, like Herefordshire, was a poor county. A few years earlier Becon had written that since the priests lacked learning so did the people for 'when the blind leadeth the blind, both fall into the ditch'. The commissioners reached much the same conclusion, recording after each of many chantries in Walsall church, 'Schools, Preachers, Poor, Nothing', adding a note that all the priests concerned were 'utterly unable to minister or assist ministration'.[4] Only ten of the

[1] *ESR*, II, pp. 92–3.

[2] *CPR Philip & Mary*, I, pp. 395–8. Schools refounded by letters patent under Mary had usually been initiated earlier and were therefore established on precisely the same lines as the Edward VI schools, among which they really belong, e.g. Leominster, Walsall, Clitheroe, cf. C. W. Stokes, *Queen Mary's Grammar School, Clitheroe*, I (Chetham Society, 1934), pp. 17, 167–72.

[3] Injunctions were issued in 1547 to impress the duty of maintaining schools on cathedral churches, evidently with the old, unreformed secular cathedrals chiefly in mind. Where no school was kept and there was no other near 'the king's majesty willeth that of the common lands and revenue of this church shall be... maintained perpetually a free grammar school'—a reaffirmation of ancient obligations (Frere, II, p. 138). The Hereford chapter, apparently unwilling so to use its revenues, later attempted to get a reversion of stipends granted to four schools in the county to finance its own (J. Strype, *Life of John Whitgift*, Oxford, 1822, I, p. 215).

[4] Since none of these could be retained a request from the earl of Warwick, lord of the manor, was passed on that a stipend of £10 be reserved for a competent minister to be appointed in due course (*ESR*, II, pp. 207–9).

eighty-five chantry priests in this county had been engaged in any sort of teaching.[1] One at Kingsley was bound by the foundation 'to teach poor men's children of the said parish grammar, and to read and sing'; but at Cannock the incumbent of a priest's service had for thirty years 'kept a grammar school and taught children of the said parish for the most part freely' though 'not bound so to do by any foundation'. None the less in the latter as in the former case a stipend was awarded. The commissioners sent in a memorandum: 'Towns in the said county wherein it is most need to have free schools: Stafford, Wolverhampton, Tamworth, Walsall, Burton-upon-Trent, Leek'. There was an endowed school at Wolverhampton, well administered by the Merchant Taylors' Company. Now backward Walsall was provided with a foundation, completed in 1554. The town of Stafford, which had a small chantry school, was quickly off the mark with representations to Sir Richard Sackville followed up by a petition; lands were granted to endow the school of an annual value of £20 in December 1550, with the requirement that in future two masters be maintained.[2]

One of the places to complain to the county commissioners of loss of an endowment at the dissolution of the monasteries was Cirencester; the parishioners represented that 'with their whole assents, driven thereunto of great necessity', they had converted a priest's service into a school and the incumbent had since very diligently applied himself in teaching children. A stipend was awarded here but no endowment in lands gained.[3] Other schools left without status at the dissolution were, however, the first to be refounded in 1550, when Bruton, Sherborne and Bury received letters patent. The list of sixteen governors in the Bury charter begins with the names of Dr William May, president of Queens' and dean of St Paul's, and Sir Nicholas Bacon, followed by those of three esquires, two gentlemen and nine yeomen.[4] Bury school was shortly provided with statutes which lay down that poor men's

[1] D. P. J. Fink, *Queen Mary's Grammar School, Walsall* (Walsall, 1954), p. 56. It seems a reasonable deduction, from the chantry certificates so far printed, that less than 10 per cent of chantry priests taught.

[2] C. G. Gilmore, *King Edward VI School, Stafford* (Oxford, 1953), pp. 12–14.

[3] *ESR*, II, pp. 84–5. There were no refoundations in Gloucestershire. Schools at Wotton-under-Edge and Chipping Camden were unaffected by the chantries act, as also the borough school of Gloucester and the recently established cathedral school.

[4] *CPR Ed. VI*, III, pp. 191, 192, 436. Of the twenty governors named for Sherborne only three were gentlemen. The Bruton charter, naming two Chekes among the governors, is given in full in Carlisle, II, pp. 412–18.

children be admitted before others and taught without partiality as soundly as the richest.[1]

That an eye was being kept on progress is suggested by a minute of the privy council of 5 June 1552, that the chancellor of augmentations be asked to certify what free schools had been erected.[2] Shortly before this, instructions had been sent to Sackville to proceed with arrangements for refounding St Alban's school and to consider a petition from Bath and give his opinion on it.[3]

St Alban's was finally established in 1553.[4] Bath received a grant of lands which belonged to the former abbey within the town, again with the assistance of the former abbot and a local petition, in July 1552.[5] In August a licence to acquire lands to bring in £40 annually for Bedford school was granted, in response to a petition of the mayor and burgesses. Here a wealthy London merchant, Sir William Harpur, was laying plans to endow the school, a former fellow of New College having been secured as master in 1548.[6]

Totnes received a grant of former monastic property to enlarge the gildhall and provide a prison and school in 1553.[7] The same year Tavistock, where there had formerly been a school in connection with the abbey, began paying £10 to a schoolmaster out of the profits of two yearly fairs granted by letters patent shortly before. This grant, gained with the assistance of the lord of the manor, Francis Russell, who had just succeeded as second earl of Bedford, was towards the relief of the poor and 'about such necessary affairs and doings as shall be most beneficial and profitable to the whole body and commonwealth of the town'.[8] Another town affected by the dissolution of a considerable abbey, though one that had apparently been in poor repair and financial shape, was Abingdon. In 1552 property which had formerly financed the repair of roads and bridges, confiscated under the chantries act, was returned and—with the aid of Sir John Mason,

[1] *VCH Suffolk*, II, pp. 314 ff.

[2] *APC*, IV, p. 68.

[3] *APC*, III, pp. 247–8, 471.

[4] Meanwhile it is recorded that Our Lady's chapel designed for the school was made over to Robert Boreman, former abbot, in consideration of £100, part of £400 to be paid by the inhabitants for this (*APC*, III, pp. 247–8).

[5] *CPR Ed. VI*, IV, pp. 439–40; K. E. Symons, *The Grammar School of Edward VI, Bath* (Bath, 1934), p. 84.

[6] He was still teaching when Harpur formally endowed the school in 1566, J. Sargeaunt, *History of Bedford School* (Bedford, 1925), pp. 4–5; *CPR Ed. VI*, IV, p. 405.

[7] *CPR Ed. VI*, V, pp. 227–8.

[8] H. P. R. Finberg, *Tavistock Abbey* (Cambridge, 1951), pp. 274–5; *CPR Ed. VI*, IV, p. 162.

privy councillor and native of the town—crown lands to the annual value of over £65 were settled to support other public services, the endowment of a Christ's Hospital and maintenance of the school kept in being since the dissolution.[1] Here, as at Bedford, a wealthy merchant completed the refoundation of the school early in Elizabeth's reign.

Schools were established elsewhere by the grant or purchase and settling of former monastic and chantry property without any official refoundation. Marlborough bought back chantry lands and a hospital in 1550 and obtained a licence to hold additional lands for a school, the master to be appointed by the duke of Somerset.[2] Great Yarmouth, following the example of Norwich, obtained a grant of a dissolved hospital for a school in 1551.[3] High Wycombe also obtained a former Augustinian hospital for its school which was initiated in the same year.[4] Lands were bought and settled on former chantry schools at Ilminster and Wellingborough in 1549, at Towcester and Penwortham in 1552, at Little Waltham in Essex in 1553.[5]

Individual benefactors also contributed new foundations. The burgesses of Southampton petitioned for a licence to hold lands to the value of £40 for a school; they had received a legacy of £100 to this end from William Capon, for long master of Jesus and briefly dean of Wolsey's Cardinal College at Ipswich.[6] Tonbridge, which twenty years before had preferred a priory to a school, gained in 1553 a foundation endowed by Sir Andrew Judd, to be under his control during his lifetime and then governed by the Skinners' Company of London.[7]

It was more difficult for remote districts, and smaller places, lacking a corporate organisation or powerful spokesmen to intercede for them, to get results. But schools were secured in a variety of ways in York-

[1] *CPR Ed. VI*, v, pp. 142–3; Richardson, pp. 290–2. The town gained incorporation in 1556.

[2] *CPR Ed. VI*, III, p. 226.

[3] Jordan, *Charities of Rural England*, p. 155.

[4] *VCH Bucks.* II, p. 210; L. J. Ashford and C. M. Howarth, *History of the Royal Grammar School, High Wycombe* (1962), pp. 13–16.

[5] *VCH Somerset*, II, p. 451; Carlisle, II, p. 226; *VCH Northants.* II, pp. 227–8; *VCH Lancs.* II, p. 210; *VCH Essex*, II, p. 553.

[6] *CPR Ed. VI*, v, p. 75. The first master secured had been usher of the school of Winchester College (C. F. Russell, *History of King Edward VI School, Southampton*, 1940, pp. 16–19). Capon had earlier been instrumental in retrieving lands for the town church by appeal to the court of augmentations (*ibid.* p. 2 n.).

[7] *CPR Ed. VI*, v, p. 223; *Records of the Skinners of London*, ed. J. J. Lambert (1933), pp. 177–81.

shire. Besides Sedbergh, refounded in 1551, a school connected with Christ's College, Giggleswick, was refounded in 1553 when Pocklington also received letters patent.[1] At Leeds the former incumbent of a chantry settled lands to endow a school in 1551. Bradford regained the original school lands in 1553 having proved that these had been left solely for a school. Beverley secured lands for the upkeep of minster and school by decree of the court of augmentations in 1552.[2] On the other hand the gild at Ripon brought difficulties on itself by passing off the gild lands as a school endowment to the chantry commissioners; when this came to light the lands were forfeit and only retrieved after considerable trouble and expense in 1553.[3] That same year the inhabitants of Thorne complained that their church was being dismantled, and received a grant of the fabric; twenty inhabitants were appointed wardens of the property threatened by 'certain greedy and malevolent men' and at the same time licensed to acquire lands to the value of £20 for a school in the town.[4] Hull provides an example of a school originally kept by a borough but later endowed in connection with a chantry; a stipend awarded in lieu of this endowment was later augmented by the borough but it did not, as other boroughs had done, secure rights over the school, and this led to some complications later.[5]

When Archbishop Rotherham's little college of four chantry priests was dissolved the two teaching singing and writing were pensioned, the one teaching grammar awarded a stipend. At Acaster where there should also have been three chantry priests teaching, according to the statutes, only one was teaching grammar and he was 'indifferently learned'; none the less he was appointed to continue teaching and also to serve the cure.[6] As for the remaining collegiate foundations—the major ones with schools had fallen in the previous reign—the superstructure of canons, clerks and choristers was removed, all being

[1] *CPR Ed. VI*, IV, pp. 97–9; V, pp. 68, 234.

[2] *VCH Yorks.* I, pp. 428, 457, 471–2.

[3] *Ibid.* p. 433; P. M. Rogers, *History of Ripon Grammar School* (Ripon, 1954), pp. 45–9. By contrast Lancaster seems successfully to have persuaded the commissioners that a water mill had been left to the borough solely to endow the school and not a chantry, though this was not so (A. L. Murray, *The Royal Grammar School, Lancaster*, Cambridge, 1951, pp. 26–7; see also L. P. Wenham, *History of Richmond School, York.*, Arbroath, 1958).

[4] *CPR Ed. VI*, V, p. 278. For the conversion of a chapel into a schoolhouse with the consent of the parish at Almondbury, see Jordan, *Charities of Rural England*, p. 318.

[5] Lawson, pp. 43–6, 48–9.

[6] *ESR*, II, pp. 298–9, 304.

pensioned, and a stipend assigned for a vicar to serve the church, as also where there was one for a master of grammar. Thus the school at Stoke-by-Clare, revived a decade earlier by Matthew Parker when he became dean of the college, had the former stipend of £10 allotted.[1] The lands of collegiate foundations which had made no contribution to education quite often went towards endowing schools, at Shrewsbury and Stafford for example.

No lands were confiscated from the London livery companies which held many allocated as an endowment for chantry priests; instead under the act, the sums payable to the latter were converted into rent charges payable to the crown. In 1550 the companies clubbed together and bought these up in a combined operation at a cost of over £18,000, under pressure from a privy council urgently in need of ready funds.[2] Schools governed by city companies therefore continued as before. And in 1552 the common council of London initiated a remarkable new foundation, Christ's Hospital, with the aid of Bishop Ridley and a grant of the former Franciscan friary from the crown.

To summarise the evidence is to find that there was a refoundation or foundation by letters patent in twenty-three English counties (six having more than one newly constituted school). In six other counties schools were augmented or re-endowed by other means. In Sussex the four main schools fell outside the provisions of the act, so also in Gloucestershire. The remaining counties were Durham and Cumberland where cathedral schools had recently been refounded, Oxfordshire which was served by Magdalen College school and other facilities in Oxford, Derbyshire where Derby school was established in 1555 according to plans initiated in Edward's reign, leaving over Huntingdonshire, Leicestershire and Rutland, Westmorland.

The royal indenture establishing Christ's Hospital commended 'the good and godly endeavours' of the mayor, commonalty and citizens of London to ensure that 'as neither the child in his infancy shall want virtuous education and bringing up, neither when the same shall grow unto full age shall lack matter whereon the same may virtuously

[1] *VCH Suffolk*, II, p. 339.

[2] Ashley, II, pp. 153–4; A. H. Johnson, *History of the Worshipful Company of Drapers of London* (Oxford, 1915), II, p. 100. For a detailed list, see *CPR Ed. VI*, III, pp. 386–401. The companies evidently secured the exemption of endowments for schools; the only one to figure in a long list is that assigned to the Mercers' Company for a priest in Farthingoe church who was also to teach (*ibid.* p. 387).

occupy himself in good occupation or science profitable to the common-weal'. When the hospital first opened its doors in the autumn of 1552, 380 children were taken in from the London streets and parishes; by Christmas, a month later, they could be marshalled for the mayor's procession, lining the roads 'from St Lawrence Lane to Cheape towards St Pauls, all in one livery of russet cotton'.[1] There were two school-masters on the foundation to teach the elements and also a writing master and music master to instruct children up to an age when they were bound apprentice. But those who showed aptitude for learning could be promoted to the grammar school attached to the hospital which, attended also by town boys paying fees, soon became one of the chief London schools.[2] This foundation, an essential link in an organised system of poor relief, served as a model for provincial towns in succeeding decades.

In general the schools officially refounded during this reign mark a new departure in that, following on what had been virtually a national survey of school provision, they were conceived of as units in an educational system serving a protestant nation. The preamble to the royal letters patent reconstituting the school of the Holy Trinity Gild at Louth as the Free Grammar School of King Edward VI 'for the education, institution and instruction of boys and youth' ran:

> We have always coveted with a most exceeding, vehement and ardent desire that good literature and discipline might be diffused and propagated, through all the parts of our kingdom as wherein the best government and administration of affairs consists; and, therefore, with no small earnestness, have we been intent on the liberal institution of youth, that it may be brought up to science, in places of our kingdom, most proper and suitable for such functions; it being, as it were the foundation and growth of our commonwealth.[3]

The statutes of another refoundation, East Retford, illustrate a new trend in the curriculum. Subscribed by Archbishop Holgate they required attendance at divine service in the parish church on every Sunday and holy day and that one of the scholars should read 'the catechism in English openly and distinctly in the body of the said parish church...as well for their own instruction as for the instruction

[1] *Christ's Hospital Book*, pp. 7–8.

[2] It had 157 pupils in 1581, 27 foundationers and 51 town boys in the lower school, 15 foundationers and 64 town boys in the upper school (E. H. Pearce, *Annals of Christ's Hospital*, 1901, pp. 24–6, 65–6).

[3] Carlisle, I, pp. 822–3.

of other young children...in the parish'.[1] The school day was to begin with a psalm and prayer and to close with a short evening prayer. Among the books prescribed are texts familiar from humanist programmes—Erasmus's *Colloquies* and *De Copia*, Cicero's familiar letters, Sallust, Virgil, Ovid; though Terence, not favoured by reformers, is omitted. But scholars were also to be taught 'the scriptures both the Old and New Testament' and the top forms were to study the Greek grammar and authors and Hebrew grammar if the master was 'expert in the same'.

A more ambitious programme which must also date from this period is set out in the statutes for the school at King's Lynn, whose representatives had so stubbornly resisted confiscation of gild lands.[2] Like the statutes of Bury school these enjoin: 'Let rich and poor have the same consideration. Let it be exhibited in teaching and everything else without distinction.' Hebrew is to be taught as well as Greek to the highest of the six forms and the authors prescribed for this stage are Homer, Sophocles and Demosthenes as well as Cicero, Virgil, Sallust, Quintus Curtius, Suetonius. The fifth form was to study Cicero and Caesar, the poems of Horace, Xenophon on the education of Cyrus, some 'orations of Socrates', and 'every Saturday the Greek Testament and Apollinarius's version of David's Psalms rendered into verse for the use of the primitive church and scholars when Julian the Apostate interdicted the poets and heathen authors to Christian children'.

Whether or not this kind of course was followed depended on the calibre of the masters available but at this time there were scholars of reputation teaching school. Alexander Nowell had since 1543 been headmaster of Westminster school where he taught Greek and introduced the regular staging of a play; his brother, Lawrence Nowell, also a scholar and reformer, was master of Sutton Coldfield school. Thomas Cooper, whose revised edition of Elyot's dictionary was to be used in innumerable schools, had become master of Magdalen College grammar school, the previous master having left to start the refounded school at Bruton in 1550. The head of Maidstone borough school in

[1] The catechism referred to was presumably that in the new prayer book. Schoolmasters were required to use this as 'the ground and foundation' of their teaching while bishops were enjoined to visit every school in their diocese annually to ensure it was properly taught and learned. The statutes are given in full in Carlisle, II, pp. 281–7.

[2] These, in the possession of the school, are headed 'Ancient Rules of this Grammar School. In the year 1662 again confirmed.'

1552 was an M.A. from King's, Thomas Cole, one of the more radical reformers.[1]

A new edition of the royal grammar was published in 1549, under the title *Brevissima Institutio*. But this now seemed over long and complex to John Foxe, tutor to the young Howards in the duchess of Richmond's household, and he prepared a brief version in the form of tables, with the help of Leonard Cox and others, particularly for the use of those embarking on Latin late in life; this, sent to William Cecil with a request for assistance, evidently achieved publication.[2] Cecil was also concerned at this time, as he was to be in later years, in securing sound masters for schools; a letter in 1551 from William Turner, recently installed as dean of Wells, promises assistance in getting a recommended master appointed there.[3] It was, incidentally, to Cecil that Ridley looked when unduly pressed by the privy council, for instance, to relinquish for lay purposes a prebend of St Paul's needed for a preacher.[4]

The education of the clergy remained a particular concern of bishops. Archbishop Holgate issued in 1552 a comprehensive educational plan for those of York Minster and also detailed instructions for building up a library as the injunctions of 1547 to cathedrals had required.[5] Other bishops made sustained efforts to raise the standard of the parish clergy for there had been no general removal of incumbents and the task was to instruct all in the reformed religion. Ridley is said to have examined every parson and curate personally and privately in his house, in order to gauge their learning, during his visitation of the diocese of London in May 1550.[6] The fiery Bishop Hooper, surveying the diocese of Gloucester, had note taken of his clergy's accomplishments; an analysis of the return shows that, of 311 examined, 171 could not say the ten commandments, 20 did not know where the Lord's Prayer was to be found, 27 could not name its author and 10 were incapable of repeating it. The bishop proclaimed that, according to St Paul, 'it is not lawful

[1] Tanner, pp. 13–14; *Athenae*, I, p. 357; Stanier, pp. 82–3; Porter, pp. 79–80.

[2] According to one account it was issued as approved by eight members of the privy council (*EGS*, pp. 254–5; J. F. Mozley, *John Foxe and his Book*, 1940, pp. 34–5).

[3] *CSPD 1547–80*, p. 33.

[4] Protesting to Cheke, Ridley urged him to 'speak for God's sake, in God's cause, unto whomsoever you think may do any good withal', naming Sir Thomas Wroth and Cecil who 'I do take for men that do fear God' (Nicholas Ridley, *Works*, Parker Society, 1843, p. 332). The plea seems to have been successful.

[5] Frere, II, pp. 310 ff.

[6] *Ibid.* p. 230.

for any man to sing or say in the church in any kind of tongue other than such as the people shall be able to understand'; it was not sufficient to speak English, there must be 'due and distinct pronunciation'.[1] Hooper enjoined all his clergy to study one book of the bible each quarter and undergo an examination in it, as also to participate in public discussion of doctrinal matters, and appointed superintendents throughout the diocese to ensure these directives were carried out.[2]

An episcopate, headed by Cranmer and including also Scory, the scholarly and radical Ponet and other like minds, was naturally interested in extending elementary instruction in English. The most direct means to this end was to raise the educational standard of the clergy and to provide new aids to teaching. In 1552 a new Latin catechism was published prepared by Bishop Ponet which appeared in English translation the following year.[3] It was issued with injunctions to 'all schoolmasters and teachers of youth' to use it, so that the 'yet unskilful and young age, having the foundations laid, both of religion and good letters, may learn godliness together with wisdom'. The method of teaching embodied was commended as follows:

> This is the plainest way of teaching, which not only in philosophy Socrates, but also in our religion Apollinarius hath used; that both by certain questions, as it were by pointing, the ignorant might be instructed: and the skilful put in remembrance, that they forget not what they have learned.

So the whole catechism was in dialogue form, the master apposing the scholar, the scholar replying. It was on this work that Alexander Nowell based the catechism studied by innumerable schoolboys in the Elizabethan age.

[1] *Ibid.* pp. 270, 308–9. Latimer complained that some called the homilies 'homelies, and indeed so they may be well called, for they are homely handled. For though the priest read them never so well, yet if the parish like them not, there is such talking and babbling in the church that nothing can be heard; and if the parish be good and the priest naught, he will so hack it and chop it, that it were as good for them to be without it, for any word that shall be understood' (*Sermons*, p. 121).

[2] The royal injunctions of 1547 had required all incumbents under the degree of B.D. to get a New Testament in Latin and English and 'diligently study the same, conferring the one with the other' and enjoined bishops to examine 'how they have profited in the study of holy scripture' (Frere, II, p. 122; cf. F. D. Price, 'Gloucester Diocese under Bishop Hooper 1551–3', *Transactions of the Bristol and Glos. Archaeological Society*, LX, 1938).

[3] According to letters patent giving licence to John Day to print, this was 'for the better instruction of youth to be taught in English schools' as had been an 'A.B.C. with the brief Catechism, already printed' (*The Two Liturgies set forth in the Reign of Edward VI*, Parker Society, 1844, pp. 487, 493–5).

In 1553 there were still school foundations formerly connected with a chantry which had not been assigned lands or tenements as an endowment. But they received the income originally given for both chantry and school in the form of a stipend and continued as before; with the important qualification that masters, freed from duties in the church, could give their whole attention to teaching. Other onetime chantry priests had been recognised as schoolmasters, on the strength of past services to teaching, and also drew a stipend from the crown. Among schools which had retained or acquired endowments by various means were all the main gild schools; and a nucleus of well-organised grammar schools, independent of any ecclesiastical institution and administered by lay bodies of governors, had been established by letters patent as Edward VI schools to serve as an example to the rest. There was still much to be done; some administrative muddles had been cleared up but others remained, nor could constructive plans be brought to completion in a few short, and very disturbed, years. But there had been effective steps towards establishing a school system to serve the needs of a protestant nation before the king's death brought abrupt changes and the reforming party disappeared from the English scene.

X

UNIVERSITY REFORM 1549–53

In the *History of Italy*, published in 1549, William Thomas—just returned from Padua, with a considerable reputation, to take up the post of clerk to the council—explained to his countrymen the great superiority of the university there. He stressed particularly the large number of gentlemen among students of all nations; though these attended 'principally under pretence of study' in fact 'all kinds of virtue may there be learned'—the ways of the world, fencing, dancing, riding. In short, Padua was 'furnished not of such students alone, as most commonly are brought up in our universities (mean men's children set to school in hope to live upon hired learning) but for the most part of noblemen's sons, and of the best gentlemen; that study more for knowledge and pleasure than for curiosity or lucre'. After careful computation Thomas had arrived at a figure of nearly fifteen hundred students, 'whereof, I dare say, a thousand at the least were gentlemen'.[1]

Oxford and Cambridge, with not many more students between them, were by comparison mere provincial universities. But since the dissolution of monastic foundations and the Cromwellian innovations they had shed some of their professional atmosphere and were giving more attention to polite learning; some at least of the colleges were more concerned with teaching and now offered facilities for boarding students under supervision. These were attracting considerably more interest than formerly. It was as necessary as ever to train competent officials, at home if possible rather than at universities abroad as had so often been the case in the past. There were also many country gentlemen who had been accustomed to look to the households of abbots and priors to train up sons but were now seeking an alternative; in so doing they lighted on colleges with rooms for hire since the departure of beneficed clergy and monks. The universities had long been used to give an educational grounding by those families in which it was a tradition to enter sons in the law. Men of a reforming turn of

[1] Quoted in Clare Howard, *English Travellers of the Renaissance* (1914), p. 53. The coats-of-arms of gentlemen attending Padua University, hung on the walls of its entrance hall according to nations, may still be seen there.

mind now desired their sons to study whether or not they were to take up a profession. Noblemen had often drawn young scholars from the university to act as tutors but there was the less reason to do this if a boy could be sent to a college where he might have both tutors and the advantage of mixing with others. This last had long been advocated as an important aspect of education and when such as Lord Wentworth, a leading upholder of reform in the ranks of the nobility, sent an heir to Cambridge, the duchess of Suffolk's sons were entered at St John's and a batch of young noblemen—some of them royal wards—was dispatched to Queens' for a time, an example was set which others were likely to follow.[1]

Indeed during the past half century the court and successful statesmen had consistently set an example, the doctrine of education for the gentry had been preached in a variety of ways, the circulation of books had greatly stimulated interests, the events of the day had driven home the need for an informed mind, and even country-bound gentlemen could hardly remain unaffected. No longer did education seem proper only to clerks, preparing to gain a livelihood by their learning; on the contrary it was beginning to be regarded as the prerogative of men of birth. Reformers moreover daily reinforced the argument that gentlemen should prepare themselves to fill offices of state, leaving the clergy free to preach and serve their cures.

On the other hand 'mean men' who had formerly set sons to learning were subject to different pressures. According to the pamphleteers economic stress prevented many a yeoman's son from remaining at school, let alone looking to a university. This apart, during the latter

[1] Lord Wentworth's heir was at St John's at the close of Henry's reign when Francis Russell, heir of the earl of Bedford, was at King's Hall (*Athenae*, I, p. 484; II, p. 532). The young noblemen entered at Queens' were Henry Hastings, heir of the earl of Huntingdon, in 1548; Henry Fitzalan, heir of the earl of Arundel, in 1549, at the age of twelve, with his fifteen-year-old brother-in-law, John, Lord Lumley (whose father had been attainted in 1537); Thomas Howard, heir of the earl of Surrey (executed in 1547), matriculated as fellow commoner in 1550 (*ibid.* III, p. 92; I, p. 548; II, p. 516; III, p. 95). Others entered at St John's in 1549 besides Henry and Charles Brandon were John Manners, second son of the earl of Rutland, with a younger brother (*ibid.* III, p. 43; II, p. 465). The heir of Lord Sheffield succeeded to the title in 1549 when at university and the only son of Lord Willoughby of Parham entered Magdalene in 1551 (*ibid.* I, p. 263; II, p. 387). There were also heirs of statesmen. Thomas Sackville, only son of Sir Richard, was at St John's (*ibid.* II, p. 484). Sir Anthony Denny's heir with a younger brother were at Pembroke in 1551 where they were tutored by Arthur Yeldart, later president of St John's, Oxford (*ibid.* II, p. 267). Sir Thomas Wroth, a strong supporter of reform, entered his heir at St John's in 1553 (*ibid.* II, p. 428).

years of Henry's reign there was little enough to encourage entry to the church. The monasteries were dissolved, the ecclesiastical system under attack, theology necessarily marked time when doctrinal questions were dangerous ground and canon law, a knowledge of which had taken many a young man far, was no longer studied. As the universities emptied there were the less regent masters to teach in the schools and hostels tended to close down so that students who did seek to reside and qualify found it harder to do so. Yet except when there were links between a school and college, as in the case of Sedbergh and St John's—and such links were as yet few—it was only by getting to the university and proving his worth that a poor student, lacking influence, could commend himself for a place on a college foundation. The student who failed to obtain such a place and lacked the support of a patron was hard put to it, at a time of rising prices, to keep his head above water.

This was the background of the sometimes contradictory complaints voiced by Latimer, which expressed a dilemma facing the reforming clergy.[1] Stressing that churchmen should not fill high offices in the state, that gentlemen should be trained for this calling—his particular target being Archbishop Holgate, president of the council of the north—Latimer demanded in January 1548:

> Why are not the noblemen and young gentlemen of England so brought up in knowledge of God and in learning, that they may be able to execute offices in the commonweal? The king hath a great many of wards, and I trow there is a Court of Wards: why is there not a school of the wards, as well as there is a court for their lands? Why are they not set in schools where they may learn?

These were points Starkey had made, but whereas Starkey had advocated specially constituted schools, reserving the universities to scholarship and the church, Latimer went on, 'Or why are they not sent to universities, that they may be able to serve the king when they come to age?' If young gentlemen were properly educated they would not later give themselves to vanities—'the only cause why noblemen be not made lord presidents, is because they have not been brought up in learning'. There was a remedy: 'appoint teachers and schoolmasters, ye that have charge of youth; and give the teachers stipends worthy their pains, that they may bring them up in grammar, in logic, in

[1] It is best to disregard an attempt to explain away the contradictions, which assumes that Latimer could not have meant what he said (Curtis, p. 69 n.).

rhetoric, in philosophy, in the civil law, and in that which I cannot leave unspoken of, the word of God'.[1] But though gentlemen's sons must be trained to rule, yeomen's sons must also be trained to preach, and if the former ousted the latter from the university without applying themselves seriously to study then all was in the melting pot. So, in April 1549 Latimer is exclaiming:

It would pity a man's heart to hear that I hear of the state of Cambridge.... There be few do study divinity, but so many as of necessity must furnish the colleges: for their livings be so small, and victuals so dear, that they tarry not there, but go other where to seek livings; and so they go about. Now there be a few gentlemen, and they study a little divinity. Alas! what is that. It will come to pass that we shall have nothing but a little English divinity, that will bring the realm into a very barbarousness and utter decay of learning. It is not that, I wis, that will keep out the supremacy of the bishop of Rome.

He went on to call on gentlemen, as Brinkelow had earlier called on merchants, to bestow as much in supporting poor scholars as they used to bestow in masses, pardons, 'purgatory-matters', to 'bestow so much godly as ye were wont to bestow ungodly' so that men might be trained for the church. 'It is a reasonable petition; for God's sake look upon it. I say no more. There be none now but great men's sons in colleges and their fathers look not to have them preachers; so every way this office of preaching is pinched at.'[2]

If Latimer overstated the case—by affirming that few studied divinity except those with places in colleges earmarked for the purpose, the others being taken up by gentlemen's sons—at least he was pinpointing a trend. The universities had always attracted the sons of noblemen and gentlemen, that is younger sons destined for the church. Now younger sons of the nobility no longer looked at all to the church since the day of princely prelates had passed.[3] Younger sons of gentlemen, though

[1] *Sermons*, pp. 68–9

[2] *Ibid.* pp. 178–9. Returning to the same point a week later Latimer found the devil at work restricting preaching. 'He stirs men up to outrageous rearing of rents, that poor men shall not be able to find their children at the schools...yea what doth he more? He gets him to the university and causeth great men and esquires to send their sons thither, and put out poor scholars that should be divines' (*ibid.* p. 203).

[3] They did not do so again until the eighteenth century, when the value of church preferments rose considerably and plurality was as rife as in earlier days. 'Our grandees', wrote Bishop Warburton in 1752, 'have at last found their way back into the Church. I only wonder they have been so long about it' (J. H. Plumb, *England in the Eighteenth Century*, 1950, p. 43).

they looked to the same kind of career as before, no longer saw entry to the church as the way to it, since key posts in government and administration were now held by laymen for the most part qualified in the common law. This necessarily had an effect, but more decisive, perhaps, in altering the atmosphere of the universities was the advent, in place of monks and clergy studying in the schools, of gentlemen's heirs who bore themselves as such, studied for 'knowledge and pleasure' and set a new tone. At the same time country gentlemen secured places in colleges for one or two sons, sometimes sent very young with their own tutor as they had formerly been dispatched to monastic houses.[1]

In an oration at the Cambridge commencement in 1547 Walter Haddon, fellow of King's and shortly to become the regius professor of civil law, said of the university he had first entered in 1533, 'never do I remember to have seen it more affluent or more thronged'. But though he welcomed the presence of sons of the nobility and gentry he found it necessary to deplore the prevailing lack of study, even in colleges, while university professors sometimes addressed a single auditor.[2] Roger Ascham, writing to Archbishop Cranmer the same year, gave his reasons for a deterioration in learning at St John's. Cambridge was overfull of mere boys, students now admitted being

> for the most part only the sons of rich men, and such as never intended to pursue their studies to that degree as to arrive at an eminent proficiency and perfection of learning, but only the better to qualify themselves for some places in the state, by a slighter and more superficial knowledge.

Inevitably this was detrimental to learning since the 'drones' kept out the poorer student 'whose whole time was spent in good studies'. Cranmer would have appreciated a point he had himself raised at Canterbury seven years before but Ascham's conclusion about elections

[1] The earliest college register to be kept, that of Caius, provides examples in the admissions of 1564. William, Thomas and Robert Drury, aged fifteen, twelve, eleven, the heir and third and fourth sons of a Suffolk esquire. William Mannock, aged nine, heir of a Suffolk esquire, and Abraham Copwood, son of an Essex esquire, aged twelve, with their tutor, a former fellow of St John's admitted fellow commoner. From the household of Rooke Green, esq., of Sampford, Essex, six boys were dispatched at once; his heir, aged nineteen, and a younger son, aged eleven, the heir of another Essex esquire and three boys of humbler parentage, two of them brothers aged sixteen and fourteen. Of all these only the last took a degree and entered the church (Venn, *Admissions to Caius College*, 1887, pp. 7–10, supplemented by *Biographical History*).

[2] Mullinger, II, pp. 87–8, 96–7.

to scholarships, based on an inside knowledge of college affairs, showed how slender was the hope that ability might be given due weight as against gentility: 'talent, learning, poverty, and discretion avail nothing in a college, when interest, favour, letters from the great, and other irregular influences exert their pressure from without'.[1]

The extent to which pensioners now pressed on the more notable colleges may, perhaps, be gauged by reference to the statutes of Trinity, drawn up in 1549 and modelled on the example and experience of St John's. This large new foundation provided for sixty scholars and the relevant statute limited the number of pensioners to fifty-four (four for the master and one for each fellow) so that they should not predominate and, in their 'rawness', obstruct the progress of the scholar's learning. This was to accept the fact that gentlemen's sons came up young and relatively unqualified, but the measure was, perhaps, a comparatively restrictive one since the 1545 statutes for St John's had permitted thirty-six pensioners as against some twenty-seven scholars on the foundation. If, as Ascham complained, scholars' places were now also awarded to young gentlemen there would have been a very great change in a college whose fellows had recently been able to engage in serious communal scholarship.[2]

The operation of the chantries act helped further to secularise the universities and benefited the colleges. Some were able to buy up parcels of land from dissolved chantries in the town to extend their sites, as formerly they had acquired monastic property. And when chantries within colleges were dissolved the income accrued to the foundation, so implementing the promise to 'augment the universities'; it was intended to go to providing additional scholarships but at Pembroke, and probably elsewhere, it went to augment the stipends of those already on the foundation.[3] Fellows, relieved of the duty of praying for the souls of founders and benefactors, now had more time for scholarly activities and the colleges took on much more of an appearance of lay educational institutions. Moreover, the statutes of Trinity proclaimed that a college should rightly be regarded as a centre for teaching students.

[1] Mullinger, II, pp. 89–90.

[2] There were greater changes to come as demand continued to rise and men did bestow money on endowing more fellowships and scholarships. By 1573 there were 58 fellows and 6 ministers, 78 scholars, 89 pensioners and 46 sizars at St John's (H. F. Howard, *An Account of the Finances of St John's College, Cambridge*, Cambridge, 1935, p. 51).

[3] Attwater, p. 38.

The lectures hitherto provided, at first in some of the newer colleges but under the Cromwellian injunctions in all, had served to supplement the arts course in the university schools and engage fellows in teaching members of their own foundation. In the Trinity statutes recent developments were taken to their logical conclusion under reforming influence.[1] The duty of teaching was placed squarely on college fellows who were required not only to lecture in hall but also to tutor the students registered with them. Each of the sixty scholars on the foundation and all pensioners must on entry register with a tutor, one of the junior fellows, who was responsible for general supervision and collecting payments due to the college as well as educational oversight. Other fellows were assigned as examiners in Greek and Latin, or as preachers whose duty it was to supervise the religious discipline and general conduct of scholars.

The statutes governing fellows' duties illustrate the hierarchical form of organisation which had gradually been developing within colleges. Not only were senior and junior fellows clearly differentiated, but eight of the former had a particular status, constituting the seniority under the master; this included a vice-master, deans responsible for religious discipline, a head lecturer to supervise studies and methods of tuition, and, if they were fellows, the regius professors. Nearly all the sixty fellowships were reserved to M.A.'s who expressed an intention to pursue studies in divinity; only two were reserved to medicine, two to civil law. This college, so settled, was almost half as rich again as King's and three times as wealthy as St John's, both of which far outpaced other colleges. But unlike King's it was closely integrated with the university and acted as a model to which other colleges, including later foundations, approximated.[2]

[1] The original Trinity statutes, writes Mullinger, 'are especially remarkable for the completeness of the organization for which they provide and the minuteness of their instructions with respect to details—characteristics justified by the theory on which the whole scheme had been conceived, as that of a foundation which, in the words of dean Peacock, "gave the first complete example of the separation of domestic and collegiate, from academical, public, and professional instruction"' (II, p. 139, citing George Peacock, *Observations on the Statutes of the University of Cambridge*, 1841, p. 35, where the detailed scheme of instruction is also outlined, pp. 5–12).

[2] Mullinger, II, pp. 138–43. Trinity seems shortly to have provided nearly a quarter of the university body. The number of members of the college in 1564 has been given as 305 as against a university total of 1267; the corresponding figures in 1583 being 393 and 1813—in which year there were 277 at St John's (W. W. R. Ball, *Trinity College*, 1906 p. 51).

The settlement of Trinity was a postscript to the full visitation of Cambridge University which took place in the spring of 1549. The visitors were all Cambridge men, including those who had been prominent in the advancement of scholarship and the propagation of reform.[1] The new code of statutes the visitors brought with them was presented to the university over the signatures of the privy council. It was accompanied by a letter which characterised the ancient statutes as 'antiquated, semi-barbarous and obscure' and underlined the need to drive out the darkness of ignorance and let in the light of true learning. 'It appertains to the kingly office', ran the introductory paragraphs, not only to protect and defend the people against foreign enemies 'but also to increase the same in virtue, to cultivate by learning' and, eliminating so far as possible that rustic and crude behaviour which is the companion of ignorance, 'to adorn and amplify with humanity and the sciences'.[2]

The new statutes envisaged the raising of standards and the recasting of the university curriculum. In particular, at a time when steps were being taken to establish grammar schools throughout the country, all grammar teaching was excluded from the universities. College authorities were enjoined to examine all entrants to ensure that they had reached the standard in Latin necessary if they were to profit from study of arts.[3] There was also to be no more teaching of logic on traditional lines. Instead the arts course outlined began with a year's study of mathematics; that is, cosmography, arithmetic, geometry,

[1] They were Nicholas Ridley (bishop of Rochester but still master of Pembroke), John Cheke (of the king's household appointed provost of King's the previous year), Dr William May (president of Queens', dean of St Paul's and master of requests), Sir Thomas Smith (now provost of Eton and a secretary of state, of the privy council); also of the privy council were the technical head of the visitorial body, Thomas Goodrich, former fellow of Jesus now bishop of Ely, and Sir William Paget, once of Trinity Hall now controller of the king's household; the remaining member being Dr Thomas Wendie, once of Gonville Hall, physician to the king (Mullinger, II, p. 110). It will be noted that of seven members only three were in orders. The fact that in Elizabeth's first visitorial body churchmen outnumbered laymen by five to four has been cited as a remarkable example of erastianism (Curtis, pp. 24–5).

[2] J. Heywood (ed.), *Collection of Statutes for the University and the Colleges of Cambridge* (1840), pp. 3–4.

[3] 'No one is to teach grammar in any college, except in Jesus College only. In every college the master, the dean, and the public lecturer are to examine each person to be admitted...before his first entering, whether he knows grammar perfectly or not', in order that none be admitted without 'sufficient proficiency in it for the learning of mathematics and dialectics' (*ibid.* pp. 31–2). The grammar school originally attached to Trinity disappeared at this point (Ball, *Cambridge Papers*, pp. 15–17).

astronomy, the texts enumerated being Pliny, Strabo, Ptolemy and Euclid, Cardan and Cuthbert Tunstall's new arithmetic. Study of mathematics was much stimulated at this time by the interest of court circles in overseas exploration. Cheke dispatched to King's from court a former fellow of the college, William Buckley, tutor to the royal pages and noted as a mathematician, to teach arithmetic and geometry; he also distributed copies of Euclid at his own expense, with a text of Xenophon that Greek might not be forgotten, at both King's and St John's.[1]

The second year of the arts course was to cover dialectic and rhetoric, with texts of Aristotle, Cicero, Quintilian and Hermogenes. Two years reading philosophy, still mainly Aristotle but supplemented by Pliny or Plato, completed the course leading to the bachelor's degree. Then the intending master of arts must study further in philosophy, astronomy, Greek. Greek studies were to cover grammar and syntax—an indication that Greek had not yet taken root in the grammar schools—and such authors as Homer, Demosthenes, Isocrates, Euripides. Masters of arts who had completed their period of teaching in the university schools—now increased to three years, presumably because of the continuing shortage of regent masters—must take up divinity and Hebrew, unless they were entering the faculties of medicine or civil law. The course for the bachelor of law was six years, with two more for the doctorate, and lecturers were required to cover not only traditional texts but also the forthcoming ecclesiastical laws of the kingdom, which Cranmer was in process of drafting. For those studying medicine the texts were still Hippocrates and Galen, but the bachelor must perform two anatomies and effect three cures before being admitted to practice and witness three more anatomies before qualifying for a doctorate. Those studying divinity must attend a theological lecture daily, dispute twice on theological questions and preach twice in Latin and once in English in St Mary's Church.

While the method of disputation was retained in all faculties, public theological disputations were to take place once a fortnight; during the visitation itself there were some notable sessions in which Ridley took a prominent part.[2] But ancient ceremonies and public processions

[1] Mulcaster, *Positions*, p. 241. Nearly all the Elizabethan mathematicians were at Cambridge; Mulcaster's interest derived from Buckley's tuition at King's, John Dee was fellow of Trinity from its foundation though he also studied abroad, Leonard Digges's son Thomas was at Queens' throughout this reign.

[2] Foxe, VI, pp. 305–35.

associated with catholicism were forbidden as also the custom of electing a 'lord of misrule' in each college at Christmas. There were the usual injunctions, common in earlier years, about student discipline and behaviour—no dicing, card playing (except at Christmas), fencing, nor idling about the town.

In university government there were no fundamental changes. Though within colleges masters, instead of being *primus inter pares*, were being accorded greater powers, in the university at large heads of houses had no special status but continued to rank according to academic degree. Officers of the university and regent masters continued to elect the vice-chancellor but a change was made in election to the chancellorship which was devolved on the whole university body including non-regents. A section of the code bore directly on the internal affairs of colleges laying down regulations designed both to improve education and curb abuses in elections, handling of funds, disposition of offices. In particular it was clearly enjoined that 'in the election of fellows and scholars, the sons of poor persons, being apt and of good abilities, are to be preferred to the sons of rich and powerful persons'[1]—a notable change of emphasis from that of Cranmer in 1540, though the difficulties of enforcement remained.

Any college statutes which conflicted with the new code were declared void, but the visitors also examined colleges individually, thoughtfully timing their visits so that a poor college was not put to the charge of entertainment.[2] At Pembroke Hall a lecturer in logic and philosophy was established on whom, with the master and dean, it devolved to examine candidates for entrance, in accordance with the new statutes. At Christ's the visitors settled claims for endowments which had long been outstanding and for one which was not honoured the college received a recompense from the king which allowed for the appointment of an additional fellow and three more scholars.[3]

A considerable time was spent in revising and amending the statutes of older colleges, such as Peterhouse and Jesus whose foundation had

[1] Heywood, p. 34.

[2] There is an account of their progress from one to another (Lamb, pp. 109–20).

[3] Attwater, p. 39; Peile, p. 53. The king also made dispositions to reimburse St John's for the loss of its original endowment many years before by granting lands yielding £100 per annum, but this was not effected (Strype, *Ecc. Mem.* II, ii, p. 22). Nor was his intention, as expressed in a draft will, to endow a new college; the plan for this 'Edward's College' survives providing for a master, twenty-three fellows and twenty-eight scholars (*CSPD 1547–80*, p. 17).

preceded the innovations at the turn of the century. A list of inmates of the latter at this time suggests that the pressure for places must as yet have been mainly on colleges with a reputation such as St John's and Queens'. Besides the eight fellows and five or six scholars on the foundation the only other residents were five graduates (one the former prior of Barnwell who farmed some of the priory's former property in Cambridge) and five other students. Not only seniors but also some of the scholars had a room to themselves and nine chambers remained empty, whereas colleges that were sought after had three or four to each chamber. But from now on Jesus, which had received no benefactions since 1519, began to expand. In 1547 two fellowships and two scholarships were added, in 1551 one fellowship and eight scholarships, in 1558 four further fellowships—so that within little more than a decade places on the foundation had more than doubled. The same development began to take place in other older colleges.[1]

Much time was, however, taken up with one specific directive, that two colleges—Trinity Hall and Clare Hall—be dissolved and in their place with their endowments a college be erected devoted to civil law.[2] With this, it was envisaged, there would be connected a permanent body of civil lawyers in London which could be at the privy council's disposal. Evidently much importance was attached to this project; a bill to amalgamate the two colleges had indeed been introduced in the Commons at an earlier stage but it had failed to pass,[3] perhaps through the influence of common lawyers who tended to react against any plan to extend the sphere of civil law. Objections now came from the master of Trinity Hall, Bishop Gardiner, confined in the Tower for contumacy in matters of religion; the two colleges once dissolved, he suggested, the next step might never be taken and in any case Trinity Hall already provided as many civil lawyers as were required.[4] Possibly this resistance prompted a change of plan for the visitors were eventually

[1] Arthur Gray, *Jesus College, Cambridge* (1902), pp. 48–9, 60. At Gonville Hall there were, in 1540, five scholarships and nine fellowships, and after Caius' refoundation in 1558, twenty-eight scholarships and twelve fellowships (Venn, *Biographical History*, III, pp. 213–18, 225–32). But not all resources were cultivated; St Catharine's had only eighteen resident in 1558 and endowment of this college only begins in 1587 (W. H. S. Jones, *A History of St. Catharine's College*, Cambridge, 1936, pp. 75, 234). For the original statutes of this college and the Edwardian visitors' revision, *ibid.* pp. 339 ff.

[2] Mullinger, II, p. 133. On the same pattern as Trinity College had replaced Michaelhouse and King's Hall.

[3] *Commons Journals*, pp. 6, 7.

[4] Thomas Fuller, *History of the University of Cambridge* (1840), p. 242.

required to dissolve only Clare and amalgamate it with Trinity Hall. This proposal in turn met with strong objections from the master and fellows concerned; declaring that they would all be forced out of their places, they sold off the college library and made dispositions to sell the plate and divide the proceeds.[1]

Faced with these objections the visitors reported back to the council while Ridley, who had not been informed of the plan in advance, wrote personally to Somerset stressing the dangers of converting a college founded for the study of God's word to study of men's laws. Clare, he said, had sent out many worthy men, not the least of whom was Latimer who was doing yeoman service against the papists; Alexander had spared a city for Homer's sake and Latimer was greater than any poet. The reply took the form of an order to proceed with the matter, but Ridley wrote again asking leave to abstain in accordance with his conscience.[2]

To this Somerset replied on 10 June. 'We would be loth any thing should be done by the king's majesty's visitors, otherwise than right and conscience might allow and approve; and visitation is to direct things to the better, not the worse, to ease consciences not to clog them.' But, as Ridley must surely know, the plan was not new; the uniting of the colleges had been proposed under Henry VIII (as Sir Edward North could tell) to provide places for scholars financed from the cathedral churches who were to study law. This had not been achieved, and the number of places for lawyers had diminished; it was not a case, as Ridley seemed to fear, of reducing places for divinity students since more of these were being provided, as at Trinity. 'If in all other colleges where lawyers be by the statutes or by the king's injunctions ye do convert them, or the more part of them, to divines, ye shall rather have more divines upon this change than ye had before.' 'We are sure', Somerset added, 'you are not ignorant how necessary a study that study of civil law is to all treaties with foreign princes and strangers, and how few there be at this present to do the king's majesty's service therein.' The council 'would the increase of divines, as well as you' but 'necessity compelleth us also to maintain the science'. Ridley might do as he would about abstaining from the decision so long as he

[1] Maldon, pp. 82–4; Wardale, pp. 42, 47–9. A running report on the visitation was forwarded to Sir Thomas Smith in London by the visitors' registrar, William Rogers, fellow of Queens'; all the correspondence is briefly calendared (*CSPD 1547–80*, pp. 14–18).

[2] Mullinger, II, p. 136; Ridley, pp. 327–30.

did not hinder the king's proceedings but took thought for the quiet promotion of the visitation in ways conducive to the 'glory of God and benefit of that university'.[1]

Ridley was subsequently recalled, though his colleagues urged he might remain until the visitation was concluded. But soon after, with the uprisings of that summer, the visitation was suspended and the amalgamation of colleges was not again attempted. Since the original university statutes had assumed a new college of civil law, amending ordinances were issued which indicate that there were still hostels—notably Nicholas Hostel—which catered mainly for civil lawyers, and these were required to concentrate on this study.[2] Later, in August 1551, a new set of statutes was drawn up for Clare; these, which again insist on teaching functions, indicate that the arts course was now covered in colleges. 'For the right administration of the college, care must especially be taken that certain persons be appointed to instruct the youth'; to this end six lecturers should be appointed, four in logic and sophistry, two to teach rhetoric and Latin literature and Greek. The first four should lecture daily, immediately after prayers, in the college hall, each having his own class appointed to him at the outset of the year; for the first three-quarters of an hour the class should be examined, then an author should be expounded for half an hour. Similar directives were laid down for lectures in 'polite' literature and the Greek language; all scholars who had learned Greek grammar were to attend the college Greek lecture except those appointed to attend the one in the university schools. There were also to be disputations in the college hall during term and declamations were to be held immediately after supper twice weekly, on Saturdays in Latin and on Tuesdays in English—a notable innovation.[3]

The Oxford visitation took place later in the year and was once more conducted mainly by Richard Cox, though there was a full commission on which Oxford men were conspicuously few.[4] Here instructions

[1] *Ibid.* pp. 505–6.

[2] Heywood, pp. 37–8. For the rest the project remained to be carried out in Elizabeth's reign when in 1567 Doctors' Commons was established in London under the aegis of Trinity Hall (Maldon, pp. 103 ff.).

[3] James Heywood (ed.), *Early Cambridge University and College Statutes* (1855), II, pp. 161–71. These statutes were subscribed by Goodrich, Cheke, May and Wendie, as was the Trinity code; for the Pembroke code, subscribed by Ridley, Cheke and May, *ibid.* pp. 179–97.

[4] It was headed by the earl of Warwick, Ridley and Paget provided a link with the Cambridge commission, and there were two educated at Oxford, William Petre of the

were evidently similar to those of the previous reign. All Souls was to be transformed into a college of civil law, New College confined to arts and divinity; but though fellows of the latter were enjoined not to enter on civil law and directives may have had their effect during the remainder of the reign they did not outlast it.

There was much outcry over the question of removing choristers from colleges and grammar teaching from the university, in particular as it related to Magdalen and its school. The college, assuming that it would lose both the demies' places on the foundation for those studying grammar and the school, protested to the privy council; the townsmen of Oxford joined their pleas, arguing that the school was a 'singular treasure, help and commodity for the education of their sons'—indeed, though this was stretching a point, 'the only school of all the shire'. The visitors had merely been trying to do what had been done at Cambridge, keep places in colleges for those qualified for university studies and relegate grammar teaching to grammar schools, as they explained to the privy council:

> We thought it good to give this injunction because it seemed not convenient that grammarians should be nourished in any college to the trouble of students and hindrance of their study, but that in every college such grammarians be converted into logicians to the intent that both the children taught in Magdalen school and other grammar schools in the realm should be encouraged unto better learning, having rooms provided for them in the university.

All this had been explained, the visitors added, but the college continued blindly to protest, maintaining 'with false surmise that we should dissolve the school, and diminish their number of students to the number of fifty or sixty, which was never intended nor thought upon'.[1] Though Magdalen may have won its point the university statutes laid down that grammar teaching was the task not of universities but of schools, while as at Cambridge the subjects and authors to be studied, time-tables to be followed and so on were set out in detail;

privy council and Richard Morison still public servant and ambassador. Those present at the visitation were Henry Holbeach (onetime prior of Buckingham College, newly elected bishop of Lincoln), Simon Heynes (former president of Queens' now dean of Exeter), Christopher Nevinson (a Cambridge civil lawyer) and Cox (Mallet, II, pp. 82–3).

[1] Frere, II, pp. 228–9 n. This was evidently missed by the historian of Magdalen school who, remarking that 'why any one wanted the school suppressed has never been explained', suggests nepotism on the part of Cox (Stanier, p. 86). The average age of the demies in the college later rose (*ibid.* p. 95).

indeed the two codes were fundamentally the same, only minor variations resulting from injunctions promulgated on the spot during the visitations.

Some fellows had fled before the visitors' approach and for these substitutes were provided while, as at Cambridge, some heads of houses were eventually replaced. But Lincoln and Exeter remained conservative strongholds and also, if to a lesser extent, Balliol, Merton, All Souls now shorn of its chantry observances and more like an educational institution. New College was divided between strong reformers and equally determined opponents but Magdalen had many ardent young adherents of reform.[1] Because there was more conflict at Oxford there was more violent action in stripping chapels of ornaments, libraries of manuscripts, instigated not by the visitors but as a result of internal dissensions; even the duke of Gloucester's collection, which had formed the core of the university library, was dispersed.[2]

Though it is unlikely that the university was as popular as Cambridge, which figured as the nursery of statesmen and churchmen of the day, numbers now evidently increased; in the summer of 1552 an assessment of masters, bachelors and others gave a figure of 761 in the colleges (nearly 200 more than seven years before) and 260 in the halls.[3] There was, however, no new model college like Trinity for Christ Church was never accorded any statutes but left under the control of the dean and chapter. As it eventually developed there were one hundred 'studentships', twenty for theologians who must take orders, forty for those studying philosophy, forty for younger scholars, or disciples; the income of £2000 supported in addition canons, chaplains, lay clerks, choristers, eight of each with other officials required by a cathedral church. Pensioners were also admitted here from the outset and though only four are recorded for 1547, when the foundation in this form was barely established, by 1553 there were nine 'high commoners' and eighteen 'second commoners' while young gentlemen from Broadgates Hall came over for tuition.[4] It was largely by this

[1] Lawrence Humfrey took his B.A. from here in 1549. Some fellows tried to secure the election of William Turner, formerly of Pembroke, as president in 1550 but Walter Haddon was appointed (*CSPD 1548–70*, pp. 31–3).

[2] Mallet, II, pp. 89–91.

[3] Magdalen is credited with 138, Christ Church with 131, New Inn Hall with 49, Hart Hall and Broadgates Hall with over 40 apiece (*ibid.* p. 94).

[4] *Ibid.* p. 41. At Queen's there were twelve not on the foundation in 1552; there were twenty in 1565, forty in 1570, seventy in 1581 (R. H. Hodgkin, *Six Centuries of an Oxford College*, Oxford, 1949, pp. 71–2).

means that the colleges, now grown richer, gained control over the remaining halls at either university which had latterly suffered from the fall in numbers. Already, or within the next few years, Merton had gained control of St Alban Hall, Exeter of Hart Hall, Oriel of St Mary Hall, New College of New Inn Hall, Queen's of St Edmund Hall.[1] Magdalen controlled the hall that had grown up in connection with its grammar school until this, reversing the current trend, attained an independent status as Magdalen Hall.

There was not heavy pressure to conform at this period. The emphasis was rather on education and persuasion and, as a result, upholders of the old order in the church could without prejudice engage openly in disputation on key tenets and need only make so much show of conformity as enabled them to keep their places. Back in the 1530's, Cranmer and Cromwell had together arranged to send teachers of sound doctrine to the universities; one of Melanchthon's followers, the Scottish reformer Alexander Alane, had been sent to Cambridge, only to meet with such violent opposition in the schools that he soon withdrew. With later measures members of the universities, like others, had been swept along, hardly recognising the full significance of the steps taken, for practical demands were made without allowing debate on the underlying questions. After 1539 there was, for all but the reforming party, a comfortable reaffirmation of former practices allowing for an assumption that, whatever the course in matters of state, there would be no fundamental doctrinal change. When, therefore, from the outset of Edward's reign radical change was forecast there seems to have been a new gathering of forces at the universities to oppose it, a hardening of opinion made all the more easy by the methods adopted.

So convinced was Cranmer of the truth and reasonableness of reformed doctrine—however much controversy there might be about particular points—that it only seemed to him necessary to make this truth plain, by clear exposition, for it to be generally acclaimed. He therefore once more put trust in preaching and teaching, in free discussion, the kind of policy Somerset also upheld.[2] This time the

[1] A. B. Emden, *An Oxford Hall*, Oxford, 1927, p. 260.

[2] Richard Morison expressed much the same view, writing to the privy council from Augsburg of catholic attitudes in France: 'They, whose religion standeth only by sufference and silence, cannot abide that it should come to a trial. Their doctrine hath no metal in it able long to abide the hammer of learned disputation' (*CSP Foreign*, p. 100).

teachers sent to the universities were not Lutherans but rather men who adhered to the more advanced doctrines promulgated by Zwingli and his successor as leader of the Swiss churches, Bullinger. So it was that Peter Martyr, arriving in Oxford as regius professor of divinity in 1549, expounded Zwinglian doctrine on the eucharist, only to raise an uproar similar to that Alane had once raised at Cambridge.

To Cambridge, as Lady Margaret professor of divinity, went a man who had been one of the leading reformers at Strasburg and taught in the reformed school there; a man who had long worked for union between the reformed churches, helped Melanchthon compile the liturgy on which the English book of common prayer was based, and, like Melanchthon, remonstrated with Henry VIII for his fall from grace in 1539. Martin Bucer arrived at the university in November 1549, when the new statutes were in force. But what forcibly struck him was that many college fellows, in foundations endowed for the education of the clergy, remained on after taking degrees without performing any positive service to learning or the church. Commenting on this in a treatise addressed to the young king on the occasion of the new year, he concluded that such men were like monks and friars, occupying places to the exclusion of needy and deserving students, and exhorted them to depart.[1] This stricture should probably be considered in conjunction with remarks made in a private letter to Calvin in Geneva a few months later, in which Bucer says the work of reformation goes very slowly, among the clergy and so at large. 'You are well aware', he writes, 'how little can be effected for the restoration of the kingdom of Christ by mere ordinances and the removal of instruments of superstition', and goes on to say that in Cambridge colleges 'by far the greater part of the fellows are either most bitter papists, or profligate epicureans, who, as far as they are able, draw over the young men to their way of thinking, and imbue them with an abhorrence of sound Christian doctrine and discipline'. For this reason the colleges, despite good endowments and statutes, did not send out 'swarms of faithful ministers' as they should.[2]

It was with the unregenerate that Bucer often had to contend in disputations in the schools and the result was not always edifying. But he also lectured, and taught privately. In the event he was only

[1] Mullinger, II, pp. 119–20.

[2] *Original Letters relative to the English Reformation*, ed. H. Robinson (Parker Society, 1847), II, pp. 546–7.

in Cambridge for little more than a year, since he died there in February, 1551, but his influence was profound. It was supplemented by others who came, also chiefly by Cranmer's agency, to advance study of the learned languages. John Tremellius, another teacher from Strasburg, lectured in Hebrew from 1549 to the close of the reign. Francis Encinas, pupil of Melanchthon, of a noble Spanish family, was Greek reader for most of 1549. Anthony Chevallier, a French nobleman who had learned Hebrew in Paris and was well known to Bucer, taught the language at Cambridge for several years and, also acted as French tutor to the Princess Elizabeth.[1] Bartholomew Traheron, a Cornishman, a friar turned reformer who had gone into exile at Zurich after 1540, taught at both universities and held the appointment of librarian to the king. Other Cambridge men forced into exile in the final years of Henry's reign had also returned, but mostly to take up influential positions; Miles Coverdale and John Hooper became first royal chaplains then bishops, William Turner physician and chaplain to Somerset before becoming dean of Wells.

The visiting teachers contributed considerably to advancing both learning and Reformation principles; their reputation and the disputations that took place on matters of key interest certainly added to the university's attractions. But all this did little to improve the position of the university schools. Bucer, in his inaugural lecture, underlined the need to maintain the standard and probity of degree courses and examinations; there were, he warned, universities in Germany where degrees might be bought for money and this had brought about their ruin as centres of learning.[2] Men of rank had long been able to buy degrees at English universities, in so far as a customary contribution made up for failure to perform the necessary exercises and reside for the required period. But the problem at this time was rather that numbers proceeding to degrees remained low. The total number recorded as admitted bachelor of arts in the six years of Edward's reign was 196 by comparison with 191 in the previous six years when the university had been at a low ebb.[3]

That academic exercises were neglected did not mean that no education was going on nor that higher studies were altogether left

[1] *Athenae*, I, pp. 292, 425. The latter afterwards taught Hebrew at the Geneva academy, returning to Cambridge in 1569; one of his then scholars, Hugh Broughton, wrote that 'men might learn more of him in a month, than others could teach in ten years' (*ibid.* pp. 306–7).

[2] Mullinger, II, p. 120.

[3] *Ibid.* pp. 88 n., 101 n.

aside. But here it must be noted that leading scholars seem to have spent a considerable time tutoring young noblemen; Henry and Charles Brandon, the young sons of the duchess of Suffolk—whose untimely death shortly after that of Bucer greatly stirred the university—were taught by Walter Haddon, the professor of civil law, by Traheron, by Bucer himself. Moreover, masters of colleges were often taken up with outside affairs and could only keep an eye on their charge from afar. Lever was a popular preacher, Ridley was never at Pembroke except when he resided during the visitation, nor was Cheke much at King's, while others were often away engaged in discussion of the new liturgy, or, like May of Queens', working on the codification of ecclesiastical laws. Leading fellows were likewise called upon. When Edmund Grindal was appointed one of Ridley's chaplains he had duties away from Pembroke and in 1550 Ascham left St John's again to join a mission to Germany led by Richard Morison.

When, in December 1550, Lever preached at Paul's Cross against 'wicked mammon' he had particular strictures to make about treatment of the universities. King Henry had done much for them, he said, relieving them of taxation, confirming their privileges, founding a notable college; but those responsible for carrying out his designs had cheated Cambridge by diverting lands and substituting impropriations.[1] It had been the chief fault of monasteries, for which they had been put down, that they held so many impropriated churches to the detriment of the parish clergy and preaching; yet, the monasteries gone, impropriations continued and the laity thrust them back as endowments on bishoprics and colleges in place of lands which they coveted for themselves, when it was the primary duty of reform 'to restore and give again all such things as have been wrongfully taken and abused'. Why, Lever asked, 'did God cause the abbeys to be destroyed but for papistical abuses? And why should not God plague the universities and bishops keeping and meddling with impropriations that be the same papistical and devilish abuses?' The universities and bishops were, indeed, to be plagued in future on this account, by temporal critics.

Lever did not mince words about losses at Cambridge. He may have had in mind the disappearance of Michaelhouse and the Physwick

[1] Lever made a scarcely veiled reference to Sir Edward North, formerly treasurer then chancellor of the court of augmentations, implying he had taken money from the university for what should have been a free gift from the king (Willis Clark, p. 9; Baker, I, pp. 132–3). And a clear accusation that Trinity should have been endowed with lands but impropriations had been substituted (*Sermons: 1550* (1895), pp. 91 ff.).

Hostel—where there had been upwards of forty scholars and of which the reformer Edward Crome had once been so excellent a principal—to make way for Trinity; but no doubt other halls or hostels had disappeared in the course of speculation in property. 'Before you did begin to be disposers of the king's liberality towards learning and poverty', he told attendant statesmen and officials, with heavy irony, there were 'in houses belonging unto the university of Cambridge, two hundred students of divinity, many very well learned; which be now all clean gone, house and man, young toward scholars, and old fatherly doctors, not one of them left'. Not only this, but a hundred other scholars who 'having rich friends or being beneficed men did live of themselves in hostels and inns be either gone away, or else fain to creep into colleges and put poor men from bare livings'. With all these gone there were only a few 'poor godly diligent students' remaining in colleges and these were 'not able to tarry and continue their study in the university for lack of exhibition and help'. Yet these, affirmed Lever, echoing Latimer and Ascham, were the only ones devoted to study; some worked from four in the morning until ten at night, sustained only by porridge and broth, without even fires to warm them, so they had 'to walk or run up and down half an hour to get a heat on their feet when they go to bed'.

Whatever reformers might say about the abuse of good intentions, the continued contumacy of many college fellows, the hardships of the poor student, there were young men at the universities at this time who received a basic education of a kind which influenced their whole outlook. In 1547 Thomas Cartwright matriculated as sizar at Clare Hall, passing on later to St John's; one of the devoted students of whom Lever spoke, he studied day and night, never allowing himself more than five hours' sleep.[1] Another young scholar entered Pembroke Hall at this time, where his tutor was John Bradford, brought in by Ridley and like Ridley to go to the stake for his beliefs in a few years; John Whitgift, though he was eventually Cartwright's greatest opponent, nevertheless always retained the mark of his early introduction to protestant doctrine. So did others, including young gentlemen from families which begin at this period to stand out as strong upholders of reform and were later patrons of puritans.[2] Even to those at school

[1] *Athenae*, II, p. 360.

[2] Many such names first figure in this reign (Knappen, p. 102). Francis Walsingham was at King's from 1548 to 1550 (Conyers Read, *Mr. Secretary Walsingham*, Oxford, 1925, I, pp. 15 ff.).

the same applied. 'I thank God my life hath been such among men, as I am neither ashamed to live, nor fear to die', wrote the historian and schoolmaster William Camden in his old age, 'being secure in Christ my saviour in whose true religion I was born and bred in the time of King Edward VI and have continued firm therein.' There were many who could say the same.[1]

The colleges of Winchester and Eton, specifically exempted from the chantries act, were also reformed by visitation during the reign. Like those at the universities they were freed from observing obits and permitted to retain the lands which had formerly endowed these and chantries. At Winchester, where it was often complained that the revenues were barely enough to support the society and there were many chantries, this marked a turning point towards a future of greater ease and prosperity. The college, visited in 1549 by a small commission, headed by the lawyer Sir James Hale, was required to regulate abuses in administration of the school and promote teaching according to reformed doctrine. The bible should be 'daily read in English distinctly and apertly at dinner and supper', and all graces and prayers 'henceforth said or sung evermore in English'. All scholars should study Erasmus's catechism on Sundays, all able to do so should buy a New Testament in English and Latin, read it on Sunday and be examined on what they had read by the warden or schoolmaster. When profane authors were read any opinions contrary to the Christian religion must be refuted. There should be four bibles in the church which boys might borrow for hall or school.[2] The statutes of the college only allowed for ten resident commoners, though boys living or lodging in the town might attend the school on payment of fees, and this number had rarely been exceeded, but from now on Winchester attracted more young gentlemen—including not a few who demanded free places on the foundation as kindred of the founder.[3]

At Eton there had probably been an increase in the number of

[1] *Original Letters of Eminent Literary Men*, p. 125. If he was no great age in King Edward's reign Camden received his first education in what was particularly Edward's school, Christ's Hospital.

[2] Frere, II, p. 151; T. F. Kirby, *Annals of Winchester College* (1892), pp. 26–7, 265.

[3] Kirby, pp. 110–16. One historian of the college infers that exemption from the chantries act, and so retention of the collegiate superstructure, was disastrous. 'For three hundred years after the Reformation Winchester as a *school* has no history to relate of any public significance'; the history is one of warden and fellows exploiting revenues as well as founder's kin seeking free facilities (J. D'E. Firth, *Winchester College*, Winchester, 1949, pp. 35, 56).

commoners since the dissolution of the monasteries. It was now further transformed by the disappearance of chantry chaplains and the advent of the new provost, Sir Thomas Smith, elected at the request of Somerset though he was not in orders. Smith created a small revolution, such as Oxford and Cambridge colleges were to experience many years on, by introducing his wife into the college, an example promptly followed by several fellows. The provost's quarters were altered to make them fit for a lay statesman and he was allowed £100 a year for the diet of his household while some £60 was found from college funds to maintain his stable. Though Eton came within the purview of the Cambridge commissioners Smith managed to stave off a visitation of what he evidently regarded as personal territory until 1552; some of the visitors then made a brief descent but shortly after a dispute prompted the appointment of an influential committee of inquiry. There is no record of the outcome except for a note in the young king's journal: 'The duke of Northumberland, the marquis of Northampton, the lord chamberlain, Mr secretary Petre, and Mr secretary Cecil, ended a matter at Eton College between the master and fellows and also took order for the amendment of certain superstitious statutes'.[1] But the headmaster of the school during this reign, William Barker, was a married man who was lenient towards his scholars and also qualified to teach Greek.[2]

In 1553 a decisive step was at length taken to remove 'dissent of opinion'; members of the universities were required formally to subscribe to the newly promulgated Forty-Two Articles when proceeding to an M.A. or degrees in divinity or before teaching in the schools. The Cambridge visitors, forwarding this order to the vice-chancellor, underlined that it was 'only right that those who had given themselves up to the study of letters and were occupied in the investigation of truth should profess that discipline which was most useful for living and most consistent with the word of God in its judgments'.[3] Little more than a month later, Edward VI was dead.

Fully implicated in the attempt to secure a protestant succession, besides standing condemned for their teaching and preaching over the past years, leading reformers at Cambridge in common with many others were forced to go into hiding or take refuge from certain retaliation abroad. By no means all went into exile; Matthew Parker

[1] Lyte, *Eton*, pp. 125–36, 159–60.

[2] *Athenae*, I, p. 275.

[3] Mullinger, II, p. 145.

was one who rode out the catholic reaction in retirement at home. But of the total of 472 known Marian exiles, nearly a fifth were one-time Cambridge men, 44 of whom had been or still were college fellows. The latter represented nine of the fifteen colleges and the largest contingent—a party of ten led by the master, Thomas Lever—left from St John's.[1]

[1] Porter, pp. 78–82, 91–8.

XI

THE LEGACY OF THE EDWARDIAN REFORMATION

The reign of Edward VI, however brief, was a distinctive period, more so perhaps than a later one that has earned a title in history. It is sometimes represented as an interlude during which little emerged but a prayer book, a time when Tudor rule all but came to grief amid factional struggle while idealists advanced impracticable schemes for a 'true commonweal'—all in all a wretched tailpiece to the Cromwellian achievement under Henry VIII.[1] When the full history of these years comes to be written a clearer picture should emerge of this turning point in mid-century. Meanwhile a study of educational policies and progress does not bear out the view that utopian ideas at one pole, unmitigated corruption and folly in government at the other, together ensured the absence of all practical achievement. Seventeenth-century reformers looked back to this reign as a springtime, and with good reason, though they lamented that its promise had yet to be realised. But though some developments were stunted under Elizabeth, other of the seeds sown bore fruit.

That the achievements have been obscured is not only because Cromwell's shadow is cast ahead but also 'the Elizabethan age' casts a long shadow behind. It is easy to evoke glamour through the persons of Sidney, Drake, Shakespeare, Raleigh and Bacon,[2] and it tends to slip from notice that the last three produced their mature work after 1603 while the literature that can justifiably be called Elizabethan—as also the work of Hooker, the historians and much else—is the product only of the last two decades of the century. As for the earlier years of Elizabeth's reign, there is little remarkable whose beginnings cannot be traced back to that of her brother. In education, not only were the university statutes, the catechism and other text-books taken over with little amendment—as was the Edwardian prayer book, but also the

[1] Henry's son, it has been suggested, the product of 'an appalling schooling', merely exercised such influence as he possessed 'in favour of disastrous policies and disastrous politicians' (Elton, *England under the Tudors*, p. 202).

[2] Rowse, p. 533.

whole pattern of refounding and endowing grammar schools administered locally under the general supervision of the state.

Again, Ascham usually figures as Queen Elizabeth's schoolmaster when he was in point of fact her tutor in 1548–9 until the atmosphere of a household proved distasteful. The book he wrote in the 1560's was, some contemporary asides apart, essentially the product of learning and teaching in the Cambridge of the Reformation and correspondence with Sturm. Ascham, it may be noted, was never in orders, nor were Cheke and Smith, both knighted in Edward's reign for scholarship turned to public ends.[1] The way was prepared at this time for a new generation of lay teachers by profession. While he was provost of Eton, Smith, carefully supervising the leasing of college lands, introduced forms of lease requiring that payment be made in part in kind, which effectively cushioned the revenues against inflation; it was in the light of this experience that he framed an act, passed in the 1570's, which literally altered the fortunes of all colleges at the universities.[2]

Most of the lay statesmen who governed the country from 1558 had tried out their powers and learned important lessons in the years from 1547 to 1553. Indeed it is at this moment, with the crown weak and noblemen at loggerheads, that there are clear signs of servants of the state endeavouring to hold things together such as Paulet and Petre, Cecil and Smith. There was also Nicholas Bacon, already recommended by Cranmer to Cromwell in 1538 as 'of such towardness in the law and of so good judgment touching Christ's religion' that he could not but make an excellent public servant,[3] while Walter Mildmay began a long career at the exchequer in 1545 holding office throughout Edward's reign when an important financial re-organisation was planned. Thomas Gresham was first employed as financial agent in 1551; he wrote to Northumberland from Antwerp of the incompetence of English merchants and the need to make an eight years' apprenticeship the rule for Merchant Adventurers, as in time it became.[4] Whatever the adverse judgements on Northumberland's psychology and personal abilities—and the subject has attracted more attention than important social trends—he fathered a progeny without which Elizabethan England would have been the duller. While Elizabeth's first two

[1] Smith was recommended by Somerset to the Eton fellows as provost even though 'not priest or doctor of divinity, or otherwise qualified as your statutes doth require... considering his other qualities the excellency whereof...far surmount the defect' (Lyte, *Eton*, p. 126).

[2] J. Strype, *Life of Sir Thomas Smith* (Oxford, 1820), pp. 145–6.

[3] Cranmer, p. 384.

[4] *CSP Foreign*, p. 263.

archbishops of Canterbury were active in Edward's reign, even the third received an education at Cambridge during it. The first president of the council in the north to make that body effective was the third earl of Huntingdon, bred at Edward's court. There was something of a school for young noblemen here, to which considerable attention was given, and this possibly inspired William Cecil to take like measures in his own household later, at a time when the court was less educative.

The royal injunctions of 1547 substituted for the doctrine of purgatory and prayers for deliverance, the duty of providing for the poor as 'a true worshipping of God, required earnestly upon pain of everlasting damnation'.[1] Support was given to plans drawn up by London's common council to deal with poverty at various levels, plans that, adapted and applied elsewhere, provided the foundation for the Elizabethan poor laws. So also forms of local government which came into prominence after the dissolutions, aided by efforts to strengthen lay parochial organisation, were later built upon and the incorporation of boroughs on the initiative of local people backed by interested gentlemen in the counties continued. While letters from the great secured election to places on school and college foundations under Edward, in later years they secured the election to parliament of college educated men.

Representation in parliament was already growing. Seven boroughs had been enfranchised under Henry, 'under Edward VI the process gathered great impetus....In all, seventeen boroughs and thirty-four members were added in this brief reign.' The dissolution of chantries not only provided many chapels for the use of schools but also placed at the disposal of the Commons the chapel of St Stephen in the palace of Westminster. 'Bringing the Commons under the same roof, figuratively speaking, as the Lords was symbolic and in many subtle ways speeded on the new age of parity between the Houses.'[2] Many matters came up for review. There were steps to rationalise parishes of a kind not taken again until the years of the commonwealth.[3] While the first

[1] Frere, II, p. 127.

[2] J. E. Neale, *The Elizabethan House of Commons* (1949), pp. 140, 364; cf. A. F. Pollard, *The Evolution of Parliament* (1934 ed.), pp. 263, 333–4.

[3] An act of 1549 uniting parishes in Lincoln provided for the amalgamation of many small stipends to provide a few of adequate amount. There had once been forty-six parish churches in the city; after the act, nine remained, the town council disposing of the fabric of superfluous churches making use of the doctrine of escheat (J. M. F. Hill, *Mediaeval Lincoln*, Cambridge, 1948, pp. 148, 286–7).

bill introduced during Edward's first parliament was characteristically 'for bringing up of poor men's children',[1] the second was a comprehensive measure of law reform; it did not get beyond a second reading, but this was 'the nearest that the common law came to a thorough overhaul by statute during the century'.[2] There is evidence of considerable freedom of discussion from the first parliament of the reign during which new blood in the episcopate changed the quality of representation in the Lords and royal intervention was lacking. In the early 1560's Sir Thomas Smith could write, 'the most high and absolute power of the realm of England consisteth in the Parliament'; he intended, of course, the crown in parliament but it was in marked contrast to Elyot's plain statement—'The best and most sure governance is by one king or prince which ruleth only for the weal of his people'.[3]

In the Edwardian age patronage centred, with noblemen in power, round the royal court, the young king standing as figurehead of a reformed kingdom. But though there was much preaching at court there were also other interests among those who regarded it as part of the kingly office, which it fell to them at this time to perform, to dispel ignorance among the people, 'to adorn and amplify' with the humanities and sciences. There was enlightened patronage of the arts to secular ends which finds expression in some of the best buildings of the century, country houses which exemplify a purer classicism than anything in England before Jones's Palladianism. Northumberland was responsible for dispatching John Shute to Italy in 1550 to 'confer with the doings of the skilful Masters in architecture and...view such ancient Monuments thereof as are yet extant'. Nor need this admixture of pure 'Renaissance' with thoroughgoing Reformation principles surprise any but those who think in categories.[4]

There was a lively interest in overseas exploration at the Edwardian court, prompted in part by the recent slump in European trade, which

[1] *Commons Journals*, p. 1.

[2] Marjorie Blatchford in *Elizabethan Government and Society* (1961), p. 201. Nor must Cranmer's revision of the ecclesiastical laws be forgotten, the remarkable *Reformatio Legum* which had its influence in Elizabeth's day (J. E. Neale, *Elizabeth I and her Parliaments*, I, 1953, p. 63).

[3] J. W. Allen, *A History of Political Thought in the Sixteenth Century* (1960 ed.), pp. 247, 264. Smith 'never refers to God as the author or giver of authority; nor does he ever refer to the Scriptures or even to natural law in any sense. He has, apparently, no conception of divine right in the Prince...' (*ibid.* p. 266).

[4] Eric Mercer, *English Art 1553–1625* (Oxford, 1962), pp. 58–68.

finds its full development later. It was in 1548 that Sebastian Cabot returned to England after long service under Spain to put his experience at the disposal of his country. In 1551 John Dee of Cambridge returned from Louvain, where he had been in conference with Mercator and other mathematicians, to provide expert assistance in planning new discoveries. The following year, under Northumberland's energetic guidance, a joint stock company was formed and a major expedition mounted in 1553 led to the formation of the Muscovy Company.[1] There were other lesser voyages and a knowledge of more distant lands was provided by the first publication of Richard Eden, a student at Queens' under Thomas Smith, who translated in 1553 a cosmography by a foreign author:

> A treatise of the New India, with other new found lands and islands, as well Eastward as Westward, as they are known and found in these our days... wherein the diligent reader may see the good success of noble and honest enterprises, by the which not only worldly riches are obtained but also God is glorified, and the Christian faith enlarged.[2]

The last phrase is typical of the times, in a work dedicated to the duke of Northumberland in 1553. The voyage undertaken the same year by Sir Hugh Willoughby and Richard Chancellor—'The new navigation and discovery of the kingdom of Moscovia, by the north east'—was written up by Clement Adams, formerly of King's College and appointed master to the king's henchmen in 1552; though it was not published until almost fifty years later, in Hakluyt's *Voyages* to which credit for these early works usually goes.[3] Books of travel of a more domestic kind also begin to appear at this time, the forerunners of a host which form an essential branch of educational literature. William Thomas followed up his history of Italy, which included an account of methods of government and was dedicated to Northumberland, with an Italian grammar published by Berthelet with Mildmay's aid in 1550. Andrew Borde's *The First Book of Introduction of Knowledge* (1548) was a traveller's guide over a wider field, extending to the Middle East, and introduced the reader briefly to various languages.[4]

Other publications bear witness to scientific and mathematical

[1] Elton, *England under the Tudors*, pp. 334–6. [2] *Athenae*, II, p. 2.

[3] *Ibid.* pp. 6–7. Adams also engraved a map of Cabot's discoveries in 1549.

[4] Published by the Early English Text Society (1870). Borde also wrote a *Breviary of Health* (1550).

interests. It was in part on travels abroad, during exile at the close of Henry's reign, that William Turner collected materials towards a notable botanical work, dedicated to Somerset his patron in 1548. An enlarged edition, *A New Herbal* (1551), gave the names of herbs in Greek, Latin, English, German, French, and Turner subsequently joined issue with the doctors who deplored this uncovering of the mysteries belonging to medicine in the vernacular tongue.[1] Robert Recorde had already embarked on this argument when dedicating a medical treatise in English to the Company of Surgeons in 1547, and in 1548 there appeared the first English text-book on anatomy written by a surgeon, Thomas Vicary, *A Treasure for Englishmen containing the anatomy of a man's body*, which long remained in use.[2]

Recorde published an enlarged edition of his successful book *Ground of Arts*, with a preface addressed to Edward VI, in 1550. It was subtitled 'an introduction for to learn to reckon with the pen or with the counters...in whole numbers or in broke...not before seen in our English tongue, by which all manner of difficult questions may safely be dissolved and assailed'.[3] This new kind of arithmetic book was furnished with many clear examples specifically designed to give 'ease to the unlearned' and written in the lively dialogue form popular from colloquies and other didactic works; two geometry text-books followed in 1551. Here was a beginning of the collaboration between expert and practitioner which was to have such far-reaching results. Moreover, there is to be discerned in Recorde's writings, as in those of Vives, a sense of the need not only to apply knowledge but to add to it, and pass on the results to a posterity which may in turn make additions; a conception of progress in this world, absent in an earlier age, which accompanied and inspired the early beginnings of experimental science.[4]

[1] Jones, pp. 50–1 n.

[2] *The Anatomy of the body of man, the edition of 1548 as re-issued by surgeons of St Bartholomew's in 1577* (E.E.T.S. 1888). John Cauis, who returned to England in 1547 and became fellow of the Royal College of Physicians, published in 1552 a treatise in English on the sweating sickness, based on direct observation of an outbreak in Shrewsbury (Brown, p. 5).

[3] F. A. Yeldham, *The Teaching of Arithmetic through Four Hundred Years* (1936), p. 31. To 'reckon with the pen', otherwise 'to cipher', involved numerals; to 'reckon with counters' was the traditional method often briefly referred to as 'to cast accompts'.

[4] S. Lilley, 'Robert Recorde and the Idea of Progress', *Renaissance and Modern Studies*, II, pp. 24–5. Recorde, a fellow of All Souls, took his M.D. at Cambridge in 1545; in 1549 he became controller of the mint at Bristol and in 1551 surveyor-general of mines and currency in Ireland. He had the reputation of skill not only in medicine and mathematics, but cosmography, mineralogy, coinage, music and Anglo-Saxon. For his

The combination of patronage centred at court and the popularisation of knowledge is a particular feature of the Edwardian age. It may, perhaps, be seen most plainly in the fostering of biblical literature and music. Musicians of the Chapel Royal such as Thomas Sternhold and Christopher Tye, who taught Edward music from early youth, produced works which were heard at court—and overtly intended to replace worldly music and poetry—but which also served the spread of education and participation in new forms of service.[1] That injunctions concerning the conduct of services, the ordering of churches, purchase of the English bible, paraphrases of the New Testament, prayer books, had their effect can be traced in the records of innumerable parishes. Badly though homilies might sometimes be read all this was an education in itself, and the prayer book was English prose of a new quality. In general, there was a marked growth in the range of vernacular literature at this time which gives additional point to the stress laid on teaching in English. It is worth enumerating more of the books that now became available, since they have received little attention as products of this age.[2]

It was probably in the first year of the reign that Sternhold published his translation of the psalms in popular ballad form, *Certain Psalms chosen out of the Psalter of David*, the first edition of a compilation which by the close of the century had been reprinted over seventy times. Robert Crowley followed this up with the whole psalter of David, addressed to 'the Christian reader' and designed to move him 'to delight in the reading and hearing of these psalms'.[3] Christopher Tye addressed

methods, F. R. Johnson and S. V. Larkey, 'Robert Recorde's mathematical teaching and the anti-Aristotelian movement', *Huntington Library Bulletin*, no. 7 (1935), pp. 59–87.

[1] John Marbeck and William Hunnis were others whose long careers began at this time, the former being entrusted by Cranmer with the task of composing music for the prayer book.

[2] The title of the comprehensive survey by L. B. Wright, *Middle Class Culture in Elizabethan England*, serves to draw what went before as well as much published in the early seventeenth century into the orbit of 'the Elizabethan age'. An inventory of the library of an Elizabethan merchant (given by W. G. Hoskins in *Elizabethan Government and Society*, pp. 184–5) enumerates, besides the bible, service books, Rastell's abridgement of the statutes issued in 1527 and Lydgate's *Fall of Princes*, Turner's *Herbal* and Hall's *Chronicle* published in Edward's reign; thus the nucleus of a middle class library was available by mid-century.

[3] Francis Seager dedicated selected psalms to his patron Lord Russell, shortly to become earl of Bedford, in 1553 (Lily B. Campbell, *Divine Poetry and Drama in Sixteenth-Century England*, Cambridge, 1959, pp. 34 ff.).

his *Acts of the Apostles* in English metre with music for lute to Edward VI; it was both for students of music and 'all Christians that cannot sing, to read the good and godly stories of the lives of Christ his Apostles'. In 1551 there appeared the first instalment of an attempt to put the whole bible into English metre, published by Crowley; it was the work of William Samuel, who described himself as a servant of Somerset and gave it as his aim to substitute for songs about feigned miracles or Robin Hood 'undoubted truths, canonical scriptures, and God's doings'.[1] William Baldwin's metrical version of the Song of Songs appeared in 1549 under the popular title *The Canticles or Ballads of Solomon*; two years earlier he had published a *Treatise of Moral Philosophy containing the sayings of the wise*, dedicated to Somerset, the forerunner of the *Mirror for Magistrates* of which he was first editor and chief contributor.[2]

Meanwhile the work of an earlier court poet who used more sophisticated techniques was first printed in 1549 when Sir Thomas Wyatt's version of the seven penitential psalms, each prefaced by a prologue of the poet 'very pleasant and profitable to the godly reader', was published by John Harrington.[3] Wyatt was one of the gentlemen praised by Becon for embracing 'not only the studies of humane letters but also the grave exercises of divine literature'. Surrey had versified the psalms during his last imprisonment and Sir Thomas Smith did likewise when confined after the palace revolution of 1549. Thomas Churchyard, who began his career as a page to the earl of Surrey, himself set up as poet at this time. That his verse, like most other writings of this period, is qualified as drab by latter-day literary critics need not concern us here; the relevant point is that Churchyard chose to write about things familiar to the people and declared his purpose not to 'weary them with a strange and stately style, nor overcharge their judgments with far fetched words or weighty devices'.[4]

When Roger Ascham wrote *The School of Shooting contained in two books*, addressed to the gentlemen and yeomen of England,[5] he took as his guide the counsel of Aristotle; that the writer should try 'to speak as the common people do, to think as wise men do', for 'so should every man understand him and the judgment of wise men

[1] *Ibid.* pp. 67, 69–70. [2] *Ibid.* pp. 57–9.

[3] Father of Sir John Harington; he also printed William Hunnis's *Certain Psalms drawn into English metre* in 1550 (Campbell, p. 35).

[4] Jones, p. 94 n.

[5] Published under the general title *Toxophilus* in 1545, *English Works*, p. xiv.

allow him'. This kind of approach which, skirting the courtly and contrived, leads directly towards the writing of Shakespeare, was consciously made by others at this time, though it was for the most part translators who set out to produce books that would be readable, understandable and instructive.

Various works by the early humanists were translated to add to such popular works as Erasmus's *Manual of the Christian Knight*, reprinted in 1548 and again in 1550. *In Praise of Folly*, 'englished' by Sir Thomas Chaloner, son of a London mercer who had won a knighthood in traditional fashion in the Scottish wars, appeared in 1549.[1] In 1551 followed Ralph Robinson's translation of More's *Utopia*, made 'at the procurement and earnest request of George Tadlow, citizen and haberdasher of London', dedicated to William Cecil, secretary of state.[2] A new edition came out that same year of Vives's *An Introduction to Wisdom*, translated earlier by Richard Morison and dedicated to Thomas Cromwell's son.[3] To these were added a translation of Zwingli's treatise 'declaring how the ingenious youth ought to be instructed and brought up unto Christ', made by Richard Argentine, schoolmaster of Ipswich, and published there in 1548, with a dedication to Edward Grimstone, later M.P. for the town.[4] Particularly intended as a contribution to educational thought and practice was William Barker's translation of the *Cyropaedia* of Xenophon, so often upheld as a model of upbringing; published in 1553 it was dedicated to the earl of Pembroke.[5]

In the more strictly educational field there were by this time English

[1] Chaloner was at St John's at the same time as Cecil and also a pupil of Cheke (*Athenae*, I, pp. 235–7). It was to him that John Withals dedicated *A Short Dictionary for Young Beginners* published by Berthelet in 1553 (STC, 25874).

[2] Robinson—educated at Grantham and Stamford schools and Corpus Christi, Cambridge, where he was fellow in 1542—was a clerk in Cecil's service. More's book had already been translated into German (1524), Italian (1548) and French (1550) (Lupton, pp. lxxi–lxxiii).

[3] The introduction made a radical contribution to the analysis of nobility, asking: 'what other thing is nobility now, but a chance, to be born of this or that gentle blood, and an opinion graft upon the foolishness of rude and unlearned people, which oftentimes is gotten by robbery and like ways. True and perfect nobility, springeth of virtue. ...Truly we be all made of like elements, and have all one god, father to us all' (Zeeveld, pp. 209–10).

[4] *Athenae*, I, p. 275. Argentine, one of a considerable group of reformers at Ipswich, also translated a sermon of Luther dedicated to Lord Wentworth and another work by a German reformer dedicated to Somerset.

[5] George B. Parks, 'William Barker, Tudor Translator', *Papers of the Bibliographical Society of America*, LI (1957), pp. 126–7.

versions of some of Erasmus's aids to study of the classics—parts of the *Adagia* and the *Apophthegmata*, certain of the colloquies.[1] New aids to studying the classics were from now on provided by translators who, repeating the humanist injunction that man should not live to himself alone, set their learning at the service of others. 'I wished many more to be partners of such sweetness, as I had partly felt myself,' wrote Nicholas Grimald in the preface to his translation of Cicero's *De Officiis* published in 1553, 'and to declare that I meant no less than I wished I laid to my helping hand'. A graduate of Christ's College, Grimald had gone on to Oxford in 1540 where he wrote the first of a number of biblical plays, one of which, dedicated to Richard Cox, was produced at Christ Church of which he became a senior member. This was in Latin and only published abroad but Grimald also wrote two plays in English, one based on Chaucer, as well as the poems which earned him a place after Wyatt and Surrey in *Tottel's Miscellany* (1557).[2] He was, too, as chaplain to Ridley, a writer of popular religious tracts while, as scholar, he translated from the Greek of Xenophon and Hesiod—in short, a typical product of this reign.

In 1550 Richard Sherry, a former headmaster of Magdalen College School, published *A Treatise of Schemes and Tropes* described as 'very profitable for the understanding of good authors, gathered out of the best grammarians and orators'; to it was appended a translation of Erasmus's treatise on bringing up children in learning from their infancy.[3] In 1551 Thomas Wilson of King's, Cambridge, dedicated to Edward VI his English logic, *The Rule of Reason*, in which he attempted 'to make logic as familiar to the English man as by divers men's industries the most part of the other liberal sciences are', because of 'the forwardness of this age, wherein the very multitude are prompt and ripe in all sciences'.[4] There were some up-to-date examples in the text of Wilson's logic:

[1] Woodward, *Erasmus*, pp. 235–9. The editor of selections from the *Adagia* reprinted in 1550 and 1552, and from the *Apophthegmata* reprinted in 1547 and 1550, was Richard Taverner, onetime canon of Cardinal College, who held the post of clerk of the signet during Edward's reign; though not in orders he was given a licence to preach throughout the kingdom in 1552 (*Athenae*, I, pp. 338–41; Howell, p. 139).

[2] Jones, p. 35; Campbell, pp. 176–81.

[3] Howell, pp. 125–32.

[4] The passage occurs in the original dedication to Edward which professes that he himself can need no instruction given his excellent grounding by Sir John Cheke and Sir Anthony Cooke. The work is discussed by Howell, as also *The Art of Reason, rightly termed, Witcraft* by Ralph Lever of St John's, written at this time though not published until 1573 (*ibid.* pp. 12–31, 57–63).

Whosoever desireth to live virtuously must marry a wife
Every true preacher of God's word desireth to live virtuously
Ergo every true preacher must marry a wife.

There followed two years later the same author's *The Art of Rhetoric for the use of all such as are studious of Eloquence*, prepared at the instigation of Northumberland and dedicated to his son Lord John Dudley.[1] It is noteworthy that writers of this time express optimism both about the spread of learning and the potentialities of the English tongue. Sherry, referring to such excellent past writers as Gower and Chaucer, stresses among recent contributors Sir Thomas Elyot, in particular the service performed by his dictionary, and 'that ornament' Sir Thomas Wyatt; he adds, 'many other there be yet living whose excellent writings do testify with us to be words apt and meet eloquently to declare our minds in all kinds of sciences'.[2]

Besides the works of Chaucer, Gower, Lydgate, now again current, Langland's *Piers Plowman* was printed in 1550 by Robert Crowley, who had taken to publishing the previous year, and reprinted twice before the year was out. Among highly contemporary publications were the sermons of Latimer and Lever printed immediately after delivery and *The Hurt of Sedition: how grievous it is to a Commonwealth or The True Subject to the Rebel* of John Cheke which was published after the uprisings of 1549. That noblemen could be well educated was proved by Henry, Lord Stafford—son of the attainted duke of Buckingham, restored in blood in Edward's reign—when he translated from the Latin a treatise by Edward Foxe who had recruited Oxford to the king's cause in 1530, *The True Difference between the Regal State and the Ecclesiastical Power* (1548).[3] Vernacular chronicles were also being added to: that of Edward Hall was first published by Richard Grafton in this reign to be prohibited in the next. In 1549 Thomas Cooper, editor of Elyot's dictionary,[4] brought up to date an *Epitome of the Chronicles* of

[1] Howell, pp. 98–110. This held the field until Ramist rhetorics were published, being reprinted in 1560, 1562, 1563, 1567 (cf. Albert J. Schmidt, 'Thomas Wilson and the Tudor Commonwealth: An Essay in Civic Humanism', *Huntington Library Quarterly*, XXIII, 1959–60).

[2] It has been pointed out that at this period 'the vernacular was almost invariably considered barbarous, or uneloquent, so that the view which Sherry reveals was most unusual; it was, indeed, prophetic of the attitude which appeared in the last two decades of the century' (Jones, p. 91).

[3] *Athenae*, I, pp. 216–17.

[4] *Bibliotheca Eliotae*, 'Eliot's Dictionary the second time enriched and more perfectly corrected' by Thomas Cooper, was published by Berthelet in 1552 (*EGS*, p. 389).

another author covering in outline the history of England and all other countries.[1]

By the close of the reign it was possible to find vernacular text-books ranging from the alphabet to the liberal arts, even to theology, for efforts were made to bring complex theological questions to public attention. Lancelot Ridley, a relative of the bishop, known for his skill in Hebrew, Greek and Latin, had published in 1540 *A Commentary in English upon St Paul's Epistles to the Ephesians* because 'few or none... go about to open by commentaries or expositions in English to the unlearned to declare the Holy Scriptures now suffered to all the people of this realm to read and study at their pleasure'. After a necessary interval in the years of reaction Ridley issued several more commentaries on other Pauline epistles and on the gospels after 1548.[2] In the 1550's Nicholas Udall, onetime master at Eton, translator of one of Erasmus's paraphrases, made a translation of the discourse on the eucharist with which Peter Martyr had so affronted Oxford University a year or so before. He attempted to simplify difficult terminology, in order that such a notable good work should not be 'kept (as it were) hidden under a bushel' but published abroad so that 'everybody may be edified as far forth as his capacity will serve'.[3] A volume intended particularly for the parish clergy was that translated from the Latin by Robert Hutten, a former student at Pembroke with William Turner—*The Sum of Divinity drawn out of the Holy Scriptures* (1548) advertised as 'very necessary for curates and young students in divinity and also meet for all Christian men and women whatsoever age they be of'. This, recommended by Turner for its plain and easy style which did not swerve from the common speech, was reprinted four times in the first decade of Elizabeth's reign.[4]

There was, of course, more partisan protestant literature, such as Grimald's *Vox populi, or the people's complaint* (1549) directed against non-resident ministers, *The image of God or lay man's book* (1550) by Roger Hutchinson, formerly of St John's now fellow of Eton, and several works by the prolific Becon including *The Principles of Christian Religion necessary to be known of the faithful* dedicated 'to the most gentle and godly disposed child Master Thomas Cecil, son to Sir

[1] The chronicles were by T. Languet, Foster Watson, *The Beginnings of the Teaching of Modern Subjects* (1909), p. 77.

[2] Jones, p. 33; *Athenae*, II, p. 354.

[3] Jones, pp. 39–40.

[4] *Athenae*, II, pp. 261–2.

William Cecil...secretary to the king's majesty'.[1] John Bale now published further tracts and his didactic plays on biblical themes were probably again acted, as they had been under Cromwell's patronage in the 1530's.[2] What with the teaching and preaching in English, services no longer in an unknown tongue and in which participation was required, the catechising and psalm singing, the books and the new ideas in the air, it is hard to understand how anyone could suppose that vernacular education suffered at this time a disastrous eclipse.

John Marbeck, who had narrowly escaped the stake in the 1540's, dedicated to the young king in 1550 *A Concordance*, 'that is to say a work wherein by the order of the letters of the ABC ye may readily find any word contained in the whole Bible'.[3] He had never, he writes, 'tasted the sweetness of learned letters' in youth, having been 'altogether brought up in your highness college in Windsor, in the study of music and playing on organs, wherein I consumed vainly the greatest part of my life'. The evidence suggests that St George's Chapel, exempted from the chantries act, paid little enough attention to education. Several visitations took place in this reign, and in 1550 it was ordered that a fit master be appointed to teach choristers 'the catechism and the principles of grammar and to write, and also to see to their manners', that a proper lodging be provided for him and that the school-room be repaired, 'the windows glazed and the floor boarded under foot'.[4]

The Edwardian age had also its model household, held up as an example, that of Sir Anthony Cooke, scholar and reformer, who had brought up a family of nine. The learning of his daughters, like that of Margaret More, became a byword and two of them in time brought up notable sons—Robert Cecil and Francis Bacon. A third was wife of Thomas Hoby who attended St John's in Cheke's day and, being the younger brother of one of Edward's ambassadors, also travelled abroad. When Hoby at length brought out a translation of Castiglione,

[1] All these were found in the possession of a former vicar choral of Beverley Minster, arraigned in 1556 for speaking publicly against transubstantiation (Dickens, pp. 227–9). There were also admonitory works in Edward's reign such as William Turner's *A Preservative...against the poison of Pelagius lately revived and stirred up again by the furious sect of Anabaptists*, dedicated to Latimer in 1551, with verses prefixed by Grimald.

[2] Campbell, pp. 226 ff., where it is argued that these were not adaptations of the old miracle play but rather pioneers of the new divine play or interlude. See also J. W. Harris, *John Bale, a study in the Minor Literature of the Reformation* (Urbana, 1940).

[3] Nichols, I, p. cccxl.

[4] Frere, II, pp. 227, 260–1.

The Book of the Courtier, on which he had long been at work, it had a prefatory letter by Cheke—sadly enough in 1561 since he fell by the wayside in Mary's reign to die of remorse—and was dedicated to Henry Hastings, heir to the earl of Huntingdon. But this admirable book found little appreciation among Elizabethan courtiers of the early 1560's, so Roger Ascham complained.[1]

The pre-eminent example, for schoolboys in particular, was of course the saintly young scholar king.[2] For the detailed guidance of youth a text-book on manners, morals and duties was provided which long continued in demand. This was *The School of Virtue and Book of Good Nurture for Children and Youth to learn their Duty by*, in the writing of which two translators of the psalms—Francis Seager and Robert Crowley—collaborated. Seager, besides providing advice of a traditional kind on daily behaviour, contributes a rhymed paraphrase on the ever current subject of birth and learning which has a different emphasis from that of Castiglione.

> Experience doth teach and show to thee plain
> That many to honour by learning attain
> That were of birth but simple and base,
> Such is the goodness of God's special grace,
> For he that to honour by virtue doth rise
> Is double happy and counted most wise.[3]

This is capped with exhortations to all estates and conditions of men to fulfil their proper functions, in the manner of the homilies. In the state, princes should seek knowledge, judges judge rightly, prelates preach purely. In the family, fathers and mothers should instruct children in virtue, children obey and honour their parents, masters do right and not use might, servants apply themselves to their duties, husbands love their wives, wives obey their husbands. In callings, let parsons and vicars look after their cures, lawyers help the poor, craftsmen be honest, landlords charge reasonable rents, merchants set reasonable prices. All subjects must live in obedience and awe of God

[1] 'I marvel this book, is no more read in the Court, than it is, seeing it is so well translated into English....And besides good precepts in books...this Court never lacked many fair examples, for young gentlemen to follow....If king Edward had lived a little longer, his only example had bred such a race of worthy learned gentlemen, as this Realm never yet did afford' (*English Works*, pp. 218–19).

[2] Strype cites one instance, *Ecc. Mem.* II, ii, p. 49.

[3] Furnivall, p. 228; a reprint of the augmented version, published in 1557.

and the law, it is the duty of the rich to look after the poor and, arriving at the very bottom of the scale, Seager bluntly enjoins:

> Ye that are poor with your state be content
> Not having wherewith to live competent.

With the spread of literacy, moralising on these lines had an assured future. Cheke had taken up much the same position in his book of 1549 when he argued that the commons were merely cutting off their own ladder to well-being—which after all some might ascend—if they attempted to confound all higher estates.[1] But while some reformers gilded the picture of a God-given hierarchy of estates by holding out the promise of a commonwealth bonded by love and mutual service, others were embarking on political thought. William Thomas, who, holding the post of clerk to the council, acted as political adviser to Edward, wrote several discourses for his use which have the same kind of rational and secular approach as the writings of Sir Thomas Smith. One of these—'Whether it be better for a commonwealth that the power be in the nobility or in the commonalty'—discusses a point familiar enough in theory since the days of Aristotle but recently raised in practice.[2]

Without following up the argument Thomas's conclusion may be noted, that the tyranny of nobility is more tolerable than that of the multitude, a single tyrant better than many; with the proviso that he would not have the commons 'so kept down as the wretched commons of some other countries are'. But, he adds, 'I would that their discipline and education should be such, that the only name of their prince should make them tremble', which can never be so if they have power themselves and fear no superior power. Indeed 'if they have but so much liberty as to talk of the prince's causes, and of the reason of laws, at once they show their desire not to be ruled; whereof groweth contempt, and consequently disobedience, the mother of all errors'. It was an attitude, fostered by the experience of the past twenty years,

[1] The real remedy was mutual love, the 'knot' of the commonwealth 'whereby divers parts be perfectly joined together in one politique body' (J. Strype, *Life of Sir John Cheke* (Oxford, 1821), pp. 40–3; J. W. Allen, p. 141).

[2] 'The people of every monarchy, or realm, is divided in two parts: the one nobility, and the other commonalty. In whom be two repugnant desires: the one to rule, and the other not to be ruled. And because the desire of them prevaileth in whom the power consisteth; therefore our question is, to whom the power is most convenient for the commonwealth' (Strype, *Ecc. Mem.* II, ii, pp. 373–7); Allen summarises Thomas's argument and his debt to and differences from Machiavelli (pp. 248–9).

that Elizabeth was to adopt even in relation to the House of Commons, while the contempt engendered by unpopular policies was skilfully diverted from the crown onto the episcopate as Cranmer had earlier argued was the judicious course.[1]

The reform of abuses in the commonwealth was the subject of a discourse by the young king—possibly written in answer to Bucer's New Year message of 1551—which found the remedy once more in education, much in the manner of Starkey, Morison and the Cromwellian injunctions of 1536.[2] 'With whatsoever thing the new vessel is imbued it will long keep the savour, meaning that for the most part men be as they be brought up', wrote Edward, a well-tutored youth, quoting from Horace. The most healing of plasters to apply to the sores of the body politic, then, is a sound training for different estates:

> Youth must be brought up, some in husbandry, some in working, graving, gilding, joining, printing, making of cloths, even from their tenderest age, to the intent that they may not when they come to man's estate loiter as they do nowadays and neglect: but think their travail sweet and honest. And for this purpose would I wish that artificers and other were either commanded to bring up their sons in like trade, or else have some places appointed them in every good town where they should be prentices, and bound to certain kind of conditions. This shall well remedy...disobedience of the lower sort, casting of seditious bills, and will clearly take away the idleness of the people.[3]

Steps were in fact initiated in London to provide an apprenticeship and training centre for the poor in the former palace of Bridewell, granted by the crown for the purpose, as part of the comprehensive scheme for poor relief finalised by the city in 1552.[4] Men of the kind who had been behind Thomas Cromwell's policies but not sufficiently influential to prevent his fall now held leading positions in the city. The master of the Merchant Taylors' Company in 1547 was Thomas Offley, among the first of Lily's pupils at St Paul's, who was noted for his

[1] 'I fear lest a grudge against the prince and his council, in such cases of religion, should gender in many of the people's hearts a faint subjection and obedience', Cranmer wrote to Cromwell in 1537—'I would fain that all the envy and grudge of the people in this matter should be put from the king and his council and that we, which be ordinaries, should take it upon us' (*Misc. Writings*, p. 347).

[2] As also did a tract of 1549 which argued that all children should be put to school from the age of four and then trained for a trade or profession under the guidance of an overseer supported out of public funds (Herrtage, pp. lxxix, xcii–xciii).

[3] Nichols, II, pp. 485–6.

[4] E. M. O'Donoghue, *Bridewell Hospital...* (1923), pp. 139–46.

benefactions.[1] The master of the Grocers' Company in 1550 was William Laxton, of the Mercers' Company Rowland Hill, both founders of schools, as also were John Gresham and William Harpur, treasurers of St Bartholomew's. Richard Grafton, printer of the prayer book and one of the innumerable editions of the bible issued in this reign, was active also in the city's affairs. It was at this time that the common council followed the precepts laid down by Vives some twenty years before. In 1550 there was an ordered census and classification of different categories of poor in each ward with plans to take in the vagabond and thriftless at Bridewell, the poor by casualty and sick at St Thomas's and St Bartholomew's, while for infant children a hospital was planned in the former Greyfriars 'where they should have meat, drink, and clothes, lodging and learning and officers to attend upon them'. Here again, as has been noted, the premises were granted by the crown and, the project once approved, a committee of thirty met daily in the gildhall to complete plans. Under Richard Grafton as treasurer circulars were sent out to parishes, 'a very fine witty and learned oration' for the use of every incumbent, collecting boxes to innholders, contribution forms to substantial householders for promises of weekly subscriptions. Finally, the money in, much of it collected by the thirty among themselves, one of these equipped the Greyfriars with '500 featherbeds and 500 pads of straw to lay under the featherbeds and as many blankets and a thousand pairs of sheets'.[2] So Christ's Hospital was born with, for the furtherance of learning to prevent the emergence of poverty, two petty teachers, writing and music masters, and a grammar school attached. It was an institution of which the city, with justice, was particularly proud, linked with the three other hospitals in an ordered system under city management.[3]

This, then, was the background against which planned educational reconstruction took place. Here the aim was to promote schools in parishes taught by curate or schoolmaster, or at the least regular

[1] He was later described by Fuller as the 'Zaccheus of London, not for his lowly stature but for his high charity in giving half of all his goods to the poor' (A. B. Beaven, *Aldermen of the City of London*, 1913, II, p. 171; Jordan, *Charities of London*, p. 333).

[2] *Christ's Hospital Book*, pp. 6–7, drawing on the account by John Howes.

[3] E. M. Leonard, *The Early History of Poor Relief* (Cambridge, 1900), pp. 36–7. Bridewell, granted in April 1553, did not get started until 1556. It provided a model for future houses of correction, including several workshops run by various craftsmen to whom children of the house were apprenticed; after the statute of 1563 became operative children of poor freemen as well as vagrants were apprenticed here (O'Donoghue, pp. 199–200).

catechising and teaching in English by incumbents, and to establish efficient grammar schools in the main towns, while insistence was laid on the teaching function of colleges at the universities within the framework of a reformed curriculum. But in considering the legacy of this age, particularly so far as the development of scholarship is concerned, it is necessary to take in its continuation from 1553 to 1558 when, while many maintained the course set in private at home, a select band resorted to the main educational centres of the Reformation on the continent. There were prominent laymen with their families as well as leading reformers among the clergy among the four hundred or more Marian exiles. As they deepened their learning, notably in Greek and Hebrew, many absorbed the teaching of Calvin who had taken over the leadership of the reforming movement since Luther's death. So also the Geneva academy, modelled after that under Sturm at Strasburg and presided over by the distinguished scholar Theodore Beza from 1559, replaced Wittenberg as the inspiration and training ground of reformers.

While there had been a first acquaintance with Calvinist doctrine in England,[1] on the continent it had spread rapidly and beyond the confines of cities. In eastern Europe an old and proud nobility—which had found the religion of German burgesses, with its servile insistence on the superior rights of princes, little to its taste—immediately took to Calvin's creed.[2] This proved in time equally attractive to the gentlemen of England as well as to many of the clergy. Calvin, who in sharp contrast to Luther wrote as a scholar and in an admirable style, made a direct appeal to the educated whether clerical or lay; to the discussion that had been in train for many years about means of government and the qualities that make men fit to govern he contributed the doctrine of the elect.[3]

[1] Bartholomew Traheron wrote from England to Bullinger in 1552: 'the greater number among us, of whom I own myself to be one, embrace the opinion of John Calvin as being perspicuous and most agreeable to holy scripture' (Porter, p. 338).

[2] 'It was not German, not even predominantly French. It was radical, uncompromising, logical, and above all republican. Its denial of any authority, papal or monarchical, over religion had a powerful appeal to a class which was fighting and winning...a war for the sovereignity of the landholders.' Most notably, it was 'a church in which at every level from the local presbytery to the national synod the pastors were elected or nominated by the laity, and where the lay elders were the dominant element' (R. R. Betts, *New Cambridge Modern History*, II, pp. 203–4).

[3] The concepts of divine election and salvation in fact had much in common with the *virtus* and *fama* of Petrarch, applied and adapted by his successors. 'Presumably the two pairs of concepts are based on the same underlying experience. There is a common

Many of the Marian exiles came at one time or another under the influence of Geneva, and the more radical made it their home. From there a group issued a declaration to 'our brethren in England'. The cause of the Marian persecution, they affirmed, was the incompleteness of the Edwardian reformation which had drawn the wrath of God upon his disobedient children, and for future guidance they set out the organisation and form of service of the Calvinist church.[1] There were others—at Strasburg and Basle, at Frankfurt where Melanchthon had extended a welcome, at Zurich on the invitation of Bullinger—who did not adopt this outlook. But even the most conservative group at Frankfurt accepted Calvin's catechism as the best medium for Christian instruction while the Geneva bible, published in English in 1557, had a far-reaching influence. This had its marginal comments, in the manner of Erasmus, which pointed the lessons including that which loomed largest for English university men—that the locusts of the apocalypse were not only heretics and monks but also 'archbishops and bishops, doctors, bachelors and masters which forsake Christ to maintain false doctrine'.[2]

From Basle, the versatile William Turner—graduate of Queens', botanist, reforming pamphleteer, recently physician to Somerset and dean of Wells—addressed a message to the young gentlemen of England. A continuation of the allegory he had begun during an earlier exile under Henry VIII—*The Hunting of the Romish Wolf*—it advanced the proposition that episcopal wealth be divided into four parts and three-quarters devoted to religious and charitable purposes; the directive that, as Colet had reminded convocation in 1512, Pope Gregory sent to Augustine in the seventh century. Turner advocated as worthy purposes the augmenting of poor livings, repair of churches and highways, establishment of schools, while the fourth part should go to superintendents of the reformed church annually elected by the clergy in place of bishops. He further proposed the liquidation of prebendaries, for which Cranmer had vainly hoped, and the turning of cathedral revenues to subsidising additional preachers and schoolmasters[3]—an objective that was eventually to be attained but not until the 1640's.

John Knox, a licensed preacher in England during Edward's reign, likewise elaborated upon projects that had then been in hand. In a

belief among successful men that their success has derived from some unusual quality in themselves' (Bolgar, p. 247).

[1] Knappen, p. 139.

[2] *Ibid.* p. 144.

[3] *Ibid.* pp. 113–14.

Brief Exhortation to England he argued that 'it is most expedient that schools be universally erected in all cities and chief towns, the oversight whereof to be committed to the magistrates and godly learned men of the said cities and towns'. Later, called upon for detailed plans for his own country when in 1560 the Scottish church broke with Rome, Knox proposed that ecclesiastical revenues be turned to the maintenance of preaching ministers, relief of the poor, the promotion of education. There should be parochial schools taught by ministers in smaller and more distant places, a grammar master in every town, and arts colleges teaching languages, logic and rhetoric in every notable town, while 'the great schools, called universities' should be 'replenished with those that be apt to learning'. Knox called for compulsory education for all estates as Starkey had once done and in terms Erasmus would have recognised. 'This must be carefully provided, that no father, of what estate or condition that ever he be, use his children at his own fantasy, especially in their youth-head; but all must be compelled to bring up their children in learning and virtue.' The rich and powerful, in particular, 'may not be permitted to suffer their children to spend their youth in vain idleness, as heretofore they have done. But they must be exhorted, and by the censure of the Church compelled to dedicate their sons, by good exercise, to the profit of the Church and to the Commonwealth.' This at their own expense, since they could afford it, while the poor must be sustained at the charge of the church; all found apt for advanced studies, whether rich or poor, 'must be charged to continue their study, so that the Commonwealth may have some comfort by them'.[1]

In the event, in Scotland as elsewhere, the nobility profited from disendowment of the church at the expense of the clergy and people, though, again, not to the exclusion of educational plans which were vital to the establishment of a reformed church and consolidation of the social order. Knox's plan aptly summarises a stage in the movement which, first inspired by the humanists, received official sanction during the years Cromwell was in power and then, checked for a time after 1539, resumed and reached a new level in the six to seven years of the Edwardian reformation. It remains to assess what was made of the legacy of this age during the second half of the century.

[1] *The Book of Discipline*, which also includes detailed plans for university reform, is printed as an appendix in W. C. Dickinson (ed.), *John Knox's History of the Reformation in Scotland* (1949), II, pp. 295–302.

PART III

THE PLACE OF EDUCATION IN THE ELIZABETHAN AGE

XII

EDUCATION AND SOCIAL CHANGE

When the reign of Edward VI is given due weight as a period of educational advance, that of Elizabeth falls into place as a predominantly conservative age. There was continued concern to promote education in ways that would ensure unity in religion and consolidation of the social order, but unity in religion was pursued at the expense of more radical reformers while legislation was also directed to preventing any rise in the social scale. Educational measures were taken within this general framework and it has sometimes been held that autocratic and restrictive control hampered development all along the line. But policies did not go without challenge, notably from those most active in the establishment of schools who were also concerned to promote teaching on reformed lines, and the evidence suggests that standards rose. In the outcome it proved impossible to control educational developments to the end of upholding the established order and they contributed much towards undermining it.

Elizabethan education has often been discussed in terms of individual founders and schools, school life and the curriculum. Less attention has been paid to the evolution of a system of schools administered locally by lay governing bodies under the general supervision of the state. This was the major change initiated at the Reformation. There was no sharp break with the past in the sense that an older system directed by the church was swept away. Rather ecclesiastical control had ceased to be a reality in the later middle ages and a variety of schools had come into being in a haphazard way. These were re-organised and adapted, once the religious superstructure had been removed, chapels quite often became schoolhouses and henceforth benefactions which would once have gone to maintain masses frequently went to extend the system of schools.

In the process humanist theories merged with reforming ideas in the formulation of educational programmes. In one sense the question at issue in the conflicts of the Elizabethan age was which would come uppermost. Here it must be noted that 'puritanism' is a category as difficult to disentangle as 'humanism' at an earlier stage; it, too, extends to cover a whole set of attitudes, a way of thought and approach to learning, not merely advocacy of the Genevan form of church government. Though there were some who actively pursued this end, and in so doing raised important political issues, it is not helpful to conceive of puritans in general as a tiresome and noisy left wing of a settled Anglican church. Rather the theology of the Elizabethan church was predominantly Calvinist and in this sense puritanism was in the mainstream of development; those called puritans were the most thoroughgoing upholders of the Reformation, whether earls or ministers of the gospel as in Edward's reign, at a time when this had yet to be secured in England. The significance of the policies advocated becomes clearer when account is taken of the revival of catholicism under the Stuarts.

In considering the effect on the schools it is once again important to dispense with the idea that a classical education is necessarily the best education, that any deviation from this must be deplored as short-sighted or narrow-minded. No one in the sixteenth and early seventeenth centuries advocated the kind of classical education that became the hallmark of aristocratic upbringing in the eighteenth century. The choice was rather between the humanist programme as modified under reforming influence—and puritan ideas extended readily to advocacy of new scientific studies—and adaptations of that programme which accorded with the outlook of the Anglican church once it became established. The point of interest is the kind of education contemporaries sought to promote, both in general and for different ranks of the social order, and in relation to this and the circumstances of the time the results achieved.

The education of the gentleman remained a matter of particular concern, and it is this aspect that has recently received most attention. It has been suggested that one of the most important developments in English life in the Elizabethan age was 'the use of the Inns of Court as finishing schools for the gentry'.[1] This was no innovation in so far as the inns had fulfilled this function during the fifteenth century, but they were evidently now used on a considerably greater scale by gentlemen who figure much more prominently on the scene. It has

[1] J. E. Neale, in a paper read in 1950, reprinted in *Essays in Elizabethan History* (1958), pp. 230–1.

also been argued that sons of the nobility and gentry progressively invaded Oxford and Cambridge in the years between 1560 and 1640 so that the universities, adapting themselves accordingly, fulfilled the function of educating future governors on humanist lines.[1] But this is to underrate the role of the inns of court and also of foreign travel which figured increasingly in the upbringing of noblemen and the more wealthy gentlemen, while the universities were adapted anew to the requirements of the church, a church much lower in status than that of the pre-Reformation years. Upbringing in the household continued to be favoured in the Elizabethan age by a nobility which was becoming more clearly separated from the growing body of gentlemen, while forms of education adopted for gentlemen's sons also differed from the recommendations of humanists who had envisaged special academies to train future governors. At the same time fresh ideas about the course of education that could best form the gentleman were canvassed, considerably in advance of those set out by, for instance, Sir Thomas Elyot in 1530. That the traditional pattern of education recommended by the latter continued in some measure to prevail is not, therefore, evidence of enlightened progress so much as of a conservative trend. The most significant development, which no one had advocated, was that gentlemen frequently sent sons to grammar school.

Attention has tended to focus on the spread of education among the gentry to the exclusion of other aspects. But it has recently been emphasised anew that wealthy merchants continued to play a major part in promoting educational expansion both by founding schools and endowing scholarships and fellowships at colleges designed to bring into being a learned clergy.[2] While gentlemen were particularly well placed to take advantage of opportunities, townsmen and yeomen in the countryside, indeed all above the swelling ranks of the poor, could profit. By no means all schools maintained at this time owed their existence to particular benefactors or influential support. As examination of the chantry certificates has suggested there was considerable local initiative in promoting education and this continued during the remainder of the century, not least in those parts of the countryside where, with the continuing high prices, standards of living

[1] Curtis, *op. cit. passim.*

[2] Attention was long ago drawn to the fact, recently documented in detail by W. K. Jordan, that between 1560 and 1650 the middle class 'poured their wealth into the endowment of education' to a greater extent than at any comparable period of English history (Godfrey Davies, *The Early Stuarts*, Oxford, 1937, p. 349).

steadily rose. Earlier Latimer, a Leicestershire man, had complained of the intolerable burdens on tenant farmers in what was one of the most heavily populated and well-cultivated districts of England. During the second half of the sixteenth century the most marked feature of the economic and social history of the English midlands was the rise of the substantial yeoman farmer,[1] and there now begin to figure yeomen founders of schools. The more numerous husbandmen, or small peasant farmers, who worked the typical mixed farms that still remained the norm also prospered if they were able to produce a surplus to dispose of in the market. Consequently schools are to be found not only in market towns but also in the more populous villages and, as education became more easily accessible to the bulk of the population, this too had its effect. Though there was much poverty in the countryside pauperism remained primarily an urban problem with which it fell to the more considerable towns to deal.[2]

To take a general view of the social scene is to recognise that at a time when commerce was expanding, professions were taking shape and the church was established on a new footing, education was becoming the key to advancement in most fields. It has been suggested in an earlier chapter that the emergence of different social groupings in the later middle ages owed much to the education indirectly acquired by engaging in new concerns, while more specific training was acquired mainly by apprenticeship to particular callings. Once an organised system of education began to take shape schools provided an initial step towards various callings, as also towards further education which itself now led to a greater variety of careers. It was a primary object of Elizabethan policies to restrict men to the callings of their fathers, to consolidate the social order by maintaining due differences between estates; accordingly there were moves to reserve certain forms of education to gentlemen at one end of the scale while at the other the children of the poor were trained to habits of useful work. But there was no means of controlling the supply of schools at a time when the demand for education was stimulated by the dissemination of reforming ideas as well as practical needs. The school system developed, rather, in response to various social pressures.

There is no need to enter here into the controversy about the rise or

[1] 'There are scores of instances in which a yeoman family rose to be gentry, and occasionally even acquired a title within two or three generations between, say, 1560 and 1630' (Hoskins, p. 151).

[2] Jordan, *Philanthropy*, p. 67.

otherwise of the gentry, and the parallel arguments about the existence or non-existence of a middle class, except to note that it is mainly in the service of one side in this dispute that assessments of developments in the gentleman's education have been advanced. Obviously, the argument runs in part, the nobility did not constitute an effete feudal estate giving way before a vigorous middle class; 'on the contrary is not their quest for learning a mark of the flexibility of Renaissance aristocrats, who, having lost the influence over the course of affairs that their bands of stout fellows afforded them, were seeking, in a measure successfully, to exercise power in a changed world through new channels?'[1] This conclusion results from counting 'at the very apex of the pyramid of gentility' the frankly *parvenu* such as Cecil and Smith who rose to become 'Renaissance aristocrats' by ability and education brought to bear at an opportune moment. There is little or no evidence that magnates of long standing compensated for the loss of feudal retainers by acquiring knowledge at school and university, and the position filled by relatively untutored noblemen in the Elizabethan age was usually that of lord lieutenant of a county which accorded status without requiring trained brains. Protagonists of the upper classes complain that the importance of the middle classes has been exaggerated by assimilating to this category all those who have middle-class antecedents, however remote or indirect. But a more remarkable sleight of hand is the writing off of the middle classes altogether by assimilating to the upper classes merchants, professional men and even the impoverished post-Reformation clergy; it is on the basis of such an analysis that the claim has been advanced that the upper classes progressively ousted others from the universities.[2]

It is important here to retain a sense of perspective, to recognise that the aristocrat and gentleman were only emerging within the traditional order in the Elizabethan age, that indeed education at this time contributed much to their formation. Meanwhile social and political theorists adapted traditional views as best they could. Sir Thomas Smith, for instance, divided the formerly single category of nobility into two, though he adhered to custom rather than contemporary reality in counting the prince in with the *nobilitas major* together

[1] Hexter, p. 69.

[2] Curtis, pp. 60–1. For a critique of this, Joan Simon, 'The Social Origins of Cambridge Students 1603–40', *Past and Present* no. 26 (1963), and see later issues for continuance of the discussion.

with all those holding baronies or higher titles; as for knights and esquires they 'go with the residue of gentlemen' in the *nobilitas minor*.[1] It was a characteristic of this period that function and authority added to status and in practice much power rested with those who, while remaining mere knights, held key offices. This was the politically active class, 'virtually the first generation of that compact yet flexible "aristocracy" which in another hundred years would elbow aside the monarchy and in the eighteenth century would enjoy a golden age of uncontested power and privilege'; but 'under Elizabeth it was still in its hesitant infancy',[2] though we are also told that 'the substantial and ancient families' among the English gentry, cemented together by intermarriage, were already at this time 'a closely integrated class', influential in innumerable ways.[3]

The 'better sort' of gentlemen in the counties, on whom government relied, were in fact relatively few.[4] For the rest the rank and file gentry, often anything but gentlemanly and speaking 'not the standardised speech of a social class but with all the rich variety of their native parts',[5] tapered off into the 'poorer sort' whose means might be narrower than those of many a townsman or yeoman farmer.[6] While gentlemen of standing could educate heirs to be such in turn, to take their places as governors on the bench of justices or in parliament, many others must perforce set their sights lower, particularly for a growing number of younger sons. The point is that wherever an opening was sought—at court or in a household, in the Commons, the law, medicine, a respectable trade, or even, as the years wore on, the church—an education was now necessary.

[1] G. W. Prothero (ed.), *Statutes and Constitutional Documents 1558–1625* (Oxford, 1949 ed.), pp. 176–7. In the 1580's Mulcaster, linking status to degree of authority, takes a more dialectical view; he places gentlemen as newcomers to the status system, as relatively speaking they were, by designating them the 'cream of the common', while the nobleman is 'the flower of gentility', the prince 'the primate and pearl of nobility' (*Positions*, p. 197).

[2] Wallace MacCaffery, 'Place and Patronage in Elizabethan Politics', *Elizabethan Government and Society*, p. 98.

[3] Neale, *Elizabethan House of Commons*, p. 315.

[4] Gentlemen who came within the system of taxation numbered less than a thousand; in 1579 Burghley listed only a hundred names 'among the inner core of county notables, peers and gentlemen'. The number of J.P.'s in 1587 was about 1500; MacCaffery, *loc. cit.* pp. 98–9.

[5] Hoskins, p. 86.

[6] These were the 'poor relations', see M. E. Finch, *The Wealth of Five Northamptonshire Families, 1540–1640* (Northamptonshire Record Society, 1956), pp. 28–30.

It is here that the development of a system of grammar schools catering for lay needs emerges clearly as the new factor in the situation. Shoulder to shoulder with the gentry in seeking suitable educational facilities, as in the past, were established tradesmen and substantial merchants who contributed much to providing these; though towards the close of the century those possessed of the greatest wealth, who in turn devoted some of it to education, were a 'new sort of men', the entrepreneurs who continued to prosper despite the efforts of legistators.[1] Other ready candidates for places in school or college were sons of the already more numerous professonal men or those aspiring to the status—solicitors, apothecaries and surgeons, for instance, as well as barristers and physicians—while there was an entirely new body of men bent on educating sons to follow in their footsteps, the married clergy. Yeomen farmers still looked mainly to the church, and so to a school and college education, as a means to the advancement of sons, though the wealthier could also favour the inns of court. In the towns there was a growing demand for a good educational grounding for sons looking to a profession, as also those entering on apprenticeships. It seems reasonable to accept the contemporary view that there was a new development of the professional middle class at this time to which education made an immediate contribution; though the picture is confused because forms of education and professions sought after by gentlemen tended to be regarded as gentlemanly, so that to engage in them to some extent conferred this rather than professional status.[2]

Only if all these factors are taken into account does the expansion of educational facilities and the impulse to make use of them—and eventually the extent of criticism of their limitations—come into focus. In the remaining chapters only three points will be followed up in an attempt to assess what was made of the legacy of the Reformation and

[1] Peter Blundell, the west country clothier who founded Tiverton School in 1599 was a great deal more wealthy than old-established Exeter merchants. Thomas Sutton, who refused a title and the honour of bequeathing his fortune to the duke of York in order to found the Charterhouse, was accounted the richest layman of his time.

[2] This, surely, is the sense of Smith's summary (echoed by Harrison or vice versa)—'whosoever studieth the laws of the realm, who studieth in the universities, who professeth liberal sciences, and to be short, who can live idly and without manual labour ...he shall be called master,...the title which men give to...gentlemen, and shall be taken for a gentleman...' (Prothero, p. 177; Sir Thomas Smith, *De Republica Anglorum*, ed. L. Alston, Cambridge, 1906, pp. 39–40). In short developing professions were taking the place of the middle estate formerly given to prayer.

so to bring this into sharper relief. First, the extent to which control was exercised over the school system in the reign of Elizabeth and the direction in which developments were influenced. Second, 'the institution of the gentleman', in the contemporary phrase, what this stood for in theory and practice. Third, the wider demand for education fostered by the protestant ethic and the development of vernacular culture; the ways in which this developed and was met.

XIII

THE ELIZABETHAN SETTLEMENT AND THE SCHOOLS

The chapel which once bore St. Mary's name
Under Elizabeth a school became;
Why not? When faith and learning are combined
Then only do we true religion find.

So runs the inscription over the door of the former Lady Chapel at St Albans which was granted and purchased for a schoolhouse under Edward VI.[1] The royal injunctions of 1559 closely followed those issued in 1547 with the additional proviso, 'No man shall take upon him to teach but such as shall be allowed by the ordinary and found meet as well for his learning and dexterity in teaching as for sober and honest conversation and also for right understanding of God's true religion'.[2] But from the outset of Elizabeth's reign, indeed throughout it, the 'right understanding of God's true religion' was the matter most in dispute. The lines on which education developed were determined not so much by the settlement negotiated in 1559 as by the conflicts to which it gave rise, set against the wider conflict throughout Europe as the Counter-Reformation gathered way. Or, to put it another way, the whole direction taken depended not merely on the broad lines of policy laid down but on the kind of measures implemented from day to day in promoting the education of the clergy and the people. In this sense it can be said that the reign of Elizabeth marked not the end of the Reformation but a first opportunity of securing it at large.

In one matter Elizabeth directly followed the example of her father. During this reign the semi-feudal status of bishops was effectively reduced on lines envisaged in the 1530's and pursued during Edward's reign. Legislation favoured unequal exchanges of lands and other methods of mulcting revenues were resumed though a due share now went to the crown.[3] Moreover, informers could make large sums

[1] *VCH Herts.* II, p. 58. [2] Frere, III, p. 21.

[3] So far were the revenues and status of the episcopate reduced that Hooker could observe at the close of the century that many gentlemen were better placed than bishops (Hill, pp. 14 ff., 207).

seeking out and reporting lands forfeit to the crown but 'concealed' from the chantry commissioners and there was much pressure to grant favourable leases; not only bishops and cathedral corporations but also colleges and schools were pestered in this respect, their endowments and revenues endangered. The queen also led the way in drawing college fellowships into the vortex of court patronage. The irregularities of Edward's reign fall into place when it is recognised that similar procedures formed part of the very fabric of political life under Elizabeth; though the fact is seldom emphasised because historians, while disposed to heap contumely on Edward's counsellors, tend to approach the Elizabethan age in a different spirit. It was William Cecil who remarked that the way to reduce the political power of the church was to reduce its wealth. Whitgift, at the receiving end, observed: 'The temporalty seek to make the clergy beggars, that we may depend upon them'.[1]

None the less the civil powers of the episcopate were built up as a support for the crown against the Commons and the more radical reformers among the clergy. Under the settlement arrived at during the first parliament of the reign the hierarchy of bishops and higher clergy was retained, with the crown as 'supreme governor', to rule over a church with a reformed doctrine, though the Edwardian prayer book was not in all respects restored.[2] While this did not go so far as many, particularly Marian exiles, had pressed, it went considerably further than the queen had intended and it was her subsequent policy to forbid the Commons to discuss ecclesiastical policy and use the episcopate as a higher civil service to carry out her own directives. One of the results was that bishops earned all the opprobrium for unpopular measures and, though there were at first many Marian exiles among them, became increasingly conservative. In the outcome another generation became persuaded that the only true church is one divorced from the civil power, and a new reforming movement took shape which sought to purify the church from within; originating at Cambridge it gathered growing support outside, not least among lawyers who were particularly alive to the dangers of a recrudescence of ecclesiastical powers. This movement Elizabeth was determined to suppress recognising, as zealous puritans often did not, that attacks on the hierarchy in effect challenged the powers of the crown.

[1] Neale, *Elizabeth I and her Parliaments*, I, p. 74; Hill, p. 27.

[2] Neale, *op. cit.* pp. 31 ff.

In this situation—at a time when influential gentlemen in the shires and many of the clergy could not be relied upon[1]—leading statesmen exercised a decisive influence. If 'Elizabethan England, as mirrored in the House of Commons, was overwhelmingly Puritan in its sympathies',[2] the Commons to a considerable extent mirrored the outlook of great patrons. These were influential not only in the counties but also in boroughs to which they now stood in much the same relation as to monasteries in former days. One representative of the new nobility who exercised an extensive parliamentary patronage was Francis Russell, second earl of Bedford, newly returned from studies in Geneva in 1558.[3] Others, who also consistently supported the puritan clergy, were the third earl of Huntingdon, married to a Dudley, and Northumberland's son, Robert Dudley, who became earl of Leicester, chancellor of Oxford university and the most influential man of the day. All these were of the privy council while gentlemen with a staunchly protestant past and much political experience—Nicholas Bacon, Thomas Smith, Walter Mildmay, Henry Sidney also married to a Dudley—were in key positions from the outset of the reign. The former ruler of Edward's household, Anthony Cooke—father-in-law of Bacon and Cecil—now took a leading part in the House of Commons. Francis Knollys, kinsman of the queen but a convinced reformer, veteran of the first Reformation parliament, also returned from exile to take a place in the privy council and an active part in events. Mildmay's brother-in-law, Francis Walsingham—student at Edwardian Cambridge and abroad during Mary's reign—was ambassador and diplomat before becoming chancellor of the duchy of Lancaster and privy councillor. All these took a close interest in educational matters; above all so did William Cecil who held the commanding positions of lord treasurer and master of the court of wards and was chancellor of Cambridge University from the first year of the reign.

Such men, professionally concerned to ensure the government and

[1] Much care had to be taken in administering the oath required under the act of supremacy. 'The royal commissioners treated...hesitating priests with patient forbearance; and the meaning of the oath was minimised by an ably worded Proclamation. We may conjecture that many of those who swore expected another turn of the always turning wheel....Among the laity there was much despondent indifference....For some time afterwards there are many country gentlemen whom the Bishops describe as "indifferent in religion"' (F. W. Maitland, in *Cambridge Modern History*, II, p. 572).

[2] Neale, *op. cit.* p. 418.

[3] 'The Bedford influence made no small contribution to the strong puritan complexion of successive parliaments' (Neale, *Elizabethan House of Commons*, p. 198).

safety of the realm, were not prepared to stand by while the most able men in the church were silenced, least of all when growing catholic influence constituted an immediate danger; rather they favoured sound preaching and teaching wherever it was to be found. As a result they indulged in what Matthew Parker—Elizabeth's first archbishop of Canterbury—despairingly denounced as 'Machiavel governance'.[1] While overtly appearing to follow the queen's directives they would in fact encourage bishops to go further with reform than she intended; at the same time they encouraged the puritans who so harried bishops, both to make reform more thorough and check too great an increase in episcopal powers. In the process they did much to ensure the development of education on reformed lines.

(1) *The ordering and establishment of schools*

At the close of Edward's reign the system of schools comprised foundations unaffected by any dissolutions including borough schools, the refoundations made by Henry, the Edwardian grammar schools and former monastic or chantry schools which continued in being because stipends were paid to their masters by the court of augmentations. Some dislocation was caused when plans to absorb the latter in the Exchequer were implemented in 1554,[2] but a much greater danger to the Edwardian schools was averted when Mary's attempts to retrieve monastic and chantry lands for their original purposes failed. The Commons made it clear that no interference with property now settled in other hands would be tolerated, offering as justification the argument that many of the lands had gone to support cathedral or school foundations and to disturb these would cause great confusion. An act passed by the first parliament of the reign in fact enabled the completion of plans in hand to refound particular schools and a few more were re-established when boroughs were incorporated. The position was further secured when Cardinal Pole, however reluctantly, gave legatine authority to the foundations of the two previous reigns.[3]

[1] Knappen, p. 239.

[2] Richardson, pp. 246–50. Recipients of stipends had to sue in the court of exchequer for a renewal and some payments ceased.

[3] Strype, *Ecc. Mem.* III, i, pp. 251–4. Pole had been forced to give an undertaking, before he was allowed to leave for England to become primate, that he would eschew policies liable to disturb a province about to come within the Hapsburg orbit through the Spanish marriage.

There was, however, a reversion to earlier methods in the schools which emphasises the extent of educational change at the Reformation. For instruction in the vernacular, designed to promote understanding of the faith, the Marian injunctions substitute an order that children be instructed 'so as they may be able to answer the priest at Mass; and help the priest to Mass as hath been accustomed'.[1] Moreover, one cathedral school was established which contrasts strongly with the king's schools of Henry's reign designed to provide a humanist course of studies to 'the glory of God and the advantage and adornment of the commonwealth'. Pole had been closely concerned in the early beginnings of the Jesuit order, one of whose main objectives was the reconstitution of education in the service of the catholic church; to this end schools, or seminaries, were advocated following a humanist course in the early stages and then the theological studies necessary for intending priests, but it was a particular aim to draw sons of the aristocracy into these and so control the upbringing of the lay governing class. The cathedral school at York, though shortlived in this form, is an early example of a policy encouraged by the Council of Trent and later made obligatory, which, indeed, inspired the training of the 'seminary priests' dispatched to reconvert Elizabeth's England. It was designed to provide recruits to the 'church militant' who would be able 'to ward off and put to flight the ravening wolves, that is, devilish men ill-understanding the Catholic faith, from the sheepfolds of the sheep entrusted to them', but it was also open to young men of birth provided they followed the discipline and used a clerkly dress.[2]

In 1557 Pole revived the ancient prerogative of bishops to grant a licence to teach, a measure which Elizabeth found it advisable to retain. During the first parliament of her reign an act was passed enabling the making of statutes for schools left incomplete under Henry, Edward or Mary, while another measure enabled dissolution of the chantries and religious houses Mary had refounded and the re-establishment of any connected schools.[3] The passage of the latter was

[1] Frere, II, p. 328.

[2] Raine, pp. 66–70; A. G. Dickens, *The Marian Reaction in the Diocese of York*, II, (1957), p. 26. Eventually the Jesuit programme, the *Ratio Studiorum* (1586, revised 1599) outlined a six year junior course to 16, a philosophical course of two to three years and a final course of four to six years in theology, much after the pattern of early medieval cathedral schools. In later years the academic level attained in these schools was to be contrasted with that in English grammar schools which developed to serve very different needs.

[3] Prothero, pp. 36–8.

the work of the Commons, the preamble denouncing catholic policies in a tone studiously avoided in government measures; had this bill not been pressed through Westminster would have remained a monastery, as reconstituted by Mary, for several more years,[1] but under the act a collegiate body was set up in 1560 to which the school was attached. The queen accordingly figures as foundress of Westminster school, though the original abbey school had been re-established under Henry, and it was now linked with the royal colleges at Oxford and Cambridge.[2] This turned out to be the best Elizabeth could do to emulate her father in the educational field. Other schools were founded in her name but usually in title of the grant or renewal of a charter; grants in aid were few and there were no refoundations on the scale of Edward's day. But there were immediate efforts to place schools on a sound footing after the disastrous interlude of Mary's reign.

It had been laid down that all masters must be qualified to teach, both by scholarship and religious views, and while there could be no general ejection of those in office it was clearly politic to replace the heads of leading schools, as well as of colleges where possible.[3] The clergy returning from exile and acquaintance with new standards of scholarship were appalled at the deterioration of the church and learning. John Jewel, back in Oxford from Zurich, found barely two supporters of reform in the place.[4] William Whittingham, returned from Geneva to become dean of Durham, spent three or four hours a day teaching in the school 'till God provide us of some that may better suffice'.[5] The Durham schoolmaster was in protective custody, so also the head of the school of Winchester College who subsequently retired to Douai allowing a suitable replacement.[6] It was no doubt through Cecil's

[1] Neale, *Elizabeth I and her Parliaments*, I, p. 73.

[2] The foundress was soon enforcing the proviso that six out of the forty foundationers be found places annually at Christ Church and Trinity which proved a heavy burden to the colleges; Whitgift, when master of Trinity, did what he could to reduce the demands (Ball, *Cambridge Papers*, pp. 48 ff.).

[3] The 'Devise for alteration of religion' drawn up before the first parliament had noted: 'The universities must not be neglected, and the hurt that the late visitation in queen Mary's time did, must be amended; likewise such colleges where children be instructed to come to the universities, as Eton and Winchester, that as well the increase hereafter as this present time be provided for' (*Somers Tracts*, 1809, I, p. 63). Archbishop Parker was particularly disturbed by the knowledge that catholic heads were despoiling college assets in expectation of going and hastened the first visitations. J. Strype, *Life of Matthew Parker* (Oxford, 1821), I, p. 82.

[4] J. Strype, *Annals of the Reformation under Elizabeth* (Oxford, 1824), I, i, p. 195.

[5] Strype, *Parker*, I, p. 268.

[6] Kirby, p. 276.

influence that his protegée William Malim, educated in Edwardian Cambridge and subsequently by travel abroad, became head of the school at Eton; Malim drew up a detailed account of the school's organisation and curriculum for the visitation of the college that took place in 1561.[1] A suitable provost was also provided in the person of William Day, fellow of King's from 1548, who in the event remained in office until 1595.

The party of learned men who descended on St Paul's school in 1559 to conduct an inspection comprised the Marian exiles Richard Cox, Robert Horne, David Whitehead and Jewel. They reported that the master was 'very weak and slender to teach such a school'; he accordingly went, for lack of Greek rather than other deficiencies, to be replaced by a man who in a few years was sending forward boys of the fifth and sixth forms to be examined in Greek.[2] This was the period when the teaching of Greek became established first in leading schools and then more widely[3] and when the introduction of annual examinations in the greater schools, presided over by scholars of note, contributed considerably to raising standards.[4] Westminster school gained a reputation for Greek after Edward Grant, associate of Ascham at Cambridge, became master in 1572 and Camden, author of what became the standard grammar, his assistant. Up to this time it had no master of note but, again through Cecil's influence, Gabriel Goodman—educated at Christ's in Edward's reign—became dean of the collegiate church and was probably chiefly responsible for the school's statutes. Here was another who remained in office some forty years.[5]

Westminster school was designed to take forty scholars on the foundation, thirty-six pensioners and town boys to make up a number of 120 with two masters in charge; but the number was evidently soon exceeded and another master engaged. It had originally been intended that the canons should act in part as tutors on the university model but this never came about.[6] The year after this royal refoundation in a

[1] Lyte, *Eton*, pp. 141 ff.; Baldwin, I, pp. 353 ff.

[2] McDonnell, pp. 77, 80, 87.

[3] *EGS*, pp. 490, 493.

[4] For the first examinations at St Paul's, McDonnell, pp. 88–9.

[5] J. Sargeaunt, *Annals of Westminster School* (1898), pp. 10–11. The statutes, usually ascribed to 1560 (*ECD*, pp. 497–525), must date from some years later since they prescribe Cordier's *Colloquies* (Baldwin, p. 380). Cf. Richard Newcome, *A Memoir of Gabriel Goodman with some Account of Ruthin School* (1825).

[6] Archbishop Parker tried the same at Canterbury but, if not busy eating as Cranmer had forecast, the prebendaries were otherwise engaged: 'as to the appointing of the scholars to be under tutors' ran the reply from the chapter, 'the same cannot be well

traditional framework the Merchant Taylors' Company of London made dispositions to establish an entirely new school over twice the size. The prime mover was the wealthy Richard Hilles, an exile for religion in Henry's day and leader of the reforming party on the court of the company, who provided £500 for the purchase of a property for the use of the school and secured the services of Richard Mulcaster as the first master.[1] The statutes of 1561 reproduced those of the chief city school under the Mercers' care, St Paul's, many of Colet's provisos being reproduced almost word for word. Of the 250 pupils a hundred, being 'poor men's sons', were to have their education free; fifty more, also designated as poor, were to pay 2*s.* 2*d.* a quarter while the quarterage was 5*s.* for the remaining hundred, 'rich or mean men's children'.[2]

Also on the court of the company at this time was Sir Thomas White, founder of St John's College at Oxford during Mary's reign, and arrangements were made to link the school with this. Since the college was barely established it was not until 1574 that the first scholars were taken[3] and by this time the school had already established a link with Pembroke, Cambridge, particularly through the medium of seven Greek scholarships founded in 1570 with a special preference for Londoners. For these Merchant Taylors' boys were soon well qualified to compete, one of the first to be successful in 1571 being Lancelot Andrewes, future master of the college and a leading scholar of his generation.[4] Under the rule of Mulcaster, son of a Cumberland squire, at Cambridge during Edward's reign then Christ Church—who added to a knowledge of Hebrew and Greek a lively interest in mathematics, music and drama—the company's school rapidly established a reputation. There were some skirmishes when Mulcaster brought his own pupils into the school at the outset but in these the company prevailed, Hilles paying an additional stipend as recompense, and it was as a burgesses school that this first developed.[5]

observed because few or none of the prebendaries or preachers are willing to take upon them the function; and that because they are seldom at home at the time of admission... and many of them for the most part of the year absent' (Strype, *Parker*, II, p. 311).

[1] F. W. M. Draper, *Four Centuries of Merchant Taylors' School* (Oxford, 1962), pp. 5, 10; Jordan, *Charities of London*, pp. 214–15.

[2] Draper, pp. 241–51.

[3] H. B. Wilson, *History of Merchant Taylors' School* (1812), I, pp. 32, 35–43, 56.

[4] Attwater, pp. 48–9. Edmund Spenser had gone up in 1569.

[5] Wilson, p. 23. The first entrants besides sons of merchant tailors were sons of a minister, plumber, leatherseller, carpenter, upholsterer, clothworker, salter, vintner, grocer, dyer, draper and wax chandler. The entries for succeeding years, though not

St Paul's provided a useful model for those formulating statutes at a time when the direction matters would take was anything but clear.[1] The royal injunctions of 1559 included the proviso that masters should 'accustom their scholars reverently to learn such sentences of Scripture as shall be most expedient to induce them to all godliness';[2] but otherwise there was little guidance. The relevant Merchant Taylors' statute specified a catechism, adding 'such a catechism as shall be approved by the Queen's majesty that now is, and by the Honourable Court of Parliament of this Realm from time to time'. But as yet none was forthcoming.

In 1562 the power to amend statutes of colleges or schools founded during Mary's reign was delegated to the High Commission, newly authorised under the act of supremacy. This was a mixed body of churchmen and laymen entrusted with responsibility for ecclesiastical jurisdiction under the crown which initially encroached considerably on episcopal functions.[3] It was directed to amend any 'enormities, disorders, defects, surplusages or wants' in the statutes of foundations settled under Mary and to devise such new rules 'as may best tend to the honour of Almighty God, the increase of virtue and unity in the same places, and the public weal and tranquillity of our realm'.[4] Archbishop Parker headed the commission nominated in 1562 which included the former exiles Edmund Grindal, now bishop of London, and Richard Cox, now bishop of Ely, while among lay members were Sir Thomas Smith, Sir Anthony Cooke, Francis Knollys. Another member was Alexander Nowell, former head of Westminster school, Marian exile, now dean of St Paul's, who frequently figures as adviser in the drawing up of statutes, notably to the London companies responsible for schools.

By 1562 Nowell had been put in charge of the important matter of producing a catechism for general use. Elizabeth's policy of letting

complete, suggest that this pattern continued (C. J. Robinson, *Register of Scholars... Merchant Taylors' School 1562–1874*, 1882, I, p. 2).

[1] They served for Northwich school initiated in Mary's reign and for Sherborne (1558), Bruton (1559) and Tideswell (1559)—founded by Robert Pursglove former prior of Guisborough, onetime pupil of Colet's school, who also founded Guisborough School in 1561 (*CPR Eliz.* I, pp. 289–90; II, p. 83)—and for the gild school of Worcester which secured a charter and the title 'royal grammar school' (1561).

[2] Frere, III, p. 21.

[3] Though by 1580 it had developed into yet another court with judicial powers largely under episcopal control (*Tudor Constitution*, pp. 217–18).

[4] Prothero, pp. 232–5.

the doctrine of the church remain obscure—a course dictated largely by inability to control the situation but which drove Archbishop Parker to distraction[1]—left a gap which was filled by Calvinist views propagated by the most learned and energetic sections of the clergy. At the convocation of 1563, during which a radical programme of doctrinal reform was defeated by only one vote,[2] it was agreed that 'there should be authorised one perfect catechism for the bringing up of the youth in godliness in the schools of the whole realm'; this it was noted 'is well nigh finished by the industry of the dean of St Paul's' and, once approved, should also be used in universities and wherever youth were 'taught their grammar in any private men's houses'.[3] This was Ponet's version, revived rather than much revised, and Nowell sent it to Cecil as approved by convocation in June.[4] But Elizabeth would have none of it and it disappeared into oblivion for years.

Influence could still be exercised on individual schools and one of the first sets of orders Nowell approved were those for Tonbridge school, adminstered by the Skinners' Company, in 1564.[5] These stipulate that 'upon the Sabbath and holy days' all scholars should 'resort in due time to divine service in the parish church' under the guidance of one at least of the masters; in subsequent years chapels or special galleries were fitted up for schoolboys in many a parish church. Careful rules were also laid down for the supervision of boarders. In order that local inhabitants should have the benefit of lodging scholars the master was limited to twelve in his house, the usher to eight. But parents intending to lodge boys in the town were adjured to take the master's advice about suitable households, while the chosen householder must promise to keep his charges from 'all unthrifty pastimes and gaming'

[1] Brook, pp. 164 ff.

[2] Strype, *Annals*, I, i, pp. 502–6.

[3] G. E. Corrie (ed.), *A Catechism...by Alexander Nowell* (Parker Society, 1853), pp. iv–vi.

[4] Seeking Cecil's support for its publication Nowell wrote that, as he well knew, a treatise of this kind was vital 'seeing the opinion beyond the seas is, that nothing touching religion is with any authority, or consent of any number of the learned, here in our country, taught or set forth', *Original Letters of Eminent Literary Men*, pp. 20–1.

[5] The company, engaged in litigation about the school lands, could not get a hearing in the Court of Wards and Liveries until it had drawn up orders for the school's governance approved by the dean of St Paul's and the archbishop of Canterbury. Nowell and Parker readily obliged—the copy of the statutes among the Parker MSS. at Cambridge has corrections by both with the latter's authorisation and the date—but litigation continued for fifty years and it took two acts of parliament to protect the school lands from a fraudulent claim. It was not an uncommon story at this time (Rivington, pp. 62–72, 82–6; Brook, p. 151).

and to lay information if they went astray, thus 'not in any point bolstering up their evil but seeking, as he ought, to have them well occupied'. All this was to accept that local grammar schools catered for a considerable number coming from far enough afield to board while also taking steps to root them in the locality.[1] The first headmaster of Tonbridge school was John Lever, younger brother of the former master of St John's newly returned from exile, and in 1574 there succeeded a notable puritan, John Stockwood.

Meanwhile, during the early years of the reign, statesmen and others in office again took a hand in the establishment of schools in counties where they had influence. Sir Gilbert Gerrard, attorney general, was instrumental in securing a school at Hoddesdon in 1560 when the town was incorporated.[2] Sir Nicholas Bacon founded Botesdale school on his manor of Redgrave in 1561.[3] Sir William Petre had an interest in Friar's School, Bangor (1561), for which Nowell later drew up statutes.[4] The assistance of James, Lord Mountjoy, was sought to refound the school at Wimborne in 1562.[5] Roger Manwood, an exchequer official, obtained letters patent for Sandwich in 1563, Archbishop Parker securing a building while funds were raised in the town of which Manwood's brother was mayor.[6] Sir Thomas Smith, now holding the deanery of Carlisle, helped to re-establish Penrith school in 1564.[7] The same year the borough of Leicester obtained an annuity from the crown to replace an endowment lost by fraud, probably with the help of the earl of Huntingdon.[8] A petition for the refoundation of Darlington school in 1567 was signed by the earl of Westmorland and the bishop of Durham, now James Pilkington.[9]

Other schools were established at the suit of the inhabitants of towns, as earlier, without mention of any particular adviser; at Mansfield and Godmanchester in 1561 and Kingston-on-Thames in 1562.[10] A school was settled in London at St Dunstan's-in-the-West at the suit of Bacon and Cecil on behalf of the parish; but there was evidently a strong legal interest in this, the majority of the sixteen governors

[1] These orders were borrowed and largely copied by the Grocers' Company when they settled Oundle school in 1572, also after many years of litigation (W. G. Walker, *History of the Oundle Schools*, 1956, pp. 71–2).

[2] *CPR Eliz.* I, p. 297. He later had much to do with Harrow school.

[3] *Ibid.* II, p. 104.

[4] *Ibid.* pp. 158–9.

[5] Clegg, pp. 75–7.

[6] Carlisle, I, pp. 594–6; Brook, pp. 150–1.

[7] Carlisle, II, p. 312.

[8] M. C. Cross, *The Free Grammar School of Leicester* (Leicester, 1953).

[9] Carlisle, I, p. 389.

[10] *CPR Eliz.* II, pp. 156, 157–8, 186–7.

being clerks of the chancery and leading lawyers appointed to have an oversight.[1] Hartlebury school was established in 1560 'by advice of the Council' and there was official action to settle schools in the Channel Islands where the Edwardian chantry commissions do not seem to have penetrated, or at any rate completed their work. A commission was appointed to visit Jersey in June 1562 to inquire into former chantry lands and 'take order for the refoundation of the two grammar schools there which are now misgoverned', drawing up rules for their government. Similar commissions were issued later in the year for Guernsey and the Isle of Wight which state that neither of these islands had any school and a grammar school was to be erected on each, endowed with 'wheat rents'.[2]

Among the chief individual benefactors were crown officials.[3] But one of the first founders to describe himself as 'yeoman' left lands for a school in Lincolnshire in 1560[4] and another Lincolnshire founder, a merchant of Alport, left £50 to be put out at interest to pay a master to teach 'the ABC and also to read both English and Latin'.[5] London merchants continue to figure; a modest foundation, endowed with £8 a year, was 'The Free School of Lawrence Sheriff of London, Grocer' (1567) intended to educate the children of Rugby and adjacent places for ever—it had a small almshouse attached as was the habit of London founders familiar with the city's measures for poor relief.[6]

[1] *CPR Eliz.* II, pp. 226–7.

[2] *CPR Eliz.* I, p. 94; II, pp. 426, 524, 622. The school at Newport was more regularly endowed in 1617 when the former chantry house and lands were made over to the mayor and burgesses by Sir Thomas Fleming (P. W. F. Erith, *A Brief History of the Ancient Grammar School at Newport, Isle of Wight*, Newport, 1950, pp. 16–23).

[3] Lord Williams of Thame, first advanced in the court of augmentations by Cromwell, owing his title to Mary, completed the foundation of an almshouse and school at Thame in 1559 (Richardson, pp. 266–70). Richard, Lord Rich, who had turned his coat under Mary and founded a chantry refounded this as Felsted school in 1564; (Andrew Clark, ed., *The Foundation Deeds of Felsted School and Charities*, Oxford, 1916). Sir Roger Cholmely, lord chief justice under Edward, displaced under Mary, founded Highgate school in 1565 (Jordan, *Charities of London*, p. 217). In 1566 by the will of Sir Roger Fulmerston, who profited largely from grants in Edward's reign, Thetford school was endowed (Jordan, *Charities of Rural England*, pp. 121–2, 157).

[4] At Moulton, *CPR Eliz.* II, p. 82.

[5] This, however, was Cecil territory and a charter obtained by William Cecil and his son Thomas transformed the foundation into a Queen Elizabeth grammar school in 1576 (Carlisle, I, p. 780).

[6] Carlisle, II, pp. 662–4; Jordan, *Charities of London*, p. 226. But this was not a great school to be credited to the Elizabethan age; only much later, like others endowed with lands in London which increased enormously in value, was it transformed into a 'public

One school in the north was given statutes with a very catholic flavour, that endowed at Kirby Stephen in 1566 by Thomas, Lord Wharton—who obtained the possessions of Shap at the dissolution, was subsequently a strong supporter of Marian policies and in 1560 displaced sixty-nine tenants to make a deer park.[1] That the north-west remained strongly catholic was a stimulus to planting protestant centres of education and Archbishop Parker provided one in Lancashire when he secured an endowment for Rochdale school in 1564.[2] Two years later the bishop of Durham—James Pilkington, who had spent Mary's reign at Zurich and Geneva, Basle and Frankfurt—founded a grammar school at Rivington; he laid down that each of the six governors must be 'a professor of pure religion and a hater of all false doctrine, popish superstition and idolatry' and that only three might be gentlemen.[3] On the other hand the former chantry school at Blackburn received a royal charter in 1567 naming fifty governors, so drawing in all the gentry who held lands in this extensive parish.[4] In 1568 a London merchant endowed a school at Blackrod,[5] and later Dean Nowell added one at Middleton, with the help of Cecil and Mildmay, and Edwin Sandys another at Hawkshead.[6]

Schoolmasters were now examined with the clergy at visitations, though many of those teaching in the early years were, in fact, incumbents.[7] But supervision was also exercised by means of special

school', by turning out scholars from the locality and almsmen (Brian Simon, *Studies in the History of Education 1780–1870*, 1960, pp. 313–17).

[1] The schoolmaster must swear not to read to pupils 'any corrupt or reprobate books or works set forth at any time contrary to the determination of the universal catholic church' and must read the ten commandments in 'the Latin tongue as is used in the realm of England for the most part' (Carlisle, II, 714–17). Mass was openly celebrated in Cumberland and Westmorland churches in the early 1560's (C. M. L. Bouch and G. P. Jones, *The Lake Counties, 1500–1830*, Manchester, 1961, pp. 43, 56, 78).

[2] Strype, *Parker*, I, pp. 362–3.

[3] M. Kay, *History of Rivington and Blackrod Grammar School* (Manchester, 1931), p. 17.

[4] Stocks, p. xii.

[5] Kay, pp. 116–17; for other Lancashire schools in the 1560's, pp. 4–5.

[6] These last and Grindal's foundation at St Bee's, Cumberland, in 1583 were endowments of a native place. But a chief mover in founding Carmarthen school in 1576 was the bishop of St David's—Richard Davies, Genevan exile, translator of the prayer book into Welsh. In 1574 Houghton-le-Spring school was endowed by Bernard Gilpin, who refused a bishopric to become 'apostle of the north'; he boarded up to twenty scholars himself when rooms in the village gave out, accepting payment only from the well-to-do (Foster Watson, *The Old Grammar Schools*, Cambridge, 1916, pp. 62–4).

[7] In the diocese of York in 1564, fifty-seven teachers were examined. Of these twenty-six (of whom nineteen were named as incumbents) were admitted to teach and

inquiries into the conduct of schools, particularly those drawing a stipend from the crown, and this could be withheld if the master's outlook was in question.[1] Returns of schools and hospitals functioning in their dioceses were from time to time requested by the crown from bishops.[2] It was presumably as a result of such inquiries that stipends which had lapsed—often in Mary's reign—were renewed, some to be paid with full arrears; a few crown grants were also made.[3] Where there were complaints of alienation of land or misuse of endowments special exchequer commissions were appointed to investigate on the spot; for instance a school was revived at Kegworth in Leicestershire in 1575, by a decree recalling the Edwardian aim of distributing schools rationally, though in less fervent terms.[4] For schools that fell within the territory of the duchy of Lancaster the duchy court acted in the same way.[5]

Schools were also handed over to boroughs as before; Reading, for example, gained control of the former monastic school in 1560.[6] But one official refoundation typifies a conservative approach by contrast with that prevailing in Edward's reign. The chantry commissioners had reported in 1548 that Salisbury was without a school (though a cathedral town) but had awarded high stipends from well-endowed

catechise, so also were six described as schoolmasters, while thirteen other schoolmasters were admitted to teach alone; six clergy and one schoolmaster were admitted to catechise in English only, two clergy and three schoolmasters were rejected as insufficient teachers (J. S. Purvis, *Tudor Parish Documents*, Cambridge, 1948, p. 104).

[1] As at Preston in 1560. *VCH Lancs.* II, p. 571.

[2] Parker returned in 1562 an account of the schools at Canterbury, Wye, Maidstone and Tenterden (Strype, *Parker*, I, pp. 227–8). In 1570 Grindal sent in returns relating to Yorkshire schools receiving stipends and the following year replies to another commission inquiring whether masters were receiving salaries, who had their appointment, whether duties had been properly performed since the first year of the reign (Leach, *Early Yorkshire Schools*, II, pp. 74–9).

[3] Stipends were renewed at Rothwell (1559), Acaster (1561), Rotherham (1561), Brailes (1564). The former chantry school at Wymondham received a grant of lands in 1559, the school at Bridgwater a stipend payable out of the tithes of the parish in 1561 (Jordan, *Charities of Rural England*, p. 156; Carlisle, I, p. 402).

[4] 'The situation is thought very apt and convenient for the purpose, and also somewhat far off and distant from any other free school, by reason whereof the children in the country thereabouts remain utterly void of good education and learning' (B. Simon, 'Leicestershire Schools 1625–40', *British Journal of Educational Studies*, III, no. 1, p. 45). Eventually methods of dealing with the abuse of charitable trusts were laid down under the poor law of 1601 (Jordan, *Philanthropy*, pp. 112–14).

[5] For instance it put together the stipends granted in 1548 to several small schools in Yorkshire to augment the centrally situated school of Pontefract in 1583 (Leach, *loc. cit.* pp. lxiii–lxiv).

[6] *CPR Eliz.* I, p. 287.

chantries to two priests teaching in the cloth towns of Bradford and Trowbridge. In 1569, on the grounds that these places did not need schools being 'but upland towns and not a resort of gentlemen and merchants', the stipends were alienated and put together to finance Salisbury school.[1]

On the other hand there is fresh evidence of a demand for schooling from those below the ranks of the privileged. In 1562 the parishioners of two Southwark parishes, who had earlier obtained the priory church of St Mary Overy for a parish church, established St Saviour's school in which both the poor and the rich 'might be freely and successfully instructed and educated in grammar'.[2] Eight years later a second school was opened in Southwark, where the population was rapidly increasing with the city's overspill into the suburbs, and St Olave's was to teach not only grammar but also 'in accidence and in other low books and in writing'.[3] From now on grammar schools, both in towns and rural parishes, frequently provided for a class of petties to be taught the elements by an usher or one of the older pupils. Local schools began, therefore, to provide an education from the earliest stages, though there were evidently many small private schools, sometimes little but dame schools, whose inefficiency was often lamented; standards were now considerably higher than in the days when it had seemed adequate to leave the teaching of children to chantry priests. In place of the latter there were now curates admitted to teach as well as parish schoolmasters who sometimes, no doubt, gave little more than an elementary grounding. An example of a foundation directed to this end is the school established by Archbishop Parker in 1569 in connection with Eastbridge Hospital, Canterbury. Here a master was appointed to teach twenty poor children to read, write and sing, and books, pens, ink and paper were provided freely; no boy might stay longer than four years in school in order to make room for others.[4]

Evidence from the Lake District, illustrates that schools which would formerly have figured as run by gilds were now administered by parish authorities. A commission sent up to investigate a dispute in the parish

[1] They added up to a total of £26. 1*s*. 8*d*. (Stowe, p. 12).

[2] The number of scholars to be taught by master and usher 'shall not be above one hundred, lest peradventure they oppressed with multitude be not able to set forward and further their charge to their honesty and the children's profit. Provided always, that none of the parish being meet and able found, shall be refused' (Carlisle, II, pp. 582–5).

[3] *Ibid*. pp. 578–9.

[4] Strype, *Parker*, I, pp. 203, 566–7.

of Crosthwaite, Cumberland, in 1571, took occasion to regularise the system of local government and financing of the school. This was one of those northern parishes governed by 'sworn men', and for time out of mind they had collected 2*d*. a year from all freeholders for the wages of the parish clerk. They were directed in future to pay the clerk a fixed wage and to use the residue to augment the schoolmaster's stipend—an indication that there was here an established parish school.[1] Kendal school in the years up to 1588 received endowments or subscriptions not only from local men who had made good in London but from 232 residents who contributed sums ranging from 2*d*. to 10*s*.[2]

Another example of local effort is Liverpool, granted a stipend in 1548, confirmed by charter in 1565, but which soon proved insufficient. Accordingly it was agreed the following year 'that it is needful to have a learned man to be our schoolmaster, for the preferment of the youth of this town, and that master mayor shall call the town together... and then to take order for his wages over and above that the queen's majesty doth allow us'. Promises for over £5 were obtained and a bachelor of arts forthwith appointed at £10 a year, though it did not prove easy to maintain payment of this salary and the levying of a rate, which was resorted to, was unpopular.[3]

There was a special incentive to transfer property to the endowment of education at this time in the attempts on the part of the crown, aided by informers, to resume lands which it might be claimed should have been forfeited under the chantries act. It was as a result of a case of this kind brought in 1567 that the burgesses of Burford set about securing the parish lands; that they had retained the majority is proved by the fact that seven of the eleven properties transferred in May 1571 to a grammar school had figured in the chantry returns. Later that year one of the leading aldermen, Simon Wisdom, endowed the school further and set out a detailed constitution for its governance. This was the same 'Simon Wisdom of Burford' who in 1530 had been charged,

[1] Other similar bodies in Lakeland parishes which come to light at this time were also responsible for schools. The body of sixteen at Holm Cultram levied rates and had the appointment of parish clerk and schoolmaster in 1568. The twenty-four of Dalton-in-Furness supervised custody of the parish funds and payments to the schoolmaster. The twenty-four of Cartmel were in 1598 responsible for the stock of the grammar school, a sum of over £65 laid out at 10 per cent interest; the school was held in the onetime priory gatehouse (Bouch and Jones, pp. 151–3).

[2] *Ibid*. p. 173.

[3] H. A. Ormerod, *The Liverpool Free School*, (Liverpool, 1951), pp. 15 ff.

during the bishop of Lincoln's inquiries into heresy in the diocese, with having the gospels, the psalter and 'the sum of Holy Scripture' in English.[1]

These examples, mostly from the first decade of the reign, illustrate that there was consolidation of the system of schools on the foundations laid in Edward's reign, if in a more conservative setting; and that there was both more local initiative and more supervision by government than is usually suggested when the credit for educational expansion is accorded chiefly to individual benefactors. There was a special pride in new schoolhouses erected mainly by public subscription. At Leicester where the twenty-four on the governing body of the town levied themselves at 2*s.* apiece and the lesser forty-eight at 1*s.*, a special entry in the hall book records the completion of plans. 'In this year, viz. the sixteenth year of the reign of our most dread sovereign lady Queen Elizabeth was the School house builded and finished. Item the same year was a new house erected and builded...appointed for the head school master to dwell in.'[2]

At the upper end of the scale were what became known as 'great schools', the most notable outside London for nearly a century being the borough school of Shrewsbury, an Edwardian foundation, later brought partially under the supervision of St John's, Cambridge. Thomas Ashton, former fellow of that college, became master here in 1561, an administrator and teacher somewhat of the type of Sturm who was called in to order the Strasburg city school. Ashton may well have been placed by the influence of the privy council; a strong Calvinist, he stood well with the earls of Bedford and Leicester, his relations with Cecil were close and he was employed on delicate political negotiations after leaving the school. In 1562 he entered on his lists 266 boys, half from outside the town and many from leading families in the surrounding counties.[3] For his work in gathering the sons of gentlemen in Wales and the Marches under sound tuition and good

[1] M. Sturge Gretton, *Burford Past and Present* (Oxford, 1920), pp. 15, 63–4; R. H. Gretton, *The Burford Records. A Study in Minor Town Government* (Oxford, 1920), pp. 547–60.

[2] Cross, p. 13.

[3] Fisher, pp. 4–7, 11–12, 21. Among the 800 boys entered during the first six years of Ashton's mastership were gentlemen's sons from Cheshire, Lancashire, Herefordshire, Rutland and Buckinghamshire but later the school drew mainly on Shropshire and north Wales. Entrance charges were graded: for sons of a peer 10*s.*, a knight 6*s.* 8*d.*, a gentleman's heir 3*s.* 4*d.* or younger sons 2*s.* 6*d.*, commoners from outside Shropshire 1*s.*, burgesses 4*d.*, other inhabitants of Shrewsbury 8*d.* (*ibid.* p. 43).

discipline, Ashton received much recognition, and in 1571 a substantial additional endowment for this school was forthcoming from the crown.

(2) *The content of education*

There was an official grammar in Elizabeth's reign as there had been earlier, printed in London.[1] Otherwise the main text-books available to schools, like theological works for the clergy and the bible itself, came from the reformed centres on the continent. Of particular importance were the colloquies of Castellion and Cordier, both of Geneva, which replaced those of Erasmus and Vives in many schools.[2] Moreover, rather than acting plays by Terence, schools staged pieces on more sober themes; Westminster school chose to present before the queen in 1565 the *Sapienta Solomnonis* of Sixt Birck, first master of the Augsburg gymnasium established in 1536.[3] Eventually the *Terentius Christianus* of Schonaeus banished the original Terence from the schoolroom; this was of catholic provenance—it was by no means only puritans who sought to purify the school curriculum.[4] While other Latin authors specified in humanist programmes found their place, Greek studies were initially directed to the scriptures; after the first readers the texts usually advocated were the catechisms of Calvin or of Nowell (translated into Greek by his nephew William Whitaker in 1573) and the New Testament. In other words, as Foster Watson pointed out, when Greek was first generally introduced into English schools it was not with a classical motive but 'as a religious instrument'[5] The same, of course, applied to Hebrew which took root in leading schools towards the close of the century. French, taught mainly by exiled Huguenots, was by the same token presented under respectably protestant auspices;

[1] The patent was a valuable one in that four double impressions annually were allowed, i.e. a print of 10,000 as against the standard edition of 1250 (*EGS*, pp. 255–6). Printing had ceased at both universities in the 1520's and was not resumed until the 1580's (*CHEL*, III, p. 427).

[2] Castellion's *Dialogues Sacrés* (1543) were based entirely on the bible—'the subject-matter thus precisely met the puritan demand for scripture-knowledge' while the book also 'satisfied the classical schoolmaster by its sound Latinity'. Cordier's *Colloquorum Scholasticorum* (1564) depicted the doings of boys in and out of school, notably sons of farmers and tradesmen, and were pervaded by the Geneva outlook (*EGS*, pp. 338–43).

[3] Chiefly responsible for giving the drama an important place in the curriculum of German schools, Birck had written vernacular biblical drama before turning to humanist Latin plays (D. Van Abbé, *Drama in Reformation Germany and Switzerland*, Melbourne, 1961, pp. 10–12).

[4] *EGS*, p. 322; Campbell, pp. 164–5.

[5] *EGS*, p. 493.

Cecil and Walsingham were the chief patrons of exiles allowed to settle in England at this time, from the Netherlands as well as France.[1]

For the first eleven years of the reign there was no prescribed catechism. But after the rising of the northern earls and the papal bull excommunicating Elizabeth, positive steps to secure protestantism could no longer be delayed; the pope had absolved English catholics from their oath of allegiance to the queen and called upon them to remove her.[2] Typical of reports reaching privy councillors from outlying counties was that sent by Ashton from Shrewsbury. 'The people in general in these parts with the greatest part of those also that be of good port show in their countenance a misliking of the state'; they also sometimes expressed it, the simple plainly, but gentlemen 'so cunningly, as no advantage can be taken of them'. Ashton urged that such dissembling be dealt with; papists found too much favour at court while there were also 'double-faced gentlemen who will be protestants in the court and in the country secret papists'.[3] It was a happy accident that the second and enlarged edition of John Foxe's *Book of Martyrs* came out in 1570, to find a place in parish churches as well as innumerable households.[4] Now, too, on the representation of the two archbishops, Nowell's catechism at length achieved publication, to be prescribed for general use by the canons of 1571—though the canons were never ratified by the queen. An English version was also published, prepared by that leading puritan in parliament, Thomas Norton, onetime tutor to the duke of Somerset's family. The opening phrase, differing little from that of Ponet, proclaimed that the young ought 'no less, yea, also much more, to be trained in good lessons to godliness than with good arts to humanity'.[5]

This was the view of a strong section of the Commons which finds expression in the act incorporating the universities passed in 1571: the

[1] Among the most popular books, which achieved a wide circulation, were those of Claudius Holyband, notably *The French Schoolmaster* (1583) (Lambley, pp. 118–19, 134–40, 143–5).

[2] Elton, *England under the Tudors*, p. 303.

[3] Fisher, pp. 429–30. His successor as schoolmaster was active in uncovering one of these (Strype, *Whitgift*, I, p. 165).

[4] And spread the view advanced by the author at an Easter sermon at Paul's Cross: 'As the bishop of Rome is wont this Good Friday, and every Good Friday, to accurse us as damned heretics, we here curse not him but pray for him, that he, with all his partakers, either may be turned to a better truth; or else, we pray thee, gracious Lord, that we never agree with him in doctrine, and that he may so curse us still, and never bless us more as he blessed us in queen Mary's time! God of his mercy keep away that blessing from us' (Mozley, p. 79).

[5] Corrie, p. 105.

preamble, referring to the 'great love and favour of the queen' insists more specifically on 'the great zeal and care that the lords and commons of the present parliament have for the maintenance of good and godly literature and the virtuous education of youth'.[1] By this act the universities became public corporations, no longer exclusively dependent on the crown for their franchises, and the Commons continued to take a close interest in their conduct. But despite the political situation the parliament of 1571 failed to secure any revision of the religious settlement.[2] It was equally in no position to prevent the adoption of a new code of statutes for Cambridge pressed through to facilitate the suppression of puritanism in the university.

Whereas in 1530 Archbishop Warham had found the regent masters at Oxford lagged behind royal demands, in the 1560's there were too many regent masters at Cambridge too far ahead of official policy. Younger members of the university had recently much increased in number.[3] Moreover, installed as Lady Margaret professor of divinity and exercising much influence was the chief theoretician of puritanism, Thomas Cartwright. The new statutes, for which John Whitgift master of Trinity was chiefly responsible, accordingly reversed the policy once advocated by Cromwell's visitors, that of giving the 'younger sort' their heads and removing heads of colleges. Instead the latter were made effective rulers of the university body. Not only were they given absolute powers in all elections to scholarships and fellowships or any other matter within their own colleges, but to them fell the privilege of nominating two persons for all university offices while other members of the university were confined to choosing between these; moreover the heads alone had the power to interpret the code that gave them such absolute rule. The first step taken when it became effective was to deprive Cartwright and dismiss him from the university. The statutes, which provoked an outcry from regent masters deprived of ancient privileges,[4] were the more suspect in that there had been no

[1] J. Heywood and T. Wright, *Cambridge University Transactions* (1854), I, pp. 50–5.

[2] Neale, *Elizabeth I and her Parliaments*, I, pp. 191 ff.

[3] The aggregate number of fellowships in colleges had increased by about a third in the early 1570's as compared with 1564. Trinity had its full complement of sixty for the first time, the number of fellows at St John's had risen from forty-three to fifty-one, at Pembroke from seventeen to thirty, at Christ's from eleven to thirteen, at Queens' from fifteen to nineteen, at Peterhouse from ten to fifteen, at Caius from eight to ten (Porter, pp. 107–8).

[4] A petition protesting against the new code, sent to Cecil as chancellor, was subscribed by 164 fellows of colleges (Porter, p. 168).

thoroughgoing purge of college heads; Caius, for example, now master of his own foundation was well known to be a catholic.[1] But there was no redress. Though Caius retired, under pressure, two years later the college remained a catholic centre under his successor up to about 1590; apart from twenty or more members during these years who later figure as recusants, seven joined the Order of Jesuits, eleven became seminary priests.[2]

While puritan influence at Cambridge was reduced in one direction there was in subsequent years a turn towards French and German scholarship which had its effect on the schools. In particular, the logic of Ramus was closely studied, the more fervently after he became a protestant martyr as victim of the massacre of St Bartholomew. Ascham had earlier rejected Ramus's criticisms of Ciceronian rhetoric and Aristotelian dialectic, observing 'He that can neither like Aristotle in logic and philosophy, nor Tully in rhetoric and eloquence will from these steps likely enough presume by like pride to mount higher, to the misliking of greater matters: that is either in religion to have a dissentious head, or in the commonwealth to have a factious heart'.[3] But others carefully studied works which exposed weaknesses in Aristotle and set out a new division of the subject matter of grammar, logic and rhetoric. Lawrence Chaderton, fellow of Christ's which was now the chief centre of puritanism, was the leading protagonist of Ramus at Cambridge, together with Gabriel Harvey also of Christ's and later Pembroke.[4] In time the university was supplying Ramists to

[1] Writing to Cecil, Edward Dering, fellow of Christ's and noted for his learning, accused Whitgift of vesting absolute powers in the hands of enemies to the true religion, citing Caius and several other heads; he enjoined, 'you that have been brought so easily to hurt God's people to do pleasure to the Pope and with so fearful statutes have proceeded to the punishment of so small offences; now make again some good statutes that may punish sin' (Strype, *Parker*, III, pp. 219–24). A petition against the dismissal of Cartwright, forwarded to Cecil, was signed by thirty-three fellows of colleges (Porter, p. 208).

[2] Venn, *Caius College*, pp. 76–85. The *Biographical History* provides information about what went on in a divided college; e.g. one Nicholas Lusher, admitted 1578, 'being dehorted from papistry by his reader...made answer that his mother had requested the master to train him up in papistry', and another John Vavasour, having offended his tutor by asking for Calvin's catechism, 'being a sober and wise young man he said...that he thought his tutor was a papist' (*loc. cit.* I, pp. 97, 99).

[3] *English Works*, pp. 243–4.

[4] Howell, pp. 178–9, 247–55. Among those to profit from their teaching were all the chief exponents of Ramism in subsequent years, Dudley Fenner, William Temple, Abraham Fraunce whose *The Lawyer's Logic* (1588) was based on an earlier manuscript incorporating some of Chaderton's exposition (*ibid.* p. 222).

grammar schools. A graduate of Trinity, William Kempe, who became master of Plymouth School, published *The Education of Children in Learning* (1588), dedicated to the corporation and intended for the information of parents as well as schoolmasters; this, setting out a method of teaching logic and rhetoric based entirely on Ramus, was followed by *The Art of Arithmetic* (1592), a translation of a treatise by Ramus dedicated to Sir Francis Drake. Another Ramist schoolmaster, from Oxford's puritan college, was Charles Butler of Magdalen who became master at Basingstoke; his rhetoric, issued in final form in 1598, remained the chief text-book for many years.[1]

During the earlier years of the reign, however, such schoolmasters were not plentiful and the nature and standard of education depended largely on the quality of the clergy. This, in turn, depended on the kind of opportunities offered by the church, as reformers consistently stressed, pointing to what was a vicious circle; there was no real incentive to education so long as the church could not provide due rewards for the educated but there could be no real reform of the church until it incorporated more educated men. It was in these circumstances that measures were taken against puritans which operated to reduce the number of competent ministers in office. In particular, the convocation of 1571 required that all incumbents subscribe to three articles signifying acceptance of the thirty-nine articles and the prayer book. Subsequent enforcement of this provision, though not at first very vigorous, led to the deprivation of a number of schoolmasters as well as clergy; though in reverse those suspended from preaching could often manage to teach, thus adding anew to the number of puritan schoolmasters.[2]

But convocation was also concerned to prescribe Nowell's catechism for general use[3] and to insist on the clergy's duty to teach children. Subsequent diocesan injunctions, following this lead, are couched in

[1] Howell, pp. 258–65.

[2] It was at this time that separatism began to develop. Robert Browne was a onetime schoolmaster who, after a forced emigration to Germany, returned in 1586 and was still conducting separatist teaching when master of St Olave's school, Southwark in 1586–8. His colleague Robert Harrison lost the mastership of Aylesham school though he had local support (Knappen, pp. 305–6, 308; Strype, *Parker*, II, pp. 335–7). John Field, the leading puritan agitator and organiser, turned to teaching for a time when suspended from preaching (Patrick Collinson, in *Elizabethan Government and Society*, p. 133).

[3] This was issued in three versions; the 'larger', the 'middle', an abridged version, and an elementary 'short catechism'. All were available in English, Latin and Greek by 1574 (*EGS*, p. 74).

terms which indicate that considerable educational development had taken place since similar injunctions were addressed to chantry priests. Thus in 1577 Richard Barnes, bishop of Durham, enjoined that all parsons, vicars and curates not licensed to preach 'shall duly, painfully and freely teach the children of their several parishes and cures to read and write; and such as they shall by good and due trial find to be apt to learn, and of pregnant capacity, then they shall exhort their parents to set them to schools and learning of the good and liberal sciences'.[1] The visitation conducted in this diocese in 1578 illustrates that the injunction of 1559 requiring that masters obtain a licence to teach was by no means always observed; several schoolmasters, even in established schools, were without one. In rural parishes masters were few enough; there were as many in the great port of Newcastle, eleven, as in several rural deaneries taken together.[2]

It was one of the strongest puritan arguments against bishops that, while they deprived men who could preach and teach, innumerable parishes were still served by an unlearned clergy some of whom had been in office throughout Mary's reign. The bishops' chief excuse for low standards was the poverty of many livings, a matter for which lay impropriators were often to blame.[3] The church at this time attracted few bequests to amend this situation; the middle class, who had earlier endowed and controlled their own chantry priests, were now tending to endow lectureships to provide for preachers outside the reach of the bishops.[4] That the church profited little from the extension of education up to 1583 is shown by the fact that only a third of incumbents were then graduates, few others had attended university for even a brief period, while only a sixth were licensed to preach.[5]

Despite the queen's preference for reducing puritan influence, in the northern counties measures were directed to eliminating catholicism. From 1572 when he became president of the council in the north—which

[1] Parents of those found 'inapt, and of no pregnant wit nor good capacity' should be encouraged to set them 'to learn husbandry, or other good crafts, that yet so they may learn to be good members to the country and commonweal' (*Injunctions...of Richard Barnes, bishop of Durham 1575–87*, Surtees Society, XXII, 1850, p. 19).

[2] *Ibid.* pp. 29 ff. Returns from Cambridgeshire parishes in the period 1576–80 provide evidence of many more local schoolmasters; but of nineteen presented for various offences at one visitation, sixteen had no licence (*VCH Cambs.* II, p. 338).

[3] Of some 9000 benefices, 1000 were worth as little as £2, only some 400 over £25, while about half brought in no more than £10 a year (Strype, *Whitgift*, I, p. 171).

[4] Jordan, *Charities of London*, p. 284.

[5] For the social and economic status of the clergy, see Hill, ch. IX and *passim*.

acted as a higher ecclesiastical commission as well as exercising civil powers—the earl of Huntingdon was actively engaged in promoting preaching and teaching on sound protestant lines, and able to depend for assistance on Edmund Grindal, installed as archbishop of York in 1570.[1] Here schoolmasters were examined for recusancy rather than refusal to subscribe and some were deprived. One of the main problems was tutors kept in catholic households. Grindal's injunctions of 1571 specify that no master be allowed to teach privately in any gentleman's house, or elsewhere, unless he be 'of good and sincere religion and conversation' and duly licensed. All teachers were enjoined to use Nowell's catechism and 'such sentences of Scripture (besides profane chaste authors) as shall be most meet to move them to the love and due reverence of God's true religion...and to induce them to all godliness and honest conversation'.[2]

In 1576 Grindal succeeded Parker as primate, at Burghley's instigation, and began to favour measures adopted in the north more at large. In particular he encouraged the 'prophesyings', monthly meetings of the clergy designed to raise the standard of education and preaching. To these Elizabeth, who saw no call for a learned clergy beyond one or two preachers for each county, was entirely opposed; in her view incumbents had best read the homilies, re-issued on the lines of those of Edward's reign with additions.[3] Since the archbishop stood firm—indeed told the queen to curb the peremptoriness of her dealings with matters bearing on religion—he was sequestered for much of his term of office and Elizabeth issued her own directives to the bishops to ban all prophesyings. But members of the privy council were of another mind and the meetings accordingly continued, at their active instigation, at any rate in some dioceses. The orders regulating those in the diocese of Chester show that schoolmasters were required to attend as well as ministers; all teachers in the district must be present at every exercise, which lasted a whole day, 'there either to write or speak' and fines were levied for non-attendance.[4]

[1] 'My lord president's good government here among us', wrote Grindal to Cecil (now Lord Burghley), who had favoured Huntingdon's appointment against some opposition, 'daily more and more discovereth the rare gifts and virtues which afore were in him, but in private life were hid from the eyes of a great number' (Strype, *Grindal*, pp. 262–3).

[2] Frere, III, pp. 270, 291.

[3] Strype, *Grindal*, p. 329.

[4] The exercises were still continuing here in 1585 under the guidance of bishop William Chaderton, onetime Lady Margaret professor of divinity at Cambridge

Leading councillors also actively supported the endowment of lecturers in the city of London and provincial boroughs.[1] The privy council itself, though forced for appearance sake to issue a general covering order for conformity at the inns of court, where there were zealous puritans, directly afterwards appointed as preacher of Lincoln's Inn a man they well knew had been expelled from a Cambridge college for obstinate non-conformity.[2] Burghley himself retained as tutor for his son Robert a leading puritan who had earlier been driven from Trinity College by Whitgift; and Walter Travers was also, despite having taken orders abroad, appointed lecturer at the Temple.[3]

It was in the same spirit that steps were taken to ensure schools were in good hands and properly run. Sir Nicholas Bacon supervised new orders for St Albans school in 1570 on much the same lines as those drawn up for Bury in the 1550's. Mildmay, in Northamptonshire, kept a close eye on Oundle school.[4] The earl of Huntingdon signed every page of the statutes for Leicester school, issued in 1574, in the drafting of which Thomas Sampson probably had a part. A Genevan exile—who had refused a bishopric and was ejected from the deanery of Christ Church during the vestiarian controversy—Sampson had been found a place as master of Wigston's Hospital, Leicester, under the earl's patronage, and as such was a visitor of the school. Its statutes, besides specifying attendance at church also required that scholars attend the weekly lecture established by the earl in the town. Those of the highest forms were also required to go 'to the divinity exercise called

(Strype, *Annals*, II, ii, p. 548; III, i, pp. 476–9). For those held in the diocese of York, and other puritan activities, Ronald A. Marchant, *The Puritans and the Church Courts in the Diocese of York, 1560–1642* (1961).

[1] 'I do all I can to get good preachers planted in the market towns of this country', wrote the earl of Huntingdon from York (F. Peck, *Desiderata Curiosa* (1779), I, p. 151). Walsingham, in his capacity as chancellor of the duchy of Lancaster, acted on similar lines (Strype, *Whitgift*, I, p. 425). For an occasion when both acted in concert to instal a suitable preacher at Leicester and secure him adequate remuneration, Joan Simon, 'The Two John Angels', *Transactions of the Leicestershire Archaeological and Historical Society*, XXXI (1955), pp. 35–6.

[2] Knappen, pp. 258, 261. This was William Charke who ended up as fellow of Eton where he was still obstinately non-conformist in 1610 (Lyte, pp. 199–200. For his expulsion from Cambridge, Heywood and Wright, pp. 123–33).

[3] Though to Whitgift he was 'one of the chief and principal authors of dissension' in the church, Travers would have had the important post of Master of the Temple in 1584 had Burghley had his way (Dawley, pp. 176–9).

[4] Carlisle, I, pp. 514–18; Walker, pp. 84, 91–2, 94.

prophesying the schoolmaster coming with them', while among the books prescribed was Calvin's catechism—in English for the petties, Latin for the middle school and finally in Greek.[1] Similar statutes were provided for the school at Ashby-de-la-Zouch, also endowed by Huntingdon, who was thus able to appoint the visitors to control it; these were the master of Wigston's Hospital, Sampson, and the vicar of Ashby, another onetime Genevan exile who led the puritan movement among the rank and file of the clergy, Anthony Gilby.

The privy council as such also intervened to adjust the curriculum of schools. In April 1582 a letter addressed to the High Commission prescribed a new text-book in Latin verse by Christopher Ocland, then master of St Olave's school, Southwark. Not only was the quality of the verse commended but also the matter which had to do in the first part with the history of England up to 1558, in the second with the reign of Elizabeth, the character of leading ministers being outlined; it was dedicated to one of Anthony Cooke's learned daughters, Lady Burghley. The council's letter described this as a book 'worthy to be read of all men, especially in common schools, where divers Heathen Poets are ordinarily read and taught, from which the youth of the realm doth rather receive infection in manners than advancement in virtue'. Encouragement had been given to authors to produce such works to replace the 'lascivious poets' and this one was 'heroical and of good instruction'. The High Commission was accordingly instructed to command the bishops to ensure the book was used in all grammar schools and an order to this effect prefaces the book as published in 1582; a reprint was required within six months.[2]

Nothing could have served better to underline the deficiencies of the English clergy than the advent in the 1580's of Jesuit missionaries, carefully educated abroad and single-mindedly devoted to their task of retrieving the English gentry for the catholic faith. Many of these were harboured in gentlemen's households under the guise of tutors but the privy council also drew attention at this time to failure adequately to supervise the schools; 'a great deal of the corruption in religion grown throughout the realm, proceedeth of lewd schoolmasters, that teach and instruct children as well publicly as privately in men's houses'.

[1] The statutes are printed in Cross, pp. 15–20.

[2] Strype, *Annals*, III, i, pp. 223–5; Watson, pp. 80–2. Among the signatories of this letter, expressing the kind of 'anti-renaissance' views often attributed to the more bigoted middle class, were Leicester, Walsingham, Knollys and Hatton (*Original Letters*, 1843, pp. 64–7).

Statutes directed to retaining subjects in due obedience now required that all schoolmasters attend church on pain of a heavy fine and bishops were instructed to enquire closely after 'backsliders' from religion in their dioceses; all schoolmasters found unfit must be 'displaced and proceeded withal as other recusants and fit and sound persons placed in their rooms'. Subsequent episcopal injunctions reflect the concern.[1]

At a time when protestantism became inescapably associated with national feeling there was a new impetus towards providing a sound education and school statutes of this period insist on prayers before opening, attendance at church on Sundays, and on occasion, taking notes of sermons.[2] It has been suggested that there was an intense, 'almost contemptuous', secularism in Elizabeth's reign, mainly in the light of the queen's own attitude and the falling away of bequests to churches.[3] But it should not be overlooked that bequests to education were essentially towards upholding 'true religion' and, if it had ceased to be a custom to bequeath sums for the upkeep of churches, there were special rates and collections to this end; they were less neglected than is usually supposed, though their appearance might be plain and workmanlike.[4] Churches were much used not only for services but for lectures which provided an education for adults, and as a gathering place on many occasions—such as thanksgivings for victory over Spain at a time when Elizabeth (whatever her personal feelings in the matter) figured as the main bulwark of the Reformation.[5] Everyone had his proper place in church, as in the world outside, as a visitation order of 1578 for the parish of Kendal illustrates; special seating is specified for the aldermen on the left side of the chancel, for J.P.'s and gentlemen in a chapel south of it, and for the schoolmaster and his scholars in a chapel to the north of the chancel with 'forms and seats round about ...convenient and seeming for the place and purpose'. At this time the parish was officially urged that all stipends 'wont to be given to the organ player and other unnecessary clerks be wholly employed to the stipend of [a] preacher' who, with the vicar, might provide 'every Sunday in the year a sermon to their great comfort and edifying'.[6]

[1] Strype, *Grindal*, pp. 377–9, 394–5, 400; *Whitgift*, I, pp. 191–3, 238.

[2] *EGS*, pp. 45–8.

[3] Jordan, *Philanthropy*, pp. 298–9.

[4] Jack Simmons, 'Brooke Church, Rutland: with Notes on Elizabethan Church-Building', *Transactions of the Leicestershire Archaeological and Historical Society*, XXXV (1959), pp. 36–55.

[5] Cf. W. Haller, *Foxe's Book of Martyrs and the Elect Nation* (1963).

[6] Bouch, pp. 221–2. For Lakeland chapels built or adapted at this time, see pp. 223–4.

An account of a boarder's life in the household of the master of Christ's Hospital grammar school gives some idea of the kind of régime many boys came under at this time.[1] David Baker entered the school in 1587 at the age of eleven to be placed as boarder 'in company with divers other gentlemen's sons, of divers parts of England' with the master and his wife. The former, educated at Eton and Cambridge, had been in office over twenty years; as he and his wife were 'both of them very zealous protestants' and 'very honest and good moral livers', their boarders were well disciplined in religion and morality. At meals the scholars gathered at a long table, with master and mistress of the house at the head, and one read a chapter from the bible before the meal began. Each evening prayers were read, and every Sunday and holy day the scholars followed their guardians to church for morning and evening service; they were often asked 'to write down the preached sermon, the which done the master would afterwards peruse it'. The sermons the boy best remembered were those of Hugh Broughton, noted as a Calvinist and Hebrew scholar, formerly of Christ's and a pupil of Anthony Chevallier who had first taught Hebrew at Cambridge in Edward's day.

Christ's Hospital, under the eye of the common council of London, was bound to be a godly school as were others governed by the livery companies. But the first book bought for Philip Sidney when he entered Shrewsbury school in 1564 had been Calvin's catechism, at Westminster Camden did what he could to bring up scholars (including heirs of Irish families sent to the school) to the true religion,[2] and there were puritan teachers up and down the country whose scholarship usually outran that of others and made them sought after. These were the writers of text-books which went into other schools; John Stockwood is an example, a great preacher of God's word as well as teacher, master at Tonbridge from 1574–87.[3] Concerned, as Colet had once been, with the early stage of education, Stockwood was author of an English accidence framed to be 'as it were dunstically plain, for the

[1] *Christ's Hospital Book*, pp. 16–18. The writer gives a dispassionate account in the third person of his early upbringing, the more interesting in that he later became a Benedictine.

[2] *Original Letters*, p. 125.

[3] He translated tracts by Bullinger and Beza and published *A Short Catechism for Householders* (1583), *A very godly and profitable sermon of the necessary properties and office of a good Magistrate* (1584), a commentary on the prophets (1594) dedicated to the earl of Huntingdon (Rivington, pp. 27–32; *Athenae*, III, pp. 24–5).

better understanding of the young ones, unto whom nothing can be made too plain'. This was published in 1590 as 'appointed by authority to be taught in all schools of her Majesty's dominions, for the great use and benefit of young beginners' and followed by a simple version of part of the official Latin grammar intended 'for the help of the weaker sort in grammar schools'.[1] Besides the regular schoolmasters there were also the incumbents teaching. The most notable writer on education in the early seventeenth century, John Brinsley, was a graduate of Christ's—among whose fellows were Edward Dering, William Perkins, Arthur Hildersham, Francis Johnson; Brinsley began his teaching career in the 1590's as curate of Kegworth, within the ambit of the earl of Huntingdon, while Hildersham succeeded Gilby as vicar of the neighbouring parish of Ashby.

When in the 1580's a system of presbyterian classes became established, drawing together congregations in some districts, members began to translate into practice the belief that all should have access to education. Thus the elders of the Dedham classis took measures to see that every child was taught to read and set up a school; a house was provided for the master and the collection taken on communion Sundays devoted to paying the fees of poor children.[2] With the rise of the classis movement measures against puritans, which had not ceased when attention turned to catholics, were intensified under the direction of Archbishop Whitgift who succeeded Grindal in 1583. The puritan programme submitted to the parliament of 1584—in support of a learned ministry and for the restraint of bishops—once more linked the expansion of education with reform of the church. Plurality and non-residence should be ended in favour of providing adequate livings for the parish clergy. The endowments of cathedrals, instead of going to maintain singing men, should be used to support preaching ministers, grammar schools and poor scholars at the universities—the kind of programme William Turner had advanced from Basle thirty years before. Moreover, if all decayed schools, were revived, if rich ecclesiastics in fact gave £10 a year to keep students of divinity at the universities (as injunctions laid down), if heads of colleges ensured that bribes were never taken and worthy scholars elected to fellowships—then there would soon be no want of godly ministers.[3]

[1] *EGS*, pp. 266–7.
[2] Knappen, p. 469.
[3] Strype, *Annals*, III, ii, pp. 279 ff.

A bill was, in fact, introduced during this parliament to curb corruption in elections to college fellowships but it was vetoed by the queen who saw this as an encroachment on the crown's prerogative and patronage. Whitgift expressing his regret to Burghley hoped that none the less action would be taken to curb abuses.[1] But he met more general criticisms with the argument that to remove high office in the church and end plurality would deprive 'learned men of their due reward', while the catholic enemy would have 'just cause to triumph when they shall see the clergy and learning generally so much disgraced and vilified by the gentry and commons of this land'.[2] Bishops had long retorted, when puritans sought to solve the economic problems of the church by removing the hierarchy, that there was another way of doing so, by retrieving the large sums pocketed by lay impropriators. Moreover, if the clergy were unlearned the fault also lay with 'corrupt patrons' who 'nowadays search not the universities for a most fit pastor, but... post up and down the country for a most gainful chapman. He that hath the biggest purse to pay largely, not he that hath the best gifts to preach learnedly is presented'.[3] It was an old complaint brought up to date.

But this same year, yet another puritan programme for reform having failed, a veteran of the Edwardian age founded a new college at Cambridge designed to ensure that swarms of faithful ministers should go out into the parishes, as Bucer had once so ardently wished. Sir Walter Mildmay set out his intentions clearly when founding Emmanuel. It was to 'render as many as possible fit for the administration of the Divine Word and Sacrament...that from this seed ground the English Church might have those that she can summon to instruct the people and undertake the office of pastors, which is a thing necessary above all others'.[4] The chapel of Emmanuel was built to face north instead of east and was never consecrated, members of the college wore no surplice, the official prayer book was left aside in favour of a special

[1] Since an act would have brought the universities into open disrepute he was glad this move had failed, Whitgift wrote (a tactful acceptance of the royal veto) but unless some action were taken this failure would aggravate malpractices—it could not be denied that it began 'to be an ordinary practice for fellows of colleges...to resign up their fellowships for sums of money' and this was a cause of much evil (Strype, *Whitgift*, I, p. 149).

[2] *Ibid.* 380–1.

[3] Hill, pp. 144–5. The comment occurs in the preface to a translation of Bullinger's *Decades* intended for the education of the clergy (Strype, *Whitgift*, I, pp. 367–8).

[4] E. S. Shuckburgh, *Emmanuel College* (1904), pp. 23–4; Knappen, pp. 469–72.

form of service and communion was taken seated. The first master Lawrence Chaderton, brought from Christ's, steered the college during a rule of thirty-six years along the course set by the founder. Modelled largely on the college ordered in Edward's reign, Trinity, Emmanuel served in turn as a model for Sidney Sussex founded by Frances, countess of Sussex, the aunt of Philip Sidney, as a 'good and godly monument for the maintenance of good learning'.[1] The two colleges established during Elizabeth's reign were, therefore, founded at Cambridge under puritan auspices.[2] Emmanuel shortly had 200 undergraduates, more than any other Cambridge college except the largest, though there were only twelve fellows to teach as against fifty to sixty at Trinity.[3]

There is also a new incisiveness in orders for the schools of these later years, drawn up now by local men. 'For as much as this school is principally ordained a seminary for bringing up of christian children...and generally is intended a school of christian instruction for virtue and manners therein to be learned of all the scholars thereof', ran the imposing statutes of the Free Grammar School of Wakefield—initiated by the Savilles, merchants turned gentlemen, in the 1590's—'therefore we will that especial care be had in the placing of a fit teacher from whom as the root the scholars are to draw the sap and juice of religion, learning and good nurture'. The master must be an M.A. and one 'withal well reported of for his knowledge, religion and life, and known to be an enemy to popish superstition, a lover and forward imbracer of God's truth, a man...diligent and painful in his own studies, of a sober and amiable carriage towards all men, able to maintain the place of a schoolmaster with dignity and gravity, given to the diligent reading of God's word'. His first charge must be 'to instruct and inform his scholars in the grounds of religion', examining them in this on Saturdays, accompanying them to church on Sundays and ensuring that notes of sermons are taken, correcting these on Monday. He should

[1] The foundress also left an annuity for a learned preacher to read two lectures weekly in Westminster Abbey and a sum to distribute among poor and godly ministers in London and the suburbs. The college was established in 1596, statutes being issued in 1598 (G. M. Edwards, *Sidney Sussex College*, 1899, pp. 18–19, 24).

[2] Oxford had profited during the reign of Mary who favoured that university and Trinity and St John's were founded there in 1555. Another college, Jesus, was endowed in 1571 by a Welshman; Elizabeth usurped the title of founder but nothing else was done to establish it and with only a small income, without statutes, it had no resident fellows until 1602 (Mallet, II, pp. 195–7).

[3] S. E. Morison, *The Founding of Harvard College*, Harvard, 1935, p. 92.

also 'in the plainest and most familiar sort teach them grammar, and the Latin and Greek tongues, reading unto them the most classic authors', detailed directives being given to this end; and the final duty laid upon him is that of 'informing his youth in good nurture and manners which are of themselves an ornament to religion and good learning'.[1]

In the closing years of the reign the great statesmen who had for so long dominated the scene disappeared one by one.[2] But shortly before his death Walsingham endowed a divinity lecture at Oxford and secured the appointment of John Rainolds—leader of the puritan party at the Hampton Court conference and one of the most influential teachers of a new generation of Oxford men.[3] In 1591 Burghley became chancellor of the university at last brought to birth in Dublin and Walter Travers was made provost, an office in which he was succeeded by an even more pronounced puritan, Henry Alvey of St John's, Cambridge.[4] In December 1595 Burghley was writing to his son from a sickbed on behalf of this college, that it be allowed (as a petition to him from twenty-three of the fellows requested) to elect its own master. 'If you shall find any intention in her majesty upon any sinister suit', he wrote, 'to prefer any other than the voices of the company shall freely choose, to beseech her majesty that at my suit (being their chancellor, and having been wholly brought up there from my age of 14 years, and now the only person living of that time and education) the statutes of the college...may not now be broken; as I hope her majesty will not in her honour and conscience do.'[5] It was a tone very different from that of his public letters to the college. Although Elizabeth actively interfered the principle of free election was retained, if not to the extent that the majority of fellows prevailed for their candidate had been the puritan Henry Alvey.[6]

The spirit of Huntingdon also lived on in the council of the north, as is illustrated by a letter addressed to the burgesses of York in 1599, which summarises a whole educational policy:

[1] Peacock, pp. 62–3, 65–6. These statutes were not actually framed until 1606; it took fifteen years to accumulate the necessary funds to establish the school for which a charter was gained in 1591 (*ibid.* pp. 18–19).

[2] Leicester died in 1588, Mildmay in 1589, Walsingham in 1590, then in 1595 Huntingdon, in 1596 Knollys, in 1598 Burghley.

[3] Mallet, II, p. 237; Read, III, pp. 438–40.

[4] J. W. Stubbs, *History of the University of Dublin* (Dublin, 1889), pp. 18–20.

[5] Peck, I, pp. 170–1.

[6] Porter, pp. 201–5.

It is the duty of all Christian magistrates to have a care of the good education of all youths and children within their charge, that they may be instructed and seasoned at the first with the true knowledge of God and His religion, whereby they are liable to become good members of the Church and commonweal and dutiful subjects of her majesty and the state.[1]

During the last decades of the reign the privy council brought pressure to bear on Whitgift—strong in the support of the queen—to modify his campaign against the puritans, in return for assistance in preventing further lay encroachment on ecclesiastical endowments and consolidation of the church.[2] Thereafter many suspended ministers were restored to their cures, efforts were turned to wiping out the classis movement and the archbishop himself launched comprehensive plans for educating the clergy similar to those initiated in the Edwardian age. This policy, applied at a time when more scholars were coming up through school and university, bore fruit. By 1598 about half the clergy held a preacher's licence, many of these being graduates, while some of the rest had attended university for a time.[3] Much might still be said about lack of education in the church but this was relative by comparison with the first twenty-five years of Elizabeth's reign. At its close attempts to secure a presbyterian system of church government had foundered and the Anglican church—now nearly half a century old, practically strengthened and gaining doctrinal support at last from Hooker's *Laws of Ecclesiastical Polity* (1597)—began to appear almost established.

None the less, during the foregoing decades Calvinism had struck deep roots. Oxford had been under the protection of the earl of Leicester for many years, and a generation later Archbishop Laud was complaining that Winchester scholars entering New College were examined chiefly in their knowledge of Calvin's *Institutes*[4]. At Cambridge the regular sermons given by William Perkins, after he relinquished his fellowship at Christ's up to his early death in 1602, were one of the chief features of university life; and the treatises of this spokesman of the new puritanism, which would prevail in the coming years, made up nearly a quarter of the 200 works published by the university press

[1] Quoted in N. Wood, p. 70.

[2] Knappen, pp. 280–1.

[3] Dawley, pp. 201–5.

[4] Rashdall and Rait, pp. 148–9. The library catalogues of Oxford theological students 'are replete with works by Calvin, Melanchthon, Peter Martyr, Zanchius, Beza, Bullinger, and other continental theologians' (Curtis, p. 162).

between 1590 and 1618.[1] Puritan preaching and discussion had been actively encouraged at the inns of court to which so many young gentlemen came up from the counties. In particular, efforts had consistently been directed to making the grammar school a reformed school. All in all there was a good deal less of a *via media* in the educational system than in the church.

[1] Porter, p. 264. When Thomas Goodwin entered Christ's in 1613 he found that 'the whole town was then filled with the discourse of the power of Mr. Perkins's ministry, still fresh in most men's memories' (Christopher Hill, *Puritanism and Revolution*, 1962 ed., p. 217).

XIV

THE INSTITUTION OF THE GENTLEMAN

The clergy had for centuries been instituted to their office. The early humanists preached 'the institution of the Christian prince' or 'Christian man', and the phrase carried over into the years of the Reformation when the prince became godly and obedience a primary duty of all Christians. In Elizabeth's reign the centre of attention was the 'institution of the gentleman'. The first tract on this theme since that of Elyot, published in 1555, in fact bore this title, and it imparts a new tone to the discussion. In the days of Henry VIII when assistance was needed to reduce the church and offices vacated by churchmen must be filled it had seemed that there was plenty of room at the top; sons of obscure gentlemen rose to high status and Elyot issued a call for further recruits. Matters looked different in the age of Elizabeth when gentlemen found less outlet upwards and at the same time became conscious of encroachments from below. This provided a strong stimulus to defining and securing their position, a position that now seemed, under God, more independent than before.

The Reformation had revived an old popular query—when Adam delved and Eve span, who was then the gentleman?—and disquisitions often go back to this beginning. The *Institution of a Gentleman*[1] finds that 'so much grace as Adam our first father received of God at his creation, so much nobility and gentry he received.' In other words, if Adam was good and of honest behaviour then he was the first gentleman; thus 'it appeareth that gentlemen took their beginning of gentle deeds'. This argument is buttressed by another. It is contended—at a time when it was generally supposed that Cambridge had been founded by King Sigbert, Oxford by King Alfred—that noblemen of the past established universities and places of study in order to 'increase virtue by way of knowledge', sending sons there to inherit 'greater

[1] By an anonymous author it is dedicated to the heir of the earl of Sussex. There is a facsimile reprint, lacking numbered pages, *The Institucion of a Gentleman*, ed. C. Whittingham (1839).

goods, that is to say, riches of the mind, than either lands or worldly possessions can bring with them'. It is thus established, in the humanist tradition, that learning is integral to gentility—with the proviso that gentlemen made it so.

In the circumstances those of low degree, by acquiring learning and applying it judiciously, can be transformed into gentlemen and even attain the highest offices; of such, says the writer, there are now very many in England. But there are also the lowborn who, merely through purchasing lands by 'certain dark augmentation practices', creep 'into the degree of worship without worthiness' and cheapen it. In this situation gentlemen must actively uphold the status, and justify the attendant privileges, by fulfilling obligations proper to them—such as serving in the wars, on embassies abroad, as justices of the peace, or keeping hospitality in the countryside and administering their estates well. They must always stand out as better than others, in all they do, so proving themselves 'worthy to possess such lands and inheritance as God hath prepared for them to the maintenance of their lives or their estates'.[1]

It is noteworthy that the prince receives little recognition here as the source of ownership of land and honour. Moreover, it is an easy step from arguments of this kind to the view that the lowborn should be prevented from purchasing lands, which confer status, and also from acquiring the kind of education favoured for gentlemen. This view is clearly advanced in a list of *Considerations* drawn up for submission to parliament at the outset of Elizabeth's reign.[2] The dispersal of monastic lands was now well under way and prosperous butchers, graziers, yeomen farmers were among those who purchased in the market; well-to-do yeomen, as in the past, also set sons to train as lawyers and seemed particularly to tread on the heels of gentlemen.[3] Accordingly

[1] Reprinted in 1568 this tract—with its division of gentlemen into those of birth and good behaviour, the 'gentle gentle' and those who rise by education and service, the 'gentle ungentle'—was frequently drawn upon by later writers.

[2] *Historical MSS. Commission, Hatfield MSS.*, I, pp. 162–5. There is no good reason to ascribe this to Cecil though it figures among his papers; it was possibly the work of a committee of lawyers which included Richard Goodrich, who was responsible for some very conservative advice at this time, and others in office under Mary (S. T. Bindoff, in *Elizabethan Government and Society*, pp. 80–1).

[3] Yeomen, wrote William Harrison in 1587, are '40*s*. freeholders, or six pounds as money goeth in our times' and usually live well. Since instead of keeping idle servants like gentlemen they employ workers who 'get both their own and part of their master's living' they often gain great wealth 'inasmuch that many of them are able and do buy

one clause of the *Considerations* proposes that yeomen be prohibited from buying lands above the value of £5, butchers and tanners above £10, merchants above £50, unless they are London aldermen who become knights and may be permitted more to support this state. At the same time the interests of gentlemen should be safeguarded by reserving suitable educational facilities for them. 'A third of the free scholarships at universities' should be set aside for 'the poorer sort of gentlemen's son' and yeomen should be prevented from entering sons at the inns of court—only those 'immediately descended from a nobleman or gentleman' should be permitted to study either common or civil law.

While there could hardly be a statute framed on these lines, the interests of gentlemen were safeguarded by the enactment of other proposals designed to keep the lower orders to their proper callings and discriminate against the entrepreneur. The *Considerations*, complaining that landowners could not get labourers at a reasonable wage because the unregulated trades provided alternative employment, proposed that old labour laws be re-enacted; and that, in addition, all but the sons of 40*s*. freeholders be prevented from entering urban trades and all but sons of men worth at least £10 a year and sons of gentlemen be excluded from entering as apprentices to merchants. This last proposal, framed entirely in the landowning interest, was evidently challenged in the Commons by borough representatives concerned to avoid restrictions on apprenticeship, for the measure eventually passed represented a modified version of the original plan.[1] None the less the Statute of Artificers of 1563 severely delimited the opportunities of different sections of the population. The seven-year apprenticeship was extended to all urban trades, which thereby secured a share in the labour market, but the suggested property qualifications of 40*s*. was introduced to restrict entry to the better trades of mercer and goldsmith and to the ranks of overseas merchants. At the same time, and this protected urban as against country industry as well as the interests of landowners seeking agricultural labour, clothiers were forbidden to take any apprentices, while entry to weaving was restricted to sons of 60*s*.

the lands of unthrifty gentlemen'; either they leave sons sufficient land to enable them to live without labour or else 'set their sons to the schools and to the universities and to the Inns of Court' and by this means make them 'to become gentlemen' (*Description of England*, pp. 132–3).

[1] Bindoff, 'The Making of the Statute of Artificers', *loc. cit.* pp. 92–3; for the main provisions of this, *Tudor Constitution*, pp. 466–70.

freeholders. This closed up the nearest outlet for the countryman's son and the measure bore particularly harshly on wage labourers; not only were they virtually bound to the soil, while powers to fix wages rested with justices of the peace who represented the employers, but their children were at the disposal of any who wished to hire them from the age of twelve.[1] A further proposal in the *Considerations*, that the vicious poor law of 1547 be revived with additions, did not come to fruition; but measures were later passed to ensure that the children of the poor were set to work while otherwise they drifted into the poorest trades as cheap unskilled labour.[2]

At the other end of the scale there were the more opportunities for gentlemen's sons; they were, of course, excluded from compulsory employment while the high property qualification on the better trades told in their favour. This last, it seemed to a commentator some years later, was devised to control gentlemen themselves from unrestricted gathering to the detriment of the commonwealth.[3] It may well have made more easily available a useful outlet for younger sons; in any case in later years a considerable proportion of London apprentices were immediate descendants of gentlemen.[4] But if younger sons were to be set up in trade they needed some capital behind them; it was also costly to train them for the law, to buy a commission in the army, even to establish them in the church when this involved buying an advowson or a right of presentation; moreover, dowries must also be found for daughters, on a considerable scale if they were to vie with the well-endowed daughters of merchants. Nothing could well prevent the accumulation and consolidation of landed property by

[1] G. Unwin, *Industrial Organisation in the Sixteenth and Seventeenth Centuries* (Oxford, 1904), pp. 138–40; *Studies in Economic History*, pp. 187, 251. Dunlop and Denman, pp. 60 ff.

[2] Justices of the peace and officers of towns were given powers to bind the children of the vagrant poor to any trade or to husbandry provided their services were demanded by a householder, a power later extended by the act of 1601 to cover the offspring of parents 'over burthened with children' who might in future become a charge (Dunlop and Denman, pp. 70, 95–8; Leonard, pp. 72–3).

[3] It was intended to ensure, it was suggested, that gentlemen 'might have some convenient means to bestow and place their younger sons in the commonwealth to live in a reasonable countenance and calling; the want whereof causeth many to be more mindful to gather for their children than to regard the state of the commonwealth' (Unwin, *Industrial Organisation*, p. 138).

[4] So longstanding links were forged anew; as Harrison remarked, gentlemen often exchanged estate with merchants and vice versa 'by a mutual conversion of the one into the other' (*Description of England*, p. 131).

provident and persistent men, the feature of the Elizabethan age by contrast with the earlier scramble for what was going and the begging of grants from the crown. There were, after all, also heirs to set up, while there was a growing tendency to settle some younger sons as well on the land.[1]

There was one other educational proposal in the *Considerations*—that 'an ordinance be made to bind the nobility to bring up their children in learning from the age of twelve to eighteen at least'. While this might seem in the spirit of Knox, the explanation added suggests a bitter memory of Edward's reign. If the old nobility are ignorant the prince is forced 'to advance new men that can serve, which for the most part neither affecting true honour, because the glory thereof descended not to them, nor yet the commonwealth (through coveting to be hastily in wealth and honour) do forget their duty and old estate and subvert the noble houses to have their rooms themselves'. This was a complaint of the rebellious northern earls of 1569 who demanded that the upstart Cecil be brought to trial, as the rebels of 1536 had called for Cromwell's head. Such a reaction served to underline from another angle the dangers of lack of a proper upbringing among the nobility. But no statute was passed to deal with a problem so closely bound up, as Starkey had divined, with the system of wardship. Since this could not be dispensed with, later plans for training the nobility to their duties took the form of advocating at least a compulsory education for royal wards. Meanwhile gentlemen made the most of their opportunities in the educational field as elsewhere.

(1) *The nobility, household education and foreign travel*

The Marian exiles had their contribution to make in the matter of educating the nobility as in that of ordering schools. Much thought had been given to problems of government in a reformed state, not least those arising from the doctrine of obedience to the prince. While reformers had earlier been single-minded in stressing this duty, despite injustices, doubts necessarily arose when it became clear that the prince could be ungodly as well as unjust. Some held that tyranny

[1] Though much remains in doubt about the distribution of former monastic and chantry lands it seems clear that, while most existing categories of landed proprietor increased their holdings and some laid the foundation of great houses, prosperous yeomen and younger sons of gentlemen notably bettered their position (Knowles, p. 399; *Tudor Constitution*, pp. 371–2).

was a punishment from God to be borne in silence, but in his *Treatise of Politic Power* (1556) John Ponet—former bishop of Winchester in exile at Strasburg—rejected this view as blasphemous; rather tyranny resulted from forsaking God and the way to return to God was to remove the tyrant. In this context Ponet advanced a notably fresh analysis of the origin and function of nobility. How, since all men are descended from Adam and Eve, did some come to be held in honour? Because of 'their virtue and love to their country. Because they revenged and delivered the oppressed people out of the hands of their governors, who abused their authority, and wickedly and tyrannously ruled over them; the people of a great and thankful mind, gave them that estimation and honour.'[1]

Ponet died in exile but others returned who had also debated the problems. Anthony Gilby reached the conclusion that Henry VIII led 'no reformation but a deformation'; and yet 'this monstrous boar must needs be called the Head of the Church, displacing Christ our only Head'. John Knox saw as the two alternatives 'that either princes be reformed and be compelled also to reform their wicked laws or else that all good men depart from their service and company'.[2] If these were the most radical views there was a more general tendency to write down duty to the prince which implied a new stress on the nobility as the shield and buckler both of the social order and the church. A clear example is the book written by Lawrence Humfrey when in exile, published in Latin in Basle in 1559 and in London, in an English version, four years later. In this he argues that it is the particular function of the nobility to act as a bulwark against the tyranny of princes on the one hand and the turbulence of the people on the other.[3]

Humfrey acknowledges at the outset the abuses of rank but finds that they are outweighed by its uses which some do not well understand. 'There be neither few, nor those altogether evil', he writes, 'that think this nobility ought to be banished and not borne in the commonwealth. And seeing some nobles infect themselves and the state, with idleness,

[1] Zeeveld, p. 358; J. W. Allen, pp. 118–20.

[2] Allen, pp. 108–9, 211.

[3] *The Nobles or of Nobilitie. The original nature, duty, right, and Christian institution thereof* (1563). There have been books on teaching and framing princes, Humfrey notes, but princes and nobles differ; the latter are subjects, more numerous and have more to do with the people. He evidently uses the category in the traditional sense to cover all men of birth, though perhaps with a bias towards the nobleman.

pleasure, sloth, licentious living and evil example, and disdainfully, proudly, and arrogantly despise their inferiors: think they ought to have no place in a right and Christian commonwealth.' Certainly, Humfrey agrees, all men are of equal right in Christ. 'But foolishly reasoneth he, who weaneth to confound the certain and several estates, to root up the limits and bounds of nature, kind, nation, kin or flock', for these are given 'by the laws of God and man'. While each estate has its duties those of the nobility are numerous and indispensable; they rule, guide, serve the prince in action and attain honour not only through their ancestors but their own contribution.

Discussion about long lineage is, therefore, brushed aside in favour of concentrating on education. Old stocks can degenerate and a new nobility may well be better than the old; what matters is that all those of status should have the necessary qualities to serve the commonwealth aright. The essential characteristics to be developed are Christian humility, justice, willingness to serve the country and, above all, sound religion. Whereas Erasmus had once assimilated the orator Cicero to God, Humfrey brings forward, with Isocrates and Demosthenes, 'the most reverend author and orator Christ Jesus with the apostles whose writings I allow ever first and last'. Indeed the scriptures, study of which Elyot had referred to maturity, are presented as a textbook in rhetoric, economics and history.[1] It is the main duty of the nobles, so schooled, to uphold the church. To them it falls to defend the true religion, not as knights once did in crusades, but by acting 'to relieve the cause of the gospel fainting and falling, to strengthen with their aid impoverished religion, to shield it forsaken with their patronage'; thereby 'both the tyranny of princes is bridled, and the rage of the common people repressed, and the pride of prelates tamed'. To this end especial care must be taken to root out all forms of superstition and 'suffer no delusion of idolatry creep into the church'.[2] This was advice that Elizabethan statesmen tended to take, while Humfrey himself—installed as president of Magdalen—put precepts into practice in educating the sons of Francis Knollys and many another young man who went on to take his place in parliament.

Calvinist ideas must, however, contend with others during the early years of Elizabeth, particularly at court where contemporary Italian fashions and courtly guides exercised a strong appeal. An earlier and sounder example was brought forward in 1561 when Castiglione's

[1] Kelso, p. 128. [2] Knappen. p. 177.

The Courtier was published in English.[1] This, which became in time almost a second bible for English gentlemen, by no means depicted a courtier dancing attendance on the throne. Rather it is the courtier who instructs and guides the prince, attempting gradually to 'distil into his mind goodness, and teach him continency, stoutness of courage, justice' leading him 'through the rough way of virtue'; indeed he leads the prince to such an extent that he almost seems 'more excellent than the prince' and for all his knowledge and wisdom to deserve a far greater and more honourable name than courtier. To the translator of this work, the travelled Sir Thomas Hoby, it seemed that to attain this degree of civilisation English gentlemen must first cultivate their own language so that 'we alone of the world may not be still counted barbarous in our tongue, as in time out of mind we have been in our manners. And so shall we perchance in time become as famous in England, as the learned men of other nations have been and presently are.'[2] To achieve this end, to bring the English language and literature to the level attained in Italy and France, became a conscious aim pursued first by a host of translators and later by writers of English poetry and prose. All this in time contributed much to the institution of the gentleman.

But in the 1560's, as Roger Ascham noted, Castiglione was left aside in favour of superficial courtly guides and the aping of foreign fashions. In response to a request from old Sir Richard Sackville—so prominent in educational matters in Edward's day—Ascham once more set out the case for learning combined with sound religion in *The Schoolmaster*. This was 'specially purposed for the private bringing up of youth in gentlemen and noblemen's houses', but Ascham, while giving much detailed advice about teaching method and the proper treatment of children, could now concede that young gentlemen 'commonly be carefully enough brought up' from seven to seventeen; Elyot had complained that education usually ended at fourteen. None the less, he repeats the stricture that young men of birth are let loose at court or abroad at the most impressionable age and then cease to study. Small wonder that lesser men's children rise to high positions, through God's providence. For 'God is a good God, and wisest in all his doings', comments Ascham sententiously, 'that will place virtue, and displace vice, in those kingdoms where he doth govern, for he knoweth

[1] It was shortly to be banned in the catholic world, first by the Spanish Inquisition in 1576, then by the papacy, being placed on the index in 1590.

[2] Castiglione, pp. 5, 265, 284–96.

that nobility without virtue and wisdom is blood indeed, but blood truly without bones and sinews; and so of itself, without the other, very weak to bear the burden of weighty affairs'. The remedy lies with well-born parents who, by ensuring that their sons attain to 'truth in religion, honesty in living, right order in learning' can see they acquire wisdom and its due reward.[1] In short the emphasis is less now on lack of education, more on the need for education of the right kind, with 'true religion' placed first.

Ascham's book was published posthumously in 1570. That same year it was again forcibly stressed, this time by Sir Humphrey Gilbert, that gentlemen were prevented from providing sons with a sound and godly education by the system of wardship. This longstanding problem had been ventilated nine years before when, on retiring after many years service as attorney to the court of wards, Sir Nicholas Bacon forwarded a plan for the better education of the royal wards to Cecil, now master of the court. The accompanying note bluntly characterises the prevailing proceedings as 'preposterous'. What matters most is the mind of the ward, then his body. 'Now, hitherto, the chief care of governance hath been had to the land, being the meanest; and to the body, being the better, very small; but to the mind, being the best, none at all, which methinks is plainly to set the cart before the horse.' His advice was that all royal wards whose lands had an annual value of over a hundred marks should be brought together from the age of nine in a special academy; there, under the governance of a warden and five masters, a regular routine could be followed, covering the teaching of modern languages as well as classics, law, music and allied arts, riding and the handling of weapons.[2]

Gilbert, concerned to canvass a more far-reaching plan,[3] insists at length on the abuses arising from the sale of wardships by the crown. Wards handed over to one who has merely purchased the right to govern their lands and arrange their marriage may fall under guardians 'either of evil religion, or insufficient qualities'. Indeed most wards, through the deficiencies of their guardians, are brought up to the 'no small grief of their friends, in idleness and lascivious pastimes, estranged from all serviceable virtues to their prince and country'; their education is meagre, either from skimping of funds or of purpose 'to abase their minds, lest being better qualified, they should disdain to stoop to the

[1] *English Works*, p. 205. [2] Bell, p. 120.

[3] *Queene Elizabethe's Achademy*, ed. F. J. Furnivall (E.E.T.S. 1869), pp. 1–12.

marriage of such purchasers' daughters'. In presenting his plan for a special academy in London for wards aged twelve to twenty, Gilbert suggests that this could also be attended by courtiers, students at the inns of court and others. This enables him to extend his case and argue that gentlemen cannot find any adequate form of education in England for their sons. If sent to university they are offered unsuitable forms of school learning and since there is no other gentlemanly quality to be acquired are likely merely to acquire licentious habits; moreover, by taking up places in colleges, they disappoint the poor of their livings and advancements. In an academy young gentlemen can be brought up together in amity, safely out of reach of corruption by papistry, and 'trained up in the knowledge of god's word'; this will 'much assuage the present grief that good and godly parents endure by that tenure of wardship for (as it is) it not only hurteth the body, but also (as it were) killeth the soul and darkeneth the eyes of reason with ignorance'. Gilbert concludes that it is both in the royal interest and a duty to promote such an education since kings become guardians and have the use of their wards' lands during minority 'principally for to train them up in virtue, which for conscience sake ought not by them to be forgotten'.

To train up young gentlemen in virtue meant to Gilbert—associate of Smith, Cecil and Leicester in 'The Society of the New Art' which prospected for and treated minerals, sailor, and briefly member of parliament—a good deal more than a classical regimen combined with study of the scriptures. It meant instruction in arithmetic and natural philosophy, cosmography and navigation, military sciences as well as arts, modern as well as ancient languages. It meant teaching history and politics and teaching them in English—the language used 'in preaching, in parliament, in council, in commission' and other public offices.[1] Civil law should also be studied supplemented by instructions from a common lawyer on the duties of the J.P. and sheriff; for anything more students could go to the inns of court. Models of fortifications, precise replicas of ships, maps, study of the stars and use of navigational

[1] 'I omit to show what ornament will thereby grow to our tongue, and how able it will appear for strength and plenty when, by such exercises, learning shall have brought unto it the choice of words, the building of sentences, the garnishments of figures, and other beauties of oratory—whereupon I have heard that the famous knight Sir John Cheke devised to have declamations, and other such exercises, sometimes in the universities performed in English' (*loc. cit.* p. 2). An indication that statutes which had laid this down were not now observed.

instruments, instruction in medicine—all these come into Gilbert's course. So also does scientific experiment, attempts 'by the fire and otherwise, to search and try out the secrets of nature'. These should be carefully recorded 'without equivocations or enigmatical phrases' and handed in each year so that later investigators may avoid mistakes and carry forward positive work 'which in time must of force bring great things to light'.

Gilbert's recognition of new potentialities to be explored stands out in all the stronger relief because he is concerned to mitigate the evils attendant on the exploitation of feudal rights, now centred in the crown. In the last analysis it turns out that it is his aim, no less, to turn the English court itself into 'an academy of philosophy and chivalry'. Whereas the early humanists had extolled the enlightenment of princes and urged the untutored gentry to emulate them, fifty years on an English gentleman is voicing advanced educational ideas and seeking to civilise the court. It is a notable change of emphasis.

Gilbert's scheme, on his own accounting, would have involved an initial outlay on equipment of £2000, buildings apart, and an annual expenditure of £3000. There was no likelihood that funds on this scale would be made available, let alone that the sale of wardships would be foregone when it added indispensably to the resources of the monarchy, and the new activities Gilbert brought to attention continued only under private auspices. But the master of the wards was by no means unconscious of the educational issues at stake, in particular the problem of re-educating the catholic nobility and the use that could be made of wardship to this end.[1] Under Cecil's direction relatively generous allowances to guardians were made out of the funds held by the court, and covenants bound them to bring up wards 'in good education, virtues and decent qualities';[2] while, according to his contemporary biographer, he 'ever endeavoured to commit wards to persons of sound religion. And preferred natural mothers, before all others, to the custody of their children'.[3] Cecil himself found time

[1] He himself advocated in the 1580's that all the children of catholics of standing be brought together in one place in every shire for their upbringing; 'education of the younger under good schoolmasters' was a much more effective means of reducing catholic influence than making martyrs (*Somers Tracts*, 1809, I, pp. 166–7).

[2] Bell, pp. 122–3; for examples of exhibitions for education, Hurstfield, pp. 115–17.

[3] Peck, I, p. 20. Lord Herbert of Cherbury describes how, when his father became mortally ill, his mother sent a relative posting to London to secure his wardship, which was successfully achieved; to offset Gilbert's picture the boy affectionately addressed his

to keep an eye on the upbringing of his friends' sons, those of the dead Cheke, for instance, and those of Smith and Chaloner when the fathers were abroad.[1]

Most notably, however, the master of the wards set up a regular school in his household for the education of sons of leading noblemen whose wardships were not sold but retained in the queen's hands. Consequently the earls of Oxford, Essex, Southampton, Rutland, Surrey, among others, came directly under the eye of a statesman conscious of the importance of training the mind and guiding the development of young nobles on whose outlook and loyalty much could depend.[2] This household school was a good deal more select than the one Bacon had envisaged, concentrating those whose inheritance amounted to £1000 or more. But it followed much the kind of programme suggested and tutors were provided of the calibre of Lawrence Nowell, noted scholar and antiquary and brother of the dean of St Pauls.[3] In the morning the young men first took exercise and were instructed in dancing, then came tuition in French and Latin, writing and drawing; in the afternoon the same subjects figured with cosmography in addition.[4] Cecil was often on the look out for teachers and books. Sir Thomas Smith tutored the earl of Oxford for a time and when later in France on an embassy was asked to send back a qualified French tutor for his former pupil who was advancing well in the tongue, a man honest in religion, civil in manners and not unpersonable; Cecil added that a competent horseman to instruct the wards would also be welcome and worth a salary of £20 a year.[5]

There was naturally much competition for a place in the lord treasurer's household; 'most of the principal gentlemen in England

guardian as 'worthy father' and signed himself 'your adopted son in name, but natural all other ways' (Lord Herbert of Cherbury, *Autobiography*, ed. Sidney L. Lee, 1886, pp. 39–40, 334–7).

[1] Cheke's sons were, of course, Cecil's nephews by his first marriage. The elder, Henry, was first tutored then sent to King's—regular progress reports going to his uncle—and after travelled abroad to train for the queen's service, to Antwerp, Genoa, Florence, Ferrara, Padua. The second son, John, was of Cecil's household (Strype, *Cheke*, pp. 138–40).

[2] Hurstfield, p. 249. A considerable number were from catholic families, the duke of Norfolk's sons, the earl of Southampton, Lord Wharton.

[3] A third Nowell brother, Robert, succeeded Bacon as attorney of the court of wards; he too was a great furtherer of education, leaving a fund to be used for aiding poor scholars which Alexander long administered.

[4] Hurstfield, pp. 255–6.

[5] Strype, *Smith*, pp. 19–20.

sought to prefer their heirs to his service'.[1] But places among the following of other leading statesmen were also sought after and wardship was a good deal less burdensome if the guardian provided a good education and later patronage.[2] But if this was the traditional form of upbringing for the nobility, the atmosphere in which it was pursued was by no means always the same as of old. Elizabeth was sparing in granting titles; among her leading statesmen Cecil alone was rewarded and then only with a barony. He would have taken the point, indeed may have been partly responsible for a policy which both husbanded the peerage and kept capable privy councillors in the Commons, but the fact remained that these neither were nor set up to be noblemen. Lord Burghley's following was but a tenth of that Wolsey had once entertained though he was the queen's first minister; to the Spanish ambassador he appeared, by comparison with the lords of the council, 'a man of mean sort', however astute.[3] His outlook, as illustrated by the maxims passed on to his son Robert, was in tune. He warns against training a boy up for the wars, since he who lives by that profession 'can hardly be an honest man and a good Christian', while 'soldiers in peace are like chimneys in summer'; he stresses that it is one thing to look after kindred and allies but superfluous dependents in the household are, of all things, to be avoided. On general tenure he concludes: 'Towards thy superiors, be humble, yet generous. With thine equals, familiar, yet respective. Towards thine inferiors show much humanity and some familiarity....The first prepares the way to advancement. The second makes thee known for a man well-bred. The third gains a good report; which, once got, is easily kept.'[4]

This was something very different from the old *noblesse oblige*. That the difference was appreciated at the time is suggested by a letter to Burghley from the ill-starred Walter Devereux, earl of Essex, shortly before his death in Ireland in 1576. He would, writes Essex, have placed his son Hereford in Burghley's household 'though the same had not been allotted to your lordship as Master of the Wards'. He wishes that his son's whole time in England during his minority may be divided in attendance on 'my lord chamberlain and you, to the end, that as he

[1] Peck, I, p. 24; Hurstfield, p. 255.

[2] Sir William Petre entertained various wards in his household over fifteen years; he found among them suitable husbands for his daughters but meantime they were brought up with his own son and some sent to university with a tutor, books and other costs provided (Emmison, pp. 126–7, 203–5, 221, 288).

[3] Neale, *Essays in Elizabethan History*, p. 175.

[4] Peck, I, pp. 47–9.

might frame himself to the example of my lord of Sussex in all the actions of his life, tending either to the wars, or to the institution of a nobleman', so 'he might also reverence your lordship for your wisdom and gravity, and lay up your counsels and advices in the treasury of his heart'.[1]

The reference here to the period of education in England draws attention to the fact that travel abroad was now an essential aspect of the institution of the nobleman. Even in the difficult days of 1581 Burghley was speeding the earl of Northumberland's son abroad, at the age of seventeen, with a stock of advice and directions.[2] By the close of the century much published advice was available about the courtly arts to be acquired on the continent, as well as the cost of travel which put it well outside the reach of most gentlemen.[3] It was of this kind of 'education' abroad, often little but a social round, that the critics complained.

But travel was also, as it had long been, a means to more serious studies preparatory to seeking office. Indeed it could now be a final stage in apprenticeship to the calling in so far as young men were required to accumulate and convey useful information—Henry Cheke, for instance, sent back regular 'observations' when on his travels in the 1570's. As various directives show what was required were accounts of cities and fortifications, of methods of government and the attitude of the people towards their prince, descriptions of ecclesiastical organisation and law courts, schools and universities and how they were run. Philip Sidney summed it up in a sentence when advising a younger brother what he was travelling for: 'your purpose is, being a gentleman born, to furnish yourself with the knowledge of such things as may be serviceable to your country'.[4]

[1] Quoted by Furnivall, p. xv.

[2] The eighth earl of Northumberland was a catholic (successor of the seventh earl executed in 1572) but had his son brought up a protestant (G. B. Harrison, ed., *Advice to his Son by Henry Percy, Ninth Earl of Northumberland*, 1930, p. 7).

[3] 'If he travel without a servant £80 is a competent proportion except he learn to ride', wrote Robert Dallington in *Method for Travel* (1598). 'If he maintain both these charges, he can be allowed no less than £150: and to allow above £200 were superfluous and to his hurt. The ordinary rate of his expense is 10 gold crowns a month for his fencing, as much his dancing, no less his reading, and 10 crowns monthly his riding except in the heat of the year. I allow him for apparel, books, travelling charges, tennis play and other extraordinary expenses' (Lambley, p. 231).

[4] Howard, pp. 30–1. It has been noted that Walsingham, handing out similar instructions, refers always to duty to the commonwealth 'but does not even once mention the obligation to serve the prince' (Hexter, p. 70). For these instructions, to his nephew, see Read, I, pp. 18–20.

Sometimes financial assistance might be forthcoming; more often, perhaps, travel was a hopeful investment and hopes were not always fulfilled.[1] In any case it was something other than the grand tour of a later date. Francis Bacon, son of the lord keeper, having spent two years at Trinity, Cambridge, registered at Gray's Inn in 1575 at the age of fifteen, but soon interrupted his legal studies to take an opportunity of visiting France in the train of an English ambassador. He spent the next two and half years in Paris and travelling in the provinces, to some purpose, and would probably have stayed longer had not his father's sudden death called for an immediate return.[2] An older traveller was Henry Wotton, of a family of diplomats, who after taking an M.A. at Oxford and coming into his inheritance at the age of twenty-two 'laid aside his books and betook himself to the useful library of Travel, and a more general conversation with mankind, employing the remaining part of his youth, his industry and fortune to adorn his mind'; his travels took him to France and Geneva for one year, to Germany for three, Italy for five,and he was thirty when he returned.[3]

The tour embarked upon by Philip Sidney, at the age of nineteen, remained a model of one planned to educational ends. Son of the lord president of the council in Wales, educated for some years at Shrewsbury school and a year or so more at Christ Church, he was dispatched on his travels with a sound protestant tutor and three servants in 1572. He travelled in the train of the lord high admiral to Paris where he came under the care of Francis Walsingham, then ambassador, and narrowly missed involvement in the massacre of St Bartholomew. Walsingham evidently planned most of the later programme which took the young man on visits to one leading protestant scholar after another; the learned publisher Andrew Wechel at Frankfurt, Henry Estienne at Heidelberg, Sturm at Strasburg and finally, at Vienna, Hubert Languet who supervised Sidney's later studies and long remained in touch in subsequent years. A tour in Hungary and then

[1] Writing in 1583 to a kinsman, John Dutton esquire, Sir Christopher Hatton informs him of the return from abroad of 'my cousin and servant your son' and that 'her majesty doth very graciously accept of the gentleman's travel...with assurance, that he will prove a man meet to be hereafter employed in service, to the benefit of his country'. Expressing his own obligation for the bestowal of the young man in his service Hatton adds 'in case I may perceive any desire in him to follow the life of a courtier...he shall have my best furtherance for his preferment' (Peck, I, p. 142).

[2] B. Farrington, *Francis Bacon* (1951), pp. 30–1; Bacon later gave sound advice on making travel an education in his essay on this topic.

[3] Izaak Walton, 'Life of Sir Henry Wotton', *Reliquiae Wottonianae* (1672).

in Italy, with a short spell at Padua University but avoidance of the dangers of Rome, preceded a return through Germany and Poland with visits to Prague and Antwerp. The whole took up nearly three years and shaped a young man whose abilities had much recognition abroad before he was well known at home.[1]

It was Sidney who became, despite all the embroidery on the theme of Gloriana, a symbol of the age, and his influence was immense. Of noble connections and combining learning with virtue—diplomat and courtier, poet and man of action who met with death on the battlefield—he long figured as an ideal to be emulated. But Castiglione's courtier come to life in Elizabethan England was no mere embodiment of 'renaissance' ideals; he was, as his education had been designed to ensure, a convinced Calvinist. Like others, Sidney wearied of the court and preferring country-house life acted as host and patron to many writers and scholars. In 1578, three years after his return from abroad, he initiated a campaign with others of like mind to launch a new English poetry; at his death in 1586 he was mourned by a company of poets. The tradition he set of an openhanded 'Maecenas' of learning and literature was carried on by his sister, the countess of Pembroke, whose household at Wilton was virtually staffed by writers. Others who emulated the Sidney example were the earl of Leicester, Sir Charles Blount (of a family once tutored by Erasmus), Sidney's former schoolfellow and lifelong friend Fulke Greville, Lord Brooke, and later Cecil's ward, the young earl of Essex in whose London house Francis Bacon wrote his early work.[2]

In an earlier age all roads had led to court or to the vast entourage of a Wolsey or a Cromwell and out from there to office. During the Reformation years learning and literary skill were largely turned to immediate polemics or practical matters. In the Elizabethan age noblemen vied with each other not only in the political field and the church but in patronage of writers and translators, dramatists and musicians, artists and architects, scientists and mathematicians. Where once classical scholars had been engaged as tutors there now figured English poets, such as Samuel Daniel, who tutored the countess of Pembroke's

[1] John Buxton, *Sir Philip Sidney and the English Renaissance* (1954), pp. 43–79. The first of many poems addressed to Sidney was by Daniel Rogers, son of a Marian martyr, active in Leiden from 1575; for this, a sketch of Sidney's activities abroad and later contacts with the continent, J. A. Dorsten, *Poets, Patrons and Professors* (1962), pp. 39–40, 48–67.

[2] Buxton, pp. 98 ff.

heir later the leading patron in his turn.[1] Mathematical tutors were quite frequently employed; Sir Nicholas Bacon retained Thomas Blundeville whose later writings were mainly designed to instruct young gentlemen of the inns of court in the use of maps, globes, instruments.[2] Walter Raleigh, a young half-brother of Humphrey Gilbert, engaged as his own 'tutor' a young mathematician of promise who soon came to the forefront. Later Thomas Hariot became chief instructor to a select society interested in natural philosophy; a society under the patronage of the earl of Northumberland which included the earl of Derby, Lord George Hunsdon, Raleigh, the poets Chapman and Marlow.[3] Again, while young classical scholars had once started on their way in the family circle of leading humanists, aspiring scientists now studied with men already established in the scientific world who owned libraries and the necessary instruments. One such was John Dee who took Thomas Digges, among others, under his care and considerably influenced his work; though Dee himself looked in vain for recognition for science in the form of endowments for a suitable research centre.[4]

Boys brought up in the country houses with different models before them developed aspirations of their own accordingly. Michael Drayton, a tanner's son who took service as page to a gentleman in the 1570's, approached the household tutor with the plea:

> Make me a poet, do it, if you can
> And you shall see, I'll quickly be a man.

The ambition was achieved before Drayton reached his early twenties and on his patron's death he was bequeathed to the care of another who

[1] That Englishmen's understandings 'are not to be built by the square of Greece and Italy' was one of the lessons imparted to the future protector of Shakespeare and Jonson, Donne and Herbert (*ibid.* pp. 239–40; cf. Edwin Haviland Miller, *The Professional Writer in Elizabethan England*, Cambridge, Mass., 1959).

[2] *M. Blundevile his exercises* (1594) included six treatises 'very necessary to be read and learned of all young gentlemen that have not been exercised in such disciplines, and yet are desirous to have knowledge as well in cosmography, astronomy, and geography, as also in the art of navigation' (E. G. R. Taylor, *The Mathematical Practitioners of Tudor and Stuart England*, Cambridge, 1954, p. 173.)

[3] G. B. Harrison, p. 10.

[4] Marie Boas, *The Scientific Renaissance, 1450–1630* (1962), pp. 241, 244. For Archbishop Parker's household out of which came 'the antiquities of Britain and divers ancient authors never before published' while many were engaged in 'making collections, transcribing, composing, painting, drawing, or some other learning or art', Strype, *Parker*, II, pp. 441 ff.

could advance his interests. Patrons also sent promising young dependents to university; Sidney's protégée Abraham Fraunce, profiting from Ramist studies at Cambridge on his patron's advice, took occasion to bring the work of English poets to attention.[1]

When this work came to light, when—following on the publications of John Lyly, grandson of the first high master of St Paul's—Spenser's poems and Sidney's heroic romances were printed, they proved to turn closely on the theme of forming the gentleman. While the *Shepherd's Calender* (1579) was dedicated to 'the noble and virtuous gentleman most worthy of all titles both of learning and chivalry, M. Philip Sidney', Spenser later wrote *The Faerie Queen*, as he explained in an accompanying letter to Raleigh, 'to fashion a gentleman or noble person in virtuous or gentle discipline'. Spenser had his own approach to this question[2] but by the 1590's this was only one of many.[3] The relevant point here is that in its new beginnings English literature was still traditionally and intentionally didactic and centrally concerned with the long-debated question of learning and virtue. While in dependence upon it there constantly accrued new educational guides in English.[4]

Sidney himself wrote *An Apology for Poetry*, eventually published in 1595, which took up the theme Vives had expounded as it was later developed by Italian humanists—on the relations of nature and art, the true use of imitation, in what learning consists and what is its proper end. 'This purifying of wit, this enriching of memory, enabling of judgment, and enlarging of conceit, which commonly we call learning', wrote Sidney, is usually directed to some immediate end, but its ultimate end must be to 'draw us to as high a perfection as our degenerate souls...can be capable of.' The highest end of learning lies 'in the knowledge of a man's self, in the ethic and politic consideration, with the end of well-doing and not of well-knowing only'. It was in this context that Sidney pressed the claims of the poet as one who most

[1] Buxton, pp. 147–8, 223–5.

[2] It is discussed by Caspari.

[3] Mulcaster could write in 1581—by which time all the relevant classics had been translated—'one might talk beyond enough and write beyond measure, that would examine what such a one saith of nobility in Greek, such a one in Latin, such in other several tongues, because the argument is so large, the use of nobility stretching so far, and so brave a subject cannot choose but minister passing brave discourses' (*Positions*, p. 195).

[4] E.g. Abraham Fraunce's *Arcadian Rhetoric* (1588) which drew examples from Sidney and Spenser; Puttenham's *Art of English Poesie* (1589); Angel Day's *English Secretary* (1592) which extended from letter writing to rhetoric.

effectively inspires the 'virtuous action' which is 'the ending end of all earthly learning'.[1]

By the close of the century the dramatists were contributing their share to the theme. The first play published over the name of William Shakespeare in 1598, *Love's Labour's Lost*, was an exercise in rhetoric in the Lyly tradition, in the course of which the author counterposed to courtly learning the owlishness of a pedantic schoolmaster. But several other plays had preceded this in print and on the stage which presented the characters in action of kings and noblemen of the past—in much the kind of way Elyot had once advocated as instructive for young gentlemen—drawing on Holinshed's chronicles of English history.[2] By 1603 *Hamlet*, in one aspect a philosophical essay on the relations between knowledge and action, the hero of which had studied at the university of Luther and Melanchthon, had been staged at both universities.[3]

By now English gentlemen could also profit from the essays of Montaigne which, in John Florio's translation, were widely read, and so learn that 'the grandeur and value of true virtue lies in the facility, the pleasure and usefulness of its practice', that things come before words, that accordingly education should be concerned with enlarging experience and cultivating the mind in action rather than poring over books.[4] English prose was also being fostered and in 1597 there appeared a first collection of ten essays in a lucid and civilised style by Francis Bacon. The initial essay 'On Studies' advised that 'to spend too much time on studies, is sloth; to use them too much for ornament, is affectation; to make judgment wholly by their rules, is the humour of a scholar; they perfect nature, and are perfected by experience'. As for various studies, 'histories make men wise; poets, witty; the

[1] Sidney, *An Apology for Poetry*, ed. H. A. Needham, pp. 13–14. For the contemporary view that poetry is 'the third great form of communication, open and popular but not fully explained by rhetoric, concise and lean but not fully explained by logic', Howell, pp. 4–5.

[2] This was cited in defence of the drama, for instance by Thomas Nashe referring to *Henry VI* as an example in 1592; the playhouses drew young gentlemen of the court and inns of court from the taverns and to see such pieces was an inspiration to degenerate contemporaries (F. E. Halliday, *The Life of Shakespeare*, 1961, p. 83).

[3] 'The younger sort takes much delight in Shakespeare's Venus and Adonis', wrote Gabriel Harvey from Cambridge, 'but his Lucrece and his tragedy of Hamlet, Prince of Denmark, have it in them, to please the wiser sort' (F. E. Halliday, *Shakespeare and his Critics*, 1949, p. 269).

[4] *The Essays of Montaigne*, trans. E. J. Trechman, I, p. 161.

mathematics, subtle, natural philosophy, deep; moral, grave, logic and rhetoric, able to contend'. More essays were gradually added to make up a volume more frequently reprinted than any other secular work, covering as it did every burning theme of the day—high office, nobility, travel, wisdom, friendship and followers, parents and children, education, honour and reputation.[1]

It was not only practised writers who circulated advice of this kind. Eminent parents drew up precepts for sons, as Cicero had done for his, and these circulated privately before finding their way into print as the poetry of the day also did. Sir Henry Sidney's letters of advice to his son as a boy were published in 1591. Raleigh addressed advice to his son on the ways of the world and tenure in society.[2] His companion in the tower—the ninth earl of Northumberland who had rounded off his own education with travel—wrote a tract which recommended in particular study of natural philosophy; not only could this make men the masters of natural forces, to the improvement of the nautical and military arts, but also it contributed to creating a 'well-fashioned mind'.[3] The 'advice to a son' became a minor literary form, a special branch of the extensive literature bearing on education and upbringing. In this matter gentlemen had now outgrown tutelage and laid down the precepts themselves.

In the process an outlook emerged contrasting with, rather than emulating, life at court which indeed became the subject of bitter comment. 'Know the court but spend not thy life there', advised Sir Walter Mildmay, 'for court is a very chargeable place. I would rather wish thee to spend the greatest part of thy life in the country than to live in this glittering misery.'[4] The complaints had become a chorus by the turn of the century. 'No more than empty words, grinning scoff, watching nights and fawning days', was how Sir John Harington summed up a lifetime looking for recognition.[5] This was hardly the true end of a humanist education. But though it is usually held that this was the period when early humanist precepts were translated into practice to shape the education of the upper classes, it is

[1] Francis Bacon, *Essays* (World's Classics), pp. 139–40; Farrington, pp. 49–50.

[2] It is printed with that of Burghley, Sidney and later writers in *Practical Wisdom: or the Manual of Life. The Counsels of Eminent Men to their Children* (1824).

[3] G. B. Harrison, p. 71.

[4] The advice was passed on by the fifth earl of Huntingdon to his son in 1613 (*Historical MSS. Commission, Hastings MSS.*, IV, p. 333).

[5] Quoted by L. Knights, *Drama and Society in the Age of Jonson* (1937), p. 328.

clear that there was a good deal more than this to the institution of the Elizabethan gentleman. As the subject passed from hand to hand a mirror was held up to practice, new models provided, additional accomplishments and spheres of learning advised, fresh duties defined.

(2) *Inns of court, universities and grammar schools*

When Richard Mulcaster addressed advice on education to the gentry in 1581 he cast mockery on humanist plans for a classical education from the nursery onwards, such as Elyot had advanced, and deplored subservience to classical guides. 'It is no proof', he declares, 'because Plato praiseth it, because Aristotle alloweth it, because Cicero commends it, because Quintilian is acquainted with it, or any other else...that therefore it is for us to use.'[1] With two decades of experience at the Merchant Taylors' school behind him and now at St Paul's, member of an emergent profession, Mulcaster is disposed to look on education as a developing science.[2] In his view it is possible to work out a balanced educational course, the best that can be devised in the light of experience, and this should be introduced universally in the schools. All children should have a careful elementary grounding—being taught to read in the vernacular, to write, draw, sing—before embarking on academic studies, and these should be supplemented by a due amount of physical exercise and training.

As for gentlemen's children, these are no different from others—'their wits be as the common, their bodies oftimes worse'—so they should follow the normal educational course; and they should follow it in a public school, if necessary accompanied by a tutor. The public school Mulcaster has in mind is no humanist academy apart but the grammar school where gentlemen can mix not only with each other but with 'the common'. He concedes that the great noble needs special treatment, tutors and upbringing at home, but why do the gentry ape their superiors in this rather than following the ranks below

[1] *Positions*, p. 11.

[2] He had studied Vives's *De Disciplinis*; referring to this at one point he writes 'if only Vives the learned Spaniard were called to be witness, he would crave pardon for his own person, as not able to come for the gout, but he would substitute for his deputy his whole twenty books of disciplines' (*ibid.* p. 259). Here a protest may be entered against the description of Mulcaster—who was at Cambridge throughout the Edwardian age before entering Christ Church—as 'a good Oxford Aristotelian' (Rowse, p. 507).

who are really liker to them and form the chief supporters of the state?[1] 'Cloistering from the common' encourages lording it above the common from the cradle, 'the overweening of one's self, not compared with others'; this makes for friction 'where the higher condemneth his inferior with scorn, and the lower doth stomach his superior with spite: the one gathering snuff, the other grudge'. Life in a school community knits bonds and is an essential aspect of a sound education. Gentlemen anyway take a particular place there since they enjoy particular advantages 'and are much bound to God for them'; they can stay on at school to the end of the course, whereas the poorer must leave early; they are not bound to particular employments, but have a free choice with 'all opportunities at will, where the common is restrained'.

Since the country so honours young gentlemen they should bestir themselves 'to serve their country honourably'. Once furnished with sound learning in what directions can they look? Mulcaster will have nothing to do with traditional appeals to martial valour. 'I do not hold Tamerlane or any barbarous and bloody invasions to be means to nobility'; nor is wealth a cause for renown 'unless it be both got by laudable means and likewise...employed upon commendable works'. But besides becoming counsellors, lawyers, physicians, gentleman can and should enter the church; though poorer than it was 'who is so impudent as not to confess that profession an honourable profession which hath God himself to father, and friend?' Young gentlemen can stand out in the professions and they ought besides to 'be better than the common in the best kind of learning'.[2]

Here the sphere of operation suitable to gentlemen is considerably widened by comparison with the tract of thirty years before which suggested that gentlemen best stand out as such by cultivating their own estate. But even Mulcaster does not mention as a suitable occupation trade, a subject which all the theorists of gentility scrupulously avoid however many young gentlemen in fact entered on apprenticeships. In trade a young man could look forward to living 'in a reason-

[1] 'For the gentleman generally, which flieth not so high, but fluttereth some little above the ordinary common, why doth he make his choice rather to be like them above, which still grow privater than to be like of them below, which can grow no lower, and yet be supporters, to stay up the whole, and liker to himself than he is to the highest?' (*Positions*, p. 189).

[2] *Ibid.* pp. 217–20. Moreover, as Humfrey had earlier stressed the duty of aiding the church, Mulcaster stresses the duty to aid learning and education whereby gentlemen can help their country 'and themselves, to all honour'.

able countenance'; it was otherwise with the church which, no longer headed by men of noble rank and offering few livings of worth, hardly seemed a suitable profession for gentlemen to adopt during most of Elizabeth's reign. On the other hand the law remained a calling of immediate use which also opened up prospects of influence and wealth; as such it is the one profession to find general acceptance in theory while in practice young gentlemen crowded into the inns of court.

Taken together the inns of court, wrote Sir Edward Coke, make up 'the most famous university for profession of the law only, or any one humane science, that is in the world'; and the 'readings and other exercises of the laws there continually used are most excellent and behooveful for attaining to knowledge of these laws'.[1] He goes on to describe the inns and their courses in detail. Some eight years' study was required before becoming an utter barrister, twelve years as a barrister before becoming a bencher and eligible to be a reader. Exercises included conferences and disputations, pleadings and putting cases in law French and English and also attendance at Westminster Hall to hear leading barristers and judges. In short the traditional course persisted virtually unchanged, though in practice it proved difficult to retain busy lawyers to act as readers and take other offices in the inns and there were many complaints that exercises were deteriorating.[2] None the less, outstanding lawyers did lecture and legal training, which bore closely on contemporary affairs in parliament and at large, was something much more than an outmoded discipline when such as Coke and Francis Bacon dealt with burning problems of the day.

Gray's Inn, Lincoln's Inn, the Temple, were enlarged and beautified at this time, as a century earlier collegiate churches had been. Entrants seem to have come up younger than formerly, many of them direct from school or tutoring in a household rather than by way of the university, to be placed under the guidance of seniors who were often relatives; families given to the law were by now almost dynasties.[3] Those who registered only for a brief period could presumably attend lectures and exercises as they would, but there were also up-to-date text-books

[1] J. H. Thomas (ed.), *Reports of Sir Edward Coke* (1826), II, pp. xxv–xxvii.

[2] Kenneth Charlton, 'Liberal Education and the Inns of Court in the Sixteenth Century', *British Journal of Educational Studies*, IX, no. 1 (1960), pp. 25–38.

[3] Registered members were not always in residence but in 1574 Gray's Inn had 220, the Middle Temple 190, the Inner Temple 189, Lincoln's Inn 160; the first was the chief resort of young gentlemen (Rowse, pp. 522–5).

prepared for their use and many other activities to engage in—from sermons in the chapels to drama in the halls and ritual celebrations during the Christmas season which persisted longer here than elsewhere. The distractions offered by the capital were near at hand and young gentlemen of the inns figured largely in London life; there was also tuition of all kinds available though the traditional courtly arts of singing, dancing, fencing most frequently find mention. Coke, therefore, can once more describe the inns, as Fortescue had done, as a centre where 'commendable exercises fit for gentlemen' are followed. When the heir of Sir William Fitzwilliam, grandson of Walter Mildmay, entered Gray's Inn in 1594 after two years or so at Emmanuel College, his expenditure on music, dancing and fencing lessons evidently accounted for more than costs of residence.[1]

Some time at the inns of court after perhaps a year or so at an Oxford or Cambridge college—an adaptation for amateurs of what had been, for such as Cecil, a serious educational course—became a recognised pattern of education for the gentleman of standing, not least those intending to enter parliament. Wealth and influence were needed to secure election, heirs were often put forward as soon as they were of suitable age, and the results are to be seen in the parliament of 1584 which was a particularly youthful one; of the total of 460 members, 300 were newcomers, most of them gentlemen.[2] It is not, therefore, so very surprising to find that over 200 members of this House of Commons had attended an inn or a university or both; only a minority, including the lawyers who played an important part in debates, had qualifications. The relative lack of information about educational background at an earlier date, as well as the changing composition of the house, make it difficult to assess the spread of this form of education among gentlemen since the outset of the reign. But comparable figures for the parliament of 1593 show an appreciable increase; in all 252 members (as against 219 in 1584) had some acquaintance with a centre of higher learning.[3] By this time the trend towards giving

[1] His chamber rent at Gray's Inn was £2. 13*s*. 4*d*. a year, commons 5*s*. 4*d*. a week. Singing lessons cost 10*s*. a month, dancing lessons 20*s*. and he also attended a 'fence school' and paid a fee for his 'entrance into music at the exchange'. By contrast the son of a family still making its way and stretched for funds lodged at a tavern in Fleet Street, to obviate the expense of rooms in the Temple and the possible burden of an expensive office there, and had no extras (Finch, pp. 26, 124).

[2] Neale, *Elizabethan House of Commons*, pp. 317–18.

[3] *Ibid.* pp. 302–5. In 1584, 164 members had been at the inns of court, 90 of whom had previously been at university; in 1593 the corresponding figures were 197 and 106.

heirs an education of this kind had been set for half a century, since the Reformation.

Clearly it was now widely accepted among gentlemen that education was a worthwhile investment. Indeed, while foreign travel was favoured in some quarters as the best way of rounding off upbringing, there was a growing tendency to regard the House of Commons—filled as it was with gentlemen's heirs—as another kind of finishing school. 'My son being willing to adapt himself for the service of his country is desirous to become a scholar in the best school of Christendom for knowledge, and experience (the parliament house of England) a desire that every father is to further in his children', wrote Sir Thomas Hasilrig of Noseley in 1625, requesting that the burgesses of Leicester adopt his son as candidate.[1] The sentiment had become something of a commonplace in the later years of Elizabeth[2] and there was more than a little basis for it. Indeed from the outset of the reign privy councillors had acted, it might almost be said, as tutors to the house. Sir Nicholas Bacon set the tone when he opened the memorable first parliament of the reign with a disquisition on the conduct of debate, expressing the hope that

> you will...in your assembly and conference clearly forbear, and, as a great enemy to good council, fly from all manner of contentions, reasonings and disputations, and all sophistical captions and frivolous arguments and quiddities, meeter for ostentation of wit, than consultation of weighty matters, comelier for scholars than counsellors; more beseeming for schools, than for parliament houses—beside that commonly they be great causes of much expense of time, and breed few good resolutions.[3]

Here spoke the father of the boy who in the 1570's found Cambridge still steeped in scholasticism, whatever changes there might have been, still dominated by a traditional philosophy 'only strong for disputations and contentions, but barren of the production of works for the benefit of the life of man'.[4]

When Gilbert declared that there was no suitable learning for gentlemen at the university and Bacon deplored the unfruitfulness of a philosophy of words they were judging from the standpoint of their own time, accepting as given the changes of the Reformation years. Though these had been material, in relation to the curriculum they

[1] *Records of the Borough of Leicester*, ed. H. Stocks (Cambridge, 1923), IV, p. 220.

[2] Neale, *op. cit.* pp. 150–1.

[3] D'Ewes, p. 12A.

[4] Farrington, pp. 23–4.

had not been fundamental; rather humanist studies had been absorbed into the old framework, the arts course being adapted to make way for rhetoric and study of classical authors while grammar was delegated to the schools.[1] Otherwise only the topmost pinnacle of the edifice of scholasticism had been removed when study of the schoolmen was banned and, while the scholastic method still reigned supreme, Aristotelian philosophy had since attained a hold greater than before. Mathematics remained a part of natural philosophy, studied side by side with metaphysics, ethics and logic and there was no place for the development of newer scientific studies for which humanist rationalism had begun to prepare the way. There was, of course, a strong trend towards study of the scriptures but, as has been pointed out, the theology of the Reformation involved a turn away from the secularism of the humanists, a reversion to explanations in terms of God's providence; this was not a backward step, like the return to Aristotle, in so far as clarification of doctrine bore closely on an understanding of politics, law, history—indeed it carried the seeds of development.[2] But it was not until the contradiction between faith and learning was 'resolved' by making a clear separation between reason and revelation—as Vives had been inclined to do and as Francis Bacon was to do for his generation—that scientific thinking in the modern sense of the term had room to develop; meanwhile scholarship in the sixteenth century was concerned rather with the clearing away of settled landmarks and the search for new viewpoints than with a clear advance on new lines.[3]

Oxford and Cambridge colleges still had something to offer to young gentlemen who did not seek a degree or intend to enter a profession; indeed they increasingly provided a useful bridge between schooling and the inns of court or travel, or where these were not contemplated themselves acted as finishing schools. Initially gentlemen's sons were sent up very young, sometimes accompanied by their own tutors, but as the schools developed younger entrants became rarer and college tutors seemed adequate; there were now many more of them, giving most of their time to teaching within colleges, and they could provide the necessary guidance in reading the classics and add polish to the often unfinished products of schooling. Fellows received pay-

[1] One of the few changes made in the Edwardian statutes at the outset of Elizabeth's reign was to eliminate mathematics in favour of rhetoric (Mullinger, II, pp. 401–3).

[2] 'The dialectic between research and controversy, between religion and learning, was given a new direction, power, and impetus by the Reformation' (Fussner, p. 20).

[3] W. P. D. Wightman, *Science and the Renaissance* (1962), I, p. 303.

ments directly from parents and reported to them on progress and behaviour; many college fellows were in fact either related or well known to gentlemen in their home counties, sometimes took successive sons under their care and visited with pupils in vacations. Such men were ready enough to promote the interests of gentlemen, rather than advancing boys of merit with nothing to offer, and complaints about the diversion of scholarships intended for the poor continued during Elizabeth's reign;[1] though the poorer sort of gentleman's son, about whom there had been some concern, quite often found a place in colleges, maintained there by a well-to-do relative with his own sons.

That gentlemen so freely used the resources of colleges at this time has been represented as a fruitful development for the universities. This was by no means necessarily so, though the main vices of patronage originated with the crown. Not only did Elizabeth place masters of colleges and nominate to fellowships and scholarships—either directly or through intermediaries—but also dispensed men from the necessary exercises for degrees over the head of the university. In 1579 the Cambridge vice-chancellor and heads registered a strong protest with their chancellor at the crown's interference whereby 'the rewards of merit and studiousness are witheld, scholars being induced to look for preferment to the favour of courtiers rather than to their true deserts at the hands of the university'.[2] But there was nothing Burghley could do, since the royal prerogative was at stake, but extract from the queen a promise that her dependents would be instructed to exercise more care in future, after which things continued as before. Dispensations meant a deterioration of standards, of the kind Bucer had warned against in Edward's day, while disciplinary problems also grew. Mulcaster administered a sharp rebuke about conferment of degrees on the unworthy, in his *Positions* dedicated to the queen, though he blamed the doctors who let unqualified candidates through.[3] Whitgift who had done all he could to give college heads overriding powers blamed them; complaining to Burghley in the late 1580's about the decay of learning at Oxford and the universal disregard of statutes he

[1] Even so large a school as Merchant Taylors with a company behind it disputed in vain over elections to scholarships at the small college of St John's, Oxford; the college openly deprecated the advancement of poor scholars and on one occasion blandly interposed the son of a benefactor to its library between a properly elected scholar and his rights (Wilson, I, pp. 135–6, 148).

[2] Mullinger, II, p. 289.

[3] *Loc. cit.* pp. 162–3.

concluded that this resulted from their intolerable carelessness—'who have authority sufficient to reform all these things but do it not'.[1] Burghley, for his part, blamed the fellows for being too obsequious and self-seeking. 'I am credibly informed', he wrote in 1587, in one of his numerous letters of admonition to Cambridge, 'by the great complaints of divers both worshipful and wise parents...that through the great stipends of tutors, and the little pains they do take in the instructing and well governing of their pupils...the poorer sort are not able to maintain their children at the university; and the richer be...corrupt with liberty and remissness'; this because 'the tutor is more afraid to displease his pupil through the desire of great gain, the which he hath by his tutorage, than the pupil is of his tutor'.[2]

While direct attempts to curb corruption failed Sir Thomas Smith's 'Act for the Maintenance of Colleges' (1576) helped to do so indirectly; under it revenues were cushioned against inflation, incomes rose and masters were bound to distribute surplus funds between fellows and scholars.[3] If greater affluence encouraged more independence of attitude, in what had been relatively poor and struggling institutions, it also helped to change semi-monastic surroundings into something more like country houses. Halls were panelled, fireplaces installed, hangings appeared on the walls, new quadrangles were built. 'As the college began to rise in building, so it declined in learning', records the seventeenth-century historian of St John's, Cambridge, paraphrasing a contemporary.[4] Another contemporary comment occurs in a drama staged in the hall of this college in 1602; that such stately buildings seemed more suitable for 'knights, lords and lawyers' than the 'ragged clerks', the 'weavers' and butchers' sons', who predominated among students.[5]

[1] Strype, *Whitgift*, I, p. 610. [2] Heywood and Wright, pp. 500–1.

[3] 'For the relief of commons' so that allowances under this head shortly exceeded the former total for commons and stipend combined; a 'most blessed and gracious statute' as Cambridge University proclaimed in 1601 (Mullinger, II, pp. 380, 385–6). In 1600, St John's had a surplus of £433 divided in the ratio of 2:1 between fellows and scholars (Howard, pp. 36–9).

[4] He adds his own observation, that the master elected under pain of the queen's displeasure in 1596—a wealthy pluralist—spent many a year looking to the new quadrangle but 'he has not (that I ever could meet with) left so much as one book to the library' (Baker, pp. 190–7).

[5] Though the play was *Return from Parnassus* (Mullinger, pp. 374, 522–3). Such presentations were 'for the exercise of young gentlemen and scholars' as Trinity put it in 1595 when seeking through Burghley to borrow robes to dress 'sundry personages of great estate' figuring in a tragedy they planned to stage (Ellis, 1825, III, pp. 32–4).

Young gentlemen brought their own manners and interests into the universities. Efforts to re-establish the clerkly pattern of dress and behaviour—to prevent the wearing of hats and ruffs, silks and satins except by young noblemen and heirs of knights who had some latitude[1]—were unavailing. Classical studies were often supplemented by reading modern authors, including courtly guides, and learning modern languages. 'Machiavelli is a great man....', wrote Gabriel Harvey from Cambridge to his friend Edmund Spenser in 1580, 'Petrarch and Boccaccio in every man's mouth; Galateo and Guazzo never so happy... the French and Italian when so highly regarded of scholars? The Latin and Greek when so lightly.' There was no more ado about surplices, said Harvey, referring to earlier puritan controversies, Cartwright was nearly forgotten. And, he added echoing Burghley, many pupils were hail-fellow-well-met with their tutors; 'some too, because forsooth they be gentlemen or great heirs, or a little neater and gayer than their fellows...their very own tutors'.[2] None the less this was the time when lectures on Ramus were filling hitherto empty lecture halls while it must also be recalled that university sermons made an important contribution to education. These at least were in English—though teaching in the vernacular had not otherwise developed since Cheke's day, as Gilbert complained—and the sermons of such as Perkins, which drew a large attendance, constituted almost a regular course in divinity.[3]

While colleges obligingly adapted themselves to cater for gentlemen's sons, at the expense of scholarship and church, gentlemen were in a position to influence schools more directly from positions on governing bodies or through powers to appoint masters. Wakefield's school building had not only the arms of the Savilles over the door but those of other gentlemen in the windows, lesser men who contributed the glazing of a window adding their names. Here instructions to the master insist on methods of teaching at length, deprecating too academic an approach. 'We do straitly in the Lord charge the schoolmaster and usher...that they do not so much hasten their scholars in the too soon climbing of their forms, especially in the too hasty going from prose into verse, and from Latin to Greek, or from Greek to Hebrew

[1] *Ibid.* pp. 24–8.

[2] *Letter-book of Gabriel Harvey 1573–80*, ed. E. J. L. Scott (Camden Society, 1874), pp. 78–80.

[3] W. J. Costello, *The Scholastic Curriculum at Early Seventeenth-Century Cambridge* (Harvard, 1958), pp. 111–12.

or logic...'; as for younger scholars the usher 'shall neither post haste them in grammar, nor dull them with exercises of writing Latin', and what he should do is detailed.[1] In 1590 an order for Blackburn school laid down 'that no English interludes or plays shall be from henceforth played or used in the same school', but a decade later comprehensive statutes advocated that, in addition to classical studies, 'the principles of Arithmetic, Geometry and Cosmography with some introduction into the sphere, are profitable' and specified the teaching of writing, ciphering, singing 'or such like' out of normal school hours. A fund was raised to endow this school the following year and the list of subscriptions has a somewhat feudal flavour; headed by the name of a justice of the Queen's bench who gave a hundred marks it goes on to list 'Sir John Southworth knight his tenants and followers £27, John Osbaldston esq. his tenants and followers £30, William Farrington esq., his own gift £10' together with lesser contributions.[2]

There were now many more competent masters about able to fulfil such directives, as has already been suggested. John Brownswerd, master at Stratford and later Macclesfield, was an accomplished Latin poet who drew many pupils; one of these, who collected his former master's writings for publication, was Thomas Newton who became in turn a poet and kept school in Cheshire and at Ilford.[3] Newton was also a physician and others of this profession who taught were Christopher Johnson, head of the school of Winchester College from 1560–71 and Thomas Cogan, master at Manchester from 1583–95.[4] Another author of text-books was John Bond, master of Taunton school in the 1580's; Francis Meres, author of *Wits' Commonwealth*, acted as schoolmaster for a spell, so also did Robert Dallington, author of one of the first travel books and later master of Charterhouse.[5] The headmaster of Southampton borough school in the 1570's, a Flemish exile Adrian à Saravia who later became a theologian of some note,

[1] Peacock, pp. 20, 66, 68.

[2] The list of governors of the school in 1586 is headed by the master of the rolls and includes sixteen other knights and esquires, thirty-four gentlemen, one vicar, thirteen with no designation; the charter assigned fifty governors but more seem to have been acquired (Stocks, pp. 37–9, 56, 67 ff., 73–4).

[3] One of his pupils was Lord Herbert of Cherbury (Anthony Wood, *Athenae Oxonienses*, ed. Bliss, II, pp. 5–6).

[4] Johnson's successors at Winchester were Thomas Bilson, later warden then bishop, and John Harmer, after professor of Greek at Oxford (Kirby, pp. 290–8).

[5] A. Wood, pp. 115, 263, 292.

boarded sixteen to twenty young gentlemen who were obliged to talk only French in his house besides being taught the language.[1]

Where masters achieved a reputation there gentlemen's sons were sent. The first extant school list for Pilkington's foundation at Rivington, for 1575–6, has 114 names including those of gentlemen's families from all over Lancashire.[2] Some schools had detailed arrangements for boarders, as the example of Tonbridge has illustrated. Sedbergh, Giggleswick and Appleby were favoured in the north, Bury and Norwich in East Anglia, Thame in Oxfordshire, Northwich in the north-west, Blandford in the south-west and many another. In addition incumbents who had a university education, particularly those known as college tutors, were much sought after as masters and not infrequently found themselves with small schools on their hands. This was the experience of John Bois of St John's, Cambridge, who was in his early thirties when he settled at Boxworth in 1596 with a reputation as a Greek scholar; he soon found it necessary to retain an assistant, both 'for the instruction of his own children and the poorer sort of the town; as also because many knights and gentlemen of quality did importune him to take their children to board with him, and to take some care of their education as well for learning as manners'.[3] An example of a private schoolmaster holding no preferment is Elias Newcomen, a Cambridge M.A. who lived near London and from the late 1570's took in twenty or thirty boarders, 'the children of worshipful persons', and sent some on regularly to university.[4]

Young gentlemen must have left school with varying degrees of accomplishment. One of the first aims of education was correct use of English.[5] David Baker was sent to Christ's Hospital from Wales to seek 'perfection in the English tongue and the right pronunciation of it';

[1] Two competent translators had their education here (Russell, pp. 34 ff.).

[2] E.g. four Pilkingtons, two Norris of Speke, a Charnock of Astley, a Dewhurst of Dewhurst, two Standishes of Duxbury, an Adlington of Adlington, an Ashton of Chilherne, a Rigby of Burgh, two Sherburns of Stonyhurst—evidently some of the catholic gentry sent sons to school after 1570. Gentlemen's sons later fell away but some of these families figure for generations, among children of the tenants of school lands and from local farmhouses. The school, like many others, had its ups and downs; it had only thirty scholars in 1613 when an inquiry found much need for reform (Kay, pp. 40–2, 62).

[3] Peck, I, p. 333.

[4] Wilson, I, pp. 78, 83; *Athenae*, III, p. 17.

[5] The only criticism of Merchant Taylors' school at the first visitation in 1562 was of the ushers 'that being northern men born, they had not taught the children to speak distinctly, or to pronounce their words so well as they ought' (Wilson, I, pp. 24–5).

he achieved this, together with a sound knowledge of the bible, but the classical teaching was less good than it might have been in the school at this time because of the master's age. None the less after three years he

> could write very true Latin, and no incongruity was to be found in it. But there was no elegancy at all in the style, he not having been taught anything as to that, but rather some barbarousness, or at least homeliness in it....He could make a Latin verse hexameter, pentameter and sapphic (but learnt no other kind of versifying) that was somewhat better in its kind, than was his prose....He could also read and understand Greek in some reasonable manner, and make a Greek verse.

There remained much polish to be added in this case which tutoring at the university may have helped to provide; David Baker was only fourteen when his father, deciding the school could do no more for him entered the boy at an Oxford college.[1] But in the established Elizabethan grammar school it was usually possible to get a sound grounding in English, the scriptures, the classics, and sometimes a good deal more—there is Ben Jonson's testimony that his methods of composition were guided by what he learned from Camden at Westminster.[2] Writing was now taught and the normal course might be supplemented by some arithmetic or cosmography, history, music, even modern languages. One of the sons of Sir John Wynn, of a leading family in north Wales, attended Bedford school where he learned French, Italian and music besides Latin, Greek and Hebrew.[3] Sir James Whitelocke, pupil under Mulcaster at Merchant Taylors, remembered the care taken to increase his skill in music by daily practice 'in singing and playing upon instruments' and recalled also the dramatic productions.[4] These, too, were an excellent means to clear and correct speaking.[5] The grammar schools must have contri-

[1] *Christ's Hospital Book*, pp. 20–1.

[2] The grammar school curriculum has been analysed in detail in relation to Shakespeare's works by Baldwin, II, *passim*.

[3] A. H. Dodd, *Life in Elizabethan England* (New York, 1961), p. 106.

[4] Bruce, p. 12.

[5] 'As a knowledge of singing is found to be of the greatest use for a clear and distinct elocution' the statutes of Westminster school specified that all boys spend two hours a week with the choristers' master (at a charge of 6*d*.). The play, which replaced the old ceremony of enthroning the boy bishop at Christmas, was also designed 'that the youth may spend Christmastide with better result and become better accustomed to proper action and pronunciation' (*ECD*, pp. 513, 519).

buted much towards developing the uniform speech of an educated class.

'Master Mulcaster's children' frequently appeared in masques and interludes before the queen, and though in time scholars no longer performed so much in public, as professional boys' companies and players took over the stage, the presentation of plays remained an essential aspect of education in the larger schools. Grammar-school pupils were also usually present to make orations on public occasions, not least when the queen's progresses took her through the kingdom or when there were other visitors of note. A play staged at Shrewsbury in 1569 throughout the Whitsuntide holiday, attended by 'great numbers of people, of noblemen and others', was greatly praised. A decade later the school was prominent in organising a welcome when the lord president of the council in Wales paid an official visit. The 360 boys marched to the nearby fields in full military order with drums, trumpets and ensigns to be reviewed; later selected scholars, wearing green and crowned with willows, delivered orations and verses in English mourning the departure of the official party as it left by barge down the river.[1]

It has been said that schoolboys had little scope for play: not even football was allowed.[2] But statutes prescribed half-days for games and exercises, often specifying shooting with bow and arrow, though football—whose contemporary horrors Elyot had so eloquently described—was not favoured.[3] The newer grammar schools were usually provided with their own fields for play near at hand and the example of Shrewsbury suggests that military training of a kind was

[1] Though the verse was not distinguished:

> And will your honour needs depart
> And must it needs be so
> Would god we could like fishes swim
> That we might with thee go. (Fisher, pp. 54–6.)

A History of Shrewsbury School from the Blakeway MSS. and many other sources (Shrewsbury, 1889), pp. 56–8, 61–6.

[2] Rowse, p. 506.

[3] The relevant statute for Leicester school, however puritan the authors, was reasonable enough, referring to the borough's common fields by the river: 'In their play they shall use honest games, and shall keep themselves in one field...appointed...by the schoolmaster, only they that exercise shooting shall be in places meet for the purpose.... They shall not swim or wade in waters; or come near to the river bank, neither shall they play in the street, nor go to alehouses, nor use any unlawful games, or break into orchards and rob gardens' (Cross, p. 20).

sometimes added to other exercises. Certainly in the early seventeenth century the future Colonel Hutchinson, one of many young gentlemen then attending Lincoln grammar school, followed with his companions a regular course of training in arms under a seasoned soldier; a training which, his wife noted later, stood him in much stead 'when the great cause of God's and England's rights came to be disputed with swords against encroaching princes'.[1] Elizabethan school founders and governors were more concerned with the encroachment of Jesuits and bent their efforts to arming scholars with sound protestant precepts. But, though there was consistent pressure in the direction of a fully reformed school, the English grammar school found more time than those in Germany for classical literature, versifying, orations. It was an education of a kind to lay the groundwork for many characteristic developments of the age.

At the outset of the sixteenth century there is little but complaint about the cultural backwardness of young men of birth, their lack of education, addiction to hunting, hawking, idle pleasures, and the irresponsibility of their parents. At its close treatises repeat the same strictures; it was impossible to write a book on gentlemen and education without them. But this literary convention masks a profound change. Country houses had attained a new level of civilisation, usually housed a tutor and sometimes sponsored a variety. University-trained men were much less rare than formerly in vicarages, while there were other well-qualified masters in charge of established local grammar schools. Young gentlemen were now to be found not only under tuition at home and in residence at colleges but also at their desks in the new school buildings up and down the country.

No courtly academies had been established; there was not the same basis for these in England as there was in France where men of birth tended to become courtiers alone and government fell to a bureaucracy. Rather the traditional form of educating the nobility continued, conditioned by continuance of the system of wardship, but its content was filled out and foreign travel added while the atmosphere of great households had also changed. If Sir Philip Sidney never went out without *The Courtier* in his pocket, Lord Burghley was never without Cicero on government, and attempts were made to merge these examples in training those whose commanding position in the social order conferred a like influence. This very position, however, undermined character

[1] Lucy Hutchinson, *Memoirs of Colonel Hutchinson* (1846), pp. 49–50.

particularly in the case of those who succeeded young and the later careers of Burghley's wards illustrate that educational efforts by no means always met with success.[1] On the other hand the education of noblemen was not entirely apart, as in a later age. Sir Henry Sidney's letter, reminding his son of the honour of Dudley blood, was addressed to Shrewsbury school and Burghley sent royal wards, as well as his own sons, to Cambridge colleges for a spell.

Both boys and girls were still sent away at an early age to be brought up in the households of others, wards or no.[2] Indeed guardianship, wardship, arranged marriages on the feudal pattern cemented links between those of affluence and status and the sale of wardships (like that of monastic lands) served to spread an interest in preservation of the system.[3] But gentlemen caught up in the system of wardship for the first time, as a consequence of purchasing lands from the crown, were outright critics.[4] Ambitious plans to mitigate its effects and promote special educational centres failed.[5] But gentlemen increasingly acted on their own account to ensure a regular course of education for sons.

Those of influence and means provided heirs with a prolonged training of the best they could devise. But younger sons must make their way in a trade or profession or in what might still be called, if with ironical overtones, the 'gentlemanly profession of serving man';[6] though here the hope was not now assistance to gain further qualifications so much as of a captaincy in the army, a patent to exploit or some other material aid to get on in the world. Some gentlemen aped their betters, as it now seemed, by providing tutoring at home. The catholic gentry, who tended to retire into their households to cultivate the old

[1] Hurstfield, pp. 258–9.

[2] Sir William Petre's daughter Thomasine was fitted out (at a cost of £10) at the age of ten to be sent to the household of the marchioness of Exeter (Emmison, p. 127).

[3] Neale, *Elizabethan House of Commons*, p. 315, Bell, p. 127.

[4] 'Many men do esteem this wardship by knights-service very unreasonable and unjust, and contrary to nature, that a freeman and gentleman should be bought and sold like an horse or an ox', as Sir Thomas Smith put it (Hurstfield, p. 110); cf. the rejection of a bill in the Commons in 1584–5 (Neale, *Elizabeth I and her Parliaments*, II (1957), pp. 91–4).

[5] There was a later scheme resembling Gilbert's in some respects to establish a special college at Ripon, backed by Huntingdon, Walsingham, Heneage, Sandys and others but (as it was noted when attempts to revive this were made in the next reign) it met only with 'fair unperformed promises from Elizabeth' (Peck, II, pp. 283 ff.).

[6] Cf. *A Health to the Gentlemanly Profession of Serving-Men* (1598), ed. A. V. Judges (Oxford, 1931).

religion, usually employed tutors;[1] though sons were often sent to university—Sandys, when archbishop of York, complained that all the popish gentlemen of Yorkshire sent their sons to Caius.[2] But gentlemen who were consolidating estates by judicious purchase and management employed regular servants rather than entertaining followers and keeping open house on traditional lines. These—indeed it would seem by the close of the century the majority of country gentlemen—sent sons to school, sometimes as boarders to a school of good repute but also, as facilities improved, to local grammar schools. As for poorer relatives, to whom obligations remained and were honoured, these, too, rather than being entertained in the household were maintained at college and school.

The habits and inclinations of gentlemen, then, chimed in with the official policy of bringing up the new generation together as dutiful servants of God and the state. And while the grammar schools contributed much towards turning the country gentry into gentlemen they themselves did not suffer in the same way as colleges from being recast in the gentleman's image; perhaps the contrary, in so far as new subjects were introduced and horizons widened. Within their walls, as Mulcaster had desired, 'the cream of the common' did come to associate with the rest so that in this sense too schools made their contribution towards moulding a common outlook. This was the specifically new development in the institution of the gentleman during Elizabeth's reign, and it went considerably further in the next, though it escaped the notice of contemporary writers of courtesy literature who tended to hand down a formula. Evidently mutual understanding was fostered between gentlemen and the ranks immediately below them, as has often been remarked. But in the long run, perhaps, this operated not so much to strengthen the established order as to consolidate forces against it. In any case post-Restoration observers saw the grammar school as a breeding ground of roundheads and regicides; ironically enough the royal foundation of Westminster gained a particularly bad name as the nursery of Henry Vane the younger, Thomas Scot and Arthur Hasilrig.[3]

[1] E.g. Sir Thomas Tresham, who kept hospitality on the old pattern in Northamptonshire, employed a schoolmaster, though later his secretary and surveyor taught the sons of the house—history, geography and arithmetic among other things (Finch, p. 185; see John Bossy, 'The Character of Elizabethan Catholicism', *Past and Present*, no. 21, April 1962).

[2] Venn, *Caius College*, pp. 77–8.

[3] Anthony Wood, III, p. 578.

XV

THE TRIUMPH OF THE VERNACULAR

'All may not pass to learning which throng thitherwards, because of the inconvenience which may ensue, by want of preferment for such a multitude', wrote Richard Mulcaster, bearing witness to the demand for education and the increase in the number of schools by 1580. Indeed he thought there were too many small schools, that fewer and better would be more serviceable, affirming that during 'her majesty's most fortunate reign' there had been more schools erected than 'all the rest be, that were before her time in the whole realm'. But necessity acted as a useful brake on educational aspirations. Parents lacked money and needed a child's help at home, or when there was no school nearby could not bear the charges of sending children far afield. This was just as well for if the many had the advantage of schooling 'they will not be content with the state which is for them, but because they have some petty smack of their book they will think any state, be it never so high to be low enough for them'. Certainly, Mulcaster concedes, 'God hath showed himself marvellous, munificent and beneficial in conferring talent on the poorer sort', but this does not mean that he has not also bestowed gifts on gentlemen, though they may have failed to use them. The needs of the commonwealth are best served by cultivating the best wits, in gentlemen at their own cost or 'by public aid if poverty pray for it', but, while the former have special responsibilities which call for education, the ordinary man 'doth not well to oppose his own particular against the public good, let his country think of him enough, and not he of himself too much'. This in a book addressed to the general reader was a neat adaptation of the usual adjurations to the nobility not to be outdone by lesser men, an injunction to the latter not to outdo their betters.[1]

The really poor did not, of course, even begin to press on the

[1] *Positions*, pp. 142 ff. Though it is doubtful how much Mulcaster's book was read; it was evidently held to rival Ascham's *Schoolmaster* and was never reprinted (*CHEL*, III, p. 435). Ascham's book was reprinted in 1589.

established grammar school. Rather they were impressed into work from an early age, or if 'idle' apprenticed to clothiers or householders to be trained while earning their keep in the process. In 1570 the city of Norwich, after finding that a tenth of the population was destitute, introduced special arrangements for children 'whose parents are not able to pay for their learning'; 'select' women were appointed in each ward to receive these children and teach them spinning or other skills so that 'labour and learning shall be easier than idleness'. Some 900 children earned 6*d.* a week under this scheme which remained in being for a decade or more.[1] As Thomas Wilson observed, referring to it, English citizens were not allowed to be idle like those in other parts of Christendom 'but every child of 6 or 7 years old is forced to some art whereby he gaineth his own living and something besides to help to enrich his parents or master'.[2]

The grammar school was also far out of reach of the labourer earning his 3*d.* a day, or the poor husbandman who fell into the category of those needing the child's help to support the family. Above this level there remained the problem of finding the wherewithal to equip a boy for learning. Schools might be called free but this meant that no charge was made for the actual teaching of local children. Incidental charges were many—entrance fees were general, so also 'voluntary' gifts to the master at certain seasons, while books, writing materials, wax candles, added up to a considerable sum.[3]

Voluntary gifts were often associated with Shrove Tuesday cock-fighting sessions which, though discredited, continued. In the Lake District, at any rate, most schools had their cockpits and in the seventeenth century 'cockpenny' varied from 6*d.* for the small school at Rydal, through 1*s.* at Ambleside, 2*s.* 6*d.* at Hawkshead, to 10*s.* at Kendal, while parents might sometimes provide extra for laying bets.[4]

[1] Dunlop and Denman, pp. 95 ff., 248–64; Leonard, pp. 105–6.

[2] *The State of England (1600)*, ed. F. J. Fisher, Camden Miscellany, XVI, Camden third series, LII (1935), p. 20.

[3] Local children paid entrance at 1*d.* or 2*d.* a quarter while 'foreigners' might pay 6*d.*, 1*s.*, 2*s.* (Stowe, pp. 93–6). According to accounts kept by Whitgift when a tutor at Trinity in the 1570's, paper was 4*d.* a quire, a bundle of pens and an inkhorn 4*d.* or 6*d.*; a Greek or Hebrew grammar cost 1*s.*, a prayer book 1*s.*, a testament 2*s.*, a bible 9*s.*; (Ball, *Cambridge Papers*, p. 37). French and arithmetic text-books sold for 7*d.* or 8*d.* to 1*s.* 4*d.*, cf. F. R. Johnson, 'Notes on English Retail Book Prices 1550–1640', *The Library*, fifth series, V (1951), pp. 83–112.

[4] Bouch and Jones, p. 152. A cockpit may still be seen next to the old schoolhouse of Heversham, built in 1613.

Once masters commanded their own dwelling house and took in pupils, especially if they achieved some reputation and became sought after, other incidental payments were likely to arise. When Peter Blundell, a wealthy cloth merchant desirous of spreading a sound protestant education, founded Tiverton school in 1599 he allocated a stipend of £50 to its master; with this—more than double what was usual in the largest schools—he must be content and ask no more 'for my meaning is, it shall be for ever a Free School and Not a School of Exaction'.[1]

This last went to the root of the problem, that stipends, like those of the clergy, remained low. It was by no means merely a matter of those awarded in 1548, which remained fixed despite inflation; since the whole income of chantries had been made over these were sometimes at quite a respectable level and onetime chantry schools, if placed where there was a demand for schooling, received local support or fresh endowments. But even landed endowments did not provide much surplus,[2] so that the master's stipend tended to remain at the sum laid down by the founder, the standard being £10.[3] It must be recalled that all stipends at this time, from the highest offices downwards, were in the nature of retainers while the real rewards of office depended on what could be picked up on the side. If Camden gathered 'a contented sufficiency' by his long labours in Westminster school, by no means all schoolmasters were in a like position, nor compensated for the lack. Heavy pressure on borough authorities were usually necessary before an increase for masters on their payroll was forthcoming. One example of successful local pressure is that on the Merchant Taylors' Company which held the endowments for Wolverhampton school, the master's salary being raised first to £10 then to £20 in 1572. But there were also schools kept as Hull borough school had been in the 1450's; Newcastle-under-Lyme in 1565 agreed to pay 'our schoolmaster 26*s.* 8*d.* for one whole year, and after as the town likes'—he had a £2 rise in 1572.[4] Gentlemen on governing bodies were no more disposed

[1] Carlisle, I, p. 340.

[2] 'The present revenues of the hospital being spent in salaries and wages to the schoolmasters and almsmen', wrote Sir John Harpur, one of the governors of Repton, to the fifth earl of Huntingdon who was another, in 1622, there was no money left to repair buildings nor 'to sue forth the fines' on hospital lands in Derbyshire and Lancashire (*H.M.C. Hastings MSS.* II, p. 60). Lands were also mishandled by governing bodies, as at Birmingham (Hutton, pp. 11–15); and Clitheroe (Stokes, pp. 13–20).

[3] Stowe, pp. 86–92.

[4] Mander, pp. 37, 44; T. Pape, *Newcastle-under-Lyme in Tudor and Early Stuart Times* (Manchester, 1938), pp. 105–6.

to offer any appreciable rise; the general trend was to keep schoolmasters, like the clergy, under and fees and extras, though putting the grammar school out of reach of many, did not make education expensive for the reasonably prosperous gentleman.[1]

Taken as a whole the Elizabethan gentry offered little in the form of endowments for schools by comparison with the benefits they received.[2] While lawyers figure as benefactors gentlemen otherwise seem more frequently to appear in the role of disappointed heirs engaged in litigation to retrieve lands bestowed on schools.[3] The founder of the free school at Harrow—a yeoman who had looked after the education of thirty poor children in his lifetime and wished to continue this support—expounded in his statutes how he had been blessed by God with considerable lands which he wished to devote to this purpose and to promoting preachers of 'good learned and godly sermons', providing dowries for poor girls, maintaining poor scholars at university and relieving the poor generally.[4] But other yeomen and gentlemen, accumulating lands to provide for their own, had none to spare for others.[5] The grammar schools depended much on the beneficence of childless men, among whom, it may be noted, bishops in time

[1] Sir John Wynne paid £13. 2*s*. 3*d*. a year for his son's education at Bedford school, covering board and all extras, including modern languages (Dodd, p. 108). The largest annual expenditure on education in the accounts of the Fitzwilliams of Northamptonshire—whose sons went to Cambridge and the inns of court—was less than one-sixteenth of a total expenditure of £900. Costs at Cambridge (at a high level) were nearly £8 a quarter (Finch, p. 125). Compare the proportionate expenditure of the second earl of Nottingham on educating sons in the first decade of the eighteenth century (H. J. Habakkuk, 'Daniel Finch, 2nd earl of Nottingham', in *Studies in Social History*, ed. J. H. Plumb (1955), pp. 166–7).

[2] In the ten counties covered by Jordan those classified as gentry contributed £53,041 for educational purposes in the eight decades 1480–1560; from 1561 to 1600, when the gentry were worth considerably more, money much less, they gave £11,120 by comparison with £72,875 left by merchants and tradesmen (*Philanthropy*, pp. 385, 387).

[3] E.g. successful claims by the founder's heirs to lands made over to Repton (*VCH Derbys.* II, p. 233), likewise at Warrington (*VCH Lancs.* II, p. 601). Even rights of presenting masters were disputed; the burgesses of Stafford sold their right to present to Henry, Lord Stafford, subsequently bought it back from his son in 1596 for £20 but nonetheless had later to buy off the grandson (Gilmore, p. 17).

[4] The statutes are of 1590 though the foundation did not take effect until 1608 after the death of the founder's widow (Carlisle, II, pp. 127–36).

[5] Dame Agnes Brudenell, a staunch protestant, expressed an intention of endowing schools, but her husband by unworthy means retained her property and his own dispositions in 1585 were concerned (as he had been in life) with the advancement 'of my house' (Wake, pp. 82, 89–90).

rarely figured; when John Whitgift did build a school and almshouses at Croydon in 1599 he was to draw accusations of profiting overmuch from the archbishopric.[1]

Merchants, growing to greater wealth than before, endowed schools generously but Mulcaster maintained—with the strong distaste so often aroused at this time by contemplation of merchant gains—that their benefactions were meagre enough by comparison with what they took from the poor.[2] At the close of the century Thomas Wilson, a knowledgeable observer, affirmed that there were London merchants worth £100,000 while at least half this sum was needed to be accounted rich; in Norwich, a city where so many were destitute, he knew at least twenty-four aldermen worth £20,000 apiece. By comparison the sum of benefactions to schools in ten of the chief counties of England in the Elizabethan age amounted to some £73,000, those to scholarships and fellowships at colleges to £27,000;[3] in all the reputed sum of one great London merchant's wealth.

Whether or not grammar schools were endowed at the expense of the poor, certainly a large proportion of the population was excluded from their benefits, leaving as the main candidates for entry sons of the more considerable yeomen farmers and burgesses, the country gentry and professional men, including ministers of the church. Scholarships were quite often attached to school foundations, either endowed at a particular college or held by the governors to pay out in aid to pupils going on to university. But there were relatively few funds to aid the poor boy to attend and remain in school.[4] It would seem that only those intended for university stayed on beyond the age of fourteen when apprenticeship began, while many may only have

[1] Dawley, pp. 221–2.

[2] 'These people by their general trades will make thousands poor; and for giving one penny to any one poor of those many thousands will be counted charitable. They will give a scholar some petty poor exhibition to seem to be religious, and under a slender veil of counterfeit liberality, hide the spoil of the ransacked poverty'; a thousand pounds gain to such, adds Mulcaster, 'bowels twenty thousand persons' (*Positions*, p. 194).

[3] Jordan, *Philanthropy*, pp. 288, 293.

[4] At Crediton the governors had £8 a year to distribute among four boys of the parish 'of the best disposition for grammatical learning'; at Lichfield six poor pupils might qualify for £1. 6*s*. 8*d*. apiece towards buying books if they also bought brooms and swept out the school (Stowe, p. 126). An Ipswich burgess left an endowment in 1598 towards buying books, ink, paper and apparel for sons of poor freemen at the borough school (Gray and Potter, pp. 51–2). At Halsham eight boys chosen by the parish officers were to be awarded £3 p.a. maintenance according to the founder's order in 1579 (Jordan, *Charities of Rural England*, p. 319).

spent a year or two in school.[1] Cathedral and collegiate schools with places on the foundation became subject to the same kind of patronage that bedevilled elections to colleges. It was the diversion of such places that so affronted Elizabethan churchmen, for where might the poorer scholar looking to take orders more justly expect assistance than from an ecclesiastical foundation? Yet, wrote Harrison, in the 1587 edition of his *Description of England*, before a scholar was nominated 'such bribage is made that poor men's children are commonly shut out, and the richer sort received...and yet, being placed, most of them study little other than histories, tables, dice and trifles, as men that make not living by their study the end of their purposes'.[2] The complaint, more strongly voiced in relation to colleges at the universities, was the more bitter in that most of the clergy were now married and making no small contribution to the increase in population.[3] Towards the close of Elizabeth's reign the prospective poor scholar was all too often the son of a minister aspiring to a good education for all his sons but lacking any ready means.

If, however, the gentry took up places and economic pressures controlled entry to established schools there were others available which enabled wider sections of the population to participate in the spread of education. Not only did boroughs come to regard a flourishing school as a sound investment and an essential mark of status but also townships, without concerning themselves about charters or rules, administered schools and did so more competently than in the past. There were, moreover, quite new opportunities for acquiring education

[1] A memorandum relating to St Olave's school, Southwark, in the 1570's notes that the usher who taught writing and ciphering had the same salary as the grammar master for 'we have now and so is like to continue many more scholars at writing than at grammar, seeing we have here great number of poor people in our parish who are not able to keep their children at grammar, but being desirous to have them taught the principles of Christian religion and to write, read and cast accompts and so to put them forth to prentice' (*VCH Surrey*, II, p. 183).

[2] This comment, sometimes dismissed as exaggerated, did not figure in the edition of 1577 and may well have been an embroidery on the preamble to the bill to curb abuses introduced in 1584 and finally passed in 1589; this recited supposed provisions 'notwithstanding it is seen and found by experience that the said elections...be many times wrought and brought to pass with money, gifts and rewards, whereby the fittest persons, are seldom or not at all preferred' (Heywood and Wright, pp. 541–8).

[3] Examples from Leicestershire in the first decade of the seventeenth century are the vicar of Cosby with thirteen children, the vicar of Peatling and the rector of Knaptoft with twelve, the parson of Enderby and the rector of Peckleton ten, the vicar of Hungarton eight (Hoskins, p. 194).

as the number of books in English steadily increased to cover a wide variety of subjects. By the close of the century the ordinary citizen without any command of Latin had access to knowledge which had earlier been reserved to those who had undergone years of schooling, and, too, to a vernacular literature reflecting the main concerns and interests of the age.

(1) *The common country schools*

When John Brinsley, a teacher from the 1590's, summarised his experience in two books published in 1612 and 1622 it was his concern to provide advice for the 'common country schools'. A graduate of Christ's College, Brinsley had first taught as curate of Kegworth in Leicestershire and then as master of the school of Ashby-de-la-Zouch under Huntingdon patronage until ejected for puritanism. Before writing his first book he made a tour of schools studying the methods used, including the Merchant Taylors' school in London. But he clearly differentiates his approach from the practice of larger schools and from that of writers who 'have specially fitted their course for the instruction of two or three alone, to be trained up in private houses, as our renowned Mr Ascham':

> Let not any man expect from me great matter, in a lofty kind of verse or prose, or eminency in declamations, orations or the like, this I leave to our worthy renowned schools of Westminster, Eton, Winchester, and the rest both in London and elsewhere, and to our schoolmasters of chief fame, whose breeding and employment in schools hath been accordingly....For myself I content me with this mercy from the Lord, and bless him for it, that I have travailed chiefly for our meaner and ruder schools.[1]

While attention has concentrated on endowed grammar schools there have been few attempts to assess the overall educational provision in any particular locality at this time, taking all the available evidence into account. But there is some information from Brinsley's county, Leicestershire. In this case no chantry certificates survive and there were few foundations; the picture that emerges is rather one of locally supported schools, some of them formerly connected with chantries but others coming to light in Elizabeth's reign in the market towns and then further afield. Thus a former chantry school at Loughborough

[1] John Brinsley, *A Consolation for our Grammar Schools*, ed. T. C. Pollock (New York, 1943), pp. 22, 25–6.

figures under the administration of the 'bridgemaster' and was held in the church, at Melton Mowbray the school was financed out of the 'town estate' and there was another school of obscure origin at Kibworth. Kegworth school was revived by an exchequer commission in 1575, while existing schools at Ashby and in the county town itself were endowed in the 1570's by the earl of Huntingdon and a former chantry school at Market Bosworth received an endowment from a London merchant in 1593. No endowments are recorded for other schools in the market towns of Billesdon, Hallaton, Lutterworth, Hinckley, the last two again being financed by the feoffees of the town lands, as also was Market Harborough until it received an endowment in 1614; and there was a school in the sizeable village of Wigston kept in a disused church which was attended by girls as well as boys.[1]

Most of these schools had a schoolhouse and two masters by the early seventeenth century when there were, in addition, some thirty other townships and villages with parish schoolmasters or curates teaching, many of whom had university degrees; at least forty-five places in the county had a school or a schoolmaster in the period 1625–40.[2] One or two Leicestershire village schools, which were evidently well established, sent the odd scholar to university direct, in other cases pupils passed on to a larger school and entered from there; most of the masters had themselves been at school in the county. This survey suggests the general direction of development; a nucleus of organised schools in the main centres, then parish schools interspersed with lesser foundations in the countryside and, on a more casual basis, curates and schoolmasters engaged in teaching whose qualifications gradually rose. There were not many graduates in the parishes in the

[1] Girls probably often attended village schools. That they sometimes attended more considerable ones is suggested by orders specifically excluding them: e.g. at Harrow, 'no girls shall be received, to be taught in the same school'. But on the seal of Uppingham and Oakham schools, founded in the 1580's, are represented four boys and two girls (Carlisle, II, pp. 132, 323). A girl figures on the Rivington School list in 1615 and two or three others in each quarter in the next two years (Kay, p. 72, cf. J. W. Adamson, '*The Illiterate Anglo-Saxon*' *and other Essays*, Cambridge, 1946, pp. 59–61).

[2] This information derives mainly from subscription books which first become available at this period. Of the sixty-two who subscribed as schoolmasters in the archdeaconry of Leicester between 1626 and 1639, forty-three were graduates and only four subscribed in English, specifying teaching only in the vernacular (B. Simon, 'Leicestershire Schools 1625–40', *British Journal of Educational Studies*, III, no. 1, 1954, p. 42–59: cf. E. H. Carter, *The Norwich Subscription Books 1637–1800*, 1937; Alan Smith, 'Schools in the Salford Hundred of Lancashire in the Seventeenth Century' thesis, Manchester University, 1955).

sixteenth century but curates were constantly exhorted to teach. Visitation returns from Cambridgeshire parishes in 1590, when information was requested on this point, record teachers in twenty (forty-five returned '*nullus*', in eighty-six cases a blank was left); incomplete returns in 1596 give twenty-two parishes with a teacher, only nine of which coincide with those named six years before.[1]

Masters of smaller schools frequently held office in the church at this period, but as time went on they tended to be masters first and as such to be appointed curate—an important reversal of the position whereby lesser incumbents taught in their spare time. Evidently the education provided in the smaller country school depended largely on the qualifications of the master, as also local demand. In so far as endowments allowed for a higher stipend, they assisted education to a higher standard; but there is no good reason to suppose that the small foundation differed materially from the school run by parish authorities. The latter were immediately interested in the quality of local schooling and jealously guarded their rights in the matter; an example is the eighteen 'sworn men' of Crosthwaite (or Keswick) who stoutly resisted the bishop of Carlisle's attempt to interfere when they dismissed an incompetent master in 1616.[2]

In practice, as has been suggested, few schools taught Latin exclusively. While some founders laid down that all entrants should be able to read and write—to read, even, both in Latin and English—others stipulated that reading and writing be taught, as also sometimes 'casting accompts'.[3] The tendency was to develop classes for petties taught by the usher in larger grammar schools while some schools which went under this name evidently catered mainly for boys entering on apprenticeships. By 1574 the borough school at Leicester had an under-usher or 'usher of the petits', with a stipend of £3. 6*s*. 8*d*., who taught in a room separate from the main school; subsequent benefactions were sometimes divided between the three masters with emphasis on

[1] *VCH Cambs.* II, p. 338.

[2] At an inquisition of that year it was stated that the eighteen had always placed and displaced the schoolmaster and made orders for the school's governance wherein 'the bishop and ordinary of the diocese, his commissary, nor chancellor, nor any other ecclesiastical ministers, have not of right had any other interest, power or authority than by the canons and ecclesiastical laws of this realm is lawfully permitted' (Carlisle, I, 179–80). It was more difficult for tenants to resist the local gentry; at Kirkham, in Lancashire, the catholic gentry obtained control over the local school for a time (Henry Fishwick, *History of the Parish of Kirkham*, Chetham Society, O.S. XCII, pp. 135–9).

[3] Stowe, pp. 104–10.

encouraging the ushers to teach writing.[1] By contrast Hull School had its first usher appointed in 1579 because of a considerable increase in the number of scholars, parents being required to pay 1*s*. towards his stipend if they could or a sum assessed by the mayor.[2] A school list for Wolverhampton school in 1609, of a kind that has rarely survived, shows that it then had two masters and sixty-nine pupils. Of these forty-one were in two forms and a petties class under the usher, and twenty-eight were in three forms under the master, though only nine of the latter were in the top two forms. It is worth noting how the forms were divided and the authors mentioned. Under the usher the petties class, with ten boys aged six to ten and one of thirteen, studied the accidence; form II, with fifteen boys aged eight to eleven, used Cato as text; form III, also with fifteen boys aged nine to thirteen, added Terence as author. Under the master, form IV entered on Cicero's *De Officiis*; this form was divided, the lower section having eight boys, aged eleven to thirteen, while in the upper section were eleven, one aged nine, two of seventeen who had just come to the school, the rest ranging from twelve to fourteen. Form V, with seven boys aged fourteen to seventeen, had entered on the Greek grammar. The 'head form' comprised only two boys of seventeen and eighteen who had just entered on the Greek testament and were reading Cicero, Horace and Virgil.[3]

A similar kind of internal organisation, ranging boys by attainment, must also have prevailed in the one-teacher school in the countryside, though here an assistant was sometimes kept or older pupils helped to teach the younger. The smaller school, near to hand, did not call for great expenditure on extras. Nor, presumably, did it provide anything like a full course of classical studies; rather the teaching of Latin must often have been confined, as indeed it seems to have been at Wolverhampton, to the official grammar supplemented by a few texts. Mulcaster argued strongly in favour of a uniform grammar, while recognising that 'Lily's' was no longer necessarily the best—for by now there was a variety of others in use. Indeed he favoured an altogether uniform curriculum in accordance with which school texts could be provided; his reason being that teachers varied widely in learning and judgment and if left at liberty to choose were likely to chop and

[1] Cross, pp. 14, 21–2, 23–4. It should be noted that masters of schools of this standing were usually forbidden to hold office in the church, though ushers were often curates.

[2] Lawson, pp. 51, 59.

[3] Mander, pp. 280–1, 373–5.

change books so that parents' purses were heavily taxed and poor men 'very sore pinched'.[1] This suggests a readiness for change that has not always been recognised. Much discussion of the curriculum of Elizabethan schools rests on collating foundation statutes, but these were not observed to the letter any more than the statutes of the realm or those of the universities. As has been suggested the more considerable grammar schools introduced additional studies of various kinds in response to demand and so also, it would seem, did lesser schools. When in the early seventeenth century more information becomes available, and professional teachers are more numerous, it is clear that these adapted the curriculum freely, making use of new books as they appeared, and increasing emphasis is now laid on the need to teach the vernacular.

Brinsley, while acknowledging his debt to the writings of 'the chief learned who have revived learning in this last age'—such as Erasmus, Melanchthon and Sturm—pays especial tribute to practising English teachers, naming Edmund Coote and 'the reverend and ancient schoolmaster Master Leech'.[2] Though Brinsley deals in detail with the teaching of Latin, Greek, even Hebrew—drawing attention to available texts of which his readers may not have heard—he devotes a long and detailed chapter at the outset of his first book to the teaching of reading in English. He insists on the importance of training children so that 'they may be able to express their minds purely and readily in our own tongue, and to increase in the practice of it'. This must be 'the chief endeavour' of masters, because most men use the native tongue both in speaking and writing, because the development of a pure language is of honour to the nation—all nations have flourished when their languages were most pure—and because among those trained in schools 'there are very few which proceed in learning, in comparison of them that follow other callings'.[3] He recommends the use of English

[1] *Positions*, pp. 263–8.

[2] Coote seems mainly to have kept a private school; he occurs as master of Bury School only for a year in 1596–7. John Leech tutored the earl of Leicester in youth and was for over forty years a tutor to gentlemen or schoolmaster (*Original Letters*, 1843, pp. 74–5). His *Book of Grammar Questions for the Help of Young Scholars*, another translation and clarification of parts of Lily, was dedicated to the puritan Robert Johnson, founder of Oakham and Uppingham schools (*EGS*, p. 267; *Athenae Oxoniensis*, II, 352).

[3] *Ludus Literarius: or the Grammar Schoole*, ed. E. T. Campagnac (1917), p. 22. Among books recommended for younger children is Seager's *School of Virtue* published in Edward's reign, reprinted in 1619.

translations of the classics[1] and names useful vocabularies and dictionaries. He warmly advocates Butler's rhetoric and advises use of a recently published manual by Perkins. For writing, masters should use the copy books 'prepared of purpose for the grammar schools' which give directions for writing Greek and Hebrew as well.[2] If ciphering is wanted there is Recorde's arithmetic or they should pass boys on to a master of the subject. But Brinsley maintains there is no reason why the ordinary schoolmaster should not teach writing adequately, even if no penman, and there follows another detailed chapter of advice. There is no evidence of stagnation here.[3]

It may be noted that there is proof that English texts not usually specified were used in school—and passed from hand to hand—in some unique survivals in the old town library of Leicester which was first brought together in 1625. A copy of Peter Martyr's *Commentarie on St Paule's Epistle to the Romans* has many names, and two quatrains with no bearing on the subject; one runs

I have invented a littel rime
Of one whose name was berrie
And also to passe away the time
Yet verie pleasant & merie.

There is a prosaic comment in George Joye's *Esposition of Daniell the Prophete* (John Day, 1550): 'John Bankes is a preti felo for the cane broke'. Cicero's *Orationes* (Lyons, 1582), also with many names, is more soberly inscribed:

In my beginning God be my good speed
In grace & virtue long for to proceed.

Among several of Erasmus's books, a copy of the *Moriae Encomium* (1522) was evidently used in school.[4]

But whether or not scriptural texts in English were used in the classroom there were always the sermons in church which grammar school pupils were bound to attend, while puritan masters favoured

[1] The list is headed by Grimald's translation of Cicero published in the 1550's (*A Consolation*, pp. 63–5).

[2] *Ludus Literarius*, p. 204; *A Consolation*, pp. 77, 79.

[3] *Ludus Literarius*, pp. 26, 27–40. This book is, in fact, cast in the form of a discussion between a traditionalist and an innovator, the former outlining accepted practice, the latter canvassing new methods and texts.

[4] All these are listed in C. Deedes, J. E. Stocks and J. L. Stocks, *The Old Town Library of Leicester* (Oxford, 1919).

attendance at lectures and monthly exercises as well, even where this was not specified in statutes. Indeed it was often the master or usher of the local grammar school who arranged repetitions of sermons for the benefit of his pupils and others; a close connection between puritan preacher and grammar school was typical of the early decades of the seventeenth century.[1]

While duly emphasising proficiency in languages Brinsley consistently urges, as Erasmus and Vives had done, that the end of education is knowledge and understanding; to read and not to understand 'is nothing else but a neglect of all good learning, and a mere abuse of the means and helps to attain the same'. It follows that the understanding and use of English must always proceed *pari passu* with learning Latin. English material can be dictated to the children, to be translated into Latin and back again; thereby they learn to spell English and exercise their writing as well. Taking notes of sermons in church, and discussing them afterwards in school, is another excellent exercise in English. It may be added that the plan of school organisation outlined, with emphasis on encouraging children to help each other, reduces puritan ideas on church government to the school level. In place of the monitors or praepositors of an Eton or a Westminster, armed with rods of office, Brinsley advocates seniors elected by the children themselves to look after classes while the master's attention is elsewhere.[2]

This was, no doubt, an exceptional teacher. Many masters of smaller schools may well have been pedants of the kind so tellingly presented by Shakespeare and other writers of the day, or only a step ahead of older pupils. But there were many puritan teachers, the trend was towards a grounding in the vernacular and this, even if supplemented by a minimum of Latin, laid the foundation for further study. The outcome is to be seen in the next generation, in such men as Lilburne, Walwyn, Overton, who left school early to take up apprenticeships but later read widely and wrote in a plain and vigorous English prose.

Meanwhile those able to stay on in school and acquire some scholarship in Latin sought a place at the university and an outlet in the church; for the ministry, if no suitable profession for the gentleman of standing, was soon absorbing younger sons once more and was the only one to which lesser men could reasonably look. As increased numbers pressed up through the schools the universities also expanded, aided by endowments to provide more places in colleges, so that after

[1] Marchant, pp. 37–8, 115. [2] *Ludus Literarius*, pp. 42, 273–4.

the turn of the century Bacon is pointing, more specifically than Mulcaster had done, to the dangers of an over-production of clerks. Much was also said of the miseries of scholars, deprived of an adequate outlet,[1] but the relevant point in our context is the access of graduates to country parishes. There were also others available with some university training for, despite more facilities at the universities, the poorer student had his work cut out to remain through the degree course and was often forced to return to his own county and seek a job in teaching to see himself through. Whitgift complained to Burghley that so many dispensations from residence were granted at Oxford that 'the greatest part of proceeders in arts yearly do not spend above a third part' of the statutory period in residence but were rather to be found in some gentleman's house or curate's place, though he recognised these were poor scholars driven by need.[2] Some never managed to return to university and graduate.[3] One who persisted was Jonathan Jephcott who, after an early schooling at Coventry, entered himself at an Oxford college at the age of 17 in the 1590's. He was advised to take a post as schoolmaster for a year and did so, using his earnings to maintain himself at Oxford, 'and when it was gone, he went and taught school for more; and thus he held on for some years'. When he did qualify and find a place as vicar he 'went every day two miles to teach school' to eke out his stipend.[4]

Teachers, therefore, constantly became available for the smaller school at a time when the demand for education was rising. At this period the wills of lesser yeomen frequently stipulate that sons be given an education 'proper to their degree and calling', that is at least education enough to understand leases though more was often in-

[1] What opportunities were open to the graduate after all his study, asked Richard Burton. 'The most parable and easy, and about which many are employed, is to teach a school, turn lecturer or curate, and for that he shall have a falconer's wages, ten pound per annum and his diet, or some small stipend, so long as he can please his patrons or the parish' *The Anatomy of Melancholy* (Everyman ed.), I, p. 306.

[2] Strype, *Whitgift*, I, p. 610. Information reaching Burghley from Cambridge at about the same time, in 1581, was that of 1950 students, 269 were in danger of leaving their studies for poverty and lack of exhibition (Strype, *Annals*, III, i, p. 74).

[3] There are instances among the Leicestershire schoolmasters. A testimonial signed by several local incumbents refers to the son of a colleague, recently deceased, who leaving a Cambridge college for want of means, was 'forced to betake himself into the country amongst us, where he hath behaved himself ever since...very studiously and commendably in teaching of children'—the next step was to take deacon's orders and seek a place as curate (*loc. cit.* p. 54).

[4] Samuel Palmer (ed.), *The Nonconformist's Memorial* (1775), I, p. 251.

tended.[1] Where there was no foundation or parish school, local farmers clubbed together and made arrangements to invite a master as towns had earlier done, taking him in to board in turn.[2] In the early seventeenth century most of the small chapels in the dales of the Lake District had their schools, held by the young men in deacon's orders, or unordained 'readers', who served the cure; and ecclesiastical visitors were sometimes scandalised to find communion tables, which had been pressed into the service of education, stained with ink.[3]

For those who had no access to a school Edmund Coote published *The English Schoolmaster* (1596) from which they could teach themselves, though it was also used in schools. That it served a need is indicated by the fact that a twenty-fifth edition appeared in 1625.[4] The book was also intended to be serviceable to tradesmen and craftsmen responsible for teaching apprentices, one of its advantages being that it could be propped up on a counting-house desk and used to hear lessons without undue interruption of work.

(2) *The third university of England*

Once again it was not only schools which acted as a powerful agent in promoting popular education. The stream of books in English, which had reached respectable proportions in Edward's reign, had by the close of the century become a flood, giving the ordinary citizen an established share in the spread of knowledge. It was not only that there were innumerable popular books in circulation—guides to domestic life and religious handbooks, chapbooks and romances especially suited to bourgeois taste, tales of travel, anthologies of the latest poetry, books on practical subjects and the wonders of science, tracts and

[1] Mildred Campbell, *The English Yeoman under Elizabeth and the Early Stuarts* (Yale, 1942), pp. 263–5.

[2] Adam Martindale bears witness to the practice in Lancashire, *The Life of Adam Martindale written by himself* (Chetham Society, O.S. IV), pp. 34–5. It long continued in outlying parts; this was how an education was first arranged for Robert Burns, son of an Ayrshire farmer, in the 1760's—later he and his brother attended a local school, in alternate weeks so that one fee covered two boys; J. R. Lockhart, *Life of Robert Burns* (Everyman, 1907), p. 4.

[3] 'Readers' lingered on here for decades because of the poverty of livings. Bishop Gastrell noted in 1717 that the curates who taught school had only 12*d*. a quarter, their 'whittlegate' (board from local families), 'harden sark' (some clothing), supplemented by cockpenny and other small returns from the schools; they also had the right to keep sheep or geese on the fells (W. G. Collingwood, *Lake District History*, Kendal, 1928, pp. 147–8).

[4] *EGS*, pp. 108, 154, 156, 177–8.

treatises of every kind—but that knowledge of the ancient world, which had had so telling an influence in moulding the outlook of the educated, was no longer locked away behind the barrier of an unknown language.[1]

Most of the translations of this age, like earlier ones, were consciously prepared with an eye to the ordinary reader. 'I framed my pen', wrote Philemon Holland, dubbed the translator general of his age, 'not to any affected phrase but to a mean and popular style, wherein, if I have called again into use some old words, let it be attributed to the love of my country language; if the sentence be not so concise, couched and knit together, as the original, loath I was to be obscure and dark.' Or again, introducing his translation of Pliny's *Natural History*, Holland advertises it as 'furnished with discourses of all matters, not appropriate to the learned only, but accommodate to the rude peasant of the country; fitted for the painful artisan of the town and city; pertinent to the bodily health of man, woman and child; and in one word, suiting with all sorts of people living in a society and commonweal'. Scholars registered strong protest at this cheapening of learning but the translators stood their ground and by the 1580's most of the major works of classical literature, including educational writings, were available in English. Translations from other languages now accrued. Learning could not be made too common, said Florio when he opened Englishmen's eyes to Montaigne: 'This mistress is like air, fire, water; the more breathed the clearer, the more extended the warmer; the more drawn the sweeter. It were inhumanity to coop her up.'[2]

Besides the many translations there were also outcrops from the schools. The Elizabethan grammar-school pupil often kept a commonplace book, in which he entered memorable and well-expressed phrases, notes about natural history, great historical figures, geographical facts—the idea popularised by Erasmus and Vives and recommended in various school orders. By 1600 there were many such books in printed form, in English. Again, the practice of taking notes at sermons became widespread under puritan influence. When the great educationist Comenius visited England in 1641 he wrote back to his community in Poland of the things that had chiefly struck him and he was particularly

[1] This and the following paragraphs draw on the comprehensive account by Louis B. Wright, *Middle Class Culture in Elizabethan England* (Chapel Hill, 1935).

[2] *Loc. cit.* pp. 349–51.

impressed by the crowded churches and the people's attention to sermons. 'A large number of the men and youths copy out the sermons with their pens', he wrote. 'Some thirty years since...they discovered an art which has now come into vogue even among the country folk, that of rapid script which they call stenography....Almost all of them acquire this art of rapid writing, as soon as they have learnt at school to read the scriptures in the vernacular. It takes them about another year to learn the art of shorthand.' Comenius added: 'They have an enormous number of books on all subjects in their own language.... There are truly not more bookstalls in Frankfurt at the time of the fair than there are here every day.'[1] It had been a very different tale at the outset of Elizabeth's reign.

London was the birthplace of all these developments. While the population was increasing throughout the country that of the capital may have more than trebled in the years between 1563 and 1624 to reach a figure of over 300,000—a significant proportion of a nation numbering between four and five millions.[2] The city, now becoming the economic centre of Europe, was the very heart of national life and London exercised a more powerful attraction than ever for ambitious young men. Whatever the restrictions imposed by statute London offered the poor and unknown the promise of making a fortune and a name; most of the aldermen and mayors in the late sixteenth century were of provincial origin and often of relatively humble parentage.

In the capital, merchants and diplomats from many countries mingled with the man in the street, ships left on voyages of discovery and returned with tales of new lands, poets held court in the taverns, playhouses staged the latest dramas. As their horizons widened Londoners grew accustomed to discussing anything and everything and there was a growing demand for reading-matter. While the provincial towns remained under the tutelage of the gentry, country gentlemen themselves were largely dependent on London for books and in London it was the bourgeoisie that set the tone. Thus no subject was considered more necessary to a gentleman's education than history, while it was also urged that teaching relate to the history of England. But it was the pride of London citizens that first gave rise to chronicles published in

[1] R. F. Young (ed.), *Comenius in England* (Oxford, 1932), p. 65. Continental printers published twice a year in spring and autumn for the bi-annual fair.

[2] Wright, p. 10. For a discussion of the complex problem of assessing population, Rowse, pp. 217–22; cf. Jordan, *Philanthropy*, pp. 26–9, where a figure of 4,200,000 in 1600 is advanced.

the vernacular. Holinshed worked in London, Grafton was a member of the Grocers' Company, Stow was a merchant tailor, so also John Speed.[1] Camden, son of a Lichfield craftsman who moved to London, studied and then taught in city schools; his *Britannia* first appeared in Latin but was soon translated by the indefatigable Holland. The common reader passed on from chronicles and the ubiquitous *Book of Martyrs* to North's translation of Plutarch's *Lives* designed for the 'common sort', and eventually more philosophical works such as Raleigh's *History of the World*.

In the matter of languages it was much the same. Italian may have been looked on as pre-eminently the courtier's language but it was very necessary to merchants trading with the Levant—and it was only one of the tongues taught and learned in the city. If French remained the most generally useful, German, Flemish, Spanish, had their claims and Arabic soon became necessary for those trading with the east. Protestant refugees from Italy and Spain contributed to the teaching of their languages, as did the French Huguenots; there were schools connected with the French church at St Anthony's Hospital and with the Dutch church at Austin Friars as well as those kept over many years in St Paul's churchyard.[2] Merchants were naturally interested in the study of languages for use rather than ornament and the more direct method of teaching used by private teachers instructing busy men, the soon common experience of acquiring another tongue, led to informed criticism of slow grammatical methods of teaching Latin; criticism, growing in volume after the turn of the century, which prepared the way for acceptance of the radical reforms advocated by Comenius and others.

Teachers of mathematics also developed methods suitable to their own subject, which differed greatly from the traditional approach, and some kept private schools. Humphrey Baker, for instance, kept a school on the north side of the Royal Exchange and took in boarders.[3]

[1] 'That the history of our country may rescue itself from the shears and stealths of tailors' was one of the objects of the royal academy for gentlemen's sons proposed in 1620 (*Archaeologia*, XXXII, 1847, p. 141).

[2] Lambley, pp. 129, 145–6, 169–70. One French schoolmistress kept school for forty years. See also Foster Watson, 'Religious Refugees and English Education', *Proceedings of the Huguenot Society*, IX (1909–11), pp. 446–9.

[3] He was author of *The Well Spring of Sciences which teacheth the perfect work and practice of Arithmetic in both whole numbers and fractions* (1562) dedicated to the Merchant Adventurers (Yeldham, pp. 51–8).

John Mellis, editor of a new edition of Recorde's *Ground of Arts*, was teaching writing, drawing and arithmetic in Southwark from about 1590. Thomas Hylles, author of *The Art of Vulgar Arithmetic* (1600), probably did the same; he produced rhymed rules for learners in English, as Buckley had done in Latin in the Edwardian age.[1] Again merchants necessarily had a close interest in mathematics and astronomy with their bearing on navigation, in geography and mapmaking, and the great companies trading overseas were the main employers of mathematicians and the first practising scientists; one such was John Dee, a friend to many sailors for whom he charted routes. The companies also aided the publication of works by men in their employ. It was when acting as publicist for the East India Company that Richard Hakluyt, son of a London merchant, completed the researches published in 1589 in *The Principal Navigations, Voyages...and Discoveries of the English Nation made by Sea or over Land to the Remote and Farthest Distant Quarters of the Earth*—a book which contributed much, like that of Foxe, to making Englishmen conscious of their nation.

Most of these men had been at Oxford or Cambridge, some had taught geography or cosmography to students—a subject which, as Gilbert's plan indicates, was now accepted as an important adjunct to the gentleman's education. But the more notable completed their education abroad and it was from London, with its great enterprises, that the impetus to further probing into scientific matters came, as distinct from discussion and some teaching as an aspect of polite education.[2] Thus Hakluyt, having lectured at Oxford with the latest maps, globes and other instruments, and published one book left for London to continue research in the archives of London companies at their expense.

1
Multiplication bends all his devotion
By folding together 2 numbers assigned
To bring forth a third in such like proportion
To one of those 2 as the other behind
Is unto an ace, which number we call,
The product or ofcum, wherever it fall.

2 'However much it remained true that most scientists were university-trained and that many scientists found positions as university teachers, the science of the later sixteenth century was not indigenous to the university. In this respect the early modern period differs markedly from the middle ages when almost all scientific discussion took place within the walls of the university, and within the framework of the standard university curriculum'; teachers preferred private lectures to university posts and when writing about the advancement of science did so in terms of various institutions but not the universities (Boas, pp. 239–41).

In 1596 the college endowed many years before by Sir Thomas Gresham was opened under the administration of the Mercers' Company and the common council of the city. Here, by the founder's express wish, lectures in the seven liberal sciences were given in English. The assistance of the universities was sought in choosing the first seven professors but these were reminded that their hearers would be merchants and other citizens and that lectures should not, therefore, be read 'after the manner of the universities'; rather the lecturer should 'cull out such heads of his subject as may best serve the good liking and capacity of the said auditory'. Consequently the liberal sciences took on a new look. The astronomy professor was to read 'the principles of the spheres and theoriques of the planets and to explain the use of common instruments for the capacity of mariners'; he was to apply this knowledge to use further by lecturing in geography and the art of navigation. The professor of geometry was to lecture during one term in arithmetic, the second in theoretical geometry, the third in practical geometry. In music lectures theory was to be covered for half an hour and the rest of the time spent in performance with voices and instruments. The lecturer in medicine was instructed to cover physiology, pathology and therapeutics. Lectures in divinity must embody 'sound handling of such controversies as concern the chief points of our Christian faith', dwelling particularly on differences between the established religion and the tenets of papists and sectaries.[1]

It became a commonplace in Elizabeth's reign to refer to the inns of court as a university, the third in the kingdom. But by the early seventeenth century it seemed to one man that it was the city of London itself that earned the title 'The Third University of England'. Sir George Buck was no bourgeois; master of the revels at court, he was proud of London's facilities for educating a man of the world.[2] Nevertheless, it is to academic learning that he first refers, to the numerous schools, small and large, teaching the liberal arts and the organised teaching available in all the recognised higher faculties—in common law at the inns of court and in civil law at Doctors' Commons, in medicine by lectures promoted by the College of Physicians, while there were innumerable theological lectures and sermons. If this was

[1] Wright, pp. 64–5; J. W. Burgon, *Life and Times of Sir Thomas Gresham* (1839), II, pp. 515–18.

[2] His tract, dedicated to Sir Edward Coke, was written in 1612 and published later as an appendix to an edition of Stow's *Annals*, ed. How (1631), pp. 1056 ff.

all there was to most universities it was only a beginning so far as London was concerned. In addition to the scientific lectures read at Gresham's College, there was another given at Leadenhall Chapel, a cosmography lecture in Blackfriars, while hydrography and navigation could be studied at Deptford. He enumerates the opportunities for learning all kinds of writing, all branches of mathematics, all languages necessary for ambassadors, agents to merchants, travellers, commerce and negotiation—including Persian, Turkish, Russian and other Slavonic tongues.

In addition, the capital could boast poets of every kind—dramatic, lyric, heroic, epic, pastoral or satirical. There were also good masters of painting; though this art, the author comments, has fallen from its ancient reputation and is accounted a mere metier of the artificer or handicraftsman so that few gentlemen adventure the practice of it. But they may have the benefit of the best musicians in the kingdom, incorporated in a society to which dancing masters too belonged, and there were besides instructors in vaulting, tumbling, rope climbing. The eminently gentlemanly art of riding was practised by the Gentlemen of the Stable Royal at Charing Cross and also taught on Clerkenwell Green and at Mile End. Teachers skilled in the use of every kind of weapon might be found, and there were regular schools where pupils could qualify for the degree of provost of defence (won at a public trial of skill) and then master of defence, which enabled them to teach in turn. The art of shooting with ordinance was taught in the Artillery Garden, without Bishopsgate, all teachers coming directly under the Master of Ordinance. Engineers expert in mining and fortification also provided instruction, as did many seasoned soldiers. There were plenty of teachers of swimming and plenty of river and water for practising it.

In advancing the concept of London as a university of all the arts and sciences the writer propagates a new idea of a university. Indeed, from the heights of classical knowledge, he effectively demolishes the medieval conception that a university is only such when a pope blesses a scholarly corporation with a bull; 'then', he remarks drily, 'had Athens been no university, for there the pope had nothing to do, as being not then in *rerum natura*'. By the early seventeenth century, therefore, there was teaching in London of all the arts and sciences Gilbert had wished to promote, not in an academy confined to gentlemen, nor within four walls, but in the city at large and in some branches very much open to citizens. The fact that there were ordinances forbidding apprentices to attend dancing, fencing and music schools suggests that they did just this, though, of course, many were young gentlemen completing their education in the third university of the kingdom.

A key point Gilbert had raised, that of promoting research and publishing findings, has no mention here, but there were circles concerned with advancing knowledge. Such was the Society of Antiquaries which began to meet regularly in the 1580's,[1] and the circle, likewise composed of men of leisure with opportunities for discussion, which met under the auspices of Henry Percy, earl of Northumberland and was interested in scientific matters. More important in this connection, and typical of the Elizabethan age, was the steady accumulation of knowledge in practice and the consequent development of a scientific attitude. When Robert Norman, mariner and compass maker, published a book in 1581 he passed over all 'tedious conjectures or imaginations' in order to base his arguments on 'experience, reason and demonstration, which are the grounds of art', and his work paved the way to the discovery of magnetism. Norman owed nothing to an established centre of learning but scholars engaged in promoting a new outlook at the universities were quick to recognise the merit of such men. Gabriel Harvey of Cambridge wrote: 'He that remembereth Humfrey Cole, a mathematical mechanician, Matthew Baker, a shipwright, John Shute, an architect, Robert Norman, a navigator, William Bourne, a gunner, John Hester, a chemist or any like cunning and subtle empiric'—and these 'will be remembered, when greater clerks shall be forgotten'—is a proud man if 'he condemn expert artisans, or any sensible industrious practitioner, howsoever unlectured in schools, or unlettered in books'; the experts, Harvey added, well knew the value of such work—'what profound mathematician, like Digges, Hariot or Dee, esteemeth not the pregnant mechanician?'[2]

This kind of defence was still very necessary in the face of aristocratic distaste for mere *métier* and the continued assault by the learned on books in English. But it was easier to challenge this attitude now that authors could point to a host of forerunners, while underlining their own obligation to pass on knowledge in turn. 'This I know full well',

[1] Fussner, pp. 92 ff. Of the forty known members all (except John Stow) were gentlemen, many being knights, two noblemen.

[2] J. D. Bernal, *Science in History* (1954), pp. 299–300.

wrote William Clowes, who had gained his experience in medicine and surgery on the battlefield and in the great London hospitals, 'that art comes to no man by succession, but by great pains, long study, much care and diligence.' Men who have thus gained knowledge rightly aim to pass it on 'that their knowledge should not die with themselves but remain unto posterity as a testimony of their love to further the travails of such as should follow them'. This, says Clowes, enumerating the workers in his particular field—both physicians and surgeons—has been the aim of many worthy men. And it is noteworthy that he gives the surgeons an honourable place, though they held no title of doctor; the raising of the surgeon's status with the development of anatomical studies helped to bridge a gap between practice and theory and doctors were very prominent among the early scientists.[1] Clowes can also call in aid gentlemen who have helped to spread medical knowledge in the vernacular, beginning with 'that worthy knight Sir Thomas Eliot', asking 'should all their knowledge, all their painful labours and all their commendable works have no better recompense but a malicious upbraiding because they are penned in English?' Finally he turns on the detractors: 'O wicked and spiteful minded men, unworthy the benefit of so good labours, not unlike in nature to the Cuckoo which devours the bird that brought her up'. It is reminiscent of Latimer and Tyndale castigating the Scotists half a century or more before.

In 1592 the significance of new achievements by comparison with the stagnation of traditional learning, was brought to notice in a short 'device', *Mr Bacon in Praise of Learning*, written in honour of the queen's birthday. 'Are we the richer by one poor invention by reason of all the learning that hath been these many hundred years?' asked Francis Bacon, and answered, 'The industry of artificers maketh some small improvement of things invented; and chance sometimes in experimenting maketh us to stumble upon somewhat which is new; but all the disputation of the learned never brought to light one effect of nature before unknown'. Two years later a similar interlude, presented at Gray's Inn at Christmas, represented a prince urged to

[1] Clowes was himself no university man but, apprenticed to a barber-surgeon, he felt as much bound to this master 'for giving me the first light and entrance into the knowledge of the noble art of surgery' as ever Alexander the Great to Aristotle. He was responsible, with other surgeons of St Bartholomew's, for reprinting Vicary's work on anatomy first published in Edward's reign (F. N. L. Poynter, ed., *Selected Writings of William Clowes*, 1948, pp. 16, 18, 161–7).

promote the conquest of the works of nature. Four great works, Bacon suggested, would be a worthy monument to any prince. The collecting of 'a most perfect and general library'. The creation of a spacious garden, with every plant and herb, a zoo for rare animals and birds, lakes for fish, to provide in a small compass 'a model of universal nature made private'. A museum of natural science and mechanical arts, 'wherein whatsoever the hand of man by exquisite art or engine hath made rare in stuff, form or motion' might be collected together and classified. A centre for experimental research—'a still-house so furnished with mills, instruments, furnaces and vessels, as may be a palace fit for a philosopher's stone'.[1] Here was the germ of ideas later to be developed at length.

Bacon was at this time seeking the help of his uncle, Burghley, to embark on a life of study. But no place was forthcoming, and leisure to write was hard to come by in that struggle for survival which faced the Elizabethan gentleman in public life, especially a younger son without resources. It was not, then, until two years after Elizabeth's death that there appeared, dedicated to her successor, *The two Books of Francis Bacon. Of the proficience and advancement of learning*. Advocating a radically new evaluation of knowledge and so education, criticising the limitations of established centres of learning, this was yet another work written in English, published in London, to be sold at the book-shop at the gate of Gray's Inn.

(3) *Humanism and puritanism*

Bacon admirably summarises the tendencies of an age while generalising its achievements in a new philosophy which bears closely on education. He is critical of humanist insistence on a return to the classics in so far as this has led 'rather towards copy than weight' and caused men to study 'words and not matter'. But, himself insisting on the study of nature and the importance of mechanical arts and sciences, he reserves a much stronger condemnation for scholastic method and subservience to ancient philosophy, taking up points broached by Vives in the 1530's. While the mechanical arts advance, being improved by the industry and intelligence of many men, scholastic learning is barren—'many wits and industries have been spent about the wit of some one, whom many times they have rather depraved than illustrated'. From

[1] Farrington, pp. 33–6.

this approach derives his criticism of university teaching methods which do not accord with needs in real life, whereas exercises should be framed 'as near as may be to the life of practice for otherwise they do pervert the motions and faculties of the mind, and not prepare them'. But to Bacon the greatest error of all is the mistaking of the ultimate end of knowledge. Men enter on learning for reasons of every kind—through curiosity, to adorn their minds, 'most times for lucre and profession'—but seldom 'to give a true account of their gift of reason for the benefit and use of men'; they fail to see knowledge as 'a rich storehouse for the glory of the Creator and the relief of man's estate'. Yet it is this, Bacon insists, that will in fact dignify and exalt knowledge, 'if contemplation and action be more nearly and straitly conjoined and united together than they have been'. His meaning, he explains, is not that knowledge must always be turned to use in some profession; he has no wish 'to call philosophy down from heaven to converse upon the earth; that is, to leave natural philosophy aside, and to apply knowledge only to manners and policy'.

But as both heaven and earth do conspire and contribute to the use and benefit of man; so the end ought to be, from both philosophies to separate and reject vain speculations, and whatsoever is empty and void, and to preserve and augment whatsoever is solid and fruitful: that knowledge may not be as a courtesan, for pleasure and vanity only, or as a bond-woman, to acquire and gain to her master's use; but as a spouse, for generation, fruit and comfort.[1]

This is no place to take issue with those who traduce Bacon's ideas and intentions, in much the same way as Colet has been traduced for failure to fit into the conceptual schema of modern scholarship. Bacon would not have been so much a man of his time if he had not epitomised its limitations as well as its achievements; but it was his signal service to make contemporaries aware of the latter, of the need for thought to make room for and direct further advance rather than continuing to turn in on itself and looking down on the world at work. Knowledge had, in fact, increasingly been applied to practical ends in the foregoing years. Metallurgical processes, in particular, had been much developed in the manufacture of household goods of all kinds and of arms for war; this had led in turn to a search for cheaper fuels

[1] *The Advancement of Learning*, ed. W. Aldis Wright (Oxford, 1873), pp. 29–30, 37, 42–3, 82.

and the discovery of new methods of mining coal. While in an earlier age objects had been designed and produced to beautify churches, production was now largely turned to providing things of use and beauty for homes—country houses were designed for the needs of those living in them, schools for the purposes of education. The introduction of new processes, the emphasis on production for use, insistently directed attention to relations between practice and knowledge hitherto unrecognised and to the direct link between the advancement of knowledge and the betterment of human life.[1]

It was Bacon's achievement, as it was Shakespeare's in another range of experience, to chart the deeper current in a tide about to flow into new and more separate channels. The first industrial age in England was short-lived and the traditional social structure, which Elizabethan legislators had been at such pains to consolidate, militated against recognition of its significance. Gentlemen who held patents were more interested in financial returns than the nature of industrial processes, merchants in command of the domestic system had no interest in developments in factory production, while contempt for *métier* precluded understanding of advances in technique which prepared the way for scientific advance. Divisions were to be accentuated in the coming decades, for once the essential scientific discoveries had been made they were vigorously exploited and interest in advancing knowledge correspondingly waned. The first generation of professional scientists had no immediate successors; rather the *virtuosi*, abandoning poetry to poets by profession, took to this field. But in general there was a trend away from learning among gentlemen for when the professions became established learning itself became, in Bacon's term, 'a bond-woman'. There had been a growing emphasis on the pleasures as opposed to the uses of knowledge and the idea that learning is integral to gentility gradually gave place to the conception of learning as an ornament. Successors of Elyot, Ascham, Gilbert, in the coming age accordingly stress, not so much the greater the learning the greater the virtue, as that too much learning lowers the dignity of rank, a general acquaintance is all that is required. The view is clearly expressed in the directions for reading drawn up by a seventeenth-century college tutor for young gentlemen under his care, at university not to acquire knowledge to apply to the benefit of their country but 'such learning

[1] J. E. Nef, *Cultural Foundations of Industrial Civilisation* (Cambridge, 1958), pp. 43–9, 60. Economic and industrial changes are summarised by Rowse, pp. 107 ff.

as may serve for delight and ornament and such as the want whereof would speak a defect of breeding'.[1] In 1628 John Earle delineated 'A Young Gentleman of the University' (as contrasted with 'A Down-Right Scholar'):

His father sent him thither because he heard there were the best fencing and dancing-schools; from these he has his education, from his tutor the over-sight....His main loitering is at the library, where he studies arms and books of honour, and turns a gentleman critic in pedigrees. Of all things he endures not to be mistaken for a scholar....But he is now gone to the inns-of-court, where he studies to forget what he learned before, his acquaintance and the fashion.[2]

Within this framework the universities were doubly bound, by their scholastic tradition and their gentlemanly connections. Cosmography might be an extra-curricular study, but natural philosophy remained grounded in Aristotle and there was no appreciation of the Baconian view; science in this sense seemed something much less than learning in any understood sense of the term. Those who sought to study medicine seriously were drawn chiefly to the university of Leiden, founded with the establishment of Dutch independence in 1575, which rapidly came to the fore. If there had been much cultivation of learning in Elizabeth's England there was little advancement of it in the centres of learning to fulfil the promise of an earlier age. Over a considerable period leading scholars had been drawn off into the political arena and when the number of qualified teachers in colleges did increase the pressure of student numbers turned attention to tutoring rather than study and research; in particular, the mounting demands of young men preparing to take their place in the world as gentlemen, who were in some ways more parasitic on the universities than the monks they had replaced. Though there were Greek and Hebrew scholars of note and devoted students, languages were not studied as they were abroad. When the young Lancelot Andrewes of Pembroke, who was particularly interested in oriental tongues, resolved to acquire a new language each year he applied to his parents in London to secure a tutor for his month's vacation and carried out the project in this way.[3] While

[1] Harris Francis Fletcher, *The Intellectual Development of John Milton*, II (Urbana, 1961), p. 647, where Holdsworth's 'Directions' are printed.

[2] *Character Writings of the Seventeenth Century*, ed. Henry Morley (1891), p. 185–6.

[3] Florence Higham, *Lancelot Andrewes* (1952), p. 13. What he could not find at Cambridge Andrewes got in Grub Street, from a man named Hopkinson, 'an obscure

Cambridge turned with profit to the logic of Ramus in the last decades of the century, at Oxford something like the old arts course crept back and Aristotle was reinstated by authority as chief of philosophers.[1] By the same token the dedicated study of the scriptures for which puritans looked was lacking.

It was one of Bacon's chief contributions to draw a clearer line than Vives had done between reason and revelation and this enabled puritans to embrace his scientific views wholeheartedly; engaged in separating the true word of God from the vanities of scholastic philosophy they could support as energetically efforts to prise science from this shell.[2] But if in this sense Bacon developed the rational humanist outlook his whole approach was also in the best protestant tradition, a tradition which, itself absorbing and adapting humanist views, 'equated charity with works done to benefit the commonwealth, or mankind'.[3] His philosophy inspired a new body of reformers who advanced practicable plans for recasting education in the light of new social needs and developments in knowledge. In republican England after 1640—when king and court had been swept away, the House of Lords abolished as useless and dangerous, bishops banished from the church—parliament seriously considered plans for educational reform on Baconian lines.[4] Once more, as in Edward's day, confiscated ecclesiastical endowments were turned to the use of schools and there were innovations at the universities where colleges, suitably purged of drones, were sometimes furnished with enthusiasts for science.

Meanwhile a sign of bourgeois coming of age at the turn of the century is the growing criticism of educational institutions. In earlier days merchant founders had felt incapable of suggesting a curriculum for the schools they established. In the Elizabethan age the London companies took a growing share, under tutelage, in running schools, administering two of the great schools besides others up and down the country. In the provinces boroughs and parishes ran schools which

and simple man for worldly affairs but expert in all the lefthand tongues, as Hebrew, Chaldean, Syrian, Arabian', to whom James Whitelocke of Oxford also went to keep up his Hebrew, acquired in a London school (Bruce, p. 13).

[1] Mallet, II, p. 147.

[2] R. F. Jones, *Ancients and Moderns* (Washington, 1936), pp. 75–6.

[3] Christopher Hill, 'Intellectual Origins of the English Revolution', *The Listener*, 7 June 1962—from the Ford Lectures due for publication in book form.

[4] D. Bush, *English Literature in the Earlier Seventeenth Century* (Oxford, 1962 ed.), pp. 13–21. Cf. Joan Simon, 'Educational Policies and Programmes, 1640–60', *Modern Quarterly*, II, no. 4 (1949), pp. 154–68.

were also necessarily responsive to public demand.[1] Brinsley describes the dissatisfied parent who complains 'my son comes on never a whit in his writing. Besides his hand is such, that it can hardly be read; he also writes so false English, that he is neither fit for trade, nor any employment wherein to use his pen.' When, he warns, 'all in a town generally, shall murmur against us, in this or the like manner, that their children do no good under us, but lose their time, and spend their friends money, being brought up idly, made fit for nothing', they will go on to ask why there should be a school at all; and may well answer 'that it were much better to turn the maintenance given to the school to bear the charges of the town for other duties and services, than so unprofitably to employ it'.[2] This was a potent argument indeed. If gentlemen were beginning to appreciate learning in relation to its uselessness, there were others to value it according to its use and the benefits it might bring.

All this prepared the ground for further endowments of schools in the decades up to 1640 and these were much more numerous than in Elizabeth's reign, reaching a peak in the years 1611–30.[3] Benefactions were also in general more purposive; it was not statesmen and bishops at this period but London merchants who consciously directed attention to outlying parts which had yet to be won for protestantism by a godly education.[4] When developments are followed through from the sixteenth to the seventeenth century it is clear that, despite the importance of the early humanists as forerunners, the school system was essentially a product of the Reformation. Nothing could well be more mistaken than the usual view, that puritanism left the English grammar school unchanged.[5] A close study of statutes, teaching methods, text-books,

[1] In response to the complaints of parents that their sons were not advancing well enough the Merchant Taylors' Company introduced a new system of probation in their school in 1607; an examination was held three times a year, exercises were done in writing in a prescribed time, scholars found inept were to be dismissed, and lists of marks drawn up for each class for future reference (Wilson, I, pp. 159 ff.).

[2] *A Consolation*, p. 43.

[3] Over a third of the funds left for schools during the whole period 1480–1660 in the ten counties covered by Jordan were left in these two decades, nearly a half in the period 1600–40 (*Philanthropy*, p. 288). Though the total amount of money is less important than the number of foundations represented—there were less great endowments of the kind that bump up figures for earlier decades, many more modestly endowed local grammar schools.

[4] Christopher Hill, 'Propagating the Gospel', *Historical Essays 1600–1750*, ed. H. E. Bell and R. L. Ollard (1963); 'Puritans and "the Dark Corners of the Land"', *T.R.H.S.* fifth series, XIII (1963).

[5] Clarke, p. 45.

no less than of general attitudes and policies, shows that at this period the grammar schools 'entered deeply into the national thought and life' and that on education as at large 'the influence of puritanism... was epoch-making'.[1] It cannot be accepted that by 1660 schools were so distributed and available that there was one 'within the reach of any poor and able boy who thirsted for knowledge and aspired to escape the grip of poverty'.[2] But if schools, however near, remained outside the reach of many it cannot be doubted that they increased enormously in number, to make up a relatively organised system, and that the content of education was transformed during the century after the Reformation. For this development the policies pursued in the Edwardian age charted the way.

Criticisms of the universities also multiply after the turn of the century when Gilbert's complaints about licentious habits, Burghley's private censures, find their echo in parliament and at large. Such objections, linked once more to criticism of ecclesiastical policies, prompted the Commons' submission to Charles I on his accession—that the universities were disastrously lax in discipline, infected with popery and in urgent need of reform; strictures sufficiently well grounded to persuade the king that the universities must be required to put their house in order.[3] No doubt Oxford and Cambridge 'did more than any other institution to develop a body of trained and cultivated men' since there were no comparable institutions; but while the old picture of them as shackled in turn 'by the Schoolmen, the men of the Renaissance, and the leaders of the Churches' evidently needed correction,[4] the newer one of lively bodies providing an enlightened humanist education hardly tallies at all points with the evidence. If the colleges put themselves out for gentlemen's sons more than has sometimes been recognised, humanist learning had failed to oust scholasticism, as Milton bears witness, recalling

[1] Foster Watson, *EGS*, pp. 530 ff.

[2] Jordan, *Charities of Rural England*, p. 165. The reference is to Norfolk, where no family lived more than twelve miles from an endowed school, but a general impression emerges from the valuable surveys by this author that the problems of providing education and overcoming poverty were virtually solved at this time.

[3] Passing on the request, the chancellor of Cambridge, the earl of Suffolk, implored heads of colleges to 'put all their brains together and be all of one mind, as one entire man, to bring home that long banished pilgrim Discipline' (D. Masson, *Life of John Milton and History of his Time*, Cambridge, 1858, I, pp. 131–2).

[4] Curtis, p. 262; the quotation is from the historian of Oxford University writing in the liberal tradition with fresh memories of the bitter struggle to throw off clerical dominance in the nineteenth century (*ibid.* pp. 8–9).

Erasmus in the vigour of his denunciation though his target was bishops rather than monks.[1]

At this period the humanist approach assisted men not merely to stand on the shoulders of their forerunners but so to apply themselves as to 'judge better over the whole round of life and nature than could Aristotle, or Plato or any of the ancients', as Vives had foreseen. But it was not in the universities that this outlook was fostered.[2] When Simonds d'Ewes decided 'to consider of employing my labours to the public good', as he completed his course at Cambridge in 1620, the resolve was his own, upheld by a few learned and godly men of his acquaintance who had encouraged his study of the scriptures. Though he had had some good tutoring, and heard many good sermons, he was glad to leave St John's College where 'swearing, drinking, rioting, and hatred of all piety and virtue under false and adulterate nicknames, did abound...and generally in all the university'.[3]

The universities, under the supervision of crown and church, were not subject to the same kind of social pressures as local grammar schools and, rather than providing the training society wanted and demanded of them, as Mr Curtis has concluded, they met certain influential demands at the expense of others. Colleges also received many more endowments in the early seventeenth century than under Elizabeth, notably from London donors intent on fostering a learned and godly ministry, but benefactions abruptly fell away when Laudian policies

[1] Gentlemen who went to universities 'to store themselves with good and solid learning', he writes in *The Reason of Church Government*, were 'there unfortunately fed with nothing else, but the scragged and thorny lectures of monkish and miserable sophistry, were sent home again with such a scholastical burr in their throats, as hath stopped and hindered all true and generous philosophy from entering, cracked their voices for ever with metaphysical gargarisms, and hath made them admire a sort of formal outside men prelatically addicted, whose unchastened and unwrought minds never yet initiated or subdued under the true lore of religion or moral virtue, which two are the best and greatest points of learning...' (*Milton's Prose*, p. 139). Nor should Milton's academic exercises be left out of account (*Milton. Private Correspondence and Academic Exercises*, ed. E. M. W. Tillyard, Cambridge, 1932; cf. W. Haller, *The Rise of Puritanism*, New York, 1938, pp. 296–305).

[2] As is well illustrated by the attitude of a Cambridge M.A. in 1633; forwarding to his former colleagues the findings of a sea captain which are startlingly at variance with received conclusions it is his first instinct to suggest that they 'find out how these observations may be reduced to Aristotle's philosophy', though there is a sign of grace in the added suggestion that it may be necessary to examine them 'by some other rules than Aristotle hath yet light upon' (Jones, *Ancients and Moderns*, pp. 75–6).

[3] *The Autobiography...of Sir Simonds D'Ewes*, ed. J. O. Halliwell (1845), I, pp. 120, 140–1.

gained the ascendant, to underline how far the universities fell short of what was wanted here.[1] That sustained efforts to introduce new studies, such as had begun in Edward's reign, failed with the passing of republican England was to their lasting detriment, for they could only return to a classical scholarship now divorced from significant social developments, becoming in time little but appendages of the Anglican establishment; it was a heavy price to pay for the transmission to modern times of 'the medieval university ideal'.[2]

The schools also had their faults but there is a clear line of development to be traced. It was here that humanist educational precepts found their most detailed application though not, as is usually held, merely in relation to teaching the classics. Vives, it will be recalled, urged schoolmasters to become 'custodians of the treasury of their language' and pay particular attention to the vernacular as an essential step towards improving educational practice. Mulcaster wrote a book on the subject *The First Part of the Elementarie which entreateth chiefly of the right writing of our English tongue* (1582), dedicated to the earl of Leicester in return for 'his special goodness and most favourable countenance these many years'. Besides advocating a sound grounding in the vernacular it was his aim, as it had been a concern of Cheke and Smith at Cambridge many years before, to regulate English orthography. Others followed suit in a variety of ways—compiling vocabularies, dictionaries, grammars—for there had been a ceaseless and exuberant development of the language and the overriding task was to reduce it to order.[3] At the same time translations of the classics, made available in growing numbers in good English, enabled less knowledgeable masters to teach both English and Latin much better than in the past, while scholarly and annotated Latin, Greek and Hebrew texts were produced specifically to fit the school course, as Mulcaster had urged was so essential to consolidate advance.

Erasmus and Vives always insisted that in the last analysis educational progress depends on schoolmasters, their grasp of teaching method and understanding of children's capacities as well as their own learning; just as they insisted, above all things, that learning is empty unless accompanied by understanding and turned to good use. Puritanism did not wither the humanist heritage, even though schools became

[1] Jordan, *Philanthropy*, pp. 293, 295–6. [2] Curtis, pp. 280–1.

[3] Jones, *Triumph of the English Language*, *passim*; de Witt T. Starnes, *Renaissance Dictionaries* (Austin, Texas, 1954).

progressively more godly, but rather developed this tradition, fostering studies as a means to the realisation of religious and social ends.[1] Looking back from the vantage point of the seventeenth century—when, following on the rift in the church, Baconian philosophy has heralded the separation of sacred and secular learning with all the developments this implied—it can be seen that the Christian humanist outlook, taken as a whole, was the last of the great medieval syntheses. Reaching England late it was not destined long to survive intact, though Erasmian views were taken up and restated to some extent by the Anglican church, not least in controversy with the more militant puritans.[2] But humanist method was literally absorbed into ways of thought, the humanist approach used and furthered in the service of contemporary needs, from which, after all, it had first arisen.

It was the original intention of this study to outline the actual course of events at the Reformation in order to correct the view that many schools were destroyed and education suffered a setback for many years; a view which finds expression in virtually every history covering the period. But to trace developments in the theory and practice of education is to arrive at more general conclusions, which are in turn at variance with accepted accounts of the main line of educational development and suggest that these lose sight of the most significant trend. It has become one of the chief contentions of this book that educational change cannot be covered merely by invoking 'the renaissance' or the energetic efforts of gentlemen to equip themselves with learning and approximate to a set pattern. Indeed the way ideas developed in practice is well illustrated by changes in the prototype. During the Henrician Reformation there was the excellent prince, placed above all others by his command of learning, and the well-schooled governor who served under him. In the Elizabethan age the main prototype to emerge was the great statesman combining courtliness with learning, status with function, superimposing on the wisdom of a Burghley the graces of a Sidney. At the same time humanist ideas were worked over with emphasis on cultivation of the vernacular, the dissemination of knowledge and the influence that learning can exercise in realising inner worth in outward life. In the process,

[1] As catholics also did; Vives was an inspiration not only to Sturm and Mulcaster but to Ignatius Loyala (Woodward, *Studies*, p. 210).

[2] R. F. Jones, 'The Humanist Defence of Learning in the early Seventeenth Century', in *Reason and Imagination*, ed. J. Mazzeo (1962), pp. 71–92.

corresponding to social developments, the statesman-courtier figure disintegrates and new prototypes emerge, as always after the event; on the one hand the 'Complete Gentleman' as depicted by Peacham, on the other Brathwait's 'English Gentleman' distinctively protestant and middle class, for a time the country gentleman of principle on the John Hampden pattern, and eventually Fuller's 'True Gentleman', a 'solid, Anglican, merchant-squire, moral without religious enthusiasm, patriotic and public-spirited, neither ill-mannered nor uneducated, neither courtly nor cultured'.[1]

This, however, is only one strand in the complex skein of educational ideas and practices which need to be more comprehensively considered. It has been seen that, with the dislocations of the early sixteenth century aggravated by the measures of the Reformation, the old doctrine of estates was revived and re-interpreted in the light of humanist ideas and current pressures; in the process emphasis was laid on the functions that fall to particular ranks in the social order and the need to prepare for those functions. This outlook later spread widely, with the dissemination of educational precepts and the operation of Elizabethan policies to find expression in what was to become an extensive literature on callings under puritan auspices. Accordingly education began to appear as a means of fitting men not merely for general but particular functions, a concept corresponding to the growing specialisation of knowledge and the development of professions—leaving a non-specialised 'liberal' education to become the hallmark of gentility, preserving the forms of a humanist education emptied of the essential content.

Meanwhile humanist insistence on the need to disseminate education had received a fresh impetus at the Reformation. Now the bible took its place before classical texts, as a book written of 'special intent and purpose', which was no less than 'the edification or amendment of the life of them that readeth and heareth it'; this book, in Cranmer's words, had in it to teach all men all things 'what they ought to believe, as also concerning themselves and all other'. From it not only an élite but men at large took ideas and attitudes which gave new point to life and shaped both thought and action—counting it true, as Erasmus had taught, 'that the only and most perfect nobleness is to be regenerate in Christ'. This outlook comprehended much of what is usually ascribed to 'the renaissance', though often juxtaposed as a contrary trend.

[1] W. E. Houghton, *The Formation of Thomas Fuller's Holy and Profane State* (Harvard. 1938), pp. 199 ff.

'Drive out fear from my heart, O my body....Laugh at the threats of disease, despise the blows of misfortune, care nor for the dark grave and go forward at Christ's summons. For Christ will be to each man a kingdom, a light, a life, a crown.' So runs the inscription on a monument erected in 1569 by Edmund Harmon, barber-surgeon and first lay owner of Burford priory, in the parish church. It was not to commemorate a death but thankfulness for the gift of a large family, beside whom are depicted in lively action the Indians of the New World, and a whole philosophy is summed up in the opening words: 'I was not; then by God's will I was born, to be a man'.

Beneath the pressures of current politics and fears of social disorder, which stimulated so much state intervention in education, there always ran a clearer stream—the deeply held belief that all God's children have the right to read and understand God's word, and, too, a duty to use the gift of grace and develop their capacities in the service of their fellow men. At the close of the sixteenth century, though there was still a long way to go, teaching was attaining a new status and there were dedicated teachers who took a pride in their profession. At this stage those who were fired with the belief that all men have the right to knowledge and who, labouring to extend education, grasped the wider implications of their work, were above all the heirs to humanist ideas.

You know well [wrote John Brinsley, addressing himself to his colleagues] that we are they to whose charge that rich treasure, both of church and commonwealth is committed in trust...and the hope of a more happy age hereafter to come. We are they who help either to make or mar all; for that all the flower of our nation, and those who become the leaders of all the rest, are committed to our education and instruction; that if we bring them up aright, there is great hope, that they shall prove goodly lights, and marks to all the rest of the land, especially to the towns and countries where they are; and clean contrarily, most woeful examples (as are everywhere to be seen) if they be spoiled through us, or for lack of our better care. As we are before them, so we may expect that they shall prove for the most part after us. We are therefore the men upon whom the flourishing of this our Canaan doth very much depend.[1]

It is the language of the bible rather than the classics, but it is the essence of the humanist message that a puritan schoolmaster here conveys, even to the common country schools.

[1] *A Consolation*, p. 45.

CHECK-LIST OF SOURCES

The list covers works referred to more than once in footnotes. Abbreviated references appear alphabetically

ALLEN, C. G. 'The Sources of "Lily's Latin Grammar". A Review of the Facts and some Further Suggestions', in *The Library*, fifth series, IX (1954).

ALLEN, J. W. *A History of Political Thought in the Sixteenth Century* (1928). London, 1960 ed.

ALLEN, P. S. *The Age of Erasmus*. Oxford, 1914.

ANSTIE SMITH, P. *A History of Education for the English Bar*. London, 1860.

APC. *Acts of the Privy Council of England*, ed. J. R. Dasent. London, 1890–1907.

ASCHAM, ROGER. *English Works of Roger Ascham*, ed. W. Aldis Wright. Cambridge, 1904.

ASHLEY, W. J. *An Introduction to English Economic History and Theory*. 2 vols., London, 1893.

Athenae. *Athenae Cantabrigiensis*, ed. C. H. and T. Cooper. 3 vols., Cambridge, 1858–61, 1913.

ATTWATER, A. *Pembroke College*, ed. S. C. Roberts. Cambridge, 1936.

BAKER, THOMAS. *History of the College of St John the Evangelist, Cambridge*. 2 vols., ed. J. E. B. Mayor, Cambridge, 1869.

BALDWIN, T. W. *William Shakspere's Small Latine and Lesse Greeke*. 2 vols., University of Illinois, Urbana, 1944.

BALL, W. W. R. *Cambridge Papers*. London, 1918.

BALL, W. W. R. *Trinity College, Cambridge*. London, 1906.

BECON, THOMAS. *The Catechism of Thomas Becon* with other pieces written by him in the reign of Edward the Sixth, ed. for the Parker Society by John Ayre. Cambridge, 1844.

BELL, H. E. *An Introduction to the History and Records of the Court of Wards and Liveries*. Cambridge, 1953.

BIRKS, MICHAEL. *Gentlemen of the Law*, London, 1960.

BLOCH, MARC. *Feudal Society* (1940). London, 1961.

BOAS, MARIE. *The Scientific Renaissance, 1450–1630*. London, 1962.

BOLGAR, R. R. *The Classical Heritage and its Beneficiaries*. Cambridge, 1954.

BOUCH, C. M. L. *Prelates and People of the Lake Counties*. A history of the diocese of Carlisle. Kendal, 1948.

BOUCH, C. M. L. AND JONES, G. P. *The Lake Counties, 1500–1830*. A social and economic history. Manchester, 1961.

BROOK, V. J. K. *A Life of Archbishop Parker.* Oxford, 1962.

BROWN, WALTER LANGDON. *Some Chapters in Cambridge Medical History.* Cambridge, 1946.

BRUCE, J. (ed.). *Liber Famelicus of Sir James Whitelocke.* Camden Society, LXX, 1858.

BURTON, E. (ed.). *Three Primers put forth in the Reign of Henry VIII.* Oxford, 1834.

BUXTON, JOHN. *Sir Philip Sidney and the English Renaissance.* London, 1954.

Cambridge Modern History. Ed. A. W. Ward, G. W. Prothero, S. Leathers; vol. II, *The Reformation* (1903), 1944 ed.

CAMPBELL, LILY B. *Divine Poetry and Drama in Sixteenth-Century England.* Cambridge, 1959.

CARLISLE, N. *A Concise Description of the Endowed Grammar Schools of England and Wales.* 2 vols., London, 1818.

CASPARI, FRITZ. *Humanism and the Social Order in Tudor England.* Chicago, 1954.

CASTIGLIONE, B. *The Book of the Courtier*, trans. Sir Thomas Hoby, ed. W. Drayton Henderson. Everyman, 1928.

CHAMBERS, R. W. *Thomas More* (1935). Penguin Books, 1963.

CHEL. *Cambridge History of English Literature.* 1902, reprint 1932.

Christ's Hospital Book, The. Published for a Committee of Old Blues. London, 1953.

CLARKE, M. L. *Classical Education in Britain, 1500–1900.* Cambridge, 1959.

CLEGG, A. L. *A History of Wimborne Minster and District.* Bournemouth, 1960.

Commons Journals. Journals of the House of Commons. Vol. I, *1547–1628.*

COOK, G. H. *Mediaeval Chantries and Chantry Chapels.* London, 1947.

CORRIE, G. E. (ed.) *A Catechism in Latin by Alexander Nowell, dean of St Paul's.* Together with the same catechism translated into English by Thomas Norton. Parker Society, Cambridge, 1853.

CPR. Calendar of Patent Rolls preserved in the Public Record Office. Edward VI, 1547–53, ed. R. H. Brodie, 5 vols. London, 1924–6, index 1929. Philip and Mary, 1553–58, ed. M. S. Guiseppi, 4 vols. London, 1936–9. Elizabeth, 1558–63, ed. J. H. Collingridge and R. B. Wersham, 2 vols. London, 1939–48.

CRANMER, THOMAS. *Miscellaneous Writings and Letters.* Ed. J. E. Cox for the Parker Society. Cambridge, 1846.

CROSS, M. C. *The Free Grammar School of Leicester.* Leicester University Department of English Local History, Occasional Papers no. 4, ed. H. P. R. Finberg. 1953.

CSPD. Calendar of State Papers, Domestic Series...1547–80. Ed. Robert Lemon, 1856.

CSP Foreign. *Calendar of State Papers, Foreign Series...1547–53*. Ed. W. B. Turnbull, 1861.

CURTIS, M. H. *Oxford and Cambridge in Transition, 1558–1642*. A study in the changing relations between the English universities and English society. Oxford, 1959.

DAWLEY, P. M. *John Whitgift and the Reformation*. London, 1955.

DE MONTMORENCY, J. E. G. *State Intervention in English Education*. A short history from the earliest times down to 1833. Cambridge, 1902.

D'EWES, SIMONDS. *The Journals of all the Parliaments during the Reign of Q. Elizabeth*.... London, 1682.

DICKENS, A. G. *Lollards and Protestants in the Diocese of York, 1509–1558*. University of Hull and Oxford, 1959.

DODD, A. H. *Life in Elizabethan England*. New York, 1961.

DUNLOP, O. J. AND DENMAN, R. D. *English Apprenticeship and Child Labour*. New York, 1912.

EBY, F. (ed.). *Early Protestant Educators*. The educational writings of Martin Luther, John Calvin and other leaders of protestant thought. New York, 1931.

ECD. *Educational Charters and Documents, 598–1909*, ed. A. F. Leach. Cambridge, 1911.

EDWARDS, K. *The English Secular Cathedrals in the Middle Ages*. Manchester, 1949.

EGS. *The English Grammar Schools to 1660*: their curriculum and practice, by Foster Watson. Cambridge, 1908.

Elizabethan Government and Society. Essays presented to Sir John Neale, ed. S. T. Bindoff, J. Hurstfield, C. H. Williams. London, 1961.

ELLIS, SIR HENRY. *Original Letters Illustrative of English History*. First series, 3 vols., London, 1825; third series, 4 vols., London, 1846.

ELTON, G. R. *The Tudor Revolution in Government*. A study of administration in the reign of Henry VIII. Cambridge, 1953.

ELTON, G. R. *England under the Tudors*. London, 1955.

EMMISON, F. G. *Tudor Secretary*. Sir William Petre at court and at home. London, 1961.

ESR. *English Schools at the Reformation*, by A. F. Leach (two parts in one volume, part II being a transcript of chantry certificates referring to education). London, 1896.

Essays in the Economic and Social History of Tudor and Stuart England in honour of R. H. Tawney, ed. F. J. Fisher. Cambridge, 1961.

FARRINGTON, BENJAMIN. *Francis Bacon. Philosopher of Industrial Science*. London, 1951.

FINCH, M. E. *The Wealth of Five Northamptonshire Families, 1540–1640*. Northamptonshire Record Society, vol. XIX. Oxford, 1956.

FINK, D. P. J. *Queen Mary's Grammar School, Walsall.* Walsall, 1954.
FISHER, GEORGE W. *Annals of Shrewsbury School.* London, 1899.
FLYNN, V. J. (ed.). *A Shorte Introduction of Grammar by William Lily.* Scholars' Facsimiles and Reprints. New York, 1945.
FORTESCUE, SIR JOHN. *De Laudibus Legum Anglie*, ed. S. B. Chrimes. Cambridge Studies in English Legal History, 1942.
FOWLER, T. *The History of Corpus Christi College.* Oxford Historical Society, 1893.
FOXE, JOHN. *Acts and Monuments*, ed. J. Pratt. 8 vols., London, 1870.
FRERE, W. H. (with KENNEDY, W. M.) *Visitation Articles and Injunctions of the Period of the Reformation.* 3 vols., Alcuin Club, XIV–XVI, 1910.
FURNIVALL, F. J. (ed.). *Early English Meals and Manners*, with introductions on education in early England. E.E.T.S. series III, 1894.
FUSSNER, F. SMITH. *The Historical Revolution.* English historical writing and thought, 1580–1640. London, 1962.
GEE, J. A. *Life and Works of Thomas Lupset.* Yale, 1928.
GILMORE, C. G. *King Edward VI School, Stafford.* Oxford, 1953.
GRAHAM, ROSE. *The Chantry Certificates for Oxfordshire*, ed. Rose Graham; and *The Edwardian Inventories of Church Goods for Oxfordshire*, ed. Rose Graham. From transcripts by T. Craib, Alcuin Club, XXIII, 1920.
GRAY, ARTHUR. *Jesus College, Cambridge.* London, 1902.
GRAY, I. E. AND POTTER, W. E. *Ipswich School, 1400–1950.* Ipswich, 1950.
GRAY, J. H. *The Queens' College.* London, 1889.
GREENSLADE, S. L. (ed.). *The Work of William Tindale.* London, 1938.
HAMILTON THOMPSON, A. *The History of the Hospital and the New College ...in the Newarke, Leicester.* Leicester, 1937.
HAMILTON THOMPSON, A. *The English Clergy and their Organisation in the Later Middle Ages.* Oxford, 1947.
HAMILTON THOMPSON, A. *Song Schools in the Middle Ages.* Church Music Society Occasional Papers, no. 14, 1942.
[See also *Visitations.*]
HARRISON, F. *Life in a Mediaeval College.* The Vicars Choral of York Minster. London, 1952.
HARRISON, G. B. (ed.). *Advice to his son by Henry Percy, Ninth Earl of Northumberland.* London, 1930.
HARRISON, W. *The Description of England.* Ed. from the first two editions of Holinshed's Chronicle A.D. 1577, 1587, by F. J. Furnivall. New Shakespeare Society, 1877.
HERRTAGE, S. J. (ed.). *Starkey's Life and Letters.* E.E.T.S. extra series, XXXII, 1878.
HEXTER, J. H. *Reappraisals in History.* London, 1961.

HEYWOOD, J. (ed.). *Collection of Statutes for the University and the Colleges of Cambridge.* London, 1840.

HEYWOOD, J. AND WRIGHT, T. (ed.). *Cambridge University Transactions during the Puritan Controversies of the 16th and 17th Centuries.* Vol. I, London, 1854.

HILL, CHRISTOPHER. *Economic Problems of the Church. From Archbishop Whitgift to the Long Parliament.* Oxford, 1956.

HISTORICAL MANUSCRIPTS COMMISSION. Hastings MSS. 4 vols., ed. Francis Bickley. 1930. Hatfield (Salisbury) MSS. I, 1888.

HOSKINS, W. G. *Provincial England.* Essays in Social and Economic History. London, 1963.

HOWARD, CLARE. *English Travellers at the Renaissance.* London, 1914.

HOWARD, H. F. *An Account of the Finances of St John's College, Cambridge.* Cambridge, 1925.

HOWELL, W. S. *Logic and Rhetoric in England, 1500–1700.* Princeton, 1956.

HURSTFIELD, JOEL. *The Queen's Wards.* Wardship and marriage under Elizabeth I. London, 1958.

HUTTON, T. W. *King Edward's School, Birmingham, 1552–1952.* Oxford, 1952.

JACOB, E. F. *The Fifteenth Century.* Oxford, 1961.

JONES, R. F. *The Triumph of the English Language.* A survey of opinions concerning the vernacular from the introduction of printing to the Restoration. Stanford and Oxford. 1953.

JORDAN, W. K. *Philanthropy in England, 1480–1660.* A study of the changing patterns of English social aspirations. London, 1959.

JORDAN, W. K. *The Charities of London, 1480–1660.* The aspirations and the achievements of the urban society. London, 1960.

JORDAN, W. K. *The Charities of Rural England, 1480–1660.* The aspirations and the achievements of the rural society. London, 1961.

KAY, M. *History of Rivington and Blackrod Grammar School.* Manchester, 1931.

KELSO, RUTH. *The Doctrine of the English Gentleman in the Sixteenth Century.* University of Illinois Studies in Language and Literature, vol. XIV, nos. 1 and 2, 1929.

KIBRE, PEARL. *Scholarly Privileges in the Middle Ages.* Mediaeval Academy of America, 1961.

KIRBY, T. F. *Annals of Winchester College.* London, 1892.

KNAPPEN, M. M. *Tudor Puritanism.* A chapter in the history of idealism. Chicago, 1939.

KNIGHT, S. *Life of Dean Colet (1723).* Oxford, 1823.

KNOWLES, M. D. *The Religious Orders in England,* vol. III. Cambridge, 1959.

L & P. Letters and Papers, Foreign and Domestic, of the Reign of Henry VIII, 1509–47. 21 vols. in 33 parts, ed. J. S. Brewer, James Gairdner, R. H. Brodie. London, 1862–1910.

LAMB, J. (ed.). *Cambridge Documents.* A collection of letters, statutes and other documents from the MS. Library of Corpus Christi College. London, 1838.

LAMBLEY, K. *The Teaching and Cultivation of the French Language in England during Tudor and Stuart Times.* Manchester, 1920.

LATIMER, HUGH. *Sermons.* Ed. G. E. Corrie for the Parker Society. Cambridge, 1844.

LATIMER, HUGH. *Sermons & Remains.* Ed. G. E. Corrie for the Parker Society. Cambridge, 1845.

LAWSON, JOHN. *A Town Grammar School through Four Centuries.* A history of Hull Grammar School against its local background. University of Hull and Oxford, 1963.

LEACH, A. F. *Early Yorkshire Schools.* Yorkshire Archaeological Society Record Series, XXVII (1899), XXXIII (1903).

LEACH, A. F. *A History of Winchester College.* London, 1899.

LEACH, A. F. *Schools of Mediaeval England.* London, 1915.
[See *ESR, ECD.*]

LEONARD, E. M. *The Early History of Poor Relief.* Cambridge, 1900.

LLOYD, A. H. *The Early History of Christ's College, Cambridge.* Cambridge, 1934.

Lords Journals. Journals of the House of Lords, vols. I and II.

LUPTON, J. H. (ed.). *The Utopia of Sir Thomas More.* Oxford, 1895.

LYTE, H. C. MAXWELL. *A History of the University of Oxford.* From the earliest times to the year 1530. London, 1886.

LYTE, H. C. MAXWELL. *A History of Eton College.* London, 1877, 2nd ed.

MCDONNELL, SIR MICHAEL. *Annals of St Paul's School.* London, 1959.

MCKISACK, M. *The Fourteenth Century.* Oxford, 1959.

MALDON, H. E. *Trinity Hall.* London, 1902.

MALLET, C. E. *A History of the University of Oxford*, vols. I, II. London, 1924.

MANDER, G. P. *A History of Wolverhampton School.* Wolverhampton, 1913.

MARCHANT, R. A. *The Puritans and the Church Courts in the Diocese of York, 1560–1642.* London, 1960.

MASON, J. E. *Gentlefolk in the Making.* Studies in the history of English courtesy literature and related topics from 1531 to 1774. Philadelphia, 1935.

MITCHELL, R. J. 'English Students at Padua, 1460–75', *T.R.H.S.*, fourth series, XIX.

MOZLEY, J. F. *John Foxe and his Book.* London, 1940.

MULCASTER, RICHARD. *Positions*, wherein those Primitive Circumstances be Examined, which are necessary for the training up of children, either for skill in their booke, or health in their bodie (1581). Reprinted for Henry Barnard and R. H. Quick. London, 1887.

MULLER, J. A. (ed.). *The Letters of Stephen Gardiner.* Cambridge, 1933.

MULLINGER, J. BASS. *The University of Cambridge; I, The Mediaeval University; II, From the Royal Injunctions of 1535 to the Accession of Charles I.* London, 1873–84.

MUMFORD, A. A. *Hugh Oldham.* London, 1936.

NEALE, J. E. *The Elizabethan House of Commons.* London, 1949.

NEALE, J. E. *Elizabeth I and her Parliaments, I, 1559–81.* London, 1953.

NEALE, J. E. *Essays in Elizabethan History.* London, 1958.

NELSON, W. *A Fifteenth Century Schoolbook.* Oxford, 1956.

New Cambridge Modern History. Vol. II. *The Reformation*, ed. G. R. Elton. 1958.

NICHOLS, J. G. (ed.). *Literary Remains of Edward VI.* 2 vols., Roxburghe Club, 1867.

O'DONOGHUE, E. M. *Bridewell Hospital, Palace, Prison, Schools.* London, 1923.

Original Letters of Eminent Literary Men. Ed. Sir Henry Ellis, Camden Society, O.S. XXIII, 1843.

ORMEROD, H. A. *The Liverpool Free School (1515–1803).* Liverpool, 1951.

PEACOCK, M. H. *A History of the Free Grammar School of Queen Elizabeth at Wakefield.* Wakefield, 1892.

PECK, FRANCIS. *Desiderata Curiosa*: or a Collection of Divers Scarce and Curious Pieces relating chiefly to matters of English History. 2 vols. in one, London, 1779.

PEILE, J. *Christ's College.* London, 1900.

POLLARD, A. F. *England under Protector Somerset.* London, 1900.

POLLARD, A. F. *Henry VIII.* London, 1905.

POLLARD, A. F. *The Political History of England, 1547–1603.* London, 1910.

POLLARD, A. F. *Wolsey.* London, 1929.

PORTER, H. C. *Reformation and Reaction in Tudor Cambridge.* Cambridge, 1958.

POWER, EILEEN. *Mediaeval English Nunneries.* Cambridge, 1922.

PROTHERO, G. W. (ed.). *Statutes and Constitutional Documents Illustrative of the Reigns of Elizabeth and James I.* Oxford, 1949 ed.

PURVIS, J. S. (ed.). *Educational Records.* Borthwick Institute of Historical Research, York, 1959.

PUTNAM, B. H. *Early Treatises in the Practice of the Justices of the Peace.* Oxford, 1924.

RAINE, A. *History of St Peter's School, York.* London, 1926.

RASHDALL, H. AND RAIT, R. *New College.* London, 1901.

READ, CONYERS. *Mr Secretary Walsingham and The Policy of Queen Elizabeth.* 3 vols., Oxford, 1925.

RICHARDSON, W. C. *History of the Court of Augmentations, 1536–54.* Louisiana University, Baton Rouge, 1961.

RIDLEY, NICHOLAS. *Works.* Ed. H. Christmas for the Parker Society. Cambridge, 1843.

RIVINGTON, S. *Tonbridge School.* London, 1925.

ROWSE, A. L. *The England of Elizabeth.* The Structure of Society. London, 1950.

RUSSELL, C. F. *A History of King Edward VI School, Southampton.* Privately printed, 1940.

SALTER, F. R. (ed.). *Some Early Tracts on Poor Relief.* London, 1926.

SARGEAUNT, J. *Annals of Westminster School.* London, 1898.

SEEBOHM, F. *The Oxford Reformers.* Colet, Erasmus and More. London 1887, 3rd ed.

SMALLEY, BERYL. *English Friars and Antiquity in the Early Fourteenth Century.* Oxford, 1960.

SMYTH, J. *Lives of the Berkeleys*, ed. J. Maclean. 3 vols. Bristol and Gloucestershire Archaeological Society, 1883.

STANIER, R. G. *Magdalen School.* Oxford, 1958, 2nd ed.

STOCKS, G. A. (ed.). *The Records of Blackburn Grammar School.* Chetham Society, N.S., vol. LXVI, 1909.

STOKES, C. W. *Queen Mary's Grammar School, Clitheroe.* Chetham Society, N.S., vol. XCII, 1934.

STOREY, R. L. *Thomas Langley and the Bishopric of Durham, 1406–37.* London, 1961.

STOW, JOHN. *Survey of London (1598).* Everyman, 1912.

STOWE, A. MONROE. *English Grammar Schools in the Reign of Queen Elizabeth.* New York, 1908.

STRYPE, JOHN. *Ecclesiastical Memorials.* 6 vols., Oxford, 1822.

STRYPE, JOHN. *Annals of the Reformation under Elizabeth.* 7 vols., Oxford, 1824.

STRYPE, JOHN. *The Life of Sir John Cheke.* Oxford, 1821.

STRYPE, JOHN. *The Life of the Learned Sir Thomas Smith.* Oxford, 1820.

STRYPE, JOHN. *The Life and Acts of Matthew Parker.* 3 vols., Oxford, 1821.

STRYPE, JOHN. *The Life and Acts of Edmund Grindal.* Oxford, 1821.

STRYPE, JOHN. *The Life and Acts of John Whitgift.* 3 vols., Oxford, 1822.

TANNER, L. E. *Westminster School.* London, 1954, 2nd ed.

TAWNEY, R. H. *The Agrarian Problem in the Sixteenth Century.* London, 1912.

The Tudor Constitution. Documents and Commentary. Ed. G. R. Elton. Cambridge, 1960.

THRUPP, SYLVIA. *The Merchant Class of Mediaeval London, 1300–1500.* Chicago, 1948.

UNWIN, G. *Industrial Organisation in the Sixteenth and Seventeenth Centuries.* Oxford, 1904.

UNWIN, G. *Studies in Economic History.* London, 1927.

VCH. Victoria County Histories. The first section comprises accounts of schools by or edited by A. F. Leach:

Bedfordshire, II, 1908.
Berkshire, II, 1907.
Buckinghamshire, II, 1908.
Derbyshire, II, 1907.
Durham, I, 1905.
Essex, I, 1907, by C. Fell-Smith.
Gloucestershire, II, 1907.
Hampshire, II, 1903.
Hertfordshire, II, 1908.
Lancashire, II, 1908, partly by H. J. Chaytor.
Lincolnshire, II, 1906.
Northamptonshire, II, 1906.
Nottinghamshire, II, 1910, partly by F. Fletcher.
Somerset, II, 1911, by T. Scott Holmes.
Suffolk, II, 1907, partly by E. P. Steele-Hutton.
Surrey, II, 1905.
Sussex, II, 1907.
Warwickshire, II, 1908.
Worcestershire, IV, 1924.
Yorkshire, I, 1907.

Cambridgeshire, II, 1948, by E. M. Hampson.
Huntingdonshire, II, 1932, by G. Parsloe.
Oxfordshire, I, 1939, by M. D. Lobel and M. Midgeley.
Rutland, I, 1908, by F. Fletcher.

VENN, J. *Admissions to Gonville and Caius College 1558–1679*. London, 1887.

VENN, J. *Biographical History of Gonville and Caius College 1349–1713*. 3 vols., Cambridge, 1887–1901.

VENN, J. *Gonville and Caius College*. London, 1901.

VENN, J. *Early Collegiate Life*. Cambridge, 1913.

Visitations of Religious Houses in the Diocese of Lincoln. Ed. A. Hamilton Thompson. Lincoln Record and Canterbury and York Society, 3 vols., 1915–27.

Vives: On Education. A Translation of the *De Tradendis Disciplinis* of Juan Luis Vives, with an introduction by Foster Watson. Cambridge, 1913.

WAKE, JOAN. *The Brudenells of Deene*. London, 1954, 2nd ed.

WALKER, W. G. *A History of the Oundle Schools*. London, 1956.

WARDALE, J. R. *Clare College*. London, 1899.

WATSON, FOSTER. *The Beginnings of the Teaching of Modern Subjects in England.* London, 1909.

[See *EGS, Vives: On Education.*]

WEINBAUM, M. *The Incorporation of Boroughs.* Manchester, 1937.

WELLS, J. *Oxford and its Colleges.* London, 1897.

WILLIS CLARK, J. *Endowments of the University of Cambridge.* Cambridge, 1904.

WILSON, H. B. *The History of Merchant Taylors' School.* 2 vols., London, 1812–14.

WOOD, ANTHONY. *Athenae Oxoniensis,* ed. P. Bliss. 4 vols., London, 1815–20.

WOOD, NORMAN. *The Reformation and English Education.* London, 1931.

WOODRUFF, C. E. AND CAPE, H. J. *Schola Regia Cantuariensis.* A History of Canterbury School commonly called the King's School. London, 1908.

WOODWARD, W. H. *Desiderius Erasmus concerning the Aims and Methods of Education.* Cambridge, 1904.

WOODWARD, W. H. *Studies in the History of Education during the Age of the Renaissance, 1400–1600.* Cambridge, 1924.

WRIGHT, LOUIS B. *Middle Class Culture in Elizabethan England.* Chapel Hill, 1935.

YELDHAM, F. A. *The Teaching of Arithmetic through Four Hundred Years.* London, 1936.

ZEEVELD, W. G. *Foundations of Tudor Policy.* Cambridge, Mass., 1948.

ADDENDA

The following books appeared after completion of the present volume

In 1964:

CHADWICK, OWEN. *The Reformation.* Pelican History of the Church, vol. III.

CLARKE, SIR GEORGE. *A History of the Royal College of Physicians,* Vol. I. Oxford.

DEWAR, MARY. *Sir Thomas Smith.* A Tudor Intellectual in Office. London.

DICKENS, A. G. *The English Reformation.* London.

ELTON, G. R. *Reformation Europe, 1517–1559.* Fontana History of Europe.

HILL, CHRISTOPHER. *Society and Puritanism in Pre-Revolutionary England.* London.

IRWIN, RAYMOND. *The Heritage of the English Library.* London.

JANE, SEARS. *John Colet and Marsilio Ficino.* Oxford.

RYAN, LAWRENCE V. *Roger Ascham.* Stanford and Oxford.

LEHMBERG, STAMFORD E. *Sir Walter Mildmay and Tudor Government.* University of Texas.

NICOLL, ALLARDYCE (ed.). 'Shakespeare in his own Age', *Shakespeare Survey 17.* Cambridge.

MANN PHILLIPS, MARGARET. *The 'Adages' of Erasmus.* Cambridge.

PORTER, H. C. (ed.). *Erasmus and Cambridge.* The Cambridge Letters of Erasmus, trans. D. F. S. Thomson. Toronto and Oxford.

SOUTHALL, RAYMOND. *The Courtly Maker.* An Essay on the Poetry of Thomas Wyatt and his Contemporaries. Oxford.

WILLIAMS, PENRY. *Life in Tudor England.* London.

In 1965:

DUNLOP, ANNIE I. *Acta Facultatis Artium Universitatis Sanctiandree, 1413–1588.* Edinburgh.

STONE, LAWRENCE. *The Crisis of the Aristocracy 1558–1641.* Oxford.

THOMPSON, C. R. (ed. and trans.). *The Colloquies of Erasmus.* Chicago.

BIBLIOGRAPHY

This covers some general works of reference, reprints of contemporary writings and documents (most of which have useful introductions), and a selection of secondary works relating to the history of education and educational institutions.

I. GENERAL BIBLIOGRAPHIES AND WORKS OF REFERENCE

The main bibliography covering the period is Conyers Read, *Bibliography of British History Tudor Period 1485–1603* (Oxford, 1959, 2nd ed.) which goes up to 1956. F. W. Bateson, *Cambridge Bibliography of English Literature*, vol. I, *600–1660* (1940) goes up to 1936 and has a useful section on education but also for much else, including autobiographies, correspondence, diaries: supplementary vol. v, ed. G. Watson (1957). The best explanatory bibliography, fully covering publications by American scholars, is in D. Bush, *English Literature in the Earlier Seventeenth Century* (Oxford, 1963, 2nd ed.). There are others in works already listed and in the Oxford histories, J. D. Mackie, *The Earlier Tudors 1485–1558* (1952), J. B. Black, *The Reign of Elizabeth* (1959, 2nd ed.).

The main more recent publications are reviewed in the *Annual Bulletins of Historical Literature* published by the Historical Association. The *Bulletin of the Institute of Historical Research Theses Supplements* list theses in progress as well as those completed. *The 23rd Report of the Historical Manuscripts Commission* for 1946–59 lists returns to the National Register of Archives which cover school deeds, minute books and other documents deposited in local record offices and those in parish custody; the changed location of other MSS is noted in the 24th Report for 1960–2. For detailed references to the reports, *Sectional List 17* (H.M.S.O., 1962).

For contemporary publications, *Short Title Catalogue of English Books 1475–1640*, ed. A. W. Pollard and G. R. Redgrave (1926, rev. ed. 1946) which can now be supplemented by Franklin B. Williams, *Index of Dedications and Commendatory Verses in English Books before 1641* (Bibliographical Society, 1963). See also the *British Museum General Catalogue of Printed Books* now nearly complete and in all major libraries.

Contemporary school books figure quite largely in W. C. Hazlitt's collections; see J. C. Gray, *A General Index to Hazlitt's Handbook and his Bibliographical Collections*, ed. W. Carew Hazlitt (London, 1893). The Librarians of the Schools and Institutes of Education have issued in duplicated form a

'Union list of books on education and educational textbooks published, or first published, in the 15th–17th centuries' (Leicester, Institute of Education, rev. ed., 1962). For relevant papers in educational journals, their annual *British Education Index* published by the Library Association since 1954. For theses, A. M. Blackwell, *Lists of Researches in Education and Educational Psychology*, published by the National Foundation for Educational Research; first list 1918–48 with supplements up to 1957.

There are short bibliographies to historical entries in *The Encyclopaedia and Dictionary of Education*, ed. Foster Watson, 4 vols. (1921), still in 1964 the only publication of its kind—reference books relating to education barely fill half a shelf in the British Museum Reading Room.

II. REPRINTS OF CONTEMPORARY WRITINGS AND DOCUMENTS

(i) *Textbooks*

For the Magdalen College grammarians, *Vulgaria of J. Stanbridge and Vulgaria of R. Whittinton*, ed. B. White (E.E.T.S., Original Series, 187, 1932); *William Horman's Vulgaria*, ed. M. R. James (Roxburghe Club, 1926); *A Fifteenth Century Schoolbook*, ed. W. Nelson (Oxford, 1956). Some other early texts, *ABC both in Latin and English: Being a Facsimile Reprint of the two Earliest Extant English Reading Books*, ed. E. S. Shuckburgh (London, 1889); *A Volume of Vocabularies...*, ed. T. Wright (privately printed, 1882, 2nd ed.) for three fifteenth-century vocabularies; *The Earliest Arithmetics in English*, ed. R. Steele (E.E.T.S., 1922).

A Shorte Introduction of Grammar by William Lily (1567 ed.), ed. V. J. Flynn, Scholars' Facsimiles and Reprints (New York, 1945). In the same series, Richard Rainolde, *The Foundacion of Rhetorike*, ed. F. R. Johnson (1945)—an English adaptation of Aphthonius's Progymnasmata; *The Eclogues of Baptista Mantuan* (1567 ed., trans. L. Turbevile), ed. Douglas Bush (1937). *The Comedy of Acolastus translated from the Latin of Fullonius by John Palsgrave*, ed. P. L. Carver (E.E.T.S., O.S., 202, 1937).

Leonard Cox, *The Arte or Crafte of Rhetoryque*, ed. F. I. Carpenter (Chicago, 1899); Richard Sherry, *A Treatise of Schemes and Tropes*, ed. H. W. Hildebrandt, Scholars' Facsimiles and Reprints (Gainseville, Florida, 1961); *Wilson's Arte of Rhetorique* (text of 1585 ed.), ed. G. H. Mair (Tudor and Stuart Library, 1909); *The Arcadian Rhetorike by Abraham Fraunce*, ed. Ethel Seaton (Luttrell Society, 1950); Henry Peacham, *The Garden of Eloquence*, ed. W. E. Crane, Scholars' Facsimiles and Reprints (1954); John Hoskins, *Directions for Speech and Style*, ed. H. H. Hudson, (Princeton, 1935).

Erasmus, *Colloquies*, trans. N. Bailey, ed. E. Johnson, 3 vols. (London, 1900); *Ten Colloquies of Erasmus*, trans. C. R. Thompson (New York, 1957);

The Earliest English Translations of Erasmus's 'Colloquia', 1536–1566, ed. Henry de Vocht (Louvain, 1928); *Proverbs or Adages gathered out of the 'Chiliades' and Englished by Richard Taverner* (1569 ed.), ed. de Witt T. Starnes, Scholars' Facsimiles and Reprints (1956). For a contemporary schoolmaster's notes on adages, *Letters and Exercises of the Elizabethan Schoolmaster John Conybeare*, ed. F. W. Conybeare (London, 1905).

J. L. Vives, *Tudor School-boy Life: the Dialogues (Linguae Latinae Exercitatio) of J. L. Vives*, trans. with an introduction by Foster Watson (London, 1908). Based in part on these are the dialogues of Hollyband, *The Elizabethan Home. Discovered in Two Dialogues by Claudius Hollyband and Peter Erondell*, ed. M. St Clair Byrne (London, 1949, 3rd ed. rev.); see also Claudius Hollyband (otherwise Saintliens), *The French Littleton. A Most Easy, Perfect and Absolute Way to Learn the French Tongue* (1609 ed.), ed. M. St Clair Byrne (Cambridge, 1953).

For prayer book catechisms *The Two Liturgies (1549, 1552) set forth in the Reign of Edward VI* (Parker Society, 1844); Everyman, 1910. G. E. Corrie's edition of Nowell's catechism. For the homilies as adapted in Elizabeth's reign, *Certain Sermons or Homilies* (London, 1938).

Examples from contemporary copybooks in Ambrose Heal, *The English Writing-Masters and their Copy Books, 1570–1800* (London, 1931); H. Jenkinson, *The Later Court Hands from the 15th to the 17th Century* (London, 1927). See also *Humanistic Script of the Fifteenth and Sixteenth Centuries* (Bodleian Library, 1962); *The Italic Hand in Tudor Cambridge*, ed. Alfred Fairbank and Bruce Dickens (London, 1963).

(ii) *Writings on education*

Colet's statutes for St Paul's and other original documents are printed as appendices to Samuel Knight's biography and in J. H. Lupton, *Life of Dean Colet* (1909, 2nd ed.).

Erasmus, *Enchiridion Militis Christiani or The Manual of the Christian Knight Replenished with Most Wholesome Precepts*, a reprint of a contemporary translation (London, 1905); trans. F. L. Battles in *Advocates of Reform*, ed. M. Spinka (Philadelphia, 1953). *The Education of a Christian Prince* with an introduction on Erasmus and on ancient and medieval political thought by L. K. Born (Columbia, 1936). *Upon the Right Method of Instruction* and *That Children should...from their Earliest Years be Trained in Virtue and Sound Learning*, trans. or paraphrased by W. H. Woodward in *Desiderius Erasmus...* (Cambridge, 1904). *In Praise of Folly*, Chaloner's translation of 1549, ed. J. E. Ashbee (1901); trans. H. H. Hudson (Princeton, 1941).

Vives, *De Ratione Studii Puerilis*, trans. Foster Watson and *The Christian Education of Women*, contemporary translation by R. Hyrd in Foster Watson (ed.), *Vives and the Renaissance Education of Women* (London, 1912); *On the Relief of the Poor*, trans. F. R. Salter in *Some Early Tracts on Poor Relief* (London, 1926); *De Tradendis Disciplinis*, trans. Foster Watson in *Vives: On Education* (Cambridge, 1913).

Baldassare Castiglione, *The Book of the Courtier* (Everyman, 1928) where other editions are listed; this is Hoby's translation, a modern version is edited by L. E. Opdycke (1901, reprint 1902). *Sadoleto on Education*, a translation of the *De Liberis recte instituendis* (1533), ed. E. T. Campagnac and E. Forbes (Oxford, 1916).

Thomas Lupset, *An Exhortation to Young Men*, in J. A. Gee, *Life and Works* (Yale, 1928); also in *Complaint and Reform in England 1436–1714*, ed. W. H. Dunham and S. Pargellis (New York, 1938) which includes other relevant tracts and extracts. Sir Thomas More, *Utopia*, R. Robynson's contemporary translation, ed. J. H. Lupton (Oxford, 1895); Everyman, 1935. *The Dialogue concerning Tyndale*, ed. W. E. Campbell (London, 1927).

Sir Thomas Elyot, *The Boke named the Governour*, ed. H. H. S. Crofts. 2 vols. (London, 1883) with full introduction covering the author's life; ed, Foster Watson (Everyman, 1907, 1937). *The Defence of Good Women*, trans. Foster Watson in *Vives and the Renaissance Education of Women* (1912); ed. E. J. Howard (Oxford, Ohio, 1941). *The Castel of Health*, ed. S. A. Tannenbaum, Scholars' Facsimiles and Reprints (New York, 1937).

Thomas Starkey, *Dialogue between Pole and Lupset*, ed. J. N. Cowper and *Life and Letters*, ed. S. J. Herrtage, in *England in the Reign of King Henry the Eighth* (E.E.T.S., Extra Series, 32, 1878); modernized version of *Dialogue*, ed. K. M. Burton (London, 1948). Richard Morison, *A Remedy for Sedition*, ed. E. M. Cox (London, 1933). There is an extract from John Cheke, *The Hurt of Sedition* in E. Nugent (ed.), *The Thought and Culture of the English Renaissance...1481–1555* (Cambridge, 1956); this includes useful extracts from earlier humanist writings and bibliographies but the section on religious treatises, ed. W. E. Campbell, treats Edward's reign from Gardiner's standpoint and the bibliography is heavily weighted in favour of catholic interpretations.

Selections from Tyndale's works are given in the volume edited by S. L. Greenslade (1938). For protestant ideas on the duties of a prince, Latimer's sermons of 1549 in *Sermons* (1844); see also *Seven Sermons before Edward VI on each Friday in Lent (1549)*, ed. E. Arber (London, 1869), Thomas Lever, *Sermons: 1550*, ed. E. Arber (London, 1871, rep. 1895), Robert Crowley, *Selected Works*, ed. J. M. Cowper (E.E.T.S., E.S., 15, 1872), and the works of Cranmer, Becon, Ridley. John Knox, *Book of Discipline* in vol. II of his *History of the Reformation of Scotland*, ed. W. C. Dickinson (London, 1949). There has been no reprint of Lawrence Humfrey, *The Nobles*, but for some extracts, and from other writings, Foster Watson, *Notices on Some Early*

English Writers on Education, with descriptions, extracts and notes, reprint from Reports of the Commissioner of Education (Washington, 1902–6).

Roger Ascham, *Toxophilus*, ed. E. Arber (1868), *The Scholemaster*, ed. J. E. B. Mayor (Cambridge, 1863). Both these with report on Germany in *English Works of Roger Ascham*, ed. W. Aldis Wright (Cambridge, 1904), also with letters in *The Whole Works of Roger Ascham*, ed. J. A. Giles (London, 1864). Sir Humphrey Gilbert, *Queene Elizabethe's Achademy*, ed. F. J. Furnivall (E.E.T.S., E.S., 8, 1869). There is a section on education in *Life in Shakespeare's England. A Book of Elizabethan Prose*, ed. J. Dover Wilson (Penguin, 1944).

Richard Mulcaster, *Positions...*, printed for H. Barnard and R. H. Quick (1887); with an appendix by R. H. Quick (London, 1888). *The First Part of the Elementarie*, ed. E. T. Campagnac (Tudor and Stuart Library, 1925). A version in modern English of the main passages from both works in James Oliphant, *The Educational Writings of Richard Mulcaster* (Glasgow, 1903). John Brinsley, *Ludus Literarius or The Grammar School*, ed. E. T. Campagnac (London, 1917), *A Consolation for Our Grammar Schooles*, ed. T. C. Pollock, Scholars' Facsimiles and Reprints (New York, 1943). See also Charles Hoole, *A New Discovery of the Old Art of Teaching Schoole in Four Small Treatises* (1660), ed. with bibliographical index by E. T. Campagnac (London, 1913). Sir Henry Wotton, *A Philosophical Survey of Education or Moral Architecture and the Aphorisms of Education*, ed. H. S. Kermode (London, 1938); Juan Huarte, *Examen de ingenios. The Examination of Men's Wits* (1594), translated from Spanish into Italian and from Italian into English by Richard Carew, Scholar's Facsimiles and Reprints (1959).

(iii) *Courtesy books, advice, etc.*

For *A Booke of Precedence* and other fragments, ed. F. J. Furnivall, and essays on early Italian and German books of courtesy by W. M. Rossetti and E. Oswald (E.E.T.S., E.S., 8, 1869). For Hugh Rhodes, *The Boke of Nurture*; Francis Seager, *The Schoole of Virtue...*; other tracts and fragments and an introduction on education in early England, *The Babees Book*, ed. F. J. Furnivall (E.E.T.S., O.S., 32, 1868), reprinted under the title *Early English Meals and Manners* (1894): see *The Babees' Book: Mediaeval Manners for the Young*; done into modern English from Dr Furnivall's texts by E. Rickert (London, 1908).

Andrew Boorde, *The First Booke of the Introduction of Knowledge, 1547...*, ed. F. J. Furnivall (E.E.T.S., E.S., 10, 1870) with advice on foreign travel. Two influential later treatises were *The Galateo of Maister John della Casa*, published in Italian in 1558, translated in 1576, ed. J. E. Spingarn (Boston, 1914) and *The Civile Conversation of M. Steeven Guazzo*, published in French in 1574, trans. in the 1580's, ed. Sir E. Sullivan, 2 vols. (London, 1925). An anonymous tract *Cyvile and Uncyvile Life* (1579) was reprinted in 1586 as *The English Courtier* (Roxburghe Club, 1868). Select passages from Antonio de Guevara, *The Diall of Princes*, trans. Thomas North, ed. K. N. Colville (London, 1919).

For a modern edition of the advice of Burghley and Raleigh, *Advice to a Son*, ed. Louis B. Wright (Cornell and Oxford, 1963). *Advice to his Son by Henry Percy, Ninth Earl of Northumberland*, ed. G. B. Harrison (London, 1930). James Cleland, *The Institution of a Young Nobleman* (1607 ed.), ed. Max Molyneux, Scholars' Facsimiles and Reprints (1948). Henry Peacham, *The Compleat Gentleman* (1622), facsimile ed. G. S. Gordon (Oxford, 1906); a modern version omitting chapters on heraldry, ed. Virgil B. Heltzel (Cornell, 1962). See G. E. Noyes, *Bibliography of Courtesy and Conduct Books in Seventeenth Century England* (New Haven, 1937).

(iv) *Biographies, diaries, letters, etc.*

The Life of Fisher, transcribed by Ronald Rayne (E.E.T.S., E.S., 117, 1921). *Thomas Wolsey late Cardinal his Life and Death written by George Cavendish his gentleman-usher* (1557), ed. Roger Lockyer (Folio Society, 1962) is the latest of many editions. William Roper, *Life of Sir Thomas More*, ed. E. V. Hitchcock (E.E.T.S., O.S., 197, 1934), *The Correspondence of Sir Thomas More*, ed. E. F. Rogers (Princeton, 1947).

Original Letters of the English Reformation, 2 vols., ed. H. Robinson (Parker Society, 1846–7) covers Edward's reign. See also *The Life and Poems of Nicholas Grimald*, ed. L. R. Merrill, Yale Studies in English, vol. LXIX (1925) which includes a letter to Cecil on the state of Oxford University in 1549, *The Works of William Thomas, Clerk of the Privy Council in the Year 1549*, ed. Abraham D'Aubant (London, 1774) and, written in 1549, *A Discourse of the Commonweal of the Realm of England*, ed. E. Lamond (Cambridge, 1893). *The Journal of King Edward's Reign written with His Own Hand* (Clarendon Historical Society, 1884) and *Literary Remains of Edward VI*, ed. Nichols.

Matthew Parker, *Correspondence*, ed. J. Bruce and T. T. Perowne (Parker Society, 1853); Edmund Grindal, *Remains*, ed. W. Nicholson (Parker Society, 1843). For the life of Burghley by a member of his household, *The Compleat Statesman* in Peck, *Desiderata Curiosa* (1779) which also has letters of the period; and see volumes edited by Sir Henry Ellis.

The Travels and Life of Sir Thomas Hoby written by Himself 1547–64, ed. E. Powell (Camden Society, 3rd series, IV, 1902); Sir Philip Sidney, *Correspondence with Hubert Languet*, ed. S. A. Pears (London, 1845); Fulke Greville, *The Life of the Renowned Sir Philip Sidney*, ed. Nowell Smith (Tudor and Stuart Library, 1907). For the household upbringing of girls, *Diary of Lady Margaret*

Hoby 1599–1608, ed. D. M. Meads (London, 1930); *The Autobiography of Edward, Lord Herbert of Cherbury*, ed. S. Lee (London, 1886); and ed. J. O. Halliwell, *The Autobiography and Personal Diary of Dr Simon Forman* (London, 1849), *The Private Diary of Dr John Dee* (Camden Society, XIX, 1842), *The Diary and Correspondence of Sir Simonds D'Ewes* 2 vols. (London, 1845).

Letter Book of Gabriel Harvey 1572–80, ed. E. J. L. Scott (Camden Society, N.S., XXXIII, 1884) and for his later writings *Elizabethan Critical Essays*, ed. G. G. Smith, 2 vols. (Oxford, 1904). *Two Elizabethan Puritan Diaries* (R. Rogers, S. Ward), ed. M. M. Knappen (Chicago, 1935).

Among recent publications *Letters of Thomas Wood Puritan, 1566–1577*, ed. P. Collinson, *Bulletin of the Institute of Historical Research*, Special Supplement no. 5 (1962) and on the concerns of a noble family *Clifford Letters of the Sixteenth Century*, ed. A. G. Dickens (London, 1962). *Journal of a Younger Brother. The Life of Thomas Platter as a Medical Student in Montpellier at the Close of the Sixteenth Century*, trans. and ed. Séan Jennett (London, 1963). *The Autobiography of Thomas Whythorne*, a teacher of music; modernized edition, ed. James M. Osborn (Oxford, 1962).

(v) *Documents*

To add to visitations of monastic houses, *Visitations of the Diocese of Lincoln, 1517–31*, ed. A. Hamilton Thompson (Lincoln Record Society, vols. 33, 35, 37, 1940–7) for the parish clergy before the Reformation; and after it, *The State of the Church in the Reigns of Elizabeth and James I*, ed. C. W. Foster (Lincoln Record Society, vol. 23, 1926). Other published ecclesiastical records are listed in bibliographies to volumes of the *Oxford History of England*, ed. Sir George Clark. For a monastic house which kept a small school *The Chronicle of Butleigh Priory, Suffolk, 1510–35*, ed. A. G. Dickens (Winchester, 1951), and for a register of foundations with the number of boys they were bound to keep, M. D. Knowles and R. N. Hadcock, *Mediaeval Religious Houses: England and Wales* (London, 1953), with *Additions and Corrections*, from *EHR*, LXXII (London, 1957). *A Small Household of the XVth Century: The Account Book of Munden's Chantry, Bridport*, ed. K. L. Wood-Legh (Manchester, 1956). For information about chantry certificates and a list of those published, by Lawrence S. Snell, *Short Guides to Records*, no. 6, Historical Association, reprinted from *History*, XLVIII, no. 164 (1963).

For the parish clerk and his duties, *The Clerk's Book of 1549*, ed. J. Wickham Legg (Henry Bradshaw Society, XXV, 1903). There are some printed volumes of churchwardens accounts beginning in the sixteenth century and a few other records, e.g. *The Vestry Minute Book of the Parish of St Margaret Lothbury 1571–1677*, ed. E. Freshfield (London, 1887). For the minutes of the Dedham Classis (with an anti-puritan introduction), *The Presbyterian Movement in the*

Reign of Queen Elizabeth, ed. R. G. Usher (Camden Society, 1905). See *Tudor Parish Documents of the Diocese of York*, ed. J. S. Purvis (Cambridge, 1948).

Tudor Economic Documents, ed. R. H. Tawney and Eileen Power, 3 vols. (London, 1924), vol. II for the poor law, vol. III pamphlets and extracts. *Extracts from the Records and Court Books of Bridewell Hospital*, ed. T. Bowen (London, 1798); *Memoranda References and Documents relating to the Royal Hospitals of the City of London*, ed. J. F. Frith (London, 1836). *John Howes MS. 1582. Being 'a brief note of the order and manner of the first erection of the three royal hospitals'*, ed. W. Lemprière (London, 1904), particularly on Christ's Hospital.

For legislation relating to the poor *Tudor Constitutional Documents*, ed. J. R. Tanner (Cambridge, 1940 ed.) which has otherwise been supplemented by *The Tudor Constitution*, ed. G. R. Elton (Cambridge, 1960). There are many contemporary documents in the various volumes by Foxe and by Strype—including *Memorials of Thomas Cranmer*, 3 vols. (Oxford, 1848–54)—and in Gilbert Burnet, *History of the Reformation*, ed. N. Pocock, 7 vols. (Oxford, 1865). See also P. F. Tytler, *England under the Reigns of Edward VI and Mary Illustrated in a Series of Original Letters*, 2 vols. (London, 1839).

(vi) *Educational records*

Educational Charters and Documents 598 to 1909, ed. A. F. Leach (Cambridge, 1911) is the only general collection, badly in need of replacement; despite the title there are only a few odd documents for the post-Reformation period. Some school statutes are printed in Carlisle, *Endowed Grammar Schools* (1818) and see two volumes published by the Worcestershire Historical Society: *The Old Order Book of Hartlebury Grammar School 1556–1752*, ed. D. Robertson (1904); *Documents illustrating early Education in Worcester*, ed. A. F. Leach (1913), also the latter's *Early Yorkshire Schools*. Other records are referred to in accounts in the *VCH* or in school histories, but the main sources of information are the reports of the Commissioners of Inquiry into Charities; for an analysis of returns relating to education, *Public Charities*. II. *Digest of Schools and Charities for Education* (1842). Reports relating to particular schools are briefly summarized with the further returns on these by the *Schools Inquiry Commission* (16 vols., 1868).

For Cambridge, C. H. Cooper, *The Annals of Cambridge*, vols. I and II (1842–3); J. Lamb (ed.), *Cambridge Documents* (1838); J. Heywood and T. Wright, *Cambridge University Transactions*, I (1854), and *The Ancient Laws of the Fifteenth Century for King's College, Cambridge and...Eton College* (London, 1850). Other translations made at the time of the movement for university reform, J. Heywood (ed.), *Collection of Statutes for the University and Colleges of*

Cambridge (1840), and *Early Cambridge University and College Statutes in the English Language* (London, 1855), two parts in one volume.

See also a seventeenth-century account, Thomas Fuller, *History of the University of Cambridge*, ed. M. Prickett and T. Wright (London, 1840). J. E. B. Mayor (ed.), *Early Statutes of St John's College* (Cambridge, 1859) and Baker's *History of St John's* (1869) in vol. I of which correspondence relating to schools administered by the college is calendared. *Masters' History of Corpus Christi*, ed. J. Lamb (London, 1831).

For Oxford, *The Foundation Statutes of Bishop Fox for Corpus Christi College*, trans. and ed. G. R. M. Ward (London, 1843) and various volumes published by the Oxford Historical Society. A. B. Emden, *A Biographical Dictionary of Members of the University of Oxford from* A.D. *1176 to 1500*, 3 vols. (1957–9).

For the Inns of Court, *Calendar of Inner Temple Records*, I. *1505–1603*, ed. F. A. Inderwick (London, 1896); *Pension Book of Gray's Inn*. I. *1569–1669*, ed. R. J. Fletcher (London, 1901); *Records of Lincoln's Inn*, I, ed. W. P. Baildon (London, 1897); *Calendar of Middle Temple Records*, I, ed. C. H. Hopwood (London, 1904). See also *Readings and Moots at the Inns of Court in the Fifteenth Century*, ed. S. E. Thorne, 2 vols. (Selden Society, 1954).

To the Caius College registers, ed. Venn, may be added *Biographical Register of Christ's College*, I, ed. John Peile (Cambridge, 1910); T. A. Walker, *A Biographical Register of Peterhouse Men*, I (Cambridge, 1927); and J. and J. A. Venn, *Alumni Cantabrigienses*, part I, vols. I–IV (Cambridge, 1922–7).

School registers often purport to begin in the sixteenth century but list only a few names taken from printed college registers for early years. Most useful are C. J. Robinson, *A Register of Scholars admitted into Merchant Taylors' School from* A.D. *1562 to 1874*, compiled from authentic sources and edited with biographical notices, vol. I (Lewes, 1882); *Shrewsbury School Regestrum Scholarium 1562–1635*, transcribed by E. Calvert (1892); *Christ's Hospital Admissions*, I. *1554–1599*, ed. G. A. Allan (London, 1937); and see *Christ's Hospital Exhibitioners to the Universities of Oxford and Cambridge 1566–1923*, ed. G. A. T. Allan (1924). For aid to particular students, *The Spending of the Money of Robert Nowell 1568–80*, ed. A. B. Grosart (Manchester, 1877).

Tonbridge School Register 1553–1820, ed. W. G. Hart (1933) has a first list in 1653; Bury in 1656, *Biographical List of Boys educated at King Edward VI Free Grammar School Bury St Edmunds 1550–1900*, ed. S. H. A. Hervey, Suffolk Green Books, XIII (1908). Also beginning at this period *The Giggleswick School Register 1499–1921*, ed. H. B. Atkinson (1922); *The Sedbergh School Register 1546–1909*, ed. B. Wilson (Leeds, 1909, 2nd ed.) consists mainly of the, quite numerous, entrants to St John's. Interesting for its marginal comments, though mainly for the post-Restoration period, *Register of the Scholars admitted to Colchester School 1636–1740*, ed. J. H. Round (Colchester, 1897);

another genuine register opening 1675, *Rugby School Register 1675–1876* (Rugby, 1867).

For a revised version of a bibliography edited by H. E. R. Hart (1931), Phyllis M. Jacobs, 'Registers of the Universities, Colleges and Schools of Great Britain and Ireland', *Bulletin of the Institute of Historical Research*, XXXVII, no. 96 (1964), pp. 185–232.

III. SECONDARY WORKS RELATING TO THE HISTORY OF EDUCATION AND EDUCATIONAL INSTITUTIONS

There are many bibliographies bearing on the early humanists on the one hand, the age of Shakespeare on the other, and in general 'the renaissance' tends to overshadow the Reformation. To redress the balance some books may be noted as a preface to this section, to add to those listed under sources.

(i) *The Reformation*

A survey by a medievalist is F. M. Powicke, *The Reformation in England* (Oxford, 1941). In the Teach Yourself History Series, K. B. McFarlane, *John Wycliffe and the Beginnings of English Non-conformity* (1952); V. J. K. Brook, *Whitgift and the English Church* (1957); A. G. Dickens, *Thomas Cromwell and the English Reformation* (1959). Also by A. G. Dickens, *Robert Holgate, Archbishop of York and President of the Council of the North, The Marian Reaction in the Diocese of York*. I. *The Clergy*. II. *The Laity*, St Anthony's Hall Publications nos. 8 (1955), 11 and 12 (1957). T. M. Parker, *The English Reformation to 1558* (Home University Library, 1950); L. Baldwin Smith, *Tudor Prelates and Politics 1536–58* (Princeton, 1953); E. G. Rupp, *Studies in the Making of the English Protestant Tradition: mainly in the Reign of Henry VIII* (Cambridge, 1947).

Heinrich Boehmer, *Martin Luther: Road to Reformation*, trans. J. W. Doberstein (New York, 1957); C. L. Manschreck, *Melanchthon. The Quiet Reformer* (New York, 1958); C. L. R. A. Hopf, *Martin Bucer and the English Reformation* (Oxford, 1946); Francis Wendel, *Calvin*, trans. Philip Mairet (London, 1963); B. Hall, *John Calvin. Humanist and Theologian*, Historical Association, General Series, 33 (1956). See also Richard M. Douglas, *Jacopo Sadoleto 1477–1547. Humanist and Reformer* (Cambridge, Mass., 1959).

The relation between early humanist and reforming ideas is covered by M. Knappen and H. C. Porter, and see Christopher Morris, *Political Thought in England, Tyndale to Hooker* (Home University Library, 1953) with useful bibliography. R. R. Bolgar, *The Classical Heritage* (1954) brings educational developments over nine centuries into perspective, and for a lucid essay on 'The Concept of the Renaissance' with extensive bibliography, Federico

Chabod, *Machiavelli and the Renaissance*, trans. David Moore (London, 1958). A standard work is W. Haller, *The Rise of Puritanism or the Way to the New Jerusalem as set forth in pulpit and press...1570–1643* (New York, 1938) and see *Foxe's Book of Martyrs and the Elect Nation* (London, 1963).

Studies which range comparatively widely are J. F. Mozley, *Coverdale and his Bibles* (London, 1953); J. W. Harris, *John Bale, a Study in the Minor Literature of the Reformation* (Urbana, 1940); and see Helen C. White, *Social Criticism in Popular Religious Literature of the 16th Century* (New York, 1944) and *The Tudor Books of Private Devotion* (University of Wisconsin, 1951). Charles C. Butterworth, *The English Primers 1529–45: their Publication and Connection with the English Bible and the Reformation in England* (University of Pennsylvania, 1952); Harold R. Willoughby, *The First Authorised English Bible and the Cranmer Preface* (Chicago, 1942); M. Maclure, *The Paul's Cross Sermons 1534–1642* (Toronto, 1958).

Some biographical studies are J. F. Mozley, *William Tyndale* (London, 1937); H. S. Darby, *Hugh Latimer* (London, 1953); Allan G. Chester, *Hugh Latimer, Apostle to the English* (Philadelphia, 1954); Jaspar Ridley, *Nicholas Ridley* (London, 1957); and, though supplemented by later work, A. F. Pollard, *Thomas Cranmer and the English Reformation* (London, 1905). See also Eustace Percy, *John Knox* (London, 1937); and G. Donaldson, *The Scottish Reformation* (Cambridge, 1960). For a biographical list of those who went into exile, part II of C. H. Garrett, *The Marian Exiles 1553–9* (Cambridge, 1938).

Three recent publications: C. H. and K. George, *The Protestant Mind of the English Reformation 1570–1640* (Princeton, 1961); W. M. Southgate, *John Jewel and the Problem of Doctrinal Authority* (Harvard, 1962); S. J. Knox, *Walter Travers: Paragon of Elizabethan Puritanism* (London, 1962). For William Perkins, W. Haller, Christopher Hill, *Puritanism and Revolution* (London, 1958), H. C. Porter ch. XII, and L. B. Wright covers the 'Treatise of Vocations' with other handbooks to domestic improvement, etc., in chs. V–VIII. For evaluation of educational aspects M. Knappen ch. XXVI, S. E. Morison, *The Founding of Harvard College* (Harvard, 1935) which covers universities in Scotland and the Netherlands as well as England; W. E. Houghton, *The Formation of Thomas Fuller's Holy and Profane State* (Harvard, 1938).

(ii) *The great households and the education of the gentleman*

There is a bibliography in A. R. Myers (ed.), *The Household of Edward IV* (Manchester, 1959); also for earlier social patterns, A. B. Ferguson, *The Indian Summer of English Chivalry* (Duke University Press, 1962) and on wardship the volumes by H. E. Bell and J. Hurstfield.

For the Tudor Age recent publications are H. A. Mason, *Humanism and Poetry in the Early Tudor Period* (London, 1959); John Stevens, *Music and Poetry in the Early Tudor Court* (London, 1961); John Leon Lievsay, *Stefano Guazzo in the English Renaissance 1575–1675* (University of North Carolina, 1961); G. K. Hunter, *John Lyly. The Humanist as Courtier* (London, 1962); John Buxton, *Elizabethan Taste* (London, 1963). Eleanor Rosenberg, *Leicester: Patron of Letters* (New York, 1955) covers activities as chancellor of Oxford; also on patronage E. H. Miller, *The Professional Writer in Elizabethan England* (Cambridge, Mass., 1959).

P. V. B. Jones, *The Household of a Tudor Nobleman* (Illinois, 1918); G. Scott Thomson, *Two Centuries of Family History: a Study in Social Development* (London, 1930)—the Russells from Dorset merchants and squires to an earldom. Some relevant biographies are C. Sturge, *Cuthbert Tunstall* (London, 1938); J. T. Sheppard, *Richard Croke* (Cambridge, 1919); Jervis Wegg, *Richard Pace, Tudor Diplomat* (London, 1932); Stanford E. Lehmberg, *Sir Thomas Elyot, Tudor Humanist* (Texas University, 1960); E. E. Reynolds, *Margaret Roper* (London, 1960). For Pole's household at Padua, W. G. Zeeveld, and W. Schenk, *Reginald Pole: Cardinal of England* (London, 1950).

There are relevant chapters in F. Emmison, *Tudor Secretary* (1961) and, though they deal mainly with public affairs, in Conyers Read's biographies of Walsingham and of Cecil, *Mr Secretary Cecil and Queen Elizabeth* (London, 1955), *Lord Burghley and Queen Elizabeth* (London, 1960). For a later master of the court of wards, R. H. Tawney, *Business and Politics under James I: Lionel Cranfield as Merchant and Minister* (Cambridge, 1958). Failing a biography of Huntingdon, M. Claire Cross, 'The Third Earl of Huntingdon and Elizabethan Leicestershire', *Transactions of the Leicestershire Archaeological and Historical Society*, XXXVI (1960) and for light on Sir Nicholas Bacon, Alan Simpson, *The Wealth of the Gentry 1540–1660* (Cambridge, 1962).

Other recent studies are Hester W. Chapman, *The Last Tudor King. A Study of Edward VI* (London, 1958); Catherine Drinker Bowen, *The Lion and the Throne. The Life and Times of Sir Edward Coke, 1552–1634* (London, 1957) and *Francis Bacon. The Temper of a Man* (London, 1963); see also J. G. Crowther, *Francis Bacon: The First Statesman of Science* (London, 1960).

There are comprehensive bibliographies of contemporary sources in R. R. Kelso; *The Doctrine of the English Gentleman* (1929) and its sequel *Doctrine for the Lady of the Renaissance* (Urbana, 1956). See also J. E. Mason, and E. N. S. Thompson *Literary Bypaths of the Renaissance* (Yale, 1924) has a chapter on the courtesy book and its disintegration into different forms in the late sixteenth century. There are essays in Ernest Barker, *Traditions of Civility* (Cambridge, 1948), and Harold Nicolson ranges round the subject in *Good Behaviour: Being A Study of Certain Types of Civility* (London, 1955).

Clare Howard, *English Travellers of the Renaissance* (1914) has a bibliography of contemporary sources; H. S. Bates, *Touring in 1600: A Study in the Development of Travel as a Means to Education* (Boston, 1912) is not as useful as it sounds. A. L. Rowse, *Raleigh and the Throckmortons* (London, 1962) has a chapter on foreign travel, and see George B. Parks 'Travel as Education', in *The Seventeenth Century. R. F. Jones Festschrift* (Stanford, 1951).

Kenneth Charlton, 'Holbein's "Ambassadors" and Sixteenth Century Education', *Journal of the History of Ideas*, XXI (1960); W. E. Houghton, 'The English Virtuoso in the Seventeenth Century', *Journal of the History of Ideas*, III (1942), and for later attitudes George C. Brauer, *The Education of a Gentleman. Theories of Gentlemanly Education in England 1660–1775* (New York, 1959).

(iii) *Apprenticeship, the poor, and life in town and country*

For gilds and apprenticeship add to the two books listed by G. Unwin, *Guilds and Companies of London* (London, 1908); W. Herbert, *The History of the Twelve Great Livery Companies of London*, 2 vols. (London, 1837). The standard work O. J. Dunlop and R. D. Denman, *English Apprenticeship and Child Labour* (London, 1912) is based mainly on municipal records with special reference to the poor. A study based on county court records, concerned mainly with economic aspects, M. G. Davies, *The Enforcement of English Apprenticeship 1563–1642. A study in Applied Mercantilism* (Harvard, 1956).

On the poor laws, Brian Tierney, *Mediaeval Poor Law. A Sketch of Canonical Theory and its Application in England* (California, 1959). The standard work, now out of date, is E. M. Leonard, *The Early History of Poor Relief* (Cambridge, 1900). For references to more recent studies, W. K. Jordan, *Philanthropy in England* (1959).

W. K. Jordan, *The Charities of Rural England* (1961) covers Bucks., Norfolk, Yorks., and three other counties are covered in his *Social Institutions in Kent 1480–1640* (Archaeologia Cantiana, vol. LXXV, 1961), *The Social Institutions of Lancashire 1480–1660* (Chetham Society, 3rd series, XI, 1962), 'The Forming of the Charitable Institutions of the West of England. A Study in the Changing Pattern of Social Aspirations in Bristol and Somerset 1480–1660', *Transactions of the American Philosophical Society* (Philadelphia, 1960). In view of the importance of these studies it should be noted that some of the conclusions have been questioned, e.g. the overall figures for benefactions at different periods since allowance is not made for inflation; cf. some reviews, D. C. Coleman, *EHR*, 2nd series, XIII; L. Stone, *History*, XLIV; T. Ashton, *History*, XLVI; G. Aylmer, *EHR*, XV.

A standard work comparable to Sylvia Thrupp, *The Merchant Class of Mediaeval London* (1948) is Mildred Campbell, *The English Yeoman under*

Elizabeth and the Early Stuarts (Yale, 1942) with a chapter on schooling and placement though mainly in the seventeenth century. E. Trotter, *Seventeenth Century Life in the Country Parish* (Cambridge, 1919) has chapters on the duties of overseers, churchwardens, etc. Alice Clark, *Working Life of Women in the Seventeenth Century* (London, 1919) for family life and domestic industry; C. L. Powell, *English Domestic Relations 1483–1653. A Study of Matrimony and Family Life in Theory and Practice* (Columbia, 1917) is chiefly on the position of women but a chapter on domestic conduct books. There are relevant chapters in D. M. Stenton, *The English Woman in History* (London, 1957) and Dorothy Gardiner, *English Girlhood at School* (Oxford, 1929).

For general background from contemporary sources, M. St Clair Byrne, *Elizabethan Life in Town and Country* (8th ed. rev., 1961). Town life is a relatively neglected subject but see recent *VCH* volume *The City of York*, ed. P. M. Tillott (1961) and relevant chapters in other volumes: J. W. F. Hill, *Tudor and Stuart Lincoln* (Cambridge, 1956); Tom Atkinson, *Elizabethan Winchester* (London, 1963). Barbara Winchester, *Tudor Family Portrait* (London, 1955) is on a merchant family; John Webb, *Great Tooley of Ipswich. Portrait of an Early Tudor Merchant* (Suffolk Record Society, 1962).

A. L. Rowse, *Tudor Cornwall. Portrait of a County* (London, 1941); W. G. Hoskins, *Essays in Leicestershire History* (Liverpool, 1950); *The Midland Peasant. The Economic and Social History of a Leicestershire Village* (London, 1957). M. W. Barley, *The English Farmhouse and Cottage* (London, 1961). M. E. Finch, *The Wealth of Five Northamptonshire Families* (1956), with a preface by H. J. Habakkuk, gives a better idea of the way of life and fortunes of gentlemen than general discussions on the subject, but references to the controversy among historians may be found here. See also Anthony P. Upton, *Sir Arthur Ingram c. 1565–1642. A Study of the Origins of an English Landed Family* (Oxford, 1961).

For the condition of the clergy, Christopher Hill, *Economic Problems of the Church* (1956). See also Glanmor Wills, *The Welsh Church from Conquest to Reformation* (Cardiff, 1962) and G. D. Owen, *Elizabethan Wales. The Social Scene* (Cardiff, 1963).

For reading habits, H. S. Bennett, *English Books and Readers 1475–1557* (Cambridge, 1952), G. B. Harrison, 'Books and Readers 1599–1603', *The Library*, 4th series, XIV (1934), and the account by L. B. Wright.

(iv) *Medieval education*

There are chapters on education by T. A. Walker in *CHEL*, II, by G. R. Potter covering the later middle ages in *Cambridge Mediaeval History*, VIII (1936); by J. W. Adamson in *The Legacy of the Middle Ages*, ed. C. H. Crump and E. F. Jacob (Oxford, 1926); by A. B. Emden in *Mediaeval England*, II, ed.

A. Lane Poole (Oxford, 1958); and in volumes of the *Oxford History of England*. See also R. W. Southern, *The Making of the Middle Ages* (London, 1953), and leading up to this H. I. Marrou, *History of Education in Antiquity*, trans. G. R. Lamb (London, 1955). A. W. Parry, *Education in England in the Middle Ages* (London, 1920) provides a useful corrective to A. F. Leach, *Schools of Mediaeval England* (1915) which includes a bibliography of this author's books and papers.

A key text recently edited in full, *John of Salisbury, The Metalogicon: a Twelfth-Century Defense of the Verbal and Logical Arts of the Trivium* with introduction and notes by Daniel D. McGarry (Berkeley, California, 1962); in the Nelson Mediaeval Classics series *The Monastic Constitutions of Lanfranc* trans. and ed. M. D. Knowles (London, 1951). Bearing closely on education is David Knowles, *The Evolution of Medieval Thought* (London, 1962) and see *The Monastic Order in England* (Cambridge, 1963, 2nd ed.), *The Religious Orders in England*, 3 vols. (Cambridge, 1950–9). For secular cathedrals and collegiate churches K. Edwards, the various volumes by and edited by A. Hamilton Thompson (bibliography, privately printed, Oxford, 1948) and G. H. Cook, *English Collegiate Churches* (London, 1959); E. F. Jacob, 'Founders and Foundations in the Middle Ages', *Bulletin of the Institute of Historical Research*, XXXV (1962) is mainly on collegiate bodies.

A general account of medieval Oxford is that by H. Maxwell Lyte. H. Rashdall, *The Universities of Europe in the Middle Ages*, ed. F. M. Powicke and A. B. Emden, 3 vols. (Oxford, 1936), vol. III on England, or his short outline in *Cambridge Mediaeval History*, VI (1929), ch. XVII. R. Rait, *Life in the Mediaeval University* (Cambridge, 1910) and see E. F. Jacob, 'English University Clerks in the later Middle Ages', added to *Essays in the Conciliar Epoch* (Manchester, 1953 ed.). For halls and hostels: A. B. Emden, *An Oxford Hall in Mediaeval Times, being the Early History of St Edmund Hall up to 1560* (Oxford, 1927); H. P. Stokes, *The Mediaeval Hostels of the University of Cambridge* (Cambridge Antiquarian Society, 1924); W. W. R. Ball, *The King's Scholars and King's Hall* (Cambridge, 1917); A. E. Stamp, *Michaelhouse* (Cambridge, 1924).

Pearl Kibre, *Scholarly Privileges in the Middle Ages* (1961) is the most recent study; Beryl Smalley, *English Friars and Antiquity* (1960) is a sequel to the comprehensive *Study of the Bible in the Middle Ages* (Oxford, 1952, 2nd ed.). For a review of other relevant works, the bibliography in F. M. Powicke, *The Thirteenth Century* (Oxford, 1953).

J. W. Adamson, *The Illiterate Anglo-Saxon and other Essays on Education Mediaeval and Modern* (Cambridge, 1946) includes a reprint of 'Literacy in England in the 15th and 16th Centuries', from *The Library*, 4th series, X (1930). C. McMahon, *Education in Fifteenth Century England* (Baltimore, 1947) is a quite useful survey. W. H. Woodward, *Vittorino da Feltre and other Humanist*

Educators: essays and versions (Cambridge, 1897) includes extracts from Vergerius, Bruni d'Arezzo, Aeneas Sylvius, Guarino. See R. Weiss, *Humanism in England in the Fifteenth Century* (London, 1957, 2nd ed.) and R. R. Bolgar.

(v) *Universities and scholarship*

C. E. Mallet, *A History of the University of Oxford*, 3 vols. (London, 1924–7), vol. II on the sixteenth and seventeenth centuries, is the standard history. A much more comprehensive account is J. B. Mullinger, *The University of Cambridge*, 3 vols. (London, 1873–1911), vol. I up to 1535, vol. II up to 1625. For a brief assessment of changes still useful is G. Peacock, *Observations on the Statutes of the University of Cambridge* (London, 1841).

The City and University of Cambridge, ed. John Roach, *VCH Cambs.* III (1959) brings the history of town and gown together. There are short histories of the colleges, varying in usefulness, in the two series 'Oxford University College Histories' and 'Cambridge College Histories' written at the turn of the century. Two have recently been revised: Arthur Gray, *Jesus College, Cambridge*, by F. Brittain (1960), H. W. C. Davis, *Balliol College*, by R. H. C. Davis and R. Hunt (Oxford, 1963). See also A. Attwater on Pembroke, W. G. Searle, *History of the Queens' College: 1446–1560*, (Cambridge Antiquarian Society, 1867–71) and A. H. Lloyd, *The Early History of Christ's College* (Cambridge, 1934).

The best account of tutoring, drawing on Holdsworth's 'Directions', is in S. E. Morison, *The Founding of Harvard College*, and of the standard course in W. T. Costello, *The Scholastic Curriculum at Early Seventeenth Century Cambridge* (Harvard, 1958), see H. F. Fletcher, *The Intellectual Development of John Milton* (Urbana, 1961), II, also J. B. Mullinger, *Cambridge Characteristics in the Seventeenth Century* (London, 1867); for comments on the renewal of scholastic influence after reversal of the Commonwealth reforms, David Ogg, *England in the Reign of Charles II* (Oxford, 1955, 2nd ed.), II. For a bid to reassess the universities' role the volume by M. H. Curtis.

Particular aspects are covered in F. C. Carpenter, *Music in the Mediaeval and Renaissance Universities* (Oklahoma, 1958)—see also Denis Stevens, *Tudor Church Music* (London, 1961)—by F. S. Boas, *University Drama in the Tudor Age* (Oxford, 1914), by W. S. Howell and K. Lambley. Relating to tutors of modern languages, F. A. Yates, *John Florio* (London, 1934) and see her *French Academies of the Sixteenth Century* (Warburg Institute, 1947). There is a great deal of information in the books by E. G. R. Taylor, *Tudor Geography 1485–1583* (London, 1930), *Tudor and Early Stuart Geography 1583–1650* (London, 1934), *The Mathematical Practitioners of Tudor and Stuart England* (Cambridge, 1954), and various relevant works are listed in D. Bush.

Recent publications are F. Smith Fussner, *The Historical Revolution* (1962);

W. P. D. Wightman, *Science and the Renaissance* (Aberdeen University Studies, 1962), vol. I a study of the emergence of the sciences in the sixteenth century, vol. II a bibliography of relevant printed books in the university library; D. Campbell, 'The Medical Curriculum of the Universities of Europe in the sixteenth century with special reference to the Arab tradition in science, medicine and history', in *Essays...in Honour of Charles Singer*, ed. E. Ashworth (London, 1963). The period is covered in T. K. Derry and Trevor I. Williams, *A Short History of Technology* (Oxford, 1960).

For legal education, W. Holdsworth, *A History of English Law* (London, 1932 ed.), vol. II, ch. V; T. F. T. Plucknett, *A Concise History of Common Law* (London, 1936); and the introductions to the records of the inns. Michael Birks, *Gentlemen of the Law* (1960) traces the solicitor's role in social life, from 1200 to the present. For the effect of legal education, J. G. A. Pocock, *The Ancient Constitution and the Feudal Law* (Cambridge, 1957).

De Witt T. Starnes, *Renaissance Dictionaries: English–Latin, Latin–English* (Austin, Texas, 1954); this covers Withals's *Shorte Dictonarie* and two other English–Latin versions issued in 1552. De Witt T. Starnes and E. W. Talbert, *Classical Myth and Legend in Renaissance Dictionaries* (Chapel Hill, 1956). H. B. Lathrop, *Translations from the Classics into English from Caxton to Chapman 1477–1630* (Madison, 1933); F. O. Matthieson, *Translation: An Elizabethan Art* (London, 1931); A. F. Clements, *Tudor Translations* (London, 1941). For licensing of books, Frederick W. Siebert, *Freedom of the Press in England 1476–1776* (Urbana, 1952). See also R. Irwin, *The Origins of the English Library* (London, 1958) and *The English Library before 1700*, ed. F. Wormald and C. E. Wright (London, 1958).

There are chapters on education and scholarship by Sir John Sandys in *Shakespeare's England*, I (Oxford, 1917) and on 'Universities, Schools and Scholarship' by W. H. Woodward in *CHEL*, III (1908) which includes other relevant articles; early seventeenth century scholarship is covered by Foster Watson in *CHEL*, VII. There is a general account of educational institutions in the final chapter of A. L. Rowse, *The England of Elizabeth* (1950). Gordon Donaldson writes on 'Education in the century of the Reformation', in *Essays on the Scottish Reformation 1573–1625*, ed. David McRoberts (Glasgow, 1962). Craig R. Thompson, *Schools in Tudor England* (Washington, 1958) and *Universities in Tudor England* (1959) are Folger Library popular booklets reprinted in *Life and Letters in Tudor and Stuart England*, ed. Louis B. Wright and Virginia A. La Mar (Cornell and Oxford, 1963). A. C. F. Beales, *Education under Penalty: English Catholic Education from the Reformation to the Fall of James II* (London, 1963) argues that there were catholic schools in Elizabethan England (apart from clandestine teaching) but the supporting evidence is questionable; see correspondence in the *Times Literary Supplement*, 7 May and 4 June 1964.

(vi) *Schools and teaching*

To add to the specialist studies by Foster Watson there is a straightforward account, with chapters on merchant founders, the Marian exiles, etc., in *The Old Grammar Schools* (Cambridge, 1916); on an unusual book prescribed for several Elizabethan schools, *The Zodiacus Vitae of Marcellus Palingenius Stellatus* (London, 1908); and for a more general discussion 'The Curriculum and Text-Books of English Schools in the First Half of the Seventeenth Century', *Transactions of the Bibliographical Society*, VI (1901), 159–67. For other titles Foster Watson, 'List of Research and Literary Work on the subject of Education', *Transactions of the Bibliographical Society* (1913); many later articles are listed in W. H. G. Armytage, 'Foster Watson 1860–1929', *British Journal of Educational Studies*, x, no. 1 (1961).

The period is covered by J. W. Adamson, *A Short History of Education* (Cambridge, 1919); N. Wood, *The Reformation and English Education* (1931) is an informative thesis taking in universities as well as schools; A. Monroe Stowe, *English Grammar Schools in the reign of Queen Elizabeth* (1908) is based mainly on collating school statutes, with a list of functioning schools; for a list of schools in being in the early seventeenth century which draws also on college entrance registers, W. A. L. Vincent, *The State and School Education 1640–60* (London, 1950). J. Howard Brown, *Elizabethan Schooldays* (Oxford, 1933) is on school life in general: see also M. St Clair Byrne, *Elizabethan Life*, ch. XII; A. H. Dodd, *Life in Elizabethan England* (London, 1962).

Erasmus's teaching methods are discussed by W. H. Woodward in *Desiderius Erasmus* (1904) and *Studies in Education...1400–1600* (1906, rep. 1924) takes in Budé, Cordier, Sadoleto and Melanchthon. S. S. Laurie covers much the same ground more generally with chapters on Rabelais and Ascham in *Studies in the History of Educational Opinion from the Renaissance* (Cambridge, 1905). For a more comprehensive account, which relates educational change to social demand, R. R. Bolgar, *The Classical Heritage*, ch. VIII; see also F. Caspari, *Humanism and the Social Order in Tudor England*.

T. W. Baldwin, *William Shakspere's Small Latine and Lesse Greeke*, 2 vols. (Urbana, 1944) covers school foundations, educational writings and different aspects of the curriculum in detail; see also *William Shakspere's Petty School* (Illinois, 1943). Another survey covering teaching methods and textbooks, H. F. Fletcher, *The Intellectual Development of John Milton. I. The Institution to 1625; from the Beginnings through Grammar School* (Urbana, 1956); see also D. L. Clark, *John Milton at St Paul's School: A Study of Ancient Rhetoric in English Renaissance Education* (New York, 1948).

G. A. Plimpton, *The Education of Shakespeare Illustrated from the School-books of his Time* (Oxford, 1933) gives title-pages and excerpts; on the same model, *The Education of Chaucer* (Oxford, 1935). On primers designated for use in school, C. C. Butterworth, 'Early Primers for the Use of Children', *Papers of the Bibliographical Society of America*, XLIII (1949) and for some plays written for schools Lily B. Campbell. Jean Robertson, *The Art of Letter Writing. An essay on the Handbooks Published in England during the Sixteenth and Seventeenth Centuries* (Liverpool, 1942). There is no study of school libraries but see R. T. D. Sayle, 'Annals of Merchant Taylors' School Library', *The Library*, 4th series, XV (1935). R. C. Christie, *The Old Church and School Libraries of Lancashire* (Chetham Society, 1885) has information but mostly for a later period.

For administrative aspects, R. Somerville, *History of the Duchy of Lancaster*. I. *1265–1603* (London, 1953); H. E. Bell, *The Court of Wards and Liveries* (1953); W. C. Richardson, *History of the Court of Augmentations* (1961); and the bibliography in *The Tudor Constitution* (1960). There is often information in borough records and see W. E. Tate, *The Parish Chest: A Study of the Records of Parochial Administration in England* (Cambridge, 1951, 2nd ed.). A useful guide, J. S. Purvis, *An Introduction to Ecclesiastical Records*, published by the Borthwick Institute of Historical Research, York.

There is much information about founders and school foundations in the volumes by W. K. Jordan, covering six counties in detail, and other regional studies of educational provision seem to be in the making. Meanwhile for a list of Yorkshire schools, P. J. Wallis and W. E. Tate, *Register of Old Yorkshire Grammar Schools*, edition in pamphlet form (Leeds, 1956).

(vii) *Histories of individual schools*

There are now many histories of schools, ranging from the scholarly study to the short pamphlet, often privately printed to celebrate a centenary and obtainable only from the school but which may draw on records in its keeping. Some have already been listed. Others are little but pious tributes to an *alma mater* particularly where latterday 'public' schools are in question, the modern image overlaying what were, until local boys were excluded, foundations serving a town or parish. The following selection is confined mainly to schools administered by boroughs or city companies which originated before or at the Reformation with particular reference to those established in the Edwardian age.

The account of Hull school by John Lawson, *A Town Grammar School through Six Centuries* (1963) breaks away from the traditional pattern—of recording benefactors, headmasters, entrants to university and eminent *alumni*—to place a school's development in its social setting. See also accounts by M. C. Cross of Leicester School, H. A. Ormerod of Liverpool, I. E. Gray and W. E. Potter of Ipswich, which draw on local records. Other histories are A. W. Thomas on *Nottingham High School 1513–1933* (Nottingham,

1957); W. A. Sampson on *Bristol Grammar School* (Bristol, 1912) and the volume by C. P. Hill (1951); H. W. Saunders on *Norwich Grammar School* (Norwich, 1932); F. V. Follett on *Worcester Royal Grammar School* (London, 1951); G. H. Martin on *Colchester Royal Grammar School 1539–1947* (Colchester Museums Committee, 1947) and A. L. Murray, *The Royal Grammar School, Lancaster* (Cambridge, 1951); R. Austin, *The Crypt School, Gloucester ...1539–1939* (Gloucester, 1939).

See also J. T. Lennox, *Sevenoaks School and its Founder 1432–1932* (Sevenoaks, 1932); B. Varley, *History of Stockport School* (Manchester, 1957, 2nd ed.); A. A. Mumford, *The Manchester Grammar School 1515–1915. A Regional Study of the Advancement of Learning in Manchester since the Reformation* (London, 1919); E. E. Dodd, *A History of the Bingley Grammar School 1529–1929* (Bradford, 1930); L. S. Knight, *Welsh Independent Grammar Schools to 1600* (Newtown, 1926) for Oswestry.

For schools run by city companies: M. J. F. McDonnell, *A History of St Paul's School* (London, 1909) supplemented by his *Annals* (1959). H. B. Wilson's two-volume history has been supplemented by F. W. M. Draper, *Four Centuries of Merchant Taylors' School 1561–1961* (Oxford, 1962). Also in this category E. H. Pearce, *Annals of Christ's Hospital* (London, 1901). For schools outside London, G. P. Mander on Wolverhampton run by the Merchant Taylors, W. G. Walker on Oundle run by the Grocers' Company, S. Rivington on Tonbridge run by the Skinners' Company (the short history by D. C. Somervell, 1947, erroneously ascribes the statutes to Mary's reign), E. Beevor (ed.), *History and Register of Aldenham School* (London, 1938, 7th ed.) under the Brewers' Company.

There is information about the administration of company schools—including the financial transactions of 1550 and the subsequent act of indemnity in respect of 'concealed lands' in 1607—in the five volumes of the *City of London Livery Companies' Commission* (1884), PP 4073.

For some Edwardian foundations and refoundations. Schools formerly connected with monastic houses: K. E. Symons, *The Grammar School of Edward VI, Bath* (Bath, 1934); J. Sargeaunt, *A History of Bedford School* (Bedford, 1925); G. Sale, *A Short History of King's School, Bruton* (1950); R. W. Elliott, *The Story of King Edward VI School, Bury St Edmunds* (1963); A. B. Gourlay, *A History of Sherborne School* (Winchester, 1951) and see A. E. Preston, *The Church and Parish of St Nicholas, Abingdon* (Oxford Historical Society, 1929); A. E. Gibbs, *Historical Records of St Albans* (St Albans, 1888).

Schools formerly administered by gilds or placed under boroughs or special governing bodies: H. L. White, *A History of Wisbech Grammar School* (Wisbech, 1939); F. Streatfield, *An Account of the Grammar School in the King's Town and Parish of Maidstone in Kent* (Oxford, 1915); C. G. Williamson, *The Royal Grammar School, Guildford: A Record and Review* (London,

1929); N. J. Wheatley (ed.), *King Edward VI School, Chelmsford* (Chelmsford, 1951); G. H. K. Burley, *History of King Edward's School, Stourbridge* (Stourbridge, 1948); *King Edward VI School, Nuneaton* (1952); *The Grammar School of King Edward VI at East Retford 1552–1952* (Retford, 1952); B. L. Deed, *History of Stamford School* (Stamford, 1954); A. M. Cook, *A Short History of Grantham School* (n.d.); J. B. Whitehead, *The History of Great Yarmouth Grammar School 1551–1951* (Gt. Yarmouth, 1951); C. Brice, *Ludlow Grammar School* (Ludlow, 1850); A. R. Stedman, *A History of Marlborough Grammar School 1550–1945* (Devizes, 1945); T. Kelly, *History of King Edward VI Grammar School, Totnes* (Totnes, 1947); G. Kennedy, *The Story of Morpeth Grammar School* (Morpeth, 1952); D. Wilmot, *A Short History of the Grammar School, Macclesfield* (Macclesfield, 1910); C. G. Gilmore, *King Edward VI School, Stafford* (Oxford, 1953) and see E. I. Fripp and R. Savage, *Minutes and Accounts of Stratford-on-Avon 1552–1620*, 3 vols. (Dugdale Society, 1921–6).

Schools which received fresh endowments, or retained old: R. T. Graham, *Ilminster Grammar School 1549–1949* (n.d.); E. A. Bell, *History of Giggleswick School 1499–1912* (Leeds, 1912); H. L. Clark and W. N. Weech, *History of Sedbergh School 1525–1925* (Sedbergh, 1925); P. C. Sands and C. M. Haworth, *History of Pocklington School* (London, 1951); A. C. Price, *A History of the Leeds Grammar School* (Leeds, 1919); A. M. Gibbon, *The Free Grammar School of Skipton-in-Craven* (Liverpool, 1947); P. W. Rogers, *A History of Ripon Grammar School* (Ripon, 1954); W. Claridge, *Origin and History of the Bradford Grammar School* (Bradford, 1882); L. P. Wenham, *History of Richmond School, Yorks* (Arbroath, 1958).

New foundations: T. W. Hutton on Birmingham; C. F. Russell on Southampton and F. L. Freeman, *A Short History of King Edward VI School, Southampton* (1954); G. W. Fisher on Shrewsbury supplemented by J. B. Oldham, *History of Shrewsbury School* (Oxford, 1952); see also Christ's Hospital and Tonbridge.

For schools planned under Edward VI, established under Mary: D. P. J. Fink on Walsall; C. W. Stokes on Clitheroe; G. P. Gollin and Roy Christian, *Derby School: A Short History* (Derby, 1954); see also H. Turpin, *Boston Grammar School 1555–1955: A Short History* (Boston, 1955).

Among early Elizabethan schools mentioned in the text: H. Barber and H. Lewis, *The History of Friar's School, Bangor* (Bangor, 1901); F. R. Raines, *Memorials of Rochdale Grammar School* (London, 1845); P. H. Reavey, *Records of the Queen Elizabeth Grammar School, Penrith*, Cumberland and Westmorland Antiquarian and Archaeological Society Tract Series, 10 (1915); J. Howard Brown, *A Short History of Thame School* (London, 1927); M. R. Craze, *Felsted School, 1564–1947* (Ipswich, 1955). Two recent publications N. R. W. Stephenson, *A Short History of Guisborough Grammar School*

(Guisborough, 1962); John Cavell and Brian Kennett, *A History of Sir Roger Manwood's School, Sandwich, 1563–1963 with a Life of the Founder* (1963).

For Leicestershire schools referred to: A. Hopewell, *The Book of Bosworth School 1320–1950* (Leicester, 1950); George Irving, *Lutterworth Grammar School* (Leicester, 1956); Bernard Elliott, *A History of Kibworth Beauchamp Grammar School* (Kibworth, 1957); T. H. Corfe, *The School on the Hill* with a chapter on the older schools of Melton by J. E. Brownlow (1960) and for Wigston, W. G. Hoskins, *The Midland Peasant* (1957).

P. J. Wallis has in preparation a preliminary list of all histories of old schools in England and Wales.

INDEX